D0848999

ELEANOR RATHBONE
and the Politics of Conscience

1. Eleanor Rathbone *c.* 1931.

ELEANOR RATHBONE
and the Politics of Conscience

Susan Pedersen

YALE UNIVERSITY PRESS
New Haven and London

SOCIETY AND THE SEXES IN THE MODERN WORLD
SERIES EDITOR, CHRISTINE STANSELL

Designed by Adam Freudenheim
Set by SNP Best-set Typesetter Ltd., Hong Kong
Printed in the United Kingdom at the University Press, Cambridge

Library of Congress Cataloging-in-Publication Data

Pedersen, Susan, 1959–
  Eleanor Rathbone and the politics of conscience / Susan Pedersen.
    p.   cm.
  Includes bibliographical references (p.) and index.
  ISBN 0-300-10245-3 (hardback : alk. paper)
    1. Rathbone, Eleanor F. (Eleanor Florence), 1872–1946.   2. Women in politics –
Great Britain – History – 20th century.   3. Great Britain – Politics and government –
20th century   4. Legislators – Great Britain – Biography.   5. Suffragists – Great Britain –
Biography.   6. Feminists – Great Britain – Biography.   I. Title.
DA566.9.R25 P43   2004
328.41'092 – dc22   2003023094

A catalogue record for this book is available from the British Library

10 9 8 7 6 5 4 3 2 1

If we had a keen vision and feeling of all ordinary human life, it would be like hearing the grass grow and the squirrel's heart beat, and we should die of that roar which lies on the other side of silence.

George Eliot, *Middlemarch*, ch. 20

Table of Contents

Illustrations

Abbreviations

BDBJ	Board of Deputies of British Jews
CMC	Children's Minimum Campaign Committee, later Children's Minimum Council
COS	Charity Organisation Society
CRS	[Liverpool] Central Relief Society
EC	Executive Committee
FES	Family Endowment Society
ILP	Independent Labour Party
LNU	League of Nations Union
LWSS	Liverpool Women's Suffrage Society
NCRNT	National Committee for Rescue from Nazi Terror
NJC	National Joint Committee for Spanish Relief
NUSEC	National Union of Societies for Equal Citizenship
NUWSS	National Union of Women's Suffrage Societies
SPSL	Society for the Protection of Science and Learning
SSFA	Soldiers' and Sailors' Families Association
SSSTSW	School of Social Science and of Training for Social Work [Liverpool]
TUC	Trades Union Congress
UAB	Unemployment Assistance Board
WSPU	Women's Social and Political Union

For abbreviations used in the Notes, see p. 388.

Acknowledgements

This book is appearing at least five years later than I intended, the blame for which is partly mine and partly Miss Rathbone's. Was any biographer ever blessed with a subject at once so admirable and so enraging? Of course she felt it was her work that mattered and the worker of no consequence at all – but was it really necessary to give so many brilliant speeches, write such volumes of engaged and acute prose, and leave among them almost nothing about her faith and friendships, desires and dreams? This biography began, then, in scavenging and importunity, a pursuit of hunches and tips, knocks on unknown doors and letters sent to addresses fifty years old. If I ever tire of writing history, I can probably take up work as a private investigator.

To those who ransacked their memories and their storage rooms, I owe a debt that this volume can only partially repay. First among these are the members of the Rathbone family, especially Eleanor's nephew, the late Dr B.L. Rathbone, who not only shared his affectionate memories of his aunt but allowed me access to a small cache of invaluable and then private papers. The late Lady Wright (Mrs Beatrice Rathbone, MP), the late Lady Warr (Hannah Mary Reynolds Rathbone), Noreen Rathbone, Jenny Rathbone and Cristina Rathbone delved into the family lore with me. Margaret Simey told me of Rathbone's work in Liverpool in the twenties; David and Diana Hopkinson recalled Rathbone's collaboration with Diana's mother, Eva Hubback; Mrs. Joan Gibson (Joan Prewer) shared memories of her years as Rathbone's secretary. Without Brian Harrison's interviews with so many of Rathbone's suffrage friends and collaborators, done in the 1970s, not only this biography but the field of British women's history would be much poorer. I am also grateful to Sir Claus Moser for insight into the experience of internment and to Frank Field, MP, for several useful conversations on the culture of the House of Commons. I never knew Mary Stocks, but her moving *Eleanor Rathbone: A Biography* (1949) remains the only source for some personal information.

Then there are the archivists and librarians, ever a historian's saviours and guides. I cannot thank warmly enough the archivists and librarians of Special

Collections and Archives at the Sydney Jones Library of the University of Liverpool, especially Adrian Allan, Maureen Watry and Katy Hooper, who have turned the copious Rathbone Family Papers into an indexed, accessible wonder, and who have taken a sympathetic interest in this project for more than a decade. Equally I must thank the Women's Library (formerly the Fawcett Library), whose archivists and collections have sustained my work for more than twenty years. I have relied on too many other archivists to list here (the appendix listing private papers consulted and acknowledging copyright gives some indication of my debt), but must thank those individuals who made privately held materials available. Deirdre Morley of the Liverpool Council of Voluntary Aid arranged access to the papers of the Council and (wonder of wonders) tracked down a copy of Stocks's now-rare biography for me to keep; Annabel Cole allowed me to consult the correspondence and papers of Rathbone's friend Margery Fry; Sir Edward Cazalet kindly checked the diaries of his uncle, Victor Cazalet, for references to Eleanor Rathbone. (There were, of course, those who refused to grant access to private papers, but I shall resist the temptation to name them as well.) Tracing the elusive Elizabeth Macadam, Rathbone's lifelong companion, proved a challenge all its own. I am grateful to Ms Sylviane Dubois of the Literary and Historical Society of Quebec and Ms Kim Arnold of the Presbyterian Church in Canada Archives for help in tracing Macadam's father, and Dr Jean McAllister for sharing memories – and, invaluably, photographs – of her great-aunt.

Writing the life of a woman who involved herself in most of the great political events of the twentieth century is a risky business. Who among us can move with assurance from the quarrels of the suffrage movement to debates over Indian constitutional reform to the calculations of the British Cabinet on the Abyssinian question? I have made, I am sure, some errors; that there are not more is because friends and colleagues have been ready with advice and (when necessary) red pens. Four people deserve special thanks – Philip Williamson for taking a razor to my chapters on the politics of the thirties, Deborah Cohen for insisting that I allow the reader a chance for empathy (and for herself reading every chapter), Chris Hilliard for heroically pruning back the rhetorical questions, Peter Mandler for two decades of intellectual companionship that has left its mark on everything I write. David Bush, Peter Clarke, Stefan Collini, Krista Cowman, Catherine Evtuhov, Anne Goldgar, Susan Grayzel, Brian Harrison, Mark Kishlansky, Seth Koven, Jon Lawrence, Fred Leventhal, Alison Light, Charles Maier, the late Colin Matthew, Andrew Muldoon, Deborah Nord, Alex Owen, Bronwyn Rae, Kim Sichel, Mrinalini Sinha, Chris Stansell, Peter Stansky, Bernard Wasserstein, Robert Webb and Geoff Wisner also commented on particular chapters. Liz Harvey became another reason to visit Liverpool, and companionably tracked Miss Rathbone with me through its history-soaked streets. Jeremy Knowles, former Dean of the Faculty of Arts and Sciences at Harvard University, helped this project without intending to by giving me, for two years, the taste and feel of a life in politics.

David Nickles and Ben Hett, then graduate students, took on the tiresome job of tracking down Rathbone's manifold letters to the press and parliamentary speeches. Nicole Raspa breezily completed her own undergraduate degree while checking notes, tracing references, fetching books, and learning much more about British politics than she ever intended. The Radcliffe Institute for Advanced Study (formerly the Bunting Institute) offered me time to write not once but twice – although the first time inadvertently, since I told them I was working on something else. Florence Ladd, Drew Faust, Judith Vichniac and two classes of institute fellows gave this project the measureless gift of their intelligence and love. Beth Humphries copy-edited the manuscript with meticulousness and restraint; Douglas Matthews distilled from it a sensible index. Adam Freudenheim of Yale University Press hauled the boat ashore with a sure hand.

'So why, with all that help, did this book take her such a long time?' Miss Rathbone would have known the answer. 'Young families like yours are delightful things,' Rathbone wrote to one of her collaborators after the birth of her daughter, 'but rather an impediment to public activities!' One could not really expect a mother to carry on with paid work, she thought – and yet, the work of motherhood too was important, deserving of time and care, remuneration and respect. Hence those long campaigns for family allowances, hence her insistent demand that marriage not deprive women of civil and citizenship rights. Like so many women today, I wanted more – my work and my family – but I needed more than family allowances to have it. Without Dana Linskill's, Heike Schmitt's and Brigitte Fehn's loving arms and generous spirits, without the caring and imaginative teachers of the Krabbelstube Becker in Munich, and the Botanic Gardens Children's Center and the German International School in Cambridge, this book could not have been written. And this is before we come to the husband – a figure Miss Rathbone viewed with such a sceptical eye! Thankfully, even Miss Rathbone could be wrong. My most loving gratitude I reserve for Tom Ertman, who not only spent hundreds of hours reading chapters and arguing with me about the possibilities and choices confronting political actors many decades ago, but also came home from the office to do the dishes and change the diapers so I could ferret in archives or just sit in front of a computer screen at home. And so, slowly, distractedly, and punctuated by the crises of a too-full life, this book inched its way to completion. Miss Rathbone would forgive its long delay. It is the work that matters, yes, but whom is the work for? We learn from example the contours of the virtuous life; haltingly but in hope we pass those lessons on to our children. For Saskia and Carl, then, lights of my life, treasures of my heart, a book about families.

Eleanor Rathbone's Family Tree (abridged)

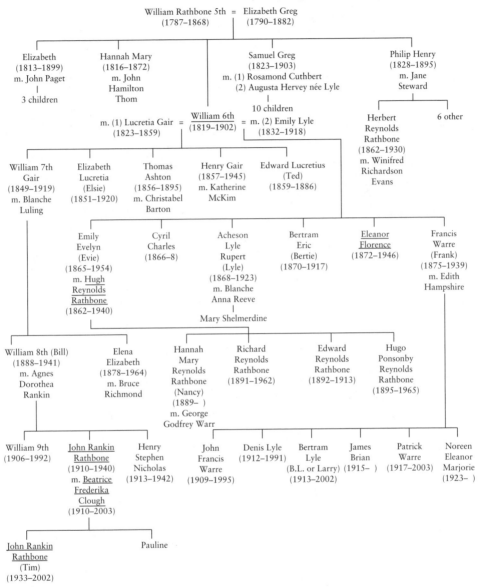

William Rathbone 5th = Elizabeth Greg
(1787–1868)   (1790–1882)

Elizabeth
(1813–1899)
m. John Paget
|
3 children

Hannah Mary
(1816–1872)
m. John
Hamilton
Thom

Samuel Greg
(1823–1903)
m. (1) Rosamond Cuthbert
(2) Augusta Hervey née Lyle
|
10 children

Philip Henry
(1828–1895)
m. Jane
Steward

Herbert
Reynolds
Rathbone
(1862–1930)
m. Winifred
Richardson
Evans

6 other

m. (1) Lucretia Gair = William 6th = m. (2) Emily Lyle
(1823–1859)   (1819–1902)   (1832–1918)

William 7th
Gair
(1849–1919)
m. Blanche
Luling

Elizabeth
Lucretia
(Elsie)
(1851–1920)

Thomas
Ashton
(1856–1895)
m. Christabel
Barton

Henry Gair
(1857–1945)
m. Katherine
McKim

Edward Lucretius
(Ted)
(1859–1886)

Emily
Evelyn
(Evie)
(1865–1954)
m. Hugh
Reynolds
Rathbone
(1862–1940)

Cyril
Charles
(1866–8)

Acheson
Lyle
Rupert
(Lyle)
(1868–1923)
m. Blanche
Anna Reeve
|
Mary Shelmerdine

Bertram
Eric
(Bertie)
(1870–1917)

Eleanor
Florence
(1872–1946)

Francis
Warre
(Frank)
(1875–1939)
m. Edith
Hampshire

William 8th (Bill)
(1888–1941)
m. Agnes
Dorothea
Rankin

Elena
Elizabeth
(1878–1964)
m. Bruce
Richmond

Hannah
Mary
Reynolds
Rathbone
(Nancy)
(1889–)
m. George
Godfrey Warr

Richard
Reynolds
Rathbone
(1891–1962)

Edward
Reynolds
Rathbone
(1892–1913)

Hugo
Ponsonby
Reynolds
Rathbone
(1895–1965)

William 9th
(1906–1992)

John Rankin
Rathbone
(1910–1940)
m. Beatrice
Frederika
Clough
(1910–2003)

Henry
Stephen
Nicholas
(1913–1942)

John
Francis
Warre
(1909–1995)

Denis Lyle
(1912–1991)

Bertram
Lyle
(B.L. or Larry)
(1913–2002)

James
Brian
(1915–)

Patrick
Warre
(1917–2003)

Noreen
Eleanor
Marjorie
(1923–)

John Rankin
Rathbone
(Tim)
(1933–2002)

Pauline

Note: Includes only immediate family and persons mentioned in the text. MPs are underlined.

Introduction

Lives Seen and Unseen

Whatever Eleanor Rathbone's constituents thought their Member of Parliament should be doing in early March of 1939, it probably wasn't what she *was* doing – which was hiring a ship to run the blockade of Spain and bring Republicans threatened with reprisal to safety. Of course, she was doing other things as well – putting together a plan to expand schoolchildren's access to free milk and meals, for example, and reviving her campaign for family allowances, which were beginning to look achievable as the prospect of war put the health of the population back on the political agenda. But in early 1939, with Franco's troops poised for final victory in Spain, Czech Jews and social democrats fleeing the territories ceded to the Nazis by the Munich accords, and Hitler poised for another eastward strike, international issues and the claims of refugees must take priority. After all, Rathbone thought, if those Spanish Republicans and Czech Jews had not actually elected her, they were nevertheless her responsibility – for would they be fleeing their homes and menaced by war if the British government had not pursued the disastrous policy of appeasement? Cabinet ministers and Foreign Office officials, who found themselves receiving deputations from any of the half-dozen refugee groups Rathbone helped to run or taking calls at all hours from the distinguished lady member, wished she didn't feel that obligation quite so deeply, didn't profess quite so fervently that 'in a democratic State, what our Government does we do.'[1] But Rathbone had spent her young womanhood in the women's suffrage movement because she was certain that political rights mattered, and because she was eager to take on the responsibilities they entailed. There are people around today who owe their lives to the strength of her convictions.

Eleanor Rathbone was sixty-seven in 1939, and had achievements to her name that no other British woman, and few political figures, could rival. Born to a wealthy, Liberal, Liverpool merchant dynasty, she had first honed her political skills – and her feminism – on the streets of that fiercely partisan port city. Between the 1890s and the First World War, Rathbone helped to establish a network of social services for women and children in Liverpool, won election as the first woman on the Liverpool City Council, and guided the region's constitutionalist suffrage movement. She also gained a national reputation as a sophisticated and radical thinker on questions of poverty. Her studies of Liverpool dock labour, and her work with local women, had convinced her that families could not be supported through wages alone. 'After all,' she wrote, 'the rearing of families is not a sort of masculine hobby, like tobacco smoking or pigeon flying'; why then support it 'by the clumsy device of paying men wage-earners more than women'?[2] Her experience during the First World War administering the benefits system through which soldiers' dependants were supported suggested a better, and more feminist, alternative. The work of mothers deserved its own remuneration; the support of children should be a collective charge.

After the war, as President of Britain's main feminist organization, the National Union of Societies for Equal Citizenship, Rathbone helped bring to fruition a series of legislative reforms that transformed women's status in the twenties. At the same time, as author of the brilliant economic treatise, *The Disinherited Family*, she launched her movement for family allowances. Elected to the Commons in 1929, she emerged as its most forthright feminist. Her hopes of an early introduction of family allowances died as the depression drove unemployment rates and spending deficits upwards, but even in these conditions Rathbone allied with medical doctors and poverty experts to improve social services and benefits for the children of the unemployed. But the subjection of women and children in other countries claimed her attention as well. When Indian constitutional reform monopolized the political agenda, she forged a cross-party Commons lobby that expanded the numbers of women enfranchised under the 1935 Government of India Act.

The deepening international crises of the thirties pushed that work to the sidelines. For five years, Rathbone spent most of her time trying to persuade her countrymen and women of the need to defend the democracies and the obligation to welcome refugees. Indeed, so closely identified was Rathbone with the refugee cause that when the British government decided to intern many Jewish refugees as 'enemy aliens' during the invasion scare of 1940, it was she who led the campaign for their release. Likewise, when news of Hitler's campaign of extermination against the Jews reached British political circles in the autumn of 1942, it was she who spearheaded the public agitation for efforts at rescue. She was met, more often than not, with irritation: officials grew tired of her importunity; junior ministers would duck into doorways when they saw her coming. But in the Commons, her courage and independence won her increasing respect. When the war made the introduction of family allowances possible, backbench MPs from all parties lined up behind her to stipulate that the new allowances be paid by statute to the mother. 'No Parliamentary career has been more useful and fruitful,' the *Manchester Guardian* insisted, on her sudden death in January 1946.[3] At once visionary and pragmatic, analytically rigorous but politically acute, she stands as both the most significant feminist thinker and the most effective woman politician of the first half of the twentieth century.

Today, however, Eleanor Rathbone is scarcely remembered. A survey of important women in political life in the first half of this century would probably place other names first. We think of Beatrice Webb, persuading cabinet ministers over dinner of the merits of Fabian socialism; of the charismatic Christabel and Emmeline Pankhurst, rousing women across the country to acts of defiance and militancy; of the witty and stylish Nancy Astor, entering the Commons as the pioneer woman MP; of the socialist firebrand Ellen Wilkinson, leading her unemployed constituents to London at the head of the Jarrow crusade. Rathbone, whose record of practical achievement outstrips any of these, comes less easily to mind. In part, this is because of her non-party stance: on the Liverpool City Council and then in Parliament Rathbone sat as an Independent – a fact that barred her from office in her own day and that has meant that no party can claim her name. In part, it is because she concentrated so much on the unglamorous work of lobbying and coalition-building – work essential to constitutional political reform but too painstaking and tedious to draw the public eye. In part, it is because she so often worked through others, briefing well-connected allies for deputations or speeches, or setting up cross-party committees to disguise her own directing hand. But in part, surely, it is because of Rathbone's own reticent personality. A more original thinker than Beatrice Webb, she left no diaries chronicling the evolution of her thought; shy and awkward in social gatherings, she worked best with a handful of like-minded collaborators and inspired respect rather than love. And yet, Rathbone's life had emotional complexities of its own – as I discovered when writing this book.

Eleanor Rathbone was a 'new woman' – that is, she was one of that first generation of women who, coming of age in the 1890s, entered politics not as dynastic matriarchs or 'political wives', but as individuals and in their own right. Rathbone was the most successful of that cohort, and had formidable advantages from the start. Blessed with a father who believed in the capacity of women, she was given an independent income and the Oxford education usually reserved for sons. When she began her career in social work and social investigation, William Rathbone's patronage and the acquaintance of Charles Booth smoothed her way. On her election to the Liverpool City Council, one brother and one cousin were already there to greet her; when she went up to London to lobby MPs on women's suffrage, she knew the ways of the House and many of its members from her father's long parliamentary career. So untroubled, indeed, might Rathbone's ascent appear, that one might paint it, as her first biographer and dear friend Mary Stocks did, as a kind of inevitable dynastic succession. Eleanor appears, in that account, as the seventh 'William Rathbone', seizing 'the flag of Lancashire liberalism' from her father, and carrying it 'out and beyond'.[4]

But Eleanor was not, of course, the seventh William Rathbone, and not just because her older half-brother already bore that name. The point is that she was female. In 1872, when she was born, her later career would have been almost unimaginable. Somerville Hall was not yet a college when she went up to Oxford to read philosophy; women could not stand for the City Council, much less for Parliament. Eleanor was well aware of these restrictions. Even in her girlhood she had worried that the 'woman's renaissance' might not last long enough to carry her with it;[5] by the time of her return from Somerville she realized that her ambitions must wait upon the women's movement at every turn. Hence her own partial repudiation of that liberal succession in which we have been too eager to place her. For all her affection for her father, Rathbone abandoned his party and his faith; she risked her City Council seat and lost one parliamentary election rather than moderate her outspoken feminism. If she sought entry into spheres once reserved for men, she did so as a political Independent, and backed by a local women's movement she did much to create.

But how, emotionally, could she do this – especially as an unmarried daughter still living in the family home? Although Stocks scarcely mentions her, Rathbone had a mother as well as a father, and a mother whose ambitions for her attractive daughter did not lie in the direction of spinsterhood and social reform. She had two older sisters who were not sent to Oxford, and a number of older brothers who were. Eleanor's father had died by the time she began her political ascendancy, but her mother was alive to see her daughter reject marriage as a prison of dependence; her less-gifted brothers heard their younger sister praised in public as their father's heir. And did even her sisters, living out more conventional models of feminine accomplishment, watch Eleanor's rise without a measure of ambivalence or pain? At the heart of the story of the 'new woman' lies a complex family drama – a story not only of the daughter's valiant conquest of hitherto male realms but equally of her rejection of the demands of family, her abandonment of a prescribed womanly sphere. For as long as they lived, Eleanor's relations with her mother were marked by fear and compunction, with her sisters by apology and gratitude. She wanted the work of wives and mothers honoured and compensated, yes, but to bring this about she had to avoid her own mother's fate and escape her own family's loving grasp.

In Rathbone's case, one woman helped her do this – Elizabeth Macadam, the Scottish social worker with whom Rathbone ran a settlement, conducted social investigations, discussed all her cares and decisions, and shared a life for more than forty years. No one embodied better than Elizabeth the ideal of female autonomy; no one did more to free Rathbone from the entanglements of family. And no one sought so assiduously to disguise her own crucial role. So uninterested was Macadam in being cast in a supporting light that she supervised Mary

Stocks's selection of materials for her biography, insisted that Stocks keep her out of the story, and made sure her own correspondence with Eleanor was burned after her death. I have been less dutiful than Stocks, who was herself less dutiful than Macadam wanted. This biography does bring Macadam in – because it must, and because times, fortunately, have changed. The personal anxieties and changing public norms that drove Macadam to burn those letters must be part of the story. But as I write these words I do so knowing that Macadam, could she read them, would rise up in protest.

This is the story, then, of public and of private achievement – of a woman who became, for a time, Britain's most accomplished and capable woman politician, and who tried to live – if with mixed success – freely and in a new way. The first story is, of course, the main theme: we trace Rathbone's life through Oxford and Liverpool, the streets and the Commons, from an early reliance on family and friends to the full independence and authority of her later years. And yet the leitmotif of the private must run through the life as well – less easily traced, only half acknowledged, but a critical foundation of Rathbone's thought and power. Through her economic writings and her political campaigns, Rathbone sought to make the hidden work of women – the work of mothers, wives and sisters – publicly visible, publicly 'count'. Writing her life, I have tried to be faithful to her teaching.

PART I

DILEMMAS OF A DUTIFUL DAUGHTER

2. The Rathbones on holiday in Scotland, 1892. Back row, left to right: William, Emily, Eleanor. Front row, left to right: Evie, Frank (with Nancy), Hugh (with Reynolds), Elsie.

When one is young and a newcomer in the world, one looks at it all in a detached way, wondering why the inhabitants take themselves and their trivial affairs so seriously, and finding one's chief interests outside it. But by degrees one warms to the world and one's fellow mortals. . . .

Eleanor Rathbone to Hilda Oakeley, n.d. [1901]

Eleanor never was young from the time she was born. . . .

Emily Rathbone to William Gair Rathbone, 13 March 1900.

Chapter 1

Snares of Wealth and Virtue

Eleanor Florence Rathbone thought herself lucky in her birth. Who would not wish to be born into wealth and virtue – to have a father known for his benevolence, a mother admired for her charm, and a raft of cousins, uncles and forebears honoured for service and standing in their bustling, vibrant town? If we were to invent the dynasty likely to produce Britain's most remarkable inter-war woman politician, we would no doubt imagine a family much like the Rathbones. But if Eleanor Rathbone was blessed at birth with wealth, position and principles, that inheritance was tempered with one less agreeable gift. For the Rathbone children grew up surrounded, almost crushed, by reminders that their wealth and position were a sacred trust, to use to the glory of God and in the service of their fellow man. Eleanor was the child who adopted her father's views most fully – but, almost by virtue of that loyalty, she developed a rather lop-sided personality, an abnormally tender moral sense grafted on to starved and almost atrophied human passions. Eleanor's experiences in her twenties – her encounter with Oxford idealism, her apprenticeship as a social worker, and her intense identification with the 'new women' of the 1890s – would deepen her commitment to a life of social service. But the initial impulse, the Dorothea-Brooke-like desire to serve, was born in childhood, founded on the search of a lonely little girl for love. Like many Victorian daughters, Eleanor Rathbone discovered early that only selflessness could win parental approbation. In time, her own conscience would be an even more vigilant judge.

Just being born a Rathbone was a grave responsibility. By the mid-nineteenth century, this Liverpool family had already constructed a dynastic myth. In Eleanor's father's generation they began to denote earlier William Rathbones, rather regally, by number, and to commission family histories; both Augustine Birrell's *Records of the Rathbone Family* and Eleanor Rathbone's own memoir of her father thus recount the lives of successive William Rathbones as a necessary precursor to any individual life.[1] Applying the Whig interpretation of history to their own past, they thought of themselves as an exemplary, progressive family: devout but not puritanical, liberal but not insurrectionary, wealthy but not grasping – a family elected to act as Liverpool's conscience, urging the city to turn from the error of its sectarian and slave-trading past and to embrace the liberal causes of free trade, religious toleration, and municipal improvement.

As is often the case, this myth contained a good deal of truth. The Rathbones were indeed a remarkable family, at once apart from and deeply engaged with their city and their time. They had been in Liverpool since the 1720s, when the second William Rathbone left Gawsworth in Cheshire to build up a business as a timber merchant; for more than 150 years thereafter Rathbone ships would sail from the port of Liverpool and Rathbone merchants trade on the Liverpool Exchange. Religious ties and strategic marriages undergirded the family's fortune. During the religious turmoil of the 1730s, the first two William Rathbones joined the Quakers, drawn perhaps by that sect's reputation for scrupulous business practices, spiritual seriousness and sturdy companionate marriages. Through alliances with the Darby and Reynolds families of Coalbrookdale and with the Liverpool Rutters, the Rathbones moved to the centre of this web of Quaker kinship and enterprise. When the fourth William Rathbone left the Quakers for the Unitarians, he merely shifted these dynastic alliances on to a larger stage. Whereas the third William Rathbone had traded largely in timber, the fourth expanded into the American trade, supplying raw cotton to Samuel Greg, who by the early nineteenth century was turning a handsome profit manufacturing cotton cloth at his new, water-powered mill at Quarry Bank.[2] His son cemented these ties by marrying Samuel's daughter Elizabeth in 1812, a link that left both families with a bewildering assortment of Samuel Greg Rathbones and William Rathbone Gregs.

Yet it was as a byword for liberalism rather than as a byword for enterprise that the Rathbones were (and wished to be) known.[3] They owed this reputation especially to the fourth William Rathbone, who used his wealth as a springboard for civic action. He helped to found the Liverpool committee of the Society for the Abolition of the Slave Trade in 1788 (a stand that made him 'a marked man' in the British capital of the trade) and together with William Roscoe, James Currie and other free-thinking radicals, he championed the causes of peace, free trade and universal suffrage to local opprobrium and against the inhospitable backdrop of the French wars. This William Rathbone also bought Greenbank, then a comfortable farmhouse some three miles beyond the edge of the town: in the next decades, the city would creep up to the edge of its gardens, and the handsomely rebuilt house serve as the headquarters of many worthy if sometimes impractical campaigns.[4] The fourth William Rathbone's son spearheaded one of the most disastrous, sacrificing the new Whig majority on the City Council after 1835 to the unpopular cause of ending the Anglican monopoly of religious instruction in the schools.[5]

Of course, some element of distortion was necessary to the Rathbone myth: as historians have discovered, the third William Rathbone was more equivocal about the evils of the slave trade than his membership in the Anti-Slavery Society would imply,[6] while the fourth William Rathbone's Jacobin and free-thinking beliefs scarcely fit the dynastic mould of a devout, improving Nonconformity.[7] Yet this inheritance was certainly one of which any child might be proud. The Rathbones were well outside those landed and aristocratic circles tarred with the brush of 'old corruption'; they survived the cataclysm of the French Revolution without losing their rationalist preferences or their historic liberalism. Nor, however, was the family more than distantly linked to that inner circle of Macaulays, Trevelyans, Arnolds and Stephens that formed, in Noel Annan's apt phrase, England's intellectual aristocracy.[8] As dissenters, the Rathbones did not go to Oxford; they did not enter law or the professions; they did not often distinguish themselves as writers, intellectuals or colonial civil servants. Acute in business, culturally philistine, determinedly provincial and a little too high-minded, they spent their reforming energies in municipal improvement and held themselves apart from the capital and its corrupting ways.

By the mid-Victorian period, they were too locally important and much too wealthy to remain on the political margins. Over the course of Eleanor's father's life, the family began negotiating the terms of its incorporation. They were fortunate, at this moment, in the character of the family patriarch, for if the earlier generations were perhaps more colourful and less consistent than their principled descendants painted them, in the figure of the sixth William Rathbone, family traditions found their epitome. William, who was born, like Victoria, in 1819 and died one year after her in 1902, managed the family's rise to national importance without ever sacrificing its indelible local ties or its reputation for fair trading, plain speaking and open-hearted benevolence. His public philanthropy stemmed from private anxiety, however, and his children grew shadowed by both inheritances.

William Rathbone followed from childhood the script laid out for the morally serious, aspiring young dissenter. Guided by his mother, the strong-minded Elizabeth Greg, William grew from a stubborn and bossy little boy to a determined and persuasive young man. Educated locally and sent for a year to Heidelberg University, the young William served a three-year apprenticeship in a firm of Bombay merchants and a clerkship with Baring Brothers before becoming, in 1842, a partner in his father's firm. Five years later, and again in the approved Unitarian fashion, he made a strategic marriage to Lucretia Gair, the daughter of Samuel Stillman Gair, his former colleague at Baring Brothers; Lucretia's brother Henry Wainwright Gair was brought into Rathbone Brothers as a partner some seven years later. Two of Lucretia's sisters would marry sons of Robert Hyde Greg, who had taken over Samuel Greg's enterprise at

Quarry Bank, while a third sister, Elizabeth, married Thomas Ashton, William's closest friend from childhood and his partner in many business ventures. Financial management, cotton supplying and cloth production were now linked together in one cosy cousinhood.

William needed those ties, for when he entered Rathbone Brothers in the early 1840s, the firm was at a crisis in its fortunes. By 1842, working capital had fallen to under £40,000 while profits had averaged only £3,000 annually for the past ten years.[9] Yet the moment was a propitious one: with the opening of the China trade, the ever-expanding demand for cotton, and the gradual stripping away of duties, opportunities were available to merchants reputable enough to win commissions and daring enough to tolerate risk. Rathbone Brothers was well placed on both counts, for although under-capitalized, the firm was respected. William and his brother Sam, who came in as a partner in 1847, could work as commission agents while building up their merchanting activities, diversifying the firm's routes and commodities to deal in tea and silks from China, coffee from Brazil and grain from Egypt. Sam travelled to China twice, establishing branch houses in Canton and Shanghai; after much bitter argument, the firm also accepted the common practice (formally proscribed in China) of using opium as the currency of trade.[10] Rathbone Brothers also acted as Liverpool agents for a line of packet steamers to America, and, in the 1850s, acquired a line of fast sailing clippers, thus winning a strong position in the Eastern trade.[11] When the cotton trade collapsed during the American Civil War, they were able to shift excess capital into securities and other commodities. By 1868, the £5,000 capital that William had invested in 1842 had become a personal fortune of £150,000 – and profits kept mounting.[12] Between 1869 and 1873, this family firm made an impressive £269,000 profit, probably the height of its prosperity.[13]

If their ethical make-up had been different, this could have been only the beginning for William and Sam. But raised as they were to see riches as a spiritual snare, the two young men greeted their unexpected success with more alarm than pleasure. Both had had devout upbringings, and William had been strongly influenced by the teachings of the Reverend John Hamilton Thom, minister of the Unitarian Chapel in Renshaw Street, who had married William's elder sister. Like his friend James Martineau, who presided over Liverpool's other main Unitarian congregation, Thom preached a doctrine that was at once profoundly liberal and deeply anxiety-inducing. Rejecting utterly the idea of man's innate sinfulness and salvation through Christ's atonement, Thom saw Christ as a moral exemplar, a 'perfect man' whose humility and sacrifice Christians must perpetually strive to emulate. Such teachings placed great emphasis upon moral behaviour in everyday life: self-scrutiny and self-sacrifice were the watchwords for a Christianity that was ethical and improving rather than evangelical or chiliastic.[14]

William and Samuel Rathbone took such teachings as a challenge and a guide. While the self-restraint required to build up a family fortune could strengthen character, and while it was surely right to try (as William put it) 'to prevent the whole family from sinking out of the position of independence and usefulness which they had held for several generations', the relentless pursuit of wealth for its own sake had no place in a moral life.[15] 'No one but the most shallow fool can suppose that it is merely [in order] that he should enjoy more than his fellows that God has given him wealth and position,' William insisted; surely they had the responsibility to use their gifts to fulfil their social duties.[16] The two brothers thus sought with 'much anxious consideration' for a 'self-acting guide' by which to regulate their spending. A 10 per cent tithe was not enough, William thought; instead, they should treat all income above that necessary for a healthy and happy family life as a 'trust', and give a healthy proportion to public objects – as much as 50 per cent, if possible.[17]

William, remarkably, did his best to live up to this rigorous standard. He and Lucretia lived modestly with three servants on an income that averaged between £700 and £1,000 per year – no small sum, of course, but a very moderate one for a Liverpool merchant prince. Over twelve years, Lucretia gave birth to five children: William Gair in 1849, Elizabeth Lucretia (Elsie) in 1851, Thomas Ashton in 1856, Henry Gair (Harry) in 1857 and Edward Lucretius (Ted) in 1859; Sam and his wife Rosamond Cuthbert also began a family. Yet parenthood, far from spurring a drive for accumulation, made William and Sam even more determined to guard against the corrosive effects of wealth. Sam, as early as 1854, said that he thought it was mere 'humbug' for them to be 'slaving our constitutions away to leave large fortunes to our children which will probably only get them into grief and debauchery', and William was equally worried about the corrupting effects of wealth.[18] 'I am filled with anxious thought & doubt as to how far I have been right in spending so much of my life & health & strength to acquire for my children means which may become temptations or in giving them indulgences which may unfit them alike for usefulness & peace here or happiness hereafter,' William wrote to his fifteen-year-old daughter Elsie in 1866.[19] Alarmed by 'the number of sons in our class who are growing up in idle listless ways', William and Sam inserted clauses in their wills instructing trustees to withhold the inheritance of any child likely to put the money to bad use.[20]

William and Sam's choices seem, from a business viewpoint, surprising; they were after all choosing to restrict the future growth of a firm they had spent their young manhood building up. Yet their reflections bring out the indelibly familial and moralistic nature of their economic ventures. They did not hanker after aristocratic status; indeed, they did not see wealth as the real goal of economic activity at all.[21] Instead, enterprise was a school for virtue, a crucible for a manly character – prudent, reliable and self-controlled. The reward for the man who had achieved these virtues was thus not wealth *per se*, but rather the standing and capacity to undertake public responsibilities. Far from believing that he had hazarded his children's patrimony, William concluded at the end of his

3. William Rathbone in 1865.

life that his decisions to give away much of his fortune and, later, to leave business for public life, right in themselves, had had the added 'great advantage that my children have had, and have, to work as I did, for their own support'.[22]

As early as the 1840s, then, William began the remarkable philanthropic career for which he was later famous. He supported domestic missions, provident funds, educational efforts and other 'improving' causes; he endowed holiday homes, paid the salaries of clergymen willing to live among the poor, and (as applicants soon realized) responded seriously to personal begging letters (some 900 of which sit, carefully investigated and indexed, among his papers in the Liverpool University Library). He was also a brilliant natural fundraiser, both because his own generosity shamed his fellow merchants into giving, and because he was endlessly optimistic, always ready to believe, as Eleanor later put it, 'that the next notorious skinflint would become a generous benefactor to education, or to nursing, if only the claims of those good causes could be effectively enough laid before him'.[23] But the catalyst for his most famous piece of social work was a devastating personal tragedy: the death of his first wife. Lucretia had never been strong, and the rapid succession of pregnancies told on her. By 1857 – the year she gave birth to Harry – she had consumption, and in 1859, shortly after giving birth to Ted, she died. William, who stayed close to his dying wife's side, was well aware of the difference that skilful nursing had made to her comfort, and now worried about the suffering of those too poor to afford such aid. Would Lucretia's nurse, a Mrs Robinson, care for such invalids if he would pay her salary? Within a few years, this experiment had blossomed into a training school for nurses, a system of professional workhouse nursing and a district nursing scheme throughout Liverpool. For one year William himself acted as one of the 'lady superintendents', accompanying the nurse faithfully on her weekly visits to her patients.[24]

He was soon aided in these tasks by his second wife. Left a widower at the age of forty with five small children, after an interval of three years William married again, still within the business and kin networks that had furnished his first bride. His second wife, Emily Lyle, was a distant cousin; the Lyles, a Londonderry family, had trading interests with the Gregs. But with his second marriage, William began moving in rather different cultural and social circles. Emily's family was Anglican and far more worldly than the high-minded Unitarian Rathbones. Her father was Lord-Lieutenant of the County; her brother and brothers-in-law were barristers, army officers and civil servants. Yet William could not have made a better choice: so successful was his second marriage that Sam, always one for keeping things in the family, sensibly married Emily's recently widowed sister Augusta in 1869, following his own first wife's death two years earlier. Both men were well into middle age and their wives were not young (Emily was thirty on marriage), but they soon had second families. Emily had six children in quick succession: Emily Evelyn (Evie) in 1865, Cyril Charles (who died in infancy) in 1866, Acheson Lyle Rupert (Lyle) in 1868, Bertram Eric (Bertie) in 1870, Eleanor Florence in 1872, and finally Francis Warre (Frank) in 1875.

William's wealth, local standing, keen sense of social duty and – not least – presentable and politically astute wife put one other role in reach. With the agreement of Sam and the three other partners, he withdrew from active management of Rathbone Brothers in 1868 and stood for Parliament as a Liberal. He won his seat easily, benefiting from the surge in Liberal Party fortunes that followed the extension of the urban franchise in 1867 and from the peculiarities of Liverpool's three-member constituency: since Liverpool voters could cast their ballots only for two members, even the locally weak Liberal Party was guaranteed one safe seat. In 1868, then, William and Emily took their young family to London, renting an imposing five-storey townhouse in Princes Gardens, a Georgian terrace where the Joseph Chamberlains also lived. Lucretia's children never lived there permanently, for the boys were at boarding-school and Elsie, now in her late teens, remained with her grandmother at Greenbank. But with a live-in staff, when they came for visits the house must have been bursting at the seams. 'Have you realized that we are now a family of *nine*, equal to the Ashtons?' Elsie wrote to her brother William Gair soon after Eleanor's birth on 12 May 1872. 'Nine always seems to me the boundary of a large family. *Eight* is moderate but nine decidedly a numerous one.'[25]

William Rathbone entered Parliament at precisely the right moment: the early Gladstonian programme of educational reform, fiscal retrenchment, Irish Church disestablishment and moderate social reform accorded perfectly with his views that government should be made at once more democratic and more 'moral'. In 1868 and again in 1874, he pledged himself wholeheartedly to the Gladstonian programme, and – in the arena of social reform especially – sought to press it further. John Vincent, no admirer of the Gladstonian Liberal Party, sees Rathbone and other 'Dissenting capitalists' – men like Samuel Morley or John Bright – as the 'heroic element in Parliamentary Liberalism', 'the one group that surprised by a fine excess'.[26] And, in a party sensitive to the need to recruit such 'new men' of wealth and local standing, William Rathbone had an easy entrée into leading Liberal circles. Family letters from the 1870s show William holding dinner parties for Gladstone, Lord Selborne and Sir Stafford Northcote; dining with Henry Fawcett, James Bryce or Benjamin Jowett; off in his carriage to a party at the Richard Potters or to Lady Waldegrave's 'At Home'; and, always, playing a leading role in Liverpool civic life.[27]

Politically unambitious, William Rathbone never sought ministerial office. Yet, in this heyday of the independent backbench MP, he was an important and reliable member, active in defence of Liverpool's mercantile interests, sensitive to working-class opinion, sympathetic to the concerns of George Howell and other trade unionists (for whom he sponsored some private bills), and astute enough to try to steer his local party away from the most extreme (and politically suicidal) proposals for temperance reform. Yet, despite his almost thirty years in Parliament, he never set much store by national legislation. Believing, in true Gladstonian fashion, that the task of government was less to solve economic or social problems than to provide a framework in which voluntary action would flourish, he looked to local administrative and philanthropic reforms to improve the character and the conditions of the people. With his long experience of civic action, and with two brothers on the Liverpool City Council, he had an expert's understanding (and a reformer's hatred) of the inefficiencies of England's patchwork system of local government, and was especially outraged that local rates, being unrelated to income, burdened the artisan and shop-keeping classes while being scarcely felt by the better off. During his years in Parliament, he supported rate reform, national grants in aid of Poor Law expenditure, and a wider municipal franchise – all of which he hoped would expand the scope of local government while also making it more accountable to those it served.[28] Yet William would never have argued that local services could replace voluntary effort, and his parliamentary years also saw an expansion of his own philanthropic activity – including the extension of district nursing to a national level (which he largely oversaw) and the founding of the University Colleges of Liverpool and North Wales (which he raised endowments for and helped to administer).[29]

By 1879, the year he turned sixty, William Rathbone could look back on a life of ardent striving and practical achievement. He had made a fortune, entered politics, and won a reputation as a benefactor to his city. Each of his children could profit from his endeavours: to each he would leave a portion of his wealth, an easy acquaintanceship with the leading lights of Victorian politics, and a untarnished reputation for probity and virtue. Surely the most impartial observer would conclude that Eleanor Rathbone was indeed lucky, born in the happy heyday of liberalism, in the best of all possible countries, to the best of all possible men.

This is the way Eleanor would have liked her story to be told – and the way Mary Stocks, her official biographer, tried to tell it. That account begins, as Eleanor's biography of her father does, with the lives of the successive William Rathbones, an opening that foregrounds Eleanor's paternal inheritance and positions her as her father's heir. And so accustomed are we to such genealogical elisions that we may not even stop to realize how very strange this particular opening is. Eleanor was, after all, neither an only child nor a boy: she was born into a family crowded with brothers, and to an energetic and strong-minded mother who had her own views about her daughters' destinies. Eleanor, in her later life, erased her mother and her siblings from her own story, but in her childhood they could not be so easily dismissed. Nor could William Rathbone's mantle be seized without some psychic cost.

For children do not live in the public, workaday world or judge their parents by the standards of the philanthropist and the political agent. They live – or at least the children of well-off Victorians lived – in nurseries and schoolrooms, under the constant supervision of nannies and governesses and the more intermittent scrutiny of their powerful parents. The view from the nursery is a radically telescoped one: the horizon is very near, and adults moving across it can entirely blot out the sun. For William Rathbone's children to profit from their advantages, they had first to survive their childhoods, to exit from the nursery door with their vulnerable egos intact. This is a difficult task at the best of times, but it was even more hazardous in a family (and a culture) prone to confuse self-assertion with selfishness. William Rathbone's daughters survived the travails of their upbringing better than his sons – and to understand why this was the case we must go back through the nursery door, and spy on those early encounters through which the growing child crafts a self to call its own.

Eleanor Rathbone never married: she was also shy, somewhat puritanical, and embarrassed when confronted with nakedness or evident sexual feeling. It would be natural for us to see such characteristics as evidence of a 'Victorian' upbringing, even as a clue to the nature of her parents' marriage. But historians have learned to be cautious when generalizing about bourgeois Victorian family life. Our easy assumptions about the sexual prudery of those bearded, frock-coated gentlemen and their crinoline-clad wives has not survived the outpouring of diaries, biographies and histories that show, if not an unbuttoned, sexually emancipated bourgeoisie, quite as much range in domestic and sexual arrangements as we can discover in our own time.[30] What distinguished the Victorian period, Michael Mason points out, was not the uniformity or repressiveness of its sexual practice, but rather an expanding 'anti-sensual mentality' – 'a widespread and principled belief that there should be discipline and unobtrusiveness in all sexual activity'.[31] This was not an ethos that required a Podsnappish recoil from any subject likely to bring a blush to the cheek of a young person; to the contrary, the idealization of restraint and moderation in sexual life was entirely compatible with both overt emotionalism and negotiation over specific sexual practices.

In William Rathbone's family, we find not the behaviour we think typical of Victorian domestic life, but one particular human drama acted out by characters trying to hold to what they thought was the approved script. Or rather, to be precise, we see two such domestic dramas, for William's two marriages and two families were very different. William's first marriage, to Lucretia Gair, was suffused with the conjugal ideals of their Nonconformist upbringings; the young couple lived on a plane of such spiritual and emotional self-abnegation that even the letters William wrote to guide his children after her death blister the page with self-reproach. Lucretia, William insisted, was a paragon among women – firm and kind to her servants, cheerful and devoted to her family, dutiful and loving to her husband, with a 'pure true lovely woman's heart and soul [that] had not been perfected without suffering'.[32] Marriage to such a being was a sacrament, an ideal state in which 'faith, patience, self-sacrifice and devotion have their perfect work' – but a state achieved, he warned his children, only if, 'from the first moment of your married life until the grave closes over one of you', the married couple walk 'with fear and trembling and constant watchfulness'.[33] In his unavailing efforts to assuage his grief, William expounded on the duties of married life, dwelling on everything from the importance of breakfasting together each morning to the injunction not to 'cease to be a lover' by becoming a husband or wife. But above all, he wrote, both sexes must learn self-sacrifice, that it was truly more blessed to give than to receive. The final test of a marriage was whether, at the death of the beloved, one could face 'that awful question – is the soul, which alone still lives, better, more loving, more fit for heaven, owing to its love for and life with me?'[34]

Our only portrait of Lucretia is the saint-like image conjured up in William's letters; we see her only as the consecrated martyr, fulfilling the duties of womanhood so perfectly that her death by consumption seems the inevitable, Dickensian end. For a portrait of William's second wife (and Eleanor's mother), we have, thankfully, more plentiful and less biased sources. True, the photographs we have of Emily show an unsmiling and even forbidding countenance, the visual embodiment of the word 'Victorian'. But the camera can lie, for friends remembered that while Emily may indeed have been (like her husband) 'a saint', she was also 'full of fun'; one son-in-law called her 'the most wonderful and fascinating woman I ever met'.[35] Vigorous, shrewd, plain-spoken and intensely practical, she was admired by her friends, revered and somewhat feared by her children and stepchildren and frankly worshipped by the middle-aged widower she had graciously consented to rescue. Having fretted alone over his children's upbringing, and deluged them with startling reminders of God's watchfulness and their own sinfulness, William found his domestic cares taken efficiently in hand. The religious intensity that had shrouded William's marriage to Lucretia fell away, for Emily declined to leave the established (or Anglican) Church of Ireland to join William's right-thinking, self-scrutinizing faith. Henceforth, the Rathbones would go their separate ways on Sunday mornings: William to Unitarian services (and by the 1880s he was attending Stopford Brooke's ultra-rationalist meetings); Emily to the Anglican cathedral; and the children wherever they wished. Eleanor went to Quaker Meeting, occasionally, and then to nothing at all.

Religious heterodoxy made for marital openness too. William, perhaps to his own surprise, fell deeply and lastingly in love with his wife – a love unencumbered this time by musings on the duties of women or fears for his wife's fragile health. Even after twenty years of marriage his letters to Emily overflow with longing for his 'darling Pet' and his 'own true love'. 'I slept in the room occupied by Henrietta Queen of Charles the First and by Alexander 1st Czar of Russia,' William wrote to Emily during one brief trip; 'I did not dream of Queen Henrietta however but of my own little queen of whom I dreamed persistently all through the night – so you see you are not absent night or day & very pleasant it is to learn that I shall so soon have you in person instead of in dreams.'[36] One young woman student who spent a holiday with the Rathbones in Devonshire and accompanied William Rathbone on his morning rides recalled that – at the age of seventy – he would clamber down from his horse to pick wild flowers for Emily.[37] Later generations of English men and women would laugh at the Victorians' supposed sexual prudishness and paint these marriages as glorified cages, but the merest glance at William and Emily's alliance confounds such characterizations. Emily believed in public work and did her share, but there

4. Emily Rathbone in 1862.

is little evidence that she found her marriage confining, enthroned as she was as the latest Rathbone matriarch, her children and servants gathered around her and her husband casting flowers at her feet.

Yet for all Emily's success as a wife, she does not seem to have influenced her children as powerfully as her husband did, partly because she paid them less mind. Despite her six pregnancies, Emily was not a deeply maternal woman. She was closer to her sisters than to her children and visited them often; she had amateur scientific interests, enjoyed going to lectures, and corresponded with an extensive collection of family retainers and friends. She was an enthusiastic member of a kennel club, and the archives at Liverpool University contain more correspondence with the servants who cared for her beloved Pekinese dogs than they do with the children's governesses and nursemaids.[38] The few letters from her children that survive are dutiful rather than affectionate; the few letters from her to them are practical and firm-minded. Emily asserted herself powerfully during Eleanor's young womanhood, but small children did not especially interest her. She turned her babies over to wet-nurses, nursemaids and governesses, devoting herself to her friendships, interests and her husband's public career. William approved those choices. 'It is necessary and happy that parents should lead a life of constant sacrifice for their children,' he had written to Elsie after Lucretia's death, 'but it is a great evil to the children where the husband is by the wife made to hold a second place.'[39] Marriage and not motherhood lay at the heart of upper-class Victorian family life; Victorian gentlewomen – and still more 'political wives' – did not arrange their lives around their children's needs.[40] In conforming to this pattern, the Rathbone family was not entirely unusual. What was unusual is that maternal distance was combined with intense paternal interest.

William's preoccupation with his children's moral health began with Lucretia's death, when for three years he bore alone the burden of ensuring (as he would have seen it) their fitness for salvation. His remarriage did not lessen his concern. Fearful of imparting the taint of 'selfishness', this most upright of men attacked every childish manifestation of egotism. 'I find it so difficult to be a companion to the boys,' William wrote anxiously to Emily in 1871 – and yet since ('as Whately puts it with reference to Christ') we modify our behaviour so as not to offend those we love, then surely 'to gain this power over one's children would seem almost our first duty'.[41] From the purest of motives, William thus used the threat of paternal unhappiness to shape his children's characters, showering them with moral lessons or, when displeased, reproving them by letter. 'If [God] has placed you where you have more advantages than others it was not that you might be vain and puffed up but that you might make use of your opportunities to fit yourself to be useful to others,' he wrote to his eldest son when he caught him being insolent to the servants – adding, 'and if you are ungrateful and forget this he will assuredly punish you for it'.[42] He tried to drill into his now-motherless children a disdain for the wealth he had piled up so successfully. '[W]hen you or Willie seem to think that you must have every whim gratified,' he wrote in 1866 to the fifteen-year-old Elsie, she should repeat her daily lesson: 'that money is a trust & that the sum that would buy the necessary pleasure or acquisition would do far far more for those less amply provided for'.[43] Not even the memory of their mother was exempt from use in this battle for his children's souls. 'I do long & pray that you may grow up pure & unselfish & energetic & courageous,' William wrote to the sixteen-year-old Ashton, who had been only three when his mother died and who must have found her disappearance bewildering. 'I trust I may never forget the vow I made by your mother's death bed that to seek & strive that you should all do so should be my first object during the remainder of my life.' 'Do help me in this,' he urged his son.[44]

Unsurprisingly, his elder children responded, throughout their lives, with guilt-ridden confessions of inadequacy or tortured professions of love. 'I am conscious of having often fallen far below the standard you have set before your children, and indeed of never having really approached it,' William Gair wrote to his father at the age of forty-one.[45] Their sense of self-worth became heavily dependent on parental approbation, and Emily did little to lighten their load. When she uncharacteristically sent Ashton a birthday letter expressing her pride and satisfaction in him, the young man, then twenty-one, responded with pathetic gratitude. 'I have no stronger conviction than this, that if I should succeed in living a life which will be satisfactory to myself and to those who take an interest in me, it will be due absolutely and entirely under God to Papa and to you, and to the home influences which you have made for us and amongst which you have brought us up,' he wrote, 'and I shall pray God to-night that in the years that are coming, if I have in any way pleased you in the past, I may be ten times more a source of pleasure to you so long as we both shall live.' Yet it is a sign of just how repressive those 'home influences' were that Ashton ended his letter with the admission that since neither he nor Emily were 'given to much expression of feeling', this was 'the very first time I have ever attempted to give any verbal expression to my love and gratitude to you'.[46]

The intense burden of expectation that William placed on his children strikes a chord familiar from such classic Victorian *Bildungsromane* as *The Way of All Flesh* or even Edmund Gosse's *Father and Son*. Yet William, for all his anxiety, was never openly despotic, and when dealing with his daughters he lightened his yoke. Unlike Leslie Stephen who, as Virginia Woolf bitterly remembered, vented his tyrannical temper and histrionic rages on his daughters in particular, William was gentler, more loving and far more indulgent with his girls. His closest relations had always been with women: he admired and loved his mother, adored his wives, and collaborated throughout his life with women reformers and philanthropists – including Florence Nightingale, who admitted her dependence upon him in a fulsome letter of condolence to Emily after his death. Yet William also favoured his daughters because he believed absolutely that men and women should be held to what feminists were later to call an 'equal moral standard', and had concluded that it was men who were not making the grade. 'Women are generally much more self sacrificing & gentle & less expecting than men,' he wrote to Elsie in 1861; 'they are so I believe naturally; but their life also is generally free from that struggle for existence which unless carefully watched hardens men's character.'[47] Determined that his boys should be 'self sacrificing' as well, William thus 'watched' them so 'carefully' as to resemble a Benthamite jailer – exhorting them to avoid 'immodest companionship', 'the excitement of wine', and, above all, any 'loose and disreputable talk about women'. 'Next to the direct influence of God through revelation and conscience, the most holy influence I know is that which pure and good women exercise over us,' he wrote to Willie in 1861; how, then, 'can anyone who knows what women may be when pure, have any part or share' in the 'sin which consigns such numbers . . . to misery and degradation?'[48]

William never ceased to chastise his sons for profligacy or laziness or to look to his daughters with pride and affection. But the younger group of children as a whole – Emily's children and the two who were mere infants at Lucretia's death – seem to have had less repressive upbringings. Happiness blunted William's feelings of anxiety; parliamentary responsibilities left him less time to write hectoring letters. Their problems were different ones: whereas the Rathbone 'senior division' may have received more paternal attention than they wanted, the younger children found themselves jockeying for position and approval. Eleanor, who entered the nursery in 1872 to find Evie, Lyle and Bertie already there, discovered almost at birth that she was not the centre of the universe and learned to watch her siblings for signs of unfair advantage. As the second youngest, she was not well placed to outwit her brothers and sister, yet even as a small child Eleanor did her best to win her parents' love.

The few brief glimpses we have of Eleanor are amusing in view of her later life, for they show a grave little girl with a strong need for approval, a child desperate to do right. When Eleanor was only three, William wrote to his wife that the little girl 'seems to retain things for meditation',[49] and Ashton, that same summer, reported an early passion for justice. When Bertie came home ill, Ashton wrote:

> I enquired the cause of his indisposition of Eleanor and she told me with great indignation, a sad tale of the miscarriage of justice. Lyle had been very naughty and had gone into the garden and eaten the *wrong peas* and given some of them to Bertie and poor Bertie had a bad pain and Lyle had none. . . .[50]

But if this precocious infant was scrutinizing and judging her brothers with her 'big serious eyes', she was also scrutinizing and judging herself. 'Miss Eleanor' had asked him whether she ought not to be going to church, her father reported to Emily a few months later, and he had told her it would be too long and tiring for 'a little body like her'. 'She is getting an awful little prig,' he wrote, 'always asking whether to do something would not be good for her.'[51]

A child so 'priggish' as to merit the label from a man like William Rathbone must have been truly insufferable; all we can hope is that these infant anxieties subsided. However preoccupied or intimidating her parents, the love and attention of her elder brothers and sisters may have made her feel more secure. Evie, Lyle, Bertie, Eleanor and Frank were petted and played with by their elder siblings, whose ideas of childish activities ran to pony rides and kite-flying rather than spiritual self-examination. Ashton, a generous-hearted and sensitive young man, grew genuinely close to his younger half-brothers and half-sisters (especially Evie), and Elsie, displaced in her father's affections by her stepmother's arrival,

5. Eleanor as a young child.

became a surrogate mother to Eleanor, Frank and Bertie.[52] Yet Eleanor, through-out her childhood, kept her reputation, if not for 'priggishness', at least for a sort of docile goodness. According to her Aunt Augusta, who often had all the chil-dren with her at a house Sam and William owned jointly in the Lake District during the summers, while Elsie was 'rather fussy' and the boys (unsurprisingly) a handful, Ellie was 'such a pet & so good', so unspoilt and so – the cardinal virtue – 'unselfish'.[53] Eleanor herself remembered the atmosphere in the Rathbone summer schoolroom as rather boisterous and intemperate,[54] and Aunt Augusta did once report to Emily about 'the instinct of teazing developing itself sadly *espe-cially* in *Ellie!*'[55] But for the most part Eleanor Rathbone's childhood seems to have passed placidly. What anxieties and trials there were (and what childhood is free of them?), no one saw fit to mention.

To the adult members of the household, and especially to William, the 1880s brought new worries. As the Liberal Party's focus shifted from peace, retrench-ment, education and reform to the murkier waters of Irish 'pacification' and

Home Rule, William Rathbone began to feel out of date. He was uncomfortable with Liverpool Liberalism's growing dependence on Irish support, certain that this alliance would ultimately weaken its position in this most sectarian and 'Orange' of towns. In 1880, aware of his reservations, the Liverpool Liberal Association de-selected him, turning instead to Lord Ramsay, the son of the Earl of Dalhousie. Ramsay was duly elected, but (as William Rathbone had expected) such deference to Irish interests simply converted Liberals into Unionists six years in advance of national trends; on Ramsay's unexpected elevation to the Lords, the seat was lost to the Tories.[56] William Rathbone himself contested South-West Lancashire in 1880 and characteristically recovered from his defeat there through fundraising efforts for the newly planned University College at Liverpool.

This local rehearsal for the Party's national crisis over Home Rule did not end William Rathbone's career any more than the final split in 1886 ended Gladstone's. A few months later, he was asked to fight a by-election in the Welsh seat of Caernarvonshire, a Liberal stronghold. Devout, chapel-going North Wales in some ways suited William Rathbone better than contentious and often corrupt Liverpool, and he served the constituency faithfully for the next fifteen years, skirting the most fervent manifestations of Welsh nationalism (and of Irish Home Rule), while supporting Church disestablishment, educational reform and the creation of a University College of North Wales.[57] Yet, severed from his former political base, his importance to the Liberal Party declined. Although he remained on the Party's Gladstonian wing, he found himself unable to vote for the Home Rule bill in 1893, and expressed himself in a painful private correspondence with his admired leader.[58] He was, by this stage, more a local than a national figure: there is little evidence in the family papers of dinner parties and confabulations like those of the early seventies.

Business worries followed hard on the heels of political disaffection. Rathbone Brothers had built its position in the heyday of shipping and general merchandising, and its ageing partners were unprepared for the cut-throat competition and increasing specialization of the 1870s and 1880s. As early as 1866, in fact, William Rathbone had worried that he and Sam had 'somewhat allowed things to drift';[59] ten years later, with William in Parliament, Sam on the City Council, and other partners tied up in subsidiary banking and trading concerns, 'drift' had turned into dissension. The London office, now in the joint hands of Thomas Lidderdale (also a director of the Bank of England) and William's eldest son William Gair Rathbone, favoured investment over trade, while the Liverpool partners, aware of Rathbone Brothers' good standing in the tea, silk and grain trades, wished to rebuild the merchanting side of the firm. Sam, now over sixty, appealed to William for help. 'Considering how much time you have devoted to the service of the country,' he wrote tartly in 1884, 'I think you might devote four or five days to the consideration of the firm's affairs at what I regard as the crisis of its destinies.'[60] And yet, once again, William and Sam saw trouble as a blessing in disguise. 'As Sam said last night,' William wrote to Emily, 'we have had unusually happy prosperous lives, and if now we have some difficult task to get through and less success and more difficulties to face, we must face them manfully and cheerfully.' Their own father had made little effort to safeguard his business for his sons, and William, unsurprisingly, thought a similar 'check in the almost too continuous flow of prosperity' could 'be good not only for myself but for the boys'. ('Sam says he sees a decided change in them already,' he reported optimistically.)[61] Hoping that adversity would make men of them, Sam and William decided to give the boys their head. In 1885, the four partners who had run Rathbone Brothers since the 1840s – William Rathbone, Samuel Greg Rathbone, Thomas Kenyon Twist and Henry Wainwright Gair – all retired. William Gair Rathbone and Thomas Lidderdale were left in charge of the London office, William's second son Ashton and one other partner in charge of the Liverpool side.

But William and Emily had other cares. Bertie, the son one year Eleanor's elder, had always been a sickly child and in the early 1880s was diagnosed as epileptic – in those days a little-understood and much-feared illness, whose victims were often sequestered from the public gaze. Throughout his childhood, Bertie was kept at home (usually at Greenbank), and William's letters from these years refer anxiously to his little son's 'twitches' and to endless, usually fruitless, consultations with specialists.[62] Worse, in the autumn of 1886, after writing happy letters about a prospective engagement to an entirely suitable 'Miss Greg', Lucretia's youngest, the sunny and charming Ted, was drowned in Derwentwater. Ted had been a partner at Ross T. Smyth, a Liverpool firm founded to take over Rathbone Brothers' trade in grain, and had been busy raising funds for the university. The only silver lining was that the tragedy brought twenty-one-year-old Evie and her cousin Hugh Reynolds Rathbone together. Hugh was also a partner at Ross T. Smyth, where, he wrote broken-heartedly to Evie, Ted had been 'more than an elder brother' to him.[63] Two years later, Hugh and Evie married.

Throughout these difficult years, Eleanor lived quietly at Princes Gardens. The nursery and schoolroom emptied as Evie married, Lyle went off to Fettes and Frank to Eton, and Bertie spent long stretches of time with Elsie at Greenbank. She had a succession of governesses but somehow none lasted very long. Evie later told Margery Fry that Eleanor deliberately tried to rid herself of these incubi;[64] she remembered only one German woman, Marianne Müller, with affection. Sheltered and often alone, Eleanor became dreamy and bookish. Her more literal-minded siblings tried to keep an eye on her – 'don't let Ellie read Matthew Arnold's *poetry*,' Ashton wrote to Evie in alarm in 1886, 'it is the most unsuitable literature possible for her'.[65] Yet Eleanor enjoyed her solitary girlhood. Many years later, she let slip that she thought the haphazard education given Victorian girls of her culture and class had had its positive side,[66] and certainly unsupervised rambling through one's father's private library seems preferable to Eton's languid snobbery or Thomas Arnold's sermons-and-cold-showers regimen for young Christian gentlemen at Rugby.

There was also one enormous compensation. With his elder sons tied up in business, Elsie and Bertie in Liverpool, Evie engaged, and the younger boys away at boarding-school, William's fatherly attention turned to Eleanor. In the evenings, when Emily was away (as she often was) visiting one of her sisters, they would read together and walk and talk in Hyde Park. And what did they discuss? 'Social duties', no doubt – the subject of William's only important book, and one he could not refrain from expounding to his children. They must have made passers-by smile, that seemingly ill-suited pair: the fresh-faced, quiet young girl with bows in her hair and her bewhiskered and voluble elderly father. But in those conversations was born an elective affinity – a bond forged of Eleanor's love and loyalty and William's startled recognition that the 'character' he had sought to cultivate in his sons had been flourishing, undetected, in this feminine soil. 'She is a strange girl,' William wrote to Emily after one such conversation. 'I wish her religious feelings were stronger & sense of reverence, still I hope she will grow & if she does take a strong religious (as contradicting a theological) turn she will be very strong for good. I will work and pray towards that end.'[67]

Chapter 2

Mothers and Mentors

To this point we have little sense of Eleanor's personality – unsurprisingly, since she lived at home and her parents rarely mentioned their least troublesome child. We know that she walked and talked with her father in Hyde Park, accompanied her parents on their sojourns to Liverpool, and was educated rather haphazardly by governesses: most probably, her life was a lonely one. In 1889, at the age of seventeen, she was sent for a year to the Kensington High School – a school that, as one of the new creations of the Girls' Public Day School Company, was supposed to offer a serious and progressive education but that Rathbone later remembered as arduous and excessively narrow.[1] At the close of that year, if the evidence of *The Times* is to be believed, she conformed to that ultimate ritual of her sex and class and was presented at Court, just before her eighteenth birthday.[2] Presentation at Court required not only unimpeachable membership in the 'right circles' but also the right dress (*décolleté* and with a four-yard train), the right headdress (with three ostrich feathers), the right deportment (curtsying to the Sovereign while inching backwards towards the door) and a mamma to see the nervous débutante through the whole thrilling (or appalling) affair.[3] It is almost impossible to imagine earnest, awkward Eleanor going through this ritual – still less embarking on the marriage market of the London 'Season' – but if Beatrice Webb could do it, presumably she could as well. Yet we know nothing of what she thought of the parties and balls she attended, chaperoned by her mother or her half-brother William's beautiful American wife.

In 1891, however, at the age of nineteen, she comes sharply into focus through her encounter with one of the great figures of late Victorian science, Oliver Lodge. Lodge, a brilliant physicist with an attractive wife and a steadily growing brood of young children, had been appointed Professor of Physics at the opening of the University College in Liverpool in 1881. Lodge was a mainstay of the British Association and an enthusiastic experimental scientist, and he was a welcome addition to Liverpool's intellectual aristocracy. Although the Rathbone family spent much of the year in London, William Rathbone's important role in the founding and direction of the college threw the two men together and they

6. Oliver Lodge with his wife and children, late 1890s.

became good friends.[4] In July 1891, William urged Lodge to join Emily, Eleanor, Frank and himself for a good holiday in the Austrian Alps. 'A miser in holidays is more shortsighted than a miser in gold, for the latter does not deteriorate, but brains do,' William wrote. Lodge must come as their guest, he insisted, since 'we . . . are not, perhaps, as economical as we might be', and thus 'should feel uncomfortable on any other terms'.[5]

Lodge accepted gratefully, and his memoirs recall the holiday as a time of unalloyed happiness. The Rathbones, for all their moderation in daily life, were great holiday-makers. They spent several weeks every winter at their villa at Alassio on the Italian Riviera and long summer holidays at a twenty-bedroom house on Lake Bassenthwaite that William Rathbone and his brother Sam owned jointly, and they occasionally rented castles in Scotland or houses in Devonshire for added variety. They were also intrepid travellers: business interests took William to America, Sam to China, and their sons to South America and India; family and business ties led to regular trips to New England; the demands of 'health' drove Harry to the Alps and Bertie, astonishingly, to Australia; and sheer curiosity took Elsie in 1880 and Emily in 1904 as far as Egypt. For the Rathbones, the holiday they shared with Oliver Lodge late in the summer of 1891 was a modest one. Emily and Eleanor, having travelled to Bayreuth for the Wagner festival, met William, Frank and Lodge at Innsbruck. From there the group went together to the Austrian province of Carinthia (Kärnten) and devoted itself to pleasure, taking regular excursions in open carriages through the mountain passes and green valleys.[6]

But for Lodge, the vacation was a magical interlude of moonlit drives and intense conversations with Eleanor, 'at that time', according to his sister, 'a very beautiful, rather dreamy girl'.[7] Lodge was a man of equally powerful intellectual and sexual drives; his memoirs admit that the sexual repression of his early years had left him, by age twenty-five, in 'a sort of raging fever'.[8] Now forty and apart from his wife – who was, during these years, almost continuously pregnant – Lodge appears to have fallen more than a little in love with Eleanor. A photograph from this trip, which Lodge retained, shows her standing between her two elderly parents; she is well dressed, unsmiling and strikingly young. She became, his memoirs claim, a 'great friend',[9] but the draft of a letter of thanks that Lodge sent to Emily on his way home reveals more perturbed feelings. 'I should like to feel that I had begun a friendship which would not lightly or briefly end,' he wrote to Emily about her daughter, 'and though that may not be possible or likely let me hereby. . . .' But here the author became troubled and the draft degenerates. What did Oliver Lodge want? A whole series of phrases are crossed out: 'she ought not to prevent a man old enough . . . an aged man . . . visiting. . . .' Lodge, evidently, wanted to see Eleanor – alone – as much as he could, but in the end, he simply asked Emily to thank Eleanor 'for her unconscious contribution to the pleasures of the time & for the help her fresh young life has been to a morose & selfmistrustful student during the best holiday he ever had, indeed almost the happiest month he ever spent'.[10]

Emily, remarkably, responded equably to what verged on a declaration of love for her daughter from a married man. And here we are confronted again with the paradoxical nature of the private life of Victorians of this milieu and class. Friendships between older men and younger women were tolerated and even encouraged in enlightened families like the Rathbones precisely because mothers felt able to trust the guidance of their spirited children to men of such respectability and standing.[11] Herbert Spencer and Beatrice Webb, Mark Pattison and Meta Bradley, Oliver Lodge and Eleanor Rathbone: there were many such unlikely Pygmalions and Galateas. The pattern was tolerable because its boundaries were understood: not until H.G. Wells shattered convention by taking his dearest friends' daughter to bed would the erotic undertones of such relationships become explicit and the relationships themselves dangerous. 'Eleanor I am sure feels flattered to have been able to contribute to the pleasure of your holiday & has much & gratefully appreciated the patience & pains you took to explain & interest her in so much so deeply interesting,' Emily rather inelegantly responded. 'I think it has opened to her a new world in many ways & it is seldom a girl has a chance of "thinking it out" on such subjects to a man of intellect and training such as yours.'[12]

7. Emily, Eleanor and William
on holiday, near Vienna, 1891.

Emily was not unaware of the dangers, though: while she did nothing to prevent the blossoming intellectual friendship between Eleanor and Oliver Lodge, she did police its borders, making sure that Lodge remained, above all, her own confidant and a family friend. When the family returned to Liverpool for the winter recess, a comical game of cat-and-mouse ensued. Lodge invited Eleanor to see his new telescope and look at the moons of the planets; Eleanor responded that her mother 'says that she would *love* to see the telescope' and that the two of them would come together.[13] Lodge sent Eleanor books, only to find them appropriated by Emily, who declined to pass on those she felt were too speculative or whose influence 'might not be good on a young mind'.[14] Lodge sent the family a set of photographs of himself with the suggestion that they choose one: Emily wrote that the family had chosen 'the 3/4 length', since 'Eleanor says it shows what a "big man he is"'. 'That may be interpreted in more ways than one,' Emily added, turning the knife, '& you may make it into a very complimentary opinion if you like.'[15] Emily then sent the photographs back, to the chagrin of Eleanor, who had to write to Lodge privately asking for a portrait of her own.[16] For the next eighteen months, the two corresponded regularly.

Eleanor's voice in this correspondence is a complex one, both extraordinarily innocent and oddly mature. The innocence is unfeigned: she does not resent her mother's interventions and makes no effort to see Lodge alone; she is able to write, astonishingly, that Lodge's energy 'oozes out of you into me' with no consciousness of the sexual connotations of her words.[17] Her letters are neither flirtatious nor coy – unlike her mother's, which evince more than a little sexual jealousy. 'Don't make her conceited!' Emily wrote to Lodge admonishingly. 'Conceit is bad & she must not overwork to justify your thinking her head worth cultivating.'[18] Yet Eleanor, while never conceited, seems to have accepted from the outset that her head was indeed worth cultivating. Although she often admits her ignorance, she trusts her own judgement; she does not seem surprised that Lodge, a busy university professor with a loving family and a wide circle of friends, should find the time to write her such long letters. Twenty years his junior, and with a few scattered years of schooling behind her, she writes back to Lodge as his equal.

And she valued his attention, having led, to this point, a rather lonely life. By the time the family returned to London in the spring of 1892, Eleanor had begun to rely on Lodge's letters to give her intellectual stimulation and some sense of an independent personality. 'It was very nice to hear so much Liverpool news,' she wrote to Lodge in March 1892. 'My sisters seldom write, and when they do, their letters are generally highly domestic, the one full of servants, the other of babies.'[19] Lodge, on the other hand, wanted to know what she was reading – and received reports on everything from Meredith, George du Maurier, Rhoda Broughton and other popular novelists, to Keats ('almost too luscious . . . for an English spring'),[20] to George Frederick Wright's *The Ice Age in North America and Its Bearings upon the Antiquity of Man*. He tried to encourage her scientific interests, sending her tickets to a lecture at the Royal Institute 'on the surface-film of Water', but was told that while it had been 'very amusing' and 'pleasantly delivered', the lecturer had 'quite omitted to explain what the film was, confining himself to its effects on its inhabitants', leaving her entirely in the dark.[21]

Lodge's motives in writing to Eleanor were mixed. A staunch supporter of women's education (he had begun his teaching career delivering lectures on mathematics to women students at Bedford College), he undoubtedly wished to encourage the daughter of his dear friends. Yet he also wrote to Eleanor because, as he told Emily, she gave him 'pleasure'. To understand the nature of that pleasure, we need to look more closely at one other aspect of Lodge's life – one that also involved a controlled form of transgression. Oliver Lodge, like Gladstone, A.J. Balfour and many other late-Victorian gentlemen, was from the 1880s intensely absorbed in metaphysical speculations about the nature and limits of the physical world. He read Frederic Myers's studies of telepathy, then arousing some scientific interest, and, having succeeded in replicating Myers's findings through experiments with several young girls in Liverpool, in 1884 joined the Society for Psychical Research.[22] From that point his interest intensified. When the famous Boston medium, Mrs Piper, came to Liverpool in 1889, Lodge welcomed her into his home (causing, his sister recalled, 'some agitation among the maids who did not appreciate the odd voices which penetrated from my brother's study every night without apparent cause').[23] The Rathbones were aware of his interest; indeed, while on holiday with them, he had made some experiments on 'thought transference' with the daughters of Count von Liro, with whom the party had stayed.[24] (William, at least, never thought much of the whole thing. There was an immense difference between the revelations transmitted 'by raps, tunes, and scents, and drapery . . . and those handed down to us through the peasants of Galilee', he told Lodge.[25])

Mediumship and spiritualist practice in the late Victorian period violated the norms of class segregation and sexual order, placing frock-coated gentleman scientists and 'spiritual' young working-class girls together in darkened rooms. Alex Owen, examining mediumship and seances with a feminist and Lacanian eye, argues that these 'darkened rooms' provided a psychic space within which late-Victorian participants could surrender their normal gendered and class-bound selves – a space in which women could express aggression, desire and other taboo feelings, and middle-class men could shed the carapace of respectability and reserve that they wore in daily life.[26] It is possible that Lodge saw Eleanor's 'dreaminess' as akin to the 'psychic faculty' he had found in the Count's daughters; certainly it is significant that he thought her contribution to his pleasure – like the medium's ability to make manifest beings from the spirit world – was an 'unconscious' one. At the least, Lodge's spiritualist interest and the interest in Eleanor were products of the same cause: the psychic need that drove Lodge and his friends into Liverpool's sweatshops to search for telepathic young girls also drove Lodge's dogged pursuit of Eleanor.

But in Eleanor Rathbone, Oliver Lodge seems to have met his match, for while she responded openly to his attention and suggestions, the very innocence and 'freshness' that Lodge found so tantalizing was also her shield. Her responses to his attempts to interest her in his metaphysical and religious speculations show an almost uncanny – although probably still 'unconscious' – ability to deflect his more dangerous gifts. Eleanor gladly read the poems of Frederic Myers when Lodge sent them to her, but while she admiringly concluded that Myers 'must be a person with large capacities for reverence and affection', she was able to discuss even the love poems placidly.[27] She dismissed novels and lectures that touched on the occult as 'interesting but disagreeable', making her rationalist preferences apparent.[28] Even Rhoda Broughton's *Nancy*, a story of a May–December marriage between a handsome and affectionate middle-aged man and an 'innocent' (and hence cruel) young girl she dismissed as 'rather amusing'.[29] And she was far too young, and much too serious, to tolerate Lodge's view that religious scepticism could be a wholesome state of mind. 'It sounds to me,' she wrote back to him:

> as though you thought scepticism & belief were mere subjective states of mind with no truth outside themselves corresponding to one of them. Whereas surely religious belief must either be well-grounded or not. You cannot think that it is not (well-grounded) because you yourself profess it. But if it is, surely it cannot be wholesome to be ignorant of truth, especially of such a truth (if it *is* truth) which has such a direct bearing on action, and which seems to transform (for those who have it) the whole of life & thought as completely . . . as sun does a country landscape, and without which the life of some people is a very pleasant episode, and of others, what F. Myers calls it, a waking nightmare. The worst finally of scepticism seems to me to be that you have no answer to give when some person, sick or unhappy or both, for whom this life is a failure, questions you with his eyes, and you feel that the merest stranger . . . is better able to help than you. If you mean merely that it is better to be sceptical than to profess belief which you have not really got, that of course, but you mean more than that don't you? Mr. Balfour said the same thing. I do not understand it.[30]

Eleanor, at this stage, could accept that religious faith might not be 'well-grounded' but not that uncertainty was a healthy state of mind. Positivist rather than romantic, she preferred knowledge – however painful – to mysticism, and in true Victorian fashion, went back to the Greeks. By the spring of 1892, she was struggling her way through Aristotle, but reported to Lodge that she was constantly coming up against subjects – mathematics, logic – of which she was ignorant. The experience nourished her incipient feminism: 'It is a great disadvantage to have been educated as a woman.'[31]

And to Lodge she confided, in May of that year, a desire she scarcely dared to mention. She had been able to convince her parents to allow her some tutoring in the classics and had been lucky enough to secure the services of Janet Case, a classical scholar who had studied at Girton, and who would go on to teach Virginia Woolf Greek some ten years later.[32] Case was a demanding and gifted teacher, passionately interested in Greek literature and philosophy and convinced of its continued relevance. She was also a role model for the young Eleanor – a woman who had found in her studies, in her friendships with other women, and in London's progressive circles a full and happy intellectual and emotional life. Case, Rathbone wrote to Lodge in May 1892, had been urging her to go to Cambridge University to attend the philosophy lectures offered by Henry Jackson and Archer Hind. 'That sort of excellent but impracticable advice always wakes in me a temporary craving for stronger drink, which has not yet subsided.' Aware of her mother's likely opposition, she warned Lodge not to say anything about the plan to Emily – on this subject alone showing a willingness to deceive.[33] The Cambridge plan was a serious one: Eleanor had actually taken the Cambridge Higher Local examination in December 1889, during her year at the Kensington High School and had passed in the third class.[34] Through the winter of 1892 and the spring of 1893, she made a serious effort to prepare herself to read philosophy, working steadily with Janet Case on her Greek. The effort involved must have been enormous for a girl with one year of formal schooling, but the prize was a worthy one. Henry Jackson was dazzling Cambridge undergraduates with his brilliant lectures on Plato and was also a strong supporter of women's education. The first Cambridge women's colleges had been founded a full decade before their Oxford sisters, and Newnham, on which Eleanor's sights were set, had almost three times as many women students as Somerville. The college was famous, too: in 1890, opponents of women's higher education were startled to learn that a Newnham student – Philippa Fawcett, the daughter of Henry Fawcett and Millicent Garrett Fawcett – had been placed above the Senior Wrangler on the Mathematics Tripos.[35] Oliver Lodge, who knew Newnham's founders Henry and Eleanor Sidgwick through the Society for Psychical Research, thought Eleanor's choice a good one, and recruited the influential Myers to write her a letter detailing the advantages of a Cambridge education.

It was to no avail: once Emily found out about the plan, she objected. If Eleanor wanted to attend lectures, she could go to Oxford, where her brothers had been and where the Warden of Somerville – 'a sensible person & by no means stupid' – could be trusted to keep an eye on her.[36] Somerville was still a hall of residence and not a college, and its rules were draconian – even meetings with brothers from neighbouring colleges were strictly supervised.[37] 'I am much bothered, not to say half distracted by the Oxford v. Cambridge question,' Eleanor wrote to Lodge unhappily in July 1893. 'I wonder what makes you think Somerville Hall more "curbed." It is evidently the general impression and is a great drawback.'[38] Emily's voluble objections had given Eleanor pause, and by September relations between mother and daughter had become so strained that William himself intervened.

'What yr mother & I are most anxious you should do,' William wrote to his youngest daughter, 'is that you should go to Oxford, Cambridge or stay at home exactly as you may think will be best for *yourself & your future happiness*; that is what we wish & what ought to decide you.' Emily, it seems, had been eager to have Eleanor at Oxford partly so that she could be a restraining influence on her younger brother Frank, who would also be there, but William thought this consideration was 'too uncertain to be allowed to weigh against whichever is most likely to promote yr own improvement & happiness'. His own concern, he wrote, was that she had been worrying over the decision for almost a year,

8. Eleanor with Ashton, around the time of the Newnham plan.

showing a weakness of mind and character that made him fear for her future happiness. She was sadly given to indecisiveness, he wrote, and 'it will mean a very unhappy wasted life if you do not cure yourself of it'. He and her mother would happily accept any decision she would make, he wrote, and would 'do our best to enable you to carry it out with comfort, hope & confidence'.[39]

William, it seems, did his best to take his daughter's part. 'I am hardly allowed to mention the subject of colleges to E.,' Emily complained to Lodge the day after William wrote his letter.[40] Yet William misunderstood the cause of Eleanor's distress. Nothing was wrong with her mind; what she was suffering from was something close to a nervous breakdown, brought on by the unbearable tension between her overwhelming desire to go to Cambridge – for which she had prepared for more than a year – and the equally powerful imperative to sacrifice her own desires to her mother's will. Emily had put Eleanor in an impossible position, insisting on the one hand that her daughter was free to make her own decision, and on the other hand that – as she complacently wrote to Lodge – Eleanor could scarcely be happy deciding 'in her own favour' against her parents' wishes.[41] In the end, worn down by moral blackmail, Eleanor 'chose' Oxford, although by the time the decision was made she was 'not in a natural state of mind at all'.[42] Emily made light of the conflict: once Eleanor had settled in Oxford, she wrote to Lodge, 'much of the "fog" in which her mind has been enveloped will clear off'.[43] Yet the core truth remained: Emily had played fast and loose with her daughter's mental health in order to control her destiny.

This episode is an extraordinarily interesting one, complicating as it does some of our most cherished assumptions about Victorian family life. Taking Virginia Woolf's case to heart, we expect to find fathers thwarting their daughters' ambitions, establishing in the domestic realm a pattern of exclusion and subordination reproduced in public life. In Eleanor's case, however, both her father and a well-known university professor supported her plan; it was her mother who wished her to subordinate intellectual endeavour to family needs. Yet both contemporary debates and recent historical works reveal that this pattern was not atypical. When the *Nineteenth Century* published a series of articles on 'The Revolt of the Daughters' one year after Eleanor went up to Oxford, all correspondents were agreed that it was the mothers who were aghast at their daughters' requests for latch-keys and liberty, the mothers against whom the daughters were revolting.[44] Olive Banks, examining the lives of prominent Victorian and Edwardian feminists, finds that fathers were more likely than mothers to support their daughters' efforts to break out of conventional female roles.[45]

And some daughters, once laden with degrees and accomplishments, retaliated. Florence Nightingale's *Cassandra*, the autobiographies of Helena Swanwick and Vera Brittain, May Sinclair's *Mary Olivier* and numerous other works pulse with rage against mothers who attempted to circumscribe their daughters' ambitions.[46] Mothers appear in such works as petty, selfish and small-minded – or, alternatively, as so enamoured of the cult of female sacrifice as to be eager to arrange not only their own but also their daughters' martyrdom. Thus Virginia Woolf was bereft by her mother's death but determined to unlearn these lessons in subordination, writing that the first task of the woman writer was 'killing the angel in the house'.[47]

But Emily, unlike William's first wife Lucretia, was not an angel in the house and for that reason must have found her daughter's bid for independence hard to bear. Emily was an intelligent woman who read voraciously and held staunchly liberal views. Far from discouraging Eleanor's intellectual ambitions, she had shared much of her early enthusiasm, facilitated her correspondence with Lodge, and accompanied her to lectures. And Emily, while remarkable, was not entirely atypical of her class. It was precisely *because* mothers had themselves so successfully entered public life, one contributor argued in the *Nineteenth Century*, that their daughters wished to do so as well; and if these 'happy, well-employed, and resourceful' mothers found their daughters' demands puzzling, they should simply ask themselves why they also found it necessary to write books and plays, to 'sit on committees here and committees there, slumming in the East, drinking tea and promoting "causes" in the West'.[48] At the heart of this generational conflict was not the question of whether education and public involvements were appropriate for women – since both mothers and daughters agreed that they were – but rather whether the daughters would, as their mothers had done, combine their new roles with maternity and family life.

And this was the crux of the matter. In upper-class circles, as Pat Jalland has shown, marriage marked not the end of independence but the beginning of adult freedoms: marriage gave a woman public recognition, domestic authority, a settlement (the income from which she often controlled herself), and sometimes – if their husbands were public men – some political influence as well.[49] Women like Emily saw no contradiction between marriage and the life of the mind; indeed, as their husbands' advisers and their daughters' instructors and guardians, their domestic and intellectual authority overlapped. Yet their daughters, in demanding education and careers hitherto reserved for sons, almost unavoidably denigrated this earlier model of womanly accomplishment, dismissing domestic education as amateurish and maternal power (because sexual) as despotic. Small wonder Victorian matriarchs reacted ambivalently to demands that, while ostensibly attacking patriarchal power, identified hitherto masculine types of authority as the only kind of authority worth having.

No issue threw these conflicts into sharper relief than that of higher education, since mothers, by the 1890s, were well aware that Newnham and Girton graduates were very unlikely to marry. 'If you're naughty, you'll have to go to Girton!' Beatrice Webb's sister Georgie Meinertzhagen warned her children, and other daughters also remembered that higher education was seen almost as a physical disfigurement, 'an intellectual smallpox . . . that would unfit them for the marriage market'.[50] So widespread were such fears that Mrs Sidgwick actually undertook to trace the subsequent lives of college-educated women, only to find that 90 per cent of her cohort did in fact remain single.[51] The fact that these single women were useful and happy did not lessen the unease of mothers, who recalled the straitened lives of 'superfluous' sisters and aunts with pain, but viewed the rise of a 'glorified spinsterhood' with apprehension.

In the end, faced with Emily's inflexible opposition to Cambridge, Eleanor gave in – but, as she herself came to realize, a defeat that still brought her one of the best educations available in England was scarcely a rout. Her own perplexity over her decision between Oxford and Cambridge, Eleanor wrote to Lodge, 'shows I suppose the perversity of human nature, as a year ago still more 3 years ago I should have thought a year at either the highest summit of earthly bliss'.[52] While Eleanor went to Oxford in a 'fog' and to some extent half-heartedly, the choice was a good one. Emily looked to Somerville to save her daughter from the questionable Mrs Sidgwick and Newnham's famous feminism, but the year after Eleanor went up the Association for the Education of Women at Oxford voted to turn Somerville Hall into Somerville College and renewed its campaign to admit women to degrees. Eleanor, the only student of her year to attempt the difficult classical curriculum of *Literae Humaniores*, found the hopes of the college pinned upon her and her ostensibly private choices transformed into part of the woman's cause.

Before entering Somerville, Eleanor gathered together the many books and papers Lodge had lent her and returned them to him, and except for a few friendly but restrained letters, their correspondence ended there.[53] Lodge had always been its instigator – Eleanor had written, only half in jest, that she found his promptness in answering her letters 'beautiful but terrible'[54] – and as she grew more intellectually confident her ability to act as the unconscious medium of Lodge's pleasure surely lessened. Lodge cannot have cherished the letters she wrote that last summer in quite the same way as he did her first happy answer to his offer to show her the moons of the planets. Despite her plea that she was 'scientifically too low down on the scale even for a foolometer', she had agreed to correct his proofs – and, possibly to Lodge's surprise, subjected his chapters on Ptolemy, Kepler and Galileo to the same critical eye he had encouraged her to turn on others.[55] 'In the Descartes portion, I observe that you assume that D's piety was "put on,"' she wrote rather priggishly, pointing out that W.L. Courtney had insisted that Descartes's mind was 'fundamentally religious'.[56] The next letter apologized for her 'cheek' in burdening him with her 'worthless & irresponsible criticisms on a subject I know nothing about',[57] but still the assurance in her voice is startling.

Oliver Lodge had written to Eleanor for his own reasons, but she had been able to transmute his complicated feelings into something she could use: intellectual guidance and the psychological strength to press her ambition beyond the range her mother thought appropriate. Yet to effect this transformation, she had to cling to a 'Victorian' innocence; only by remaining 'unconscious' of Lodge's erotic desires was she able to claim his knowledge without surrendering her will. This pattern of behaviour was useful but evasive; it allowed her to develop her mind, but left her emotionally in a state of suspended animation. Somerville would change all of that. In this sequestered community, Eleanor found both intellectual sustenance and a new kind of friendship – a friendship based on the emerging common identity and shared values of its aspiring young women students. In her girlhood, Eleanor's closest relationships had been with older men – her father, Oliver Lodge – and while her Oxford studies with a series of prominent liberal-minded dons would in some ways prolong this pattern, in important ways her new female friendships would challenge its premises. At Somerville, Eleanor would learn to look at the world from a new standpoint, that of the emancipated 'new women' of the nineties. This group would form the reference point for her politics for the next forty years.

Chapter 3

Philosophy and Feminism

Somerville College was fourteen years old when the twenty-one-year-old Eleanor arrived there in the autumn of 1893, but the campaign for women's education at Oxford dated from the 1860s, when a liberal-minded group of dons brought their heterodox ideas and (worse) their wives into its masculine halls. Fellows of Oxford colleges were traditionally required to resign their positions on marriage, but with Liberal governments in office and a second commission on university reform in the offing, progressive dons and some of the more enlightened colleges were balking at this stipulation. When the eminent idealist philosopher T.H. Green married Charlotte Symonds in 1871, Balliol promptly reappointed him. The brilliant Mandell Creighton, later Bishop of London, was also permitted to retain his fellowship at Merton when he married Louise von Glehn in 1872 – although the less brilliant Humphry Ward had to resign his fellowship at Brasenose in order to marry Mary Arnold that same year.

These married dons and their artistic, clever wives brought a new style to Oxford. Intellectual life moved from the colleges to their homes, where mixed gatherings of young men and women met to discuss Ruskin and Morris, Unitarianism and politics. It wasn't long before the wives began to hope for something more. Garnering support from their husbands and other well-placed sympathizers, Charlotte Green, Louise Creighton, Mary Ward and Mrs Max Müller set up a committee to organize lectures for women in 1873; four years later, the more ambitious Association for the Education of Women was founded, with the object of establishing a hall of residence. Quarrels over religious affiliation developed, and in the end, two halls were opened: Lady Margaret Hall, which was explicitly Anglican, and a non-denominational hall named after the nineteenth-century astronomer and mathematician, Mary Somerville. Under Mary Ward's supervision, Walton Manor on the Woodstock Road, ten minutes from Broad Street and the busy heart of Oxford, was refitted with Morris wallpaper and furniture from Heal's, and welcomed its first twelve residents in October 1879.[1]

9. Somerville College, 1896. Eleanor is in the third row, eighth from left; Miss Maitland in the second row, middle.

The earnest young academic wives who founded Somerville would not have thought of themselves as feminists – indeed, Mary Ward went on to lead the anti-suffrage movement. The Cambridge women's colleges were, if anything, negative examples: 'hardly any of us were at all on fire for woman suffrage,' remembered Ward,[2] while her ally Mark Pattison, according to an early twentieth-century historian of the university, 'begged his coadjutors to avoid, if possible, in matters of dress and demeanour too close an approximation to what he regarded as a Girton or a Newnham type'.[3] He must have been comforted by Somerville's first choice of Principal, Miss Madeleine Shaw Lefevre, who could not have been a more decisive contrast to Girton's combative Emily Davies or Newnham's businesslike Mrs Sidgwick. Socially distinguished, accomplished rather than educated and most indubitably a 'lady', she charmed and disarmed Somerville's enemies. Initially, the Association for the Education of Women had been forced to organize separate lectures for students from both halls, but after five years, it was possible to send them to normal undergraduate lectures. Gradually, the final examination in the honours schools opened – a process culminating in 1888, when women were first allowed to take 'Greats', the second and final examination in the classical school of *Literae Humaniores*. By the time Miss Shaw Lefevre stepped down in 1889, many women students were following precisely the same course of study and taking precisely the same examinations as were male undergraduates – although the university neither granted them degrees nor admitted them to membership.

This was quite an achievement for the gracious Miss Shaw Lefevre, and when the Somerville Council chose Agnes Catherine Maitland as her successor, they anticipated that she would be equally diplomatic. Miss Maitland, known to her students as 'the Warden', resembled, according to Vera Brittain, 'a glorified bursar rather than a college principal'.[4] She was in her late thirties when appointed, and was probably already known to the Rathbones, since she hailed from Liverpool and had for a time worked for the Women's Liberal Association there. Certainly she violated no assumptions of appropriate roles for Victorian womanhood. Privately educated, she had written manuals of domestic economy, cookbooks and children's stories, and had acted as a school inspector in Liverpool. No scholar, she was someone whom parents could trust with the supervision of their daughters.

Yet under her unlikely leadership Somerville came into its own. Miss Maitland, despite her mild manner, 'quite frankly wanted Somerville to inherit the earth', the college's early historians remembered,[5] and she had the determination, tact and administrative skill to set the process in motion. She clarified the relationship between the college and the Association for the Education of Women, making it clear that the days of the latter's responsibility for instruction were over. She began recruiting Somerville's own teaching staff, hiring young women who had themselves recently earned firsts in modern history, modern languages, or other schools. And, finally, she oversaw an ambitious building programme to accommodate the college's growing numbers. Eleanor, in residence from 1893 until 1896, would have watched the college actually growing around her: nineteen students' rooms and a music room were added to the West Building during 1894, and a new wing built on to the Old Hall the following year.[6]

Such growth notwithstanding, the women's colleges were in Oxford on sufferance, as Miss Maitland well understood, and she was as vigilant as Miss Shaw Lefevre had been to ensure that nothing would be done to jeopardize their future. Until the very year Eleanor arrived, women students were chaperoned when attending lectures: early Somerville students remembered vividly the placid knitting figures at the back of the lecture halls, living monuments of what they themselves were struggling not to be. Girls were required to consult the Principal before accepting invitations from friends and were forbidden to be out of college gates after sunset without leave. Friends of the college were on constant alert for impropriety. 'On more than one occasion the remark has been made to me that girls who reside in Oxford Halls are allowed to visit at College Rooms with very insufficient chaperonage,' reported L.T. Meade, writing in the *Lady's Pictorial* in

1892. She was pleased to inform her readers, however, that Miss Maitland had assured her that even when visiting their brothers girls were accompanied by a trusted and responsible chaperon. 'Every possible care is taken of these girls,' Meade continued, 'and rules for their guidance, without being at all strict or in any sense severe, are so emphatic and so rigidly enforced, that the most careful parent need not be afraid to trust his daughter to the guidance which awaits her at Somerville Hall.'[7]

Severe as such regulations might be, they were intended to protect the reputation of the students and the college alike. Yet the 'new women' of the nineties found them increasingly irksome. 'We did feel that some of the college rules were a nuisance,' Rathbone recalled some fifty years later, and 'being a cheeky lot', they launched two campaigns: one to be allowed to attend balls, provided they were back in college by 11 p.m. ('the battle of the balls'), and the second to be allowed to receive undergraduate brothers in their own rooms rather than in a dreadful common reception room ('the battle of the brothers').[8] It was Eleanor, at the meeting of the Junior Common Room in January 1895, who seconded the resolution requesting that the college allow students to attend dances if the rules about the college closing time were not violated.[9] 'We are in any case already subjected of necessity to a large number of restrictions from which undergraduate members of the university are free,' the students' petition to the College Council stated, 'and we feel it hard that we who can claim to have shown ourselves not to be easily distracted from our work are placed under legislation.'[10] Fifty years later, Eleanor admitted that the petition was 'pompously worded', and remembered 'listening with burning ears to the shouts of laughter which came from the Council Chamber while, as we rightly suspected, it was being read'.[11] Modest compromises were secured on both fronts, with Miss Maitland empowered to give the students leave at her own discretion.

In some ways, Eleanor seems the most unlikely person to have joined in these early students' revolts. She does not seem to have enjoyed the balls she attended during her two London seasons, and her desire to receive her brother Frank in her own room scarcely seems a strong enough motive to launch her into college politics. On another level, however, her position was entirely expected. Having always been treated (to paraphrase Jane Austen) as a rational creature rather than an alluring female, Eleanor probably found such supervision unexpected and morally distasteful – if, that is, she took any notice of it at all. Lettice Ilbert, for one, recalled that Rathbone smoked constantly in her rooms and wandered about the college freely after hours – and that Miss Maitland, who lived right below Eleanor and certainly smelt the fumes, made no move to stop her.[12] A few years later, another daughter of a wealthy and cosmopolitan family, Margaret Haig Thomas, later Viscountess Rhondda, would leave Somerville in disgust after finding the food inedible and the girls provincial, but Eleanor – whose tastes were far more puritanical – came to love it. Having initially thought to go to Newnham only for a year, she remained as Somerville for the full three. 'The work is interesting and Oxford itself fascinating beyond anything,' she wrote to Oliver Lodge after several terms of residence. She had agreed with his conclusions about the relative merits of an Oxford and a Cambridge education, she wrote; but nevertheless, 'I do not think I regret coming here now'.[13]

In the event, Oxford gave Eleanor two educations, both of which would prove essential training for the challenges of her later life. The first education was in *Literae Humaniores*, that combination of classics, philosophy and ancient history that had for generations provided England's scholars and statesmen with a common vocabulary and the firm belief that one could derive lessons for Indian administration from Roman experiences nearly two millennia earlier. By the end of the century, Oxford's classical school was coming under criticism from those who felt that a curriculum devoid of science, mathematics or living foreign languages was scarcely likely to produce the kinds of men needed to cope with German ascendancy and growing global competition,[14] but at least until the First World War, the school retained its reputation as the best training ground for statesmen. Rejecting a narrow scholasticism, Oxford's philosophers and ancient historians retorted that Greek and Roman history and thought were the root of modern political arrangements: thus David George Ritchie, one of Eleanor's tutors, and a prolific writer on both philosophical and social questions, characteristically thought that 'the first condition of a right understanding of our institutions and ways of thinking and of a sane progress in politics and philosophy is the study of the growth of our civilisation . . . from its roots in ancient Greek life and speculation'.[15] While 'Greats' certainly tested students on Latin and Greek translation, they could also be asked to discuss the relative success of the Greeks and the Romans in drawing foreign elements into their spheres of influence, or the importance of sea power to the maintenance of domestic freedom – both subjects of absorbing interest to British statesmen managing colonial empires. Moral philosophy questions – on the nature of the state, the foundations of ethics, or the dilemmas of majoritarianism – were even more transparently designed to make a political elite reflect on its responsibilities.[16]

Few women students had the classical training necessary to attempt Greats, and Eleanor, while better prepared than most women, was certainly less well prepared than the most mediocre public-school boy. Simply by embarking on this challenge, she was regarded by her fellow students 'with admiration not unmixed with awe', and quickly became known as 'the Philosopher'.[17] Yet however difficult Greats might be, the select band of women who tried it had one distinct advantage. Precisely because they were pioneers, and because Somerville had no classical tutors of its own, professors and tutors sympathetic to the women's cause considered it a point of honour to help them in their work. Her deficient Greek notwithstanding, Eleanor was tutored by some of the most eminent philosophers and historians at Oxford. She began reading philosophy in the winter of 1894 with Ritchie, then a fellow of Jesus College, and continued with him for the spring. The following year she studied logic and moral philosophy with Charles Cannan of Trinity, a scholar of Aristotle, and Greek history with Reginald Macan of University College. During the summer and autumn of 1895, Henry Pelham, Camden Professor of Ancient History and President of Trinity, himself took her for Roman history, while Edward Caird, Jowett's successor as Master of Balliol, tutored her in Plato.

Studying Aristotle with Charles Cannan or Plato with the Master of Balliol could have been a rather intimidating enterprise. Certainly Hilda Oakeley, who entered Somerville one year after Eleanor and who also decided – partly on Eleanor's recommendation – to try for Greats, found reading with Caird to be 'a rather formidable experience, partly on account of his impressive but baffling silences'.[18] For Eleanor, however, this form of instruction was a familiar one, replicating as it did both her discussions with her father about social duties and her epistolary apprenticeship under Oliver Lodge. And her tutors, like Lodge, clearly thought 'her mind worth cultivating'. Ritchie was struck from the first by Eleanor's 'considerable power of independent thinking', and both Pelham and Caird remarked on her unusually thoughtful approach.[19] She was not just cramming – she was genuinely interested in her work, finding that it spoke to those very questions about individual action and the nature of the good that she had discussed with Lodge two years earlier.

To understand what Eleanor took from her readings and tutorials we must recall not only that the Greats curriculum was wider than is often assumed – leavening Plato and Aristotle with Hume, Kant, Mill and other modern philosophers – but also that both the ancients and the moderns were filtered through the lens of philosophical idealism – that potent blend of rationalism, neo-Hegelianism and liberal meliorism that, through the medium of T.H. Green, influenced a generation of Oxford undergraduates. As a tutor at Balliol in the 1860s, Green had found himself able neither to accept the miraculous claims of Christianity nor to reject its moral precepts; through his tutorial teaching, lectures, writings and occasional lay sermons, he gradually worked out a creed that, by founding ethics in a constantly evolving 'society', provided quite as powerful an impetus to altruistic social action. Of course, as Stefan Collini rightly notes, Green's influence lay not in his originality, but rather in the fact that both his concerns and his solutions were so very typical of his time; his moral philosophy 'was an exceptionally systematic expression of the sensibility which found something repugnant in even the hint of self-regarding actions'.[20] This sensibility found its most complete exposition in *Robert Elsmere*, Mrs Humphry Ward's famous bestseller of 1888, in which a young clergyman, having lost his faith, reconstructs an alternative ethic of social service out of his work with the poor of East London and the teachings of a 'Professor Grey' (a thinly disguised T.H. Green). And by the time *Robert Elsmere* appeared, Arnold Toynbee had already lived out its precepts, dying in the service of the poor in the East End, and a generation of Balliol students – Bernard Bosanquet, C.S. Loch, H. Scott Holland, Herbert Llewellyn Smith, A.H.D. Acland, and many others – were busy attempting the reformation of 'character' through the ethical societies, the settlement houses, the Christian Socialist movement, the Charity Organisation Society and the pages of the quarterly periodicals.[21]

By the year Eleanor arrived at Oxford, Toynbee had been dead for ten years and Green for eleven. Civic idealism was falling out of favour with Oxford and Cambridge undergraduates, who would find aesthetics and the cult of friendship more attractive than Green's relentless subordination of any private pleasures to the common good. The religious nonconformity that had made Green such an unconventional figure in the 1860s was now commonplace. Caird, who had, like Green, been a member of the London Ethical Society and other rationalist groups, placidly followed his practice of declining to take Holy Orders while delivering occasional lay sermons, and others – including Eleanor's tutor David Ritchie – were more straightforwardly agnostic.[22] The political coherence of academic liberalism had also been shattered by the late 1880s, as some convinced liberals broke with Gladstone over Irish Home Rule.[23] Yet for those Oxford dons who retained their commitment to radicalism, Green remained the philosophical guide and moral exemplar. Ritchie's biographer named Green and Toynbee as the two main influences on his life,[24] while Caird, who had been Green's collaborator at Oxford in the 1860s, continued to urge upon his students a life of social action – advising the young William Beveridge, who in 1903 went from a Balliol first to the sub-wardenship of Toynbee Hall, 'to go and discover why, with so much wealth in Britain, there continues to be so much poverty and how poverty can be cured'.[25] Through her studies with Caird and Ritchie in particular, Eleanor would have become familiar with the main tenets of idealism. And, in view of her later career, two aspects of their philosophy merit some consideration.

First, philosophical idealists broke with traditional liberals in their optimism about democracy and the extent to which they were willing to embrace the state. Their perspective on such issues arose out of their deeply 'social' view of human nature and of ethics. Accepting, as John Stuart Mill did, that societies evolve and progress, they argued that human character must adapt to society. Plato, David Ritchie argued in his study of 1902, had understood this, realizing that 'the good man is not necessarily the good citizen of any and every state'.[26] It was this belief in the civilizing and character-building effect of social interaction that led idealists to support a dense and prolific civic and organizational life. Collective bodies – trade unions, social clubs, political associations and so on – which appear in some earlier liberal thought as possible bearers of sectional 'sinister interests', became, in an almost Durkheimian fashion, schools of civic virtue. John MacCunn, Professor of Philosophy at the University of Liverpool (and Rathbone's later collaborator at its School for Training in Social Work) argued that Green saw institutions as 'material embodiment[s] of some settled plan', whose value in any particular case could be measured by 'what it is doing for the wills and characters of those who, in union of thought, sentiment and purpose, *are* the institution through participation in its life'.[27]

Yet unlike earlier liberal thinkers, who tended to see a vital associational life and an empowered state as to some extent in conflict, some followers of Green tended to treat the state only as the 'supreme institution',[28] upon whose shoulders the ultimate responsibility for cultivating an enlightened citizenry rested, and whose actions could be judged accordingly. The state, David Ritchie wrote in 1891, 'has, as its end, the realisation of the best life by the individual'; state intervention was allowable, then, if the measure proposed would 'tend to the greater well-being, physical, intellectual, moral, of mankind'.[29] By establishing this standard of human improvement with which to measure both the public utility of private associations and state policy itself, Ritchie argued, Green had improved upon Mill, for:

> while Mill would *ultimately* have brought the question back to some consideration of pleasures and pains, Green would have insisted that the social expediency [of, for example, the extension of the franchise] was determined ultimately, not by the probable effects on the greatest number of pleasures of an individual consistent with other individuals, but on the scope given to the individual for exercising all his capacities of self-development, all true self-development implying, however, the well-being of a community; for man, as we often repeat without fully understanding what we say, is essentially 'a social animal'.[30]

The state, in other words, could act as both the expression and the cultivator of the enlightened popular will, as both the means of attaining an ideal and that ideal end itself – a position Ritchie refused to view as logically fallacious, since 'the abstract logic of mathematics or of mechanics is not applicable to what is organic or more than organic'.[31]

The influence of Hegel is evident here, but so too is the optimism of the 1880s: noting the demise of sinecures, patronage and the Corn Laws, idealists were convinced that the Gladstonian state, founded on equal justice and meritocratic inclusion, could avoid the twin dangers of elite appropriation and majoritarian pandering. *Laissez-faire*, the principle of the supreme rationality of the market, formerly seen as a fundamental law, was historicized by Ritchie into a policy appropriate for specific historical conditions (now past); likewise Green, speaking to a Liberal Party organization, denied that freedom of contract and free disposal of property were absolute rights, since neither property nor contract could exist apart from society.[32] With Green, Melvin Richter points out, such arguments were formulated very largely in support of conventional Liberal policies – state education, public health legislation, temperance reform, and Irish land reform – designed to produce a better educated, moral and self-reliant citizenry,[33] but, once abstractly theorized, they were capable of almost endless expansion. In Ritchie's hands, for example, Green's ideas blended with the language of evolution to produce a justification for almost unlimited state action. 'If we can foresee what will tend towards the common welfare and adopt it,' Ritchie wrote, 'we shall save our society from going to ruin by external attack or internal dissolution' – a formula that brought him to the brink of socialism.[34]

Not that their optimism about state action led idealists to denigrate individual effort: on the contrary (and this is the second point), they tended to argue that precisely because a moralized state would offer its citizens greater opportunities for self-realization, it could demand both their loyalty and their devoted participation. If ethics were indeed inherently social, then only through social activity – or, in other words, through politics – could men determine and realize the common good. Civic action – which embraced not only expressly political activity but equally work with voluntary organizations – was viewed as a means of developing character both in the self and in others; among this generation of Victorian intellectuals, Stefan Collini aptly notes, ' "selfishness" came to be regarded at the Mark of the Beast morally speaking, the category which contained the root of all moral failing'.[35] Quite typically believing that a university fellowship scarcely absolved one from the duties of citizenship, liberal dons were active in local politics and various forms of voluntary service. T.H. Green, famously, had gone straight from a poll that declared his election to the Oxford Town Council to lecture on *The Critique of Pure Reason*;[36] Pelham served as the President of the local Liberal Association; and Caird, while Professor of Moral Philosophy at Glasgow University, had given his energies to a breathtaking array of reforming causes – from efforts to organize ill-paid women workers into trade unions, to the founding of an extension programme and a women's college, to the establishment of a settlement, modelled on Toynbee Hall, designed to bring students and working men together.[37] There was no limit to what the citizen owed the community, and those members who had greater gifts or blessings than their fellows owed most of all. Ritchie, characteristically, made use of classical analogy. 'The Athenian citizen should be ready to die for Athens,' he explained, 'because Athens offers so glorious a life of freedom to the Athenian citizen.'[38]

This was the creed that Pelham, Ritchie, Caird and others sought to impart to their students, through their teaching and through their lives. Women students, already accustomed to subordinate personal desire to various definitions of 'duty', were especially susceptible to a doctrine that would at once free them from an exclusively domestic role and provide them with an alternative and even more worthy 'calling'. One could even argue that it was through these new female devotees that the flagging idealist movement was given a new lease on life. Hilda Oakeley said that Greats succeeded in turning her from a contemplative to an active life; in time, she would become the Warden of London's Passmore Edwards settlement, originally founded by none other than Mrs Humphry Ward.[39] Barbara Bradby, Eleanor's partner in tutorials with Caird, together with her husband J.L. Hammond, also went on to devote herself equally to impassioned scholarship and reforming causes. And while Eleanor herself left no tribute to her Oxford tutors, in some ways her entire life can stand as an answer to their teaching. The optimism about state action and the stress on individual and voluntary service – always slightly in tension but always equally present – that informed their teaching became the two basic principles of her own public work.

Yet Eleanor came to give these principles a very different twist. The political campaigns and social reforms that absorbed her for much of her life can be seen, in a sense, as an effort to reconcile the advanced liberalism of Green, Caird, Ritchie – and indeed her father – with her own ambitions: to imagine a state that would enhance the citizenship of women as well as men, and require of both sexes their best efforts at social service. Eleanor, in other words, held many of the same ideals about active citizenship that her tutors held, but she was able to imagine the abstract citizen as female. Her ability to make this imaginative leap was due in part to the relative egalitarianism of her own family and the wider ferment over the 'woman question' in the 1890s, but it was also cultivated and sustained by her fellow students – by the conversations and conflicts through which this generation of 'new women' sought to work out their values and their destinies. This was her second education at Oxford: her education in friendship and feminism.

For Eleanor, this was all quite new: except for her single year at the Kensington High School, she had spent very little time among girls her own age. Somerville, however, was a community made up entirely of women, most of them very young: its students danced, acted, sang, debated and played hockey behind thick hedges and college gates. Even coeducational discussion of shared scholarly interests was almost impossible. With the exception of Caird's famous 'Balliol breakfasts', which brought his male and female philosophy students together ('rather an ordeal,' Hilda Oakeley remembered),[40] Eleanor had almost no contact with undergraduate men during her years at Oxford. Segregation of this kind bred an identification with her peers, and at Somerville, for the first time, Eleanor made close and lasting friends, including Hilda Oakeley, Barbara Bradby, Margery Fry, from the famous intellectual clan of the Frys, and Lettice Ilbert, the daughter of the legal scholar and parliamentary counsel Sir Courtenay Ilbert and later wife of H.A.L. Fisher – who wrote thankfully to her sisters that Eleanor 'looks as if she ought to be extremely good, & she's not'.[41]

Not that Eleanor ever cultivated a wide circle of friends: while some of her fellow students took to her immediately, finding her 'unselfconscious' and 'devoid of "side"',[42] to the majority she seems to have been a rather aloof figure. She couldn't take part in their enthusiastic chatter about hockey and games, and the early women's colleges in any case discouraged informality; only after long acquaintance would one student have dreamt of calling another by her first name.[43] The Rathbones' social prominence also made ready intimacy difficult. While most Somerville students came from 'cultivated homes', Lucy Kempson, one year Eleanor's junior, recalled, 'few belonged to families like the Rathbones, the Frys & the Ilberts with whom public events were part of daily life'. Coming from a household of great wealth, and with the leading lights of the Liberal Party regular visitors in her home, Eleanor must have found many of her fellow students naïve and unformed. 'It was something of a shattering honour to sit next to her at dinner,' Kempson remembered, 'for small talk was not her forte, and we felt that something was expected of us.' She was probably trying to be kind, Kempson admitted, but she did approach her juniors rather with 'the attitude of the scientist examining with interest & curiosity the varieties of the species!'[44]

Among a small group of young women as serious-minded as herself, however, a close intellectual companionship developed. In January 1894, at the beginning of her second term, Eleanor helped to form a discussion group on social subjects – the A.P.s, known by its members to stand for 'Associated Prigs'. The group agreed to restrict membership to seven, with resigning members replaced by unanimously endorsed invitations, and to leave both choice and treatment of the subjects for discussion 'perfectly free'. Their discussions encompassed both the practical and the theoretical: they canvassed parish work and the Poor Law, but also the *Fabian Essays on Socialism*, Benjamin Kidd's *Social Evolution*, Tolstoyan spiritualism and Comtian positivism. They discussed Church disestablishment (which Eleanor naturally favoured), but also the nature of free will and the publications of the London Ethical Society. At times they expressed frustration at their own ignorance; during a discussion of wealth and luxury, 'introduced by Miss Rathbone', the group 'tried in vain to fathom the economic effects of complete simplicity of life and seemed to be of opinion that it would be a pity were there not some few people living in luxury'.[45]

College societies of this sort were an essential part of male undergraduate life and could leave their imprint on a generation: one need only think of the way the Cambridge Apostles wove G.E. Moore's philosophy, aestheticism and, sometimes, homosexuality, into late Victorian cultural life. The A.P.s were less important and ephemeral, but no other society can have been so relentlessly high-minded; in this sense, the group's chosen name was apt. Not for the new women of the 1890s the aestheticism and sexual knowingness of their male contemporaries or the ironic detachment of the emancipated women students of the 1920s. 'Duty' remained their watchword: several discussions were taken up with such riveting topics as the problems of agricultural labour or rival methods of poor relief, and the task of determining their own social responsibilities was never far from their minds. At the eleventh meeting, for example, in November 1894, they discussed their responsibility 'to what are known as "fallen women"', and while one A.P. contended that 'the present industrial system was largely respon-sible', another actually worried that they themselves, 'by the pursuit of an intel-lectual life exclusively were making themselves still more responsible for the evil'. This rather idiosyncratic argument didn't impel any of the A.P.s to abandon the life of the mind for altruistic sexual service, but other discussions reveal a simi-larly sharp awareness of their vulnerability to charges of selfishness. In June 1895, when discussing the potentially frivolous subject of dress, both sides of the debate supported their arguments with appeals to duty – thus, while a minority felt that they should dress simply so as to protest against 'the costliness of dress of the present day', the majority held 'that we as women students should dress as well as possible, lest, among other considerations, carelessness in this matter should bring discredit on the cause of women's education'.[46]

Discussions like these strengthened students' sense of collective identity, pro-ducing the unique blend of public feminism and private separatism that gave the Edwardian women's movement its strength. Discussing coeducation, the A.P.s unsurprisingly concluded that they favoured mixed universities but women's col-leges – a solution that would preserve the mixture of educational equality and emotional segregation under which they themselves had flourished. Yet their sen-sibility, like that fostered by the women's colleges more broadly, was Victorian rather than modern: while they eagerly discussed women's public duties and rights, they left questions of marriage and sexuality strictly out of bounds. Outside the universities, as the 'woman question' grew in urgency, groups of men and women began to meet together to discuss the best way to achieve not only public good but private happiness. In the 1880s and the 1890s, the Men and Women's Club, the Fabian Society, the Souls, and a variety of other coteries were all attempting to find a sexual ethic that would reconcile erotic attachment with intellectual growth, marriage with personal independence. Eugenics, sexology, psychoanalysis and other ostensible sciences drew attention partly because they offered various 'quick fixes' for these seemingly insoluble problems. But for women who abjured marriage – and as critics charged, most university-educated women did tend to abjure it – none of these discussions seemed relevant. Since they did not intend to live with men, they did not need to understand them. They wanted public equality, not a renegotiation of domestic roles.

Eleanor's feminism, awakened by her attempt to read Aristotle before she entered Oxford, was nourished by this environment. As one of the first genera-tion of women educated like their brothers, she increasingly came to believe that she should have the same rights – or, as she would have seen it, the same respon-sibilities and the same opportunities for service. It was this view that led her to object to the college's regulations about chaperonage; it was this that had made her, according to Margery Fry, already a strong suffragist.[47] In this safe but stimulating company of women, she became able to ask new questions of her work, subjecting the philosophy texts she was discussing with Caird to a second, feminist, analysis. In February 1896, for example, she read the A.P.s some passages from Plato on the status of women in the Republic, and the meeting turned into a general discussion of the position of women.[48] And in the spring of that year Eleanor, Barbara Bradby, Hilda Oakeley and a fourth friend rented a farm together near Godalming in Surrey, where they could 'talk philosophically at all our spare moments and some we ought not to spare', smoke to their hearts' content, and explore the 'delightfully wild & open & lonely' countryside – sometimes on bicycles and in search of a strayed member of their party (usually Eleanor, whose sense of direction, like her philosophical bent, was rather unworldly). In this unknown Arcadia, amid 'such seas of moorland, & infinities of blue, & witch-haunted fir woods' (as Oakeley rhapsodically described it), they debated everything from 'things in themselves or immortality' to the conditions of 'lady shopgirls & dressmakers'.[49] The rigour of Oxford was leavened by the romance of friendship: Eleanor's two educations had come together.

Astonishingly, philosophy and feminism came together that year for her tutors as well, who found themselves leading a campaign to convince the university to open the BA degree to women. Eleanor had been taught by men deeply committed to the cause of women's education: both Pelham and Caird served on the Council of Somerville College, and Pelham was, from 1894, its President. During Eleanor's second year at Oxford, the councils of the Association for the Education of Women, St Hugh's and Somerville – although not that of Lady Margaret Hall – had agreed to ask the university to admit qualified women to the BA, and the Hebdomadal Council, in effect the 'cabinet' of the university, was soon deluged with petitions and memorials from women teachers, women's associations and supporters of the women's cause. During the autumn of 1895, women headmistresses, principals and tutors gave evidence to a special committee convened to consider whether women students suffered any particular hardship by being barred from degrees. In February 1896, that committee, having found itself unable to agree on any course of action, merely recommended that different resolutions be placed before Congregation, the governing body of which all Oxford MAs living within one mile of the university were voting members. A whole series of possible outcomes – from full degrees for women to the exclusion of women from Oxford and the founding of a new 'women's university' – was vetted in *The Times* and discussed throughout the colleges. Supporters of the full admission of women met in Balliol, presumably with Caird's blessing; opponents met at All Souls. The undergraduates, justifying the low opinion the women students held of them, defeated an Oxford Union motion to favour degrees for women by a majority of three to one.[50] Throughout this controversy, Eleanor was working well: her brother Frank wrote delightedly to William Rathbone that Caird thought her capable of getting a First.[51]

In the end, both Eleanor and her tutors were in for a disappointment. Congregation, meeting on 3 March 1896, rejected the proposal to grant BA degrees to women by 215 to 140.[52] One week later, a further series of half-measures – which supporters of the women's cause thought inadequate and opponents the thin end of the wedge – were defeated as well. To the great relief of the women's colleges, a resolution dreamt up by their opponents favouring special examinations and certificates for women alone was also narrowly defeated, with Pelham warning Congregation against granting 'diplomas which would only mislead the public and in the course of a few years would reflect great discredit on the University'. Caird, who had opposed the half-measures on the grounds that 'he and the advocates of the woman's movement would rather have nothing at all than only a part', predicted that degrees would be granted within a few years, but in fact the university's decision held until 1921.[53]

Eleanor, sitting Greats with 142 other Oxford students that June, failed to achieve the First for which her tutors had hoped.[54] There had been signs of trouble all along: Eleanor 'was not a very good scholar', Pelham admitted; her Greek and Latin were never entirely up to the task at hand. As early as the spring of 1895, Charles Cannan worried that she was 'too much distressed by merely specialist difficulties'; she would be a perfectly safe First 'if she would write faster and despise the examiners'. A year later, he still worried that while her work was always first class, 'she may not be able to do her best work in the hurry of the schools'.[55] And his prediction proved correct. Eleanor's hand seized up while writing, making her usual 'dreadful scrawl' almost entirely illegible; the examiners insisted that she return to Oxford and dictate the entire corpus to a typist. According to a close friend, Eleanor found the task of dictating in cold blood essays she herself found inadequate one of the most agonizing experiences of her life. Lucy Kempson, writing to Margery Fry that July, reported that Eleanor ('the Philosopher') 'was awfully cut up because she thinks she's pretty sure not to get a First'.[56] Although one of her philosophy papers was whispered to be the best of the year, the translations must have been mediocre, since the examiners in the end gave her a Second.[57]

There is no doubt that this result was a dreadful disappointment. Although such setbacks may seem trivial in retrospect, they had consequences. Eleanor had not, to this point, decided on a life of social action and may well have hoped to remain at Oxford. Margery Fry recalled that Eleanor had thought that to be Principal of Somerville was the one worthy ambition in a world in which most significant careers were closed to women;[58] a second-class degree would have barred her from this path. It was Emily Penrose, who had achieved a First in Greats four years before Eleanor's effort, who succeeded Miss Maitland as Principal in 1907. Worse, Eleanor felt she had let both the college and the cause down. Miss Maitland could only partially reassure her. 'It is no use to say I am not disappointed,' the Principal wrote, but Eleanor should remember that 'your tutors know and have told me that your powers and knowledge were both first class'. Charles Cannan also offered to write 'a very strong testimonial': 'I can say generally that I have the highest possible opinion of your philosophical ability; I scarcely think I have ever had more able essays from any pupil.' But such personal tributes could not alter official results, and Miss Maitland's recommendation that Eleanor rejoice 'for the sake of the cause as well as herself' in Barbara Bradby's triumphant double First must have been a little galling.[59]

And what was to come next? Margery Fry remembered walking in the gardens at Somerville with Eleanor shortly before Eleanor went down and discussing the future with her. They were wondering, she recalled, 'whether there was anything worthwhile to be ambitious about'. Their tutors – and still more their fellow students – had convinced them that they did indeed have abilities worth developing, and their own desire for public careers had been stimulated by their thoughtful debates over current issues. Yet their sex remained a barrier, and they concluded in frustration that since 'Parliament was shut to us, and practically everything was shut to us . . . [t]here was nothing worthwhile to be ambitious about'.[60]

What is remarkable about this scenario is not Eleanor and Margery's pessimism (which was passing), but their absolute identification with the group of educated single women to whom the college catered, and their equally powerful conviction that the public careers closed to this group were the only worthwhile focus of their ambitions. In 1891 and 1892, Eleanor had felt herself torn between her mother and Oliver Lodge – her loyalty to the former undermined by her desire for intellectual independence, and her ability to learn from Lodge complicated by his evident erotic interest. Somerville resolved this tension, offering an alternative likewise to male mentorship and maternal dominance. Women's colleges balanced public egalitarianism with private separatism: by accepting the university's established academic arrangements, they proclaimed their students the intellectual equals of men, but by founding separate residential and cultural communities built around female friendship, they made actual, living men (other than tutors) virtually irrelevant. Eleanor found this world both stimulating and fulfilling: after Somerville, she would cast her lot unambiguously with the educated, and determinedly single, new women of the nineties.

Having gained so much, Eleanor became a loyal friend of the college, donating generously to its appeals and serving on its Council between 1899 and 1908. Yet her two main legacies – which, appropriately, recognized her two quite different educations – are almost unknown. The first made her gratitude for her formal education apparent: for two years after her return to Liverpool, Eleanor gave fifty pounds – approximately a quarter of her private annual income – to help support a particularly gifted student. Preferring, like all the Rathbones, to do good by stealth, she insisted that the college preserve her anonymity, and to this day the provenance of Somerville's first research studentship remains unacknowledged.[61] Yet it is Eleanor's second legacy that is perhaps the more surprising. Having discovered the intellectual vitality and emotional warmth to be found in a community of educated women, she could not bear to leave Somerville for ever. At a meeting of the college on 15 June 1895, she thus proposed that a dinner be held each November for all current and old students.[62] The male colleges all held Gaudys, and henceforth Somerville would do so as well – the ritual celebration Dorothy L. Sayers would so brilliantly memorialize in her novel, *Gaudy Night*.

Chapter 4

Her Father's Daughter

When Eleanor left Oxford in 1896, she returned not to London but to Greenbank, her home for the next twenty-two years. William Rathbone had finally left Parliament in 1895: seventy-six years old and increasingly deaf, he found the debates harassing and difficult to follow. He was, in any case, weighed down by business and private cares. Rathbone Brothers was again in trouble, and this time it faced the crisis with its human and financial resources much diminished. Having fathered eight sons and lost only one in infancy, William perhaps could be forgiven for having imagined his patrimony safe; by 1896, however, not one son could be relied on to carry on. Ted, one of William's hopes, had been drowned in 1886, and in 1895 Thomas Ashton, then thirty-eight, died of blood poisoning. Ashton, alone among Lucretia's sons, had settled permanently in Liverpool, where he became a partner in the Liverpool branch of Rathbone Brothers and carried on the family's local philanthropic traditions. His death left William devastated.

Five sons remained, of course, but somehow none of them seemed quite as satisfactory as the ones who had died. Lucretia's sons simply kept their distance. The eldest, William Gair, refused his father's pleas to return to Liverpool to carry on the family name, and his lovely and artistic wife was unwilling to trade London society for the worthy pursuits of her Liverpool in-laws. Harry, more creatively, took refuge in his 'delicate' constitution, living with his American wife in a succession of continental resorts and watering spots, far from his father's monitory eye. And Emily's sons were proving even more troublesome. Bertie's epilepsy was worse and he was drinking; after a long and unsuccessful campaign by his parents to force amendment of life, he was moved to a cottage in Chester, where he lived under constant care.[1] Lyle kept to the Rathbone script in public – training as an engineer and serving on the Liverpool City Council – but he struck even family friends as 'rather rougher than the rest of the family', drinking too much, pottering about with motor cars and marrying a cheerful widow whom he affectionately called 'the missis'.[2] The fact that Frank was also 'supping between meals' struck William as the last straw: a pledge was extracted from the young man to

10. Greenbank.

'be specially careful . . . with regard to drink', and he was summarily dispatched to South America to manage the Rathbone trading interests from the River Plate.[3]

One can imagine William's consternation – but while to lose three sons is a misfortune, to lose all eight seems like carelessness. Much has been written of the restrictions Victorian patriarchs placed on their daughters; less attention has been given to the psychic strains they placed on their sons. No child wants a saint for a father, but Victorian assumptions left sons less equipped than daughters to cope with paternal holiness. And certainly William Rathbone's sons were, by the 1890s, withering under his inflexible moral scrutiny. The heart-breaking letters they had written as children gravely thanking William and Emily for their guidance and care had given way to more complex efforts to preserve their independence. It was William's bad luck to lose Ashton, his most meticulous and responsible son, but it was his own shining moral example that drove his other children away.

All but his daughters, who remained clustered around the family home, devoted to the domestic and political causes their parents held dear. Even in the late 1880s, when William first shared his fears for his younger sons with Ashton, he had been quick to admit that his daughters caused him no such anxiety.[4] After Ashton's death, he came to rely on them even more closely. The faithful Elsie, now in her forties, remained at Greenbank, absorbed in the running of the household (a task Emily left in her hands) and with district visiting for the Liverpool Central Relief Society. Evie helpfully provided a surrogate son: she had married her second cousin, Hugh Reynolds Rathbone, in 1888, and the couple and their four young children lived just a few minutes from Greenbank. Hugh was a partner in the Liverpool grain merchandising firm of Ross T. Smyth and took over the task of guiding Rathbone Brothers during these troubled years. The firm had emerged from the crisis of the eighties in a weakened condition. William Gair and the London partners had very nearly transformed it into an investment house, a trend deepened by the sale of the company fleet in 1889 and Ashton's death six years later. By the mid-nineties, it was clear that this strategy had been a poor one: in 1897 unwise speculations in foreign stocks almost brought the firm down alto-gether. William and Hugh were forced to intervene, closing the London office, cushioning William Gair with family money, and putting the Liverpool office under the supervision of Hugh's firm, Ross T. Smyth.[5] William does not seem to have blamed his eldest son for this crisis, but he was certainly frustrated by William Gair's unwillingness to rein in his expenses (and his expensive wife) after its collapse. In 1900, William bluntly warned his son that the almost £20,000 required to clear William Gair's business and personal debt amounted to his full share of his inheritance, and that he must persuade Blanche to economize.[6] Hugh, by contrast, righteously believed (as he once wrote Emily) that 'the secret of finan-cial and I would almost say family happiness is *lots of sinking funds*'[7] and watched his profligate brothers-in-law with a concerned and disapproving eye. And William and Emily came to see Hugh and Evie – rather than William Gair and Blanche – as their successors.

With Elsie managing Greenbank, and Hugh watching the business, two of William's concerns were in good hands. But William also had his civic responsi-bilities to attend to. He continued to serve on the University College Council, on the boards of various nursing and hospital associations, on the Executive of the Central Relief Society, and as a Toxteth guardian – riding to the meetings of the latter four times a week. Most of the other family members had their civic duties too: Lyle was also on the Executive of the Central Relief Society, Hugh was active in the University, Emily (perhaps with Bertie in mind) had founded an invalid children's association, and Elsie helped to run district nursing. Yet none of William's children had made philanthropic and social work their major concern; none was absorbed, as he was, with the moral as well as practical questions of how men and women of wealth and privilege could fulfil their social responsi-bilities. He turned, then, to Eleanor – just back from Oxford and able, he hoped, to help him to work out his ideas on the future of philanthropic work in Liverpool.

We do not know whether this project was exactly to Eleanor's taste. She returned from Oxford afire for philosophy and feminism. Eager to try her hand at writing, she had convinced Miss Maitland and Charlotte Green to give her introductions to the editors of the *Cornhill* and a few other literary and political periodicals. She also hoped to follow Miss Maitland's injunction to use her talents and powers 'to open doors for other women'.[8] Within a year of her return, she had joined a local branch of the Women's Industrial Council, become the honorary secretary of the Liverpool Women's Suffrage Society, and was on the National Executive of the National Union of Women's Suffrage Societies. Yet while her father's philanthropic concerns may not have been entirely her own, between 1896 and 1902 she became his most reliable assistant and collaborator. And whatever the frustrations this position might have involved, its compensations proved enormous: Eleanor won her father's confidence absolutely and used his authority to enhance both her family position and her feminist causes.

At William's urging, immediately upon her return Eleanor began working as a 'friendly visitor' for the Liverpool Central Relief Society, the local equivalent of the London-based Charity Organisation Society, which he had helped to found (six years before its London cousin) in 1863. The Central Relief Society, like the more famous COS, sought to relieve distress while avoiding 'pauperisation': the aim was to assist families in times of crisis while also inculcating those habits of thrift that would keep them independent of such aid in the future. Yet William Rathbone, while certainly approving these principles, had become critical of the Society's bureaucratic and 'unfriendly' practices. Long impressed by the use of volunteer almoners in philanthropic work in some German towns, in 1887 he convinced the Local Government Board and the Liverpool and London charity societies to send investigators to examine the system. Following that investigation, the Liverpool CRS had set up district offices run by volunteer friendly visitors. Ten years later, and now back in Liverpool, William Rathbone was eager to know how the system was working.[9]

Eleanor Rathbone's first effort at social analysis was thus a study of the operation of the system of friendly visitors, written for her father in March 1897. It was a damning document. After taking charge of a number of cases over the past four months, she had come to the conclusion 'that we do little permanent good' and might even be doing 'some positive harm'. Sympathetic but untrained friendly visitors simply took applicants at their word, making only cursory investigations into their claims; the committee, dealing with dozens of cases at each meeting, fell back on small weekly 'in-kind' doles of fuel or food. Such aid kept the families of casual labourers from starvation, but it did nothing more – indeed, she charged, it removed the inducement to save, deterred applicants from attempting any more permanent change, and perhaps even sustained the evils of casual labour and low pay. This was, of course, precisely the logic espoused by Edwin Chadwick more than half a century earlier, leading Mary Stocks to conclude that Rathbone's ideas were, at this stage, entirely within the moral universe of the Poor Law

Report of 1834. Rathbone was, she wrote, 'articulating at the unripe age of twenty-five the social outlook which Octavia Hill defended in a rearguard action at the age of seventy'.[10]

One can see Stocks's point. Rathbone treated Liverpool's disordered, chaotic labour market simply as a given: the idea that one might reform the labour market to deliver decent wages rather than reform labourers' behaviour to take account of their fluctuation, although soon a cornerstone of Rathbone's thought, never appears. And yet, for all her stress on the need to devise ways to encourage 'thrift' (the society should, she suggested, act as a savings bank for those it helped, thus training casual labourers to save during flush weeks for the lean weeks to come), this was not her only or main concern. The London COS, she pointed out, offered 'really effective help to good cases', providing the kind of training and equipment that could give the applicant 'a chance of making a fresh start'. The Liverpool committees never did that: she couldn't think of a single case in which a visitor suggested buying tools for a man or a mangle for a woman, or paying for schooling or training for a boy or girl. But this, surely, was what they should be doing: investigating cases thoroughly and, whenever possibly, intervening intensively so as to make permanent improvement possible.[11]

The Liverpool CRS heard her out. She presented her ideas about ways to encourage thrift to its Executive Committee in October 1897, and to the members and chairmen of the Society's various district committees one month later.[12] More creatively, she began to use her own North Toxteth Committee as a testing ground, working with Florence Melly, its long-standing secretary (and a family relation) to reform its practice. North Toxteth became, under Eleanor and Miss Melly's guidance, one of the most active of the Society's committees: in 1896–7, its fourteen volunteer friendly visitors investigated some 258 cases and made 2,000 visits; the following year, the number of cases investigated had risen to 315. In 1897 – and here the influence of Eleanor is already evident – they began meeting fortnightly rather than monthly and coordinating their work with the relieving officers, practices which increased their local knowledge and the reliability of their decisions; they also brought Rathbone's 'savings' scheme into operation, although with mixed success.[13] And, while they continued to have harsh words for the 'undeserving', they were actually fairly generous: in 1897–8, 73 per cent of those applying for aid had been assisted (even though almost half of those were later found to be either 'undeserving' or 'unsuitable') and when confronted with 'very sad cases' the committee tended (as they apologetically admitted) to 'relieve somewhat largely'. But – following Rathbone's lead – they wanted to go further, hoping to become 'an agency for permanently benefitting, and not merely for relieving from temporary discomfort, the deserving poor'.[14]

But could that ambition be realized? The North Toxteth Committee thought that it could, and in 1897–8 they spent a good portion of their report discussing one specific case, which they clearly saw as a model for social work in the future. In November 1897, a young man with a wife and two children had come before the committee. He had 'sunk into the lowest state of destitution and ill-health', and had become 'too delicate to do any work which would bring him a living wage'. There had seemed no alternative but the workhouse, but the friendly visitor had found a little work for the wife and chosen to intervene intensively, relieving the case at the rate of some four to eight shillings per week for six months. The children were sent for a healthy country holiday, and the man was taught, 'also through the Friendly Visitor', the occupation of bicycle-cleaning. Members of the committee arranged for bicycles to clean, and by November 1898 he was earning over a pound a week. 'Since the application, a year ago, the whole circumstances of the family are entirely changed for the better.'[15]

This was Eleanor's case, and it was an important one, both for this family (which was effectively helped by an agency often seen as an expression of middle-class hegemony)[16] and for Eleanor herself. Far from applying a set of rigid rules, Eleanor had intervened systematically but imaginatively, crafting a strategy to get the entire family off the ground. The Society's financial resources helped, but even more important were the couple's own determination and Eleanor's dogged (and year-long) attention. In this experience we can see the roots of later principles. Although Rathbone came to believe that the state should make more of an effort to prevent such distress, she never lost her faith in 'friendly visiting', never grew to believe that public agencies and local government officials could entirely substitute for that personal 'gift of self'. Socialists, trade unionists, working-class women's organizations and professionalizing social workers (including, sometimes, Rathbone herself) would later condemn the amateurism of friendly visitors and their often patronizing tone, but Rathbone never thought voluntary workers should be entirely superseded. From her use of visitors to administer allowances for soldiers' wives during the First World War, to her role in the founding of the Citizens' Advice Bureau to help people cope with the bombings of the Second, Rathbone constantly sought to find ways to make room for voluntary effort in public life. Certainly the teachings of her father and the idealist philosophers who tutored her at Oxford predisposed her to see such personal service as an essential duty of citizenship, but it was her own experience that convinced her of the truth of their words.

In giving of her time and energy, Eleanor got something back: social work, she discovered, was not merely sociologically interesting, it was spiritually and morally enriching. As had T.H. Green, Eleanor found in her work with the sick, workless and unfortunate of North Toxteth some respite from the philosophical and metaphysical questions that had troubled her for years. For Eleanor had returned from Oxford with her spiritual anxieties unquieted. Although she went down in June 1896, in December of that year she returned to lead a discussion with her 'Associated Prigs' on how far a belief in miracles was essential to Christianity. She returned again in February 1897 for a session on the relationship between the physical and mental worlds, and one final time in May to debate whether it was immoral to hold beliefs not based on inquiry undertaken in a scientific spirit. Eleanor took the trouble to travel back to Oxford because her friends meant a great deal to her. She was lonely in Liverpool; her family and the circle of social workers among whom she had begun moving had not succeeded in replacing Hilda Oakeley and Margery Fry. But she returned for these particular discussions – rather than for the meetings on more prosaic political and social questions – because it was spiritual and religious questions that were keeping her (like so many eminent Victorians) awake at night.

These anxieties began to dissolve as her immersion in social work deepened. Hilda Oakeley, after visiting her in 1898, perceptively remarked that Eleanor was a 'wonderfully satisfactory philosopher' because she could express her creed 'on her way to C.O.S. meetings or suffrage, or school committees' as clearly as she had at Oxford,[17] but in fact such practical work lessened her need for contemplation. So by 1901, when Oakeley (now in Canada) suggested reviving an epistolary philosophical collaboration, Eleanor was not really tempted. After some five years of 'practical work', Eleanor wrote to Oakeley, she had 'got out of the habit' of philosophical speculation, and had grown very 'utilitarian'. 'It is nearly always in connection with some practical problem that I think of the ultimate problems, and it is for their bearing on people's lives that I care for them,' she wrote, and 'I don't know that I would wish it otherwise.' She had in any case come to doubt 'whether philosophic methods (i.e. metaphysical and logical) are the right way to accomplish any increase of knowledge at all'; rather, perhaps the great philosophical questions – 'nature of time and space, personality, freewill, etc., etc.' – should be attacked by the 'pick and shovel of physiological psychology and physics'. She couldn't get rid of the suspicion that Plato and Aristotle had really gone as far as possible to work out metaphysical problems; the formulations of later metaphysicians (a group that would have included her erstwhile teacher Edward Caird), being incapable of scientific proof, seemed merely 'either pseudo-science or words, words, words'. And this would no longer content her:

To the great questions which one used to take a pleasure in debating for debate's sake, I feel I must have a definite clear-cut, and, if possible scientifically probable answer – or at least an answer which really satisfies my mind and fits in with the rest of one's store of ascertained truth. Short of that I am rather sick of 'larger hopes' and dim, vast visions of something inexplicable and great, and prefer an outspoken rational scepticism (i.e. a positive acknowledgment from my reason that it has not got the *materials* for solution or the ability for solution, and that it has therefore ceased to worry).

Eleanor had turned to philosophy partly because she wanted answers; by 1901, however, and with *Literae Humaniores* behind her, she no longer believed they existed.

But this had in some ways ceased to trouble her, since she had finally discovered an alternative foundation for a moral life. Even in her early correspondence with Oliver Lodge, Eleanor had found religious scepticism troubling more for moral than spiritual reasons: it was because religion offered believers an effective guide to life, rather than a reliable hope of a hereafter, that she feared the consequences of scepticism. But what the idealists had taught her – and what, still more, she learned through her own social and charitable work – was that social life could itself provide a school for morality; concern for one's fellow human beings, rather than the hope of heaven, could be the foundation for ethics. Implicitly admitting just how lonely her childhood had been, she traced in an abstract, third-person voice, the history of her own gradual engagement. 'When one is young and a newcomer in the world,' she wrote:

one looks at it all in a detached way, wondering why the inhabitants take themselves and their trivial affairs so seriously, and finding one's chief interests outside it. But by degrees one warms to the world and one's fellow mortals, and the danger becomes that one should lose the power of detaching oneself to the extent necessary for serving it most effectively. Of course, this does mean that one almost inevitably has one's sense of proportion spoiled – and in a world where everyone was as well off as oneself, the utilitarian spirit might be a thing to fight against. But in *such* a world with all its wrongs shouting in one's ears and every miserable face claiming kinship, how can one be *sorry* that it is no longer easy to shut one's ears and revel in thought for thought's sake.

Eleanor's famous 'dreaminess' had broken down, and the world had intruded with a vengeance.

Far from measuring the world by ideal standards, she now measured the value of philosophic thought by 'utilitarian' (by which she meant practical) ones. Consequences of ideas and actions should be judged not in terms of their influence on other ideas, but rather for their impact on the most prosaic aspects of life. Work that makes 'a great difference to a very few lives' was 'quite as important, quite as interesting' as work that makes 'a very small difference to a great many lives', and 'that is why I like the despised C.O.S. work so much':

If one's large schemes fail, if dock labour is never properly organized, or the executive power better guided, or any question of philosophy elucidated, it will be a satisfaction at the end of life to know that, at any rate, some poor bicycle-maker and his wife and children were set on their legs and saved from the House and made respectable citizens through my agency.

Ten years after her initial quarrel with Lodge over whether religious scepticism could be a wholesome state of mind, Eleanor had come to share his view. But while Lodge had turned to science to find an alternative creed, Eleanor turned – like many of her generation – to society, discovering in human interaction itself a sufficient basis and motive for the ethical life.[18]

Of course, living with doubt was not easy, especially during the two years Eleanor watched her father dying. 'I confess that the reason I especially care for [the scientific study of] "personality",' she wrote to Oakeley, 'is for the light it might throw on personal immortality. A whole world living in a baseless hope seems to me more and more tragic.'[19] William had seemed almost immortal: on 4 April 1899, he had even dictated a brief 'Memo on Experience as to Hard Work', in which he expostulated against those friends who had urged him, now over eighty, to slow down. Probably the best antidote to physical breakdown was hard work, he argued; it was only when men combined 'plentiful work with good living' that they burned the candle at both ends.[20] But in the autumn of that year William had a severe attack of eczema – a harassing complaint that left much of his body bandaged. He was soon up again, but in the spring of 1900 he had another attack and in August, while on holiday in Scotland with his family, he came down with jaundice and had to be brought back home. For the last eighteen months of his life, he was virtually bedridden; when his eczema was very bad he was unable even to feed himself.

According to Eleanor's account, he bore this cross stoically, feeling 'that there was no humiliation in suffering the common lot of humanity'.[21] With the aid of a secretary, he tried to keep up with his correspondence and turned to Eleanor to help him draft his letters and memoranda. In a letter to Emily, then on holiday with Eleanor, William admitted his reliance on the pair of them: 'I have found quite a new power with you to advise & clear my ideas & her power to put them in a forcible form.'[22] Eleanor, moved, wrote back to her 'dear Papa' humbly offering her services. 'It is a real & unmixed pleasure to me to work for you,' she wrote. 'If you have any bits of work, literary or practical, within my powers that you would like done, now or in the future, I hope you will tell me of them. I have seen so much of your work now, that I think I could manage a fair imitation'.[23]

During the final year of her father's life, Eleanor thus gave up most of her other concerns – including her feminist efforts – to devote herself to the issues with which he was most concerned. In the archives of Liverpool University sit the documents of that service: William's endless letters to the mayor or the Medical Officer of Health proposing fresh improvements in municipal services, his appeals to wealthy friends for further endowments for the University College or the District Nursing Association, were often drafted on Liverpool Women's Suffrage Society stationery, in Eleanor's spidery and awkward hand. It was at his suggestion that Eleanor began investigating the problem of casual labour at the Liverpool docks – a problem which he believed, rightly, to be both a major cause of the poverty of the city's workers and curable. She obeyed out of love for him although she didn't 'see much good in it at present'.[24] She should have trusted his judgement: two years after his death, this study would make her name and serve as a basis for local reform efforts. And although she left the actual decisions about his treatment to the doctors and Elsie, she spent several hours each evening reading him novels and memoirs – a shared pleasure that left her amused but touched by his gullible and childlike sensibility. 'Anything that savoured of irony and cynicism was repulsive to him, and to have read him a book that "ended badly" would have been an impossible cruelty: he was too ingenuous a novel reader to have become hardened to imaginary griefs.'[25] Together they worked their way through instructive biographies and old-fashioned fiction until his health failed utterly. On 6 March 1902, two months short of Eleanor's thirtieth birthday, he died.

He had been, and would continue to be, the most important man in her life: no one can possibly grasp her character and politics without understanding the nature of her relationship with her father. In her girlhood, William had been her confidant and guide; the pattern of male mentorship that guided her young womanhood – her relations with Oliver Lodge, with her Oxford tutors – was merely the shadow of that initial affinity. By her return from Oxford, Eleanor had outgrown this pattern, but she bent her neck to the yoke humbly, recognizing her father's moral – and not patriarchal – authority. William, for his part, reciprocated, consulting her on his plans, deferring to her judgements, and – convinced of her reliability – settling enough money on her to make her financially independent.

And, crucially, he nurtured and authorized her feminism. William was not a strong suffragist, but he had (unsuccessfully) urged the appointment of women as Poor Law guardians in 1886, believing that 'lady members would be much more firm in matters of public business' than men were.[26] Uncomfortable (as Eleanor was) with the language of rights, William saw virtue rather than sex as the basis of authority. When his sons began shirking their responsibilities and squandering their talents, their differential privileges and rights seemed indefensible. Eleanor thus did not have to reject her father to become a feminist; on the contrary, it was easy to justify it in her father's terms. Politically his protégée, she remained psychologically his child; his death, if anything, fixed his presence in her mind as the model of the good citizen and, still more, the virtuous man. Like Mrs Fawcett, whose faith in male probity was sustained by her memory of her husband, Eleanor had her father's image to remind her that a male life of righteousness was possible; equally, she had the counter-example of her brothers to justify her harsh criticism of male backsliding. Identifying with her father's values against her brothers' rebellions, small wonder Eleanor remained, emotionally and intellectually, a Victorian, turning on the inadequate men of her generation their failure to live up to the standard that she and her father had shared.

William's death ended Eleanor's apprenticeship but it did not end their relationship: there were two posthumous tributes to the strength of that filial tie. The first acknowledgement was the one that William made through his will: a document remarkable for its equally careful weighing of financial interest and moral deserts. William's estate was valued at slightly over a quarter of a million pounds: at the turn of the century well under one hundred persons per year would leave estates of this size.[27] As was typical of the very wealthy, William left most of his money in trusts. Less conventional, however, were the designation of the trustees and the division of the property itself. Although William Gair, Hugh and Lyle were named executors of the estate, the trustees were chosen entirely from the Liverpool clan, with Emily and the trusted Elsie, rather than William Gair, joining Hugh and Lyle, and Emily retaining the deciding vote in cases of disagreement.[28]

Emily herself was dealt with generously: £87,000 was held for her in trust, and her marriage settlement was confirmed at £3,250 per year; she was also to live at Greenbank until her death. William, who had at Evie's marriage expressed his frustration at the fact that the law did not treat women entirely equally in matters of property, attempted in his provisions for his children to correct these flaws.[29] All of the children of his second marriage save Bertie were left precisely equal amounts: Evie and Lyle, who had received £10,000 as marriage settlements, were given an additional £5,000 in trust; Eleanor, upon whom William had settled the equivalent of a marriage portion in 1898, also received £5,000; Frank, as yet unmarried, was likewise to receive a marriage portion and an additional £5,000. More interesting, however, were the stipulations governing the four siblings' moneys. While Lyle and Frank's entire settlements were held in trust, William avowed his faith in his daughters, leaving the trustees free to turn their capital over to them for their absolute use.[30]

The division of the residual capital, expected to amount to some £30,000, also reflected William's final views as to the relative merits and claims of his children. This amount was divided into thirteen shares. William Gair, as the eldest son, received three shares – but so did Hugh and Evie, and in calculating William Gair's share the trustees were instructed (as William had warned his son) to take into account the funds handed over during the demise of the London office. William's faith in Eleanor was affirmed: she received precisely the same share – two thirteenths – as her brothers Lyle and Frank. Elsie, despite the substantial sums she had received from her dead mother's estate, received one share.[31] The invalid Bertie was not granted a share, but an astounding £25,000 was set aside for his care. Henry Gair, who was living abroad and who had received £10,000 in trust on his marriage, received only the comparatively paltry sum of £2,000 outright.

In a letter written in 1892 about an earlier version of the will, William explained his choices. He had given 'unusual powers to trustees and guardians', he admitted, but not because he preferred one child over another. Rather, he had feared he might die 'before some of my children are old enough & of established character to be wisely trusted with considerable means, which they might use to their own injury & that of others, or be encouraged by their possession in a life of idleness & self-indulgence, which I hold to be fatal alike to virtue or true happiness'.[32] The final will, signed on 15 August 1898, seems to have moderated some of the earlier provisions: Lyle, for example, whose behaviour had long distressed William, must have mended his ways, since he was given considerable responsibilities as a trustee. Nevertheless, it was clear that Evie's exemplary husband Hugh had supplanted William Gair: it was Hugh who was named in the will as 'the Resident Head in his generation of our family', Hugh whose 'wise counsel and aid' were credited with helping William to cope with 'the increased labour and thought which my brother's illness and son's death brought upon me and which without such assistance might have proved too much for my age and strength', and Hugh and Evie who were designated to live at Greenbank after Emily's death. And William's daughters had, as a group, displaced his sons, being entrusted to manage not only their own but also in some cases their brothers' moneys.

William Rathbone's death made Eleanor independent; more important, it set her free. While establishing her equality with her brothers, William had not saddled her with the kinds of financial responsibilities Hugh, Evie, Emily and Elsie would bear. Yet Eleanor did not, in 1902, move to London or throw herself into a life of public work; rather, she chose to become the interpreter of her father's teachings and the guardian of his legacy. Already deeply involved in his social projects, and – alone among her siblings – having the time for the task, she decided to write his biography. The project took her two years, and was a considerable achievement, both in literary and in psychological terms. On one level a restrained and moving account of one eminent Victorian, the book was also an adroit – if unintended – response to the inevitable question of what was to be done about Eleanor. Through her writing, Eleanor mastered her grief, defined her own position and principles, and laid out her programme for her life. And, by effacing the rest of her family's presence in her father's life and work, she routed her brothers completely, establishing herself as his political heir.

Immediately after her father's death, Eleanor had been comforted by her feeling that his influence on those around him 'had never been so strong and vivid and far-reaching'; although his bodily presence was gone, she wrote to Hilda Oakeley, the force of his personality remained, as others sought to 'absorb into their own characters what was beautiful and good and magnetic in his'. But she had been unable to hold on to this reassurance, especially given her own longstanding doubts about personal immortality. 'As time goes by, and one's commonplace moods return,' she wrote to Oakeley, 'the sense of blankness and emptiness gets worse.' The project began, then, almost as a type of therapy, a way of coping with feelings of impotence and aimlessness. She did not yet know whether she would actually write the memoir, she told Oakeley, but she had begun collecting materials – although at this stage she did not want Oakeley to mention the project to anyone.[33]

As her family and friends learned of her plan, matters grew more complicated, for Emily was both supportive and interfering, and some of William's prominent friends (fearing, Eleanor reported, that she would be unable to do a 'sufficiently pretentious' job) offered to read over particular chapters as well.[34] ('I simply loathe the idea of those three bigwigs reading my prosy stuff,' Eleanor wrote to William Gair, but felt 'in the interest of the book' that she couldn't refuse.)[35] Yet, mindful of her father's dislike of artifice, she strove for Charlotte Brontë's 'perfect simplicity & sincerity' of style.[36] In simple and unadorned language, she surveyed her father's many initiatives – his founding of district nursing, his role in the establishment of the University College, his efforts to humanize charitable work. William would only have tolerated a biography, she was sure, if 'it might encourage others, especially young men and women in his own city, to trace out for themselves more definitely and to follow more boldly, a life of public usefulness'.[37] It was for these young men and women, and for 'his fellow-citizens in Liverpool, his former constituents in Wales, and his fellow-workers and friends everywhere', that she wrote her book.[38]

Yet Eleanor wrote this memoir for herself as well. According to Noel Annan, Leslie Stephen turned to the practice of biography – and ultimately created the *Dictionary of National Biography* – partly in order to discover an alternative model for the moral life once religious belief had gone.[39] Eleanor, having already decided that she preferred an 'outspoken rational scepticism' to further metaphysical speculation, also found that biography allowed her to construct a genealogy of morals. Family letters showed that her own great-grandfather had considered Christianity a proper subject for 'a strictly rigorous and rational examination', while even her father, devout as he was, cared 'a great deal for the ethical and spiritual side of religious teaching and very little for questions of doctrine'.[40] Like many Unitarians, he rejected utterly the idea of the atonement, finding Christ's death to offer not propitiation but an example, 'teaching us self-sacrifice of everything – ourselves if need be, as indeed it must be – in life and death as his disciples'.[41] The test of a man's worth was not the profession of faith but rather the moral life: a view Eleanor could, Elsmere-like, cling to long after faith had gone.

By this measure, her father's life was an exemplary one. The 'utilitarianism' Eleanor had confessed to Hilda Oakeley deepened as she began examining the words and works of her illustrious forebears. Reviewing the family history made her newly conscious of her legacy: in a formulation that Mary Stocks would repeat in her biography of Eleanor herself half a century later, she wrote that her father's, grandfather's and great-grandfather's lives seemed 'to be but a single life extended over three generations'.[42] Yet not all of these William Rathbones had used their talents wisely: one could not examine the life of her great-grandfather, the cultivated and free-thinking fourth William Rathbone, she wrote, 'without being struck by the contrast between the smallness of his achievement and the great impression which his character and abilities seem to have made upon those who knew him'.[43] By contrast, her father had the 'genius of common sense';[44] although he had loved to read history and political science, 'knowledge was always to him a means, and not an end', a chance to discover principles which he could put into practice in his daily life.[45] 'Great are the uses of mediocrity,' her father had written when estimating the value of his own life; and while Eleanor would not have accepted his evaluation, she agreed with his view that people of modest ability could, with perseverance, do great things.[46]

The biography did more than confirm Eleanor's preference for a life of practical public service: it also showed her precisely how to go about her task. Reading the biography today, and with some knowledge of her later life, it is impossible not to recognize Eleanor herself in her portrait of her father. Whether she stressed those features of his character that she herself possessed, or whether she unconsciously wrote the biography as a blueprint for her later life, the parallels are striking. Some are trivial – both adopted smoking as their only vice[47] – but others were more profound. Political principles and strategies later associated with Eleanor Rathbone – the unwillingness to accept political honours, the vigilant defence of parliamentary prerogatives, the tendency to disguise her authorship of proposals or legislation in order to maximize their chance of passage, the practice of exaggerating demands in order to leave a margin for bargaining – all appear as William Rathbone's defining political traits.[48]

Yet one aspect of William Rathbone's life – and indeed of his political work – went unmentioned. For all the attention to the family tradition of public service, the actual family bustle and commotion that Eleanor grew up among never appear. William Rathbone's close relationship to his mother is acknowledged, his reliance on his brother Sam discussed, but his own wives and children receive scarcely a mention. Although Eleanor used William's letters to Emily, the affection and camaraderie that spill out from their pages were wiped away, and Emily herself was mentioned only in passing and never by name.[49] More strikingly, although all of William's sons save Bertie served an apprenticeship with Rathbone

Brothers or an associated firm, only the careers of Ashton and Teddy, safely out of the way, were discussed. This was, of course, in keeping with the family ethos: what living Rathbone child, with William's lessons in self-sacrifice still ringing in their ears, could possibly have demanded inclusion? Eleanor wrote her father's life almost as if he had been – as she would remain – single, as if her mother and siblings never existed.

In a paragraph in the preface that she deleted before publication, Eleanor explained her decision to write such a determinedly 'public' life. A biographer writing about 'a very near relation' had, she thought, two choices: either to write explicitly from the standpoint of the relationship, or to ignore that relationship altogether. She had chosen the latter course: 'that is to say, I have tried, probably I have often failed . . . never to let myself say anything or refrain from saying anything other than I should have done if the relationship had not existed'.[50] This was a difficult standard, and a few of William's friends thought she fulfilled it only too well. Sir Edward Fry, her friend Margery's father, remembered that some of his contemporaries found its impartiality shocking, while the Shakespearean scholar A.C. Bradley regretted that she had 'not been able to use all the language of enthusiasm that a stranger would have permitted himself'.[51] Reviewers, however, thought the biography 'a model of good sense and good taste', and praised the author's modesty and restraint. What they failed to notice was that by effacing her family so effectively from the story, she was able to claim her father's legacy and make it her own.[52]

The years after Eleanor's return from Somerville were hard ones. She was living, once again, as an unmarried daughter at home, forced to adapt her ambitions to the family's needs. She was lonely, she missed her Somerville friends, and she had been thwarted in her ambition to take up literary or journalistic work. Her letters reveal both her isolation and, implicitly, her irritation with her family's demands: thus when Somerville College began discussing the conditions for a new research fellowship in 1901, Eleanor wrote to Margery Fry recommending that the Fellow be required to hold the award for a full three years. 'I don't think the Council realizes quite the position many women are in towards their families,' she wrote, 'nor what advantage to the Fellow herself strict regulation may be, to enable her to resist domestic pressure.'[53]

But if the endless demands and bustle of family life seemed at times harassing, Eleanor's scrupulous performance of her daughterly duties also had its rewards. Her brothers had abdicated, died or turned to milder pursuits in the face of her father's inflexible virtue; she had persevered, and found their positions there for the taking. By 1905, the year that her memoir of her father was published, she was ready to claim her inheritance. Alone among her siblings, she had neither established business responsibilities nor pressing domestic ties, and her advantages were remarkable. She came from the city's premier liberal family; she was independently wealthy; she had had the best education available to woman or man. She had her father's dying blessing, her mother's approbation, and a doting elder sister to look after her domestic needs. This was her chance, and she had the wit to seize it. She was thirty-three.

Coda

Emily Alone

What becomes of the family matriarch when the patriarch leaves the stage? Elsie had Greenbank to look after, Evie her young family to raise, Eleanor her 'cases' to visit and her chapters to draft. But Emily, who had been William's closest confidante and companion, the desire of his eyes, found herself at a loose end. She had plenty of money and servants to spare: for all William's exhortations to thrift on the part of his sons, he confirmed Emily's settlement at more than £3,000 a year. And, he stipulated, she had Greenbank to live in until she died.

But was this what she wanted? With six years at Greenbank behind her, she wasn't sure. Emily had felt (she admitted) 'a little queer' about the family's return to Liverpool in 1895, certain she would miss the bustle and society of London.[1] And, especially once Lyle married and Frank had been sent abroad, she did find life at Greenbank with her husband, stepdaughter and daughter 'very quiet and dull'. 'Eleanor', she complained pointedly, 'never was young from the time she was born', and both she and Elsie were busy all day long. Only William, with his vitality and projects, had kept the whole family going.[2] Now he was dead, and she – of Greenbank's three mistresses – had the fewest local interests to occupy her. She was seventy, but she felt younger, and was not inclined towards do-gooding.[3] She had always been a wanderer, making frequent trips to her family in Londonderry and taking long holidays with William and her children in Italy, Austria or Switzerland, and in Scotland or the Lake District, at least once a year. Who would accompany her now?

Hugh and Evie stepped in, bearing Emily and Eleanor off to Spain for a long rest soon after William's death. Elsie and Eleanor also went with Emily and some family friends on a long trip to the West Indies one year later. But Elsie and Eleanor both had (thank God) their 'social duties', the one force that could, in the Rathbone scale of values, outweigh maternal will. Emily thus went further afield without them, making for Egypt with her sister Augusta (now also widowed) in 1904, and (as ever) travelling back and forth to Ireland and London, the continent and the North.

Sometimes, Eleanor went along. As a young woman, Eleanor's feeling for her domineering, charismatic mother was (in the words of one perceptive Somerville friend) 'best described by Holy Fear'; now, she felt sympathy and a kind of compunction.[4] She went with Emily, her brother Lyle and her sister-in-law Blanche to Sicily in 1906; she and Elizabeth Macadam accompanied Emily to Greece in 1907.[5] As her public obligations proliferated, she made sure to save time for Emily; during the war years, working almost around the clock, she kept her Sundays free. She did not, would not, give up that public work, and Emily would no longer ask her: that battle was over, hard-fought, hard-won. And yet: who is to say that Eleanor's long campaigns to make motherhood honoured and rewarded were not tribute of a kind?

PART II

THE FREEDOM OF THE CITY

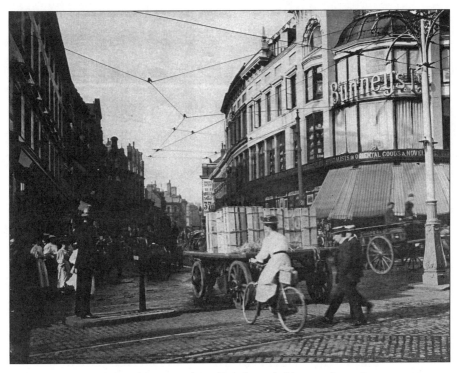

11. Young woman bicycling through Liverpool, 1908.

... to make a centre in Liverpool for all people who have wider interests than those they are surrounded by, to prove that life in the provinces could be as rich & full as life in London, to try to mould the city into new ways & to really identify *ourselves* with its life as some return for what it has done for *me* and my forebears ...

Eleanor Rathbone to Elizabeth Macadam, 5 May 1919

Chapter 5

Enter Miss Macadam

A daughter blessed by election, then, and following in her father's footsteps? The first, certainly: but within a year the paternal influence seems less overpowering; new pathways appear. On Eleanor's desk, the draft chapters of biography and statistics on dock labour lie unattended; Emily and Elsie sit down to their quiet dinners alone. 'I am deriving much enjoyment from a new friendship,' Eleanor wrote to Hilda Oakeley some time in 1903.[1] She had met Elizabeth Macadam, a Scottish social worker almost exactly her own age, newly hired as the Warden of the Victoria women's settlement.

This is the beginning of a love story, but one that is hard to describe – a story of two women's love for one another, for the women's community of which they were a part, and for the overworked, impoverished and resourceful women among whom they lived. For the next dozen years, meeting almost daily, Rathbone and Macadam sought to build relations of 'friendship', and then of political collaboration, between idealistic women 'settlers' and the dockers' wives, hawkers and charwomen of Liverpool's crowded slums. They had some success but gained something as well – careers, analyses, and a partnership that lasted the rest of their lives.

For Eleanor, these were rich and rewarding years. She came out of her father's shadow to develop an independent political base; she worked out the rudiments of the feminist economic analysis that would later make her famous. The few photographs or descriptions we have of her during those years tell the story: no longer abstracted, she looks straight at the camera. Having never put much value on pleasure, she found herself, against expectation, happy – content in a whirlwind of work, secure in her partnership with her new-found friend. Elizabeth, confident, strong-minded and independent, offered the emotionally diffident Eleanor friendship and an occupation when Rathbone most needed it. It was a gift that Eleanor repaid with love and loyalty for the rest of her life.

To write about Elizabeth Macadam is a challenge all its own, for she did all she could to evade the historian's eye. She left no papers and expected no memorials, and most of her close friends and relations died before her. Worse, almost all the letters Eleanor and Elizabeth wrote to each other were burned after their deaths, and Macadam, unwilling to be portrayed only as Rathbone's domestic partner, prevented Mary Stocks from including more than rudimentary details of the friendship in her biography.[2] We are driven, then, to public records and a few family accounts in order to piece together Macadam's family background and the nature of the two women's early friendship.

Elizabeth Macadam was born in October 1871 in the Free Church manse in a small village north of Glasgow to a Presbyterian clergyman and his young, American-born wife. Her father, Thomas Macadam, was the son of Aberdeenshire farmers; her mother, Lizzie Whyte, had a more unusual background.[3] Lizzie's father John Whyte had grown up in Kirriemuir, north of Dundee, but – having got a local girl pregnant – left the town under a cloud. The child of that illicit union, Alexander Whyte, born in 1836, achieved not merely respectability but fame, becoming one of Scotland's most important clergymen. By the time John Whyte – now a New York merchant with a wife and daughter – re-established contact with his son in 1857, Alexander had abandoned his trade of shoemaking to become a teacher; the next decade would see him accumulate degrees from King's College, Aberdeen, and New College, Edinburgh. In 1866, he landed the plum post of minister at Free St John's in Glasgow; and, being single, was looking for a female relative to keep house for him at the manse. Who better than Lizzie? 'The love and aid of a little, loving, working sister would greatly further me in my work,' the new minister wrote to his young American half-sister.[4] In the autumn of 1867 Lizzie duly arrived in Glasgow to act as Alexander's secretary and as mistress of his house. There she met Thomas Macadam, a friend of Whyte's from college days, who was about to take a pastorship at Chryston, not far from Glasgow.

Thomas Macadam and Lizzie Whyte were married in Edinburgh in October 1870 and then returned to Chryston, where Elizabeth was born a year later. Two more children soon joined her in the nursery: a second daughter, Margaret, usually called May, in 1873, and a son, Alexander Whyte, named for his uncle, in 1874. In 1880, Thomas Macadam resigned this post and accepted a pastorship with a Presbyterian congregation in Strathroy, Ontario, Canada; Lizzie and the three children joined him two years later. Elizabeth thus attended the High School in Strathroy; there, she also lost her mother and little brother. Lizzie Macadam's death left her half-brother Alexander Whyte 'bereft . . . above measure', but it surely devastated her husband and adolescent daughters still more.[5]

Thomas Macadam remained in Canada after his wife's death, taking a position in 1889 as Professor of Political Philosophy at Morrin College, a small Presbyterian school in Quebec City.[6] Both of his daughters attended classes there: thus, in 1892, when Eleanor Rathbone was reading ancient philosophy and

12. Elizabeth Macadam (standing, left) with Ian Ross, her sister Margaret, and Ian's family.

history at Oxford, Elizabeth Macadam may have been studying the same texts in Quebec.[7] The family lived quietly with a maid of all work in a modest house in the St Louis Ward in Quebec City until at least 1894, when Macadam resigned.[8] He must then have moved to Toronto, for Free Church records report his death there in 1899.[9] Yet Elizabeth and Margaret had returned to Scotland several years earlier, initially to the home of their uncle Alexander, now married and minister at Free St George's, Edinburgh. Perhaps Thomas Macadam felt that his daughters would profit from the high-minded but cultured atmosphere of the famous clergyman's home; perhaps he hoped they would find either professions or husbands in this wider social world. Margaret had musical and artistic interests and both young women were 'eagerly interested in social and public work'; certainly Whyte, who was active in Liberal politics and in social work in Edinburgh, would have introduced his nieces to a wide circle of friends.[10] One of these was a young minister named Ian Ross, who had studied in Germany and with Eleanor Rathbone's mentor Edward Caird at Glasgow University, and had served for a time as Whyte's assistant minister. In 1897, Ian Ross married

Elizabeth's sister Margaret, who then left Edinburgh to join her husband in his ministry to a Highland congregation.

This brief family history, culled from public records and memorials to illustrious clergymen, does not tell us much about the young Elizabeth. Yet it discloses several important things: her Scottishness, her Presbyterianism, and the fact that she (like Eleanor) was raised in households in which religious belief and philosophical inquiry were seen as compatible. Friends in later life recalled that Macadam's religious and regional loyalties stayed with her: throughout her life, she kept both her Presbyterian faith – in spite of Eleanor's own scepticism – and a strong regional patriotism. Macadam regularly travelled to Edinburgh to visit her uncle and his family and retired there after Rathbone died; she also left a portion of her estate in a trust to enable Presbyterian clergymen and their wives to take trips to Palestine.[11] One daughter of a friend described Elizabeth Macadam as 'very Scots', by which she meant that she had both a kind of Gaelic charm, enchanting children with stories and play, and a certain puritanical rigidity. More than one hapless child recalled having to apologize to Elizabeth Macadam for thoughtless or ill-mannered behaviour.[12]

But the most remarkable aspect of Macadam's early life, and the aspect that most shaped her personality and principles, was her independence. Orphaned from her twenties, she was forced to be self-supporting. Although she was always welcome in her uncle's home in Edinburgh, and may also have contracted (and broken) an early engagement there,[13] around the time of her sister's marriage she left Scotland, relatives and marriage prospects behind. Determined to have a profession of her own, she spent some time 'training in Kinder Garten work' in Germany[14] and volunteered for a spell at the Canning Town women's settlement in London. With little money of her own, however, Macadam – unlike many young women who turned to social work in the 1890s – could not afford to pay for board at a settlement house indefinitely. But to command a salary in a field full of voluntary workers she knew she would need contacts and training. The place that could provide both was the Women's University Settlement in South London, founded in 1887, which had built up a reputation for innovative social work. In 1898, Macadam applied for one of the newly established Pfeiffer scholarships at the settlement, telling the committee there that she could not afford to come unless she was awarded a scholarship or a paid post.[15] In time she held both: she was the Pfeiffer Scholar from April 1898 until April 1899[16] and then remained at the settlement for a further three years, running an evening school for about one hundred adolescents on a salary paid by the local School Board.[17]

Macadam flourished at the settlement, attending lectures on economics and civic administration, learning the basics of social casework, and helping to run clubs and classes.[18] From Margaret Sewell, the settlement's inspirational warden, and other experienced social workers, she gained a firm belief in the indispensability of such practical training and an equally powerful commitment to the ideals of 'friendship' and civic action across class lines. Of course, settlers' offers of 'friendship' were not always welcome: Miss H.J. Gow, who supervised Macadam's work as a district visitor, spoke of the 'sore sense of helplessness given by unopened doors', of being asked (perceptively) 'for whose benefit we come, our own or theirs'.[19] Yet by their emphasis on the twin ideals of 'professionalism' and 'friendship', women settlers tried to dissociate themselves from the patronizing figure of the 'Lady Bountiful'. And some, including Miss Gow, thought 'friendship' even more important than a strict adherence to the rules of scientific philanthropy. Admitting that local people often found the Charity Organization Society 'machine-like and heartless', she justified – on the grounds of friendship – the giving of material aid even to those whom the COS considered 'unhelpable'.

In joining the settlers' cause, Macadam was following a path trod by many young, educated women: most of Eleanor Rathbone's friends from Somerville, for example, worked for a time in a settlement. Yet not all of these converts took to the life so happily. A letter from Hilda Oakeley captures well the sense of shock and alienation she felt on leaving Somerville – 'that well-loved country where "social work" and "problems of the day" are glorified into subjects for the A.P.s to worry over' – to enter a universe in which such problems were frighteningly real. It was all very well to visit a settlement and admire its work, Oakeley wrote to Margery Fry, but 'as soon as it is suggested that I should take charge of a little Evening School, and "organize," and be ready at a particular time every evening to turn on a flow of spirits and pretend that I think this a cheery work, and that large and beautiful things are to be somehow performed through musical drill and carpentry and gymnastics, . . . how my heart slides below the floor, and I seem dead'.[20]

But Oakeley was, after all, a philosopher, a gloomy and shy young woman much disposed to musing on the meaning of life. Elizabeth Macadam was a much more positive character. She was, the settlement *Report* noted, exceptionally good at working with the 'rough young boys and girls' who came to its classes.[21] Her decisive nature kept her from discouragement, and in any case she did genuinely believe that 'large and beautiful things' could grow out of 'musical drill and carpentry and gymnastics'. Classes in recitation or mathematics could awaken a 'desire for higher things', she thought; better, if students were allowed to manage the school themselves, they would learn responsibility. In a passage that could have been penned by one of Eleanor's philosophy tutors at Oxford, Macadam wrote: 'Our great hope is that good membership of our community may be a stepping-stone to a better citizenship in the future'.[22]

Macadam's four years at the Women's University Settlement gave her just what she needed: training, mentors, and the ability to earn her own living. She also found what Eleanor Rathbone discovered at Somerville – friends with whom to share her plans and her pleasures. Many settlement workers developed close and even passionate friendships: the quiet rooms and labours of settlement life allowed such ties to flourish. Elizabeth Macadam grew close to one young woman in particular, Emily Oliver Jones, who had arrived at the settlement around the same time. The two friends trained together but developed different areas of expertise, with Macadam concentrating on work with children and Emily Jones on relief work. But Emily Jones was from Liverpool, and wished to return there: like Rathbone, she was born to one of the great Unitarian clans that dominated its Liberal Party and its philanthropic institutions. It was surely through Emily Jones that Macadam learned of the Victoria Settlement's need for a new warden, and the prospect of collaborating with her friend made the idea of a move an exciting one. After six unsalaried and dilettantish wardens, the Victoria Settlement could also see the advantages of a trained head and lured Macadam with the promise of a tiny but symbolically significant salary of £30 per year. It was not Eleanor Rathbone, then, but Emily Jones, who brought Macadam to Liverpool at the end of 1902.[23]

What Macadam and Jones found there was a city with problems severe enough to satisfy the most intrepid urban explorer, and a community of women eager to tackle them. True, Liverpool was a less romantic destination than the East End of London: it had no W.T. Stead or George Gissing to chronicle its daily life, no Arnold Toynbee drawing Balliol graduates into service of the poor, no Eleanor Marx or Annie Besant preaching socialism and sexual emancipation. Even Charles Booth, a native son, had deserted its docklands to make his name in the capital. Yet Liverpool offered much the same mix of extreme poverty, ethnic heterogeneity and sexual danger that appalled (and attracted) London's urban explorers. Like London, like Manchester, the city's population had exploded in the nineteenth century: already a bustling port city of 77,000 in 1801, Liverpool grew almost fivefold to 375,000 by 1851, and doubled again to 700,000 by 1901.[24] A magnet by the eighteenth century for Lancashire's enterprising and destitute alike, during the famine years of the 1840s the city found itself the first port of call for successive waves of Irish immigrants. Some 300,000 came during 1847 alone, escaping across the Irish Sea to land, ragged and starving, on Liverpool's docks.[25] Most of the Irish immigrants of the forties passed on to America or other destinations, but a sizeable proportion stayed: by the 1850s and 1860s, in some of the dockside areas, over 40 per cent of the permanent population were Irish-born, and if that figure declined to 7 per cent overall by 1901, a much larger proportion could still claim Irish descent and ties.[26] Smaller migrant communities sprang up as well – of Russian Jews escaping the pogroms of the 1880s, of Chinese seamen, of black ex-slaves in the eighteenth century and West African and West Indian sailors in the twentieth.[27]

The port was the magnet and lifeblood of this population. Liverpool handled almost half of all commercial tonnage entering Britain by the mid-nineteenth century: docks lined both sides of the Mersey, even squeezing out the older ship-building yards. An army of clerks laboured in the counting houses that multiplied behind the docks, and the building trades struggled to keep pace with the ever-expanding demand for warehouses and terraces, but a very large section of the labour force was casual. By the turn of the century, there were almost 20,000 dockers, most of whom rarely worked a full week – and these were only a fraction of those dependent on the health of the port. Certainly Liverpool had its sweatshops, but the manufacturing sector was under-developed as was the market for women's work. Married women in particular were forced to the economic margins, earning the odd shilling by hawking, charring or keeping lodging-houses – or by offering those sexual or semi-legal services that flourish wherever seamen congregate.

Just as the port determined the city's population and economic structure, it affected its urban geography and social relations. Casual labourers had to live within walking distance of their work, a condition that strained beyond bearing Liverpool's overcrowded housing stock. Although the city could boast its own local Chadwicks and Simons, heroic doctors and engineers who in the mid-Victorian period fought cholera and infant mortality with sewers, drains and paved streets, so long as immigration increased and the docks were hiring, the intractable problem of overcrowding remained.[28] By the 1880s the Liverpool Corporation owned as much as one-third of the parish and had seen its statutory powers to demolish insanitary dwellings and rebuild steadily expand, but some 70,000 people were still living in damp cellars, crumbling tenements or other houses deemed unfit for habitation.[29] Yet for all their poverty, Liverpool's courts and streets throbbed with life – with hawkers, delivery men, noisy children and shawl-clad women, on their daily rounds to the pawnshop or the shops, or simply taking a break from their losing indoor battle with damp, vermin and dirt.

Liverpool's shipowners and merchants lived on the edge of this urban congestion, but with every wave of immigrants they retreated further. Over the second half of the nineteenth century, even the most civic-minded deserted the lovely Georgian terraces near the heart of the city for more salubrious villas near Prince's Park on the southern edge of town. In the 1890s, the Renshaw Street Unitarian congregation moved from the heart of Liverpool to a new Arts and Crafts church near Sefton Park on Ullet Road, where assorted scions of the Rathbone, Melly, Holt, Booth and Muspratt clans also built new homes. Politically progressive as such families might be, they were intensely socially exclusive: Gervas Huxley, who joined the Booth Steamship Company in 1918, remembered that even after the First World War Liverpool's merchant princes formed a 'society wholly independent of London, both more exclusive and more formal, where powdered footmen and knee breeches were still employed for grand occasions in the wealthiest mansions'.[30] The philanthropic efforts of their status-conscious wives appear to a modern (or postmodern) eye to be almost inconceivably transparent in their appropriation of urban problems to serve other ends. Let us pause, for example, before the spectacle of a nine-course banquet held in 1907 to raise funds to protect young Irish girls from 'smooth-tongued villains' likely to lead them astray. Almost all members of Liverpool fashionable society (if not the high-minded Rathbones) were there, and the *Daily Post* spent seven paragraphs describing Lady Russell's 'primrose satin with a tunic and vest of filmy black lace and knots of turquoise blue velvet', Mrs Macfarlane's 'dainty white taffeta, draped with lace and chiffon', and several dozen other alluring outfits – protection of working-class purity offering, it seems, an unrivalled opportunity for elite sexual display.[31]

Exceptionally stratified in ethnic and social terms, Liverpool developed a structure and style of politics more reminiscent of Chicago or Boston than of Manchester or Leeds. For in those Victorian years when Gladstonian Liberals began to cast their political lot with a newly enfranchised and respectable working class, Liverpool exhibited the spectacle of a politics organized along ethnic and sectarian lines – a politics that pitted a fiercely Protestant popular Conservatism against an improbable alliance of dissenting plutocrats and desperately poor Irish immigrants. Backed by working men's clubs and demagogic clergymen, for most of the nineteenth century the Conservatives easily held the upper hand, leaving the city with a reputation for riot, excess and disorder unequalled by any other British town.[32] The great Liberal families were too remote and too wedded to the causes of fiscal retrenchment and religious toleration to appeal to Liverpool's Protestant working men: to their bewilderment, successive waves of democratization brought them no political success. Nor, however, was the city noted for those improving, cooperative and ethical movements that served in other places as the bases for the formation of an independent socialist politics. While it could rival London's East End as a textbook case of the problems of casual labour, urban overcrowding and ethnic confusion, it had neither a well-developed workers' movement nor the kind of bohemian subculture within which Fabian Society branches and radical clubs flourished.

Liverpool thus seems inhospitable territory for the formation of a progressive politics. Yet precisely because this radical culture was weak and social life deeply segregated along gender lines, a rather different form of progressive politics became possible. For what Liverpool had was a long and distinguished tradition of innovative women reformers – a tradition that crossed sectarian and class divides. Kitty Wilkinson, who founded the nation's first municipal washhouse during the cholera epidemic of 1832; Agnes Jones, the pioneer of district nursing; Fanny Calder, who developed the teaching of domestic science; Louisa Birt, founder of Liverpool's sheltering homes for runaway children; and a host of other women had over the years found ample scope for their energies in Liverpool's slums. By the 1890s, moreover, in Liverpool as in London, a new generation of educated single women were revolutionizing the theory and practice of urban social work. Eager to find purposeful activity and often frustrated by the restrictiveness of their lives, these propertied daughters dedicated themselves to voluntary work, visiting workhouses, managing board schools or running girls' clubs. Even the Central Relief Society, long in male hands, agreed in the 1890s to begin enrolling women as 'friendly visitors'. That same decade saw women first appointed as sanitary inspectors and elected to boards of guardians and school boards. When Macadam and Jones arrived in 1902, then, they joined a small but growing band of dedicated, largely single women who had found their purpose and calling in the Liverpool slums.[33]

At the heart of their efforts lay the institution Macadam was to take over: the Victoria Settlement, a residential house for women social workers in the working-class district of Everton. Liverpool had no men's settlement, but the city's reform-minded women were more ambitious: they wanted a 'centre' for their activities and a residence for those daughters of good family eager to live among those they wished to serve. In May 1897, at the home of Lydia Booth, the American-born and civic-minded wife of the shipping magnate Alfred Booth, a plan was hatched. Two graduates of Cheltenham Ladies' College volunteered to act as co-heads: Edith Sing, the daughter of a prominent Liverpool citizen who had worked in a London settlement, and Dr Lilias Hamilton, who had a medical degree from Brussels and the added cachet of having worked as medical adviser to the Emir of Afghanistan. The two women rented a large house at 322 Netherfield Road and begged or borrowed enough furniture to make it habitable, and in March 1898 the settlement opened its doors. Volunteers quickly got to work, organizing girls' clubs, a dispensary for women and children and the first classes for crippled children offered in Liverpool: in the first annual report they appealed for a cart and donkey to fetch the children to class.[34]

Yet despite its high profile and early success, the settlement was plagued almost from its opening by financial problems, revolving leadership, and the lack of a coherent philosophy. Six wardens came and went in the first five years of its existence, and although the house could accommodate five residents, rooms were often empty. The dispensary was flourishing, with some 4,000 visits annually by its fourth year, and the classes for invalid children were so successful that the School Board took them over (with settlement workers' help) in 1900.[35] Such work was a drop in the ocean, however, and for the most part the settlement functioned merely as a meeting place for workers engaged in disparate efforts. Particularly troubling was its lack of a specific *raison d'être*, any philosophy by which to integrate itself into the normal life of the district. Settlement workers acted as collectors for the District Provident Society and referred cases of distress to the Poor Law guardians, but beyond that they appeared to have no clear idea of what they were to do.

We find a vivid portrait of these early difficulties in the letters of Maude Royden, later famous as a suffragist and preacher, but who was in 1900 another idealistic daughter of good family, eager to find some means of being of use after her return from Lady Margaret Hall. Royden, from a Conservative and Anglican family of Liverpool shipowners, spent eighteen months working at the settlement (but living at home), and gave a vivid portrait of its joys and frustrations in her letters to her great friend Kathleen Courtney. Royden began in October 1900 as a collector of penny savings for the District Provident Society in the tangle of streets between the settlement and the docks. Remarkably, she felt neither afraid nor self-conscious: she admired the humour and friendliness of the women who answered her knocks and was undeterred by police warnings about the violence of the area and her own shocked discovery of the dire conditions of many of its dwellings ('cellars, you know, and all sorts of horrors').[36] What did bother her was the assumption of class superiority at the heart of her 'friendly visiting'. '*I* shouldn't be grateful if Lady Warwick e.g. came to see me every week, to get me to put a few shillings into a provident fund,' she wrote to Courtney. 'I should be mad. . . .'[37] Nor, when she began club work, was she surprised that the girls found its regime of games and singing boring. Given the choice, she admitted frankly, she too 'would infinitely prefer to loaf in the streets with a (presumably) attractive young man'.[38]

Royden dealt with her qualms through high spirits and empathy. She was not judgmental, and some of her encounters would have made the theorists of the Charity Organisation Society turn pale. When one docker's widow confessed that she had squandered every penny of the £300 she had received for her husband's death, Royden thought it was 'grand that, just for once, she had the chance to do so!' The woman recounted some of the things she had bought, and she and Maude 'laughed like hyenas'.[39] But Royden was also frustrated by the inadequacy of the settlement's theories and programmes in the face of the poverty around them. She was, she admitted, 'an idiot at grasping the difference between the deserving and the un-!'[40] and Miss Dolphin, the current Warden, did not seem able to enlighten her. All of the women looked '*unspeakably* poor' to her, and she could understand why they would 'drink like fiends': 'Poor, poor dears! I should drink if I lived in Lancaster Street.'[41] The constant injunction against any aid that would lead to 'demoralization' baffled her:

> I can think of nothing but the dangers of 'giving'. They appear to me so great as to be almost paralysing. You mustn't give money; or clothes. If you help them to get work, wouldn't it be better for their independence of character if they got it for themselves? It seems to me that the only people worth helping are the ones who don't need it.[42]

She had no trouble making friends in the slums, but was realistic enough to doubt that her friendship alone could 'uplift' its inhabitants. Perhaps she was simply missing something, she thought. 'I wish I could train under the COS,' she wrote to Courtney in December 1900, 'but there is no COS in Liverpool.'[43]

Of course, Eleanor Rathbone was, at this very moment, only a mile or so away, working with Florence Melly and the East Toxteth district committee of the Central Relief Society, and wrestling precisely with that dilemma of how to provide genuine and lasting help without 'demoralizing' character. Elizabeth Macadam and Emily Jones were in London, learning the rules of district visiting under the watchful eye of Miss Gow. Royden had left Liverpool for the world of feminist politics in London by the time these three converged on the Victoria Settlement in 1902, but they brought the training and method that she had longed for with them. Together, Macadam, Rathbone and Jones would transform the institution that Royden had found so rewarding and so frustrating.

Elizabeth Macadam's plan for the Victoria Settlement was ambitious but simple: she wanted to turn it into a model of its kind, a worthy Northern cousin of the London institution at which she trained. First, she had to improve its financial position and recruit more volunteers. She held 'at homes' for women students from Liverpool University – as the University College became in 1903 – who by 1903 numbered almost 400[44] and spoke at teas given by prominent women, in the hope of drawing ever more daughters of good family (and the family purses behind them) into the settlement's work.[45] Her prize catch was Eleanor Rathbone, who had taken her mother on a long trip to the West Indies just before Christmas 1902,[46] but was back in Liverpool, and much in need of friendship and activity, some six months later. Rathbone met Macadam soon after her return, and for Rathbone, clearly, the meeting was decisive: until the revival of the suffrage movement on Merseyside around 1909, the settlement would be Eleanor's main concern.[47] Rathbone accepted its honorary secretaryship in 1904, and when she stepped down in 1915, Evie's daughter Nancy succeeded her.

With the recruitment of Eleanor Rathbone, direction of the settlement fell into the hands of a female triumvirate. Macadam, as Warden, always played the dominant role, yet Rathbone and Emily Jones were also crucial to its programmes. Jones, who like Macadam lived at the settlement, ran its relief operations; Rathbone took charge of its social investigations. Both women, and especially Rathbone, also drew on family money to bail out the settlement at crucial junctures. It was Eleanor who arranged for a move to new and larger quarters in Everton in 1904, Eleanor's mother who donated the money for a garden there that same year, and Eleanor's aunt Augusta who endowed a scholarship for training. Eleanor herself provided fairly constant infusions of funds during those early years, and as the settlement's reach expanded, her contributions and those of her family did so as well.[48] In 1901, the settlement had run on £500 per year and had some forty volunteer workers; by 1910, the year that

Macadam stepped down as Warden, its budget had grown to £1,300 and the *Annual Report* listed sixteen separate branches of work, from girls' clubs to a legal advice service, each with its own staff of volunteers, some in the dozens.[49]

Yet Macadam, Rathbone and Jones also altered the settlement's direction, steering it towards those twin goals of professionalization and cross-class 'friendship' that Macadam and Jones had learned in London. With her belief that 'uncertain hap-hazard efforts [were] worse than none at all', Macadam was shocked to find that the settlement's workers received little or no training; almost immediately, the three women began planning a remedy.[50] Several prominent university men (and Rathbone family friends) – including the Vice-Chancellor Sir Alfred Dale, Professor of Political Economy E.K. Gonner, and Professor of Philosophy John MacCunn – offered to help, and in 1905 the School of Social Science and Training for Social Work opened.[51] It was run from the settlement, and its relationship to the university in those early days, Macadam remembered, was 'rather that of a poor and uninteresting relation.'[52] Yet, despite this marginal status, the school prospered. Frederick D'Aeth, who would collaborate closely with Rathbone and Macadam over the next ten years, came in 1905 as a tutor, and by 1906, the school was offering a challenging two-year course combining lectures with 'practical work'. Some of the university's most distinguished faculty (including Gonner, MacCunn and the historian Ramsay Muir) offered courses on sociology, philosophy and history,[53] while Rathbone lectured on civic administration, Macadam on voluntary efforts, and D'Aeth on the Poor Law.

A familiar blend of philosophical idealism and municipal socialism suffused their instruction, for this was the tradition in which MacCunn, D'Aeth, Rathbone and Macadam had all been educated. MacCunn, who had studied with Caird at Glasgow and with T.H. Green at Oxford, summarized beautifully the principles that guided the school's work. The end of human action, MacCunn told its students, must be to increase the public good; but how could such betterment be brought about? Obviously, he said, 'he who would act with effect must act in association': only through association could human action be 'broadened into civic patriotism' and intensified by sympathy. Good citizenship, to put it simply, could not be taught: only through collective action, ideally at the municipal level, would individuals grow in conscience and capacity. His faith in the moral effect of common action led MacCunn to dismiss old liberal arguments against state intervention. Working collectively, guided by their heightened social sympathies, local citizens could be trusted to use state powers for the common good.[54]

In keeping with these principles, the new school placed great emphasis on 'practical work', through which, after all, such cross-class collective action could be fostered. In the early years, students kept case records, served under school managers, helped young people find apprenticeships, ran the settlement's clubs, and spent six months developing a particular specialization; later, they often also worked for the Labour Exchange or some other new municipal service.[55]

Macadam, as director, insisted that students became familiar with independent working-class institutions: one could scarcely consider a student properly trained, she wrote, 'if his practical work had been confined entirely to relief work and the problems of destitution, and he had seen nothing of such constructive modern movements as Friendly Societies, the Co-operative Stores, and the Workers' Educational Association'.[56] Since (as Macadam put it) the school should act as 'a centre of light and knowledge, not only for the educated few but for the whole town',[57] special courses were offered for Poor Law officers, district nurses, domestic science teachers and, in time, other municipal workers.[58]

Macadam became thoroughly absorbed in the School, and by 1910 wished to resign as the Victoria Settlement's Warden to devote herself to it full-time. Eleanor and other wealthy donors raised a fund to endow a new lectureship to be held jointly at the university and the settlement,[59] and in 1911 Macadam was appointed as Lecturer in the Methods and Practice of Social Work at the modest but respectable salary of £200 per year. Under her guidance and the university's wing, the school grew in size and sophistication. By 1912–13, 241 students were enrolled in its general course of study and another 200 were attending specialized courses.[60] The university still refused to grant a degree in social work, but every year a hardy handful of students sat the school's own examinations, which were administered in 1913 by the impressive team of E.J. Urwick, Tooke Professor of Economics at King's College, London; Clement Attlee, then at the London School of Economics; and Maurice Birley, Warden of Toynbee Hall. To Macadam's great pride, most of these diploma students were women who had already completed a university degree and had chosen social work as a definite career.[61] Cicely Phelps, who became a child welfare officer for the London County Council, Cicely Leadley-Brown, who served as a welfare supervisor in the First World War, and many other social workers got their start in the programme established by Macadam and her allies at the settlement and at the university.

With its emphasis on training, the settlement in 1910 had moved some distance away from the amateurism that had so troubled Maude Royden. Under Macadam's direction, it also attempted to deal with the other problem Royden identified, the lack of a clear rationale for its existence. The first wardens and residents had tended to use a familiar language of female mission to the degraded and outcast when describing their work: as Dr Lilias Hamilton put it, they hoped 'to plant in a centre of vice, squalor and misery, a little oasis of education, refinement, and sympathy, to try (to use a Scriptural phrase) to introduce a little leaven which in time – a very long time of course – may leaven the whole lump'.[62] Macadam, by contrast, while sharing the desire 'to bring the lives of the two classes vaguely called "rich and poor" into more natural and more friendly relation with each other',[63] was uncomfortable with this language of *noblesse oblige*. The settlement, she insisted, was in the first instance simply another house, whose inhabitants should 'share as good citizens and neighbours' in the normal life of the district.[64]

What this meant in practice was that Macadam steadily built up – even favoured – those branches of work that did not involve material aid, and sought to turn those that did – such as the dispensary, the holiday funds, even the work with invalid children – into self-supporting social services. This led her to make some decisions that seem harsh in retrospect, insisting, for example, that local women make at least token payments for dispensary visits and other services.[65] Yet Macadam was convinced that ideals of independence were just as precious to the working as to the middle class. She was not ungenerous; she had, rather, a remarkably non-pathological view of working-class life. Only if the 'relief' element of the settlement's work was minimized, she thought, could middle-class and working-class women collaborate across class lines. No one rejoiced more wholeheartedly in the success of the settlement's clubs, gardening shows and dance classes, or was prouder when women from the surrounding streets began to take over the running of programmes. 'This is as it should be,' she commented, 'and we hope more and more that our relation with our neighbours will become that of fellow-workers and friends rather than the old-fashioned one of helpers and helped.'[66]

The settlement's growing aversion to 'relief' and its emphasis on a distinctly female mode of cross-class activism rubbed some of the older philanthropic organizations the wrong way. In 1905, Rathbone, Macadam and Emily Jones had all joined the Everton district committee of the Central Relief Society, using that branch to train students at the School of Social Science in casework methods; by 1908, however, they had come to dislike the CRS's narrow and exclusive focus on relief. Although Emily Jones would remain on the Everton committee, students were henceforth trained under her supervision at a new 'Office of Friendly Help' set up at the settlement to provide 'advice and information on behalf of the poor of our part of the town'.[67] A thousand local people used the office in its first year, and while it did not itself give out aid, referring all relief cases to the Central Relief Society or the boards of guardians, it did help applicants to locate the resources they needed, sending the unemployed to the Labour Exchange or to workrooms set up by the city's Distress Committee, and finding medical, legal and educational help for those who needed it.[68]

'Friendly help', however, was not enough: after years of residential work and home visiting, settlement workers understood that poor women needed more resources. In breaking with the Central Relief Society, then, Rathbone and Macadam were signalling not their disapproval of material aid *per se* but their loyalty to the idea that charitable effort in the future must develop in a more professional direction, and in partnership with an expanded local state. This was a view shared by virtually all members of the Royal Commission on the Poor Laws, and when the Commission's majority urged the establishment of municipal bodies to coordinate voluntary effort in every major town, Liverpool's progressives saw their chance. In 1909, with the support of a new Liberal mayor, Rathbone, Frederick D'Aeth and other progressives founded a 'Council of Voluntary Aid', which proposed to coordinate the work of all voluntary organizations in the city, and to maintain a central register of all recipients of *both* poor relief and charitable aid. Not everyone approved: some philanthropists objected to the blend of aid and 'inquisition',[69] while Labour guardians protested against any effort 'to show on how little people's body and soul could be kept together'.[70] With both central government support and strong local backing, however, the new council grew rapidly. By 1913, it was coordinating the efforts of more than a hundred affiliated charities, and its register contained details of over 47,000 'cases'.[71] And while the Council owed its success very largely to D'Aeth, who acted as its secretary for almost two dozen years, Rathbone, Macadam and Emily Jones also played important roles in the organization's early days – Rathbone by helping to fund D'Aeth's salary for a period of five years, and all three on the various council committees dealing with its general direction, with child welfare, and with the relief of distress.[72]

Yet all three women saw such charitable coordination as only half the battle, coming by 1910 to favour a substantial expansion in statutory municipal services. Even Macadam's views turned round: while in 1906 she had been sceptical even of the value of free school meals,[73] by 1910 she was telling the Annual Conference of Charity Organisation Societies that social workers should greet the trend towards statist social reform with 'hopefulness'.[74] Partly, of course, settlers were simply mirroring wider changes in attitudes that followed the foundation of the Labour Party and the 1906 Liberal electoral landslide. Yet the state also lost its terrors as it feminized, incorporating women into new municipal bodies and absorbing institutions that settlement workers had inaugurated. Even as early as 1905, the City Council had co-opted Rathbone and two other women 'experienced in the relief of distress' on to the new Distress Committee established under the Unemployed Workmen's Act, and had delegated to them the task of establishing programmes to deal with unemployed women.[75] With easy access to City Hall, settlement workers became accustomed to cooperating with Poor Law authorities, council committees and local schools. By 1910, the year Macadam stepped down as Warden, an impressive number of settlement house innovations – from the early classes for crippled children, now under the School Board, to the Skilled Apprenticeship and Registry Committee, now a sub-committee of the Labour Exchange – had become public services. Macadam rejoiced in this development, not only because it gave women a foothold within the state itself, but also because it freed the settlement to take on 'a kind of roving commission over the whole field of social welfare'.[76] 'Relieved of much of the curative work which is being more and more undertaken by public departments or special associations,' she wrote, 'the future Settlement, will, we hope, be able to give increasing prominence to schemes of constructive social effort.'[77]

There was one final reason for Macadam's new faith in local government – and this was that reforming women, and women with close ties to the settlement, were themselves winning election to local government. Women who paid local rates, a small group made up largely of widows, were eligible by the late Victorian period to vote in the local elections for boards of guardians, school boards and city councils; women were also eligible for election as School Board members or (if ratepayers) as guardians.[78] By the turn of the century, elected women, although few in number, had become an accepted presence; even such a determined opponent of women's parliamentary franchise as Mrs Humphry Ward agreed that women would bring special insight to local problems of poverty and child welfare. Liverpool saw its first women guardians and School Board members in the 1890s, and the settlement sought to increase their numbers. Thus in 1908, when a woman candidate stood 'as a woman and not as a party candidate' for the West Derby Board of Guardians, they vigorously supported her successful campaign.[79] One year later, in October 1909, the settlement workers seized a still-greater opportunity. Women ratepayers having just received the right to stand for the City Council, Eleanor Rathbone decided to contest a seat that had fallen vacant in Granby Ward on the death of its Liberal incumbent. Granby's neat Victorian terraces lay between the university and Greenbank; its clerks and respectable artisans consistently returned Liberals. Eleanor, already well known in the district, could scarcely have found a more promising seat.

She left little to chance, however, relying on suffragist and reforming women to canvass for her and on her powerful family to smooth her way. Eleanor stood, in good feminist fashion, as an Independent, but her brother Lyle and her cousin Herbert sat on the Council as Liberals and she had the support of some prominent Conservative women as well. In a rare moment of cross-party agreement, then, both parties stood aside to give her a straight fight against a socialist, Francis Welland. There were, of course, some objections: one disgruntled Liberal wrote repeatedly to the *Post* to complain (fairly enough) that 'too much capital is being made of the simple use of the name of Rathbone',[80] and Eleanor herself told her mother that both parties were 'very cross at not having a candidate of their own' and were 'grumbling at me and at each other'.[81] Outflanked by Welland on her left, Rathbone ran a moderate campaign, stressing her long experience with municipal affairs, her support for improved educational and social provision, and the need to have someone on the Council 'who could speak from a woman's point of view'.[82] She won decisively, polling 1,066 votes to her opponent's 516, and took particular pride in the fact that – as she told a luncheon of the Women's Local Government Society – while only 43 per cent of the men had turned out to vote, some 74 per cent of women electors had done so.[83] One year later, when her seat was up for re-election under the normal three-year rotation, the Conservatives – having discovered her true political stripes – sought to unseat her.[84] This time, with no opponent to her left, Rathbone was free to nail her progressive colours to the mast. She was not a socialist in the sense in which the word was employed by the Liverpool Labour Party, she admitted to her supporters in a speech shortly before that second election;

but if it was Socialism to believe that there was much wrong in the present social conditions, that the rich were too rich and the poor too poor, that every worker who did a fair day's work should receive a fair day's wage, a wage upon which he or she could live and not merely exist; that the City Council should set the example of being a model employer, that drastic action should be taken against unsanitary slums, and that there should be a gradual effort to level up the conditions as to housing, education, opportunities for holidays and recreation, hours of labour and rates of wages – if to hold these views was Socialism, then she was a Socialist (applause).[85]

Once again, she won decisively in a straight fight. Rathbone held Granby Ward as an Independent until her resignation in 1935, and only once during those years – in 1926 – was her seat contested.[86]

Rathbone voted largely with the progressive bloc on the Council and bore her share of committee work, enthusiastically supporting Liverpool's ambitious-housing plans. During those early years, however, as the only woman on the 120-member Council, she also kept a 'watching brief' on all issues concerning women and children, repeatedly pressing for better pay for women municipal employees.[87] There were only fourteen women city councillors across all of England and Wales in 1909; in joining this pioneering group (which included, in Manchester, her cousin and fellow suffragist Margaret Ashton), Rathbone moved into the public eye. Yet for all its symbolic importance, Rathbone's work as a city councillor never absorbed even a fraction of her time. What this position gave her, rather, was access and a public platform – access for those settlement workers and reforming women whose energy had placed her there, and a platform from which she could promote their causes. By 1910, then, the year of Rathbone's second municipal election victory and of Macadam's resignation as Warden, the settlement had more than proved itself, having won for women, as activists and as clients, a foothold within civic institutions and the local state.

Rathbone's social investigations and civic activities will soon claim our attention, for through them she developed the theories that would shape her later politics. Before turning to her work, however, it is worth noting how important the settlement house was to the lives of the young women who ran its programmes and lived in its halls. Although settlers sought 'friendship' with their

13. Election leaflet, 1910.

GRANBY WARD

MUNICIPAL ELECTION, November 1st, 1910.

Miss ELEANOR RATHBONE,

THE INDEPENDENT CANDIDATE.

Supported by the following among others : -

ALDERMAN SIR WILLIAM BOWRING, BART., J.P.	REV. H. H. MATTHEW.
DR. BICKERTON.	JOHN MORRIS, Esq., J.P., C.C.
BURTON W. EILLS, Esq., C.C.	A. LYLE RATHBONE, Esq., C.C.
ALEXANDER GUTHRIE, Esq.	H. R. RATHBONE, Esq., C.C.
CANON HARFORD.	W. B. STODDART, Esq., J.P.
A. E. JACOB, Esq., C.C.	MRS. EGERTON STEWART-BROWN.
JOHN JAPP, Esq., J.P., C.C.	MISS F. L. CALDER.
T. HARRISON JONES, Esq., J.P., C.C.	MISS GEORGIANA CROSFIELD, P.L.G.
HUGH JONES, Esq.	DR. MARY BIRRELL DAVIES.
WILLIAM JONES, Esq., P.L.G.	MRS. ELLIS, P.L.G.
JOHN LEA, Esq., J.P., C.C.	MISS E. C. GREENE.
	MISS FLORENCE MELLY.

Committee Room :—85, Granby Street. Open 10 a.m. to 9-30 p.m.

Hon. Secretary of Miss Eleanor Rathbone's Election Committee :
Miss OLIVE JAPP, 9, Alexandra Drive.

neighbours, they often found it among themselves: the settlement house became a forcing ground not only of social reform but of women's ambitions, collaborations and partnerships. In the world of the settlement, public work and private alliances were intertwined; social service and career advancement could proceed together.

In her teaching and in her person, Elizabeth Macadam brought these ideals together. People who came to know Macadam in London during the last decades of her life often remembered her as a difficult, even bossy woman.[88] ('Has she done social work?' Marjorie Green, secretary of the Family Endowment Society asked Rathbone's secretary on first meeting Macadam. 'Yes, well, I've been social-worked-over.')[89] But the very qualities that they found so irritating – her perfectionism, her domineering personality, her tendency, as the secretary of the Charity Organisation Society C.S. Loch put it, to approach issues 'rather in a robust . . .

than in a sentimental way'[90] – were, in those early years, real assets. Macadam's ambition, her strength of mind, and above all her independence, offered a powerful model for that generation of young women of good family who lived and worked under her supervision. And like many charismatic teachers, she bonded powerfully with her students, becoming, the settlement's report mourned on her resignation, 'not only a wise guide but a very real friend'. That report, probably written by Rathbone, praised Macadam's 'practical wisdom', 'organising ability', 'unfailing tact' and 'great personal charm'; it was her abilities that had made the settlement a success, its rooms always full, its programmes always expanding.[91]

To none of these young women was her friendship and example so important as to Rathbone herself. Eleanor had always had problems making friends. Her wealth, formidable intelligence and social reserve put people off. Even Margery Fry, who invited Eleanor and Hilda Oakeley to visit her during the summer holidays in 1898, confessed herself 'never absolutely free from fear of her' and dreaded the 'conversational bombs' she expected Rathbone to drop at the family dinner table.[92] Only a few – including eventually Fry – discovered that she was anything but proud; she was, rather, shy and a little socially incompetent. She recognized this failing with some grief. 'I am not really good at any form of social intercourse and nothing can cure that,' she once wrote to Elizabeth. 'I don't seem able to get inside the ring fence of any other personality or to let them inside mine.'[93]

But Elizabeth – attractive, sharp-tongued and undeferential – broke through Eleanor's 'ring fence' simply by ignoring its presence. Macadam and Rathbone seem from the outset to have spoken easily and without constraint; and to the amazement of Eleanor's family, their formidable relative let Macadam manage and chide her. Perhaps it was all those years of social work, but Elizabeth seemed to recognize from the first that Eleanor needed not more respect and admiration, but affection, argument, even a little bullying. Eleanor loved Elizabeth, we might say, because Elizabeth was not in awe of her, because Elizabeth – like her father – demanded a good deal of her, and because Elizabeth (unlike most of her friends) made her feel fully human.

Elizabeth thus brought Eleanor her first taste of emotional fulfilment since William's death, while also giving her some respite from her own demanding kin. For all Rathbone's wealth and influence, she was still an unmarried daughter living at home, still seen in dynastic rather than individual terms. Macadam, by contrast, was a self-supporting woman who, after she resigned as Warden in 1911, lived in her own house on a working-class street. Eleanor stayed at that house on occasion – when Elizabeth would, as she intriguingly put it, 'take care of Eleanor'.[94] The two friends also took long holidays together, including to Greece with Eleanor's mother in March 1907; and to the Lake District one summer, where they alarmed their old friends John and Florence MacCunn with the fervour of their support for women's suffrage.[95]

But while Macadam lived only a stone's throw from Greenbank and main-tained amicable relations with Eleanor's many relations, she resisted being turned into yet another Rathbone family retainer. Certainly B.L. Rathbone, Eleanor's nephew, thought that Macadam kept her distance in order to keep her self-respect: she couldn't bear to be patronized and was, the children of her friends recalled, intensely sensitive to slights.[96] Through her own hard work, she had become a person of some local influence, with a modest national reputation, and both Rathbone and Macadam were careful to make sure that their friendship did nothing to jeopardize that standing. Macadam's career, indeed the maintenance of separate public identities, was central to the happiness of this partnership. Having chosen spinsterhood precisely because they rejected a world in which a woman's worth was measured largely by her personal relations with men, they insisted that their own authority stem from professional qualification and work alone.

Few records remain from that time, and there is much that we can no longer discover about this friendship. What evidence there is – Rathbone's prudishness, her puzzled interrogation of a lesbian niece in the 1940s, her obvious anatomi-cal ignorance when campaigning against the practice of clitoridectomy in the 1920s, and the two women's separate bedrooms in the house they later shared – suggests it was never actively sexual.[97] But even to ask the question this way is to distort the matter: it is our post-Freudian culture that has questioned the depth of emotional attachments unaccompanied by physical desire. Raised as Victorians, Macadam and Rathbone would have seen things very differently; years of social work may well have led them to view sexual passion and sexual aggression as male attributes women were better off without. Having demon-strated, they thought, that marriage was not essential to a woman's life, they were discomfited by the later elevation of sex into an essential human need, and by the propensity in the 1920s to interpret female friendships in such terms.

Eleanor Rathbone and Elizabeth Macadam negotiated the conditions of their partnership at a feminist but pre-Freudian moment – a time when Victorian marriage was newly open to criticism, but the categories of alternative sexual practice not yet fixed. We cannot say for certain how Eleanor and Elizabeth, in their most private moments, lived; what we do know is that they chose to present this friendship – much as Sidney and Beatrice Webb did their marriage – as a partnership of equals for the social good: public service and not private pleasure was the measure of its success. Yet private pleasure there surely was as well, espe-cially for Rathbone, who had great difficulty enjoying anything she felt was not for a higher purpose. Friendship thus enabled Eleanor to satisfy her emotional needs while building her career: a happy resolution that many might envy.

Rathbone's happiness as an independent woman, blessed by friendship and wedded to public work, shines out in one brief sketch we find of her during these years. This is found in the diary of Winifred Richardson Evans, who in 1907 was about to marry Eleanor's cousin Herbert Reynolds Rathbone, then a well-established barrister and a powerful Liberal voice on the City Council. Winifred was not a sympathetic observer: she was about to become one of Liverpool's most important political wives and had little interest in spinsters. It was the family matriarchs, and especially the 'small, bright, clever' Evie, who drew her admiration: Winifred was impressed by Evie's pretty clothes and the ease with which she ran her household and kept her argumentative husband happy. But she was taken to Greenbank as well, and to a meeting at the Town Hall in support of the Victoria Settlement at which Eleanor spoke, and jotted down brief but clear-eyed sketches of the Greenbank sisters. Elsie, then over fifty, struck Winifred as 'rather lonely', looking 'thin and colourless, rather ill-in-health . . . & as if she *might* be peevish'. She looked, in other words, just the way a spinster was supposed to look, and Winifred dutifully felt sorry for her. Eleanor, then thirty-five, offered a distinct contrast:

Very firm, vigorous, strongminded, clearheaded, energetic & womansrightful – with hard red cheeks. Talks very well & knows a lot – & wrote a life of her father William Rathbone. She is awfully sane & is quite sure she is in the right (which she may be) but she does not attract me very much.[98]

All of the married woman's ambivalence towards the 'new woman' is apparent in this brief sketch. Eleanor, as Winifred perceived, had achieved independence while remaining single, while remaining a daughter living at home. Her authority derived in part from her family but even more, by now, from her own political achievements and her place within the community of independent women. Through the settlement, through Elizabeth Macadam, Eleanor was able to return to that company of 'glorified spinsters' that she had first encountered at Oxford. Drawing on the support of that community, and with Elizabeth at her side, she would turn her mind to her city and its manifold problems. Having herself painfully achieved her intellectual and emotional independence, she would go on to develop a new feminist analysis of women's oppression, one that placed the problem of dependence at its heart.

Chapter 6

Must Mothers be Poor?

By an unspoken agreement, Elizabeth Macadam and Emily Jones left one branch of settlement house work to Eleanor. The task of social investigation – of counting and classifying and writing reports – was peculiarly hers from the outset. And this was as Eleanor wished it, for even before Macadam and Jones arrived, she had already begun, painfully, to train herself as a social scientist. Her Oxford education had given her a philosophical foundation, but in many areas – statistics, modern history – she felt woefully ignorant. Yet, like the young Beatrice Potter, who had struggled to master political economy even though she found it '*hateful* – most hateful drudgery',[1] Rathbone was determined to overcome her own antipathy and family distractions to acquire the knowledge she needed. 'I am reading political questions and try to write a little every day for practice,' she wrote to Margery Fry in August 1898, although she was forced to admit that these efforts often didn't 'get beyond a few sentences'.[2] And like Beatrice Webb, she tested her new knowledge in the streets, collaborating first with her father and then with fellow workers at the women's settlement to study the conditions of women's work, the organization of dock labour, the household budgets of casual labourers and widows and a host of other problems.

Yet, unlike Beatrice Webb, Eleanor Rathbone embarked on her social investigations as a feminist, concerned to see women as autonomous beings, apart from their relations to men. A thread runs from those early inquiries to *The Disinherited Family*, Rathbone's later masterpiece: the thread of Rathbone's insistent focus on the problem of women's economic dependence. Those economic institutions – the labour market, the wage system – that Webb examined for their irrationality and class bias, Rathbone looked at rather differently, as part of an economic structure that assumed and enforced women's economic marginality. Tentatively, she began to develop her own economic analysis, one that would locate poverty and inequality as much in the relations of marriage and parenthood as in the relations of production. And from this feminist social science stemmed a feminist politics – a politics that made a case for the state support of women's maternal and household work.

But this is to begin at the end of the story: not until the First World War would Rathbone begin publicly campaigning for state 'endowment' of motherhood. More than a dozen years of social investigation and social work came first. Only after studying the market for women's work did she conclude that wage-earning could never emancipate wives; only after years in the voluntary sector did she come to argue for state intervention. In the course of that long conversion, she left few corners of Liverpool's economy unexplored. Through its dockyards and factories, courtyards and streets, Rathbone pursued the demon of women's dependence.

But why dependence, exactly? Why not violence, ill health, ridicule, overwork or some of the other disabilities from which women were then (and are still) suffering? In part, of course, Eleanor simply accepted the equation of economic independence with individual selfhood that lay at the foundation of liberal thought. The ability to support oneself, generations of Liberals argued, was the test equally of moral virtue and of political capacity – and if most measured female virtue differently, others were not so sure. Only the ability to earn one's living protected women from abuse by men, Mill argued in *The Subjection of Women*; bereft of such capacity, women turned to marriage not for companionship and love, but as (as Charlotte Lucas so famously put it), as their 'pleasantest preservative from want'. Eleanor grew up with these two texts and quoted them freely: Mill was her philosophical lodestar, Austen her favourite novelist. But the reason these insights spoke to her was because they so perfectly reflected the principles that had shaped her own young life. No man was more concerned to see his sons achieve 'independence' than William Rathbone, none more vigilant about the marriage settlements of his daughters, none more determined to treat all his children equally. Eleanor, unusually, grew up in a family where the patrimony was evenly divided, where the 'family fortune' was thought to belong to the family as a whole. How could she not be outraged to find that most women had no such 'inheritance', that every single shilling they touched had to be bargained from a man? All other subjections, she was sure, derived from that fundamental inequality. But why were women so economically vulnerable? How was the economy ordered, and what was women's place in it? If she could answer these questions, she thought, she could wrestle the demon of dependence to the ground.

She began not with housewives but with women workers. Like most students of political economy (and like many young women seeking an independent life), Eleanor looked first to the labour market to offer women a measure of autonomy. On her return from Somerville, she joined the Women's Industrial Council, which had been set up in 1894 to investigate and improve the working conditions of women. Led by a group of London-based women, including the Fabian socialists Clementina Black and B.L. Hutchins, and Ramsay MacDonald's wife Margaret, the Women's Industrial Council quickly established a reputation for reliable investigation and intelligent advocacy. Whilst its numbers remained small, a core of women interested in industrial issues, among them Eleanor's old friend from Oxford, Barbara Bradby (later Hammond), soon joined its ranks.[3] When Eleanor joined, a Liverpool branch was already in existence, although it was soon torn (possibly at Eleanor's instigation) between the trade unionist agenda of its founder, Mrs Jeannie Mole, and the desire of Eleanor and others to concentrate on social investigation. We know almost nothing about this quarrel, but Mole clearly lost: by 1897 she was active in another society organizing women workers, and the Liverpool Women's Industrial Council was in Eleanor's hands.[4]

Eleanor Rathbone's first social investigations were thus modest and practical surveys of Liverpool's women workers. A first traced the fate of 385 girls leaving school and found that few undertook any form of training;[5] a second, published in the *Women's Industrial News* in September 1900, examined women's work in cigar-making. Even in this early, brief report, Rathbone recognized the ways in which sex segregation of the workforce interacted with marriage to disadvantage women. With a seven-year apprenticeship and two or three years' practice necessary to achieve dexterity, cigar-makers were considered 'skilled'. How, then, could one explain their exceptionally low wages? They were not unionized, true, but a second problem was the prevailing assumption of their individual, rather than family, needs. Single women were satisfied with a wage of twelve to fifteen shillings, Rathbone wrote, while married women were thought to need only a supplementary wage. Although she did not at this stage spell out the implications of her findings, they were clear: marriage, whether anticipated or actual, weakened women's bargaining power at work.[6]

But the Women's Industrial Council was determined to change this state of affairs – 'to promote by all means in its power the recognition of the need of girls to receive technical and trade training . . . and to see that the needs of girls receive attention proportionate to that bestowed on boys'.[7] Rathbone and her colleagues gamely threw themselves into this task, setting up a committee at the settlement to arrange apprenticeships for young people and founding an 'Association of Trained Charwomen' to try to secure work at decent wages for this most exploited class. When the City Council co-opted Eleanor on to the municipal Distress Committee set up under the Unemployed Workmen's Act in 1905, she and the other two women on the committee also set up a sewing room for those women (mostly widows with young children) who came to the Distress Committee for help.[8]

Yet, valuable as these efforts were, they were also deeply frustrating. 'Considering the amount of work that has been involved', Rathbone admitted in 1908, the results achieved by the Skilled Apprenticeship Committee 'appear as discouraging as they well could be'. Among that year's thousands of school-leavers, a mere 218 had consulted the committee, which had succeeded in placing only 26 boys and 10 girls.[9] The situation of girls remained especially distressing:

the Women's Industrial Council could find only a very few courses – one in dress-making and one in hairdressing – open to girls who wanted to learn a trade.[10] Yet that lack of training, of any skill to fall back on, came back to haunt widows or women with unemployed or unreliable husbands. While the Association of Trained Charwomen gave its members 'a certain feeling of dignity and . . . an interest in the conditions of their trade',[11] its efforts were frustrated by the over-supply of desperate women willing to do the work at almost any wage.[12] And the Distress Committee's workrooms, although a crucial last resort, could offer only temporary help to a particularly needy few.

Moreover, the Liverpool Women's Industrial Council had been foiled in their one attempt to open a new branch of work to women, in the process learning a lesson about the complexities of women's economic situation that Rathbone, at least, never forgot. Some time in 1905 or early 1906, they organized a class in upholstery, hoping to bring women into some well-paid parts of the trade. Yet when they consulted the women's upholstery union, they found that its members opposed the class. They were related to the men in the upholstery trade, the women explained, and did not want to jeopardize men's position by learning any process not already accepted as 'women's work'.[13] Deferring to their desires, the Council abandoned their project – but if even the women's unions would not defend women's claims to work, Rathbone wondered, how could wage-earning ever become a reasonable path to economic independence?

Rathbone brought her concerns to the 1907 annual conference of the National Union of Women Workers, an umbrella organization of women active in volun-tary and philanthropic work. In the discussion following a paper by Mary Macarthur, the charismatic leader of the women's trade union movement, Rathbone mentioned her Liverpool experience and asked whether cross-sex union solidarity was really in the interests of women workers. 'One does not wish to set up sex antagonism, and it is perfectly right that women should be loyal to their men comrades,' she said, 'but at the same time they should see to it . . . that they are not confined to the unskilled branches of their work.'[14] Macarthur, however, would have none of this. 'I deprecate this introduction of sex antago-nism into the subject,' she retorted; 'the interests of men and women in industry are identical.' If men and women fought against each other, only the employer would benefit. 'The unscrupulous employer welcomes antagonism between the men and women in his employment.'[15]

This argument between Rathbone and Macarthur was merely one version of a quarrel over the respective merits of sex and class solidarity that divided both the women's and the trade union movements. Strict egalitarian feminists, such as Millicent Fawcett, objected to the labour laws, professional rules and trade union customs that barred women from many branches of work, while women trade unionists like Mary Macarthur and Margaret Bondfield insisted that women workers must earn acceptance by refusing to undercut men. The Women's

Industrial Council, composed of educated women seeking to reconcile feminism and socialism, found itself divided. While Clementina Black defended married women's work and argued for statutory minimum wages, Margaret MacDonald, convinced that married women had no business in the workforce anyway, looked forward to the day when men's successful organizing for higher wages would simply force women out.[16]

In quarrels like these, Rathbone started out entirely on Black's side.[17] But her experience with the cigar-makers, charwomen and upholsterers disillusioned her, leading her to doubt that wage-earning would ever offer most women economic independence. Everything – the labour market, the trade union movement, even their own culture and expectations – conspired to tell girls that they had no future in the workplace, to force them back into the 'women's sphere' of the home. Very well then, Rathbone thought: if marriage was supposed to provide for women, she would investigate whether it actually did so. By 1909, Rathbone and the Liverpool Women's Industrial Council were studying the conditions not of wage-earning women but of housewives, of those seeking to meet their needs through the 'family wages' paid to working men.

Of course, by this point Rathbone already knew that the 'family wage' was illusory, having documented its mythic status in a study, initially begun with her father, into the pay and conditions of Liverpool's dockers. The great London dock strike of 1889 and the almost simultaneous appearance of the first volumes of Charles Booth's survey of East London life and labour had awoken a middle-class public to the dockers' plight; in the next few years, Booth and other social reformers would begin developing schemes to rationalize dockyard labour.[18] In Liverpool, a first proposal by Booth to create a pool of registered workers was shipwrecked on the twin rocks of employers' reluctance to limit their supply (or oversupply) of labour and dockers' fear of losing easy access to work.[19] Yet William Rathbone had followed these efforts eagerly, and after his return to Liverpool in 1895 set up meetings between Booth and leading employers to try again. When these efforts again failed, he planned himself to lay out the case for reform – and, as his health deteriorated, turned to Eleanor to help him. From shipowners, foremen, dockers and union leaders (with whom William was on good terms), the two collected wage and employment statistics, information on hiring practices, and opinions about decasualization schemes.[20] Eleanor was absorbed in the work of the Women's Industrial Council and found her father's project a bit tedious. Since William died before the writing had even begun, she could have given it up.

But she didn't. In 1904, as she was writing her father's biography, she wrote up the inquiry on her own. This was an audacious decision, one with great potential benefits but also considerable risks. For dock labour was not like cigar-making: it was deemed the most profound of Britain's labour problems, the subject on which its most famous social investigators – Charles Booth, Beatrice Webb – had cut their teeth. Rathbone had the Booth inquiry in front of her as she worked through her statistics; her awareness that it provided the standard by which she would be judged accounts, probably, for the modest tone in which she presented her efforts. Her father had set the questions for the inquiry, she stated. She had not been able find answers to all of them but hoped 'at least to indicate the directions in which answers may be looked for'.[21]

Was this false modesty? Some forty closely printed, tightly argued and exhaustively documented pages followed. Professions of 'amateurism' notwithstanding, the *Report of an Inquiry into the Conditions of Dock Labour at the Liverpool Docks* is in fact the most professional of Rathbone's social investigations and remains the most reliable source of information on the market for casual labour in Edwardian Liverpool.[22] The picture she painted was not a comforting one. Although 'certainly not less than 20,000' men sought work at the separate hiring stands that dotted the quays, many of these men were chronically underemployed, averaging no more than a three-day week.[23] Liverpool's endemic poverty was one result, but casual labour also left its mark on the culture of the port and on the lives and character of thousands of individual men. Dockers 'adapted the habits of their lives only too well to the conditions of their work', preferring spells of intense work interrupted by bouts of 'complete idleness'. For the younger ones in particular this 'sense of being "their own masters"' offered 'some compensation for the irregularity of their earnings'. But, Rathbone pointed out, no such freedom was enjoyed by their wives, who were forced 'to plan out the expenditure of a weekly income that zig-zags in this bewildering way'. 'It is by the wives and children that the hardship of irregular earnings are felt most keenly.'[24] Already Eleanor's eyes were being drawn to the women and children clustered around the men.

Rathbone's inquiry catalysed another round of meetings between employers and labourers, but mutual distrust was still too strong.[25] Not until 1912, after the Liberal government had made decasualization a priority, did Ministry of Labour officials gratefully return to Rathbone's work when crafting Liverpool's first comprehensive dock registration scheme.[26] Her inquiry thus did eventually play its part in the long struggle to rationalize dock labour, but it had a more immediate effect on her own career, bringing her to the attention of those London-based reformers determined to go beyond investigation to action. By 1907, at the age of thirty-five, she was enough of an expert to be invited to give evidence to the Royal Commission on the Poor Laws, then conducting its famous hearings in London. There, she was asked for her frank advice on how best to attack casual labour, 'as we know you have worked with great success and for a long time in Liverpool'.[27] Rathbone was happy to comply. In her evidence, she stressed the link between male casual labour and family poverty, and spelt out recommendations she had hitherto been too circumspect to offer.

Casual labour wasn't just inefficient, Rathbone told the Commissioners, it also deformed workers' character and poisoned their domestic life. All the incentives built into casual labour were bad: the system offered 'no inducement to sobriety'; it discouraged enrolment in friendly societies; it aged workers prematurely; and it made boys reluctant to enter apprenticeships. Worst of all was its effect on family life. The hard-drinking, free-wheeling culture of the port victimized wives and children in particular, for dockers tended to give only the smallest weekly sum to their wives for household expenses, 'all above this sum being spent by the husband on his pleasures'.[28] Burdened with children and usually unable to earn, wives were powerless to respond. They were the unseen victims of economic downturns and spousal neglect alike.

Eleanor, however, saw them; at the settlement, she walked and worked among them. Thus in 1907, the year of her evidence to the Poor Law Commission, she began another investigation. Much was known of the industrial side of the problem of dock labour, she noted, but no special study had been made of those workers' domestic conditions.[29] A 'Joint Research Committee' was thus set up by the six organizations wishing to collaborate on such a project (the Liverpool branches of the Christian Social Union, the Fabian Society and the National Union of Women Workers; the Liverpool Economic and Statistical Society; the Liverpool Women's Industrial Council; and the Victoria Settlement) and a plan of action agreed. Once again – as with dock labour – Rathbone found herself in good company. Across Britain, government officials, local authorities and social investigators were observing and quantifying working-class life as never before. Seebohm Rowntree's comprehensive study of poverty in York, published in 1901, had reminded people that poverty was a provincial as well as a London problem, and had also – through its establishment of two 'poverty lines' and its careful allocation of York's population into separate categories – set a new standard for social research.[30] A distinct 'women's tradition' in social investigation was also developing, as women 'settlers' and socialists milked their working-class neighbours for the secrets of their domestic lives. Many of the classic women's studies would appear in the years immediately before or after the First World War – including the Fabian Women's Group's study of Lambeth housewives, *Round about a Pound a Week*, and Anna Martin's *Nineteenth Century* articles on housewives in Rotherhithe – but already in 1907, Florence Bell, wife of the ironmaster Sir Hugh Bell, had contributed *At the Works*, a detailed study of the households of her husband's employees in Middlesbrough.[31]

Rathbone and her colleagues drew upon (or anticipated) these studies. Like Rowntree, they were concerned less with wage levels than with consumption, and thus with the level of the 'housekeeping money' managed by the wife. Like the later Fabian women investigators, however, they were attempting not a comprehensive urban survey but a portrait of how one particular group of families lived. They thus began by preparing weekly 'budget books' with pages for income and expenditure, dispatching some thirteen social workers (twelve of them women) to visit local housewives and appeal for their help. Many understandably refused, whether because they were 'poor scholars' (as they euphemistically put it) or because they found the request meddlesome, but some had 'strong views about the disadvantages of the casual labourer's lot' and positively wanted to help. The inquiry depended on their cooperation; given the trouble involved, Rathbone noted, 'one wonders rather at the compliance of the few than at the refusal of the many to contribute their budgets for the information of the public'. 'It would be interesting,' she added drily, 'if an investigator could be found brave enough, to attempt to carry out the same inquiry in a middle-class suburb of Liverpool.'[32]

This was a troublesome, painstaking investigation. More than half of those who promised to keep the budget books dropped out; after a year, the committee had only 429 weekly budgets from some 40 families. And yet, even this small sample yielded some striking findings. Two-thirds of the families in which budgets were kept for at least four weeks were living below Rowntree's most stringent poverty line.[33] Their homes were overcrowded, cheerless and sometimes dirty; their diets meagre and almost entirely lacking in milk, green vegetables and fruit. And yet, Rathbone insisted, one could not just blame the ignorance of mothers: 'on the whole one is more astonished at the amount some of them accomplish in their homes with so poor an equipment, and at the high level of devotion, patience and cheerfulness they reach, than at the deficiencies of others'.[34] What one should note, instead, was the ways in which irregular earnings heightened wives' difficulties. 'I wouldn't care if it was only little he earned, if only it was regular,' was reportedly the dominant view.[35] Since rent was a constant, and most households sought to make payments for burial insurance (chilling testimony to their own estimate of their risks), the quality and quantity of the most elastic item in the budget – food – varied enormously. Yet housewives, obviously, had to feed their families even during slack periods: how, then, did they cope?

Few were able to make up shortfalls by earning: although sixteen of forty did bring something into the household by charring, hawking or washing, in only six of these cases were their earnings more than 'trifling'.[36] Nor could they draw on savings, few ever having had enough of a surplus to put money aside. The great majority of wives, then, turned to the only local figures who would help, smoothing out 'the curve of income and expenditure . . . by the help of the pawnbroker, or money-lender, or both'.[37] Pawning, which one historian has calculated was resorted to by the average working-class family every fortnight,[38] was not felt to be shameful. As one woman typically put it, she 'had no mercy for those who put themselves into the hands of money-lenders, but thought no-one could bring up a family like hers without occasional pledging'.[39] And Rathbone, who herself once pawned a gold watch (albeit in Macadam's name) when caught without ready cash on holiday,[40] considered the distinction 'amply justified'.[41] The moneylender, usually a local woman, charged exorbitant rates of interest for very small loans; by carrying such debts over weeks or months, many housewives paid their value in interest many times over.

Published in 1909, *How the Casual Labourer Lives* can stand as an early analysis of the credit arrangements of the poor. Yet, in comparison with Rowntree's *Poverty*, and still more the inquiries by Lady Bell and the Fabian Women's Group, the study disappoints. Given its tiny sample, the committee tried too hard to be 'scientific': its report consisted largely of case summaries and tables of aggregate data on income, expenditure and diet. Rathbone's perceptive analysis of this material was confined to an introduction, and even this was remarkable for what it left out. Rathbone did note the privation and physical debility of wives in particular, and pointed out that marital affection seemed to last only until 'it has accomplished the primary end for which Nature intended it'.[42] But, unlike Maud Pember Reeves, author of the Fabian study, who paid close attention to the husband's monopolization of the family food,[43] unlike Lady Bell, who noted that wife-beating was 'not so entirely a thing of the past as some of us would like to think',[44] Rathbone did not give special emphasis to women's victimization at the hands of their husbands. Such evidence can be found in the interstices of the Liverpool inquiry – in the words of one woman, for example, who said she 'dare not fill in the book, because if her husband saw how much money she was borrowing he'd "hammer" her'[45] – but the report does not stress men's contribution to their wives' problems. There is little hint here of Rathbone's later insistence that men's desire for domestic power lay at the root of women's economic dependence. Instead, the report located failures of 'character' in the system of casual labour, which did everything 'to foster the formation of bad habits and nothing to encourage the formation of good ones'.[46]

The report's recommendations disappoint as well. Rathbone, like Charles Booth and Beatrice Webb (and unlike such strict voluntarists as Octavia Hill and Helen Bosanquet), believed that social investigation should serve 'as a basis for policy prescription',[47] but there is little suggestion here of the bold thinking that would mark her later work. The report called for further inquiry into the problems of pawnbroking and moneylending; it urged that casual labourers be allowed to bank a portion of their earnings with the firm to be drawn on in slack weeks. Yet while it admitted that 'more drastic remedies are needed', it could suggest only that a fresh attempt be made at decasualization.[48] In 1907, Rathbone had told the Poor Law Commission bluntly that since private enterprise had failed the docks should simply be brought under public control,[49] but did not repeat that recommendation here. Reform of the labour market was envisaged, but not reform of the wage system itself. Within a year or two, however, Rathbone would begin thinking of ways to put an independent income directly in the housewife's hands.

The breakthrough came in 1912, when Rathbone published two landmark pieces, a pamphlet entitled *The Problem of Women's Wages*, and a shorter article on 'The Economic Position of Married Women' in the suffrage journal *Common Cause*. The studies of cigar-makers and charwomen, dockers and dockers' wives, had documented but not explained women's economic powerlessness; they had suggested a relationship between women's labour market and domestic situations, but had left that relationship unanalysed. The essays published in 1912, however, theorize that connection, offering a complex analysis of the relationship between marriage and the market, production and reproduction, public and private subjection. After years of 'practical work', Rathbone suddenly found her voice.

What made this breakthrough possible? Not some new idea or insight, for as Rathbone herself recalled she began puzzling through the connection between women's low pay and the dependence of wives and children in a paper written for her 'Associated Prigs' at Somerville many years earlier. The enabling factor was, instead, political and circumstantial – something had happened to make Rathbone feel able to rework and publish these essays *now*. That 'something' was the women's suffrage movement. The campaign for the vote was at its height in these immediate pre-war years: women felt themselves poised on the brink of political power. Suddenly, the world seemed malleable. In the wake of women's enfranchisement, suffragists imagined, even the most entrenched institutions – marriage, the market economy – could be purged of their male bias, transformed through feminist practice and feminist thought. Rathbone, who spearheaded the suffrage campaign in Liverpool, began looking at her society with new eyes – as a political system, organized to perpetuate male dominance but open equally to revision.

The Problem of Women's Wages began by posing a common question. How, Rathbone asked, could one explain the fact that women were paid less than men not only absolutely but relative to the respective value of their work? Experts pointed to a range of factors – women's smaller subsistence needs, their partial support by men, their lack of skill and their lack of union organization – but all of these, Rathbone concluded, were merely aspects of a more fundamental 'cause of causes'.[50] The reason men demanded more, needed more, expected more and were granted more was because they did – in the aggregate if not individually – have 'families to keep'. Since married women as a rule withdrew from wage-earning after marriage, 'the great bulk of the *financial* cost of rearing fresh generations has to come out of the earnings of the male parent'.[51] Men thus exerted themselves, individually and collectively, to earn a 'family wage', while women were usually paid, and often expected, an amount adequate at most for one person. Thus while men and women were not explicitly paid unequally, all factors – from union pressures to the press of basic needs, from educational practices to expectations – tended to exaggerate the differential between the wages of women and men. 'All the factors in the problem of women's wage,' Rathbone concluded:

have their root in the one set of facts common to women as apart from men; viz., their functions as childbearers and housewives, and the economic depen- dance [*sic*] of themselves and their children on the male parent which, under present social arrangements, the proper performance of those functions entails. In simpler words, the difference between the wages of men and women is due to the different consequences which marriage has for the two sexes.[52]

In tracing unequal pay to the root of the domestic division of labour itself, Rathbone might have been accused of over-complicating the issue, transforming what could be a remediable wrong into an inevitability. She was aware of the danger. 'It may be said that if my argument proves anything,' she admitted, 'it proves that the lowness of woman's wages, being based on fundamental and unalterable circumstances of sex, must itself, in this best of possible worlds, be inevitable and right.'[53] But another, more radical, conclusion was possible. Making a clear distinction between what we would today call the social circum- stances of 'gender' and biological sex, Rathbone pointed out that 'the circum- stances of sex are not unalterable, although the fact of sex is'. Children might need care and support, but they did not need to be cared for by dependent mothers or supported by the male wage. 'The arrangement by which the cost of rearing fresh generations is thrown as a rule upon the male parent, is not the only possible, nor even the only existing one.'[54]

The question, then, was simply whether this arrangement was desirable, and Rathbone proceeded to point out its many disadvantages. The ideal of the male family wage created 'a very real antagonism of interests between men and women workers, *qua workers*', for men would go to almost any lengths to protect their jobs and wages from competition from women. It also caused great hardship among those women workers who *did* – against conventional wisdom – have dependants to support. Worst of all, however, was the fact that the system left the well-being of hard-working mothers to the goodwill of men. This, to Rathbone, was rank injustice, for if 'the man in getting his wages is paid, not for his own work alone but for the work of his wife as child-bearer, nurse and house- keeper',[55] then those wages were by rights hers as well. Yet few people saw things this way, and – believing that 'a man has a right to do what he likes with his own' – turned a blind eye to 'a great deal of suffering and degeneracy, physical, mental and moral, among the women and children of the industrial classes'.[56] The system of paying for maternity through the wages of men, she concluded, might be 'satisfactory alike to masculine sentiment and to masculine love of power', but it left mothers entirely at the mercy of men.[57]

Was some better arrangement possible? If more women were in the labour force, Rathbone speculated, the effect would certainly be to raise women's wages and lower men's. But another solution was also possible, and 'in the opinion of the present writer, in this other way lies the best hope of solving, not only the problem of women's wages, but several other difficult social problems'.[58] This 'other way' was 'the device rather unfortunately called payment of motherhood' – a solution that would grant mothers the recognition they deserved and abolish any justification for unequal pay.[59] 'It appears then,' Rathbone concluded in *The Problem of Women's Wages*, 'that the efforts of those who desire to bring about equality of wages between the sexes had best be directed to hastening the large social change here indicated.'[60]

Rathbone's analysis of the connection between the household and the market is a landmark in the development in her thought, and can be seen as a significant contribution to feminist thought more broadly. Rathbone was not the first to look at marriage as an economic institution, or to point to the ways in which motherhood forced women into dependence, for the great tradition of socialist-feminist writings – from Friedrich Engels's *Origins of the Family, Private Property and the State* to Olive Schreiner's *Woman and Labour* – had also made those points. She was not alone in seeking to puzzle out real and practical solutions to the problem of marital dependence, as feminists, Fabian socialists, working-women's organizations and even practical politicians were also debating the rival advantages for mothers of wage-earning, legal reform or the introduction of new state entitlements. Nor was she the first to look to the 'endowment of motherhood', although this phrase could mean anything from the Women's Co-operative Guild's proposals to build up maternal health and welfare services to the plan – propounded by H.G. Wells in novel and tract – to put the entire population of mothers on the national payroll.[61] Yet Rathbone's analysis of these issues does mark an intellectual breakthrough for feminism, and for three reasons.

First and most importantly, Rathbone did not treat the issue of women's economic dependence in isolation, instead embedding her analysis within a broader theorization of the remuneration of socially necessary work. Feminists had often pointed out that married women's dependence was a problem *in itself*; what Rathbone did was to point to the connection between that domestic dependence and the organization of the distributive system. To put it another way, what Rathbone did was less to uncover the particular problem of the mother's lack of payment than to reinterpret the economy as a whole *from the standpoint of that insight*. Perceiving the worlds of social production and reproduction as a single economic system, she located what she felt to be a fatal flaw in the system – the economic dependence of mothers – and teased out the relations that produced it.

Second, however, Rathbone conducted that larger investigation from a rigorously feminist perspective. Ignoring the cross-cutting division of class, Rathbone's analysis was concerned *only* with the axis of sex. As she saw it, the problem was not the level of men's pay, but that one group of persons (all men) were being paid through the wage system for the work that a quite different group (mothers) were doing. Put simply, women's wages were being paid to men. It was this fundamental insight that made Rathbone's analysis so radical but also, later, so controversial, for unlike many other advocates of 'endowment of motherhood' Rathbone never implied that justice to women could be achieved solely through some class-based redistribution or through the generosity of that amorphous entity, 'the state'. Rather, to give mothers their just reward, men would have to give something up. Whatever the distribution of wealth between the classes, income must be redistributed across gender lines.

But if all men would lose, all women – and not just mothers – would gain. This was the third strength of her argument: that it recognized, and sought to reconcile, the rival interests of single women and married women, the waged and the unwaged. The single, independent 'new women' of the 1890s had often thought of married women simply as (in Schreiner's famous phrase) 'sex-parasites', living in indolence off the labours of men, morally indistinguishable from prostitutes in their reliance on sexual services to earn their bread.[62] Measures like endowment, in this view, would simply confirm married women in sexual subjection, deterring them from the honourable path of wage-earning. After years in the Liverpool slums, however, Rathbone could recognize the class bias in this perspective. Housewives, to her mind, *were* workers; they just weren't paid for their work. Wage-earning and endowment were thus not conflicting strategies: they were solutions for different women, or women in different stages of life. Moreover, she argued, because the dependence of wives justified women's lower pay, endowment and equal pay would actually be mutually reinforcing. With married women paid for their work, wage-earners (including women) could be paid equally without reference to 'family needs'.

Intellectually sophisticated as this argument was, it did not meet with much support, for reasons Rathbone should have anticipated. In acknowledging that most married women were in fact unwaged and supported by men, and that 'in the normal case, the financial cost of rearing the new generation is defrayed wholly or mainly out of the earnings of the male parent',[63] Rathbone admitted that there was – in the absence of endowment – a kind of rough justice in unequal pay. But any questioning of equal pay – any suggestion that it might not serve the needs of *all* women – was anathema to feminists. *Common Cause*, antici-pating protest, explained that they published her essay not because they accepted her analysis but 'because it is a clear and reasoned statement of a view generally very ill-expressed and more usual perhaps among anti-suffragists than suffra-gists'.[64] And the objections were quick to come in. The working-class suffragist Ada Nield Chew and one W.A. Elkin protested that men owed their higher wages to their better training and organization and not to any recognition of their family responsibilities; Maude Royden insisted that feminists should never agree to women receiving lower pay than men for comparable work.[65] Yet none of these criticisms, Rathbone retorted, really answered her main point, which was that 'so long as the maintenance of the mothers and children of the nation has . . . to be met out of the wages of the male parent', it was 'not only inevitable . . . but right and fair' that his wage should be a 'family' wage and his wife's right to a share of it enforced by law.[66] Rathbone, in fact, did not accept the first condition – that wives and children must be supported by men's wages – but she did believe that, if they *were* to be thus supported, their share of a 'family wage' should be enforced.

But was Rathbone too quick to accept a conventional sexual division of labour, to accept that married women would normally withdraw from the labour force and devote themselves to an exclusively domestic role? Certainly from today's standpoint Royden's principled defence of equal access to work and equal pay, or Chew's insistence on women's ability to combine motherhood with wage-earning, might seem more appealing. Yet Rathbone's stance had (and has) the merit of recognizing domestic labour and childrearing as *work*; it also better reflected contemporary working-class preferences. The second half of the nine-teenth century – the period in which a movement arose among single, educated women for access to careers – saw a steady retreat of married working-class women from the formal workforce, with the percentage returned as 'occupied' in the census falling from 25 per cent in 1851 to 10 per cent in 1901.[67] Sustained by protective legislation, union restrictions, rising male wages and a pervasive rhetoric of domesticity, by 1900 the male breadwinner norm was established as an ideal, and to a considerable extent as a reality, within working-class life. Not only trade unions but even the new working-class women's organizations – the Women's Labour League, the Women's Co-operative Guild – largely accepted that ideal. What these women's organizations did not accept, however, was the idea that the housewife, with her endless rounds of meals to cook and laundry to wash, was, somehow, a 'parasite'. 'The wife contributes by her work in the family equally with the husband,' the Women's Co-operative Guild resolved in 1910, and 'some form of economic independence' should thus be assured to her.[68]

Rathbone thought endowment was the answer. But this was a radical idea in the years before the First World War; it is still a radical (and largely rejected) idea today. Rathbone approached it cautiously. She was, after all, a practical politi-cian – a city councillor, with a seat on numerous public committees. She did not have H.G. Wells's freedom to propose reforms without considering their popu-larity or cost. She had also worked with voluntary institutions long enough to believe that small-scale experiment should precede any comprehensive measure. In 1911, then, she began where she could, with two communities of women who had found that 'family wage' to be particularly unreliable. In the years before the war, she returned to social investigation, but social investigation with a differ-ence. Now, she knew exactly what policy she wished to advocate, and in one case at least had the political clout to effect it.

Her first case was that of seamen's wives – the wives of stewards, firemen and other shipboard workers hired by the large shipping firms. In 1910, the Liverpool

Women's Industrial Council began to look into their case. Most seamen were paid monthly, and while the Merchant Shipping Acts of 1894 and 1906 allowed them to allot up to half of their pay to their wives, such allotments were purely voluntary. Some wives were thus left penniless when their husbands shipped off, and even those who drew allotments had to contend with monthly payment; often they were forced to turn to the moneylender or the Poor Law. For Rathbone and for Emma Mahler, a fellow suffragist who interviewed many of the wives, the situation demanded immediate action: 'Surely a seaman should be not merely permitted but obliged by the law to make some provision for the maintenance of his wife and young children before he takes himself out of the country for a period of many weeks or months,' they wrote in their pamphlet, *Payment of Seamen*, published in 1911.[69] A seaman should be able to allot up to two-thirds of his wages, and to have that money paid weekly; moreover, if he neglected to make such provision, his wife should be able to apply to a magistrate and have an allotment granted, without having to turn to the Poor Law.

Rathbone and Mahler then organized a campaign, publishing the results of their inquiry in *Common Cause*, the *Women's Industrial News*, and, crucially, the populist and Tory *Liverpool Courier*.[70] They were supported by Charles Booth and by Richard Holt, a Liverpool Liberal MP who managed to steer an amendment through Parliament allowing for larger allotments and more regular payments. In January 1912, at a 'well-attended meeting' in the Liverpool Town Hall, Mahler thanked Holt for his help while Rathbone and Charles Booth urged shipowners to encourage their employees to make allotments. Joseph Cotter, President of the National Union of Ships' Stewards, Cooks, Butchers and Bakers, also lent his support, saying that he only wished that the Act had made allotments compulsory.[71] His union had favoured extending the allotment system for years, he wrote to the *Courier*, thanking Mahler and Rathbone 'for the grand fight they have put up on behalf of the seamen's wives and children'.[72] In this restricted case, and with the backing of the men themselves, Rathbone and Mahler secured a partial disaggregation of the male family wage.

But in her second case, that of widows, Rathbone faced stiffer opposition, for here she was pressing the claim of mothers not on their individual husband's wage but rather on the collective 'social wage' as a whole. Rathbone and the settlement leaders had been trying to improve the situation of widows for many years. Their students visited those who applied for relief and, in keeping with Poor Law policies, sought to find them work, occasionally even placing young children in an orphanage to allow the mother to earn.[73] Yet the settlement workers detested these policies: the widows, they noted, could usually only turn to charring, and their incomes, even when supplemented with the shilling per head allowed by the guardians, were far from adequate.[74] By 1907, Rathbone had already had enough. In evidence to the Poor Law Commission, she argued that needy widows should be dealt with quite differently: their relief should be much more generous and administered by women officers, apart from other Poor Law cases. After all, she told a sceptical C.S. Loch, a widow's poverty was not her fault; nor could any working-class man, 'however provident he may be', be expected to save enough to support a wife and a family of young children for years after his death.[75] To Octavia Hill's argument that 'one would rather encourage the spirit of independence', Rathbone retorted that, however independent their spirit, poor women could find little work in Liverpool.[76] And these women *were*, in any case, working: they were caring for children, behaviour considered meritorious in women who had not had the misfortune to lose their husbands. In the case of widows, Rathbone implied, the moral assumptions that underpinned the Poor Law and the Charity Organisation Society – that the market would sort out the diligent and prudent from the lazy and profligate – simply did not hold. The Commission, in the end, agreed with her. Dr Ethel Williams, one of its own investigators, had found Liverpool's West Derby union to be one of the worst in the nation; Liverpool's guardians also confessed that they granted out-relief readily but at utterly inadequate rates, counting on the charities to step in to make up the difference.[77] The Commission's Majority and Minority Reports both recommended that relief for widows be increased and administration improved.[78]

Rathbone and the members of the Liverpool Women's Industrial Council were jubilant and wished to publicize Williams's scandalous findings. They held off out of fear of offending the guardians further, but by the spring of 1913 thought they had waited long enough. They therefore published a study of some 40 cases from the Parish of Liverpool, 18 from West Derby and 19 from Toxteth (Liverpool's three Poor Law unions), demonstrating the extent to which widows' income still fell below a scale of minimum needs. Cicely Leadley-Brown, at this stage Rathbone's right-hand woman in both the Liverpool Women's Suffrage Society and at the settlement, gathered most of the data. Rathbone, once again, wrote the report.

It was a shot across the bow. Not only did the report resurrect in selective and pithy quotation the Royal Commission's charges, but it insisted that the local response had been at best half-hearted. Rates of poor relief had remained very low, and with minuscule earnings, the widows were terribly poor: 56 of the 77 households studied in the report were below Rowntree's poverty line. Those boards of guardians that had attempted reform had done a poor job. The Parish of Liverpool, the report noted, had raised rates but hadn't improved supervision; in West Derby the guardians had made the even worse mistake of improving administration while maintaining low rates, as if good advice could make up for proper food. As Rathbone wrote:

It is hard for a woman to be an efficient housewife and parent while she is living under conditions of extreme penury – obliged to live in an insanitary house because it is cheap; waging a continual war with the vermin which infests such houses; unable to spend anything on repairs and replacements of household gear unless she takes it off the weekly food money; limited in the use of soap, soda and even hot water, because of the cost of coal; with no pennies to spare for the postage or tram rides that would keep up her own and her children's intercourse with relatives at a distance, or give them a day's holiday in the parks or on the sands, or enable her to frequent the Labour Exchange to seek better work for herself and the elder boys and girls; and trying through it all to earn part of the family income as well as to administer it. The astonishing thing to us is not that so many women fail to grapple with the problem successfully, but that any succeed.[79]

Effective poor relief, Rathbone concluded, required *both* higher rates and better 'supervision'.

Rathbone's report was published in March 1914 and caused an immediate furore. The clerk of the Toxteth Board of Guardians professed himself 'in a rage'.[80] Eleanor's family, long associated with the Toxteth guardians, may well have been embarrassed, and even the executive committee of the Council of Voluntary Aid, on which Macadam and Emily Jones both sat, publicly dissociated itself from the report.[81] Rathbone insisted that the study had been misread: she had not intended to attack the guardians, but rather to make the case for removing widows with children from the Poor Law entirely.[82] 'If the widow is keeping her home and her children properly,' Rathbone wrote in a more plain-spoken version of her report published in *Common Cause*, 'she is carrying out her part of the implied marriage contract. She is not a failure because she cannot carry out her husband's part as well.'[83] And given her meritorious fulfilment of socially useful work, she was entitled to public support – to the continued payment of that portion of her husband's pay which had, in Rathbone's view, always been paid to him on the assumption of her work. It should be recognized, she argued, 'that a widow who is doing her duty by her young children, tending them, washing, sewing, and cooking for them, is not a pensioner upon the bounty of the State, but is earning the money which she draws from it by services just as valuable to the community as those of a dock-labourer, a plumber or a soldier, perhaps even not much less valuable than those of the Relieving Officer or Poor Law Guardian who now browbeats or patronizes her'.[84] Motherhood and child-care, in other words, should be recognized as a 'job'. The widow with young children should be granted not relief but a 'contract of service', through which the state would provide adequate maintenance, 'binding the mother in exchange to bring up her children in such an environment as would make it likely that they should grow up into normally healthy and useful citizens'.[85] She should, to put it another way, be 'endowed'.

Arguments like these did nothing to placate the Poor Law guardians, but by 1914 Rathbone did not really care. Her actions had a new edge to them; after years working in the voluntary sector, she had become impatient. For she had developed not only an economic analysis but also a political analysis: she had arrived at an explanation for *why* governments were willing to 'insure' workers against sickness or unemployment, but cared so little for widows. 'The reason that the claim of widows for different treatment has been so long unrecognised is clearly not far to seek,' she wrote in her report. 'All widows are women, and none of them therefore are Parliamentary voters.'[86] Political disfranchisement allowed economic 'disinheritance' to continue; not until women gained the vote would they be able to right these historic wrongs. True, widows themselves might not lead the charge, for they 'carry to an extreme that misnamed virtue of patience, which is so often a real crime against the community'. But, she added, 'their wrongs cry aloud for redress, to those who have ears to hear them'.[87]

Educated women, activist women, must lead that fight. Fifteen years of social investigation had convinced Rathbone that women needed to alter the economics of marriage itself, so that the work of wives and mothers would be properly valued. But even in 1914, while she had adopted as her ideal the endowment of *all* mothers, only the more restricted demand of widows' pensions struck her as practically achievable. Within a very few years, however, women's enfranchisement and an expanding wartime state would give her a new sense of possibility.

Chapter 7

Claiming Citizenship

Reserved and analytical as she was, Eleanor took to social investigation naturally. Politics was, for her, much less comfortable terrain. Shy with strangers, awkward in groups, and principled to the point of rigidity, she was unpromising political material. And yet, as William's daughter, she knew that politics mattered; she had been a suffragist from girlhood. When she returned to Liverpool in 1896 she immediately joined the Liverpool Women's Suffrage Society (LWSS), formed some two years earlier, and became a member of the Executive of the National Union of Women's Suffrage Societies on its formation as well. For the next twenty-two years, Rathbone would shape the constitutionalist suffrage movement on Merseyside and become a dominant figure within the national suffrage movement.

The suffrage movement – or 'the cause', as its supporters affectionately called it – was demanding and exhausting, but it was also exhilarating, inspiring and fun. It was also the best of teachers: as she came to realize, Rathbone learned almost everything she knew about politics from her twenty years in its ranks. These were not lessons about women's capacities or rights, exactly, for she had never had doubts about these. Rather, they were lessons in political strategy and political practice – in how to balance ethics and expediency, principle and pragmatism, the need to remain true to one's ideals and the need to get something done. The two tenets that would guide Rathbone's later political work – her determination never to let an impossible ideal get in the way of an achievable good, and her commitment to 'democracy' as political process rather than as abstract principle – were hammered out through the meetings, campaigns and debates of the suffrage movement.

Two conflicts tested her courage and shaped her convictions. The first was the conflict between the 'constitutionalist' and 'militant' wings of the movement: between those law-abiding 'suffragists' of Mrs Fawcett's National Union, who pursued their goal through lobbying, canvassing and (in time) mass demonstrations, and the 'suffragettes' of Emmeline and Christabel Pankhurst's Women's Social and Political Union (WSPU). Rathbone learned much from the militant example but remained firmly in the constitutionalist camp. The second conflict, however, cost her more anguish. Between 1912 and 1914 Rathbone became the main internal critic of the constitutionalists' growing alliance with the Labour Party – a stance that placed her on a collision course with some of her oldest friends in the movement. Only during the war would she rebuild her position, but in an organization now riven by divisions and crises.

The Liverpool Women's Suffrage Society was a dozen years old when the militant movement arrived on Merseyside, but it hadn't made much of a mark.[1] Founded in 1894 by those same Liberal wives who lent their support to the Victoria Settlement, the LWSS resembled an elite women's club. Its supporters in the 1890s included Lydia Booth, wife of the shipowner Alfred Booth (and sister-in-law of Charles Booth), Edith Bright, wife of the Liberal merchant Allan Bright, and Nessie Stewart-Brown, sister of the Liberal MP Max Muspratt and member of the Executive of the Women's National Liberal Federation.[2] Eleanor took over the honorary secretaryship when she joined in 1896, but for friendship and adventure, for the romance of the streets, she (and other young women) looked to the settlement. The LWSS canvassed local MPs and hosted the occasional drawing-room meeting, but beyond that found very little to do.

The Pankhursts put an end to this impasse. Late in 1903, just 30 miles away in Manchester, Christabel and Emmeline founded the Women's Social and Political Union and began an energetic campaign to make women's suffrage a central Independent Labour Party demand. Some Liverpool suffragists, eager to build just such a feminist and socialist alliance, followed their work with envy and admiration. By 1905, dissension was building within the Liverpool Women's Suffrage Society, and at the annual meeting it exploded. After twelve months in the Society, Alice Morrissey of the Independent Labour Party reported, she was feeling 'very much disappointed': she had wanted to join a 'real live organization', but unless the Society began to hold meetings for working-class women all over the town, it would never make any headway. Mr Buxton, also of the ILP, agreed, criticizing especially the practice of electing the Executive Committee as a slate and the utter absence of working-class women in the Society's leadership. Rathbone bore the brunt of the attack, and when she asked the ILP members to withdraw their proposal to scrap the slate and hold a ballot instead, promising that they could negotiate new arrangements in private, Buxton was understandably outraged. 'They had had too much backdoor influence in the past,' he pointed out; nor should leadership positions 'be reserved to ladies of a particular class'. He didn't care if they had been (as Rathbone charged) 'discourteous'. Soon after this controversy, Morrissey formed a local branch of the WSPU.[3]

Suffragette militancy began a few months later, and once again Rathbone was caught off guard. The first sign of a storm came in October 1905, when Christabel Pankhurst and Annie Kenney stood up during a speech by Lord Grey to ask whether the Liberal government – now seeking an electoral mandate for a broad platform of social reform – would give the vote to women. This was in Manchester, but on 9 January 1906, when the new Prime Minister, Sir Henry Campbell-Bannerman, addressed a meeting of local Liberals at Liverpool's Sun Hall, nine women in succession interrupted him. The troublemakers were unceremoniously bundled out of the hall, and Eleanor quickly wrote to the *Liverpool Post* to dissociate the Liverpool Women's Suffrage Society from the protest.[4] But the militants didn't go away. For the next seven years the staid old Liverpool Women's Suffrage Society found itself in awkward competition with the flamboyant and unpredictable WSPU.

They were in good company: all over England, established suffrage organizations found themselves scrambling to cope with the shifting political landscape and popular interest created by the WSPU. Initially, the militants' flair and vigour gave the constitutionalists a much-needed push. Accustomed only to private lobbying, they too began marching: thus in 1907, a year after the WSPU's first London processions, Mrs Fawcett (as Millicent Fawcett, widow of the Liberal cabinet minister Henry Fawcett was always called) and Lady Frances Balfour led several thousand mackintosh-clad suffragists through the February rain to Parliament – a literal baptism which became known as the 'Mud March'. They too began holding outdoor meetings in Hyde Park and provincial towns; they too began hiring paid organizers. And while the National Union couldn't match the size and splendour of the suffragette demonstrations until after 1910, it did grow rapidly, from 31 affiliated societies in 1907, to 130 in 1909, to over 200 one year later.[5]

The Liverpool Women's Suffrage Society illustrates this dynamic well, for after 1907 Rathbone too set the local movement on a new track. She never condoned law-breaking, but she did recognize opportunity when she saw it and began shifting the movement's tactics and broadening its base. She began to recruit vigorously, looking beyond the benevolent and liberal matrons who had initially backed the cause to those women students and well-to-do daughters active in the settlement's programmes. Jessie Beavan, sister of the child welfare advocate Margaret Beavan, left settlement work for suffrage; so too did Edith Eskrigge, who had pioneered the settlement's disabled children's classes. Evelyn Deakin brought access to prominent Conservative circles; Cicely Leadley-Brown brought wealth, panache, and a much-needed motor car. Jane Colquitt, daughter of a sea captain, was another young recruit blessed with high spirits and a talent for public speaking. Suddenly, the LWSS began to look younger, more energetic, less dependent on prominent men, and a good deal freer of Liberal party ties.

This new leadership remained predominantly middle class, but Rathbone also followed the WSPU in bringing the cause out of the drawing room and into public halls and the streets. She drew especially on the talents of Selina Cooper, a working-class suffragist from Nelson in Lancashire, who had been hired in 1906 as a paid organizer by the National Union. In 1907 Rathbone advertised Cooper to local trade unions as a speaker on women workers' attitudes towards suffrage,[6] and thereafter Cooper often came to Liverpool to help with meetings, election campaigns, and tours of surrounding villages and towns. Throughout 1908, Walter Lyon Blease, a law student and enthusiastic supporter of the women's cause, shared the platform with Rathbone, Stewart-Brown, Cooper and sometimes the odd 'militant' as well at public meetings that drew audiences in the hundreds;[7] that September, the Society held its first major outdoor demonstration outside Liverpool's imposing St George's Hall.[8] Activity of this kind, which featured speeches by sympathetic men as well as by women of all classes, reinforced the LWSS's message that the vote was a tool in a wider battle for social reform. Women were demanding the vote, Rathbone told a large outdoor audience at one public meeting in 1910, 'as much in the interests of men as of women. They wanted it for the good of the whole community.'[9]

But to reach that 'whole community' suffragists had to climb up on soapboxes in its streets and dockyards – a task that took courage in this rough and even violent town. Cicely Leadley-Brown was slashed in the face by a stick, to the 'great indignation' of the listening dockers, while speaking outdoors in 1910,[10] and when Liverpool suffragists later embarked on speaking tours in rural areas they found themselves threatened by hazards ranging from inclement weather to irate untethered cattle to local stone-throwing hooligans uninterested in the fine distinctions between militants and non-militants.[11] For the young women of good family who made up the bulk of the LWSS's activists, it could not have been easy, as Maude Royden put it, to 'stand up on a chair on a street corner . . . and say to two children and a dog, "People of England!" ',[12] but as their experience grew, so did their confidence and enthusiasm. 'I wish Lord Cromer or any anti-suffragist who professes to believe that the electors are strongly against women's suffrage could be present at any of these humble meetings, when we simply drive up in wagonette or motor to some street corner where people are wont to congregate on a fine summer's evening and are in a few minutes surrounded by a crowd,' Rathbone wrote to *The Times*. Not only did these crowds eagerly pass suffragist resolutions, but they asked intelligent questions: 'Of the dispositions to "jeer and sneer" in this most conservative and not particularly tolerant town I have never seen a trace.'[13]

The LWSS also intervened in local elections, investigating candidates' stance on suffrage and supporting those who were favourable. During one by-election in July 1910 in the safely Conservative working-class district of Kirkdale, the LWSS campaigned vigorously for Alexander Cameron, a local socialist who was also a firm friend of women's suffrage, holding some twenty-nine open-air meetings over eight days. They had to face competition from rival tariff reform or free trade speakers, but as Cicely Leadley-Brown reported proudly in *Common Cause*, 'if there wasn't enough audience to go round – well, it wasn't we who went

14. Liverpool suffragists during the Kirkdale election campaign, 1910. Left to right: Emily Chubb, Jane Colquitt, Eleanor Rathbone, unknown, Edith Eskrigge (?). In car: Cicely Leadley-Brown, Selina Cooper.

without'.[14] The Unionists held the seat only narrowly, and were furious to find that 'a lady like Miss Rathbone' would 'stand on a lorry spouting to working-men at the docks'.[15] Yet Rathbone, who masterminded the Kirkdale campaign, was delighted. 'Nothing could seem less likely than that Kirkdale is in advance of the rest of England on this or any question,' she pointed out, yet 'the electorate is almost universally friendly to our cause'.[16] A photograph of the electioneering team, including Colquitt, Rathbone, Cooper, Leadley-Brown, and the famous motor car, survives from that campaign – seven determined women in respectable hats.

In moving in this populist direction, the constitutionalist LWSS were blatantly copying the successful tactics of their militant sisters – although, as Rathbone admitted, the LWSS was still not able to draw the kinds of crowds that turned out to see the charismatic Christabel and Emmeline Pankhurst during their flying visits in 1909 and 1910.[17] What the constitutionalists would not do, however, was condone WSPU members' harassment of government ministers or illegal acts, of which Liverpool saw its fair share. Several famous WSPU incidents took place in Liverpool, from the disruption of the August 1909 visit by Richard Haldane, then Secretary of State for War, to a symbolic attack on Prime Minister H.H. Asquith's car during the election campaign that December, to Lady Constance Lytton's famous arrest and forcible feeding in Walton Gaol in January 1910 while disguised as 'Jane Warton, Seamstress'.[18] The Lytton case in particular caused a great public outcry, but Rathbone continued to repudiate militancy – a stance that drew a reprimand from Christabel Pankhurst. 'I am sure you will agree with me,' Christabel wrote pompously:

> that those who have not had personal experience of forcible feeding and prison conditions generally, and have never even had any personal intercourse with those who have been in prison, are not really qualified to express any opinion upon the matter. Certainly they are not entitled to write to the newspapers in defence of the authorities. Before any Suffragist takes such a step as this, she ought to go to prison herself, and learn from her own experience what has been undergone by her predecessors.[19]

Eleanor, however, was unrepentant, and continued to denounce militant tactics in her speeches – to the annoyance of Walter Lyon Blease, who had become romantically involved with one of the militant organizers and understood their resentment of the 'aristocratic temper' of such 'old Liverpool families' as the Rathbones.[20] Rathbone's political opponents called her a 'suffragette' anyway, painting her as a one-issue extremist during her City Council election campaigns,[21] and while she tried to deflect these charges, she admitted that she was willing to risk her seat in Granby Ward because 'she placed women's suffrage before anything else'.[22] So too, of course, did the militants, whose local organization reached its most successful point in 1909 and 1910, under the imaginative leadership of its organizer Ada Flatman.[23]

The balance finally shifted in the constitutionalists' favour after 1911, following the collapse of the long cross-party parliamentary initiative in favour of a limited bill. This initiative was born of a uniquely difficult parliamentary situation: while a good deal of support for women's suffrage existed in the Commons, no party (except, after 1912, Labour) was willing to adopt the issue. Moreover, while there were many more suffragist MPs on the Liberal than on the Conservative benches, Asquith as Prime Minister was a confirmed 'anti' and was further hampered after the January 1910 election by his dependence on the Irish vote. Women's suffrage supporters in the Commons responded to this impasse by forming a cross-party alliance, chaired by the Earl of Lytton and masterminded by the strong suffragist H.N. Brailsford. Their solution – a 'Conciliation Bill' which would have enfranchised the one million or so women who, as local householders and ratepayers, already possessed the municipal vote – became the main focus of suffragist hopes for two years.

Complex negotiations surrounded the Conciliation Bill, which passed its second readings handily during both the 1910 and 1911 sessions. Yet for the bill to become law, the government had to agree to grant parliamentary time – no easy hurdle for its supporters to clear, given Asquith's intransigence and the government's packed legislative schedule. Crucially, however, while Asquith would not promise this in 1910 and resisted as best he could in 1911, until late 1911 the bill's prospects were strong enough to keep the militants on board. Except for a few months' relapse after the announcement of the dissolution of Parliament in November 1910 (which automatically killed the bill for that session), the WSPU kept their peace. And to the constitutionalists Asquith offered one tempting carrot, implying that the bill's fate would depend on the government's sense of its popular support.[24]

This challenge brought out the constitutionalists' best. Throughout 1910 and 1911, while the government fought two inconclusive elections over the Parliament Act and the Conciliation Bill worked its way through the Commons, the National Union turned to the public. The Liverpool Society threw itself into this effort, canvassing those local women likely to be enfranchised,[25] and holding demonstrations and vigils following crucial votes.[26] They travelled to London for a mass meeting in Hyde Park in July 1910, and went down again in June 1911 for a 40,000-strong joint militant and constitutionalist procession – a procession which revealed that supporters of the National Union now far outnumbered members of the WSPU.[27] In a move that demonstrated real political skill, Rathbone brought a petition from Liverpool's women ratepayers to the City Council, and convinced her fellow councillors – over the objections of Archibald Salvidge, Liverpool's powerful Tory boss – to pass a resolution urging the government to give the bill parliamentary time.[28]

15. The West Lancashire Federation caravan touring rural areas. Edith Eskrigge seated nearest the tent.

Most impressively, however, the LWSS took their message on the road, seeking new converts in the surrounding region. In the spring of 1910, they began canvassing nearby West Lancashire towns; by the autumn, they had four organizers active in Preston, West Cheshire and North Wales. That autumn, they organized eleven chapters into a new 'West Lancashire, West Cheshire and North Wales Federation', with Rathbone as its chairman, and began an ambitious programme of expansion. In the spring of 1911, a Welsh-speaking suffragist in tow, Eskrigge and Rathbone held meetings throughout North Wales – which Eleanor's father had represented in Parliament some twenty years earlier – while Leadley-Brown and another organizer ventured 'in some trepidation, as three members of the WSPU attempting to hold a meeting there had been mobbed',[29] further south into Montgomeryshire. That summer and again in the summer of 1912, Federation organizers made speaking tours, culminating in August 1912 with a van tour by six speakers.[30]

Their efforts bore fruit: by 1912, the West Lancashire Federation had 27 chapters, with two more in formation, had held some 385 meetings, and was busy extracting pro-suffrage resolutions from town councils, trade unions and party associations throughout the region.[31] Their growth, moreover, was only part of a broader expansion of the National Union as a whole: from some 200 affiliated societies in 1910 to 42,000 members in 400 societies in 1912.[32]

The WSPU, for the first time, could not match this record. Although the militants remained active during the truce, after the reversion to militancy at the end of 1911 their organization entered a period of decline. Problems in Parliament catalysed the WSPU's final phase of radicalization. In November 1911, Asquith announced that while the government would provide time for the Conciliation Bill in the next session, it intended to introduce a wider manhood suffrage bill as well, to which a women's suffrage amendment could – if support merited – be attached. Asquith's announcement caused consternation even among constitutionalists, who feared that the prospect of a wider bill would deter Liberals from supporting the Conciliation Bill; the militants declared that Asquith had betrayed them.[33] They began a campaign of window-smashing and other property damage, and by early 1913 had moved on to arson. The government would give in only when compelled to by force: any attempt to court public opinion was over. Militants caused several hundreds of thousands of pounds' damage to selected houses, churches, exhibitions and pavilions, but alienated much of the public, leading to a tapering off of both adherents and donations to the WSPU.[34] The Liverpool WSPU did its best to buck this trend, but its level of activity declined as well.[35]

Mrs Fawcett and the National Union's leadership quickly denounced these attacks, and in Liverpool, Rathbone and the LWSS leaders followed suit. They wrote immediately to the *Liverpool Post* to disavow the WSPU's window-breaking campaign;[36] when the suffragettes turned to arson, Rathbone and other prominent men and women charged that the militants had become 'the most serious enemies of the suffrage cause'.[37] Local WSPU members were angry and disgusted. 'I hear Miss Rathbone has been repudiating us again,' Dr Alice Ker, a Birkenhead suffragette, wrote to her daughters from prison in London after one window-smashing raid. 'I can't understand the National Union; they are really taking the Government's part against us.'[38]

But in fact Rathbone and the constitutionalists were not taking 'the government's part'. Rather, they were seeking to protect a mass movement, painfully constructed over the past five years, from the militants' depredations. Even the passionately committed Blease, by this point, thought the militants out of hand,[39] and in the countryside their actions were deeply unpopular. During the period of the truce, Edith Eskrigge reported that in heavily Liberal North Wales 'nine out of every ten people who have expressed agreement with our aims would not have even listened to me for a minute, had I not first explained that I was "non-militant",'[40] and these difficulties worsened after the truce was called off. Organizing efforts in Caernarvon flagged in the spring of 1912 after the window-smashing campaign,[41] and the suffrage society in Chorley fell into disarray after the WSPU burned Sir William Lever's summer house nearby.[42]

Yet, unlike the militants, who had difficulty continuing their activities except in urban areas, the West Lancashire Federation suffragists continued their rural

campaigns. BY REASON NOT FORCE read one placard on the speakers' van
that Colquitt and others took round rural areas in the summer of 1912; LAW
ABIDING proclaimed the banner they carried to London in the National Union's
Pilgrimage the following summer.[43] They continued to concentrate on open-air
meetings – now usually without suffragette competition[44] – and were delighted
to find, as Eskrigge did in North Wales, 'men, women and children ready to stand
and listen for as long as we would talk'.[45] In the spring of 1913, the Federation acquired a motor car to get to even more remote areas,[46] and that August
held a summer school in North Wales to train speakers – who then were sent
out to 'practise' on local residents.[47] Members also took part in the National
Union's last and most impressive major public demonstration, the six-week
suffrage pilgrimage of the summer of 1913. Joining a group that had set out on
18 June from Carlisle, suffragists from Liverpool, Lancashire and Wales marched,
banners flying and bands playing, towards London, where they met up with other
regional contingents for a huge public meeting.[48] That autumn saw the Liverpool

16. Liverpool suffragists walking to London in the pilgrimage of 1913.

suffragists hard at work drumming up support within local trade unions: by February 1914, Eskrigge reported that some 155 had passed pro-suffrage resolutions.[49]

At the outbreak of the war, with the WSPU in disarray, both the Federation and the Liverpool Society were at a peak of activity, carrying on their public speaking and recruiting large numbers of new members.[50] Their work, in those final pre-war years, perfectly reflected their political ideas. Constitutionalists had always argued, against the militants, that women were an essential part of the nation, part of a broad democratic public from which all political legitimacy derived. In talking to that public, they won its support; in walking through their nation, they made it their own.

The Liverpool suffragists' long effort to build up popular support and surmount the militant challenge was driven by Eleanor Rathbone's energies and shaped by her ideas. Yet the experience of running the Liverpool Society refined these ideas in turn, cementing her core view on how to operate effectively *and* ethically in politics. It would be easy to dismiss these ideas simply as 'pragmatism', yet such a label does not do Rathbone justice, for while she certainly accepted the need for careful political calculation, she never adopted particular tactics simply in order to safeguard her political position. Like the Pankhursts, she never lost sight of the final goal; unlike these rivals, however, she insisted that the *means* the movement adopted must be in themselves justifiable and likely to advance the cause. Christabel and Emmeline Pankhurst did not think in this way. For them, all means were just in pursuit of a just cause, and any setbacks were not their fault: they were responsible neither for the reaction against militancy that led Liberals to desert the Conciliation Bill in 1912, still less for the fall-off in popular support following the arson campaign. For Rathbone, by contrast, purity of motive was not enough: suffragists, as political actors, must always balance means and ends, must always judge the likely consequences of their actions in conditions not of their making. 'We have to deal with the situation as it is, and not as it ought to be,' she wrote in *Common Cause* in 1912, urging suffragists to remain committed to 'methods of conciliation'.[51]

Rathbone's commitment to 'conciliation' was motivated in part by her belief that militancy was counterproductive, likely only to anger the public and weaken support for suffrage. Yet her commitment to what the great German sociologist Max Weber called an 'ethic of responsibility' also reflected her views on the character of 'the cause'.[52] For the Pankhursts, the struggle for the vote was a contest for political power: they saw themselves as pitted *against* the government in a just war – a war in which the wider public played at best a secondary role. If that public supported WSPU actions, well and good. If not, their disaffection was not a matter of concern. As Emmeline Pankhurst explained in early February 1913:

We are not destroying Orchid Houses, breaking windows, cutting telegraph wires, injuring golf greens, in order to win the approval of the people who were attacked. If the general public were pleased with what we are doing, that would be a proof that our warfare is ineffective. We don't intend that you should be pleased.[53]

For Rathbone, by contrast, 'public opinion' was crucial – far more critical, in fact, than the passing whims of political leaders. And here we get to the heart of her political theory. Since legitimate authority derived, in her view, from the people as a whole, any reforming movement needed popular support, and she held fast to the liberal's faith that any truly democratic measure would win public backing in the end. No task was as important, then, as that of cultivating support for the cause: hence Rathbone's willingness to spar in public with Mrs Humphry Ward about the results of rival canvasses,[54] hence her arguments, on the National Union's Executive and in the pages of *Common Cause*, for ever-greater efforts to collect signatures and petitions,[55] and hence her determination, when the Union's Executive became too caught up with parliamentary machinations, to commit the Liverpool society to renewed popular appeals.[56]

This belief in popular sovereignty would stay with Rathbone: it would lead her, over some reservations, to support Indian constitutional reform in the 1930s and would drive her campaigns to rouse 'public opinion' against the policy of appeasement. Of course, in those later years, Rathbone would also be forced to grapple with the problem that a democracy could in fact opt for anti-democratic solutions – could wish to cede authority to demagogues and dictators, could tyrannize minorities or espouse racism. Yet, true to her idealist education, Rathbone saw such problems as a sign of *incomplete* democracy and not of democracy's failure: only a populace unaccustomed to political rights would either have unrealistic ideas of their usefulness or would value them lightly. Like John Stuart Mill, like Alexis de Tocqueville, Rathbone thus viewed democracy less as an abstract ideal than as a continuously unfolding practice. By exercising the rights of the citizen, a democratic public grew in capacity and virtue.

And among that virtuous citizenry, Rathbone counted women. Here, as well, her thinking contrasts with militant ideas. For the Pankhursts, women were quite literally 'outlaws': excluded from the franchise, they were not bound by legal, tax or property arrangements they had no part in making. In burning buildings, in flouting the law, militants exposed not only their own exclusion but the total illegitimacy of a masculinist social order. For Rathbone, such absolutist reasoning made no sense. Wealthy, locally prominent, and a city councillor, she viewed the WSPU's claims about all women's utter subjection sceptically; everywhere, she thought, suffragists were demonstrating their influence and capacity. Indeed, it was precisely because she saw the movement as itself an education in citizenship that she defended such time-consuming local activities as house-to-house canvasses.[57] Citizenship, in other words, was not something simply withheld or conferred. It was, rather (as the Oxford idealists had always taught), a relationship, a web of practices and duties binding individuals together in a more perfect social whole.

While the Pankhursts enacted the drama of women's exclusion, then, Rathbone demonstrated their centrality. In 1913, five years before women first exercised the parliamentary vote, the LWSS founded a new 'Women's Citizen's Association', with Rathbone as President and Jane Colquitt as secretary.[58] Organized on a ward basis, the association proposed to run non-party women candidates in local elections while supporting the suffrage cause; by the outbreak of the war, it had over a thousand members.[59] Women, this new organization implied, were already citizens – and when Parliament belatedly recognized that fact, they would be poised to take their rightful place within it.

And yet, for all her circumspection, for all her 'conciliation', didn't the militants move her? How could she watch their theatrical processions, read their harrowing tales of arrest and forcible feeding, hear their wagons of released prisoners trundle jubilantly through the streets, and not feel some pull, some twinge of regret that she was not of their number? While deploring the militants' tactics, other constitutionalist leaders – Mrs Fawcett, Frances Balfour – thought them brave beyond measure and sometimes said so.[60] Eleanor, however, paid no such tributes. Many years later, in a few commemorative speeches, she too would acknowledge their 'indispensable', revivifying role.[61] As an MP she would recount the story of Emily Wilding Davison's 'suffragette' suicide to groups of schoolgirls visiting the Commons, impressing upon them the lengths to which women had gone to achieve their freedom.[62] But if militancy had electrified the movement, Rathbone later thought, it had also come 'within an inch' of wrecking it, 'perhaps for a generation'. The militants certainly had courage, but 'it requires . . . something better than courage to resist all temptation to quicken the pace by succumbing to the dangerous doctrine that the end justifies the means'. Better, she thought, to try to hold to 'the Kantian maxim of statesmanship: "Act so that the maxim of thy action might become law universal." '[63] On the streets of Liverpool, Eleanor still carried the teachings of Balliol's Caird with her.

Transforming the National Union into a mass movement was the first precondition for the success of 'the cause'; patient negotiation and parliamentary lobbying was the second. Here as well, Rathbone played a major role. The National Union was, in the first instance, a federation of local societies, and its devolved and democratic structure gave regional organizations and their leaders considerable autonomy. Margaret Ashton in Manchester, Isabella Ford in Leeds, Margaret Heitland in Cambridge, Helen Fraser in Glasgow, Chrystal Macmillan in Edinburgh and Helen Ward in London led large and well-financed local movements. Delegates from these societies met twice yearly 'in Council' to set policy and elect an executive committee, which invariably included important regional leaders as well as the organization's London-based officers.

Rathbone attended virtually every council as one of the delegates of the Liverpool society. As West Lancashire's most prominent feminist, she was also elected without fail to the Union's Executive. Wealthy, well-connected, and (after 1909) one of a mere handful of women elected local councillors, she was a formidable political asset. Familiar from girlhood with the culture and practices of the House of Commons, she was a natural choice for parliamentary deputations. During the Union's campaigns around the Conciliation and Reform Bills, she travelled regularly to London to lobby MPs.[64] But while she was a respected member of that suffragist inner circle, after 1912 a rift developed between Rathbone and some of her colleagues. In the most narrow sense, this was a conflict about the Union's emerging alliance with the Labour Party – an alliance that Rathbone came to see as politically inexpedient and out of keeping with the Union's historic non-party stance.[65] Yet broader issues were also at stake, as Rathbone found herself seeking to balance, once again, pragmatic considerations and a commitment to democratic process.

Tensions began to emerge in the months following Asquith's announcement, on 7 November 1911, that the Liberal government planned to introduce a wider manhood suffrage bill and would allow debate on a women's suffrage amendment. The Women's Social and Political Union, as we have seen, greeted this announcement with outrage and resumed militancy. Eleanor, however, saw things differently. While she had no confidence in Asquith, she recognized that many sincere suffragist Liberals disliked the elitism of the Conciliation Bill, which would have enfranchised only those one million women who themselves met the property qualification. The proposed women's suffrage amendment to the Reform Bill, by contrast, would enfranchise some six or seven million women householders and wives of householders: was it not then the better alternative? When Christabel wrote to the *Manchester Guardian* to justify the WSPU's renewal of militancy, then, Eleanor retorted that suffragists should instead 'turn the instrument of humiliation' – the planned Reform Bill – 'into the instrument of victory'.[66]

Yet it was not simply added numbers that made the prospect of the Reform Bill, in Rathbone's view, 'incomparably superior to the Conciliation Bill, more satisfactory to us as Suffragists, as feminists and as political thinkers, likely to work out better in practice and based on a sounder and more logical theory'.[67] The proposed amendment appealed to her, rather, because it coincided perfectly with her campaigns in Liverpool to improve married women's economic standing and citizenship rights. The Conciliation Bill would have done nothing on that front: in effect, it would have sharpened the division between those single women and widows able to qualify for the vote as 'householders' and married women who (since their husbands were designated the 'householder') could not. But the proposed suffrage amendment would dissolve that difference. 'The secret charm, the unintended boon' of the proposed amendment, Rathbone wrote, was that it would enfranchise married women on the basis of their husband's residential qualification as well, thus implicitly admitting 'that the status of a married woman is really in equity that of a joint householder, even when the house is taken in the husband's name'.[68] Reiterating points (and even paragraphs) from *The Problem of Women's Wages*, she argued that so long as women devoted them-selves to housework and childcare, men's wages should in be treated as equally the property of the wife and the rights of the householder conferred on both spouses. Given the fact that the bill would grants such rights, shouldn't the suf-frage organizations cooperate with Liberal members and support it?

Unfortunately for Eleanor, many in the National Union did not see things in this light. Having been accustomed to see marriage as a state of 'sex-parasitism', many feminists were frankly revolted by the prospect of a 'wife's vote',[69] and some disagreed with Rathbone's pragmatic analysis as well. The Reform Bill, they thought, was a ruse by the devious Asquith to weaken Liberal support for the Conciliation Bill, since Liberals might now vote against the Conciliation Bill in the uncertain hope of something better.[70] When the bill duly failed in March 1912 – defeated, in part, through the defection of Liberals ostensibly committed to women's suffrage – even Mrs Fawcett's patience was exhausted. Now sceptical of the value of individual MPs' pledges, she came round to the view – shared by the powerful triumvirate of Kathleen Courtney, the Union's honorary secretary, Catherine Marshall, who was in charge of much of its parliamentary work, and H.N. Brailsford, the moving spirit behind the Conciliation Committee – that in the future the Union must demonstrate its ability to threaten the Liberal majority and to punish those MPs who had failed them.[71]

Thus was born the suffragist–Labour alliance. Since the Labour Party was the only party formally committed to women's suffrage, and since all Labour members had loyally supported the Conciliation Bill, on 2 May 1912 the Executive decided to back a new plan to support Labour candidates against Liberal anti-suffragists in by-elections.[72] The policy had much to recommend it. By helping to return Labour members, it would reward the one party that had loyally supported 'the cause'; by punishing Liberal backsliders, it would put pressure on the Party to adopt a women's suffrage plank. No one, at this stage, anticipated that the Labour Party – which had a rudimentary organizational structure and a mere forty-two seats – could bring about the passage of a bill. The aim was to use Labour as a stick to beat the Liberals.

But would this strategy work? Eleanor Rathbone wasn't sure. She and 'all the more intelligent of [her] Committee'[73] feared that the new policy would simply alienate Liberal supporters and (since three-way contests tended to split the pro-gressive vote) benefit Conservatives. The Liverpool suffragists also had local reasons to oppose a strongly anti-Liberal line. Most were (like Rathbone) Liberals by family affiliation; many were active in other Liberal causes and had spent years opposing the Conservative Party's local stranglehold; they also knew how strongly Liberal North Wales resented attacks on the party of Gladstone and Lloyd George. With Fawcett, Courtney and Marshall strongly behind it, however, a special council overrode Rathbone's objections. Henceforth, the Union would support Labour candidates in by-election contests against unsatisfactory Liberals.[74]

Beginning in 1912, then, the National Union followed a rather complex political strategy. On the one hand, they set up a new 'Election Fighting Fund', sending funds and organizers to support Labour in four by-election contests that year. On the other hand, they continued the painstaking work of canvassing Members of Parliament and collecting evidence of public support for the women's suffrage amendment to the Reform Bill, promised in 1913. On the Executive Committee and in articles in *Common Cause*, Rathbone stressed the importance of this latter work. 'Some people may be inclined to protest that it ought not to be necessary to adopt these methods . . . at this late stage in our long struggle,' she admitted, but such criticism was 'beside the point': with militancy cutting into popular support, suffragists needed every possible adherent, every possible parliamentary vote.[75] In January 1913, however, to the suffragists' dismay, the Speaker of the House ruled that women's suffrage was too significant a change to be dealt with by amendment. The embarrassed Liberal government then withdrew the bill entirely, driving the WSPU further towards factionalism and arson and leaving the National Union, for the first time in several years, without any hopeful legislation in the offing.

What was to be done? Their patience exhausted, the bulk of the Union's Executive favoured extending the Labour alliance to target all Liberal by-election candidates, regardless of the candidate's views on women's suffrage. Once again, Rathbone dissented. The policy of attacking Liberals was unlikely to turn either 'lukewarm friends' in the Commons or indifferent voters into committed suffragists, she argued in a private memo: 'If we want to impress the average Liberal elector with the truth that Women's Suffrage is an essential part of Liberalism, surely it is an odd way of going about it to show him Women's Suffrage and Liberalism always ranged at opposite sides at elections.' More seriously, she charged, the policy would most likely backfire. Supposing the National Union did succeed in damaging the narrow Liberal majority – what then? If the Liberal government fell, the Conservatives would come in, reducing the chances for a suffrage bill further.[76] However frustrating suffragists might find the current situation, with the Conservatives even less sympathetic and Labour very weak, any policy that would alienate Liberal supporters was bound to hurt 'the cause'.

Rathbone made these arguments at the Council held on 27 and 28 February 1913, but the delegates, shaken by the demise of the Reform Bill and out of patience with the Liberals, strongly endorsed the majority Executive view. It was a waste of time to support private members' bills; only a government measure would now do. Furthermore, since the current government wouldn't propose such a measure, the Union should seek to shorten its life by supporting Labour at all by-elections – with the single proviso that suffragist 'tried friends' would not be actively opposed if they had been 'first in the field'. The Council also began to define the NUWSS's policy for the general election expected in 1915 at the latest, agreeing to target anti-suffragist ministers and defend Labour seats.[77] Throughout 1913 and 1914, then, the work of the Election Fighting Fund expanded, with Fund organizers helping Labour fight a further four by-elections and beginning work in some two dozen constituencies where Labour's prospects were good.[78]

Rathbone thought this strategy reckless and almost certainly counterproductive, and, for the first time, considered resigning from the Executive. Catherine Marshall was able to dissuade her,[79] but her reservations were widely shared. The National Union had always been a broad church, drawing women of all parties together; now, under pressure to adopt a uniformly pro-Labour stance, underlying fissures came to the surface. Thus, while the policy was popular in areas (such as Manchester or the North-east) with a tradition of suffragist–Labour cooperation, it was greeted with consternation in many societies with long-standing Liberal ties or where support for Labour was likely to – or, in some by-elections, did – lead to the return of a Conservative 'anti'. Some local affiliates (among them the South Wales Federation and Rathbone's West Lancashire Federation) requested that their area be exempted from the new policy; others (such as the Scottish Federation and the London society) that the Executive be required to consult with local branches before supporting Labour in their areas.[80] The ban on giving electoral support to even the most loyal Liberal MPs bred resentment, resignations and defections to a new Liberal Women's Suffrage Union, founded in 1913.[81] Even the Union's most faithful friends in Parliament, such as the Liberal W.H. Dickinson, became disaffected.[82] Ray Strachey of the powerful London Society worried that the suffrage message itself was being compromised. 'Our organizers now talk pure socialism instead of suffrage, & the Ex[ecutive], in this effort to keep on good terms with the Labour Party, seems to be prepared to go to almost any length,' she wrote to her husband. 'The whole policy is unpopular in many places, & makes us lose quantities of money & friends, & I am quite sure the N.U. as a whole doesn't want to be too deeply committed. . . . So I believe the Council will have to make a stand.'[83]

These tensions came to a head early in 1914, and, once again, Rathbone found herself in the thick of the fight. Some in the Independent Labour Party had begun to worry about the reliability of the suffragists' support, and three of the National Union's officials had been dispatched to the ILP conference at Glasgow to calm their fears. Once there, however, the officials not only reiterated the Union's support for Labour's by-election candidates – as specified in the resolutions passed at the Council in February 1913 – but also began to define its general election stance. Even *were* the Liberals to pledge themselves to women's suffrage, they promised, it would now be 'impossible for the N.U. to oppose Labour Candidates while the Labour Party retains its present attitude towards women's suffrage, *that is to say it would not support Liberal candidates in any constituency where a Labour Candidate was standing'.*[84]

Rathbone, who had missed a special Executive Committee meeting called to consider the crisis with the ILP, was appalled. She had been trying, unsuccessfully, to convince the Executive to *narrow* the Election Fighting Fund's scope;[85] instead, these officials were planning to expand it further. Worse, in making general election pledges, she told the Executive on 5 February, the delegation had exceeded its mandate. The bulk of the Executive disagreed with her; this time, however, Eleanor did not accept defeat. She and her Liverpool colleagues decided to bring the issue to the Council to be held the following week, and in preparation circularized other societies opposed to the 'anti-government policy' of the Union. '[A]lthough the General Election policy may finally and in detail be decided at a future Special Council Meeting,' the circular warned, 'much of the work now being actually done by the Election Fighting Fund Committee is work in preparation for the General Election and is committing the N.U. practically irrevocably, to a line of action intended to secure the defeat of the Liberal Candidate.'[86] Rathbone and the Liverpool branch thus brought a resolution to the Council that would bar the Fund from constituencies where an increase in the Labour poll would most likely lead to the return of a Unionist (unless the Liberal candidate was also an 'anti'), and even though the resolution was strenuously opposed by the Executive, it failed by only five votes.[87] On 5 March, Rathbone met with a small group of sympathizers (including the newly elected Executive Committee members Margery Corbett Ashby, Mrs Cross and Mrs Haverfield) to consider further action. She informed the whole Executive that afternoon of their meeting.

This time, it was the Executive's turn to be appalled. Catherine Marshall and Maude Royden led the attack, insisting that Executive Committee members were not free to foment opposition to existing policy. Lady Frances Balfour, not one to mince words, told Rathbone that she could not conceive of anything 'more disastrous or more disloyal to the Union' than her actions; Mrs Fawcett thought that the move could split the Union. Under this onslaught, Rathbone retorted that her committee wished not to alter the present by-election policy but merely to prevent its extension to the general election, but the Executive refused to accept this distinction. The Union *had* no general election policy, Kathleen Courtney insisted, and by opposing one line of development Rathbone was hampering its future freedom. Even the by-election policy could suffer, Helena Swanwick continued, and this policy did have the Council's sanction. Uncertain how to proceed, the Executive agreed to return to the issue at the next meeting.[88] But, as Rathbone discovered, opinion was already hardening. Mrs Fawcett wrote to her to say that she had been 'very much perturbed' by Rathbone and her colleagues' actions and regarded the whole matter as 'most serious'.[89]

Whether because of some political or family crisis or because she now found the prospect too painful, Rathbone did not attend the next meeting of the Executive. The task of defending the dissenters' actions was left, quite unfairly, to Corbett Ashby, Haverfield and Cross, and in Rathbone's absence the Executive had few scruples about condemning their work. The majority continued, rather contradictorily, to condemn Rathbone's efforts to prevent the extension of the Union's by-election policy to the general election, and to insist that (the pledges to the ILP notwithstanding) the Union had no general election policy anyway. 'In view of the gravity of the situation created by the part taken by four members of the Executive Committee', they resolved, the next Council, scheduled for July, should be moved forward to April or May.[90]

This was the worst internal crisis faced by the National Union in the pre-war years. Yet once Frances Balfour used the word 'disloyal' and Mrs Fawcett raised the spectre of the Union's break-up, its outcome was set: Rathbone and her compatriots would be branded as schismatics and defeated. But were they really at fault? Certainly fundamental questions of policy and of process were at stake in this conflict, but they quickly became entangled with personal issues. As this happened, Rathbone's emerging strengths and weaknesses as a politician were revealed.

On the most basic level, the conflict was about strategy. Was the Labour alliance bringing women's suffrage any closer? Within the National Union, views differed. Frances Balfour, an early sceptic, by 1914 thought it had forced the government to take the Union seriously;[91] Rathbone, by contrast, thought it had actually weakened Liberal support. Views also differed on whether the policy was worth pursuing even if it alienated Liberals. As Rathbone told the Executive on 15 January, she considered such a prospect 'suicidal'.[92] By early 1914, however, both Fawcett and Marshall thought that a Conservative government could not possibly be worse than a Liberal government still led by Asquith.[93]

Evidence suggests Rathbone's fears were well grounded. The Election Fighting Fund was used to support eight Labour candidates in by-elections between 1912 and 1914, seven in seats previously held by Liberals and one by Labour. In none of these contests was the Labour candidate successful. In four cases, however, the Labour poll was significant enough to harm the Liberal and lead to a Conservative victory. Insofar as the policy was *intended* to threaten Liberals, then, one must conclude it was successful.[94] Yet, just as Rathbone charged, there is little evidence that Liberal losses made the Party any more sympathetic, or that Conservatives became more reliable as Liberals grew alienated; at no point did a majority of Conservative MPs support even such a limited measure as the Conciliation Bill. Had the alliance with Labour been extended to the next election, then, it would probably have contributed to some Conservative and possibly some Labour victories, but with a negligible impact on legislative hopes. Of course, the alliance also had other effects, furthering the construction of a new 'socialist-feminism' in those areas (like Manchester, but unlike Liverpool) with a strong socialist tradition. Indeed, it was for this reason that Executive Committee members with strong socialist leanings (especially Isabella Ford, Helena Swanwick, and increasingly Margaret Ashton) – and, following them, some historians – found these last phases of suffragist activity so appealing.[95] Whether they brought the suffrage movement closer to victory in 1914 than in 1912 is quite another matter.[96]

During the conflict of March 1914, however, these strategic questions quickly became entangled with a second set of issues, as questions of strategy shaded into quarrels over where the authority to set – or to oppose – policy lay. Both sides made strong procedural claims. Rathbone's critics argued, quite understandably, that members of the Executive did not have the right to organize opposition to decisions that the Executive had endorsed by a proper majority vote; Rathbone, for her part, retorted that some decisions were not the Executive's to make. The National Union had a highly democratic structure, with policy set by branch representatives meeting twice yearly in Council. The Executive was not to exceed directives of the Council – yet this, Rathbone argued, was what they had been doing.[97] With her powerful commitment to the Liverpool movement and hence to a federal structure, Rathbone thus saw herself as *defending* the democratic authority of the Council; when the Executive turned around and accused her of seeking to frame a general election policy before the Council could meet, she was understandably shocked. It was precisely because she believed that the pledges made to the ILP in Glasgow in January 1914 had gone beyond the Council's mandate that she had written to branches directly. Covert and ill-advised her actions undoubtedly were, but she believed (and the legalistically minded Chrystal Macmillan agreed with her) that the Union's officials had usurped the Council's democratic powers.[98]

She had a point. As early as October 1912, Marshall had written to the Labour Party outlining a plan to extend EFF work into constituencies important to Labour in the next general election, at a moment when the Council had agreed only to a by-election strategy.[99] Of course, negotiation of this kind is inevitable in politics: problems arise and must be addressed as events develop; no electoral strategy can be outlined entirely through biannual conferences. But in light of Marshall's negotiations and the Executive's decision in January 1914 not to support any candidate except Labour *in every seat Labour contested*, Rathbone's opponents were disingenuous in arguing that no general election policy existed.

Neither the strategic nor the procedural questions much mattered, however, once a third aspect of the conflict – personal feeling – surfaced. And here Rathbone showed her weakness. However sensible her strategic considerations, however justified her procedural arguments, she failed to take account of something less tangible: the shock that a tightly knit community of collaborators would feel upon learning of dissension within the ranks. By the time she realized her error, it was too late: too much had been said in anger at those March meetings to prevent hurt feelings and mistrust all round. Eleanor tried to keep the political question to the fore, telling the Executive that she would rather face a vote of censure at the outset so that questions of policy could then be discussed on their merits. 'Very important questions of policy ought not to be mixed up with personalities,' she insisted, or else 'the whole issue would be prejudiced and the discussion on future policy would be biased'.[100] She was right to be apprehensive. Meeting on 28 and 29 April, the Council rallied round its Executive, effectively censuring Rathbone and her allies by barring members of the Executive from advocating any course of action not endorsed by its majority.

Nevertheless, when it came to electoral policy, there was a noticeable shift in tone. True, the Council approved the pledges given to the ILP; surprisingly, however, it also passed a completely incompatible resolution sponsored by Courtney and Marshall urging the Union to consider helping 'tried friends', regardless of party, in three-cornered contests.[101] Perhaps the conflict with Rathbone had finally brought home to Courtney and Marshall the extent of dissatisfaction over the Labour alliance; perhaps they had begun to realize that a Conservative victory would scarcely deliver the vote into women's hands. Certainly in the few months before the outbreak of war, and as evidence of branch discontent flooded in, Marshall began to change her tune.[102] In July 1914, reporting 'much anxiety and unrest' within the branches about the Union's electoral policy, she recommended that the Executive discuss alternative strategies.[103]

But Rathbone was not there to welcome this shift. Immediately after the April Council, she and her three allies resigned from the Executive; they could scarcely have done otherwise. Indeed, so strong was Rathbone's 'feeling of sick distaste for the whole machinery of N.U. organisation' that she planned to give up the presidency of her beloved West Lancashire Federation as well. 'Remember I have had 17 years of it,' she wrote to Edith Eskrigge, who had sought to dissuade her.[104] Mrs Fawcett, watching the departures felt relieved. 'I feel with you that it was much better to bring the whole difference of point of view between us and the 4 into the open and have it out,' she wrote to Catherine Marshall's mother, Caroline. 'The only one of the 4 that I really regret is Miss Rathbone. The other three I part with, without a sigh.'[105]

This was the worst political crisis of Eleanor's life and one of the worst personal ones. She was forty-two, and had given the women's suffrage movement almost eighteen years of her life. She had been on the Union's Executive virtually since its formation, had helped to shape its policy, had participated in its most important lobbying efforts and deputations, and had written regularly for *Common Cause*. Over these long years, she had come to have real affection for some of her suffrage colleagues. Emotionally reserved as she was, she would never have told them what their collaboration meant to her, but she was deeply wounded when women she viewed as personal friends publicly chastised and lectured her. Millicent Fawcett, in fact, had noticed Rathbone's real perturbation that April ('very often,' she told Caroline Marshall, 'she could hardly get her words out'), but absurdly concluded that Rathbone's 'overstrain' was caused by 'illness at home' rather than by Fawcett's own vindictive behaviour.[106] Although Courtney, Marshall and Margaret Ashton all wrote to Eleanor to assure her that they had never questioned her loyalty, Rathbone could not forget the tone of the remarks made to her.[107]

The letter she wrote to Marshall in response to her overture shows clearly the depth of her hurt. She had been unable to speak about 'this hateful subject' when the two had met in the autumn, but thought that she should at least explain why she felt unable to return to the Executive, as Marshall had asked her to do. What particularly bothered her, she made clear, was that during the conflict 'the impression was conveyed to a great part of the Council . . . that I had done a rather underhand and treacherous thing; that at the very moment I was being elected on to our Executive to carry out a certain policy, I was plotting a move to undermine that policy'. 'I don't believe that in cool blood any of you who worked with me on the Executive really believe that I am that sort of person,' she wrote, but why then had they allowed such a charge to be put 'in the plainest and grossest terms' without repudiating it? 'That being so,' she continued:

> it does not seem to me that it would be consistent with the decencies of public life, or possible as a matter of personal feeling, for me to ask to be allowed to rejoin you. If after all those years, you thought it necessary to read me in public such a lesson in the elements of political morality . . . then I think you should choose colleagues whom you can trust, people whose reputation has not been, justly or unjustly, smirched.

She also felt responsible, she added, for the fate of her three collaborators. 'I don't think the Council was at all ungenerous to me,' she concluded,

> considering how much in the wrong they thought me. But a certain remark made to me first by Mrs Fawcett and repeated to me from various sources, as though it has gone the round of the Union, to the effect that people were sorry to lose me, but that no-one regretted the others, has rankled very much. It seems to me either very unfeeling or very obtuse, considering what a small share of the responsibility was theirs and what a heavy penalty they paid.

'How could I ask to be restored to favour again,' she concluded, 'knowing that if they whom I led into this difficulty, made the same request, it would probably be rejected?'[108]

In fact, Rathbone would be 'restored to favour', not that January but a few months later, after a final bitter conflict over the Union's policy towards the war had decimated and demoralized its leadership. She would rebuild her relationships with Mrs Fawcett and with Kathleen Courtney (although these two were themselves now not on speaking terms), and would mastermind the complex political negotiations that finally brought parliamentary and local government votes to most women over thirty. In April 1914, however, when she resigned from the Executive Committee, she could not have foreseen this future. Under attack in Liverpool for her report on widows' pensions and now off the National Union's Executive, Eleanor had had a hard and troubling spring. She retreated with Elizabeth to the Lake District to recuperate. They were there that first week in August when the guns began sounding.

Chapter 8

Time of Trial

When Eleanor and Elizabeth heard of Britain's declaration of war, they hurried back to Liverpool. They had no thought but that they should help. Eleanor, bruised from her suffrage battles, was eager to do something useful; Elizabeth was always at her best in a crisis. Certainly there was plenty to do. The government's first call for volunteers had gone out, and some 35,000 of the city's men (including a quarter of its dockers) would answer it almost immediately.[1] This was the pageant of those first days of war – the crush at the recruiting stations, the tearful parting scenes, Liverpool's Conservative and Liberal politicians outdoing one another in patriotic oratory. But there were also more private and desperate dramas, played out in thousands of individual homes, retailed by the wives who thronged the settlement. Suddenly and inexplicably food prices had shot up[2]; and if the City Council had managed to bring these quickly under control, the labour market and the government's plans for military families were still in disarray. Eleanor and Elizabeth had spent enough time studying working-class budgets and talking to working-class housewives to know what that meant: hungry children, unpaid rents, desperate trips to the moneylender and the pawnshop. Perhaps they had a few sharp words with Eleanor's cousin Herbert Rathbone, the outgoing Liberal mayor; perhaps they were just the obvious people for City Hall to turn to in a crisis. At any rate, within a few weeks, Eleanor emerged at the head of a 'Town Hall Soldiers' and Sailors' Families' Organization' charged with the task of assisting military families.

For the first two years of the war, this 'war work' took almost all of Rathbone's time. She did not resent this; indeed, she only wished she could do more. 'For the first time in my life,' she wrote to Catherine Marshall a year into the war, 'I would give the world to be able to migrate into a man's skin – the vulgarest little cockney Tommy Atkins would do.'[3] Her fervour is worth noting, for by this point some intellectuals and feminists (including Marshall) strongly disagreed. How do we understand Rathbone's unflagging patriotism, especially in a war that claimed so many lives? Her Liverpool location was part of it, for the city rallied to the war fiercely and across class and party lines, and Rathbone, in her work, would come in daily contact with the devastated families of some of the 13,500 local men who lost their lives. But this is not the sum of it, for if Liverpool was jingoistic, Rathbone was not: she had, with her father, opposed the Boer War, and in 1920 would speak out bravely against Lloyd George's brutal terror in Ireland.[4] Instead, her patriotism was of a piece with her politics. Like many liberals, she saw the war with Germany as a *just war*, fought to defend democracy from "Prussianism" and the rule of force. Like her close friend Mary Stocks, she thought Germany's 'monstrous, wicked, unprovoked' attack on Belgium had left Britain no choice but to act,[5] and her feminism made her determined to play her part. Since only in those countries with a deep commitment to the protection of individual liberties could feminism flourish, she argued towards the end of the war, the fate of feminism 'stands or falls with the fate of our nation'. War work was not, then, a diversion from feminism's true purpose, but an extension of its 'common cause'.[6]

Within a few months of its outbreak, and as the feminist movement began splintering, Rathbone would make her thoughts public. In August and September, however, she spent no time at all on justifications, for she found herself in charge of an almost unimaginable range of social problems. She was to safeguard the well-being of soldiers' families, yes – but how on earth was she to do this? Prime Minister Asquith had announced that all soldiers' families would now be eligible for those maintenance payments (called 'separation allowances') the army had hitherto paid only to a small number of 'official' military wives, but, as is often the case, wartime rhetoric far outstripped administrative capacity. In July 1914, a mere one thousand soldiers' wives received such allowances; by September, as many as half a million were entitled. But the War Office's clerks had no idea who these wives were and no way of dealing with them: they had no lists of dependants, no claim forms, no agreed rates of benefit and (virtually) no staff. Thus, while the Office managed to issue guidelines on rates and entitlement, it turned to voluntary organizations and the town councils to build an administrative apparatus from the ground up.

Luckily for Liverpool (or at least for its working-class wives), Eleanor and Elizabeth had expansive networks of family, feminists and friends on which to draw. Within weeks, Edith Eskrigge and other suffragists had set up some two dozen district offices; Macadam and the settlement had pitched in with rudimentary training; as many as a thousand suffragists, settlement workers, students, and simply ordinary citizens had volunteered to help. Those volunteers began the painstaking work of helping Liverpool's many thousands of entitled wives and mothers fill out claim forms, but – aware of families' often desperate straits – they also visited households, assessed needs, advanced payments or simply gave outright aid. With thousands of new cases each week and War Office reimbursements only trickling in, the new organization was soon short of funds.[7] They appealed to Eleanor's cousin Herbert, now in the last days of his mayoralty, who

– to the fury of Liverpool Conservatives – transferred some £20,000 of locally subscribed funds to Rathbone's committee.[8] Herbert and Eleanor then affiliated the organization with the national Soldiers' and Sailors' Families' Association (SSFA), a much-respected philanthropic association now designated the government's agent for the administration of allowances throughout the country.

These moves stabilized the new organization and strengthened Eleanor's position, but they also brought her into debates over national policy-making. For the whole matter of pensions and allowances was, by late 1914, bitterly disputed. Voluntary organizations may have been the only bodies capable of handling the payments crisis, but many Labour and Liberal politicians understandably objected to private charities administering public funds in what was turning into a 'people's war'. The Liberal government responded by raising rates across the board and by arranging to pay all basic allowances – which were graduated according to the size of the family – directly to the woman through the Post Office. Yet local SSFA chapters continued to handle the processes of establishing and investigating claims; their voluntary workers also visited families and paid out a host of supplementary allowances for special hardships. Left-leaning politicians were quick to denounce this reliance on home visits and voluntary workers as inefficient, inquisitorial and offensive, and to demand a uniform flat-rate system administered directly by the state. In November 1914 the government thus turned the whole problem over to a small but powerful Commons select committee, on which Lloyd George and Bonar Law both sat. Throughout that winter, the committee heard testimony from service ministers, philanthropists, local authorities and labour organizations.[9]

In January 1915, Rathbone travelled down to London to explain the Liverpool system and give the committee her views. Her organization, by this stage, had 17,000 families on its books: each family was visited weekly by one of some 700 voluntary workers, and while these families drew their basic allowance through the Post Office, many were given supplementary grants out of the organization's funds. The operation ran smoothly and Eleanor intended to defend it, but the committee gave her a rough ride. Eleanor couldn't have known it, but she'd been set up in advance. Lord Derby, the local Conservative magnate, still smarting from Herbert's transfer of funds, had written to warn Bonar Law that the Liverpool Soldiers' and Sailors' Families Organization had been 'packed by the suffragettes'; Eleanor, for all her 'extraordinary good work', was 'a rabid suffragette' and not to be trusted.[10] Bonar Law, tipped off, painted the Liverpool operation as 'practically ... a new scheme of separation allowances', dangerously independent of government control – and Liverpool's Lord Mayor, in attendance as the committee's nominal head, did nothing to back up his 'Honorary Organising Secretary'. 'Miss Rathbone seeks to have a rather larger control of the ladies' element in the administration than Lord Derby and myself,' he admitted. 'I thought it was that,' Bonar Law replied.[11] George Barnes, sitting on the Committee for Labour (and later in effect Rathbone's boss as Minister of Pensions), made it clear that socialists didn't think much of 'home visits' by charitable ladies anyway.[12]

But Rathbone refused to give ground. She agreed entirely that the government should pay out the basic allowances itself, but she made a ringing defence of SSFA administration in general and her own Liverpool organization in particular. The SSFA, she pointed out, had saved the government from 'an appalling public scandal' in the early months of the war by stepping in to handle administration and advance payments. Her female voluntary workers were at once more professional and more sympathetic than the male pensions officers who were handling soldiers' mothers' claims; their weekly visits, she told Barnes, were 'very often more important' than monetary help and were by no means resented. Such visits established 'a feeling of community of interest' among women of different classes and gave soldiers' wives an advocate to turn to in times of trouble. The government had not been fair to voluntary workers, she told the committee bluntly, and if new public bodies were to be set up, they should be required to co-opt 'a reasonable number of women, by which we do not mean one woman on each committee'.[13]

One can certainly understand Rathbone's chagrin. Her organization was neither inefficient nor arbitrary; its workers had put in tens of thousands of unpaid hours only to hear themselves denounced or ridiculed. The outcry against voluntary control, Rathbone thought, was a blind for anti-feminism: to turn administration over to 'the state' was, conveniently, to take it out of (still vote-less) women's hands. And yet, with Rathbone's organization laid out before them, one can appreciate Bonar Law's and Barnes's apprehensions as well. For Rathbone's organization was not merely aiding women, it was also – in that very process – effacing men. Where once working-class wives had to turn to their husbands for economic aid or political representation, they now had to turn to the woman 'visitor'; supplementary payments – and their denial – were in her powerful hands. Labour leaders objected that voluntary workers were inquisitive and meddlesome (as some undoubtedly were), but they would not have been mollified had they learned that most were (as Rathbone claimed) generous and sympathetic. They did not wish to see a feminized state, still less to imagine that sex could prove as powerful a foundation for sympathy and service as family loyalty or even class. Small wonder Barnes and Bonar Law alike found Rathbone's model of cross-class woman-centred social work threatening, a challenge to male domestic dominance and male political power alike.

In 1915, the government divested the SSFA of its administrative powers, turning over administration first to a new statutory committee and then, when that failed to perform, to a new Ministry of Pensions. Yet Rathbone and the voluntary workers managed to ride out these changes, adjusting to new directives while keeping their hands on the reins. Thus, once she thought state control inevitable, Rathbone – again as a feminist – pragmatically urged the Soldiers' and Sailors' Families Association to come to terms. 'I think we must make it quite clear from the first that we are not a party of kindly busybodies who will do odd jobs that the local committees cannot find time to do for themselves,' she told a conference of the national organization in 1916, 'but that we have the experience on which they ought to draw'. It was unlikely that any new public bodies would be able to do without the SSFA workers' expertise, she thought, and local voluntary associations should thus insist on 'complete absorption'.[14] And this is, in essence, what happened. Local branches of the SSFA were often asked to administer the (now publicly funded) supplementary grants, becoming subcommittees of local war pensions committees. They did sometimes feel, Rathbone recalled, as though 'the human side of their work was being . . . drained away or smothered under a mass of highly complex regulations', but they carried on.[15] Co-opted by first one public authority and then another, Rathbone, Eskrigge and their allies ran the allowance system in Liverpool until the early 1920s.

Why did Rathbone care so much about separation allowances and work so hard to keep their administration in female hands? To be sure, she was protective of the reputation and positions of her female colleagues and wished to win them a foothold in the local state. But Rathbone wanted to keep her hands on this work for a second reason: because she had come to see it as a test and vindication of her economic ideas. Separation allowances were not particularly generous, but they were regular, proportional to the size of the family, and paid to the women themselves. For the wives of Liverpool's casual workers, then, they marked a decisive break with the vicissitudes of the male wage. True, a wife was entitled by virtue of her husband's enlistment and not her own needs or services, but with the man many miles away, the money came to feel very much like 'a statutory payment . . . in respect of her functions as wife and mother'. Perhaps the War Office had not intended to conduct 'the greatest experiment that the world has ever seen in the State endowment of maternity', Rathbone wrote in *Common Cause* in the spring of 1916, but in effect this was what it had done. More than a million wives, and untold millions of children, were being supported through separation allowances; for one slice of the population, the male 'family wage' was no more. 'Students of social economics' should take note, Rathbone wrote, for they could now assess the likely results of a national endowment system.[16]

In the midst of war, then, the Liverpool Women's Industrial Council conducted one final investigation. Rathbone, Emma Mahler and their assistants consulted local police and the health, housing and education authorities; they spoke with settlement workers, pawnbrokers and district nurses; they examined statistics on public drunkenness and convictions for child abuse and neglect. All these authorities – and all the available data – were agreed: 'children are better cared for and look healthier than in prewar days'; 'separation allowances have raised the character and conditions in the homes amongst the poorer recipients'.[17] Although the wartime restrictions on pub hours and the expansion of child welfare services had certainly helped, Mahler argued in the *Englishwoman*, 'we would submit that the regular and more adequate income, and the greater economic independence of women' lay at the root of these improvements.[18]

For Rathbone, 'greater economic independence' was the key to the whole question. For years she had been acutely aware of the terrible personal vulnerability and economic powerlessness of working-class wives; nothing heartened her more than evidence of their growing well-being and confidence. The psychological effects of direct payment were, Rathbone noted in *Common Cause*, quite as important as the economic effects: 'the sense of security, of ease, of dignity that they are tasting for the first time in their lives, is one of the very few good things that the ill-wind of the war has brought'. How would these women take it, she asked 'when the war is over and they are asked to go back to their old status of dependency'? She hoped 'that the seeds of "divine discontent" will have been implanted in them too deeply to be eradicated'. If so, she promised, 'we feminists will then find our opportunity'.[19]

Of course, for feminists to seize any post-war opportunity there had to be a feminist movement, and by early 1915 that seemed open to doubt. All over England, suffrage societies had turned to war work or fallen into abeyance. The national organizations were also in disarray. The Pankhursts, to general surprise, had supported the war as militantly as they had the vote (and let the WSPU fade away), while on the Executive of the National Union complex divisions emerged. Precisely because suffragists had always claimed that feminism and militarism were fundamentally opposed, precisely because they had argued that enfranchised women would insist that 'moral force' and not 'physical force' be used to resolve international disputes, some felt that women should not be so quick to rally to war. Initially, in line with Mrs Fawcett's views, the Union had devoted itself to relief work. But perhaps it could best serve the country by urging negotiation and settlement?

By November, the dispute was out in the open. Helena Swanwick, Catherine Marshall, Maude Royden, Kathleen Courtney, and Eleanor's cousin Margaret Ashton – all Rathbone's opponents from the conflict over the Labour alliance – thought the Union should begin to work for international conciliation. Mrs Fawcett, by contrast, insisted that since 'the British Empire is fighting the battle of representative government and progressive democracy all over the world', suffragists had an obligation to support the government.[20] The pages of *Common Cause* were thrown open to the debate, which did nothing to calm tempers, and the Councils held in November 1914 and February 1915 were riven by debates over the war. In March the rift worsened, when the Executive Committee considered whether or not to send delegates to a Women's Peace Conference in the

Hague. Mrs Fawcett and Frances Balfour thought this proposal frankly trea-
sonous and told their younger colleagues so.[21] Hurt and shocked, these members
would not attack Fawcett openly; instead, by April 1915, fully half of the
Executive – including Ashton, Ford, Royden, Courtney, Swanwick and Marshall
– had resigned.

Rathbone, busy with her soldiers' wives and no longer on the Executive, first
watched this battle from the sidelines. She did not attend the November meeting
of the Union's Council, but when she heard an account of the debate from her
Liverpool colleagues she wrote to Marshall in consternation. She was appalled
by the prospect of a rift, she wrote, fearing that this would mean 'the break up
of the Union and also probably, the break up of Mrs. Fawcett'.[22] As the crisis
worsened, she overcame her own hurt feelings to return to the fray. She attended
the Council held in February 1915 on the Union's policy towards the war, where,
together with Ray Strachey, she supported Fawcett's efforts to define the organization's role as one of supporting the national effort rather than working for an
international settlement. And in June of that year, with the Executive reduced to
a disoriented rump, Rathbone agreed to offer herself for election.

Watching her former adversaries brought low, Rathbone might have felt vin-
dicated. Yet she didn't return to this fight in a spirit of vengeance. She knew just
how it felt to be expelled from a movement to which one had devoted decades
of work. Moreover, unlike Ray Strachey – who frankly thought the resignation
of the pacifist wing 'a marvellous triumph'[23] – Rathbone saw the split as a terrible mistake, driven by the resigners' desire to convert the National Union to a
purpose for which it had not been intended. Marshall and Courtney might argue
that pacifism was a necessary part of feminism, Rathbone wrote that May in
Common Cause, but many in the Union would never accept this view; worse, by
forcing the question they were endangering (as they had with the Labour alliance)
the 'broad church' character of the Union. True, to aid the war effort the Union
had to 'abandon the vision (if we knew our own sex so little as ever to cherish
it) of womanhood united on behalf of peace and goodwill'[24] – but in doing
so, feminists would only be facing facts. Feminists would always be divided
among themselves on all matters except women's emancipation, Rathbone
argued, and should accept those disagreements as fruitful. However difficult
it was to learn to live with difference, 'the chances are that the policy and
the activities that emerge out of the dust and friction of our controversies will
be suited to the conditions of the world we live in, which is not, after all, a homo-
geneous world'.[25]

Rathbone thus argued for compromise, for a pragmatic acceptance by the
pacifist wing of the limited nature of the Union's mandate. They should also
remember their mutual respect and affection; that, she said, as Elizabeth Bennet
had said of Darcy, they 'would never enjoy quarrelling with anyone else half so
well'.[26] Yet by the time she made these arguments, the damage had been done.

The resigners would not back down, and a further special council, convened in Birmingham that June, decisively backed Mrs Fawcett. Ray Strachey took over from Marshall as parliamentary secretary (a job she saw as 'just filling a breach & keeping out some poisonous pacifists'),[27] and new elections brought some old and new faces – including Rathbone – on to the Executive.[28]

Eleanor rejoined a changed and traumatized group. The resignations may have been necessary – since, as Ray Strachey perceptively realized, 'the bulk of the stodgy members' were always firmly behind Fawcett[29] – but they had ravaged the suffrage leadership. Marshall, Courtney, Royden and Swanwick had coordinated the Union's strategy and propaganda for years; their exit left a leadership vacuum at the top of the movement. None of the loyalists left on the Executive in April (a rump that Ray Strachey's husband Oliver privately characterized as 'very silly & bad')[30] really had the sense or stature to take their place, while most of the new replacements (a group that included Rathbone's old and new allies Margery Corbett Ashby and Mary Stocks) lacked hard political experience. Initially, this didn't much matter, for agitation for the vote had been put on hold by the war, and the Executive spent most of its time trying to limit the scope of the Labour alliance, for which there was now little enthusiasm.[31] But at the end of 1915 suffrage suddenly came back on the agenda.

Eleanor Rathbone, as the most prominent and politically astute member of the Executive, found herself crafting the movement's response. It was a delicate situation. The Union had said that it would not raise the suffrage question during the war, but it had assumed that the whole issue would then be shelved until peacetime. In 1915, however, members of the government, and Sir Edward Carson in particular, raised the embarrassing problem that some soldiers were still not enfranchised and most would no longer meet the residency requirements for the vote. Carson thus proposed new legislation to enable all soldiers to vote at the next election. Suffragists were left in a quandary. They did not wish to seem disloyal, but feared that any new 'men's bill' would wreck even their post-war chances. In the spring of 1916, then, at Rathbone's urging, the Union's Executive set up a 'Consultative Committee on Women's Suffrage' with other franchise organizations – although her proposals to include Labour women's organizations, the breakaway pacifists, and later even Mrs Pankhurst, were defeated.[32] On that committee (which she chaired), and with Ray Strachey on the Union's Executive, Rathbone tried to defend women's interests without giving cause for charges of opportunism.

She proceeded cautiously. Suffragists had not raised the franchise issue, the National Union pointed out; the government itself had done so. They had no objection to legislation easing residency requirements for already-enfranchised soldiers, they said carefully, but if whole new classes of men were to be given the vote, they would insist on some attention to women's claims.[33] Slowly, the machinery of the suffrage movement was reactivated, and in early November

Rathbone told the Executive Committee that the time for action had come. The government had turned the franchise question, once again, over to a committee of MPs chaired by the Speaker of the House; she thought it likely that that conference would recommend votes for soldiers and sailors but leave the women's suffrage question open. Suffragists thus needed, again, to demonstrate popular support for their cause.[34] By late 1916 the Union was once again planning deputations, holding demonstrations, and lobbying. They did their best, but they were unhappy about the way the new rhetoric of war service had shifted the ground under them. That winter they approached Carson through an intermediary to see whether he would at least be willing to include women on active service in such a 'service' franchise (he was not),[35] and in January Rathbone even tried drafting such a franchise on her own, defining service 'not on a militarist basis, but . . . taken to include child-bearing and wage-earning'.[36]

Fortunately, suffragists were never quite driven to this essentialist corner, but when the Speaker's conference proposals emerged a few weeks later, they struck many suffragists as just as peculiar. For, as so often happens in political life, in Parliament some mixture of prejudice and expediency had prevailed, with arguments about fundamental rights and state service both going by the board. The National Union's old ally W.H. Dickinson, many years later, recalled that when the conference got around to discussing women's suffrage, MPs simply took a set of informal votes; once they discovered that the committee had *both* a majority in favour of some measure of women's suffrage *and* a majority opposed to complete equality, they cast around for a basis on which to limit women's franchise. Age prevailed: by setting an age qualification at thirty for women, they would get a largely married female electorate of, in their view, a reasonable but not overwhelming size.[37]

Suffragists greeted these proposals with consternation. 'You know, as well as we do, how much the unmarried woman worker needs enfranchisement,' Ray Strachey wrote to Dickinson, 'and how doubtfully we cannot but look upon the suggested age limits'.[38] Yet at the urging of their allies in the Commons, and out of a concern that any opposition might sink the bill altogether, in the end the National Union backed this compromise.[39] The government then came round, leaving Britain, for ten years, with an electorate peculiarly composed of all adult men over twenty-one (except conscientious objectors), all soldiers over eighteen, and those eight million women who were both over the age of thirty and themselves qualified for (or married to a man qualified for) the local franchise. This was certainly a substantial political change – but in light of war conditions, could suffragists have done better?

This question is hard to answer, but there is some reason to think the Union's caution justified. Wartime support for women's suffrage, while broad, was never very deep: many conversions were (like Asquith's) superficial, driven as much by a lack of stomach for a long parliamentary fight as by any new appreciation of women's capacities. MPs had, after all, little difficulty excluding women under thirty – precisely the group most involved in war work – and uniformly urged suffragists to accept this compromise. Fearful of being labelled unpatriotic, and conscious of their own organizational weakness after internal dissension and two years of war ('we are a horridly feeble lot,' Ray Strachey wrote to Oliver),[40] suffragists understandably grasped at the bird in the hand.

Rathbone was instrumental in shaping this conciliatory strategy. Yet she did so out of pragmatism rather than preference, aware of suffragists' new difficulties in arguing their case. The suffrage cause had been so simple before the war: with their victimization and subordination everywhere visible, it had been easy to argue for women's emancipation. The war, by squandering men's lives so ruthlessly, made those arguments seem hollow; as Mrs Humphry Ward wrote in *The Times*, any comparison between the work and sacrifices of men and women now seemed 'merely grotesque'.[41] Rathbone, always Ward's doughtiest opponent, tried to respond. Women did not base their claims on their sufferings, she retorted. The vote was 'not a sort of D.S.O.' It was, rather, 'merely the symbol of the responsibilities of ordinary citizenship, which requires every one to serve the country according to the measures of his or her opportunity, and to make sacrifices for it, if the call comes for that'.[42] Yet for all her brave words Rathbone too was horrified by the endless lists of casualties and like many women came to feel a kind of survivor's guilt. Believing that the risks of citizenship *should* in fact be borne equally, she went so far as to propose the conscription of women, and in this war (as in the next one) refused an honour for services that, in her view, could not compare with the sacrifices of the lowliest private soldier.[43]

Both pragmatism and humility thus predisposed Rathbone to conciliation. Yet on one issue, almost overlooked at the time but of great practical importance, she was willing to run some risks. This was the matter of women's local government franchise. Qualification for the local vote was, before the war, based not on sex but on one's status as a householder or owner of business property, but since men were considered the 'householder' of all property a couple occupied jointly, effectively only that small number of women (largely spinsters and widows) who held property in their own right were enfranchised. Rathbone, with her firm belief that wives contributed equally to the family's well-being, had always thought the designation of the husband as 'householder' unfair, and was pleased that the government's bill, by granting the parliamentary vote both to women over thirty who themselves met the local property qualification and to those who were married to men who did so, went some distance to equalize those rights. Unfortunately, however, the bill contained no such provision for the *local* government franchise: in local elections, the 'household' would continue to be represented by the husband alone. Oddly, then, while most married women over thirty would vote for their Member of Parliament if the bill passed, the vast majority would still not vote for their own local councillors.

In March 1917, Rathbone alerted her feminist colleagues to this anomaly. She knew they risked being branded as opportunistic or disloyal, but since even the 'antis' had been in favour of extending the local government franchise, she thought they might raise this issue safely. 'It seems to me difficult to exaggerate the good that will result from the adding of five or six million of married working women to the municipal register,' she pointed out. Herself a local councillor, she knew how little time and thought local authorities gave to maternal and infant welfare; only the 'driving force' of working-class mothers would push them to take on social reform.[44] And poorer women, she was convinced, would come to understand and use their power. 'Make the hardest driven working housewife realise that there is a direct connection between her use of the municipal vote and the punctual emptying of her own ashbin,' she wrote, 'next rouse in her a sense of her responsibility for the ashbins of her neighbours, and you will have taken the first step towards making her an intelligent citizen and keen politician.'[45] The women's organizations *must* try to amend the bill so that the local franchise would mirror the new national franchise.

Yet when Rathbone brought this argument to the National Union and the Women's Local Government Society that spring, she found herself rebuffed. Feminists were opposed to 'fancy franchises', one member of the Union's Executive told her bluntly,[46] and even those who were sympathetic (among them Mrs Fawcett) thought they should not risk endangering the bill.[47] The Women's Local Government Society, citing its long-standing objection to any qualifications based on sex or marriage, simply told Rathbone (and, for good measure, the Home Secretary and the Prime Minister) that they were opposed to any extension to wives.[48] With the women's societies indifferent or opposed and the government insisting that no changes to the bill would be allowed, any prospect of movement on this front seemed negligible.

But Rathbone simply refused to take no for an answer. She considered the arguments of the Women's Local Government Society anything but feminist, and in an acrimonious interview that April told them so.[49] Enfranchising wives whose husbands were local electors wouldn't place a premium on marriage, she insisted; it would merely remedy the initial injustice by which husbands but not wives were considered 'householders' in the first place. Once again, then, she struck out on her own, looking to the House of Commons for a sympathetic ear.[50] There, she found a group of members, led by the faithful Liberal suffragist Sir Charles Roberts, willing to propose her change. The government put the whips on against all amendments anyway, but at the bill's second reading in May 1917 MPs across party lines rallied in favour of this one exception.

Caught on the sidelines of what was now a popular cause, the National Union Executive finally came round, and dragged the reluctant Women's Local Government Society behind it.[51] In the summer and autumn of 1917, suffrage societies finally began lobbying for the amendment; and Labour and working women's organizations lent their support.[52] Rathbone left nothing to chance, urging sympathetic MPs to lobby ministers and leading a final deputation on 14 November.[53] 'To enfranchise a woman politically without extending a similar franchise to her municipally,' Rathbone told the Home Secretary Sir George Cave, would be 'like giving her the heart, but not the legs and arms'.[54]

On 20 November 1917, the Roberts amendment was proposed in the House, and even the most adamant 'antis' spoke in its favour. Cave, admitting that support was overwhelming, took off the government whips, and the amendment was carried without a division.[55] Two days later, the Union's Executive thanked Rathbone with a round of applause. Without her 'indefatigable enthusiasm', Fawcett said, this reform might not have been accomplished – an encomium that was surely an understatement.[56] When Rathbone raised the issue of the local franchise, no suffrage organization supported her and the government promised to oppose any change. Only her absolute unwillingness to let the matter rest forced MPs, the women's organizations and (eventually) the government to concede to women this symbolically insignificant but practically essential right. Certainly the local government franchise would have been amended in time, but who can say when? As it was, the 1918 Representation of the People Act not only gave the parliamentary vote to some eight million women over thirty, it also quadrupled the female local government electorate. In the inter-war years, as economic collapse and financial retrenchment strained local services, that electorate – and the local councillors who served it – would, as Rathbone expected, act as one crucial safeguard of women's interests.

Throughout the middle years of the war, Eleanor travelled regularly to London for meetings of the National Union Executive and of the SSFA. At first, she stayed at the Lyceum Club, but then Emily – bored in Liverpool and now unable to travel abroad – took a house in Queen's Gate. Eleanor, presumably, stayed there, but she may have stayed with Elizabeth Macadam as well. For Elizabeth was in London too – brought there in 1916 by Seebohm Rowntree, now Director of a new Welfare Department at the Ministry of Munitions, to help set up training programmes for factory welfare workers. Macadam was a pioneer in this field: even before the war, she had sent Liverpool students to local factories to observe their health and safety provisions, and early in the war had founded the first training scheme in Liverpool. Macadam thus took leave from her Liverpool lectureship to help build up the field of industrial welfare – a line of work, she insisted, that was quite distinct from philanthropy and which working-class women could take up quite as successfully as women of the middle class.[57]

But if work and friendship started Rathbone's weekly sojourns in London, by 1917 her political ambitions were keeping her there. For, as she realized, the war had centralized policy-making further: as the state expanded, London's importance did so as well. Especially under Lloyd George, new ministries and committees seemed to appear almost weekly – including, in July 1917, a Ministry of Reconstruction. Just what the new Ministry was to 'reconstruct,' and how, wasn't entirely clear, but Rathbone had her own suggestions. In many ways, the war had challenged male domestic dominance, for not only had women's employment opportunities expanded, but millions of women had spent the war years managing their families on their own. With women's suffrage agreed as well, women were suddenly on the agenda: they were a legitimate political interest, a policy area, a problem. Could the 'male-breadwinner' family be put back together again? Would working-class women go back to their old status of dependence? Rathbone, we know, didn't see why they should – and in the allowance system in Liverpool she had found a workable alternative. By 1917 even the *Economic Journal* was willing to publish her arguments for family endowment.[58] Now, Rathbone thought, was the moment to make a practical proposal.

Thus was born the 'Family Endowment Committee', a seven-person cabal of convinced supporters. Its membership is interesting, for it shows that Rathbone – the committee's moving spirit – had managed to gain the confidence of feminists on both sides of the wartime divide. Maude Royden and Kathleen Courtney, for example, had opposed Rathbone during the pre-war Labour alliance and had resigned over Fawcett's 'pro-war' stance – and yet both took part in this effort. A third member, the radical journalist H.N. Brailsford, had masterminded the campaign for the women's suffrage 'conciliation bill'. Mary Stocks, a young Manchester-based don's wife with a degree in economic history, was a wartime recruit to the National Union's Executive and would become one of Rathbone's closest friends. The last two, Emil and Elinor Burns, were fellow social scientists from Liverpool and acted as the committee's secretaries. All but Rathbone were Labour supporters.

Throughout the late autumn and winter of 1917 this little group of colleagues met under Courtney's chairmanship at the 1917 Club in Garrick Street to hammer out a practical plan. Early in the spring of 1918 they published *Equal Pay and the Family: A Proposal for the National Endowment of Motherhood*. Exploiting the current debate over women's wages, they claimed (following Rathbone) that endowment would further the cause of equal pay, but their main concern was with the rights and status of mothers. The main barrier to women's equality, they argued, was the dependence of the mother, who – despite her own 'service to Society in making a home and rearing children' – was still 'the uncharted servant of the future, who receives from her husband, at *his* discretion, a share in *his* wages'. 'Few of us realise,' they pointed out, 'how constantly and subtly this half-conscious, but ever-present sense of the economic dependence of the woman upon the man corrodes her personality, checks her development, and stunts her mind, even while she is still a girl, with marriage only as yet a prospect.' Insisting that 'there can be no real independence whether for man or woman, without economic independence', the committee concluded that the care of young children must become a form of paid work. Even were it reasonable to expect women with school-aged children to earn, those with children under five were surely 'fully occupied'. They therefore proposed endowing all mothers with children under five, and those children, at an annual cost of some £144 million – a price tag that would rise to £240 million if the children's allowance were continued to the age of fifteen.[59]

Figures like these would have astounded any pre-war Chancellor, for even the lower amount approached that for total annual central government spending in the years before the war. Yet the wartime state had expanded radically, and by 1918 separation allowances alone were costing around £100 million per year. Moreover, with continental regimes crumbling and politicians eyeing the new and untested 'women's vote' anxiously, even utopian schemes appeared possible. Although at this stage only really a group of friends, the Family Endowment Committee was invited to give evidence to the War Cabinet Committee on Women in Industry (which had been appointed to advise on women's post-war economic position) and to a National Birth-Rate Commission established to consider problems of population. Significantly, many of the women's organizations and industrial unions interviewed by the former body spontaneously supported endowment,[60] and the Fabian-influenced Ministry of Reconstruction began considering the matter as well. By the end of 1918, anyone interested in the questions of equal pay and child welfare would have heard the arguments for endowment.

Eleanor Rathbone was only one voice in this debate, but she was already the most influential. She was also the most instrumental: having identified family endowment as the most important potential social reform, she was not above adapting her arguments to suit her audience. When writing to *The Times* in August 1918, then, she gave a laundry list of reasons – from industrial efficiency to public health – to support it. Yet even here, when trying to frame her argument conservatively, Rathbone could not disguise her feminism. 'After all,' she wrote, 'the rearing of families is not a sort of masculine hobby, like tobacco smoking or pigeon flying'; why then should it be paid for 'by the clumsy device of paying men wage-earners more than women'?[61] Her core aim remained to effect a transfer of income from men to women.

The campaign for family endowment would take many twists and turns over the next twenty-five years, as political circumstances changed and new audiences and allies emerged. But because Rathbone saw family endowment through feminist eyes, the conversion of her own fellow feminists was always her first priority. In 1918, she could feel optimistic on this score. Both working women's organizations and the big battalions of the suffrage movement expressed new appreciation for the problems of mothers, and *Common Cause*, the house organ of the National Union of Women's Suffrage Societies, kept a lively debate open. With the vote at least partly won, women – and women's organizations – would be choosing new issues, new reforms for which to fight. Eleanor was determined that family endowment would be one of them.

In launching the campaign for family endowment, Eleanor opened a new chapter in her life, one marked by information-gathering, campaigning, lobbying, and endless expert testimony. Another chapter closed: although she remained active in Liverpool social reform and local government, she would no longer guide the Liverpool Women's Industrial Council or dispatch young women to gather budgets and wage statistics, interview Poor Law widows or soldiers' wives. Why, she had asked herself in 1896, did poverty afflict women in particular; and what, moreover, could be done about it? Her attempt to answer this question had led her through Liverpool's dockyards and slums, sweatshops and council houses, but now she had her answer. Eleanor's years as a social investigator were over.

Sociological insight is born of the marriage of empathy and reason – of the ability to see human behaviour as both individual and aggregate, to detect the pattern and logic in the web of human relationships, and even (if one is visionary and determined) to pinpoint the threads that must be unpicked and rewoven to pattern society in a different way. Beatrice Webb, who had trod Rathbone's path from investigation to politics before her, also possessed that unique gift of insight – yet only Rathbone scrutinized the tapestry with women's interests particularly in mind. Webb, by contrast, found her work as the sole socialist member of the 1918 War Cabinet Committee on Women in Industry boring,[62] and while she also concluded that women's low wages were due in large part to prejudice alone (a factor she called 'the principle of the vested interest of the male') this discovery did not really arouse her outrage. Critical of her fellow committee members' endorsement of sex-based pay differentials but unwilling to condemn conventional patterns of family life *tout court*, Webb in her minority report envisaged standard rates capable of supporting a couple supplemented by state-funded children's allowances to meet differential child dependency needs.[63]

In time, pragmatic considerations would drive Rathbone towards similar proposals. In 1918, however, she thought this just not good enough. Certainly children should be a public charge, but it was women's dependence and powerlessness that had engaged her intelligence and her heart, and which she now thought it possible to end. Throughout the Edwardian years Rathbone's very feminism had led her to view statist arguments with ambivalence: too often, she thought, 'state control' meant control over voteless women by enfranchised and empowered men. By 1918, however, Rathbone thought differently. For not only had the state expanded during wartime, it had also feminized: women had become citizens and administrators, able to shape the new political world. Endowment of motherhood might just be within reach. In 1918, she faced the future with optimism.

Elsie Makes her Will

17. Elsie Rathbone.

Remarkably, Eleanor's immediate family escaped the war unscathed. But with almost everyone tied up in war work, Greenbank grew quiet. Eleanor, rushed off her feet with suffrage and soldiers' wives, was scarcely ever home. Hugh and Evie, down the road, were consumed with anxiety about Reynolds, their son at the front. Emily, still energetic and frankly bored, had taken herself off to London.

Elsie, now in her sixties and left (as ever) to manage the house, grew reflective.

Her family seemed to be coming apart. As a child, Elsie had been close to her brothers, the sons of William's first marriage, and had done her best to comfort them after their mother's death. But Ashton and Ted had died young, Harry had escaped to Italy, and her beloved Willie had – in the way of brothers – gone off to school and work and left her behind. For years, her plaintive letters had followed him, recounting the family's doings and asking for news.[1] 'People seem gradually to drift away from their sisters,' she had written on the eve of his marriage, 'but I could not bear that'.[2] But bear it she must, for William Gair and (still more) his wife Blanche found little time in their glittering London life for a provincial spinster with a penchant for good works.

Liverpool, then, reclaimed her. Born too soon for the 'new woman's' life of suffrage and social work, she lived out the Victorian daughter's fate. For forty years (as one brother recalled) she 'hovered about the house, thinking of & planning for the comfort, well-being and pleasure of every inmate . . . always thinking of everybody & never of herself'.[3] When family members came to visit Greenbank, she was there to greet them; when one became sick, she flew to their side. They took her for granted, she knew – but she had no other life and could never be far from her father. She, and not Emily, took over the job of keeping up William's philanthropic bequests; the reputation of a house known for hospitality was left in her capable hands.

But even the selfless have moments of assertion; even they might wish to make some mark. In March 1917, as the casualty lists lengthened, Elsie made her will. Or, to put it differently, for just one moment she sat in judgment. Elsie had always shared William's view that the family wealth was a trust, to be used for the good of others, and she had come to share his disillusion with his sons as well. But she loved and admired Eleanor, supporting her campaigns and causes with donations and advice. Looking around her, Elsie had no trouble deciding on her siblings' merits – and she used her will, as her father had done before her, to lay down the moral law. Although she left £5,000 each to Frank and Eleanor, and £3,000 each to Lyle, Harry and William Gair, only Frank and Eleanor received their share outright. Lyle's and Harry's were 'family endowments', conditional upon their continued marriage to their current wives; moreover, in March 1919, shortly after William Gair's eldest son Bill left his wife for another woman, she added a codicil retracting her eldest brother's portion.[4] Yet, she did not protect all her sisters or sisters-in-law equally. Surprisingly, Evie – after Emily's death the family matriarch, responsible for Greenbank – was left nothing at all to help her with this task. Instead, the bulk of Elsie's property was left to the woman who needed it least but whom she trusted most. In an astonishing gesture of sisterly – and spinsterly – solidarity, Elsie left a substantial house near Greenbank, her share in the family's Italian villa, all of her personal effects, and the residue of her estate to Eleanor 'and her heirs' absolutely.[5]

This was not an impetuous act. Elsie was an excellent manager: she knew what money could do. Probably unknown to her brothers, Elsie was the richest of her siblings, for the simple reason that she spent very little and had lived all of her life at home. Her portion of her dead mother's settlement and her legacy from her father did not go (as William Gair's and Harry's did) on London houses, European travel or expensive wives; the money just sat there, mostly in shipping shares. In 1917, when Elsie stipulated the size of her bequests, those shares were already worth a lot – and over the next three years their value would mushroom. When Elsie died, at the height of the post-war boom, she left almost £100,000. Since the bequests accounted for only half of that, Eleanor, as the 'residuary legatee' as well as a major beneficiary, came into a fortune.

As we watch Elsie sign the will and return to household tasks, then, one mystery resolves itself: the mystery of where Eleanor Rathbone's money came from. Eleanor, during her Liverpool years, was already well-off: she had had £15,000 from William's various bequests and may have had as much as another £5,000 from other family sources; her total income was probably not less than £1,000 per year. This was a great deal for an abstemious spinster living at home, certainly enough to allow her to give generously (as she did) to suffrage and social causes. Yet it could not have supported the kind of political career she later had. Everyone working with Eleanor Rathbone in the years between the wars knew that she was a wealthy woman, and it is important that she was: her money paid for houses in Westminster and Liverpool; kept printing presses and pamphlets flowing; and supported of a host of cooks, maids, researchers, typists, secretaries and, later, worthy refugees. Three houses, two staffs, and untold numbers of campaigns and donations later, Rathbone still left almost £100,000 on her death in 1946.[6] Elsie's money had borne fruit beyond her wildest expectation.

This is an unexpected finding, but it is somehow fitting. William was an important figure in Victorian politics, and when Eleanor's career took off everyone saw her as his heir. Eleanor colluded in this, writing his life and paying tribute to his example. But the money, which never lies, tells another story. Eleanor may have owed her early training and first political opportunities to her father, but her national career became possible because Elsie – this elderly, puritanical and overlooked spinster – was willing, against convention, to declare her own brothers unworthy and leave her unencumbered half-sister a fortune. Eleanor spent the next twenty-eight years justifying Elsie's trust.

PART III

A NEW FEMINISM IN THE MAKING

18. Suffragists outside Parliament on the occasion of the royal assent to the Equal Franchise Act, 2 July 1928. Macadam is in a light coat and scarf, front, fifth from right; Mrs Fawcett is to her right.

It is a fatal thing for a woman's organisation to get the reputation of being 'anti-man,' and I would not for worlds bring that reproach on the N.U.S.E.C. But I knew a wise old lady who was fond of repeating: 'The more I see of some people the better I like my dog'; and after every experience of men's politics and administration my feeling is: 'The more I see of some men, especially politicians, the less I want women to adopt all their methods and standards of value.'

Rathbone, 'Patience and Impatience', Address to the NUSEC Council, 6 March 1923

Chapter 9

Choosing Elizabeth

In life as in fiction, even the quieter heroines have their dramatic moments. Dorothea Brooke, in the mausoleum of her husband's house, weighed her love for Will Ladislaw against the claims of wealth and family, and – in the best novelistic tradition – followed her heart. Eleanor Rathbone always reminded her friend Margery Fry of the figure of Dorothea – although it was Dorothea's ardent wish to do good and not her romantic destiny that Fry had in mind.[1] But Eleanor Rathbone also faced her decisive moment, when love and loyalty hung in the balance.

Emily Rathbone's death in March 1918 precipitated the crisis, for it forced Eleanor to consider how she would in future live. Except for three brief years at Somerville, Eleanor had spent all of her forty-six years in her mother's house. The two women had made their peace after their battles of the 1890s: Emily grew to take pride in her youngest daughter's accomplishments, and supported Eleanor's career with her usual blunt comments and ready cash. Now Emily was gone, and the Rathbone clan, gathered in force at Greenbank two months later, agreed that the house should pass to Evie and Hugh, as both William and Emily had hoped.[2]

Where then was Eleanor to go? She had money enough to live independently, having inherited another £5,000 and considerable personal effects under her mother's will.[3] Her family, on the other hand, expected her to live with Elsie, who was close to her younger half-sister and who was looking forward – finally, at the age of sixty-seven – to acquiring her own home. But for Eleanor the situation was not so simple, for Emily's death made another long-held dream possible. Eleanor and Elizabeth Macadam had shared so many parts of their lives for years: now, in their mid-forties, they might finally share a home. But where would that home be? After several years in London with the Ministry of Munitions, Elizabeth returned to Liverpool at the end of the war; yet no sooner had she settled back into her old position at the Liverpool School of Social Work than she was offered the secretaryship of a newly constituted Joint University Council for Social Studies. The hitch was that the Council was based in the capital: Elizabeth would have to move permanently to London.

In the year in which Eleanor lost her mother, then, she faced the prospect of losing Elizabeth as well. Elizabeth had always been ambitious, and the move would be good for her career. Her ambitions for the settlement and the School of Social Work had been realized: while continually rewarding, her work there no longer seemed new. At the Joint University Council, by contrast, she thought she would be able to expand and shape training programmes for social workers throughout the country. This was just the kind of challenge Elizabeth relished. The only thing holding her back was the friendship she had built with Eleanor – a relationship neither she nor Eleanor knew quite how to weigh in the balance against the prospect of a London life.

Neither Eleanor nor Elizabeth was capable of talking comfortably about their feelings, and their discussion that winter must have been elliptical in the extreme – Elizabeth seeking to extract the confession that Eleanor did genuinely want her to stay in Liverpool, and Eleanor stolidly insisting that Elizabeth follow the path most likely to help her career. A day of reflection after one particularly painful discussion brought Eleanor to her senses, however, and drove her to confess, finally and fully, just how much Elizabeth meant to her. On the evening of 5 March 1919, she wrote the following letter, the only full expression of her feelings for Elizabeth that we have.

My dearest,

I am desperately anxious that you should make the right decision as to your work, unbiased by personal considerations.

But I don't want you to have *wrong* impressions & I thought perhaps in my anxiety to leave you free I have made you think that I am indifferent personally, as to whether you are in London or Liverpool, or rather that I think the advantages are about equally balanced. This is not quite so. *Provided that I felt certain* that Liverpool would give you equally fair scope for your powers & therefore equal happiness & contentment in the knowledge of your usefulness, *I would infinitely rather have you in Liverpool*. There are great disadvantages in a divided life, especially as one grows older. To share a home together, to make Elsie happy & take care of her as she all her life has taken care of others, to make a centre in Liverpool for all people who have wider interests than those they are surrounded by, to prove that life in the provinces could be as rich & full as life in London, to try to mould the city into new ways & to really identify *ourselves* with its life as some return for what it has done for *me* and my forebears (I see it as one-sided there) – to have peaceful weekends by sea and river – it would all be a happiness too great to seem possible. *But only if it means an equal happiness for you.* And it is solely because I know that you cannot just by willing it thus, *make* it mean that, that I want you to put this side of things behind you in making your decision & to choose the work that seems to call you, not necessarily the loudest at the moment, but with the most permanently compelling call.

Oh my dear, my dear. If you knew how much your life, your cares, your future, your happiness meant to me at bottom, you would not think me the self-absorbed creature I seem. I can be happy with you in London or in Liverpool, but the first essential is that you should find yourself reaching your powers and fulfilling them.

Yours, ER[4]

This is an extraordinarily revealing letter, especially for a woman who was, in her own words, 'so bad at expressing affection'.[5] What shines out from these lines is not only Eleanor's deep affection for Elizabeth, but also her profound commitment to her friend's career and her rejection of any arrangement that would have required Elizabeth to sacrifice her ambitions for Eleanor. Eleanor was trying hard to avoid emotional blackmail: she did not want Elizabeth to remain in Liverpool, she said, unless that would make Elizabeth 'equally happy'; she did not threaten Elizabeth with a loss of friendship and love. Eleanor had not been planning to leave Liverpool at the end of the First World War: she was still on the City Council, full of plans for the expansion of voluntary social work in the city. Yet, 'I can be happy with you in London or in Liverpool', she wrote, making it clear that whatever the 'disadvantages of a divided life', it was she, and not Elizabeth, who would bear them.

Left entirely free, Elizabeth Macadam did in fact decide to leave Liverpool in 1919. Perhaps she didn't relish sharing a house with Elsie; perhaps she felt that, if she stayed in Liverpool, she would never be able to escape the too-powerful Rathbone name. She had never been willing to take Eleanor on her family's terms, and, having proven her power as a counter-attraction, her relationship with the Liverpool clan deteriorated. Although Elizabeth did come to Liverpool with Eleanor for some meetings and family visits, B.L. Rathbone recalled that his aunt Evie and Elizabeth Macadam 'rather fought over Eleanor'.[6] The family never quite forgave Eleanor for leaving Liverpool, and they certainly didn't forgive Elizabeth Macadam. 'We didn't like her,' Evie's daughter Nancy recalled. 'She took Eleanor away from us.'[7]

She was quite right, for Eleanor was as good as her word. In 1919, in preparation for their 'divided life', Eleanor and Elizabeth bought a London house – 50 Romney Street, an old refurbished terraced house off Smith Square, within easy walking distance of the Houses of Parliament. But Eleanor was still on the City Council in Liverpool and needed a Liverpool house in which to work and entertain; she also genuinely loved Elsie and understood how much she owed her. In June 1919, she thus also joined Elsie in her move from Greenbank to Whitegables, a comfortable villa on the outskirts of Liverpool with which Elsie was 'very well satisfied'.[8] Sadly, this solution lasted only eighteen months, for Elsie became ill while visiting her brother Harry in Vevey in the summer of 1920 and died that November.[9] Eleanor, whose love for Elsie was unmixed with the fear she felt for her mother, was left 'very much unhinged and tired'[10] to face another Liverpool move. But Elsie had left Eleanor not just a fortune but another house as well – Oakfield, a comfortable eighteenth-century villa just at the gates of Greenbank, which had been in the family for generations. Oakfield was larger than Romney Street and a good deal more comfortable; it had the drawing rooms and gardens needed for the gatherings Eleanor hosted. From 1920 until 1929, Eleanor lived for part of each month at Oakfield.

Yet it was Romney Street that became Eleanor's emotional home, and, if the address on most of her surviving correspondence is any guide, her primary residence. Rathbone and Macadam lived there together (eventually taking over number 52 as well) until the blitz bombed them out in 1940 – and even then they only moved around the corner. They were in this new flat in Tufton Court in 1944, when the V2 rockets started hitting London, and could not be budged. 'You see nothing would induce Aunt E. to leave London while Elizabeth remains,' Eleanor's niece reported to her mother, '& nothing would induce the latter to leave the flat all unguarded – for the door is off I believe, not to speak of windows.'[11] They were inseparable, as married as the most married couple could ever be – and were newly ensconced in a house in Hampstead when Eleanor died suddenly of a stroke eighteen months later.

Their partnership had lasted because, at the crucial moment, Eleanor was willing to take a good deal of trouble to preserve it. It would have been much easier at this stage to let Elizabeth move to London alone, for in 1919 family expectations, sisterly love, an important local career and strong local pride bound Eleanor to Liverpool. Perhaps it was only just, then, that the decision to commute to London proved a blessing in disguise. Although Eleanor's ideas about pensions and poverty had been formed in Liverpool, the war had turned these into national rather than local concerns: henceforth, policy would be made in London, and those who would shape it had to live there too. The pressure groups, lobbying campaigns and strategy sessions that came to fill Rathbone's life could be run much more easily from a cramped Westminster house than from a spacious Liverpool villa – and those same activities gave her the contacts she needed. With a house in hailing distance of Westminster, Macadam beside her, and (after 1920) Elsie's money to smooth her way, Eleanor was perfectly poised to try for a national political career.

The Liverpool ties remained, of course, but with time they gradually weakened. Bertie had also died in 1917 and Lyle would follow in 1923. By the mid-twenties, the Liverpool clan would be comprised of three family clusters: Hugh and Evie at Greenbank; Eleanor's cousin Herbert, still on the City Council, and his wife Winifred; and the growing family of Eleanor's youngest brother Frank, who was absorbed in the thankless task of keeping the much-reduced firm of Rathbone Brothers afloat. In theory, Eleanor's household at Oakfield constituted a fourth cluster – but at least half of Eleanor's political life and almost all of her heart was in London, with Elizabeth.

How can we understand this partnership, which would endure for the rest of Eleanor's life? We must see it in both general and specific terms – as a form of female friendship common among the 'new women' of the 1890s, and as a unique arrangement that reflected these particular women's needs. Like many women of their generation, Eleanor and Elizabeth saw spinsterhood as the prerequisite for a meaningful public career. Almost all of the women who had influenced them in their youth – Janet Case, Agnes Maitland, Margaret Sewell – were confirmed spinsters; most of the women they worked with at the settlement or in the women's suffrage movement were single as well. Married women, after all, could scarcely live in settlement houses, or devote themselves full-time to public work. For 'new women', then, marriage seemed the lesser option, one that would involve not only new private responsibilities but also the end of meaningful public work.

'New women' did form close emotional bonds, however; they just did so with other women. Many of Eleanor Rathbone's peers developed close and loving friendships, often lasting for a lifetime. Yet these women did not see such friendships as an alternative form of marriage exactly, and only partly because they were often not openly sexual. Rather, female partnerships were felt to be different because, unlike marriage, they were organized to foster, and not to undermine, women's political and social ambitions. Like the heroines in George Gissing's *The Odd Women*, 'new women' looked to female friends not simply for private companionship and pleasure, but to affirm their public ambitions and ideals. May Staveley and Dorothy Scott at the Birmingham Settlement, Emmeline Pethick and Mary Neal at their 'Espérance' girls' club, Sylvia Pankhurst and Norah Smyth at the East London Federation of Suffragettes, and a host of other female partnerships sustained – and were sustained by – the wider demand of single women for a place in public life.

By 1919, when Rathbone and Macadam finally set up house together, the heyday of such friendships had passed. The suffrage struggle was over, and the backlash against women's friendships had begun. Yet Rathbone and Macadam remained 'new women' to the end, and continued to define their friendship as an equal partnership in the cause of social reform. It was precisely because they believed, as Rathbone had put it, that 'happiness and contentment' came not from personal ties but from 'a knowledge of [one's] usefulness' that neither woman had been willing to see Macadam sacrifice career ambitions for friendship. The first premise of their move to London was thus that their partnership would help both women to 'reach their powers'.

So both women threw themselves into their work: Macadam into the organization of the voluntary sector and Rathbone into the running of the National Union of Societies for Equal Citizenship and the Family Endowment Society. Each woman also sought to make a name as a writer on social questions. Rathbone published her magnum opus, *The Disinherited Family*, in 1924, and Macadam's study of training for social work, *The Equipment of the Social Worker*,[12] appeared one year later. Romney Street became a centre of hospitality for a developing political network – a network that was, especially during the 1920s, almost entirely female. Mary Stocks, who helped to run the family endowment campaign, regularly came down from Manchester to stay, and Eva Hubback, Eleanor's right hand during her years at the National Union of Societies for Equal Citizenship, dropped in and out – as did visitors to the NUSEC offices, which were just around the corner in Dean's Yard. Elizabeth's sister May and her husband Ian Ross usually came for a week's visit once or twice a year, and after Eleanor moved permanently to London her brother Frank's family visited regularly as well. Old friends from Oxford – Hilda Oakeley, May Staveley, and the Hammonds – were always welcome. 'This house is like a person, I think, so full of individuality and character,' May Staveley wrote in Elizabeth's visitors' book in October 1920.[13]

Even the two women's pleasures were, especially in those early days, an enhancement of their work. True, Rathbone and Macadam continued the old Rathbone practice of taking holidays in the country, and then invited friends and family to visit them. In Easter 1924, for example, they borrowed Hugh and Evie's holiday house near Keswick and took Eva Hubback, Mary Stocks, Evie's daughter Nancy Warr and the three women's young children with them. They played with the children by day and discussed feminism and family allowances in the evenings. Eleanor, however, also spent a good deal of time 'ensconced in her drawing room . . . surrounded by Blue Books and puffing Turkish cigarettes',[14] and in fact most holidays were working holidays. As Eleanor's secretary remembered, Rathbone and Macadam would often 'take a house in the country and work and work and work, or go abroad and work and work and work; it was always work'.[15]

And as 'new women' should, Macadam and Rathbone kept quite a simple household – especially in comparison with the formality and grandeur of Rathbone's childhood homes. Mrs Wilson, their formidable cook-housekeeper, made sure that visitors to Romney Street ate well, but when it came to personal comfort, Rathbone had a puritanical streak. A soft touch for all good causes, she spent very little on herself, professing herself willing to put up 'at any local pub' when out electioneering for friends, and was only persuaded when in her forties to stop travelling third class.[16] Other members of the household sometimes found that puritanism discomfiting. Marjorie Green recalled that Rathbone once got it into her head that the household should try to live within the food budget rec-

19. Visitors to Eleanor and Elizabeth's holiday house in Scotland, September 1930. Left to right: Barbara Hammond, John Stocks, Mary Stocks, Eleanor, Elizabeth, J.L. Hammond. Seated: S. Alexander.

ommended by the British Medical Association as a minimum standard to be used when calculating unemployment pay. 'There was a great to-do in the kitchen about it,' Green remembered, and Macadam had to be pressed into service to dissuade her.[17]

In its puritanism and high-mindedness, Rathbone and Macadam's partnership exemplified the ideals of the generation of 'new women' with which they identified. In other respects, however, their relationship was specific and remarkable, particularly in the degree to which Macadam accommodated herself to Rathbone's domestic and emotional helplessness. For Eleanor, in one important respect, was not a 'new woman' at all: she had always had servants and sisters to look after her, and was no more capable of managing on her own than the average man. Macadam, by contrast, had lived independently or at a settlement for years: she was practical, well organized, and – in her own words – 'liked the housekeeping'.[18] Macadam thus took charge of all domestic matters from the outset. Moving from a house managed by Elsie to a house managed by Elizabeth, Eleanor never had to hire or fire servants, arrange for repairs or order meals

– much less cook them: 'I doubt she ever touched a saucepan in her life,' the daughter of a close friend recalled.[19]

As she had done for years, Macadam also 'took care of Eleanor', seeing to it, as Margery Fry recalled, 'that Eleanor should not forget her meals, or go about in rags'.[20] Many of Eleanor's friends thought such supervision necessary: even as a girl Eleanor had been 'dreamy', and as an adult her forgetfulness about personal matters became legendary. At Somerville, her fellow students were amused by her seeming indifference to mealtimes, games and regulations alike; in Liverpool, co-workers learned to gather up her purse and umbrella after her meetings; in London, the taxi company had standing instructions to retrieve her pearls from the cab and return them to Romney Street; and friends blessed by a visit invariably had to post some errant possession back to her.[21] Yet, as her secretaries and friends noticed, Rathbone was not feckless and forgetful in all areas of life: her written work was rigorous and precise; she chaired meetings well; and if she kept her friends waiting, she arrived on time at City Council meetings, parliamentary debates, and the endless political confabulations, demonstrations and deputations that filled her days. She was, in other words, selectively forgetful, prone to overlook only those things that Elizabeth could be trusted to remember for her.

Mary Stocks explained this apparent contradiction by suggesting that Rathbone simply refused to bother with the 'irrelevant or trivial'[22] – and certainly Rathbone's domestic incompetence, like that of generations of husbands, conveniently freed her from all household responsibilities. Yet Rathbone had always insisted that housework was *not* trivial, and one secretary recalled that Rathbone was actually very embarrassed about her own incompetence. She never managed to reform, however – and surely the reason for her continued untidiness and personal disorganization is an emotional one: she liked – at least subconsciously – to have Elizabeth take care of her. In the privacy of their relationship, like an overlooked child, she was naughty almost for the pleasure of being scolded. As Stocks recalled:

Ever fresh in the mind of one of her friends is the picture of Elizabeth's revolt at the appearance of Eleanor emerging at the zero moment of a departure from Dorset with a large stone, a coil of derelict rope and an unseemly paper bag containing loose cigarettes. Why, oh why, had she elected to add these final items to an already variegated baggage train? Her answer was simple: the stone was a nice shape. The rope might come in useful at some future date for bathing. The cigarettes had to be put somewhere and the bag was ready to hand.[23]

In unguarded moments like these, we see the pattern of this partnership exposed. Elizabeth was not charmed by Eleanor's dottiness, but it did make her

feel capable and needed: together, the two developed a comfortably argumentative pattern that would have seemed familiar to anyone who has lived, as the
French say, *en couple*. Role specialization shaded into role play, with Macadam
taking on the persona of the 'practical one' and Rathbone that of the abstract
thinker – a pattern that had mirrored their contributions to the work of the
Victoria Settlement. In the household context, this was in some ways a gendered
pattern, for Rathbone, with her domestic incompetence and emotional inarticu-
lateness, did have many characteristics conventionally coded as masculine. Yet it
brought both women a measure of real emotional fulfilment.

Just how happy the life with Macadam made Rathbone is clear from reminis-
cences of friends and from the evidence of her health and appearance during these
years. Historians of women have noted that Victorian women sometimes used ill
health and vapours almost as a physical protest against the constraints of their
time; along similar lines, we can see Eleanor's rude good health as an expression
of her contentment with her life. As her involvements proliferated, she taxed her
body severely – with long hours at the House of Commons, endless cigarettes
and, particularly in the 1930s, strenuous foreign travel. Yet she proved to be
extraordinarily physically tough: she never got sick, could sleep in any position,
and would eat almost anything. She also became adventurous: in the twenties,
she and Elizabeth learned to drive and kept a car thereafter; in 1934, a green
Elizabeth by her side, she took her first aeroplane journey (to Palestine), and pronounced it happily 'certainly *the* way of travelling'.[24] When she, Lady Layton and
the Duchess of Atholl spent three weeks in Southeastern Europe in February 1937
– when Rathbone was sixty-five – they saved time by making most of their long
train journeys overnight, a gruelling schedule that had no effect on Rathbone's
formidable constitution.[25]

Living the life of the glorified spinster, Rathbone began to look the part as
well. As a young woman, Eleanor had dressed well, minding Emily's and Elsie's
instructions and keeping to the norms of her class. We see that from the pictures:
the lace-work sleeves and linen scarf of her suit on holiday in Austria in
1891; the improbable feathery collar on her blouse in the Somerville portrait.
Contemporaries at Somerville, to the amusement of friends who knew her in later
life, recalled that she had lovely clothes. But Eleanor in fact always thought
clothes a nuisance and had a bluestocking's dislike for fussy materials and petticoats. 'Oh, ridiculous child, how you're dressed,' Eleanor exclaimed one day,
watching her brother Lyle's little step-daughter Mary Shelmerdine descend the
Greenbank stairs in beribboned frock and multiple petticoats – and Mary was
taken into Eleanor's room to change. But on her second trip down Mary met
Aunt Elsie, who had firm views on proper dress for little girls, and was brought
back upstairs to retrieve the discarded petticoats.[26]

So long as Elsie lived, Eleanor at least looked respectable. But after Elsie died
and the war banished for ever the constrictions of Edwardian dress, she took to

wearing clothes that could at best be called serviceable. Elizabeth checked her over every morning to make sure her stockings weren't on inside out or her clothes back-to-front, but no one could make Eleanor dress elaborately. 'I don't "dress," I wear clothes,' Eleanor once told Margery Fry honestly,[27] and from the war years until her death, photographs show her in a sort of uniform: a drop-waisted black suit with a mid-calf skirt, white blouse, low-heeled buckled Mary Janes – and pearls, if the occasion was a formal one.

Clad in her regulation black, smoking constantly but healthy as a horse, Eleanor Rathbone had thus become by the 1920s what she had always wanted to be: a vigorous spinster politician, devoted to her work and contented in her partnership with a like-minded friend. In London if not in Liverpool, she and Macadam lived the life she had sketched out in her fateful letter – and it had brought her, as she had told Macadam it would, 'a happiness too great to seem possible'.

But there was a serpent in the garden – or rather, two serpents, coiled around the roots of these intertwined lives, quiet much of the time but occasionally showing their fangs. The first was the serpent of resentment, deadly in a relationship founded on the premiss of equality. From their Liverpool days, Eleanor and Elizabeth's friendship had been finely balanced: if Eleanor was better educated and wealthier and had better political ties, Elizabeth had her training, her salary and her position at the school and the settlement to bolster her sense of self-worth. Both women valued that equality: having deliberately rejected a model of private life in which women sacrifice their ambitions to men, they were determined to have separate – and equal – public careers. It was that very commitment that had taken them to London in the first place.

But things did not go quite as they anticipated. They had moved to London largely for Elizabeth's career, but the reconstruction efforts that she had thought would draw on the services of trained women like herself were decimated after the economic downturn of the early twenties, and her work for the Joint University Council for Social Studies never took as much time as she had expected. Eleanor, by contrast, had causes enough to spare. Gradually, Elizabeth's organizational affiliations came to reflect Eleanor's commitments and loyalties: thus when Rathbone became President of the National Union of Societies for Equal Citizenship after Millicent Fawcett's resignation in 1919, Macadam became its secretary, and, later, the editor of its paper – although she had never sat on the National Union's Executive nor really been closely involved in the suffrage struggle. Elizabeth also played a part in the work of the Family Endowment Society, which was busy propagandizing about the need for children's allowances.

The problem, of course, was that these were Eleanor's causes, driven by her convictions and funded by her money, and Macadam's position within them was always tenuous. Both women thus wanted Macadam to maintain her own independent career: 'Eleanor was always so anxious that Elizabeth Macadam should do her own work on social science and be recognized in her own right,' Mary Stocks remembered.[28] And Elizabeth certainly wanted that recognition as well. She kept abreast of developments in the fields of social work and voluntary service and in 1934 brought out *The New Philanthropy*, an impressive study of the complex and evolving relations between statutory and philanthropic efforts.[29] That study remains well worth reading today, for its visionary understanding of the benefits *and* costs of the move towards state provision and a culture of entitlement, and its sensitive defence of some place for voluntary effort even in the most developed 'welfare state'.

Hard as Elizabeth tried, however, Eleanor's career increasingly overshadowed her own – and in fact, through the dynamics of their own relationship, both women contributed to Macadam's marginalization. It wasn't only that Eleanor became much more important and famous than Elizabeth, although this was unquestionably true; it was also that the patterns of their partnership made the problem more acute. Elizabeth may have genuinely liked managing Romney Street, but it did cut into her career; Eleanor may have been genuinely domestically incompetent, but her incapacity burdened Macadam further. Their arrangements may have been driven by their abilities and emotional needs, but they did accord Elizabeth the feminine and supportive role.

Rathbone's election to Parliament in 1929 worsened this problem. Representing a constituency in Parliament was really a two-person job: most MPs relied on their wives to nurse their constituencies in their absence, host social events, and organize their domestic life. Beatrice Rathbone, later Lady Wright, who married Eleanor's half-brother William Gair's grandson John Rankin Rathbone in 1932, recalled spending much time in her husband's Cornwall constituency both before and after he won the seat for the Conservatives in 1935.[30] (Wright also took over her husband's seat when he was killed on active service in 1940, so from 1935 until 1945 there were two Rathbones in Parliament.) Some women MPs – including Nancy Astor and the Duchess of Atholl – had equally supportive spouses to help them with this work, but many were single and had to turn to secretaries or friends to step into the breach. 'What I need is a wife,' the Labour MP Ellen Wilkinson admitted – although she could at least count on her own ebullient personality when dealing with the social side of her job.[31] Eleanor Rathbone lacked Wilkinson's charisma, but she did have, in effect, a 'wife'. Elizabeth rose to the occasion. Macadam planned Eleanor's crucial, successful 1929 parliamentary campaign, drafted some of her correspondence, and organized the occasional 'at homes' or teas that Rathbone hosted. Rathbone's secretary remembered that Macadam 'managed Eleanor . . . just the way a sensible wife would',[32] and Rathbone relied on her judgement. She had an inferiority complex about social interactions, Marjorie Green recalled, and felt she had to have Macadam there on any social occasion.[33]

Rathbone's election to Parliament thus deepened the tendency in their partnership to identify Eleanor with the masculine and Elizabeth with the feminine role. What the two friends were doing, in fact, was conforming to a pattern common to married couples in political life – a pattern that had served William and Emily during William Rathbone's long parliamentary career. Yet neither woman could acknowledge publicly the degree to which Macadam had become, in effect, Rathbone's 'political wife' – and less because of their sensitivity about private matters than because of their deep and profound commitment to equal careers. Thus unlike William Rathbone, who fully and gratefully acknowledged his dependence on Emily, Eleanor and Elizabeth continued to pretend that Macadam's first concern was her career in social work. Since they saw the role of 'wife' as a lesser one, a trap that glorified spinsters had managed to escape, they refused to acknowledge the extent to which Macadam was taken up by such work. No matter how much effort Macadam was putting into Eleanor's career, Rathbone never described her as 'my secretary', 'my companion', or still less 'my housekeeper', although acquaintances came to see her as all of these things. When she did refer to Macadam, it was always as 'the friend with whom I share a house' or as an expert on social questions. It was as such an expert – and not as her companion – that Eleanor got the Foreign Office to issue diplomatic credentials to Elizabeth when they travelled together to Palestine in September 1934.[34]

But the world, of course, didn't see her that way. So famous was Rathbone by the late 1930s that anyone in her orbit was seen only in relation to her. Macadam's career became, to the outside world, almost invisible. Eleanor's niece Noreen (Frank's daughter), who saw a good deal of the two women while working as a social worker in London during the Second World War, and who found Macadam kind, sympathetic, and much more approachable than her preoccupied aunt, recalled how angry she became when Rathbone's friends, secretaries and even her own family would speak of or treat Macadam as a kind of glorified housekeeper. They passed this view down to posterity: when Macadam died, her obituary in the *Manchester Guardian*, probably written by Mary Stocks, mentioned Macadam's early work in Liverpool but then dwelt very largely on the partnership with Rathbone – a partnership in which, in the view of the writer, Macadam provided 'a well-ordered domestic background' in exchange for 'contact with [Rathbone's] master mind'.[35]

Macadam thus spent the years of Rathbone's parliamentary career caught in a terrible double bind. She did the work of a political wife, but neither she nor Rathbone really acknowledged those efforts; her own career suffered, and few of the visitors to Romney Street had much interest in it anyway. This impossible situation made her short-tempered and irritable: Rathbone's friends and co-workers would remember her as 'a difficult woman in many ways', 'tiresome' and 'meddlesome', and with 'prickles all over her'.[36] Some thought she was simply envious: 'I think Elizabeth Macadam was sometimes annoyed at the fact that she was living with a woman much greater than herself,' Mary Stocks said cruelly.[37]

In fact Elizabeth never resented Eleanor's success, of which she was extremely proud. What she resented was the implication that her own career didn't matter, that she should be content to be remembered as the servant to Rathbone's 'greatness', that she should be grateful to blacken her boots. Eleanor's nephew B.L. Rathbone, who saw a good deal of his aunt during the 1930s, came to understand how Elizabeth Macadam felt. 'The best phrase I can use is that she didn't want to be regarded as just a hanger-on,' he said. 'She didn't want anybody to regard her as a kind of high-class servant.'[38] With this evaluation of her worth confronting her, it is small wonder Macadam would try to keep her name out of Stocks's biography, that she would insist on the destruction of their correspondence. Elizabeth Macadam did play the role of the 'political wife', but it was pride, and not humility, that made her reject this view of her identity. This obstinate woman may have played a much smaller role than Eleanor Rathbone in the construction of the British welfare state – but she did play a part, and wished to be remembered for that alone.

There was a second serpent in the garden, however – a second reason why Macadam may have wanted to shield this relationship from the historian's eye. This was the serpent of knowledge – of the new science of naming and managing errant sexual ways.[39] When Rathbone and Macadam had first become friends in the years before the First World War, female partnerships had not yet been labelled and categorized by the psychological expert, had not yet fallen under the fascinated eye of a prurient public. The occasional mamma (not Emily) might worry about her daughter's devotion to a school friend, the occasional doctor inveigh against unnatural attachments, but for the most part relations between women aroused little concern.[40]

The First World War changed all that. Now, women's friendships were a subject for discussion. They were, it seemed, not quite 'healthy', possibly even perverse. Not that they had suddenly, radically, changed: rather, what had changed were popular attitudes to sex, with sexual intercourse now upheld as central – even vital – to human health and happiness. Of course, this focus on sex wasn't new. Havelock Ellis and Karl Pearson had been busy for a decade, cataloguing the behaviours of the 'normal' and the 'invert' alike, and inventing the new science of sexology through which diverse human practices would be measured and analysed. Freethinkers and Fabians, likewise, had forced a new frankness about sex – especially H.G. Wells, who sought to introduce not only his avid readers but a good number of his female friends to the pleasures of the sexual life.

But the war pushed things further, shattering once and for all the decent conventions of Victorianism and making the new teachings about sex respectable.

Along with three-quarters of a million men, a host of nineteenth-century ideals died in that war. Just as conscription put paid to the ideal of a volunteer force, so the need for ever more shells shattered the ideal of women in the home, and the romance of the uniform the ideal of sexual purity. Young women gained more freedoms: a girl could meet a man without a chaperon (if middle-class) or have a drink in a pub (if working-class) without being considered 'loose' – and even 'loose' behaviour seemed, if not commendable, at least understandable. The study of sexual practice, which had been very much a minority and intellectual interest, quite outside the bounds of respectable middle-class life, became a matter for governmental and public concern.[41]

For a younger generation of feminists, regrouping after the war, this shift could be both emancipating and unsettling. The focus on sex seemed to offer women the chance to have it all; to join, as men did, public work to a 'complete' private life. Even before the war, in new journals like the *Freewoman*, in novels like Olive Schreiner's *The Story of an African Farm*, some were beginning to argue for a new feminism of free labour and free love, and some brave women – Dora Russell and Sylvia Pankhurst among them – sought to live their lives by its dictates. And if their enthusiastic embrace of unmarried motherhood was too radical for many of their generation, Marie Stopes's writings on the importance of sexual knowledge and family planning within marriage, and her campaigns to introduce birth control to a mass public, did strike a chord with a wider audience.[42]

For the older generation, however, this new frankness seemed a step backwards. Late Victorian feminism had always been high-minded: feminists had argued for the superiority of moral force over physical force, and – as the veteran sexual purity activist Alison Neilans put it – for a 'levelling up' of men's standard of sexual morality 'into line with that accepted as right and desirable for women'. They were disconcerted to see the opposite happening, as male experts and (worse) young women began to argue that an enthusiastic response to – rather than freedom from – male sexual demands would 'emancipate' women. Even birth control, to this older generation, had been a double-edged sword: while it could free women from excessive child-bearing, it also ended any check on 'immorality', leaving women even more vulnerable to sexual pressures. By the 1930s, however, pre-war feminists understood that mores had loosened for good. As Neilans wrote in 1936, 'the end of the double standard is definitely in sight, but it is not ending in the way anticipated by the pioneers who fought for it'.[43]

Worst of all, these new sexual discourses and conventions placed spinsters, hitherto the heart and soul of the women's movement, very much on the defensive. For if sexual intercourse was essential to psychological and physiological health, as Stopes, Ellis and others claimed, then those women who were chaste were running a grave risk. By the 1930s, the novelist Winifred Holtby protested, educated opinion – from Freudian psychologists to the followers of D.H.

Lawrence – seemed determined to show that frustration and prudishness, neu-roses and even insanity were the spinster's likely fate.[44] Nor would any cure – except marriage – avail them. When one spinster wrote to Marie Stopes asking if there was any legitimate form of sexual expression open to the unmarried woman, Stopes could only advise her to emigrate in search of a husband or fall back on the old remedy of hot baths.[45]

And one blessing of the spinster life – the female friendship – stood particu-larly condemned, for in these relationships, freely chosen and emotionally intense, experts now saw the shadow of perversion, the threatening suggestion of les-bianism. Novels of the time trace the transformation clearly: in Clemence Dane's *Regiment of Women* (1917), Dorothy L. Sayers's *Unnatural Death* (1927) and even Radclyffe Hall's *The Well of Loneliness* (1928), the pre-war figure of the 'new woman' spinster, dedicated to her work, has given way to that of the per-verted, man-hating lesbian, warped and twisted in her emotions and seducing younger women away from the path of normal married life.[46] True, for some women of the avant-garde – among them Vita Sackville-West, Hilda Matheson of the BBC, the novelists Sylvia Townsend Warner and Ivy Compton-Burnett, and, Eleanor would discover, her own niece Noreen – the new category of les-bianism offered at least some recognition of their identity and desires; for others, however, it caused annoyance and anxiety. The charge of lesbianism, suddenly, was one that friends felt they had to answer: thus Vera Brittain, who lived with Winifred Holtby as a young woman and during portions of her marriage and wrote a loving tribute to that friendship after Holtby's early death, felt compelled to make clear that the two were not lesbians.[47]

But what of the 'new woman' of the 1890s, who had, after all, deliberately abjured marriage for a life of public service and turned to female friendships for emotional support and love? These women were in their fifties by the 1920s, and many must have found the new drive towards categorization baffling. By meas-uring all relationships against some idealized heterosexual standard, Eleanor Rathbone's parliamentary colleague Edith Picton-Turbervill insisted, 'experts' had profoundly misunderstood female friendships. Different in some ways they might be, but they were not for that reason 'silly and unwholesome': 'women's strong attachments can be . . . as deep, as beautiful, and as exhilarating as any human relationship'. 'Agony of separation is not confined to lovers, husbands and wives,' Picton-Turbervill wrote, 'nor is the strongest love necessarily connected with physical union.' Having herself refused an offer of marriage and having lived con-tentedly with women friends through her many years of social and political work, she wrote 'with a ring of challenge': 'Let me here confess that I have been deeply attached to women, but I have never lost my heart to a man'.[48]

Eleanor Rathbone and Elizabeth Macadam's relationship exemplified that 'strong attachment' Picton-Turbervill valued, and they too were distressed by the stigmatizing of such ties. Yet they responded only with silence: unlike Picton-Turbervill, neither Rathbone nor Macadam ever publicly defended female friendships, nor did they publicly acknowledge the extent of their own emotional bond. Instead, as they watched the women's community in which they lived being labelled repressive, deviant or perverse, they covered their tracks. Although their correspondence would have revealed the emotional depth of their friendship, they made sure that no one could read these documents. Rathbone left Macadam all her manuscripts at her death, and Macadam – certain she was complying with Rathbone's wishes as well – allowed Stocks to quote only a few neutral passages. At her insistence, the correspondence was then burnt. Only through oversight did a single letter survive.

I – the biographer – find Macadam's erasure of the record frustrating; yet I'm forced to admit that Rathbone would certainly have approved. For in living with Macadam, Rathbone had not sought to validate alternative sexualities but to show that women could find happiness outside the confines of sex altogether. Certainly Rathbone's writings and campaigns can be read as protests against the tyranny of sex: her efforts to reform the conditions of marriage, to grant wives a measure of economic independence, to prevent child marriage in India, and to combat the traffic in women in the Far East were all driven by her desire to free women from what she saw as a predatory masculine force. She did not associate sex either with emotion or with pleasure, for women at least, and could sometimes be, as a result, surprisingly obtuse. Eleanor's niece Noreen, for example, recalled how mortified she was when she tried to explain her own lesbianism to her aunt. Noreen's mother Edith had discovered her daughter's homosexuality and (her husband Frank having died in 1939) had insisted that Eleanor call the young woman in and give her a talking-to. But Noreen, to her embarassment, found that she had to face not only a scolding but also sheer bewilderment. 'She hadn't a clue,' Noreen recalled; 'she really couldn't understand why anyone would go to bed with anyone if they didn't want to procreate a child.' Noreen stammered and tried to explain, but the gulf between the emancipation of the 1890s and that of the 1940s was just too great. Eleanor rejected the new view of sex as a source of female pleasure or an essential human need and resented the influence of those who promulgated it. She would never have accepted the idea that her relationship with Macadam should be understood in such terms.[49]

Yet my discomfort with this interpretation remains, for there is a danger in giving Rathbone and Macadam the last word. They were, after all, so emotionally inarticulate – and Rathbone, for all her public maturity, was an infant in all matters of the heart. We cannot, then, leave this friendship behind without acknowledging that Rathbone is a poor guide to her own emotional terrain: raised to repress her feelings, by adulthood she had become incapable almost of acknowledging them. Unaccustomed to self-scrutiny, she would never have questioned her own motives. Whatever its subliminal content, she would have understood her love for Macadam in non-sexual – even anti-sexual – terms. Not for her Picton-Turbervill's open defence of the importance of intimate friendships in women's lives.

Was, then, 'something else' present, some feeling that Rathbone herself had difficulty even acknowledging? We cannot know, of course – and yet there is a tension there, an emotional imbalance that ran against every public measure of the two women's worth. For while Rathbone may have been the famous one, in every relationship there are other measures of value, economies of need and desire hidden from the public eye. And in this scale, Macadam was unquestionably the dominant partner. Elizabeth, after all, had been willing to leave Liverpool in 1919 and to let Eleanor decide whether to follow her, making clear her willingness to strike out – if necessary – on her own. Eleanor, on the other hand, would never have let Elizabeth go – for the simple reason that she needed Elizabeth far more than Elizabeth needed her. Mary Stocks recognized this basic emotional inequality. It was fortunate that Eleanor had died first, she told Brian Harrison, 'because I don't think Eleanor could have lived without Elizabeth but Elizabeth was able to live quite happily in Edinburgh without Eleanor'.[50]

This is the heart of the matter: Elizabeth was necessary to Eleanor's life. Eleanor chose Elizabeth for ever, with no thought of looking back. Before such love, some questions must give way – among them our inevitable and prurient queries about sexual life. For our very questions reveal our incomprehension, being built on assumptions about the body and its claims that Eleanor would not have shared. At crucial moments of her young womanhood, Eleanor's 'innocence' had shielded her: she was able to profit from Oliver Lodge's infatuation precisely because she remained 'unconscious' of its sexual undertones; she was able to write her father's biography without mentioning her mother because she refused to acknowledge her parents' powerful erotic tie. Her friendship with Macadam was of a piece with this earlier pattern. By divorcing love from physicality, she had emotional stability without emotional turmoil; she could also continue to discount women's sexual desire (while acknowledging men's sexual predation) in her analyses of political and social problems. Had she had more sympathy for the common frailties of life, more awareness of the ways in which passion and need complicate most relationships, she might have spoken with Macadam more openly, and lived with her differently – but then her analysis might have lost some of its crispness, her feminism its edge. By rejecting 'sex' as an acceptable foundation for any lifelong partnership, she could see marriage's economic underpinnings plain.

Chapter 10

What Future for Feminism?

In 1918, this London life was only a dream. Eleanor was still in Liverpool, living with Elsie at Greenbank. But with the war finally, amazingly, over, she felt oddly at sea. 'Eleanor is in the throes of indecision,' Elsie reported to her niece Elena Richmond in a letter written only a few days after the Armistice. A few weeks earlier, the House had rushed through a bill giving women the right to sit in Parliament; now, the National Union was asking Eleanor to seek election. 'I think it would in some ways be a good thing,' Elsie confided. Eleanor 'has slaved over her SSFA night and day for so long'. A change would do her good.[1]

The prospect is intriguing: what if Eleanor Rathbone, not Nancy Astor, had become the first woman MP? She would have had an uphill fight, surely, but with money, contacts and a sterling record of war work in Liverpool, she would have stood a chance. Women would have had a doughty, much-needed champion as Parliament began turning against them; her country would remember her name. But Eleanor calculated otherwise: the House might bring prestige, but how much could one really get done there? 'She would fret over the way time is wasted and private members can get no bills through,' Elsie admitted, 'and she does not suffer fools gladly.'[2] Eleanor decided not to stand.

Instead, she and Elizabeth offered their services to Violet Markham, who was contesting her brother's former constituency of Mansfield in Nottinghamshire as an Independent Liberal.[3] Markham was amazed by the offer. She had been an 'anti' before the war and had only recently converted: Eleanor, she thought, had every reason to dislike her.[4] But Eleanor admired Markham's stalwart support of women's employment during the war, and she and Elizabeth happily put in a few days stumping for their former opponent. Markham was one of seventeen women who managed to find seats to contest in 1918 – a group that included those other Rathbone sparring partners, Christabel Pankhurst and Mary Macarthur. Rathbone, like other feminists, felt optimistic about their chances. All parties were scrambling to recruit women in the wake of the suffrage victory; Ray Strachey, holding the fort as the National Union's parliamentary secretary was besieged by politicians courting favour or asking advice.[5] Women, it seemed, would help plan the post-war world.

The election results brought Rathbone back to earth with a bump. Markham polled a mere 4,000 of 38,000 votes; worse, of the seventeen women candidates, only the Countess Markiewicz was elected (and, as a Sinn Feiner, refused to take her seat). Rathbone was devastated, shocking Elizabeth profoundly by mourning even Christabel's defeat. 'I am dreadfully disappointed – not only about you & all the women candidates, but about the whole election,' she wrote to Markham. She and Elizabeth had thought an ambitious programme of social and civil reform in the offing; now, watching the all-male, Conservative-dominated House of Commons assemble, they realized that their battles were only beginning. Yet Rathbone confessed that she felt 'rather perplexed as to what course progressive women should take'. Should activist women simply join the Labour Party, thus lending their support to the one clearly progressive party, or should they instead 'try to strengthen the non-party spirit among women and run as independents'? Whatever strategy they chose, Rathbone knew that a unified feminist movement was more necessary than ever: 'Us women who want certain definite reforms will have to pool our resources as far as possible & organize, organize, organize.'[6]

Eleanor was thinking aloud, for this was now her dilemma. Mrs Fawcett had made it clear that she intended to step down as NUWSS President once the war was over. At the National Union's first post-war Council in March 1919, Rathbone defeated Mrs. H.A.L. Fisher (formerly Lettice Ilbert, her old Somerville friend), to replace Fawcett as President.[7] For Eleanor, this was a triumph and a challenge. With the WSPU defunct and other organizations embattled, the National Union – now renamed the National Union of Societies for Equal Citizenship (NUSEC) – was the main hope for feminism, the headquarters of the movement. Eleanor would be responsible for its guidance for the next ten years.

Her leadership was controversial at the time, and has left historians and feminists arguing ever since.[8] For Rathbone was not a typical organization president: she was uncompromising, visionary, and far better at drafting memos than at shaking hands. As President, then, she did more than simply mediate, she exhorted and bullied, schemed and *led*, seeking to persuade her organization – and women in Britain more generally – of her vision of sexual equality. Feminism, Rathbone thought, could only revitalize itself, could perhaps only survive, if it moved beyond its historical determination to win access to those jobs and activities that had been the preserve of men and began to grapple with a social system that continued – unjustly, frustratingly – to denigrate women's contributions. To do so, she insisted, they must take account of motherhood – and not motherhood as a brief biological event, but rather as a form of labour and service that would absorb many women for much of their adult lives. If women could become mothers only by sacrificing economic independence and political participation, 'equality' remained a chimera and 'feminism' a failure. Rathbone's leadership was controversial, to put it simply, not because she tried to tack a set of welfare reforms on to feminism's egalitarian agenda, but because she sought to redefine the goals and content of 'feminism' itself.

Rathbone's ideas, later known as 'the New Feminism', were already apparent in early 1918, when the National Union met to hammer out a post-war programme. Already, opinion was divided between those (among them Ray Strachey and Helen Ward) who thought the Union should concentrate on equal franchise and equal opportunity and those (like Kathleen Courtney) who wished to see feminists take on the whole field of post-war social reform. Rathbone tried, initially, to straddle both camps. The National Union should keep to the sphere marked out by its history, she wrote in a programmatic article that February, 'the sphere of feminism'. But this sphere was not a narrow one, for 'equality is not a synonym for "identity"'. Certainly some issues of concern to women – peace, temperance – would fall outside that mandate, but many other pressing questions could fall within it, including endowment of motherhood.[9] Courtney approved this attempt to 'stretch the equality formula to mean much which one would not naturally expect', but she doubted Rathbone could bring the Union with her.[10] At first, however, a fragile compromise prevailed. At its council meeting that March, the NUSEC agreed to work for equal suffrage and 'all other such reforms . . . as are necessary to secure a real equality of liberties, status and opportunities between men and women' – including widows' pensions, equal guardianship rights, and the admission of women to Parliament and the legal profession. Endowment, while not endorsed, was recommended for study as 'a reform needing immediate consideration'.[11] Rathbone, in 1918, would have felt cautiously optimistic.

But by 1919, when her presidency began, the tide had already turned. The Conservative-dominated Coalition was far too worried about labour to pay much attention to women; trade unionists at home and revolutionaries abroad preoccupied their nervous minds.[12] Women, when considered at all, became pawns in a strategy of stabilization. One of the first measures passed by the reconstruction parliament was the Restoration of Prewar Practices Act, a measure that fulfilled the wartime pledges to the trade unions by effectively removing women from better-paid industrial work. Those much-lauded women war workers suddenly found themselves unwanted: by 1921, the proportion of women in the labour force was no higher than it had been in 1911. Now unemployed, they looked (with ex-servicemen) to a new 'out-of-work' donation and to a hastily expanded system of unemployment benefits, but the former was purely temporary and women's access to the latter soon narrowed, as officials began disallowing claims by women who refused to take poorly paid domestic service jobs.[13] Whether as servants or wives, women were to go 'back home', and politicians' rhetoric moved sharply against those who, whether by choice or need, found it difficult to do so.

Yet that 'home' – imagined during the war almost as a public space, with the mother patriotically raising children for the nation – contracted as well. Separation allowances faded away as soldiers returned from the front; pressures from Treasury officials and angry ratepayers forced a rollback in social spending in Whitehall and the towns alike. Chancellors in the early 1920s could not find money for such pressing causes as civilian widows' pensions, much less for utopian schemes like family endowment.

The NUSEC and other feminist organizations watched these moves with consternation but found it hard to respond. Many local suffrage societies had folded during the war, and as affiliations dwindled, the NUSEC was forced to cut back drastically on spending and staff.[14] The Union faced a leadership vacuum as well, when Fawcett, Frances Balfour and Margaret Ashton stepped down after the suffrage victory, and Swanwick, Royden and Marshall were lost to the pacifist cause. Party organizations also cut into the movement's strength, for all parties recruited women vigorously in the wake of the suffrage victory – although their enthusiasm rarely extended to backing egalitarian reforms or to offering women winnable parliamentary seats. To feminists' distress, even their old ally the Labour Party thought the cross-party women's organizations a threat, urging its women supporters to devote themselves to Labour organizations alone.[15] Political independence and sex-based loyalty had given the pre-war women's movement its strength: in the 'rage of party' those same qualities became liabilities. Waves of enthusiastic women Independents were defeated in those first post-war municipal elections; if they re-emerged, much chastened, they did so under party flags.

Worst of all, feminists found themselves struggling with a new popular mood. In the years before the war, marching through London in their white dresses and wide hats, suffragists appeared brave and spirited, pure and dedicated; now their ideals seemed as dated as their dress. As Vera Brittain later remarked, once even partial suffrage was won, feminists had to contend with a chorus of voices telling them that further demands were not only unnecessary but 'hysterical'; psychoanalysis, now entering popular consciousness, supplied easy labels for ageing women jealous of men's rights.[16] 'New women' before the war had often spurned marriage for a life of friendship and service; for a later generation, with the supply of marriageable men decimated and independent incomes eaten up by inflation and debt, paid work often seemed a melancholy necessity rather than a glorious cause. With new ideals of femininity and sexual fulfilment proclaimed in every cinema and advice column, the suffrage generation's preference for single-sex societies and socializing undoubtedly struck some young women as mawkish and unmodern. Already by 1921, Rathbone admitted, 'the whole woman's movement' had become 'very unpopular'.[17]

What was the leader of Britain's largest feminist organization to do? Rathbone first tried to stop the organizational rot. She raised a guarantee fund to put *Common Cause*, now edited by Ray Strachey and renamed the *Woman's Leader*, on a stable financial footing; she helped to organize summer schools to discuss the movement's methods and aims. But the more serious challenge was to define feminism's purpose and renew its appeal now that the vote was (partially) won. The public may have been reassured to find 'that the woman's vote is not going to spell either sex warfare or national disaster', Rathbone told the 1920 NUSEC Council, but she was not: 'we do not want the woman's vote to be acceptable because it is possible to say of it that it has made no perceptible difference to politics'. For women, she insisted, had something distinctive to offer, something different from the 'bottled vintage bought at the party wine-shop'. The new feminist politics must 'bubble freshly out of women's own personalities and be impregnated with the salt of their own experiences'.[18]

When Rathbone thought of those experiences, she thought of Liverpool's working-class mothers. Colleagues (and later historians) who dismissed Rathbone's 'new feminism' as a misguided accommodation to a resurgent rhetoric of hearth and home or (worse) as a deliberate repudiation of feminism's foundational egalitarian goals overlooked the harsh local realities in which it was envisioned.[19] For Rathbone lived through those chaotic and disillusioning postwar years at least partly in Liverpool: throughout the 1920s, the city remained her point of reference for questions of politics and social reform. In Liverpool, the Armistice brought renewed violence and sectarianism, followed by renewed poverty and hopelessness, in its wake. There were race riots in Liverpool in 1919; troops and tanks were brought in during the police strike that same year.[20] The economic downturn in the early twenties hit the city hard. Work was short for the demobilized soldiers now tramping its streets, and housing was shorter still. Yet, in Liverpool as elsewhere, soldiers were given first claim – a policy that shifted the burdens of unemployment and poverty on to those even less able to bear them.

Rathbone – still Liverpool's most prominent woman politician – tried to keep women from losing out utterly in this scramble for jobs, entitlements and aid. She accepted the presidency of the ward-based Women Citizens' Association founded to strengthen women's municipal representation and voice and remained on the City Council, where, in the 1920s, another half-dozen women – among them the child welfare advocate Margaret Beavan and Rathbone's suffrage allies Nessie Stewart-Brown and Mabel Fletcher – finally joined her. Those women councillors fought hard (and sometimes against their parties) to protect the city's educational and welfare services from spending cuts;[21] Rathbone also tried to salvage the voluntary services that she and Macadam had built up before and during the war. Together with Macadam, Frederick D'Aeth, Charles Booth and other allies from the Council of Voluntary Aid, in late 1918 she converted the 'Offices of Friendly Help' at the men's and women's settlements into two branches of a new organization, persuaded Elsie to fund a third office, and convinced

Dorothy Keeling, then head of the Bradford Guild of Help, to come to Liverpool to run all three. The resulting Personal Services Society was soon coordinating the efforts of several hundred volunteers and would become a pioneer of family casework and a font of initiatives ranging from marriage counselling to legal aid to social programmes for the aged or disabled.[22]

Rathbone and Keeling also collaborated to replenish the supply of young women willing to embark on a career in social work. Margaret Simey, who trained as a sociologist in the twenties (and volunteered at the settlement) recalled just how inspiring Rathbone, Keeling and other pre-war feminists appeared to those young women unable to find either jobs or husbands after the war. The whole world seemed to consider them superfluous, Simey remembered – but then 'this whole regiment of splendid women . . . hove on our horizon, and they didn't care a dump about not being married; they'd come to terms with spinsterhood'. She and her friends, Simey thought, had never quite lived up to that example; most of them eventually married and put their families first. Yet Simey never forgot that early training in politics. When she inherited Rathbone's old City Council seat in Granby in the 1960s, she drew on lessons in public speaking and procedure learned in Eleanor's drawing room some forty years earlier.[23]

Rathbone didn't just try to preserve a sphere for women's political and social action, she served within its ranks as well. Already a member of the local War Pensions Committee, when the first women were appointed to the magistracy in 1920 she became a Justice of the Peace for the County of Lancashire as well. A letter Rathbone wrote to *Common Cause* in November 1919 gives us some insight into what these appointments involved. A routine afternoon of work at the offices of the War Pensions Committee, she reported, had included encounters with a hard-working but poverty-stricken widow with six children who had just been sacked by the Post Office to make way for a demobilized soldier, and with an estranged soldier's wife whose husband had taken the couple's children away and deposited them with his mistress. In the first case, she noted, she had tried to convince the widow to:

> let me recommend her to the Guardians for Out Relief, reminding her that she had been a ratepayer and must look upon it as insurance money, etc. But 'No one related to me or my husband has ever come to *that*.' I next suggested tailoring, and found that though she had never learnt it she 'had always made all the children's clothes, including the boy's suits' (i.e. in the intervals of post office sorting and all the other work needful for six children!) I sent a visitor to see her home, which she found spotlessly clean but showing evidences of painful poverty. . . . Mrs. H. has now started work at a wholesale clothiers, at a commencing wages of 30s. a week; not a large income for the maintenance of six children, but I am applying for an S. and S.F.A. [Soldiers' and Sailors' Families Association] grant to supplement it.

In this case, then, Eleanor managed to secure a mix of work and entitlements that would preserve the woman's independence and self-respect; in the second case, however, she found herself stymied. Although she took legal advice on the woman's behalf, 'it was to the effect that the father has the right to put the children to board with whom he pleases'.[24] In both cases, however, she used her contacts across the city – with the guardians, with employers, with legal experts, with philanthropic bodies – to try to craft reasonable survival strategies for poor women.

Rathbone wrote this letter to *Common Cause* not to provide us with a window into her life as a busy local politician (although it does do that) but rather to convince her readers of the continued need for feminist activism. The widows' pensions and guardianship rights demanded by the NUSEC would have made all the difference to these women's lives, she pointed out, and those 'satisfied and prosperous individuals' who claimed to find such reforms out of date or boring should be 'brought up against the facts of life as they affect the poorer section of working and married women'.[25] In the fights over the NUSEC's platform, Rathbone was often accused of putting 'social welfare' before feminism, but the merest glance at her life during this period explains why she found such a distinction absurd. Sacked from their wartime jobs, often responsible for children, and now bereft of the allowances that had sustained them during the war, Liverpool's working-class mothers had gained little from the suffrage victory. No task was thus more urgent (or more 'feminist') than to craft a political platform that would emancipate them as well. She was startled to find that not all of her fellow feminists shared her sense of urgency. 'I am feeling rather disillusioned about women,' Rathbone told the 1921 NUSEC council meeting – about 'women in general, and even those that form the NUSEC in particular'. Suffragists had always 'found it good propaganda to speak and write of the wrongs of the sweated woman worker, the unhappily married wife, and the Poor Law widow', since such arguments 'had more weight with the public than the mere reiteration of the intolerable fact that their own gardeners and coachmen had votes and that they themselves had none'. But now that the vote was won, she charged, many former suffragists appeared to have forgotten their implicit promise to right these terrible social wrongs.[26]

Worst of all, in her view, they declined to range themselves behind family endowment, that broad redistributive agenda that Rathbone thought essential to married women's emancipation. Watching separation allowances dry up while Liverpool fell into recession was, for Rathbone, a deeply shocking experience. Women bore the brunt of such 'returns to normalcy': not only were their standards of nutrition, health and housing relentlessly forced down, but they were also pushed back into the degrading habits of dependence – to the wheedling and cadging life of the overworked but unwaged wife – that many had hoped to leave behind for ever. 'Endowing' such women had never seemed more obvious or urgent, and Rathbone, Mary Stocks and other advocates spent much of the early 1920s trying to persuade the feminist movement (not to mention anyone else who would listen) to take on this issue. They kept up a running debate over endowment in the pages of the *Woman's Leader*, discussed it at NUSEC summer schools and conferences, and at the 1919 and 1920 councils succeeded in passing resolutions recommending that branches study the subject. Yet powerful voices within the women's movement vehemently objected to endowment, whether because they worried (with Fawcett) that it would destroy the father's will to work or because they insisted (like the working-class feminist Ada Nield Chew) that even servantless working-class wives should be forced out of the intellectually stultifying world of the home. At the 1921 Council matters came to a head, and after an impassioned debate, a proposal to place endowment on the Union's immediate programme failed by three votes. Rathbone thus found herself leading an organization unwilling to support what she believed to be 'the greatest social reform now before the country'[27] – a situation that one delegate admitted was 'no doubt a difficult one, especially for so energetic and forceful a personality as Miss Rathbone'.[28]

Committed as she was to the NUSEC's democratic traditions, Rathbone accepted the Council's decision. She did, however, begin limiting the time and energy she spent on an organization with – as she saw it – such a narrow view of feminism. After 1921 Rathbone spent much more time working up the campaign for family endowment than she did succouring the NUSEC: these were the years in which she surveyed foreign family allowance systems, wrote *The Disinherited Family*, cultivated sympathetic intellectuals and politicians, and launched the Family Endowment Society. Her shift in focus is understandable, for she genuinely believed family endowment to be a core feminist demand, as crucial to economic emancipation as the vote was to political emancipation. But the NUSEC did suffer from having a president whose main commitments were elsewhere, who felt more enthusiasm for reforms *not* on the Union's programme than for those on it, and who did not hesitate to chastise her fellow feminists for not sharing her view. In Rathbone, the NUSEC had a leader of great intellectual stature and with a clear vision of what feminism should be, but without that combination of charm and manipulative skill that helps to keep fragmented political movements together.

Nor did Rathbone's organizational style help, for if her rhetoric was expansive her administrative style was not: under her leadership, the Union's official positions came to be held by a small inner circle of trusted collaborators and friends. The wide powers of the Union's officers had been troublesome even before the war, but became a real problem in the 1920s, when the Union's agenda became more complex and the ability of its democratic structure to control it much weaker. Thus, while the Council still formally set policy, much of the Union's real work was done by a group that called itself, only partly tongue-in-cheek, the 'Big

Four' – a clique comprised not only of Rathbone and Eva Hubback, who replaced Strachey as parliamentary secretary in 1920 (and then held the position until 1927), but also of Macadam and Mary Stocks. Although Macadam had been only peripherally involved in the suffrage movement before the war, she was quickly co-opted on to the NUSEC Executive, and in the early twenties served as honorary secretary and (briefly) as honorary treasurer; she and Stocks also jointly edited the *Woman's Leader* for some years.

Eleanor found this a comfortable arrangement. She had collaborated with Macadam for years. After July 1923, when the Union's offices moved just around the corner from Romney Street to Dean's Yard, she and Elizabeth were able to pop in on the secretaries as needed while continuing to do their own work at home. Rathbone also grew very close to Hubback and Stocks, coming to see them almost as family. Of a younger generation, these two women virtually incarnated the 'new feminism'. Both had been only briefly involved in the suffrage move-ment; both had trained as economists, Hubback at Newnham and Stocks at the London School of Economics; both had young children and identified closely with Rathbone's determination to orient feminism towards working-class mothers. Both, finally, had watched their husbands go off to war, a war from which Bill Hubback had never returned, leaving Eva as the sole support for three young children. The two were temperamentally different, but in their motherhood, their comfortable rapport with men, and their tendency to see women's oppression more in economic than sexual terms, they marked a real shift from the pre-war generation – a shift well in keeping with Rathbone's interests and thought.

For the rest of Rathbone's life, Hubback and Stocks would remain – after Macadam – her closest friends. Eleanor came to see Hubback almost as a second self. Born to a wealthy, benevolent, observant but assimilated Jewish family not unlike the Unitarian Rathbones, Eva resembled Eleanor in her seriousness of purpose and reflective cast of mind. She also shared Rathbone's political instincts – she too was dogged in pursuit but pragmatically capable of compromise – and Eleanor came to trust her judgement absolutely.[29] If Eva became Eleanor's strong right arm, the attractive and witty Mary Stocks became the daughter Eleanor could never have: one secretary remembered that Rathbone softened visibly even when Stocks entered the room.[30] Stocks's relationship with Macadam was, in con-sequence, the more delicate – but all four women were at ease with one another, with joint holidays and outings continuing long after the NUSEC days had passed. Yet however sustaining these new friendships were for Eleanor, they were not equally beneficial to the NUSEC. For Hubback and Stocks were not exactly independent voices. Both were firmly in Eleanor's corner, admiring her unre-servedly and seeking to protect her from overwork and (more damagingly) from criticism.

They also left her with little reason to reach out to other, less like-minded, allies. One lost potential collaborator was Margaret Haig Thomas, Viscountess

Rhondda, who had been a suffragette before the war and after it briefly considered throwing in her lot with the NUSEC. Rhondda had spent the war years managing her father's considerable business empire and the immediate post-war years trying to defend women's employment rights; strong-minded, well-connected, very wealthy and staunchly feminist, she had a great deal to offer.[31] But after early encounters with the 'Big Four' Rhondda instead founded her own 'equalitarian' organization, the Six Point Group, and her own paper, *Time and Tide*, a political weekly that published some of the 1920s' most brilliant women writers (including Winifred Holtby, Vera Brittain, Ellen Wilkinson and Rebecca West) and that easily outshone the more pedestrian *Woman's Leader*. Mary Stocks, many years later, remembered this conflict as a narrow escape – Rhondda, she said, had been dictatorial and had wanted to take over the NUSEC paper entirely[32] – but Rathbone's usual ally Margery Corbett Ashby remembered things differently. Corbett Ashby recalled being very angry at the leadership's unwillingness to accommodate Rhondda, a failure that deprived the NUSEC of some vital modern voices and left a legacy of bad feeling between rival feminist leaderships.[33] By 1924 even Ray Strachey, Rathbone's right-hand woman during the crucial early reconstruction period, confessed to a 'dislike of the way they do things now' and to missing 'all the old war horses' who had 'gone off into the League of Nations Union'.[34]

Rhondda and Strachey were only the most famous recruits put off by the NUSEC's clubby atmosphere and outdated practices. In an acute (and unpublished) sketch revealingly entitled 'Committees versus Professions', Vera Brittain pinpointed perfectly the bases – philosophical and generational – of a wider disaffection. 'Oh, I couldn't possibly join *that*!' she recounted one 'hard-working young journalist' exclaiming when asked why she didn't belong to the NUSEC; it was 'composed of leisured women' who wouldn't understand her point of view.[35] Rathbone and Macadam, of course, didn't think of themselves as 'leisured': they were independent and active, busy about public work from morning till night. But for a younger generation of 'independent women', a generation sick of appeals to self-sacrifice and with few illusions about the hardness of the world, earning one's living – and not endless committee work – was the *sine qua non* of feminism. Rhondda, for all her wealth, understood that: she too thought the work was everything, and that her wartime management of her father's business and her successful proprietorship of *Time and Tide* did more for feminism than anything she could say. The NUSEC, with its mid-morning committee meetings and maternalist focus, excluded these women while deploring their apathy and indifference.

And yet, for all its stuffiness, the NUSEC scored some notable victories under Rathbone's leadership. They were largely legislative victories, and were won not through marches and public meetings but rather by turning the NUSEC into (as the 1920 *Annual Report* put it) 'primarily a machine for securing legislative reforms'.[36] Already in 1918 the Union had a wish-list of parliamentary acts – including equal guardianship and divorce, equal franchise and widows' pensions – and its leadership pursued those goals with energy and intelligence. Its 'Status of Wives and Mothers' subcommittee, on which Rathbone, Hubback and Stocks all sat, met regularly throughout the early twenties to plan the campaigns, but in practice Rathbone and Hubback – who proved an exceptionally talented political lobbyist – did much of the work. They arranged for bills to be drafted (often under Chrystal Macmillan's meticulous eye), found parliamentary sponsors, sent deputations to ministers and party leaders, wrote letters to the press, and elicited resolutions from the sixty or more still-active local societies. When a government fell and brought their best-laid plans down with it, they began the whole process again.

Unspectacular and painstaking as such work was, it proved a crucial catalyst for reform. For while the NUSEC's own bills were rarely allowed to pass, both Labour and Conservative governments were eager to court housewives' votes and were sympathetic to measures that would lessen women's domestic subjugation without challenging men's industrial and professional privileges. They tended, then, to respond to feminists' bills by introducing versions of their own – and the NUSEC, always ready to grasp the bird in the hand, usually came to terms. Thus, while the 1924 Labour government refused to allow the NUSEC's Guardianship of Infants bill to go forward, it did invite Hubback and the Liberal MP Margaret Wintringham (who had sponsored the bill) to a series of cabinet committee meetings to hammer out a new, government-backed, compromise.[37] Similarly, while neither Labour nor the Conservatives were willing to introduce state-funded 'pensions' for mothers raising children alone, Neville Chamberlain, Baldwin's exceptionally diligent and astute Minister of Health, did craft an insurance-based scheme of pensions for civilian widows. Little of the 'women's legislation' of the 1920s came in exactly the form the NUSEC wanted, but it did improve women's access to pensions, divorce, the guardianship of children, and separation and maintenance from abusive husbands.[38] By 1925, Rathbone was able to claim that 'some hundreds of thousands of women whose names are unknown to us and ours to them will have cause, though they know it not, to bless the National Union for Equal Citizenship'.[39]

Rathbone's much-criticized 'welfarism', her insistent focus on the debilities of unwaged wives, played a crucial role in this achievement. For in steering NUSEC towards legislative campaigns for women's domestic rights, Rathbone was not only making a strategic adjustment to the times but also playing to her own strengths. No one knew the details of custody law, insurance regulations or summary jurisdiction so well; no one had a better grasp of parliamentary practice; no one was a more intelligent political strategist or better prepared. Ministers learned not to underestimate her knowledge or persistence. Typically, when Neville Chamberlain told members of a women's deputation that they had simply not understood the nature of the government's widows' pensions bill, he excluded 'your remarks, Miss Rathbone', from these criticisms. The deputation then turned into a highly technical debate between the two about possible insurance contributions and benefits for different groups of men and women, and Chamberlain was impressed enough to instruct his civil servants to investigate her proposals further.[40] In concentrating on domestic legislation, then, the NUSEC chose the field in which its claims to expertise were strongest and its chance of success best. The record of feminist legislation in the 1920s is tribute to the intelligence of that strategy.

But by 1925, Rathbone was feeling restive. *The Disinherited Family* had appeared to warm reviews, and the Family Endowment Society was growing: it was time, she thought, to make another bid for feminist support. NUSEC officers were still tied up with bills on guardianship, widows' pensions, equal franchise, and maintenance for separated wives, she reported to the NUSEC Council in her sixth presidential address on 11 March 1925 (an address revealingly entitled, 'The Old and the New Feminism'), but 'this time we feel with considerable confidence that we shall see *finis* written to some of these stories'. About half the Union's programme looked likely to be accomplished within the next few years: thus, '[t]he time has come to take stock and decide what next'. They could continue to 'chant the gospel of sex equality' at the 'inattentive ears of employers and Trade Unionists' even if that programme was 'not likely to arouse much enthusiasm or attract new recruits'. Or, alternatively, they could move in a new direction. With women 'virtually free', Rathbone said, the NUSEC could finally say:

At last we have done with the boring business of measuring everything that women want, or that is offered to them by men's standards, to see if it is exactly up to sample. At last we can stop looking at all our problems through men's eyes and discussing them in men's phraseology. We can demand what we want for women, not because it is what men have got, but because it is what women need to fulfil the potentialities of their own natures and to adjust themselves to the circumstances of their own lives.

Practically, this meant that the NUSEC should begin to take on those questions which, precisely because they fell within 'women's sphere', were so often neglected. Family endowment, birth control and housing might not involve issues of sex equality in a narrow sense, but they were 'questions which women must think out for themselves and mould to their own patterns' if they were to achieve 'real freedom . . . to shape their own destinies'.[41]

Rathbone's audience heard this speech as a challenge. After four years' respite, family endowment was back on its agenda, as was the question of a married woman's right to receive birth control information at public clinics. Both measures were expected to be controversial, and proponents and opponents of endowment had been carrying on a fierce correspondence in the columns of Rhondda's *Time and Tide*. But while the endowment debate in particular was a hot one – kicked off by Rathbone and Fawcett and followed by a raft of five-minute speeches pro and con – both resolutions passed easily.[42] Fawcett might insist that endowment would weaken parental responsibility, others that it would dilute the egalitarian message, but with domesticity resurgent and maternalist measures under consideration across Western states, these arguments sounded simply out of date.[43] There were costs in having forced the issue, though. To Rathbone's unhappiness, Fawcett felt strongly enough to resign from the NUSEC and from the Board of the *Woman's Leader*, although in contrast to 1915 – when she had turned her back for ever on her pacifist former friends – she took care to avoid any personal rift. She remembered Rathbone's support during the terrible wartime disputes and had already assured Eleanor that 'no difference of opinion will ever break our affectionate friendship'.[44]

In terms of the NUSEC's day-to-day work, neither of these decisions meant very much. The Union's Executive left the job of campaigning for endowment to the Family Endowment Society and birth control work to other organizations. Hubback and the staff at headquarters concentrated on the NUSEC's parliamentary bills and the franchise question, pausing only to organize deputations and marshal support for women police and other feminist demands. But the decisions were symbolically significant, for they publicly committed the NUSEC to a particular interpretation of what it meant to be a feminist. And this 'new feminist' vision, with its determination to 'extend its fighting front over so large a class, over so grievously oppressed a class of women as the working mothers',[45] *was* controversial, especially after 1926, when its supporters pushed family endowment and birth control not simply on to the Union's overall list of objects but on to its immediate programme.[46] A portion of the Union's membership watched these moves uneasily, and when Rathbone, Stocks and the Labour supporter Barbara Ayrton Gould tried to get the Union to rethink its adamantly egalitarian stance on labour legislation, *Time and Tide* became openly critical. It was now clear that the Union contained a number of people, unfortunately concentrated among its leadership, who were 'first philanthropists or sociologists or internationalists or party politicians, and only secondarily, if at all, feminists'. The 1926 Council had 'marked the beginning of a big cleavage of opinion within the Union', *Time and Tide* warned, 'and the subject of that cleavage is feminism'.[47] For the next two years, British feminists engaged in one final great debate – a debate over what it meant to be a feminist.

Rathbone was happy to meet Rhondda head-on. The *Time and Tide* article, she wrote, revealed 'so complete (I am tempted to say wilful) a misunderstanding of those criticized' that she wondered whether it was even worthwhile to respond. She did, though, providing us with one of her clearest and most compelling expositions of the ideas behind the 'new feminism'. As she saw it, she wrote:

> the women's movement comprises a large number of reforms, all of which are 'feminism', but only some of them 'equality.' The 'equality' reforms are necessary and immensely important. They consist in breaking away the fetters and restrictions which prevent women from developing their capacities and doing their best work. But this aim of enabling women to be and to do their best will not have been accomplished even when every sex barrier has fallen.

To reach that goal, something more was necessary: a constructive effort by women to remake the world to serve and sustain their interests and needs. Family endowment and birth control were essential to this effort. 'We regard family allowances and knowledge of birth control,' she wrote:

> not as a side show or excrescence on feminism, but as part of its very core. We see the great majority of women engaged during the best years of their lives in the vastly important work of keeping homes and bearing and rearing children. These women work as hard as any wage-earners, yet legally their economic position is that of serfs. Most of them have not a penny in the world that is legally their own. In spite of their own actual and their children's potential value to the community, neither they nor their children have any share of their own in its resources. They are expected to be kept somehow out of the share of the men: a share no larger than that which the childless man is free to spend on his amusement. If a man chooses to indulge in a luxury of keeping a wife and children, or dogs, or pigeons, he must refrain from starving or ill-treating them. Otherwise he is free to spend his income as he pleases. Further, although no economic provision is made for the children, the mother responsible for their care is shut out by her poverty from the knowledge that would enable her to control and space their births, knowledge that is at the disposal of every woman able to pay for it.

It was in order 'to remedy these injustices, these grotesque maladjustments of values', Rathbone concluded, that the NUSEC had 'by large majorities' placed both reforms on its immediate programme.[48]

But the quarrel did not end there. Two months later, it broke out again at the tenth conference of the International Women's Suffrage Alliance in Paris, which both Rathbone and Rhondda attended on behalf of their respective organizations. Rathbone had high hopes of that conference, having spent some time cultivating its members' awareness of and support for the principle of family endowment. But this issue was sidelined by a virulent fight over whether the United States' National Women's Party should be granted affiliation in the face of strenuous objections by the Alliance's long-standing American affiliate, the League of Women Voters. The Women's Party was – like Rhondda's Six Point Group – strictly egalitarian, while the League was increasingly caught up in civic education and social reform. The International Women's Suffrage Alliance's Board (on which Rathbone sat) rejected the Women's Party application, but neither the Women's Party nor the conference accepted that decision easily. The British delegates were particularly unhappy: nine of the twelve voted against the Board's decision, with only Rathbone and two others supporting it.[49] Perhaps in punishment, the equalitarians turned out in force to defeat Rathbone's family allowances proposal,[50] and Rhondda was so incensed that she withdrew the Six Point Group's own request for affiliation.[51] 'The real reason for [your] exclusion is that you are feminists,' Rhondda told the Women's Party delegates at a luncheon she hosted in their honour. 'Therefore the sight of you makes the social welfarers shiver.' But the Six Point Group would stand beside them. 'We are one body. We are the feminists of the world.'[52]

Rathbone's 'new feminists' found this definitional exclusiveness, this circling of the wagons, enraging. 'By what logic, other than the logic of an unquestioning acceptance of masculine standards of value,' the *Woman's Leader* stormed, had 'equalitarians' decided to limit their definition of feminism to equality within hitherto masculine spheres – a definition that would consider women's entry into the boxing ring but not improving the status of motherhood as a 'feminist' reform? 'We prefer to define feminism,' it retorted, as ' "the demand of women that the whole structure and movement of society shall reflect in a proportionate degree their experiences, their needs, and their aspirations". '[53] Put this way, 'new feminism' seemed almost incontestable – but Winifred Holtby, writing in the *Yorkshire Post*, had the best response. 'New feminists' were assuming that women needed, above all, to express their special 'point of view'; old feminists, by contrast, believed in 'the primary importance of the human being'. Of course sex differentiation was important, Holtby admitted, but 'Old Feminists believe that hitherto it has been allowed too wide a lordship'. Their aim was to *reduce* such differences, to restrict 'to as small a field as possible the isolated action of women, in order that elsewhere both sexes may work together for the good of the community'. Worthy reforms such as family allowances – and Holtby had already come out in their favour[54] – concerned men as well as women, and should be pursued jointly.[55]

Here – in Rathbone's language and Holtby's reservations – we can begin to grasp the essence of the quarrel. For Rathbone, feminism was a movement to emancipate 'women' – a group in which, judging from her persistent use of the third person plural ('their natures', 'their lives'), she could never quite include herself. Indeed, wealthy and privileged from birth, she had the grace to recognize that the difficulties faced by working-class mothers were *not* her own, and the moral imagination to feel an obligation to address them anyway. But for Holtby

– as for Vera Brittain, Lady Rhondda, and that small group of women determined on careers and achievement – feminism was a movement of personal emancipation, fuelled by the drive to throw off hateful restrictions and stereotypes and to take on whatever one might like, be it mathematics or motor cars. Domestic life struck such women as a handicap, an irritation; the idea that 'housewifery' could be an adequate career, still less a foundation for economic reward and public honour, seemed to them ridiculous. After all, as Rose Macaulay quipped, no one would want on their tombstone the motto 'I have kept house'. 'Let the house go unkept,' she advised. 'Let it go to the devil, and see what happens when it gets there. Surely a house unkept cannot be so distressing as a life unlived.'[56]

Fine words for a bohemian spinster, Rathbone might have retorted: what did this have to do with the mother of five in a tenement house on Merseyside? Precious little, the 'old feminist' might have admitted, but this was not the point. Feminism should always range itself behind those women, however marginal or embattled, seeking to press beyond conventional sex roles; seeking, indeed, to deny the relevance of sex altogether. Unequal pay, the solicitation laws, the marriage bar, even the whole apparatus of chivalry and politeness were anathema to women seeking to be recognized as, simply, *human*. Holtby's point that she was 'an Old Feminist, because I dislike everything that feminism implies', like Virginia Woolf's later fantasy of throwing the very word 'feminist' on to the pyre, makes sense in this light.[57] Not even motherhood need plunge women into 'the present nightmare of domesticity', Vera Brittain insisted; a better means of reconciling work and parenthood was surely not 'beyond the ingenuity of civilized mankind'. If both spouses kept their professions, and domestic responsibilities were shared or collectivized, not merely the undervaluing of women's work but the gendered division of labour itself could disappear.[58]

Dilemmas over how to balance motherhood and work, about how to recognize the sexes' common humanity while accommodating the demands of a persistent, imposed, 'difference', still preoccupy women and women's movements today. Such arguments are never 'won'; sometimes, however (and this was one such time), the partisans on each side will not agree to disagree. In the run-up to the 1927 Council, the *Woman's Leader* upped the stakes, asking its readers for their views on the question, 'What is Equality?' Over the next weeks, the words flew. By refusing to recognize real differences between men's and women's lives, Rathbone charged, equalitarians accepted 'a pitifully narrow definition of equality'. By focusing on women's conditions rather than their rights, retorted Elizabeth Abbott, 'new feminists' patronizingly treated women as a class apart. A few moderates tried to calm things down. Helen Ward objected to the 'new feminists' denigration of the claim to equality, which had after all sustained feminism for years, but insisted that the NUSEC could and should also take up issues which did not fit well into that egalitarian frame. Edith How-Martyn also found herself agreeing with Abbott's strict definition of equality but supporting the

NUSEC's effort to improve the lives of the vast majority of women. Fair enough, countered Dorothy, Lady Balfour of Burleigh, but the Union must keep its priorities clear. Enthusiastic as she was about endowment, she would prefer to see it removed from the programme rather than blunt 'the keen edge of our Equality sword'.[59]

By the 1927 Council, both sides were determined to have it out. The main fight took place over protective legislation, the question that, two years earlier, the *Manchester Guardian* had predicted would 'in the future lead to the greatest conflict of opinion in women's organisations'.[60] The previous year the Union had affirmed its opposition to any sex-specific protective legislation, but Rathbone unwisely did not let the matter rest. True, she had her reasons. The trade union movement counted protective legislation as one of its most impressive achievements and found the NUSEC's stance frankly offensive; Labour leaders anxious to recruit women members could thus paint feminism as a class-based movement eager to return women and children to the mines. For Rathbone, who spent the late 1920s trying to convert the labour movement to the cause of family endowment, that inflexibility had become a serious problem. She did not actually want the NUSEC to support unequal legislation; what she wanted was a conciliatory gesture, one that would signal to labour organizations that organized feminism was sensitive to their concerns. Her carefully worded amendment to the resolu-

20. NUSEC Council, March 1927. Behind table, left to right: Margery Corbett Ashby (seated), Chrystal Macmillan (?), Eleanor, Eva Hubback.

tion on protective legislation thus accepted the goal of equal labour legislation but urged the Union to take into account the opinions of the women workers concerned, as well as the interests of the community and the likely chances of success, when deciding how to proceed in a given case.

In the heightened atmosphere of the 1927 Council, however, this seemed akin to treason. Rathbone's amendment was blisteringly attacked, in the end passing by a single vote. A second controversial resolution raised the stakes, proposing that the Council distinguish between the *primary* goal of securing 'a real equality of liberties, status and opportunity between men and women' and its secondary function of securing 'such reforms . . . as are necessary to make it possible for women adequately to discharge their function as citizens' – the rubric under which family allowances were usually placed. But the Executive, while accepting this resolution, tabled an amendment defining family allowances, the provision of birth control information and equality within the League of Nations as all essential to 'real equality' for women, and hence as part of that first and primary aim. When this passed by a large majority, the equalitarians again moved to declare these three goals less important than the other aims of an equal franchise, more women in Parliament, an equal moral standard and equal pay. When this final amendment lost decisively, 11 of the 24 members of the Executive – the bulk of the equalitarian wing – resigned.[61]

Both sides then had their say, in the feminist weeklies and in the national press.[62] All were agreed on the importance of an equal franchise,[63] but otherwise the resigners did not mince words. The demand 'that regulations of the conditions and hours of work shall be based on the nature of the occupation and not on the sex of the worker' was a 'long established and fundamental' feminist policy, they wrote. To acquiesce in Rathbone's effort to 'whittle down this demand' would, in their view, have been 'a betrayal of the women's movement, for which we have been working, some of us for more than thirty years'.[64] *Time and Tide* put the matter even more starkly. The National Union's Executive was 'no longer a feminist body', being now 'in complete control of the Social Reformers'.[65]

This was the worst crisis faced by the National Union since the ill-fated split over the war in 1915. As in that earlier conflict, the resigners included some of the Executive's most important members, among them Chrystal Macmillan, who had been part of that inner circle since 1910, Dorothy Balfour, the Union's honorary secretary, and Winifred Soddy, its long-suffering honorary treasurer. Moreover, in 1927 the Union was much less able to survive such a split. No eager new recruits clamoured to replace the resigners, and some old stalwarts – among them Ray Strachey – refused to serve as well.[66] A new Executive was, somehow, cobbled together, and the 'new feminist' faction put a brave – or foolhardy – face on it, with Mary Stocks privately admitting to Marie Stopes that she was 'not altogether sorry to be rid of' the equalitarians.[67] *Time and Tide*'s judgement, though typically harsh, was more accurate. 'New feminists' might count this as a victory, but 'another such victory and we are undone'.[68]

Rathbone was the principal architect of 'new feminism' and the author of the crucial and offending amendment: was she responsible for this fiasco? True, the equalitarians were not blameless: they too were far from conciliatory, and their ally *Time and Tide* played a particularly irresponsible, gadfly role. But Rathbone *was* the NUSEC's President, and the job of maintaining unity, of crafting compromises, surely rested with her. And here she failed. As an intellectual leader, Rathbone was unparalleled: 'new feminism' was the only coherent programme for feminism to appear during the inter-war years, providing the women's movement with a *raison d'être* in the decade after emancipation. As a tactician and political leader, however, Rathbone had some faults, and this conflict brought them to the fore.

For, simply on a strategic level, Rathbone should never have pressed the issue of protective legislation. Not only did she alienate the equalitarian wing, but she also damaged her own 'new feminist' cause. After all, 'new feminism' was, before 1927, ascendant. Against expectations, the NUSEC had rallied behind the campaigns for birth control information and for endowment, with many equalitarian colleagues even lending their names to the Family Endowment Society. They did so not because they accepted Rathbone's definition of feminism but because they agreed that endowment and birth control could make the lives of married women better, and because they knew the value of a unified feminist stance. Protective legislation was, however, different: it was not a 'new' issue about which feminists had yet to make up their minds, and it directly offended the principle of equality. Many, probably even most ordinary members, favoured the Union's longstanding policy of clear opposition, for – as one observer astutely noted – Rathbone's amendment passed only because some of the rank and file felt that she was 'too fiercely assailed in the ardour of the fray' and rallied to their President's defence.[69] Nor was there much advantage to be gained by revision, since whatever the NUSEC's views, they simply didn't count for much. Policy-makers in London or Geneva accepted that the labour movement spoke for women workers, while Labour leaders concerned to keep 'their' women out of feminism's clutches were unlikely to be mollified by Rathbone's careful phrasing. By pressing this question, then, Rathbone miscalculated badly, forcing a rift that seriously weakened the NUSEC and the 'new feminist' cause.

This strategic miscalculation revealed another, in a sense more serious, weakness: a failure of imagination and human understanding. Eleanor Rathbone was intellectually impressive, administratively gifted and often politically astute; what she was not, however, was clubbable or warm. Surrounded as she was by Hubback, Stocks, Macadam and other like-minded friends, and temperamentally unsuited to the confidences that would have kept her better informed, she misjudged the depth of feeling on this issue and made too little effort to conciliate it. In 1915, during the devastating wartime split, Rathbone had reminded the Union that diversity was a source of strength: a society composed only of those who agree on everything, she warned, 'tends to become a mutually admiring, self-complacent, narrow-minded coterie, out of touch with realities, and with other minds, and therefore unable to shape events or to influence mankind'.[70] If she remembered her own wise words in 1927, however, she seemed unable to act on them. She would not compromise her principles on a relatively minor issue in order to keep those who disagreed with them on board; she was unable to rise above the fray, as an organization's president should do. That inflexibility, that singleness of purpose, would serve her well during many long parliamentary campaigns, but they were not assets here. The political leader, Max Weber once wrote, needs both passion and a sense of proportion. Rathbone's convictions were always held with passion, but on this occasion her sense of proportion deserted her.

Fortunately, the damage stayed within bounds, for the simple reason that women's suffrage – the one issue that could trump all other conflicts – was once again on the agenda. The NUSEC always gave this issue top priority and had been particularly disappointed when the 1924 Labour government failed to introduce a government bill. When Stanley Baldwin's Conservative government came in, they pressed further, organizing public meetings (some 200 by 1927), writing letters, and working with Ellen Wilkinson and Nancy Astor to raise the issue in the House of Commons. That effort was just gathering steam when the NUSEC rift happened, so (at least in public) both sides made peace. Helen Ward, who had voted against Rathbone's amendment but had *not* resigned, managed to bring all the main feminist organizations together in an Equal Franchise Council, which collectively planned one final great public meeting at the Queen's Hall in March 1928.

Baldwin himself attended that meeting, listened to grateful tributes and assured feminists that their cause was all but won. He himself was not 'in the least' alarmed by the prospect of an equal franchise: 'I have faith in a free democracy. I rejoice in its advent, and I believe that the public life of this country will be enriched by the step which we are taking.'[71] But for all Baldwin's generous words, cabinet records make clear that the government was not persuaded by the feminist campaign. Not only were most cabinet members personally unenthusiastic about women's suffrage, but the party agents were unanimously opposed: according to J.C.C. Davidson, the party chairman, 'supporters of equal franchise were a very small if very vocal minority and commanded no general support'.[72] The problem was that Baldwin had implied (and the Home Secretary Joynson-Hicks had confirmed in the House) that the Conservative Party intended to equalize the franchise in the current parliamentary session[73] – and while Churchill argued forcefully in Cabinet that the government should simply ignore such pledges,[74] this was too much for Baldwin's sense of honour. Having reluctantly concluded that it would be impossible to grant an 'equal franchise' by lowering the voting age for women to twenty-five and raising it for men,[75] the government quietly passed the Equal Franchise Bill.

The feminist movement rallied for this final suffrage campaign; NUSEC's annual council meeting in 1928 was the largest since 1919. The equalitarian wing still hoped to stage a comeback: they had not resigned in 1927 from the Union itself, only from its Executive, and planned to raise the issue of protective legislation again.[76] Somehow, that promised reconsideration never came. When the 1928 council meeting decided to postpone this controversial matter until the franchise issue was resolved, the equalitarians withdrew their names from nomination for the Executive.[77] But by the 1929 meeting, when Rathbone turned the presidency over to Margery Corbett Ashby, it was too late. Yet more local societies folded after the franchise victory, and the Executive, wholly in 'new feminist' hands, moved in an even less equalitarian direction. Largely at Hubback's instigation, in late 1928 the NUSEC began building up civic associations along the lines of the rural Women's Institutes in medium-sized towns, but these new 'Townswomen's Guilds', while soon outstripping the local Societies for Equal Citizenship in size and wealth, never had the same staunchly feminist orientation.[78] By the early 1930s the National Union had become a 'National Council for Equal Citizenship', with a single part-time secretary and a budget of some hundreds of pounds a year, while the *Woman's Leader* shrank to a monthly and was then absorbed into the *Townswoman*.

Divisions within the women's movement contributed to this decline, but they did not cause it, nor can Rathbone's 'new feminism' be blamed for the NUSEC's demise. The equalitarian organizations fared no better, dwindling in size and relying on a few ageing enthusiasts to keep afloat.[79] All the trends of the thirties – economic contraction, the defeat of the left, the rise of fascism – were unfriendly to feminism, and the movement was also the victim of a generational shift. Those last equal franchise demonstrations were remarkable partly because, as one doughty campaigner admitted, their participants' 'average age was probably 73½'.[80] Rathbone recognized this problem but could do little about it: she 'barely even knew the names' of prominent women likely to appeal to 'the flapper generation'.[81] Feminism survived in the 1930s, then, but less as a movement than as a few unquenchable, individual voices, those of Nancy Astor, Winifred Holtby, Vera Brittain, Ellen Wilkinson – and, always, Eleanor Rathbone.

In the middle of that 'devil's decade', two of these women looked back. Winifred Holtby and Eleanor Rathbone had been on different sides of the 'new feminism' argument. Eleanor Rathbone, independently wealthy, progressive, but 'Victorian' in formation and faith, had sought to extend an Edwardian 'new liberal' vision of social citizenship to women of all classes; Winifred Holtby, twenty years younger, self-supporting, and 'modern', thought feminism a movement for individual self-realization and rights. Yet when the two women paused to assess the movement's achievements, they found themselves unable to disentangle those competing ideals. Those who say that the women's vote changed nothing don't know what they are talking about, Holtby wrote bluntly on the occasion of King George V's jubilee celebrations in 1935. 'I have seen a revolution in social and moral values which has transformed the world I live in. It is a direct result of that challenge to opinion which we call the women's movement.' It wasn't just 'that legally married mothers are now allowed to be their children's guardians, that grounds for divorce (although still ridiculously and indecently inadequate) are equal for men and women, that birth control is no longer an unmentionable horror but an accepted instrument of civilization, that maternal mortality is no longer an obscene joke but a matter for national regret and persistent effort'. All those were important, but were a sign of something still more significant: 'I mean that a world has changed'.[82] It had changed sufficiently for Holtby to concentrate, not on women's rights but on 'the work in which my real interests lie, the study of inter-race relationships, the writing of novels and so forth'.[83] And this she did, completing her two greatest novels – the anti-imperialist satire, *Mandoa, Mandoa!*, and the elegiac *South Riding* – in the years before her death in 1935 at the young age of thirty-seven.

Rathbone had had something to do with every one of those reforms Holtby listed. In 1936, writing in *Our Freedom and Its Results*, a volume of feminist essays edited by Ray Strachey and published by Virginia and Leonard Woolf's Hogarth Press, she too insisted that political equality had improved women's lives in concrete and measurable ways. Yet, like Holtby, she sensed a less tangible but more profound transformation, an intimation of that end to the dominion of 'sex' at which feminism – especially 'old feminism' – had always aimed. Perhaps the main consequence of enfranchisement, she hazarded, had been to weaken women's identification with their own sex: the post-war years had shown that 'those who expect women's contribution to be something completely *sui generis*, utterly different from the contribution of men, will be disappointed', and that in 'five-sixths or nine-tenths' of cases, women's concerns and activities would scarcely differ from men's. Remarkably, the architect of 'new feminism' did not lament this. 'We are citizens as well as women': the foundational purpose of the women's movement was to combat a social system where women's life chances were determined by sex alone.[84]

And yet, Rathbone thought, even as they grasped those new opportunities for equal citizenship, women would carry with them the lessons and skills they had learned in their long struggle. The 'harvest of the women's movement', she told her audience at a lecture of this title at Bedford College in 1935, was not only rights and opportunities but also experience and capacity. The campaign for the vote had taught women the art of politics, to be patient but importunate, idealistic but full of guile. 'There are reformers,' she said, whose idea of taking a citadel is to march round it blowing trumpets, and when that fails to batter it with rams, if necessary with their own heads. We sometimes used the battering-ram, but if the wall proved too strong for us, we withdrew a little and investigated every possible method of overcoming that wall, by climbing over it, or tunnelling under it, or perhaps labouring to dislodge a stone at a time, so that just a few invaders could creep through. And we acquired by experience a certain *flair* which told us when a charge of dynamite would come in useful and when it was better to rely on the methods of the skilled engineer.

Those skills, that fortitude, was feminism's legacy. And if women applied all they had learned to the problems of suffering and poverty, disease and war, what further transformation in human society might not be possible? Decades in the future, she promised, the cause of feminism would still be bearing fruit. 'I shall not live to see the end of it, nor perhaps will even the youngest member of my present audience.'[85]

Chapter 11

Feuds about the Family

Eleanor Rathbone came to the cause of family endowment through social work, not politics, but knew that politics was the only means to make that ideal a reality. Just how hard a political fight that might be became apparent in 1922, when she made her first bid for Parliament. Only two women had entered the Commons by that date, and if Nancy Astor and Margaret Wintringham could be considered feminists, both had arrived there with their party's blessing and to fill a husband's now vacant seat. Rathbone had neither husband nor party, but she had an independent political base in Liverpool and powerful enough connections to force other progressive contenders from the ring. Albeit with bad grace, then ('this lady always plays for herself and yet can spoil every other person's chances,' the Liberal merchant Richard Durning Holt noted sourly in his diary),[1] in 1922 Liverpool's Liberal and Labour parties stood aside to allow her a straight fight in the East Toxteth division against the sitting Conservative, James Rankin, a wealthy local merchant (and, awkwardly, a relation by marriage) who had held the seat without contest in 1918.[2]

Rathbone knew she was the underdog. 'When I think of the task of trying to make a breach in the serried ranks of Tory domination in this city,' she told a crowded meeting of her supporters at the outset of her campaign, 'I am bound to say that, middle-aged woman as I am, I feel like a very inadequate David going out to do battle with Goliath.'[3] And yet even *The Times* thought the contest worth watching.[4] Rathbone was the city's most prominent woman politician, a vocal advocate of municipal house-building, and the architect of the system of wartime allowances and post-war 'voluntary aid' on which some portion of the electorate relied. Her settlement workers and suffragists put together a formidable canvassing machine, and her family came out in force to stump for her.[5] And while Eleanor usually disliked electioneering – hating the need, as she put it, to 'oil the wheels with pounds and pounds of the best butter'[6] – this time she had fun tramping the district and shaking hands. 'It is wonderful how she is known and admired,' Elizabeth Macadam wrote to Eleanor's niece, Elena Richmond. Elizabeth looked forward to bringing Eleanor back to London '– shall I say victorious?!' 'I think my faith rises quite to that.'[7]

21. Rathbone campaigning in East Toxteth, 1922.

Yet on the eve of the poll, disaster struck. In this most sectarian and politically unscrupulous of towns, an anonymous eleventh-hour leaflet appeared, warning voters – and bachelors and childless men in particular – that Rathbone was the advocate of a dangerous and socialistic scheme to regulate wages not according to the efforts and skills of men at work, but according to the number of children borne by the wife.[8] Rathbone quickly denounced this 'electioneering dodge', pointing out that she supported not differential wages but additional benefits for mothers and children, but her complex views were easily caricatured by her opponents, and the attacks continued.[9] Sir Archibald Salvidge, Liverpool's adept Conservative party boss, denied that he had issued the leaflet, but called it an 'able and talented dissection' of Rathbone's desire to tax single men to support married men's families. Her views amounted to 'Socialism run mad in its worst form', Sir Archibald charged, adding: 'What the Britisher wants is freedom, and I say a man who has earned his weekly money has a right to spend it as he thinks.'[10] Some voters, evidently, agreed, for Rankin was returned by a poll of 15,149 to Rathbone's 9,984.[11]

Eleanor's friends were quick to denounce Salvidge, seeing this ploy as yet another example of Liverpool's notorious popular Toryism. Yet Salvidge was, in a sense, right: Eleanor Rathbone did wish to rework the distributive system to adjust family income to family size; she did imagine a polity in which the work of mothers would be rewarded. Moreover, on more than one occasion she had admitted that some of that money for mothers must come from childless men. In the *Manchester Guardian* in February 1921, with the country in the grip of 'retrenchment', she argued that the custom of paying for motherhood out of wages was 'grossly extravagant' as well as cruel to those with children: 'bachelors and elderly men get far more than they need, while families are stinted when the father is in work and starved when he is unemployed'.[12] Or, as she put it in a frank letter to the *Woman's Leader* that same spring: 'We have got to economise somehow. Why not economise on bachelors?'[13]

With her own abstemious habits and passion for self-sacrifice, Rathbone might have thought this sort of argument convincing, but East Toxteth's respectable male householders understandably saw things differently. Of course, about a third of the electorate was now female, and these new voters may have found 'endowment' appealing; it was, after all, a platform fashioned from their wartime experiences, designed to meet their needs. And given the circumstances, Rathbone had done remarkably well in East Toxteth, a safe-as-houses Conservative seat, one that would prove immune to Labour's growing local popularity in the 1930s and resist even its 1945 landslide. Yet Eleanor took the results as a sign, and did not contest a Liverpool seat again. In 1910 Rathbone had risked her City Council seat because she 'placed women's suffrage before anything else';[14] this time, she sacrificed her electoral appeal for endowment.

Indeed, in some ways her advocacy of family endowment was a greater risk, for the policy had, in the early twenties, few well-placed advocates. It was seen as an issue for cranks and utopians, 'unsound' in every way. Supporting endowment left Rathbone open to ridicule and attack, especially from those who found it unseemly that a well-to-do spinster should have such decided views about the proper foundation for working-class family life. That anti-feminist hostility never entirely abated: as late as 1942, one fellow MP sneered that Rathbone had 'wasted her life advocating family allowances', perhaps finding it 'a good enough substitute for the absence of a family'.[15] But by 1930, if many still found the prospect of family endowment objectionable, they could not simply dismiss it, for the issue had been forced on to the political agenda. And at the centre of that debate we find Eleanor – arguing and scheming, making converts and making plans.

Eleanor Rathbone never ceased to consider family endowment a 'women's question', but she knew that a reform of this magnitude needed more powerful backers if it was to be taken seriously. As the economic situation worsened in the early 1920s, then, Rathbone began to urge family endowment less as a measure of justice for mothers than as a practical means of safeguarding living standards in a period of retrenchment. British employers would be able to meet working-class needs while also reining in production costs if they distributed their wage bill not only in the form of wages but also (as in France) in the form of family allowances, Rathbone argued in a prominent article in *The Times* that May – and to her delight Lord Askwith, the renowned wartime industrial arbitrator, wrote in to agree with her.[16] Few industrialists, it is true, paid much heed; the Federation of British Industries, when she approached them, scarcely acknowledged her letter.[17] But the Conservative MP Sir Arthur Steel-Maitland and the prominent eugenicist C. Dampier Whetham helped Rathbone arrange for a meeting in the House of Commons that July,[18] and the publisher Edward Arnold, who was 'much struck' by Rathbone's letters to *The Times*, approached her about a possible book.[19] For the next few years, Rathbone spent a good portion of her time on research. She learned all she could about the functioning of allowance systems in government services and particular industries on the continent (France especially), contacted employers and trade unionists abroad to learn their opinions of such systems, and worked her way through population and national income statistics to figure out the likely cost and scope of a British scheme. In March 1924 Edward Arnold published the work that made her name – a book that Hugh Dalton, later a Labour Chancellor of the Exchequer but then at the London School of Economics, saw as 'one of the outstanding contributions to economic literature since the war'.[20]

Rathbone's *The Disinherited Family* belongs (if is rarely placed) alongside Henry George's *Progress and Poverty* or J.A. Hobson's *Imperialism* on that special shelf reserved for writings that genuinely lead their readers to see fundamental social and economic structures in a new light. Rathbone began her book with a simple observation. Although the family remained the most important social institution – the agency through which children were nurtured and socialized, the centre of most people's emotional life – its claims as an economic unit had been 'not so much disparaged or negatived as ignored'.[21] Economists normally considered only that (largely male) portion of the population directly involved in remunerated work; the (largely female) labour through which that working population was itself produced and made productive rarely drew their eyes. Indeed, when experts and politicians did address 'the family' they again began with men. Those eager to improve working-class living standards, for example, tended to treat poverty entirely as a question of wage levels, often following Seebohm Rowntree in arguing for a basic male wage capable of supporting a five-person family. None of these experts began by analysing Britain's families as they actually existed; none really asked whether such a 'family wage' was either obtainable or *would* meet family needs. Marshalling statistics on national income and dependency, Rathbone did so – constructing, in the process, a virtually unanswerable case for family allowances.

How, to begin with, were Britain's families really constituted? More than a quarter of the households of adult working men were comprised only of bachelors or widowers and a second quarter consisted of married couples without children under the age of fourteen. Slightly under half included dependent children: some 16.6 per cent had one dependent child, 13 per cent had two, 9.9 per cent had more than three, and a mere 8.8 per cent contained precisely those three dependent children assumed to constitute the norm. Should a five-person male family wage be introduced, then, it would suffice or more than suffice for the needs of nine out of ten working men's households – a figure that Rathbone admitted 'may seem at first glance to be "not so bad"'.[22] But 'contentment will vanish on closer inspection', she promised, for while workers with more than three dependent children might comprise only a tenth of all households, those units contained a large proportion of all working-class children. Under a male 'family wage', then, bachelors and childless men would enjoy an income capable of sustaining many millions of 'phantom children' while some 40 per cent of real children at any given moment – and some 53 per cent of all children for at least five years of their lives – would still live in poverty. Nor was this ideal 'family wage' – hitherto the hope of the labour movement and social reformers alike – achievable anyway. Drawing on the work of the reputed statisticians Arthur Bowley and Josiah Stamp, Rathbone pointed out that even if all incomes above £160 per year were confiscated by the state, the amount available for redistribution would still fall short of that needed to pay all working men enough to support a family of five. Perhaps, then, reformers should rethink their approach, beginning not with some hypothetical average family but rather with the needs of those families that actually existed. If neither the 'family wage' nor the most radical redistribution of income could eradicate family poverty, it was time to try a simpler solution: 'direct provision for the costs of child maintenance through family allowances'.[23]

The second half of the book described this solution in detail. All schemes of family allowances would redistribute income from the childless to those with children (and, if paid to women, from men to women), but within this rubric many variations were possible. Family allowances could be funded through taxation or out of a portion of the wage bill; they could be universal or limited by occupation or income; they could be graduated to favour larger or smaller families; they could include an allowance for the caregiver/mother or be granted for children alone. Rathbone sought to describe the relative advantages of these various options impartially, and was able to point to existing schemes. Many states after the First World War wished to foster industrial growth while also guaranteeing a basic level of well-being; many had turned – or had seen particular industries turn – to such initiatives as family allowances. Some seventy pages of the book summarized these various foreign developments, with special attention paid to France, where family allowance schemes had been introduced after the war by industrial consortia seeking to conciliate pro-natalist opinion while restraining wage demands, and to Australia, where a detailed examination of the prospects for paying a male family wage had led to legislative proposals for family allowances. With support growing and actual schemes spreading, Rathbone could claim that family endowment was no longer a utopian idea. It was the future – and it worked.

With its statistical underpinning and focus on policy, *The Disinherited Family* might be thought a dry read, but it is not. It is Rathbone's best book, vividly written and enlivened by moments of sardonic wit remote from her usual high-minded tone. She could not, for example, quite refrain from poking fun at the great care with which the seven men who made up the Australian Royal Commission on the Basic Wage – 'the three representatives of the great bodies of employers in Australia and the three representatives of its federated unions and the distinguished lawyer who presided' – considered 'whether the supposititious wife of the typical Australian workman should be allowed six blouses a year (two silk, two voile, and two cambric or winceyette) as claimed by the Federated Unions; or only three (one silk, one voile, one cambric or winceyette) as suggested by the employers'.[24] But it isn't only the prose style that makes *The Disinherited Family* a good read; it is also the eye-opening portrait she offers of working-class family life. Rathbone understood that this was in some ways the most important part of the book: as she shrewdly noted, while no one ever tried to refute her economic arguments, 'every unfavourable commentator has simply walked straight past them' to raise a host of moral objections to any interference in family life. Rathbone thus fought back in kind: to evaluate such objections, one would also need to examine 'how the present wage system works out from a social and moral point of view'; only then could one 'discuss the relative merits of the two systems'.[25] After making her economic case, then, and before going on to outline foreign and possible British schemes, Rathbone spent another seventy pages detailing the consequences of the current practice of supporting families, somehow or other, through wages paid to men.

Did her critics fear that endowment would destroy work incentives or lessen paternal responsibility? Consider, then, the effects on men – men as workers, men as fathers – of the practice of paying bachelors and family men precisely the same wage. Men became accustomed when single to levels of personal freedom and personal spending that could not be sustained when they married: those able to unlearn those lessons worked themselves to exhaustion to keep their families fed and clothed; those unable to do so simply kept up their old habits and forced their children to go without. In too many instances, and with the bombastic support of men like Sir Archibald Salvidge, men saw their wages as 'their exclusive property . . . which they are free to spend at will on keeping a wife or backing a winner'.[26] Most working-class households lived at two separate standards: one for the husband and father, whose food often cost more than the rest of the family's combined, and a second for the mother and children. In part, Rathbone admitted, this was a prudent domestic strategy, for the man's strength had to be kept up, but it also reflected an acceptance of 'male predominance' so widespread as to go almost unnoticed.

But if men were forced into overworking or insensitivity by the pressure of family needs, Rathbone argued, how much worse were the effects on children and (still more) women. Drawing on her own knowledge and the sensitive accounts of working-class women's lives written by Anna Martin, Leonora Eyles, and the members of the Women's Co-operative Guild, Rathbone sketched the endless work, monotonous diet, terrible anxiety and chronic ill health with which working-class women daily contended. And these were simply the common hazards of family life on a pound a week; how much worse the wife's lot when the husband drank or ill-treated her. 'Imagine what the life of the woman must be like,' Rathbone urged:

> shut up all day in two or three tiny, airless, sunless rooms; with children always with her and always more to do for them than she can possibly manage; seeing them hungry and cold and ailing and with no money to buy for them what they need; trying to keep clean without soap or cleaning materials; liable to be inspected at any time by school visitors, health visitors and district visitors, who blame her for her failure to make bricks without straw; never certain whether the little money her husband has given her this week may not be less or nothing next week; generally expecting her next confinement or recovering from the last one; always over-tired; always suffering from an ailment in some part of the body, rheumatism, dragging pains, nausea, swollen feet, aching back, bad teeth, bad eyes; dreading her husband's return from work at night, his blows and curses. Then the nights! . . . It is clear that what J.S. Mill described as 'the lowest degradation of a human being, that of being made the instrument of an animal function contrary to her inclinations,' is still enforced by a good many men on their wives as part of the price they are expected to pay for being kept by them.[27]

Their oppression (and Rathbone always saw sexual vulnerability and the widely accepted doctrine of 'marital rights' as a key aspect of that oppression) was not less for being dispersed throughout millions of isolated homes. Marital dependence, like slavery, might be economic at heart, but it was also (like slavery) borne on the body, lived out in labour and pain, physical and sexual.

Of course, social investigators had said much of this before; in her studies of dockers' families, Rathbone had said some of it herself. What made *The Disinherited Family* different, what lifted it from the realm of social investigation to the realm of social theory, was its analytic power – the fact that Rathbone was able to see the logic behind, and even propose an explanation for, the way the distributive system functioned. And this is where her feminism entered. For Rathbone paid little attention to class inequality; the injustice of a system that enabled some to live well off inheritance while others lived badly off wages scarcely detained her. Such divisions struck her as simply a distraction from a more fundamental economic division, the division of sex. The core logic of the distributive system as she described it was a gendered logic: male dominance was the essence of an economic order that 'pays tribute in plenty of sugary phrases to the value of [the mother's] services, but . . . parcels out all its wealth among those who provide it with land, or capital, or services of brain and hand other than hers'.[28] Nor was that 'logic' an inadvertent by-product of other historical forces; it was one of the reasons for the system's very shape. 'Among the strongest instincts of human nature is the desire of power, of domination, of being looked up to and admired,' she wrote. 'Through all ages and in all countries, with a few insignificant exceptions known to anthropologists, men even the humblest and most oppressed have found scope for the satisfaction of this desire in their power over their wives and children.' That masculine will to power (a trait Rathbone labelled, unblushingly, 'the Turk complex') could take different forms in different times – but was it 'fantastic to suggest' that in the nineteenth century, as men relinquished legal and political power over their wives, they took unconscious comfort in the fact that their economic power over their families was, if anything, growing? 'I am not suggesting that men value this power because, in the vast majority of cases, they have any desire to abuse it,' Rathbone wrote. 'But it is easy to see what satisfaction the institution of the dependent family gives to all sorts and conditions of men – to the tyrannous man what opportunities of tyranny, to the selfish of self-indulgences, to the generous of preening himself in the sunshine of his own generosity, to the chivalrous of feeling himself the protector of the weak.'[29] Small wonder that men showed such attachment to the ideal of the family wage; small wonder they found the prospect of direct provision 'distasteful, for reasons they do not care to analyse'.[30] But analyse it they must, for those who would reject family endowment – a system which could raise all families out of poverty – only for such sentimental and fundamentally selfish reasons 'are incurring a great responsibility'. 'A man has no right to want to keep half the world in purgatory, because he enjoys playing redeemer to his own wife and children.'[31]

The Disinherited Family marked, for Rathbone, the end of a long road – the road that had stretched from those early investigations into the earnings and lives of dockers' families, through the analysis of women's wages, and into the administrative realm of allowances for soldiers' wives. Everything she had to say about family policy she said in this book: while she would bring out a briefer analysis in 1927 and write a Penguin Special on the case for family allowances in 1940, neither of these works would approach this achievement.[32] Nor did any other writer better it. A raft of scholarly treatises were written between the wars on the tricky question of the relationship of wages to family needs, but no study matched Rathbone's in statistical virtuosity, social sympathy and intellectual power. Mary Stocks grasped the nature of Rathbone's achievement. 'Looking back at the history of economic thought,' she wrote in 1927, 'I can find no contribution of equal magnitude from the brain of any other woman. Other women have interpreted man-made economics. Miss Rathbone has stamped the science of economics with an indelible feminist mark.'[33] The book was updated and reprinted by the more congenial firm of George Allen and Unwin that year; a new edition was brought out after the Second World War; when 'second wave' feminists began campaigning for 'Wages for Housework' it was reprinted again.[34] From its publication until today, whenever feminist philosophers or economists take up the question of women's poverty and powerlessness, they find themselves returning to Rathbone's brilliant work.[35]

But Rathbone didn't write *The Disinherited Family* for feminists or for posterity. She wrote it for the powerful of her day, seeking to persuade them that an adequate income for each and every family could be 'realizable here and now'. This was the reason she had 'ventured to criticize economists on their own ground'; this was why she bolstered her case with statistics and evidence from the most unimpeachable authorities.[36] To her delight and relief, her efforts paid off: more than any other feminist treatise before or since, the book was accepted as a serious contribution to economic thought. It was reviewed widely, especially by economists, and while some of this comment was hostile – with Alexander Gray of Aberdeen University and D.H. MacGregor of Oxford writing lengthy rebuttals or debating Rathbone on the BBC[37] – most credited Rathbone with having built up a powerful logical case. Some even professed themselves converted on the spot. 'I've been reading *The Disinherited Family*,' William Beveridge, then Director of the London School of Economics, wrote to Graham Wallas, 'i.e. the case for distributing part of the total national income not as profits, interests, salaries and wages, but as "family allowances." The book has converted me, and if you read it, will, I believe, convert you and others.'[38]

The word 'convert' is an apt one, for (as Beveridge soon found out), he had joined in a crusade. Soon after those first reviews were published, Rathbone began building up a political movement.[39] She re-established the old Family Endowment Committee as a new, much more broadly based Family Endowment Society (FES), recruiting as many well-regarded economists and experts as 'vice-presidents' or members of its 'Council' as she could. Beveridge was one catch, as were the liberal academics Gilbert Murray and Ramsay Muir, the Conservative MPs Arthur Steel-Maitland and Francis Fremantle, the socialists H.N. Brailsford and Barbara Drake, and even the eugenicists R.A. Fisher and Dampier Whetham. Churchmen, lawyers, medical men and even such sometime Rathbone critics as Ray Strachey and Viscountess Rhondda (who was happy to support family

22. Family Endowment
Society leaflet, 1930.

Price 1d.

THE FAMILY ENDOWMENT SOCIETY

UTOPIA CALLING!

Miss E. F. Rathbone, M.P.

A Plea for Family Allowances from
an Address Broadcast by Miss
Eleanor Rathbone, M.P., from
Northern Stations on February 11th,
1930

endowment as long as it wasn't labelled a 'feminist' reform) also found a place
on the FES's Council.

This rather disparate group could coexist amicably because the Society advocated only 'a more adequate method than at present of making provision for
families'[40] and not any particular scheme: socialists favouring tax-funded grants
to mothers and industrialists intrigued by continental efforts to use allowances
to restrain wages never had to come to terms. Rathbone preferred it that way:
proprietary about the movement, she was anxious to keep it from being hijacked
by any one party or creed. A small Executive Committee chaired by Kathleen
Courtney and including Macadam, Hubback and Stocks actually ran the Society;
a few enthusiasts – Stocks, Hubback, the Society's honorary secretary Olga
Vlasto, the insurance expert Joseph L. Cohen, and of course Rathbone – did most
of its considerable public speaking and wrote most of its literature.[41] Rathbone
herself kept up a steady stream of letters to the press, briefs for government

bodies, specialist essays and (in time) BBC broadcasts; she also met most of the Society's operating expenses out of her own pocket.

Masquerading as a broad-based political movement, the FES was to some extent just the NUSEC inner circle under a different name. And yet, Rathbone was not quite candid when she assured Beveridge that council members were recruited only as 'names' and not expected to do anything at all.[42] They were expected to offer entrée: column inches in the journals they edited, a place at the table when questions of economic policy were discussed. Few fulfilled that charge as handsomely as Beveridge, who secured an invitation for Rathbone to give evidence to the Royal Commission on the Coal Industry in 1925, hosted a major conference at the London School of Economics one year later, and even introduced a scheme of allowances for the school's staff which she could point to and publicize. But some other members proved almost as useful. R.A. Fisher forced a debate over endowment on to the agenda of the Eugenics Society; H.N. Brailsford brought her ideas before the leadership of the Independent Labour Party and her words to the readers of the *New Leader*; E.D. Simon and Ramsay Muir played a similar role for the Liberals. Although never a Fabian, Rathbone needed no lessons in the strategy of 'permeation'.

Her own expanding political commitments offered opportunities too. Rathbone's international research gave her a wide knowledge of child welfare policies; through regular attendance at the congresses of the International Women's Suffrage Alliance, she had excellent contacts abroad. In early 1925, then, when the League of Nations gave its Advisory Committee on the Traffic in Women and Children new responsibilities for child welfare, a number of international women's organizations – including the International Women's Suffrage Alliance, the Young Women's Christian Association and the International Federation of University Women – joined together to secure her appointment as an 'assessor' to the committee. Within a few weeks, Rathbone had written to Rachel Crowdy, the formidable head of the League's Social Questions section, to suggest that the committee investigate family allowances and other economic provisions for children;[43] when the committee met in May, she persuaded them to collaborate with the International Labour Organization on this inquiry. Through the 1920s, these international bodies collected information on family allowances – a development that allowed Rathbone to cite international support for such schemes and that relieved her of some of the burden of tracking foreign developments.[44]

These efforts turned 'family endowment' into a live issue. Already by 1926, the Family Endowment Society was reporting a steady growth in requests for literature and speakers. Most audiences now had some preliminary acquaintance with the question, and numerous bodies – including the Women's Liberal Federation, the Independent Labour Party, the Women's Co-operative Guild and the National Union of Teachers – had it under consideration.[45] Two years later, the situation seemed yet more hopeful. The Liberal Party's 'Yellow Book' on industrial policy published in anticipation of an election campaign recommended – citing Rathbone's work – that family allowances be considered in selected industries.[46] Better yet, the Labour Party and the Trades Union Congress – the two bodies most concerned to protect wages – had begun an investigation. Support for family allowances featured in many election addresses in 1929, the Society reported; its three organizers found themselves swamped with work.[47]

Rathbone deserves credit for this accomplishment, but the Society's limitations can also be traced to her door. For if her willingness to welcome allies from all parts of the political spectrum gained attention for her cause, it also left it curiously adrift, particularly attractive to intellectuals and experts of no fixed political abode, yet vulnerable to misinterpretation or appropriation beyond these restricted circles. Only a small number of people felt (as Rathbone did) that a redistribution of income from the childless to those with children was desirable *in itself*; only a few probably grasped that a new distributive principle (and not just some worthy programme for children) was at stake. Most other audiences judged endowment by other criteria: not for its efficacy in meeting children's needs, but for its possible impact on their own favourite causes, whether population growth or population restriction, economic expansion or wage restraint, women's emancipation or the enhancement of male authority. And here, of course, the devil was in the detail, for different sorts of 'endowment' would promote very different (even antithetical) ends.

Take, for example, the interesting case of the reception of Rathbone's campaign by those whose main preoccupation was with the size and (as they saw it) the 'quality' of the population. Since endowment meant, in essence, paying for children, Rathbone knew that its impact on population would always be a major concern. In the late 1930s, partly under Eva Hubback's influence, Rathbone would argue that family allowances could reverse Britain's projected decline in population; in 1924, however, with unemployment rampant and the prospect of war remote, such concerns were far from her (or her reader's) mind. The objection she had to answer was, instead, that endowment would lead to an 'indiscriminate' increase in births, especially lower down the social scale. The higher-than-average fertility of the poor was already of obsessive interest to the Eugenics Society – that coterie of scientific and military gentlemen who invariably equated genetic 'fitness' with membership of that class to which they themselves belonged. Rathbone was willing to go some distance to answer their concerns. In *The Disinherited Family*, she agreed that the differential birth rate was 'disquieting' and claimed, rather ingeniously, that allowances would probably narrow that gap. Those in more comfortable circumstances were likely to deliberately restrict births, she noted; by increasing the family's self-respect and comfort, allowances might then deter excessive child-bearing among the lowest strata while enabling the already prudent to have an additional, desired, child.[48] When invited to speak to the Eugenics Society in November 1924, she repeated these arguments, even endorsing the ideal of a graduated system in order to preserve (as with social security) existing differentials between classes.[49]

But not all of the Eugenics Society's members were persuaded. No one would be made more prudent 'by the removal of some of the inducement to prudence', Leonard Darwin retorted in the discussion following Rathbone's talk: if allowances were paid to poorer families, they probably would have yet more children – and allowances would enable more of those children to survive. Darwin thought that would be disastrous. Rathbone had argued that allowances offered society 'a hand . . . on the tiller of maternity', he noted; if so, then the Eugenics Society must work 'to insure that the tiller of maternity is turned in the right direction'. But would a democracy ever accept 'that all men are not born equal', or ever tailor family allowances to eugenic ideals?[50] Darwin, clearly, doubted that – and many in the Eugenics Society shared his reservations. Thus, while the Eugenics Society (largely at R.A. Fisher's urging) supported income tax rebates for children and family allowances paid by occupation and at differential rates, the Society consistently opposed any state-funded flat-rate scheme.[51] Their support for allowances, in other words, was strictly conditional on their ability to make them serve their own goals. Such allies cannot have made Rathbone entirely comfortable. The eradication of child poverty (*all* child poverty) was one of her two fundamental aims (the other was the emancipation of mothers), and in *The Disinherited Family* she dismissed as 'contemptible' the attitude of those middle-class people who, well-off themselves, opposed alleviating the hardship of others on the grounds that such hardship might build character: 'I do not myself approve of these arrangements for making the sufferings of children a lash for their fathers' backs'.[52] Most eugenicists had no such compunctions.

The debate on the 'eugenic' implications of endowment shows the fragility of much support for Rathbone's cause, but it also reveals how very quickly arguments over population policy became, in Britain, arguments about class. In other countries, this was not so. In France, for example, pro-natalists eager to replenish their country's empty crèches in the face of a more populous Germany were quite indifferent to the social class from which such children would come; in Germany in the 1930s, racial preoccupations far outweighed concerns of class. But in Britain in the 1920s, class was the master category, its allegiances swamping all others, its nuances marking all aspects of social life. When discussing questions of population, then, and (still more) when discussing their likely impact on wages, Rathbone found herself – awkwardly, inevitably – enmeshed in the politics of class.

Would family allowances benefit the working or the 'capitalist' class? From the outset, Rathbone resisted posing the question in this way. The purpose of family endowment, she thought, was to equalize income across gender, and not across class, lines. And yet, as she came to realize, most practical experiments in family endowment – and the wildfire spread of employer-funded family allowances in France in particular – had been undertaken without much attention to women and with labour relations in mind. True, some French pioneers were driven by pro-natalist or Catholic teachings; for the most part, however, they saw allowances – which were paid by employer-controlled funds set up to equalize costs among firms in a given region or industry – as a means of restraining wage demands and stabilizing workforces in a period of inflation. French trade unions viewed such developments with ambivalence but were powerless to arrest them; in time, they came to argue for state control of the allowance system rather than for its abolition.[53] Rathbone followed French developments closely, and in *The Disinherited Family* gave a fair account of their operation. She could not grasp the extent of French employers' anti-union ambitions (since they did not admit those publicly), but what evidence there was of employer manipulation she included, even recounting how one French consortium had withheld allowance payments as a punishment for a one-day strike. And yet, revealingly, she insisted that such 'incidental uses' were 'not essential', stressing instead the tendency of some large funds to pay the allowance to the wife and noting that union opposition had abated.[54] Foreign evidence, Rathbone thought, supported her view that family endowment was, in itself, 'class-neutral': it was simply a better and more equitable way to distribute some portion of the wage.

Rathbone thus sought to publicize French employers' example, hoping that British employers might wish to follow their lead. Britain faced labour conditions quite as chaotic as those in France; it also had industries, notably mining, incapable of balancing the books while paying a 'living wage'. Yet, only the odd industrialist or two (Steel-Maitland being the prize catch) joined the Family Endowment Society; not until the late 1930s did a significant number of large or progressive firms pioneer schemes. Instead, interest came primarily from liberal economists and intellectuals seeking to damp down the smouldering labour conflicts of the 1920s. One of the most intractable such conflicts was in mining; it was in mining, consequently, that family allowances received their most serious consideration. Beveridge, once again, played a crucial role, arranging for Rathbone to bring a proposal before the Royal Commission charged with the impossible task of restoring the mining industry to unsubsidized efficiency.[55] Rathbone did so gladly: for years she had argued that mining – with its deep economic problems, clearly distinct workforce, and relatively high burden of child dependency – would benefit from an allowance scheme.[56] Current mining wages left one-fifth of all miners' children below Rowntree's most stringent poverty line, Rathbone told the Commission, but if one paid out even a small proportion of the total wage bill in allowances, one would lift all those children out of poverty.[57]

The Commission took the point, recommending that 'irrespective of the level of wages' some system of children's allowances be introduced.[58]

Of course, this recommendation, along with all the others, was overtaken by events, as miners and mine-owners marched inexorably towards the General Strike. But the Family Endowment Society did not let the matter die – and, in this case, moved beyond its usual lobbying and networking to try to elicit popular support. In the terrible year following the General Strike, FES organizers travelled through Yorkshire, Scotland and South Wales, handing out leaflets and talking to miners and their wives. Rathbone met with half a dozen regional executives of the Miners' Federation and was greatly impressed: they were, she wrote to Beveridge, 'the most intelligent working class audiences I have ever addressed', quick to see the real advantages and difficulties of allowances, and willing to contemplate even some sacrifices in order to make more adequate provision for children.[59] In 1928 the Miners' Federation resolved in favour of children's allowances, but only if funded out of taxation and not out of wages.[60]

This was not a programme that the Eugenics Society (for example) would favour, but it did make the FES's inner circle more comfortable. Most of them, Stocks and Courtney especially, were Labour supporters or of 'leftish' views; and saw 'endowment' as a way to reconcile justice to mothers with the labour movement's historic commitment to defend working-class living standards. They had noticed how enthusiastically working-class women at Labour conferences in the early 1920s followed discussions of endowment or 'mothers' pensions', and had been gratified in 1924 when the Independent Labour Party – at this stage still an important force – invited Rathbone to present the case for family allowances to its summer school.[61] By 1925, the ILP had a small expert committee (which included J.A. Hobson and H.N. Brailsford) examining how to secure a 'living wage'; by 1926, the committee thought it had the answer. Britain's economic problems (and working-class poverty) stemmed, the ILP's Living Wage Commission argued, from an over-reliance on foreign trade and a neglect of those domestic industries catering to working-class needs. Tax-funded children's allowances, however, could be part of the solution, since such income transfers would reduce family poverty and jump-start the economy in crucial domestic sectors.[62] That same year, the ILP asked the Labour Party to place family allowances on its immediate legislative agenda.[63]

Thus was born the Labour Party and Trade Union Congress's Joint Committee on the Living Wage, an inquiry set up to investigate the entire ILP proposal but which turned instead into a three-year battle over family allowances. Rathbone found the initial signs encouraging. The committee was chaired by Margaret Bondfield and included Ellen Wilkinson (already known to be a strong supporter), while some of the most important members of the Trades Union Congress's General Council and the Party's National Executive – among them the Labour

Party's chairman Arthur Henderson and the TUC's General Secretary Walter Citrine – also agreed to serve. The committee worked hard, taking evidence from groups inside and outside the labour movement, including Rathbone for the Family Endowment Society and Mary Stocks for the NUSEC. They understood that they were doing all this work for a reason, for as Henderson told the party conference, if the committee was favourable allowances could appear in the Party's manifesto for the forthcoming election.[64] The hopes of the FES ran high.

And so on 26 January 1928, in a spirit of optimism, Rathbone and three FES colleagues came to give evidence to the Joint Committee on the Living Wage. Rathbone gave one of her best performances. The Family Endowment Society supported the principle of better provision for families and had no view on the question of whether that provision should come from taxation or out of a redistribution of wages, she pointed out;[65] but in this roomful of progressives, and pressed by Citrine and Henderson, she made her own preferences clear. 'Personally I am decidedly in favour of a national scheme as the ultimate objective,'[66] she told Citrine; although she would support any measure that would ease the situation of family men in selected industries (such as mining), she would regret seeing a national system develop along French lines. Questioned closely on the sensitive issue of the likely impact on wages, Rathbone responded both intelligently and honestly. She did not – as some socialist supporters would do – make the absurd claim that allowances never had, and could never have, any impact on wages. As she pointed out, allowances would have to be paid for somehow, and 'there is no source of income you can name out of which family allowances could be paid that could not conceivably be paid in the way of increased wages'.[67] But she urged the committee to consider the case on its merits. What socialists should ask, she argued, was firstly whether the *total* share of income going to the working class would increase, and secondly whether the overall well-being of that class would increase – and to both of those questions Rathbone could give a resounding 'yes'. Any system funded even partially out of taxation or insurance would increase the total working-class piece of the pie. Moreover, since wages themselves depended less on employers' views of their workers' needs than on 'the real product of the industry and on the bargaining power of the parties',[68] such increases would probably not affect wages. Finally and most importantly, however, whatever the size of that working-class share, it would do more good, provide more real comfort and happiness, if it were distributed through wages *and* allowances rather than through wages alone. Convinced that family allowances were in the interests of the working class *as a whole*, Rathbone and her colleagues thought they could trust to socialist ideals and class feeling to bring the labour movement on board.[69]

Slowly, these hopes soured. By the spring, it was whispered that the committee was divided, and while only a minority of trade unionist members opposed allowances, this group appeared to include Citrine and the committee's theoretically impartial secretary, Walter Milne-Bailey. Milne-Bailey's summing up of the evidence in an interim report in the summer of 1928 was so biased and misleading that several committee members and witnesses (including the usually pliant Marion Phillips, the Party's chief woman officer) protested. Entirely out of the blue, that interim report presented the labour movement with a choice *between* family allowances and a laundry list of other social services; it also claimed – in defiance of the clearly stated views of the Labour Women's Conference and the Women's Co-operative Guild – that Labour women generally preferred the latter option. Probably to Citrine's and Milne-Bailey's surprise, however, a majority of the committee refused to accept this 'social services' alternative; what this majority would not do, however, was to act without the consent of the TUC. And that consent never came. The trade unionists on the committee consulted the TUC General Council; the General Council circularized affiliated unions – and then, when a majority of those unions reported back in support of allowances, still came down on the 'social services' side. By this point it was May 1930, the election had come and gone, and while there was now a Labour government in office, it was much too beset by the unemployment crisis to have any interest in new social spending. Aware of substantial support within the movement for allowances, the Party Executive did ask the TUC to continue the investigation, but Citrine flatly refused. Labour would not return to the issue of allowances until the Second World War.[70]

Rathbone was dreadfully disappointed, and from the moment she read Milne-Bailey's interim report, furious as well. Not only had her own evidence been misused, she wrote angrily, but the report contained assertions about allowances' likely impact on wages and about foreign developments that had been amply refuted by the FES.[71] Initially, Rathbone made these criticisms privately, but as the General Council dug in its heels the FES began to carry a running commentary on its errors in the Society's *Monthly Notes*.[72] More dangerously, Rathbone also tried to exploit the divisions within the movement, persuading Beveridge and other allies to sign a letter calling on the TUC to publish the committee's favourable *majority* report, and helping to set up a 'Labour Family Allowances Group' to demonstrate internal labour movement support.[73]

All of these tactics backfired. Rathbone thought she could bring the pressure of 'public opinion' to bear on the trade union movement, but Walter Citrine and Ernest Bevin – always the movement's most influential voices – didn't much care what William Beveridge and his liberal friends thought. Nor did Rathbone's hectoring letters help. In August 1928 Milne-Bailey told Margaret Bondfield that he had no intention of listening to Rathbone's bullying,[74] and the Trade Union Group in the Commons likewise went out of its way to condemn the 'sharp practice' of the FES.[75] Many years later, when the General Council of the TUC finally fell in behind allowances, Citrine admitted that its earlier opposition had, if anything, been hardened by its encounters with the ILP, not to mention the FES,[76] both of which were seen as troublesome bands of middle-class intellectuals with no practical experience of industrial affairs. As guardians of trade union interests, Citrine and Bevin considered not whether allowances would aid working-class children or even increase the share of income going to 'the working class' as a whole (the issues Rathbone thought they should focus on) but rather whether they would in any way compromise the power of the union movement or the level of the wage. Both had reservations on these points and concluded that since allowance systems might affect bargaining in unanticipated ways, the safest strategy was to keep shy of them.

Although defensive and less than solidaristic, this was not an unreasonable position, but Rathbone could never quite understand it. She had no interest in the health of the trade union movement and no particular attachment to the system of collective bargaining; indeed, having watched the craft unions collude to exclude women before and during the First World War, she had come to see trade unionism almost entirely as a means of defending male privilege. Milne-Bailey's machinations over allowances simply confirmed her in that view: as Ellen Wilkinson perceptively noted, Rathbone refused to worry too much about the impact of allowances on wages because she had 'a shrewd conviction that if she and those like her look after the women the men will, as usual, look after their own interests adequately'.[77] To her mind, the TUC veto merely demonstrated, once again, the power of the 'Turk complex' – of that essential masculine will to power.

She was not, of course, entirely wrong. Confronted with the history of women's domestic subjection – a history that Rathbone herself did so much to bring to light – one is driven, almost inevitably, to see the sexes locked in a struggle for power, and to see men's superior economic position as just one tool in that fight. Yet, one can also understand why working-class men (like middle-class men) found such explanations offensive. For Rathbone was attacking not only the economic bases of male power but also the foundations of male self-respect; she cast doubt not only on men's *ability* but also (and more shockingly) on their *willingness* to maintain their wives. The trade union MP Rhys Davies, Rathbone's bitterest opponent, grasped this: allowances, he insisted, were an objectionable sort of 'truck system' cooked up by the 'ardent feminist' who 'distrusts the father to do his duty to his wife and children'.[78] Rathbone might retort that she had reasons for her mistrust, but her statistics on differential food consumption within families – not to mention her heavy ironies about the difficulty men seemed to have in deciding whether to keep pigeons or keep their wives – unquestionably grated. Responsible husbands, after all, denied themselves much in order to support their families and felt a measure of pride for doing so; a hard-won 'family wage' was seen, in most working-class communities, as a sign of male virtue and the basis of a comely and ordered family life. Eleanor was not wrong to see this economic structure as a crucial foundation of male power, but she underestimated its cultural and ethical reach. Her own father had seen his business activity as a means of guaranteeing his family's independence and comfort, and many working-class men viewed skilled and well-paid jobs in much the same way. Quite understandably, they resented Rathbone's propensity to see the 'family wage' only as a cloak for male domination.

Rathbone's persistent attention to sex bias made for touchy relations with the Labour Party and helps us to understand Rathbone's non-party stance. Most of her close friends and allies were Labour supporters; on the Liverpool City Council (and, later, in Parliament) she almost always supported the Labour bloc. For all that, though, she would never join the Labour Party – and not only because she relished her independence. Rather, she thought Labour – like all parties – hopelessly male dominated, interested in women's issues and women leaders only if they helped the Party capture the 'woman's vote'. Marion Phillips, Rathbone thought, played that role to perfection. 'The special mission of this type of woman in the eyes of the men of her own political party and consequently of her own,' Rathbone wrote in *The Disinherited Family* (and with Phillips clearly in mind) was 'to marshal the women voters behind the party banner and to prevent their energies being "dissipated" or their minds "confused" by mingling with women of other parties . . . and so discovering the bond between them'.[79] Rathbone clashed repeatedly with Phillips over Labour's unwillingness to collaborate with the NUSEC in the 1920s, but was certain such proscriptions couldn't last for ever. Even 'less advanced and articulate' working-class women were developing 'a very unmistakable sense of sex-grievance as well as class-grievance'; 'the development of this sense of sex grievance into a sense of sex solidarity and an articulate demand for the economic independence of women is . . . only a matter of time'.[80] Rathbone hoped to stoke those grievances until they became incendiary.

The labour movement's negative decision on allowances – and, still more, the world recession – effectively blocked any prospect of a national scheme for more than a decade. Rathbone saw the way the wind was blowing and scaled back the Family Endowment Society's operations. She did not, however, think its years of intense activity had been wasted, nor believe that her strategic emphases had been wrong. Family endowment would conceivably have aroused more interest among employers if presented as a means of reducing wages or controlling workers; it could perhaps have won more support among trade unionists if allowances were – like other social benefits – to be paid *to* the working man. But to make these arguments Rathbone would have had to abandon her core progressive and feminist beliefs, and this she flatly refused to do. She had founded the FES to win support for her cause beyond those feminist and philanthropic circles within which she moved, but she could never quite hide the ideas behind its birth. Many found her feminism unpalatable, but so completely did she 'own' this issue that other understandings of endowment were inevitably pushed to the sidelines. In the 1930s, Rathbone would marshal new arguments and find new supporters for family allowances, but the movement would never entirely lose its radical, feminist edge. Family allowances would come in on her terms, she had decided, or not at all.

Chapter 12

Most Independent Member

Eleanor Rathbone worked so hard on family endowment in the late 1920s because she thought it might have a chance of success. With party rivalry at its height, leaders and strategists were casting about for electorally appealing policies. None opted for family allowances, but all parties concentrated on domestic and economic issues in the run-up to the 1929 election, and all kept an anxious eye on women under thirty, who would cast their votes for the first time. Labour had reason to be optimistic: it had a 'young' image, an experienced leader, and a comprehensive (and uncosted) blueprint for an emergency attack on the scourge of unemployment. But the Liberals, reunited under Lloyd George, also promised to 'conquer unemployment' (and steal Labour's thunder) with a proto-Keynesian package of investment and public works. Even the Conservatives, while urging the public to resist Lloyd George's 'stunts' and plump for 'safety first', stressed their own commitment to economic revival and public works; they could moreover point to equal franchise legislation and Neville Chamberlain's list of accomplishments (from widows' pensions to Poor Law abolition) as Minister of Health when courting women voters.[1] A record number of Britons went to the polls on 30 May, and this time no one had any real idea how it would all come out.

Rathbone waited for the results anxiously, for she was again a candidate. With women's questions so often before the House, and so few feminists there to speak to them, Rathbone had been itching to try again. True, she still wouldn't join a party, but might another strategy be possible? Some time in the mid-1920s, she turned a calculating eye on the university seats. England's ancient universities had long been represented in Parliament, and as the number of universities grew in the nineteenth century, so too had the number of university seats. Graduates of the respective universities were eligible to vote for these seats (provided they took the trouble to register), and given the class composition of most university graduates and the decline of the Liberal Party, by 1918 most of the twelve were Conservative strongholds. In 1924, however, the University of London had been won by an idiosyncratic academic Independent, and Rathbone thought that the constituency of which her own Liverpool University formed a part seemed even more hopeful. The two-member constituency of Combined English Universities had been added in 1918 to give some representation to the new provincial universities of Birmingham, Bristol, Leeds, Liverpool, Manchester, Reading and Sheffield, along with the University of Durham. These universities' graduate constituents were a good deal more progressive than Oxford and Cambridge graduates, and a steadily growing proportion (although still a minority) were women. The Liberal Party had thus been able to hold one of the Combined English Universities seats throughout the twenties, and the Labour vote was growing as well. Rathbone – with her record of intellectual achievement and her long-standing ties to Liverpool University – might appeal to just such voters. Her friends made sure she staked her claim early. In July 1928 *The Times* reported that she had accepted an invitation to stand;[2] the following winter a powerful committee of professors and lecturers gathered pledges on her behalf.[3] And when Baldwin dissolved Parliament in the spring of 1929, Rathbone – against the gentlemanly tradition of avoiding electioneering in university seats – travelled to the various university towns to explain her candidacy. Those meetings were smallish and quiet, and while 'no one seemed to bother much about the sex of the candidate', women outnumbered men.[4] Audiences seemed pleased by Rathbone's non-party status and attracted by her record of intellectual and practical achievement, but no one knew whether this particular venture would go further. Only thirteen women – none of them Independents – had made their way into Parliament since women's enfranchisement in 1918.

But when the election results began coming in, it was clear that the country had seen a shift in mood. The Conservatives and Labour had polled roughly the same number of votes, but Labour had more seats. Baldwin therefore resigned, and on 5 June 1929 Ramsay MacDonald formed his second minority government. That government included Margaret Bondfield, who as Minister of Labour became Britain's first woman cabinet minister. And while the 'flapper election' hadn't quite fulfilled feminist hopes, the number of women MPs – although still tiny – increased, with nine Labour women, three Conservatives and one Liberal entering the House. On 4 June the *Manchester Guardian* announced that Rathbone would be joining them; to her own surprise and delight, she found that – in university after university – she had led the poll.[5] Elections in the university seats used the system of the 'transferable vote', in which electors ranked choices and a victorious candidate's 'extra' votes were distributed among those second choices, and since Eleanor was a less attractive 'second choice' in the end she came in second, slightly behind the Conservative but well ahead of the Liberal candidate. But this meant that she was now an MP, joining Martin Conway, a Conservative former Professor of Art who had held the partner seat since 1918. She missed the first two weeks of the session, since she was off in Berlin for the Congress of the International Alliance of Women, but on 27 June she was sworn in and took her place in the chamber, choosing a seat just behind the Liberals – quite possibly the spot where her father had sat some thirty-five years earlier.

Rathbone's election made for some changes in the ménage at Romney Street. Eleanor would now have to be in London continuously during the parliamentary session from November until June. She would need more support and more space. Up to this point, she had kept much of her library and her secretary at her spacious Liverpool house. In London, where the National Union of Societies for Equal Citizenship and the Family Endowment Society each had a paid staff, she had made do with some help from Evie's married daughter, Nancy Warr. But now, Elizabeth insisted, Eleanor would need a real secretary. Unfortunately, there was no space to house this useful person. Romney Street, although a convenient stone's throw from the Commons (Rathbone would be able to pop home for dinner most nights) had been built to house a single family and was already bursting at the seams. Nor did Eleanor's Liverpool secretary have any interest in moving to London.

Within a few months, all this had been sorted out. Doris Hardman (later Cox), untrained but enthusiastic, was hired as Rathbone's secretary and an office rented for her over a nearby dairy. Hardman never quite knew why she got the job when the NUSEC's capable parliamentary secretary had wanted it, but she perceptively guessed that Eleanor – who after all had Macadam fussing over her – just didn't want another efficient person taking her in charge. In the event, Hardman and Rathbone suited each other well. Hardman was young, flexible and eager to learn. She didn't mind picking up after her formidable but absent-minded boss and would cheerfully meet Rathbone at all hours in the Commons lobby to take dictation. ('You should be grateful,' Elizabeth told her. 'Lady Astor dictates her letters through the lavatory door.') The whole operation was a bit scattershot, Hardman recalled, for neither of them knew how long the current parliament would last, but the mere fact that Rathbone had a full-time secretary set her apart from at least some of the Labour women MPs, who struggled with their voluminous mailbags entirely on their own.[6]

With money, space, a surrogate 'political wife' and ample secretarial help, Rathbone had the supports in place for a productive parliamentary career. She also had her own unique advantages: long experience in parliamentary lobbying, wide knowledge in many areas of social policy, a rugged constitution and a fine analytical mind. But she faced some daunting challenges. In three ways, she was 'exceptional': she was female; she was a political independent; and she sat for a university seat. Any one of these three could render an MP marginal or irrelevant. Eleanor's time in the Commons – and, even more, the length of that time – would depend on whether, and how quickly, she could make this unusual situation work to her advantage.

Of these three disabilities, sex might seem the worst one. After all, men still out-numbered women in the House by a factor of more than forty to one. At no point between 1919 and 1929 were there more than nine women in the Commons, and if that figure rose to a high of fourteen or fifteen between 1929 and 1935, after the 1935 election the numbers actually went down. Thelma Cazalet, who entered the House at a by-election in 1931, recalled that there was still 'something slightly freakish about a woman M.P.'; her male colleagues used to point her out to their friends 'as though I were a sort of giant panda'.[7] Few expressed their resentment as openly as Winston Churchill, who – the legend went – had told Lady Astor that he felt as if she had entered his bathroom when he was undefended by so much as a sponge ('nonsense, Winston, you're not attractive enough to have fears of this sort,' she had replied),[8] but many responded with an amused tolerance or with that exaggerated chivalry that often cloaks contempt. There were some staunch friends to women too, of course, but also plenty of instances of what, today, we would call sexual harassment. The diminutive red-haired Labour member Ellen Wilkinson had to endure prolonged cheering when she entered the chamber in a striking green dress, and the press accounts of women MPs' maiden speeches read like coverage of débutantes' presentation at Court. The private facilities for the women MPs weren't all that much worse than those for their male colleagues – they had a small shared room for reading and correspondence and in 1931 finally gained a room in which to change and have a bath – but the ostensibly 'public' facilities were far from welcoming. Only gradually did the dining rooms of the House open to them, and the smoking room – where, as several of them remarked, crucial lobbying was often done[9] – remained strictly off limits. They were MPs, yes, but they were also women, and the House never quite let them forget it.[10]

The first few among them adapted in different ways. Nancy Astor, the pioneer, thought her mere presence would be affront enough and tried to be sartorially unobjectionable. She looked demure, in her neat black suits and tricorn hat, but – as the House quickly learned – she was brave and irrepressible, adept at verbal repartee and willing to resort to less orthodox methods when that failed (she once seized an opponent's coat-tails to prevent him from rising).[11] Doing her best to promote her favourite causes of temperance and child welfare she felt, she told friends, like a voice crying in the wilderness – except that her wilderness some-times answered back! The women who followed her had an easier time. Margaret Wintringham, a Liberal who had taken over her well-liked husband's seat in 1921, had a placid, comfortable manner and was easily accepted; the Liberal Mabel Philipson, who likewise succeeded her husband in 1923, could take advan-tage of her experience and popularity as a stage actress. Others won a place through competence and loyalty. Katharine, Duchess of Atholl, a Conservative elected for Perthshire in 1923, proved so meticulous and reliable that Stanley Baldwin made her a junior minister eleven months later, and several of Labour's first women members – Susan Lawrence, Margaret Bondfield – were veteran activists with strong party reputations. Astor, whose party feelings were pretty weak, cheerfully joined Ellen Wilkinson in harrying the Baldwin government on equal franchise, and occasionally women members banded together on narrow welfare questions (boots for schoolchildren, for example) but such cross-party cooperation was the exception. For the most part, women hoped that loyalty to party would wash out the stain of sex.

Except, of course, for Eleanor, who had no party and wouldn't have thought much of this strategy anyway. In her election address, Rathbone had argued that her years of 'special study of the needs and wishes of women' were an asset and not a disqualification for Parliament,[12] and her election was celebrated even within the 'equalitarian' camp as a great victory for feminism.[13] Alone among the women MPs, then, Rathbone embraced her 'disability', proclaiming her loyalty to the women's movement and later even telling the House that she was a 'whole-hearted feminist', a '100 percent feminist'.[14] She made a real effort to reach women voters, giving several BBC talks (at Hilda Matheson's invitation) aimed at women listeners and writing a column for the *Woman's Leader* under the pen-name of 'Cross Bench'.[15] Two of her first parliamentary interventions were about the politically untouchable subjects of British women's access to birth control and (amazingly) the practice of clitoridectomy in Africa,[16] and she teamed up with Ellen Wilkinson and other women supporters to press that key feminist demand – the right of women to retain their nationality on marriage. For seventeen years, Rathbone never failed to defend the cause of 'equal citizenship' or to rise to defend women from charges of political apathy or economic incapacity.

One might have expected her feminism to have destroyed her: after all, few men would welcome lectures from a spinster on the injustices suffered by their daughters and wives. And yet, while Rathbone did sometimes face sarcastic comments about her 'obviously well-informed' views on marriage, she actually came in for surprisingly little sexist abuse.[17] Partly, of course, she was safe because she was middle-aged and (frankly) uninteresting to look at: with her uniform of shapeless black dresses and her bag bulging with files, she looked, as Ellen Wilkinson remarked affectionately, like 'what she is, a great public institution'.[18] But she also took care to master the facts: if she didn't have Nancy Astor's gift of witty badinage or her willingness to be charmingly outrageous, she also lacked Astor's habit of blundering in unprepared. True, she had a tendency to talk too fast – in the thick of debate, the words would tumble out one after another – but she was consistent, logical and not easily distracted. Edith Picton-Turbervill likened her to a 'sledge-hammer' driving her points home; hostile interruptions (and on some questions, such as family allowances, she had to face these regularly) never threw her off.[19] She could trade quotations from Mill, correct members' Latin, and explain demographic predictions or the intricacies of unemployment assistance regulations without losing her grip. Only very rarely (and very unconvincingly) would anyone accuse Rathbone of a 'female' abhorrence of logic.[20]

And here – with her opponents' inability to brand her as 'female' – we get to the heart of the matter. Rathbone could speak feminism and emerge unscathed because her style was so 'unfeminine'. If anything, in her preference for rational argument and her careful avoidance of personal attack, she behaved in ways more commonly thought of as male. That ambiguous style had been part of Rathbone's aura from young womanhood: Margery Fry, for example, described Rathbone's manners at Somerville as 'gentlemanly',[21] and her colleagues in the suffrage movement also occasionally spoke of her in masculine terms.[22] Rathbone would not have thought of it that way – it was an article of faith to her that women were as capable of reasoned argument as men – but in a culture prone to code reason as male and emotion as female, Rathbone's style (and sometimes her language) placed her firmly on one side. In an exchange widely and delightedly reported in the press, Rathbone once chastised Aneurin Bevan for 'cattish displays of feline malice' – derogatory and distinctly gendered language no one would have dared use against Rathbone herself.[23] She 'despises . . . feminine wiles', Wilkinson said in 1930, an insight that helps explain why Rathbone's relations with Astor were never very close (for all Astor's willingness to leap to Rathbone's defence).[24] One Conservative member praised, instead, the 'manly forthrightness' of her speeches; the *Manchester Guardian* correspondent was struck by the 'masculine solidity' of her mind.[25]

But if Rathbone's formidable intellect and 'masculine' style spared her some of the ridicule her feminism might otherwise have aroused, they didn't exactly endear her to the House. She may have been the only woman MP who could say (as she did when arguing for women's right to keep their nationality on marriage) that when she looked around at her fellow members she wondered 'that any woman wants to marry anybody',[26] but Olympian distance of this sort could easily put people off. Male Conservative MPs would never have clubbed together to buy Eleanor an electric cooker (as they did for their fiery opponent, Ellen Wilkinson), and if Astor tried members' patience with her incessant interruptions, she at least put on a good show. Eleanor, by contrast, was sometimes thought 'a bit of a bore': shy and awkward in personal settings, in political exchanges she could be strident and (as Doris Hardman recalled) 'sort of governessy'.[27] Her political independence compounded this risk, for being free of party she could not count on the whips to rein her in and (if necessary) shut her up. Rathbone's sex may have been less of a disability than one might have expected, but her independence was more of one: she would need to hone her political skills if her parliamentary career were to last longer than a session.

Certainly an 'independent' member seemed an oddity in 1929. With Labour and Conservatives fairly even in strength, and the Liberals holding the balance of power, party cohesion should have been at a premium. But all three party leaders were having great trouble controlling their ranks. MacDonald spent two years struggling with escalating attacks from a restive left wing comprised of portions of the Independent Labour Party and, in time, the worried TUC Group and the breakaway Mosleyites; Baldwin was preoccupied with divisions over protection and then an out-and-out revolt from a Churchillian right angry at his support for Indian conciliation; Lloyd George struggled to hold together a 'centre party' in a parliamentary system structured to force a division into two opposing blocs.[28] Amid this rage of party, small wonder a newly minted Independent had trouble making herself heard. Rathbone spoke up on women's issues and on housing (the subject of her maiden speech),[29] but her tendency to turn speeches on house subsidies or unemployment assistance into disquisitions on the need for a system of family allowances often led Colonel Fitzroy, the Speaker of the House ('a walking frigidaire towards any idea coming from a woman M.P.,'[30] Thelma Cazalet-Keir recalled) to intervene. Rathbone was repeatedly ruled out of order and forced to sit down.[31]

But in late 1930, after eighteen exciting if frustrating months, the Labour government suddenly handed Rathbone what looked at first like a noose but turned out to be a lifeline. Right before the Christmas recess, it introduced an Electoral Reform Bill which would, among other things, have abolished the university seats altogether. Given its dependence on Liberal support to stay in power, the Labour government had little choice but to agree to Liberal demands for some measure of electoral reform. The Liberal Party, having watched its numbers in Parliament steadily decline, favoured proportional representation; the Labour Party was not willing to go that far, but did offer the alternative of the transferable vote. In return, however, Labour wanted to abolish all vestiges of plural voting and any seats dependent on such privileges. The university seats were one obvious target. There were twelve such seats, and since most had returned Conservatives steadily throughout the 1920s, neither Labour nor the Liberal Party would be sorry to see them go.

Rathbone thus faced the prospect of being ousted. Worse, her expulsion would be on democratic grounds and at the hands of those two parties with whom she usually agreed. Could she, in good faith, argue against such a bill? Interestingly, she could – and 'independence' came to her rescue. During the winter of 1930–31 Rathbone brought the Vice-Chancellors and university members together to plan a campaign and circularized her own constituents to enlist support for university representation.[32] In the spring, when the bill came before Parliament, she was ready. Her first argument had to do with her understanding of the nature of democratic representation itself. The abolition of university representation was proposed, she noted, on democratic grounds. But the great theorists of liberal democracy had never asserted that universal suffrage would produce a genuinely 'representative' Parliament, one that would be 'broadly based upon the people's will', without some safeguards 'for the fair representation of minorities'. Even Mill had worried about the 'tyranny' of class interests; even the Irish historian William Lecky warned of the sycophancy and demagoguery to which mass politics was prone. But here, Rathbone argued, the university franchise could play a role. The value of such a franchise was not (as Mill had it) plural voting *per se*: university graduates didn't especially deserve – in themselves – to receive extra votes. They did, however, deserve to have learning and education *matter* – and these would matter, she pointed out, only if voters who embodied such values were grouped into constituencies of their own. Class-based parties could be trusted to defend the interests of capital and labour: the extra votes handed out to property-owners were (she agreed) indefensible. But class-based parties would never put a premium on impartial knowledge and expertise – values that were represented, however imperfectly, through the university vote.[33]

Of course one could retort – and some Labour members did – that the historical record was not on Rathbone's side. The university seats were Conservative strongholds; in practice if not in theory they bolstered a class-based Tory dominance that Labour was determined to break. But was that linkage inevitable? 'Do not make the mistake of judging the future by the past.' For the universities, Rathbone knew, were changing. The majority of students at her own civic universities came up through the state system; as many as half were on some form of aid.[34] Those younger graduates were looking for something different: for freedom 'from the ascendancy of party wire-pullers', for representatives 'with a more independent point of view'.[35] 'It has always been my dream . . . that we should be able to cut away this vital connection between party politics and university representation,' Rathbone told the House – and, from conversations with her own constituents, she thought that goal within reach. In an argument that justified the university seats but that also made them hostage to her own ideal of 'independence', Rathbone rhetorically transformed these seats into a haven – possibly the last haven – for the election of members free of party ties.[36] Amazingly, the argument worked. As Rathbone reported in the *Woman's Leader*, 'the huddled flock of University M.P.s awaiting the sacrificial knife . . . never for a moment expected salvation from the House of Commons',[37] but to their astonishment they found it. To the disgust of their whips, enough Labour and Liberal members abstained on the clause abolishing the university seats to secure its defeat by a scant margin of four.

Rathbone's argument about the progressive potential of the university vote played some role in this outcome; it also turned Combined English Universities into her own personal 'safe seat'. The University of Durham awarded her an honorary MA in 1930, and in December 1931 – having watched her lead the poll in the October election – Liverpool University cited her as 'at once a champion and a justification' of the university vote and made her an honorary Doctor of Laws.[38] Diligent constituency work cemented this loyalty. Traditionally, the university

MPs were an indolent lot, rarely electioneering and making little effort to discover and represent particular university concerns. But Rathbone changed that, keeping in close touch with 'her' universities, taking care to keep abreast of any matters affecting graduates, and speaking regularly to alumni and student associations. In January 1933 she began sending her constituents an annual letter and continued that practice until 1940 – an innovation that allowed her to dissipate some of the dislike felt for her anti-appeasement stance. Those letters usually ended with an invitation to visit her in Romney Street and an offer to secure tickets to a parliamentary debate – a degree of hospitality and personal attentiveness that must have been rare not only in university MPs but in MPs in general. In 1935, having played a prominent role in the debates over Indian devolution, she was returned unopposed.

Prophecy created fulfilment, as Rathbone's argument about the logical link between independence and university representation began to affect other contests as well. In 1935, in a move that the psephologist David Butler has called 'the turn of the tide', the literary journalist A.P. Herbert won one of the University of Oxford seats as an Independent.[39] By-elections in 1937 produced two more Independents, with Sir Arthur Salter, then Gladstone Professor of Government, winning the second Oxford seat after Lord Hugh Cecil's retirement and T.E. Harvey (with Rathbone's endorsement)[40] taking the second Combined English Universities seat away from the Conservatives. Rathbone rejoiced: she set the fashion, she told a group of Durham graduates, but now all four of the candidates contesting a Scottish Universities by-election were standing as Independents.[41] By 1945 – the year when Rathbone gained more 'first preference' votes than all five of the other candidates for her seat together – Independents won fully seven of the twelve university seats.

With representatives of this quality, the Independents developed a kind of party spirit of their own. A.P. Herbert recalled feeling, on crucial votes, that he ought not to '"let the Independents down" by voting without due thought and care'. Their votes, he thought, served a crucial diagnostic role: when the parties were 'furiously raging together', votes cast free of partisan considerations could show party leaders 'which way the pure air of free opinion blows'.[42] Sir Arthur Salter agreed: especially in the late 1930s, when Chamberlain's whips did all they could to prevent Conservatives from expressing objections to appeasement, the speeches of the Independents – and, still more, their reception by ostensibly loyal Conservatives – could throw 'a new light . . . on the real opinion of the House'.[43] Rathbone, obviously, felt this way as well. Thus, even though she knew her vote would never affect any particular outcome, she made a point of voting on major resolutions and controversial pieces of legislation and of explaining the reasons for her adherence or dissent. She also routinely used her independence to claim the prerogative of introducing uncomfortable information or asking awkward questions. 'What is the use of university representation if university representatives cannot speak the truth as they see it?' she asked in December 1944, when drawing the House's attention to the awkward fact that its gallant Soviet ally appeared to be carrying out massive deportations of Poles in the East.[44]

The House only sometimes paid heed. Even her most admiring colleagues admitted that Rathbone never became popular in Parliament; many members continued to find themselves 'a little repelled by her forceful manner of expressing her opinions'.[45] Yet, by the mid-1930s she had become an accepted House institution – a bore, at times, surely, but one whose integrity and independence were beyond question. Rathbone's successful defence of university representation and (still more) her insistence that these seats should serve as conduits for impartial inquiry and the application of expertise were crucial to that standing. Political independence and her university seat should have made Rathbone politically vulnerable or irrelevant; instead, they gave her a place and a platform all her own.

But Rathbone hadn't entered the House to speak: she intended to get things done. Just what she wanted done changed after the Nazi seizure of power in 1933 and (even more) after the Abyssinian crisis of 1935, when fears for peace, parliamentary government and Europe's beleaguered democracies possessed her. During her first two parliaments, however, Rathbone spent most of her time on 'family matters', and especially on her long-standing effort to enhance the economic standing and political rights of 'disinherited' women and children. One aspect of that work – her engagement with the issue of child marriage in India – was so sustained that it must be treated on its own. But it had a domestic side as well, as she cast about for ways to bring her ideals of married women's equality and family endowment just a little bit closer.

What could an Independent backbencher do? Family endowment had not featured on Labour's election manifesto and, in any case, those election commitments were falling by the wayside as the government struggled to cope with the economic situation. But the Labour government did bring forward legislation to raise the school-leaving age and to expand subsidies for house-building, and on both of these issues, Rathbone thought, some modest supports for dependent children could be inserted into Labour's proposals.[46] On housing especially, Rathbone had well-thought-out and original plans, shaped by twenty years of experience on the Liverpool Housing Committee. Faced by serious housing shortages and a needy low-wage population, the Liverpool Corporation had pursued an activist policy, constructing some 20,000 subsidized homes during that first post-war decade. Rathbone had supported aggressive house-building, but had become quite critical of the arbitrary ways in which houses were allocated and subsidies used.[47] The Corporation's subsidies lowered house prices and rents across the board, she noted, but tenants' needs were not uniform: older or childless couples could often afford 'market rents', while families with many dependent children often couldn't pay even subsidized rents and drifted back to the slums.[48] Why not, then, use the subsidy differently – to lower the rents of larger families by introducing a 'rebate' for each minor child?[49] Rathbone began canvassing this proposal in the Liverpool City Council, in the newspapers, and in correspondence with the chairmen of other local housing authorities; once in Parliament, she teamed up with Ernest Simon, the long-time chairman of Manchester's Housing Committee and a personal friend, to try to amend Labour's housing bill in this 'pro-family' direction. Their amendment was not accepted, but the government did agree to allow local authorities themselves to use subsidies to 'rebate' rents.[50]

It was a modest beginning, but one that already shows a characteristic Rathbone technique. Throughout her years in Parliament, and to a degree unusual for a backbench MP, Rathbone tried to shape legislation, especially by introducing amendments. Some of these were feminist in intent, mandating representation of women on particular government bodies or opposing discriminatory legislation, and whilst they often failed, Rathbone also scored some successes. She and the Duchess of Atholl managed to have a bar on discrimination by sex added to a Labour resolution on colonial policy in 1930; despite complaints that they would thereby turn local authorities into 'matrimonial causes' bureaux, Labour also accepted her amendment stipulating that a proposed child maintenance allowance could be paid either to the father or the mother.[51] In that first parliament, Rathbone also introduced a private bill, long desired by the National Union of Societies for Equal Citizenship, limiting a man's ability to will his property to a third party without providing for his spouse or children, and while that bill was not permitted to proceed, a modified version was finally passed (after many tries) in 1938.[52] In the 1930s, Rathbone would mount much more complex amending campaigns (mobilizing the Conservative women MPs in 1934, for example, to expand the 'women's clauses' of the Government of India Bill), but these early efforts give us some intimation of things to come.

We also see Rathbone wielding the other tool of the backbench MP, the parliamentary question. Most backbench MPs (stars like Churchill, of course, excepted) couldn't count on their fellows (much less ministers) to come to listen to their speeches; during 'question time', however, they could confront ministers directly, and sometimes in front of a full House. Almost from the start, Rathbone was a master of the parliamentary question, using it to publicize issues, extract embarrassing information, or even force concessions. A fair number of the almost sixty questions Rathbone asked during the period of the second Labour government were aimed at forcing ministers to act to combat child marriage in India (or at least to own up to inaction), but she asked questions about housing and child welfare as well. Once again, this was a foretaste of things to come. Rathbone made only a dozen or so major speeches a year during the first years of the National government, but her barrage of parliamentary questions continued. By the mid-1930s, she was asking two or more each week and on some sensitive subjects – British policy towards Abyssinia, for example, or the extent of British knowledge of German and Italian violations of the non-intervention pact in Spain – she proved absolutely unrelenting, feeding questions to amenable but less hard-working colleagues as well. Worse, having her own sources of information and being immune to party discipline, she proved extraordinarily hard to shut up. Sometimes the mere threat of a parliamentary question was enough to force ministers or officials to see her.

Most of this lay in the future: apart from the housing bill, the Labour government offered Rathbone few chances to promote her social policy goals. Instead, she found herself watching (and, in her 'Cross Bench' column, chronicling) the bitter fratricidal struggle developing between the Cabinet and the renegade Independent Labour Party over the government's orthodox economic policy. Her sympathies were with the ILP: she had been persuaded by ILP claims that one could jump-start the economy by redistributing income towards working-class households; like the ILP, she was willing to fund social programmes through steep inheritance taxes and thought Philip Snowden's first budget much too timid.[53] And yet Rathbone was not a socialist: she wanted meaningful child welfare policies, not class-conscious government. When James Maxton finally brought the ILP's Living Wage Bill to the Commons in February 1931 stripped of the child allowances that had been a core component of their plan, she told him shortly that a 'living wage' was impossible without child allowances and declined to support it.[54] And while Rathbone joined the ILP renegades in their doomed attack on the government's July austerity measures, she did so only to defend married women and on feminist grounds.

Rathbone's intervention was one small stream in the cascade of criticism that was, by summer 1931, drenching the Labour government. With the numbers of unemployed more than double what they had been in 1929 and the unemployment fund kept afloat only by government borrowing, virtually all politicians outside the Labour Party were urging some cutback in insurance benefits. The ILP, by contrast, was appalled by Margaret Bondfield's willingness to contemplate 'economies'. In her columns in the *Woman's Leader*, Rathbone paid tribute to Bondfield's grace and stoicism in the face of daily, unrelenting attack. But when Bondfield finally unveiled a stopgap solution – an 'anomalies bill' introducing special regulations for groups (in particular seasonal workers, short-time workers and married women) alleged to be claiming benefit while not genuinely looking for work – Rathbone grew anxious. She knew how hard it was for married women to find work at all: many industries had reinstated the marriage bar or were sacking married women at the first signs of economic trouble. Why, exactly, were married women being singled out for further punitive attention? Rathbone asked Bondfield privately, and when Bondfield would only repeat that married women were particularly prone to 'abuse' the insurance fund, she tabled an amendment to delete the married women's clause entirely.[55] No other MP, however radical their beliefs, appears to have thought it worthwhile to do this. Rathbone's old 'equalitarian' opponents, who had been so quick to label her a social worker more interested in welfare than in rights, couldn't have found a better ally.

Rathbone thus took part in a famous all-night sitting of the House on 15 July – a sitting that was (as Rathbone noted in her Cross Bench column) 'almost wholly a family quarrel within the Labour Party'.[56] Conservatives and Liberals happily went to bed, but the Independent Labour Party decided it had nothing left to lose and forced the government to division after division in opposition to Bondfield's bill. Rathbone's amendment came up at 4.30 a.m. Any married woman receiving unemployment benefit already had to satisfy very harsh conditions, Rathbone pointed out; what evidence there was suggested not that married women were 'abusing' the fund but rather that they were being singled out as scapegoats. The ILP's disaffected leaders and a few feminists rose to support her attack. Married women had a perfect right to benefit and were already being denied in shoals, Cynthia Mosley declared. 'I am more glad than I can say that I have had an opportunity of sitting up all night to oppose the Bill.' Labour was reviving the 'bad old principle' of defining women by marital status, Ellen Wilkinson added – a private matter that should have nothing to do with their employment rights. Scandalously, Bondfield retorted that married women workers actually supported the bill, and Rathbone's amendment was easily defeated[57] – although Bondfield, after further lobbying, agreed to exempt women whose husbands were dead or incapacitated.[58] But Rathbone had been right to be apprehensive. Within a few weeks, under new regulations requiring married women to prove not only that they were 'normally' employed but that they had some hope of finding employment (an impossibly cruel condition to impose during a sustained period of unemployment), almost three-quarters of all married women claiming benefit had been disallowed. Most probably never managed to claim again.[59]

The Anomalies Act was a particularly discreditable piece of legislation and lowered Rathbone's opinion of the Labour government. For two years she had usually voted on the government side – opposing, for example, Baldwin's April 1931 no-confidence motion on Labour's handling of the economy.[60] But in the August financial crisis, when MacDonald formed a National government and the Liberals and Conservatives joined in its support, Rathbone did so as well. She was more than a little ambivalent. The propensity of the members of the former Labour Cabinet – now divided between the opposition and government benches – to spend their time in acrimonious 'back-chat' over the August crisis made her 'thoroughly sick', and she worried that neither side seemed to know quite what to do. When Keynes and the Bank of England adviser Henry Clay came to explain the economic crisis to a 'motley' audience of ex-Chancellors and backbenchers, she wrote in the *Woman's Leader*, the 'rival physicians differed not greatly in their diagnosis of the nation's economic sickness, but utterly in their prescriptions for its treatment'.[61] She had more confidence in Keynes, but the National government thought otherwise – and Rathbone tried to support it. During September, she voted for most of the government's 'economy' legislation, but the 10 per cent cut in unemployment benefit was more than she could stomach. Of course she was anxious 'to support this Government in restoring public confidence', she told the House, but when it came to cutting benefits for the unemployed 'she came to a dead stop'. On this issue, as on teachers' salaries and reductions in children's tax rebates, Rathbone voted with the Labour rump. If further economies were necessary, she repeated, a higher income tax was a better place to look.[62] Reluctantly – albeit (in electoral terms) prudently – she pledged support for the government in the October election. But her goals, she admitted to her constituents, were closer to those of the fallen Labour government.[63]

The swollen majority of the new National government appalled her. Rathbone had loved the years of the second Labour government. Like many shy people, she relished inclusion in a charged and vibrant world. She warmed to the 1929 Parliament's infectious 'school-boy' spirit, the uncomfortable all-night sittings which took on the character 'of a family party', the 'outbursts of song in the lobbies . . . and last-minute hospitalities on the Terrace' when the session finally broke up.[64] She admired the courage and principles of Ellen Wilkinson and the fire-eating Clydesiders and mourned when they lost their seats. The new Parliament seemed tame by comparison: 'Ah, Miss, it's so dull . . . it's like a cemetery without even a corpse in it', she recalled one Commons policeman lamenting.[65] The intake of 1931 – to her mind 'prosperous young men who have come almost straight from college' – didn't impress her. They took part in debates on unemployment, education and housing with impunity; but, she asked pointedly, 'what do they know of the lives of working-class people?'[66]

She did her best to educate them. She spoke less about domestic issues in the 1931 Parliament, partly because she (like many MPs) became deeply absorbed in Indian constitutional reform, but also because she understood how pointless it was, in a period of financial stringency, to detain the House with long disquisitions on family endowment. But she used her knowledge of the intricacies of housing legislation to good effect, urging local authorities to use subsidies to rebate rents for families with dependent children and alerting ill-informed Ministry of Health officials when some did so.[67] She kept track of the impact of the crackdown on insurance as well, and in a chamber now bereft of Labour women members, made a special effort to remind MPs of its cost for working-class women. The Anomalies Act, she pointed out, had changed 'the whole principle of contributory insurance as it affects women': employed women, if they were so rash as to marry, had 'the privilege of contributing towards insurance but very little chance indeed of receiving any benefit'.[68] When the National government singled out married women in health insurance as well, segregating them in a special pool with distinct rates and benefits, she exploded. If married women claimed sickness benefit at a higher rate, it was because they alone bore children: their debilitating 'double day', not some sort of malingering, accounted for their claims. Rathbone thought married women deserved independent entitlements: instead, she watched them lose the few economic rights they had. 'The economists used to talk of the Economic Man, who responded solely to economic considerations,' she told the House bitterly. But 'if there is an Economic Woman, she must be a spinster, because no Economic Woman of the working class would be such a fool as to get married'.[69] Throughout the 1930s, Rathbone asked question after question about discrimination against married women in insurance: since the answers never satisfied her, she always promised to raise the matter again, and always did.[70]

Were these interventions only of symbolic importance? To a degree, yes – for no government was less likely to pass feminist legislation. Yet Rathbone did manage to be more than a gadfly, finding collaborators with whom to pursue her social policy campaigns. Indeed, the third and last tool of Rathbone's parliamentary practice – the cross-party, semi-formal, single-issue committee of backbenchers – came into its own during the 1931 Parliament. True, Rathbone, Atholl and Josiah Wedgwood had put together a cross-party 'Committee for the Protection of Coloured Women in the Crown Colonies' during the second Labour government, but it was after 1931 that such Rathbone-inspired pressure groups proliferated. The new Conservative MPs included women – among them Thelma Cazalet, Irene Ward and Mavis Tate – who proved more independent-minded than anticipated, and the peculiar shape of the 1931 Parliament favoured cross-party collaboration. As Harold Macmillan recalled, with the National government's majority so large, party discipline faltered and 'many debates took on an unaccustomed tone of non-partisanship'.[71] Yet the huge Conservative majority also left younger members like Macmillan at a loose end: ambitious, but with little hope of joining an already over-full front bench, they roamed about the Commons looking for something useful to do. Some of those returned in the 1931 landslide for marginal and often working-class seats felt the stirrings of social conscience. Macmillan, returned for Stockton-on-Tees after briefly losing his seat, was a fierce defender of his impoverished constituents; Bob Boothby kept an eye out for matters affecting his beloved Aberdeenshire fishermen. Both found the National government's regressive social policies repellent.

In the early 1930s, it was hard to do much to counter them. The government's majority was just too large, its critics too divided, its mandate too overwhelming. But, as the unemployment figures kept climbing, reaching their peak at just under three million during winter 1932–3, left-leaning social scientists felt uncomfortable. And, when uncomfortable, they investigated. The sociology departments of Rathbone's civic universities were at the forefront of this drive towards documentation, setting in motion studies of working-class living standards in many towns (including Liverpool). The professional associations were not far behind. The study of nutrition was progressing, and in November 1933 the British Medical Association (BMA) published a landmark inquiry laying out – and, more important, costing – the requirements of a healthy diet.[72] Unfortunately for the government, that report appeared just before the Commons began to debate a comprehensive bill aimed at reforming the entire system for maintaining the unemployed. And in this coincidence, Rathbone saw a glimmer of opportunity.

The National government's unemployment bill, introduced in September 1933, was intended to restore the actuarial and moral 'soundness' of the system of maintaining the unemployed by establishing a clear distinction between a rights-based system of unemployment insurance (from which an unemployed worker could draw benefit for a fixed period by virtue of contributions) and a new needs-based system of 'unemployment assistance' which would sustain the long-term unemployed. That distinction between insurance and relief had been lost in the labour dislocation and unrest that followed the First World War; in the 1920s, successive governments had extended payments to those whose entitlement was exhausted while relying on strict administration to pare the numbers down. The Insurance Fund, unsurprisingly, fell chronically into deficit, and in its economy measures of 1931, the National government cut benefits by 10 per cent and introduced a much-hated 'means test' for the longer-term unemployed. But Chamberlain and the Treasury officials wished to go further: they greatly disliked the continued use of an insurance fund to support men whose entitlement had lapsed, and resented the fact that, with local authorities administering the system, benefit levels tended to vary by local political complexion. The bill thus sought to take unemployment relief 'out of politics' by creating two new bodies – the Unemployment Insurance Statutory Committee and the Unemployment Assistance Board – to take over the local authorities' tasks. And yet, however administered, the system had to sustain the families of the unemployed. Were the aims of administrative efficiency and reasonable maintenance reconcilable?[73]

Rathbone feared they were not, anticipating that the government's desire to cut costs and discipline the localities would undermine any possibility of reasonable maintenance for the unemployed. In particular, she worried about the children. She had kept abreast of the new nutrition studies that were documenting the deficiencies in children's diets; from her work with the relief committee of the Council of Voluntary Aid in Liverpool she knew just how undernourished poor children often were. Thus, after the publication of the British Medical Association study and with the unemployment bill before the House, she mobilized. She knew all the 'poverty experts' already; more creatively, she recruited socially conscious young Conservatives like Macmillan and Boothby, bringing these unlikely allies together at a meeting in the Commons on 15 February 1934.[74] The resulting Children's Minimum Campaign Committee which later became the Children's Minimum Council (CMC) had one simple goal: to ensure that no child was

23. Liverpool children, 1934.

deprived of adequate food and necessities just because its parents were poor. A few days later, Rathbone and the Liberal Geoffrey Mander introduced an amendment to the bill instructing the Unemployment Assistance Board to take into account 'the minimum requirements of healthy physical subsistence' when setting rates, and while the amendment was rejected, the Minister of Labour, Sir Henry Betterton, did promise that the Board would do just that.[75] The CMC then flooded the newly appointed Board with evidence of malnutrition among children and advice about adequate benefit scales,[76] and sent deputations to MacDonald, the Board of Education and the Ministry of Health arguing for measures ranging from Rathbone's pet panacea of child rent rebates to expanded provision of free milk and meals in schools.[77] A raft of distinguished parliamentarians, medical men and public intellectuals, as well as most of the nation's child welfare organizations, pledged their support, but – as with the Family Endowment Society – the actual work was left in a very few hands. Rathbone shifted her talented young co-worker Marjorie Green from the Family Endowment Society to build the new organization up; Rathbone, Green and Eva Hubback together did the research, drafted the literature, enlisted the supporters, and planned the deputations.

To any effect? When the House discussed the relief scales set by the new Unemployment Assistance Board in December 1934, Rathbone implied that the committee's lobbying had led the UAB to improve rates for children in particular,[78] and minutes of the UAB meetings suggest she was right. Some members of the Board, especially Violet Markham, shared Rathbone's concerns about families with children. Thus, while the Board adopted a low flat rate for the childless couple, it set allowances for children above the level paid by the unemployment insurance system (which soon afterwards raised children's rates as well).[79] Yet the proposed rates of benefit were still deplorably low; moreover (Betterton's promise notwithstanding) the government steadfastly refused to disclose just how the UAB had arrived at its scales.[80] John Macnicol, surveying this history, concludes that the CMC – which survived as an anti-poverty pressure group until the Second World War – was almost completely unsuccessful in the face of a government determined to resist efforts to come up with a statutory poverty line.[81] Rathbone would almost have agreed. From her speeches in the Commons, it is clear that she was enraged by the government's penny-pinching attitude. MPs, she stormed, should 'compare the condition of their own children with the condition of the children of the poor', should imagine how they would feel if asked to support their own children on a few shillings a week.[82] With the economic situation improving, with British farmers complaining of a crisis of overproduction, surely the government could keep children at least above 'the bitter waters of poverty'.[83]

Nevertheless, the Children's Minimum Committee did matter – although as much for the ways it shaped understandings of the problem of family poverty and helped solidify an emerging policy consensus as for any practical achievement. Those practical achievements were not negligible. CMC lobbying, and not simply the government's desire to placate the agricultural lobby and reduce embarrassing milk surpluses, led to the introduction of a 'milk in schools scheme' in late 1934 that halved the price of milk for schoolchildren and tripled the numbers of children participating (to about half of all school-aged children).[84] CMC pressure also drove the Board of Education to press local authorities to expand provision of school meals and the Ministry of Health to pay some attention to the spread of rent-rebate schemes. What the government would not do, however, was simply provide *free* milk and meals for all schoolchildren or even all children below a fixed 'poverty line'. To do so, one Board of Education official minuted, 'would be to admit that the allowances under the Unemployment Insurance Acts and other forms of relief are insufficient to keep even the ordinary child in good health' – an admission that the government 'would presumably be unwilling to make'.[85] By 1939, although one quarter of school-age children lived in households below the CMC's carefully calculated poverty line, only 10 per cent of children received their milk ration entirely free, and only 2 per cent got free meals as well.[86]

Rathbone and the CMC found this unacceptable. Throughout the 1930s, they relentlessly exposed the gap between any reasonably 'scientific' estimate of minimum needs and the benefits paid to the unemployed; equally importantly, they helped people understand why that gap existed. Because unemployment benefits were to be based on subsistence needs, they perforce included children's allowances – and since wages did not, a subsistence allowance for a large family could well exceed an unskilled wage. The Unemployment Assistance Board, as Rathbone recognized, was acutely aware of this problem: as the Board's secretary told his colleagues, 'it is very difficult to construct a scale which allows a sufficient sum for the normal family and yet keeps the family of say five children below the unskilled wage rate'.[87] In their drive to maintain 'work incentives', the Board thus ground benefits down below subsistence – a solution that led to a serious public outcry and made some board members (especially Markham) quite uncomfortable. The unemployed and their children were not the only victims of this system: even more terrible, Rathbone thought, was what the 'wage–benefit overlap' revealed about the situation of those actually employed. For if the government found itself unable to grant even subsistence relief to large families for fear of destroying work incentives, what did this say about the welfare of those children whose parents were in work? As Rathbone had always insisted, wages were clearly not meeting 'family needs'; children of working as well as unemployed fathers were often living in poverty.

In the dilemmas faced by officials deciding unemployment policy, Rathbone thus grounded the argument for family allowances. If one wanted to peg benefits to 'subsistence needs' while maintaining the 'gap' between wages and benefits even for family men, one needed to introduce children's allowances not only for the unemployed but across the board. Those who had read *The Disinherited Family* would have known that already, but only the depression and the fierce public debates over rates of unemployment benefit that followed drove that lesson home. Rathbone's Children's Minimum Committee helped to make that argument, and with William Beveridge and Mary Stocks on the Unemployment Insurance Statutory Committee and Violet Markham on the Unemployment Assistance Board, they could be sure it would be understood. Indeed, by the late 1930s, both bodies had confessed publicly that they found it impossible to square any hope of paying adequate rates of benefit with their desire to maintain incentives for fathers of large families to work; the only solution was a system of family allowances.[88]

The debates over unemployment relief in the 1930s thus strengthened Rathbone's case, but they also altered the character of her movement. In the 1920s, family endowment had been a feminist and left-wing cause; now, it became part of a Commons-based anti-poverty alliance. Increasingly, Rathbone found herself feeding information to reform-minded young Conservatives like Macmillan, Boothby or Duncan Sandys; in the late thirties, the idiosyncratic imperialist Leo Amery lent his support as well. Amery proved a recruit worth having. He willingly trotted off to the London School of Economics in March 1938 to eat fried cod and suet pudding at a CMC 'fivepenny lunch' featuring meals affordable on the BMA scale of allowances but beyond the reach of the unemployed (the other options were mince and tripe, prompting one wag to say he'd eat the mince and listen to the tripe); in the twelve months before the war he spoke to the BMA, the Insurance Debating Society, the Fabian Society, and several other political and religious associations on the need for family allowances.[89] A vigilant Treasury made sure that matters never went further, but by the late thirties Rathbone had a small but committed band of supporters in the Commons, who let no opportunity pass to point out the costs to children's health, work incentives, and sometimes even population growth of Britain's failure to introduce a comprehensive system of family allowances.

If Rathbone's cross-party contacts gave new life to the family allowances movement, they gave her new political opportunities as well. Respected for her knowledge about social questions and free of party ties, she was a natural ally for those Liberals, left-leaning Conservatives, and intellectuals growing sceptical of orthodox economic ideas and committed to some measure of social reform. Already known to Harold Macmillan from the Children's Minimum campaign, she was one of only sixteen MPs to sign his June 1935 platform of expansionist economic policies and social reforms, *The Next Five Years*; when Lloyd George – having announced a 'New Deal for Britain' – set up 'Councils of Action' to press for a programme of defence of the League of Nations and socio-economic reform, Rathbone helped to launch that movement and joined its executive committee as well.[90] 'Anti-poverty' allies eased her entry into still other, less traditionally 'female' areas. It is remarkable how many of those CMC supporters reappear (as Rathbone does) within those groups and cabals growing sceptical of Chamberlain's foreign policy, how easily criticism of the National government's social policies shaded into criticism of appeasement. Some of Rathbone's younger colleagues were close to Churchill (Boothby, and Churchill's son-in-law Sandys in particular); others, like Macmillan or Harold Nicolson, simply followed their own star. Rathbone, in gaining the trust of these men, won the right to be heard on foreign policy and gained some allies for later campaigns in defence of refugees and aliens. Men like Amery, Macmillan, Boothby and Nicolson never became confidants or friends: they were urbane and clubbable, while she was socially awkward and (as Nicolson remarked) 'much preferred bluebooks to parties'.[91] But they shared her concerns, were willing to go along to the odd meeting or deputation, and knew she would take care of the boring business of getting the facts and figures straight. In casting her lot with this still marginal but critical group, Rathbone helped her career and her causes more than she could have known.

Rathbone's anti-poverty campaigns of the mid-1930s reveal her Commons practice perfectly: they also capture her career at a key, transitional moment. When elected to Parliament, Rathbone was known mostly as a feminist and social reformer, but by the late thirties she had become a crucial voice on imperial and international issues as well. The children's campaigns didn't simply fill the interval between these two phases; they helped make the latter, more expansive, work possible. This was not only because they gave Rathbone new allies and contacts; it was also because they affected her point of view. From her young womanhood, Rathbone saw with 'gendered' eyes: focusing on the figure of the overworked and dependent wife, she had scarcely noticed the children clustered around her. In the early 1930s, however, children moved centre stage: they became not simply the grounds for the mother's claims but entitled citizens. This shift in focus was partly strategic, for while 'family endowment' might seem dangerously feminist or socialistic, men and women, left and right, could unite behind the banner of expanded services for children. And yet, might Rathbone's new interest in children – or, rather, her new ability to *see* children as independent, rights-bearing citizens – have had personal roots as well?

For in the 1920s children became, really for the first time, a part of Rathbone's life. In her young womanhood, children had not interested her: Evie's daughter Nancy recalled that, until she became interested in Somerville, 'aunt Eleanor' paid her no attention at all. But as Eleanor grew older she found herself drawn to children. Young families were 'comforting to an elderly person like me', she wrote to Stocks, especially now that her own family members were 'dropping out almost as quickly as if they were playing a game of musical chairs'.[92] Eva Hubback's children and Mary's 'little Stockings' thus went with their mothers to visit Eleanor and Elizabeth in their holiday cottages, and after the London house was expanded in 1932, Frank's wife Edith often brought her 'young Franks' for days at a time. To Nancy's amazement, those young cousins found her redoubtable aunt 'very jolly'. Unlike their mother, she was not fussy and had absolutely no interest in whether they were clean; like them, she had a sweet tooth and would happily share a 'children's tea'. And although she was an erratic presence as an aunt, forgetting birthdays and dispensing pound notes straight from her purse at Christmas ('very vulgar, I know,' she said cheerfully), she developed a real love for her young nephews and niece and took their part in crucial family quarrels. Frank's eldest son Jack, later Director of the National Trust, lived across the street from Elizabeth and Eleanor for a time and revived her atrophied interest in music; Noreen, Frank's youngest, followed aunt Eleanor and Elizabeth's example and went into social work; Larry (B.L. Rathbone), the favourite, was grateful that Eleanor prevented his father from placing him directly in the firm after he finished school and arranged instead for a course of study at the London School of Economics. (There, he joined his aunt's efforts to charter and supply food ships running the blockade of Spain – efforts he recalled with a half-proud, half-ashamed wonder more than fifty years later.)[93]

Eleanor never lost her feminism, but these new relationships and experiences left their mark. Working, often, with men, and with her brother's sons growing up around her, her mistrust of 'the dingy human male'[94] dissipated. She became an easier collaborator, and her sympathies widened. No longer alert only to women's voices and women's pain, she became, friends recalled, abnormally sensitive to all reports of suffering. Could it be, Rathbone had asked in her final presidential address to the NUSEC in 1929, that there was 'a wave-length set up by human suffering, to which the minds of women give a specially good reception', perhaps because women have traditionally spent so much of their time listening to and caring for others? Could it be 'that among the results of the new citizenship of women . . . will be a changed attitude on the part of society towards human happiness and suffering, especially towards the happiness and suffering of its less powerful and articulate members'?[95] Certainly Rathbone had, in the 1930s, a productive intolerance of the pain of children, whether in the Liverpool streets she knew so well or in countries and continents thousands of miles away.

Chapter 13

The Difference Empire Makes

Hundreds and hundreds of hours of parliamentary time were spent on Indian questions during the early 1930s. Eleanor contributed her share to that debate, although less by her own speeches than by asking questions or tabling amendments that caused the government (and her fellow members) considerable trouble and time. This was just as she intended. Ever since the summer of 1927, when she had opened Katherine Mayo's controversial bestseller, *Mother India*, uncharacteristically chucked it across the room in disgust, and then – with gritted teeth – read to the finish, Eleanor had been unable to wipe Mayo's images of Indian girls' suffering and subjection from her mind.[1] She had quickly gathered the National Union's Executive together to discuss what they could do,[2] and soon had her own answer. She decided to run for Parliament, she told her niece Elena Richmond, so that she could 'keep the woman question alive' when the House began its anticipated consideration of India's future constitution.[3] She did so, telling the House truthfully in 1933 that 'for the last four years I have lived almost night and day with this question'.[4]

The book that started all the trouble, Katherine Mayo's *Mother India*, was written to disturb. Mayo, an American muckraker and feminist with racist views, had already written defences of the New York State police and of American involvement in the Philippines when she decided to tackle what she thought to be a dangerous romanticization of the East. Mayo knew that Indian independence was on the table, and her book landed like a bomb in an already tense political world. Ostensibly an exposé of Indian sexual and cultural norms, the book was also a comprehensive assault on the nationalist case. India's political subjection and poverty rested, Mayo insisted, on a 'rock-bottom physical base'.[5] Through lurid, almost pornographic, descriptions of raped child wives and diseased child mothers, crippled children and 'devitalized' men, Mayo sought to persuade the reader of India's ineluctable and unchangeable backwardness – and hence of its incapacity for self-rule. *Mother India* was an immediate, runaway bestseller in the United States and Britain and a subject of passionate protest within India and among those sympathetic to the cause of Indian independence.[6]

Puritanical and sensitive as she was, Rathbone was horrified by Mayo's graphic revelations. But she also felt, oddly, *grateful* – thankful to Mayo for uncovering yet another instance of female subjection and apologetic about her own earlier ignorance. Her earliest letters to Mayo are deferential, almost servile. She took Mayo's advice about speakers on Indian questions, passed on nuggets of praise (such as the report that 'the whole Cabinet' had been 'deeply impressed' by Mayo's book), and dismissed Indian criticisms of the book as 'extraordinarily unconvincing' and even 'hysterical'. 'I am tired of pointing out that you did not profess to give a complete picture, and that when the sanitary inspector gives a report on one's drains, one does not quarrel with him because he fails to dilate on the beauty of one's herbaceous border,' she wrote to Mayo, echoing Gandhi's famous review of *Mother India* as a 'drain inspector's report'.[7] A year later, she came out publicly in Mayo's defence. In their understandable outrage at Mayo's obvious 'violent dislike and contempt for the Hindu', she wrote in the *Hibbert Journal* in January 1929, critics were overlooking the simple fact that child marriage truly existed, and '[w]hich is the more important – the hurt feelings of the race-conscious, educated, articulate Hindu, or the millions of tortured bodies and wasted lives upon whose secrets Miss Mayo's book has shed its ray?'[8] After all, what difference did it make 'who has been responsible in the past for this huge mass of long-drawn-out, continually renewed, unnecessary physical and mental suffering?' The question was how to prevent it in the future.[9]

Rathbone wanted to find the answer to that question, but was, in 1929, remarkably ill equipped to do so. Although her own fortune derived from Rathbone Brothers' profitable trade in the East, although many progressive women (including her new Commons colleague Edith Picton-Turbervill) had spent years as missionaries or teachers in India,[10] and although Edwardian feminists had routinely pointed to Indian women's purported degradation as an argument for their own enfranchisement,[11] Eleanor had, thus far, taken very little interest in empire. She had, however, lived within the linked worlds of political liberalism and constitutional feminism all of her life, and when she thought about empire she fell back almost instinctively on Millian ideas. Like Mill, she tended to differentiate societies by 'stage' of civilization; like Mill, she considered the status of women to be the best index of that civilizational stage; like Mill, she thought British rule defensible if it forced backward societies up those civilizational rungs. Given this framework, small wonder Rathbone assumed both that the 'uplift' of Indian women could be kept apart from (even should precede) any further move towards democracy, and that British women – being already 'emancipated' – should lead that effort. Unencumbered by much knowledge but with all her moral outrage intact, shortly after her election she called a conference, at which British women were to plan the salvation of their Indian sisters.

But that conference proved her undoing – or, seen differently, began her political re-education. Several politically active Indian women, including the

Indian feminist and social reformer Dhanvanthi Rama Rao, heard of the event and came along: there, they found themselves confronted by a roster of British speakers and a literature table displaying Rathbone's article in Mayo's defence. They were, Rama Rao recalled, profoundly offended. Educated Indian women had been combating 'social evils' for years, Rama Rao pointed out in an intervention from the floor: why, then, had conference organizers neither consulted Indian women nor arranged for any to speak; why, moreover, was Rathbone in the chair – a woman who had written publicly in Katherine Mayo's defence?[12] Rathbone, stung, took Rama Rao 'somewhat severely . . . to task', but Kathleen Simon and Emmeline Pethick-Lawrence insisted that Rama Rao be heard.[13] The London dailies gave the conflict prominent coverage, and Rama Rao, Hannah Sen, Emily Lutyens and some ten other women also wrote to *The Times* that Rathbone had 'forfeited Indian confidence by her close association with Miss Mayo' and would only promote 'racial cleavage' by proceeding in this patronizing way.[14]

The criticism left Eleanor privately heartsick and scrambling to restore her credibility. She had only meant to help, she retorted feebly in *The Times*; she also paid tribute to the 'courageous and outspoken report' on child marriage issued by the Joshi Committee of the Indian Legislative Assembly.[15] But the mud stuck, and it was, in a sense, deserved. Imaginatively, strategically, and in terms of simple human warmth, Rathbone had fallen short, and the more reliable of her friends probably told her so. Sensibly, then, she turned her projected survey of Indian women's conditions over to her friend Ann Caton and, for a time, held her tongue. Indeed, having discovered that Indian reformers had led the campaign to pass the 1929 Child Marriage Restraint Act (the Sarda Act), and unable to find out much about its enforcement, she began to wonder whether there might be truth in Rama Rao's claim that the Government of India was to blame for India's social problems. She thus turned her attention homeward, peppering William Wedgwood Benn, the new Secretary of State for India in the Labour government, with letters requesting information about the government's enforcement of the Sarda Act.

But if Rama Rao taught Rathbone a first lesson in the politics of empire, Benn gave her a second. For, Labour minister though he was, Benn prevaricated, stonewalled and threatened, warning Rathbone in May 1930 that she was 'doing the greatest possible disservice to His Majesty's Government, to the Government of India and ultimately to the cause which you have at heart' by proposing to ask further parliamentary questions.[16] For a few months, then, Rathbone held off, but when it became clear that neither Benn nor the Government of India intended to tell her anything about their enforcement plans (no doubt because they hadn't any), she lost patience. The Sarda Act had ostensibly banned marriage of girls below the age of fourteen and boys below the age of eighteen; in practice, however, it had merely spurred a great wave of early marriages, as parents rushed to finalize their plans before the ostensible enforcement date.

Rathbone, watching this fiasco, was horrified. 'Child marriage,' she wrote bitterly to Benn, 'seems to be regarded as a quite minor point which can safely be left to some future date and must not be allowed to run the slightest risk of embarrassing the Government or anyone else.'[17] On 17 July 1930, Rathbone circularized her fellow MPs on the failures of the Sarda Act; a few months later, she followed up with a letter to *The Times*.[18]

As those interventions make clear, Rathbone initially saw the problem as one of governance: given government legislation and nationalists' support, she was convinced that human practice could change. The furore over constitutional reform struck her simply as a road-block: 'I do feel rather distracted at the thought of all the wretched little brides who are likely to be sacrificed on the altar of India's political aspirations during the next few years,'[19] she wrote to her collaborator Mabel Hartog in May 1930. Already, however, Rathbone's confidence in Britain's commitment to a 'progressive' imperialism hung in the balance, and six months later – with the Government of India still stonewalling – it was in tatters. In the summer of 1931 Rathbone began, tentatively, to reach out to Indian women. She wrote first to Muthulakshmi Reddi, a medical doctor and former deputy president of the Madras Legislative Council, whose speeches on social questions she had read and admired,[20] and to Radhabai Subbarayan, a non-Congress moderate involved in the constitutional negotiations.[21] Both women told her that Indian women's organizations found their reform efforts hampered by the government's indifference and their own political subjection: 'If women and the depressed classes are given freedom, power and responsibility,' Reddi said pointedly, 'I am sure they would very soon learn how to rectify the present social evils.'[22] Rathbone was ready to hear her. 'There is only one safeguard for any one section of people who are differentiated from others, whether by race or creed or colour or sex,' she had already told the Commons that January, 'and that is the safeguard of their full and real participation in the working of self-governing institutions.'[23]

Rathbone's dawning conviction that democracy might serve – in India as in Britain – as the foundation for social reform launched her into the heart of debates over Indian constitutional reform and returned her to views she had had since girlhood. She had, after all, faced a presumed tension between 'good government' and 'self-government' before – when anti-suffragists argued that women's horizons were too narrow for them to be entrusted with the vote, or fellow suffragists preferred a narrow, class-based franchise to a more risky struggle for a wider democratic vote – and had always come down on the democratic side. Now she began to make the same argument across the imperial and racial divide. By doing so, however, she made her differences with Katherine Mayo clear. As Rathbone never quite understood, Mayo had concentrated on the conditions of women in *Mother India* not because she was particularly concerned about women but because she thought – rightly – that the focus on sex would sell: Mayo's real aim was, as she told one friend in 1926, 'to give my own countrymen plain, spade's-a-spade reasons for ... the imperative necessity ... that Britain should stand firm in India'.[24] For Mayo, the sexual violence and degeneracy of Indian (or, as she saw it, Hindu) men was not evidence (as it was for Rathbone) of the ubiquity of sexual oppression; it was, rather, a mark of Indian men's particular racial inferiority and 'difference'. There was a fundamental gulf between the 'Oriental and Occidental mentalities', Mayo insisted, and the former was entirely unsuited to self-rule. 'I doubt there is a single Hindu who could stand up against his surroundings, atmosphere, his traditions and the demands of his friends ... to be able to administer any measure of reform, especially if it involves money, without the *controlling and supporting hand of a Briton over him*,' she had written to Rathbone in 1927,[25] and she never changed her mind. Mayo continued to have her British followers – women who, like Nancy Astor, shared Mayo's core political goal. 'Anybody who breaks up the anti-British propaganda over India,' Astor wrote to Mayo on the publication of Mayo's *Volume Two*, 'is doing civilization a service'.[26]

By 1931, however, Rathbone saw things differently. 'I shall be for ever grateful to you for opening my own eyes and those of the world to a neglected responsibility,' Rathbone wrote to Mayo, but she could not agree that Indian social reformers were insincere or the British blameless.[27] The writing of the Joshi report 'in the teeth of religious orthodoxy on the one hand and sensitive national feeling on the other', she insisted in a second article in the *Hibbert Journal*, 'must have required great courage',[28] and that courage was a sign of political maturity. 'Hence has come about the paradox, that one of the most terrible documents ever published by a people about themselves is, nevertheless, one of the most hopeful auguries of that people's future fitness for self-government'.[29] In 1929 Rathbone had thought constitutional reform must wait upon social reform; by 1931, she had changed her mind. Self-government was coming, she told the Commons in December 1931, and while it was 'not for British women to dictate to Indian women as to how they shall use the power so entrusted to them', it *was* British women's responsibility to make sure that Indian women *did* receive their share. Having themselves done so little to improve social conditions,

> Perhaps the last service we can render to India is to see that we hand over the estate to those who will manage it in future in as good a condition as possible, and, above all, to see that we hand it over to the guardianship of those who shall be really representative of the people of India, not a narrow oligarchy of class or caste or sex. ... Only when the political question is settled will those who care for the real India be free to turn their attention to those ends to which constitution making is only the means, that of bringing about conditions in India which will secure the happiness and prosperity of the whole people, the common people. ...[30]

No doubt to Mayo's horror, her most fervent British convert had come down on the opposite side.

Child marriage in India was Rathbone's first and most deeply felt imperial cause, but her involvements quickly proliferated. A number of imperial issues captured the attention of politically active women in 1929, and Rathbone played some role in most of these. First, a bitter controversy about the status of indentured girls in Hong Kong re-emerged. In the early 1920s, British feminists and anti-slavery reformers (a Commander and Mrs Haslewood in particular) had insisted that such indenture was a form of slavery; after a fierce campaign, in 1923 the Colonial Office had agreed to force the Hong Kong government to register and protect such girls.[31] Now, however, Clara Haslewood and her feminist allies had learned that this promise had never been kept and they returned to the warpath. They were joined by Nina Boyle of the Women's Freedom League, who had lived for some years in South Africa and had become convinced that some Africans' practice of cementing marriage arrangements through the payment of a 'bride price' was a form of slavery. Boyle had tried to interest the League of Nations in such instances of 'domestic slavery' in the early twenties but without success; in 1929 she too decided to try again. Finally, the Duchess of Atholl had heard through Church of Scotland missionary friends about the practice of clitoridec-tomy in Kenya. Atholl sat in Parliament as a Conservative and was anything but a feminist: she was, however, genuinely distressed by what she had heard and determined to do what she could.[32]

Rathbone was happy to help on the parliamentary front. With Atholl and the staunch humanitarian activist Josiah Wedgwood, she formed a small all-party 'Committee for the Protection of Coloured Women in the Crown Colonies'. Eight other MPs joined as well, including the new Labour women members Edith Picton-Turbervill and Ethel Bentham, former Conservative Colonial Under-Secretary William Ormsby-Gore, Rathbone's later ally on refugee questions Victor Cazalet, and the young R.A. Butler, who acted as secretary. Leaving the question of Hong Kong's indentured girls to the Anti-Slavery Society and the indefatigable Haslewoods, the committee concentrated on African practices of clitoridectomy and bride price, meeting during the autumn and winter of 1929 and 1930 to hear evidence from a number of women missionaries to Kenya, the director of Kenya's health services, the anthropologist Louis Leakey, anti-colonial critic William MacGregor Ross, and even Johnstone (later Jomo) Kenyatta, who was in London to bring the grievances of the Kikuyu Central Association before the Colonial Office. Most of these witnesses warned the committee that clitoridectomy could not be easily combated, being central to many African belief systems and often a crucial marker of adulthood.[33] They did confirm, however, that the practice was widespread, painful, and often medically damaging, and for Rathbone, Atholl and Wedgwood that was enough.

In December 1929 they asked Sidney Webb, now Colonial Secretary in the new Labour government, to appoint a select committee to look into the status of African women in general and the practice of clitoridectomy in particular. Webb refused, although he did agree to send any questions they might have on to African governors.[34] One week later the three raised their concerns in a vote on adjournment in the House.

This took some courage, for Rathbone in particular. Not only was she a new member and a woman, but she was also – unlike Atholl – a spinster and a feminist. Rathbone's own secretaries found her new obsession with 'these rather horrifying almost gynaecological things that she knew nothing about' embarrassing and unseemly;[35] how much more, then, must male MPs have winked and nudged when these two severe women in late middle age stood up in a debate over Labour's imperial policy to discuss genital mutilation. Yet Atholl and Rathbone proceeded bravely, Atholl outlining the prevalence and severity of this 'pre-marriage initiation rite', Rathbone quelling an attempt by the Independent Labour Party leader James Maxton to have Atholl ruled out of order. 'The position of the native women' in many African tribes, Rathbone told the House, was 'one of sheer slavery'. Labour was committed to a policy of trusteeship, and to the development of native self-governing institutions, and this was all to the good, but the 'champions of the native races' should also remember the 'old principle that there is no slavery under the British flag'. 'Let them take this message to the men of the native races,' Rathbone charged: 'There can be no equal citizenship between coloured men and white men till there is equal citizenship between coloured men and coloured women.'[36]

This debate took place late at night in a thinly attended House, but it was, as the *Woman's Leader* insisted, of real significance. A few months earlier, the *Leader* had published a series of articles by Nina Boyle denouncing the League, the Colonial Office and the humanitarian societies for ignoring the enslavement of women; now, with the same issues raised on the floor of the House, 1929 might go down in history as 'the year in which the conscience of feminism overflowed into imperial channels'.[37] 'Our own grievances . . . seem to sink into a strange insignificance in comparison with the unspeakable and hitherto unspoken grievances of some hundred thousands of our women fellow subjects,' the paper added a few weeks later. 'Can feminist weapons rust or feminist energies flag while such wrongs remain unredressed – or, for that matter, uninvestigated?'[38]

Rathbone, of course, had concluded that they could not; it is quite likely that she herself penned that rhetorical question. She spoke with Boyle, Atholl and Haslewood at a conference on 'domestic slavery in the British empire' in February 1930, and joined in deputations to press for a government campaign to improve women's status and for the appointment of women to the Colonial Office and the Slavery Commission of the League.[39] When talking to colonial officials, Rathbone shamelessly played the imperial card. English women were in a difficult position when confronted with customs like bride price, she told Sidney Webb in a meeting in April. If they publicized such practices, 'the effect can only be to damage the prestige of this country in the eyes of foreigners' – and yet, she warned, 'there must come a time when their feelings as British subjects must give place to their feelings as women'. For the good name of the empire, the government ought to do all in its power to combat such customs.[40]

Webb and his under-secretaries were sympathetic to a point. The Labour government did promulgate laws outlawing the practice of transferring children for cash, and began registering and overseeing such children in Hong Kong and Malaya. Webb and Lord Cecil, Britain's delegate to the League, also supported the proposal to revive a slavery commission in Geneva and were (to the distress of their officials) not unwilling to see it take up questions of the status of women. But officials and politicians agreed that a women's committee in Geneva or a woman adviser in the Colonial Office would be 'awful to contemplate' and were also understandably reluctant to contemplate a root-and-branch assault on African marriage customs.[41] Colonial governors were even less enthusiastic: asked to comment on Rathbone and Atholl's concerns, most defended bride price as a kind of surety for good treatment by the husband and dismissed clitoridectomy as either not practised in their territory or as too firmly rooted in religion and custom to be abolished. What African women needed, Donald Cameron of Tanganyika argued, was not a set of alien regulations, but improved economic infrastructure and social services – better access to markets, more remunerative cash cropping, and more hospitals and dispensaries. Officials in London were delighted, for the responses presented British colonial administration as both progressive and culturally sensitive, reforming and realistic. After prudently suppressing the one or two responses that had argued for a much tougher attack on clitoridectomy, they published the whole correspondence.[42]

The colonial governors thus told Rathbone and her humanitarian allies roughly what Louis Leakey had told her parliamentary committee: that African cultures were complex and varied, and that their gender relations should not be understood in Western terms. But if officials and scholars joined together to administer this lesson, in the case of Rathbone at least it never quite took. In the governors' responses Rathbone found enough evidence of the transfer of women without their consent to keep her going; she sent her secretaries off to the London School of Economics to hear lectures on anthropology and to the London Library to collect (as Marjorie Green recalled) some 'rather gruesome books about sex habits of African women'.[43] From these sources came yet another memo arguing that the status of women transferred without their consent must be considered 'one of, or closely analogous to' slavery,[44] and yet another deputation. If legislation was not possible, Rathbone told the new Conservative Colonial Secretary Sir Philip Cunliffe Lister in May 1932, feminists at least wanted to know that medical and educational services for women were being built up. Cunliffe Lister would not reassure her. In the wake of the 1931 financial crisis, colonial administration was everywhere retrenching.[45]

Beyond forcing the publication of some information on colonial social policy, then, Rathbone's African interventions accomplished little. Yet they tell us a great deal about her own views. Consistently, Rathbone resisted both anthropological explanations and racial reasoning: while she came to accept the difficulties of meddling with 'customs', she never agreed that such an attempt should not be made. The emerging discourse of cultural relativism, the effort to see indigenous cultures as functional and even admirable, never really touched her. This was not, however, because she was in some simple terms a racist, but rather because she saw the world almost entirely in gendered terms. 'Men all over the world are much the same,' she told one Indian feminist;[46] given the chance, they would always keep women in subjection. African women's situation was simply a particularly dire illustration of that old, old story. Nor would an empire run by men 'uplift' such women; only the power of feminism could do so. British women thus had a responsibility towards colonized women less because of Britain's imperial sovereignty (although Rathbone did use this language) than because of their fellow-feeling with 'less fortunate women everywhere'.[47] After all, as Rathbone told the women's conference in February 1930, if the women's organizations didn't take up the question of domestic slavery, 'I don't know who is going to do it'.[48]

Rathbone's belief in the universality of 'sex antagonism' certainly made her culturally insensitive and sometimes overbearing. Only rarely and with difficulty could she see British institutions and practices as particular rather than universal; only occasionally did she express much interest in non-European cultural forms. Yet that very 'insensitivity' was a source of strength, for it preserved Rathbone from the seductions of 'difference' at a moment when 'difference' was often understood in racial terms. Thus, unlike Katherine Mayo, unlike Nancy Astor (who refused to sign Rathbone's memos because she was not 'entirely confident as to the advisability of equal political rights for different races'),[49] Rathbone never accepted that democracy and individualism were specifically 'Western' concepts. While she continued, throughout the 1930s, to ask occasional parliamentary questions about social services for African women and to draw attention to instances in which women were disposed of by husbands or fathers against their will, she also emerged in 1935 as one of Haile Selassie's most impassioned defenders. Rathbone's involvements in Africa, then, never undermined her belief that parliamentary democracy and sexual equality were universal ideals – the highest and best to which humankind could aspire.

But how to export these ideals? By 1931, this question was on many people's minds. For Indian constitutional reform was now decisively on the table, and had – thanks to Mayo – become inextricably entwined with social questions. Indian nationalists had turned Mayo on her head: the 'social evils' Mayo cited as insurmountable barriers to self-government became, in their account, evidence of British imperial misgovernment and of the need for self-rule. Rathbone accepted that argument, but she gave it a feminist twist. For if those 'social evils' harmed women in particular, it was women who needed political power: the new constitution should shift power not only from Britons to Indians but also from Indian men to Indian women. This made sense to the reform-minded Conservatives in Britain involved in framing the new constitutional arrangements: they too tended to focus on India's complex social divisions and to become caught up in bean-counting exercises aimed at giving each possible 'interest' some slice of the political pie. They did not ask whether such an approach would make any sense to India's organized women.

To understand Rathbone's interventions in the process of Indian constitutional reform, we must first remind ourselves of the major milestones. Under the 1919 Government of India Act, India's constitutional arrangements were to be reviewed after ten years: the Indian Statutory Commission (an all-party parliamentary commission led by the Liberal, Sir John Simon) was thus appointed in the autumn of 1927. The Commission reported in May 1930 but Indian protests against its exclusively British composition, the election of a Labour government in 1929, and Lord Irwin's viceregal declaration endorsing dominion status for India, meant that it had by that point already been superseded. Instead, the Labour Prime Minister Ramsay MacDonald, supported by the Conservative leader Stanley Baldwin, agreed to a 'Round Table' method of proceeding, whereby prominent Indian politicians were brought to London to confer on the terms of devolution. Hostility from the Conservative Party's right wing, periodic boycotts by the Congress Party, and even replacement of a Labour by a National government in 1931 notwithstanding, a fragile alliance of cross-party British centrists and Indian moderates kept the process on track, and three Round Tables had been held by 1932. At that point cooperation broke down. A White Paper outlining the government's position was issued (in March 1933), and a Joint Select Committee of the Commons and the Lords appointed to give it legislative shape. That committee sat for some eighteen months, ultimately reporting in November 1934. After another six months of parliamentary debate and amendment, the 1935 Government of India Bill became law.[50]

Eleanor Rathbone took part in every stage of this process: this was the cause on which she honed her parliamentary skills and perfected the art of balancing lobbying with extra-parliamentary agitation. She kept up a private correspondence with every major British participant, from Sir John Simon and Wedgwood Benn in 1930 and 1931 to Secretary of State for India Sir Samuel Hoare and under-secretaries Lord Lothian and R.A. Butler during the period of the National government. In spite of her non-party stance, she established her right to be heard, and was the only British woman to give evidence on her own (and not some organization's) account to the Joint Select Committee. She kept in touch with most of the major Indian feminist leaders (even those with whom she disagreed) and met privately with the pivotal Indian 'moderates' as well. She was the force behind the creation of the formidable British Committee for Indian Women's Franchise and drafted much of its literature, including speeches appropriate to audiences of different political stripes.[51] She organized the women MPs (although not the diehard Atholl) to support her goals, arranged for parliamentary questions, memoranda, deputations and private lobbying, and masterminded the tabling of some twenty amendments. By 1935, government ministers found themselves warning the House against giving way to her eloquence,[52] and it is certainly because of her tenacity that on women's questions alone did changes to the bill move in a progressive direction in those final months when the government was busy appeasing its restive right wing. The incorporation of women into the 1935 constitution – and, still more, the *form* that incorporation took – thus had a great deal to do with Rathbone's representations.

This is the case because Rathbone never lost sight of her goal, never changed that goal, and never dropped the ball. From 1930 until 1935 her aim was the same: to secure the widest possible franchise for women and the largest number of seats for women in the new constitution. She also decided early on what she felt would be the best approach. In 1929, women held the provincial franchise in India on the same terms as men: because that franchise was property based, however, and few women held property in their own right, formal equality resulted in an electorate with a male–female ratio of twenty to one. Rathbone, recalling her suffrage experience, thought she had an answer. As early as March 1930, she told Sir John Simon that the easiest way to expand the women's electorate would be to consider wives joint owners of property, and enfranchise them on their husband's qualification. To expand the number of women representatives, she suggested that women not only be free to contest seats in provincial and federal assemblies but also should have some reserved for them. Only then would they have the power to address the serious problems besetting their sex.[53]

Simon was personally sympathetic, and when the Commission reported in May 1930 it included not only the much-quoted statement that the Indian women's movement was 'the key to progress'[54] but also a cautious endorsement of the idea of special franchise for wives of qualified men.[55] Rathbone, meanwhile, pulled together a small group of collaborators – among them the liberal educationalist Philip Hartog and his wife Mabel, Dorothea Layton, the ubiquitous Margery Corbett Ashby and Eva Hubback, and such sympathetic women MPs as Edith Picton-Turbervill and Nancy Astor. Some of these allies had already written (certainly with Rathbone's consent and possibly at her instigation) to Ramsay MacDonald or Wedgwood Benn putting forward her name as a delegate to the Round Table conference;[56] when she was not appointed, the group took up the usual tactics of memo-writing and deputations. Repeatedly, these returned to the twin panaceas of a 'wife's franchise' and reserved seats.[57]

These were, Rathbone thought, achievable goals. But they were not those of the Indian feminist movement. Although Reddi, among others, had in the past voiced some support for reserved seats, in the spring of 1931 all three of the main Indian women's organizations – the Women's Indian Association, the National Council of Women in India, and, most importantly, the All-India Women's Conference – agreed to a strictly egalitarian platform of universal adult suffrage and no reservation of seats.[58] Indian women's organizations were proud of the fact that they had convinced all but one provincial legislature to extend the franchise to women on the same terms as men, especially since they had accomplished this at a time when British women still suffered from age-based franchise restrictions. They recognized, of course, that few women had been able to qualify under this ostensibly 'sex-blind' standard, but insisted that the way forward was to remove the property qualification for *both* sexes rather than to jettison the principle of a sex-blind franchise entirely. In their own response to the Round Table conference, then, the three main Indian women's organizations called for adult suffrage without any special property, literacy or marriage qualifications, and without distinction of sex.[59]

Rathbone was taken aback. 'It seems to me very important that any proposals put forward by the women's movement in India should not only be desirable in themselves, but so carefully thought out that they cannot be laughed aside as impracticable,' she wrote to Reddi in May 1931. If the women's organizations stood out for adult suffrage (a demand that she thought, rightly, would never be considered), they would simply be dismissed as irrelevant,[60] but if they were willing to compromise, something might actually be gained. By January 1932, Rathbone was worried enough about the situation to take an unusual step. The Franchise subcommittee of the Round Table conference had endorsed her idea of special electoral qualifications for women,[61] and a committee chaired by Lord Lothian was about to set out for India to consult provincial governments and political organizations. Rathbone (who had hoped to be appointed to the committee) simply decided to go too. She was, she wrote to Subbarayan, 'very anxious to see things for myself' and hoped that she might 'be able to do something to dispel the suspicion of me which I know exists among those Indian women whom I encounter'.[62] Perhaps if she spoke to them personally, she would be able to bring them round.

Thus it was that, at the age of fifty-nine and accompanied by Hilda Gray, the wife of a Presbyterian minister with long experience in India, Eleanor Rathbone made her first trip to the East. Never willing to pass up a chance at lobbying, she travelled on the same boat as the Franchise subcommittee but was disappointed to find that 'the most important of them don't seem to hang about much'. Once in India she struck out on her own, travelling by train from Bombay to Madras and then across India to Nagpur, Lucknow, Calcutta and Lahore in a determined, six-week effort to canvass Indian (and especially Indian women's) views. This was not an easy task: she was regarded by some women in Bombay, she reported, as 'a spy and an "English K. Mayo"'. But her way was smoothed a bit by Subbarayan (with whose family she stayed in Madras), as well as by her own determination to clear the air. In Bombay, for example, she simply told the local feminist leaders that she had heard what they thought about her, and wanted to have it out; in Calcutta, she reported that 'one of the best . . . visits' was to a 'vociferous group of Congress-sympathizing ladies'. She had her own views but was willing to listen – and, as a result, met with Mrs Hamid Ali of the All India Women's Conference in Bombay, Reddi in Madras, the Nehrus in Lucknow. She went to receptions and meetings, hunted down governors, officials, and members of provincial franchise committees, and addressed the students at a women's college in Calcutta and members of a ladies' club in Nagpur.[63]

Those meetings opened her eyes to the intensity of nationalist feeling and the brutality of the British official response. Eager to hear the 'Indians' point of view', Eleanor found herself regaled with 'almost incredible' stories of official repression. These left her 'greatly perturbed': in terms 'of the completely arbitrary powers given to the police and the suddenness and secrecy with which they act', India seemed like Russia under the Tsar.[64] The Indian National Congress's position of 'non-cooperation', with which she had not been in sympathy, now seemed understandable. On her return she wrote to Ramsay MacDonald giving details of such abuses and arguing for a new approach to Gandhi.[65] As she told the Commons a few weeks later, with all the main Congress leaders behind bars, with even the ordinary sympathizer 'clapped into prison . . . for a purely technical offence', with 'every method of expressing . . . sympathy with the national movement' proscribed, small wonder India was in a state of 'sizzling discontent'. An acceptable constitutional settlement could never come out of this atmosphere; one needed to restore open consultation. And to do so, one must ease up on the emergency ordinances. After all, 'what is the plan of the Government? You cannot keep people in prison for ever.'[66]

The India trip also completed Rathbone's divorce from Katherine Mayo, whose Mother India she now recognized to be a deeply biased book. Although Rathbone had used it as a guidebook in India, going to see the temples of Kali and festivals in Benares that had so repelled Mayo, she had found that she responded differently. The temples of Kali, she thought, had a 'pleasant and pretty side which K.M. might have said more about – the little platters of fruit and garlands of flowers for offerings'. And Mayo had certainly 'exaggerate[d] the unpleasant side and ignore[d] the beautiful part' of Benares; as she remarked drily, '[a]s idolatry goes, river worship seems rather a natural and touching form of it'.[67] Rathbone had begun to distance herself from Mayo well before her India trip, but her travels widened the gulf. The India that Mayo had described as rife with dirt and disease, sadism and sensuality, Rathbone found to be a place of beauty and charm, idealism and conviction. Social problems abounded, she knew – but everywhere she turned, she found educated men and women eager to tackle them.

But if her Indian trip confirmed her belief that the time for devolution had come, it did not really shift her views about the demands that Indian women should make. The feminist organizations' dogged adherence to adult suffrage still struck her as stubborn and self-defeating. Rather fancifully, then, she began to question whether these organizations really represented more than 'a small body of opinion'; surely most activist Indian women 'really want reservation and special franchise qualifications'. True, she admitted to Lord Lothian, a majority did oppose the 'wife's franchise' and co-option as a method of filling reserved seats, but she thought their opposition based 'on ill-thought-out grounds, from which I could easily have dislodged them if I had had more time'.[68] This was not what Lothian's committee had heard from Mrs Rustomji Farudsonji, Vice-President of the All-India Women's Conference,[69] but they still took Rathbone's word. Using language virtually lifted from Rathbone, that committee recommended both some reservation of seats for women and two special women's qualifications – simple literacy (as opposed to the upper primary certificate required of men) and marriage to a man meeting the property qualification for the Federal Assembly vote – designed to raise the proportion of women in the electorate from 5 per cent to about 20 per cent.[70]

This was roughly what Rathbone had thought possible (at this stage), and she considered it a victory. But the Indian women's organizations were furious. They sent off angry letters to Hoare and MacDonald,[71] and – in a clever counter-move – brought their outrage to Rathbone's feminist home turf. The idea of a wifehood or widowhood franchise, one Indian delegate told a conference of the feminist British Commonwealth League meeting in London that summer, was 'ludicrous': 'it would give a new lease of life to the old male notion of women's *dependency* on man and as such it is repugnant to the educated and thinking women of India'. Some British 'equalitarians', already at odds with Rathbone for her espousal of 'new feminism', agreed. As a Miss Barry of the St Joan's Social and Political Alliance said: 'It seems to me . . . nothing short of impertinence for any outside body to dictate to Indian women what it thinks would be best for them. What should we have thought if Indian women had come to this country and when we were asking for equal enfranchisement with men had suggested that what we should have would be some sort of fancy franchise?'[72]

These words were aimed directly at Rathbone. Yet she continued to play her dangerous game. She kept up her contacts with Indian feminist leaders, especially Reddi and Rajkumari Amrit Kaur, President of the All India Women's Conference and the most articulate defender of the 'no special treatment' stance. She asked their opinions and scrupulously passed on their views, even hosting lunches at which they would meet the relevant ministers and politicians. She did this gladly: Rathbone genuinely admired Amrit Kaur's sharp mind and strong principles (this was, after all, a woman able to trade Latin aphorisms with Eton-educated Conservative parliamentarians) and believed that Indian women had every right to state their own case. Yet she also claimed to speak for 'Indian women', and she exploited her Commons position, her friendship with Subbarayan, her wide political contacts, and divisions within Indian feminism to keep special franchises and reserved seats on the table as the core 'feminist' demands. Thus, when the All-India Women's Conference sent Amrit Kaur and Mrs Hamid Ali to London to persuade the Joint Select Committee to abandon the 'wife's vote', Rathbone mobilized Subbarayan, her sister Sarala Ray, and Begum Shah Nawaz, who between them put together two petitions signed by several hundred women in favour of the Lothian proposals.[73] They also produced another Indian witness ('you will have to coach her,' Sarala Ray warned Rathbone)[74] to give conflicting evidence.[75]

Why did Rathbone go to these lengths to defend proposals that were, at best, controversial, and at worst positively disliked by a good portion of those she was claiming to represent? Two considerations pushed her in this direction. The first was, quite simply, her pragmatism. Rathbone understood that the British government would never concede adult suffrage; she also knew that the Government of India was deeply hostile to women's political involvement. When the Indian women's organizations reiterated their support for adult suffrage and proposed to boycott any reserved seats, then, she worried (as she told Reddi) that they would just 'play into the hands of the worst reactionaries both in your country and in mine'.[76] She was quite right, for the Government of India did gratefully cite Indian women's preference for 'a common franchise with men' when urging Westminster to drop any special women's franchise[77] – and the government White Paper, while not going that far, did drop the 'literacy' women's franchise and stipulate that wives should be required to 'apply' for their votes.[78] Such an 'application' process would wipe out more than half of the projected female electorate, Lothian protested to Hoare,[79] but Hoare retorted that there was really nothing he could do. 'There is no part of the White Paper that has given more trouble than the paragraphs about the women's vote,' he told Lothian: almost every provincial government opposed the literacy qualification and insisted on application for the wife's vote.[80] Rathbone had thought that the Indian women's organizations would 'come round'. That they would prefer no bread at all to the half-loaf of a wife's franchise and reserved seats was something she was entirely unable to understand.

And this was the case, second, because she suffered from the illusion of familiarity: this conflict was (she thought) about women's suffrage, a subject on which she could claim unrivalled expertise. Her positions are comprehensible, then, if we recognize the extent to which she interpreted all Indian positions and dilemmas not as shaped by racial, cultural, or even national difference, but through the lens of her own experiences as a feminist politician. Rathbone had, after all, negotiated a 'wife's' local government franchise in the 1918 Representation of the People Act; as a university member, she herself sat for a type of 'reserved seat'. When she confronted the All-India Women's Conference's 'strict egalitarianism', or heard arguments denigrating wives' political capacities, Rathbone tended to hear echoes of debates she had been having for years. Subbarayan shouldn't be too depressed about the women's organizations' 'impractical' line, Rathbone wrote to her as early as May 1931: 'We had much the same difficulties to encounter here from our own extremists.'[81] British feminists had also opposed the wife's vote when first introduced, she assured Reddi, but it had accomplished what it intended – which had been to enfranchise as large a number of women as possible.[82] Although herself the ultimate 'non-militant', Rathbone also drew on the suffragette legacy, warning Wedgwood Benn that with 'twenty years' experience in the suffrage movement', she knew plenty of 'blatant methods of getting the facts across the footlights'.[83] In a campaign she thought of as 'great fun . . . like sniffing the old suffrage atmosphere again',[84] Rathbone's old ally Ray Strachey helped conjure up the spectre of 'not only a suffrage agitation, but a militant agitation' to strike fear in the government's timid heart.[85]

This was pure fantasy, of course, for Indian women were not about to embark on militancy in order to win the unsought prize of the wife's vote. They were 'militants' already, in what they thought was a much greater national cause.[86] And yet this language of feminist solidarity mattered, for it justified and enabled (to herself and others) Rathbone's own prominent role. She was not motivated by 'any spirit of interference', Rathbone wrote to Reddi in May 1931; she and other British women merely wished to feel 'that the experience we have accumulated in our own struggle is of benefit to others'.[87] 'You may think that it is not for an Englishwoman to make these suggestions,' she wrote to Amrit Kaur about the child marriage question on another occasion. 'But where sufferings and injustices affecting women are concerned, I as an old suffragist simply cannot remember or bother about national distinctions.'[88] Rathbone's loyalty to the memory of the suffrage movement had its charming side – leading her, for example, to send her Indian correspondents copies of Sylvia Pankhurst's *The Suffragette Movement* as presents – but it also made her seriously myopic. Only someone blind to all power imbalances save those of sex could have said to women active in a nationalist cause that she 'trust[ed] you may never have to go through such a long and weary struggle as we had'.[89]

Dr Muthulakshmi Reddi and Rajkumari Amrit Kaur did Rathbone the honour of arguing with her. They always answered her letters; they always spoke their minds. Repeatedly, Rathbone sought to persuade them of the universality of sexual antagonism and the importance of feminist solidarity: 'It seems to me,' she wrote to Reddi, 'opposed to all the principles of democracy and unjust in every way, that under a pretence of nominal equality, women should be put off with a negligible proportion of both votes and seats': adequate numbers were the real goal.[90] But Reddi and Amrit Kaur both disagreed. 'Quality' was more important than 'quantity';[91] rural women under the thumb of their husbands would not be allies in the cause of social reform.[92] When they finally agreed to propose an alternative limited franchise, then, they suggested enfranchising literate and urban women;[93] to the very end they expressed their 'deep indignation at the wifehood qualification which has been imposed on us in spite of repeated protests'.[94] Their stance shows the investment Indian activists had in the claim to modernity, but it was also a sign of their own 'pragmatism' – of their concern to maintain a powerful and united women's movement. Even Subbarayan and Shah Nawaz, much criticized by their compatriots for their participation in the Round Table process, told Rathbone that this must be a priority. Reserved seats organized along communal lines would divide a hitherto united movement and hence actually retard women's progress, Subbarayan warned; Shah Nawaz brought the message home by simply refusing to stand in a 'Muslim' constituency.[95] Rathbone, always slow to realize that a woman might not represent 'women', never quite grasped the depth of their feeling.

Nor did she entirely realize that, for most of her correspondents, the 'women's clauses' of the India bill were not the major concern. 'Women are far too nationally minded now to accept any favours for themselves to the detriment of their country's interests,' Amrit Kaur wrote to Rathbone in February 1935: given Congress support for social reform, women need not prepare for struggle against their countrymen.[96] They desired, instead, a constitution that would promote a genuinely 'national' consciousness – and here the bill, with its separate electorates and special reservations, fell dramatically short. Gently but unambiguously, Amrit Kaur told Rathbone that she was part of the problem, for British ministers had consistently listened to Rathbone and her British women's lobby rather than to the Indian women's organizations. Confronting Rathbone's preference for 'working to get what we can as we can and making it a basis for more',[97] Amrit Kaur said that she did not 'quite agree' with her: 'In a free country like yours – yes – but in a subject country – no – because a start on the wrong basis means disaster ab initio.'[98] Their argument was not simply about tactics: it was about the ultimate goal itself. Political fragmentation and national division, if structured into the constitution, might never be overcome.

Rathbone never fully understood this, for she could never see India as a conquered and occupied country (as nationalists did) rather than as an adopted infant being raised painfully to adulthood. From 1933 until 1935, then, Rathbone campaigned to shape and then to amend the Government of India Bill in ways that she thought of as feminist but that India's most prominent women's organizations found deeply problematic. She became a thorn in the government's flesh, for almost all the women MPs, most of the important British women's organizations, and a powerful lobby of prominent liberals and reformers supported her efforts; only a few organizations – the British Commonwealth League, the International League for Peace and Freedom – objected that too little attention had been paid to Indian women's own views.[99] And it was Rathbone's arguments – and not those of the Indian feminists – that carried the day. Pressure from the British women's lobby, echoed by the Joint Select Committee itself, forced London to approach Delhi for further concessions: in the end, many of the provinces reluctantly did dispense with the requirement that eligible wives 'apply' for their votes and reduced their educational qualification to simple literacy for women alone – although (to Indian feminists' horror) women's reserved seats *were* introduced along communal lines. The form in which women were incorporated into the new Indian constitution, then, was profoundly influenced by Rathbone's interventions.

One could read this story as an exercise in 'feminist imperialism' or cultural condescension, and certainly some historians have been inclined to see it in such terms.[100] Yet the story is more complicated, for while Rathbone did hold some valuable cards – she had the credentials and connections, she was the one in Parliament – her room to manoeuvre was, as she knew, seriously limited. She could influence the ways in which women figured in the bill; she could not alter the nature of the bill itself. She could, in other words, work to have women included in that long list of identifiable 'interests' – castes and classes, princes and provinces, regions and religions – granted recognition and political representation; she could not do much about the decision to treat devolution as an exercise in political containment (rather than national consolidation) in the first place. Yet it was the bill's wider logic – its determination to fragment political identities and hence to retard the development of national consciousness and (especially) impede Congress dominance – that Indian progressives so deplored. Amrit Kaur certainly understood that logic, and recoiled from it.

But, in the end, so too did Rathbone. For, after spending almost five years working on its shaping, Rathbone voted *against* the India bill in its crucial second reading. She did so with some uncertainty, for she still felt that it was, from the standpoint of women, a step forward. Amrit Kaur had, however, asked her to 'ponder wisely before voting for a constitution which is definitely contrary to the wishes of educated men and women of India', and in this instance she deferred to their views.[101] She herself found the bill's solicitude towards the autocratic princely states profoundly offensive; she was also swayed by the fact that 'many of those Indians whose judgment I most respect would rather have no Bill at all than this Bill'.[102] Her gesture may have seemed quixotic (she went on to vote for the third reading),[103] but it relieved her feelings: just because she had worked (and would still work) to make a profoundly undemocratic bill less undemocratic, she didn't need to pretend that she approved it. Before we conclude that Rathbone was simply a pawn in the hands of a government bent on undermining Congress power, we should remember this moment – the moment Rathbone walked into the lobby on the opposition side, and then, characteristically, returned with another sheaf of improving amendments. These were the acts of someone able to be both an idealist and a pragmatist – able to hold to her faith in the ideals of self-government but insist on the right of women, always, to play a central part.

But what of the issue of child marriage – the cause that had brought Rathbone to support devolution in the first place? Rathbone never lost sight of this question. While in India, she had asked provincial governors and officials how they were responding to Wedgwood Benn's inquiry into the administration of the Sarda Act, only to learn that no governor had ever heard of such an inquiry;[104] enraged, on her return she continued her barrage of letters and parliamentary questions (by July 1933, she had asked eleven questions on the enforcement of the Sarda Act alone). Her speeches in the House, her evidence to the Select Committee, and indeed virtually all the leaflets and propaganda issued by the British Committee for Indian Women's Franchise cited child marriage as the reason women needed a wider franchise. Moreover, as early as 1931 Rathbone had warned cabinet ministers that she might, if not satisfied by the government's reforming efforts, 'revert to "Mayo tactics"' and publish a muckraking book of her own. Since they never did satisfy her, early in 1934 she brought out *Child Marriage: The Indian Minotaur*, complete with a reproduction of G.F. Watt's painting of the Minotaur on the cover (a painting, aptly enough, done for W.T. Stead's 'Maiden Tribute' campaign so many years ago). Prices were kept down and review copies copiously sent out in Britain and in India, but the book had, as the Lucknow *Pioneer* noted, 'a very quiet reception'.[105]

Rathbone was not best pleased. She had taken great care, in writing the book, to be 'scrupulously fair'.[106] She made clear that early marriage was practised by Muslims as well as Hindus, thus avoiding Mayo's anti-Hindu line; she also spread blame liberally, reserving much of her fire for a supine British establishment. And, most important, she explicitly confronted the question of her own position as an Englishwoman commenting on an Indian question. Reviewers in Britain and India praised that openness. Rathbone wrote, said the *Spectator*, 'not as a European lecturing Asiatics but as one human being sympathizing with another;'[107] Miss Rathbone, reported *Stri Dharma*, 'feels as one with the Indian women, those who suffer as well as those who are trying to fight this evil'.[108] The Indian reformers to whom Rathbone sent the book – Reddi, Amrit Kaur, Mrs Hamid Ali, Sarala Ray, Lakshmi Menon, and the Begum Shah Nawaz, among others – echoed these views. 'I do not see anything in it that should hurt the feelings of any Indian women,' wrote Amrit Kaur.[109] 'I will not misunderstand you now,' added Reddi, 'as I have known you personally.'[110]

What Rathbone had not anticipated, however, was that her hard-won sensitivity, her determination to pay tribute to Indian reformers and to load British administrators with their share of the blame, would hardly appeal to Mayo's many fans. For by locating 'difference' firmly in the realm of sex rather than race, by attributing child marriage not to Indian racial degeneracy but to the dominance and oppression of men across cultural lines, Rathbone removed the grounds for a straightforwardly imperialist response. After all, it wasn't human-itarianism that had retired colonels and matrons in Tunbridge Wells devouring Mayo's book: it was the enticing spectacle of those broken brown bodies, those ravaged Indian children crawling towards mission hospitals and white lady doctors to die. *Child Marriage* offered no such uncomplicated pleasures, and those in search of them left the book alone.

Not that Rathbone gave up: she continued to plague the government with parliamentary questions; she asked her Indian correspondents to consider the suggestions in her book (they did); she offered to raise money to pay an organ-izer to build up an anti-child marriage campaign (they refused).[111] They already had 'Sarda committees' working in almost every constituency, Mrs Hamid Ali reported to Rathbone, but those committees were much hampered by the defi-ciencies of the Sarda Act, which – though very useful in shaping public opinion – was almost useless as an enforcement measure.[112] Rathbone took the point. She had noted in her book the need to amend the Act to allow courts to issue injunc-tions against marriages and to investigate cases on their own account, and had been in touch with the Indian labour leader N.M. Joshi about the possibility of an amending bill. Joshi promised to find a sponsor, and in early 1935 Rathbone had a bill drafted. 'I think it might prejudice the Bill's chances if it was supposed that it was engineered by English People,' Rathbone wrote to Joshi, suggesting he keep her name out of it.[113] He did so: a Congress Party member agreed to introduce the bill and was never told of Rathbone's part in it; the AIWC then worked up a pro-bill campaign, innocently enlisting her aid in lobbying. Then the legislative mills began their slow grind. By 1938, when the bill finally passed, Rathbone was caught up in efforts to support Republican Spain and had lost track of it.

Eleanor Rathbone spent much of the period of the National government on impe-rial questions, to real political effect. Oddly, though, those involvements never really dented the cast of her mind. In 1935 she remained what she had been in 1927: a meliorist feminist and liberal, convinced of the universal applicability of progressive ideals and eager to spread the twin goods of parliamentary institu-tions and women's emancipation around the world. Indeed, if the Indian cam-paigns did anything, they made Eleanor even more sceptical of arguments about racial difference. Katherine Mayo did her best to convince Rathbone that India's subjection (like Britain's domination) was racially justified, even natural, but Rathbone was never persuaded. Having met Indian social reformers and battled with British ministers, she was unable to see the former as degenerates and libertines and the latter as moral exemplars. Instead, idealism and cynicism, progress and reaction, seemed to her everywhere in evidence, and everywhere in contest. This realization stripped imperialism of its humanitarian cloak. No longer able to assume that her country always followed the path of right, Rathbone sought to bolster the forces of social progress wherever they might be found.

These campaigns brought Rathbone another step closer to the role she would adopt in the late 1930s – the role of an independent defender of democratic ideals, increasingly at odds with a government she felt would not promote them. But precisely because Rathbone was able in the Indian case to support self-determination without (in effect) accepting cultural relativism, her resolution left some difficult questions unexplored. For if Indian devolution was justifiable because Indians had demonstrated their commitment to liberal conceptions of modernity and social reform, was it inappropriate where elites would not make such a commitment? What was to be done when nationalist movements or cultures would not adapt to 'modern' or Western norms? When ideals of self-determination and ideals of social modernity came into conflict, on which side should one come down?

For the most part, Rathbone avoided such questions. In one illuminating instance, however, we see her face them directly. In September 1934, during the parliamentary recess and before the India bill debates, Rathbone and Macadam took a five-week trip together to Palestine. The trip was partly pleasure. Macadam had just completed *The New Philanthropy*, her magisterial survey of the evolution of Britain's social services, and probably felt she deserved a real holiday. But Rathbone had also become caught up in a fight with the Colonial Office over a proposed municipal franchise bill for Palestine that would, effectively, disfranchise those women who had won the vote in Jewish areas in the wake of the First World War. Jewish feminists, organized into a Palestine Women's Equal Rights Association, were furious, and British feminists rallied to their cause. Throughout 1933 and 1934, Rathbone kept up a correspondence with their President, one Mrs Rosa Welt Strauss, and bombarded the Colonial Office with letters, deputations and parliamentary questions.[114] Officials, predictably, retorted that they were merely deferring to the 'strong objections ... entertained, not only by Moslems, but also by certain Jews, to the participation of women in public affairs',[115] but Rathbone had developed a healthy scepticism of such arguments. In what was becoming her usual *modus operandi*, she decided to travel to Palestine to see for herself.

Early in the morning of 11 September, after a flight over the Nile and the desert, Eleanor and Elizabeth landed in Gaza, rented a car, and drove forty miles to Jerusalem. They put up at the American Hostel and threw themselves into energetic sightseeing. They explored Jerusalem, visited the excavations at Jericho, swam in the Red Sea, and tramped through Nazareth and Bethlehem, Bethesda and Hebron, bibles in hand. They toured Tiberias, Capernaum and Damascus;

they drove through Lebanon. These were memorable, magical days, especially for Elizabeth, who had never lost her childhood religious faith, and who would leave money in her will for impoverished clergy couples wanting to make such a pilgrimage.

But they didn't just admire the old, they saw the new as well. As a prominent MP, Eleanor's visit was a matter of some importance – and, as she discovered to her consternation, almost all the settlers she met wanted immediately to know which side she was on. Eleanor was eager to be fair and went out of her way to see 'both sides', but – given her personality, connections and ideals – the contest was an unequal one. She had already come to know and like Rosa Welt Strauss; she also felt immediately at home with 'Mrs. Goldie Myerson' (later, of course, Golda Meir), who took her to see some of the projects of the Jewish Agency for Palestine. Eleanor was greatly impressed by the settlements and schools, scientific institutions and farms; by contrast, her trip to some Arab villages was a disaster. Her guides would not let her touch the feast that had been laboriously prepared, and Eleanor further dismayed her hosts by asking to see the women's quarters. She thought them dirty and squalid, and – being already exercised about child marriage in Palestine[116] – was not surprised that the census had revealed a population with a serious preponderance of men. Such statistics, she told the Grand Mufti himself in a carefully arranged interview, showed that Arabs took better care of boys. The Palestinian district officer interpreting for her was appalled by her rudeness, and the interview ended abruptly, leaving Rathbone with a rooted dislike for the Mufti that she never lost. 'Would it matter to the progress of civilization if all the Arabs were drowned in the Mediterranean?' Rathbone meditatively asked Margaret Nixon, the government official assigned to chaperon her, on a drive to Jaffa and Tel Aviv. Nixon hotly defended Arab culture, and Rathbone reluctantly agreed, but she had, as Nixon recalled, 'showed her bias'.[117]

Hence her revealing speech, early in October, in a crowded Jerusalem lecture hall. Rathbone did little public speaking in Palestine, but she had agreed to address Rosa Strauss's Palestine Women's Equal Rights Association about the British women's movement. She began, as she often did, by insisting on the importance of the suffrage victory, and on the need for both 'equalitarian' and 'new feminist' reforms. Unusually, however, Rathbone then went on to discuss a third new effort by British women's organizations – the effort to spread feminist ideals to other women in the empire, 'or, as I prefer to call it, the British Commonwealth of Nations'. Even though 'nations and races stand divided from one another by a number of vertical, upstanding walls, by political frontiers and economic rivalries and antagonisms of race and religion', the commonality of sex remained, cutting 'right through these vertical walls, enabling women belonging to rival and even hostile races to hold out their hands to each other'. Together, women could combat the 'common enemy of masculine predominance' wherever it might be found.

But what if women did not consider 'masculine predominance' the main enemy? What if women were divided from one another not only by race and religion and nationality but possibly even by feminism – by that claim to universality that wore, so often, an aggressively Western face? The Indian women's movement's deep commitment to modernity (and British officials' hidebound conservatism) had allowed Rathbone to duck this question: Palestine, however, made her face it head-on. In many ways, she said, 'the women of the Jewish community here seem to have gone further ahead than the women of any other race anywhere': they had achieved a real equality of opportunity in all spheres of work 'such as I have no where else seen equalled'. But they were 'surrounded with women' – Arab women – 'whose limbs are still in the shackles of a traditional subjection'. Jewish women should not be content with this situation: just as British women had worked to emancipate Indian women, so should Jewish women share the benefits of emancipation with their Arab sisters.

Rathbone returned, once again, to the classic Millian stance: insisting on the universality of her progressive ideals, even as she yoked them to particular national projects or forms. And this position led her, as it had led Mill, to a kind of imperialism – an imperialism of 'progress', or of social reform. Mill, after all, had thought British dominion in India justified because it would push India up the ladder of civilizations, and while Eleanor had come to doubt British officials' devotion to these ideals, she had few such reservations about the Zionists she met. She saw in Zionism, then, what she would have liked (but was not able) to see in British imperialism: the determination to spread progressive ideals – including sexual egalitarianism – from West to East.

Rathbone ended her speech on an unusually personal note. She had been reading, she reported, Arnold Toynbee's *A Study of History*, in which Toynbee sought to compare the world's great civilizations and to puzzle out the reasons for their progress or decay. The book had made her wonder how she should understand the Zionist experiment under way around her. Could this be the 'first day's progress of a new civilization', and, if so, what were its distinctive elements? How much did it draw on Western and Eastern European ideals, and would it be infected by 'disease germs' brought from those cultures? Rathbone, clearly, thought patriarchy the worst such 'germ', but the evidence she had seen left her feeling 'very optimistic' on that score. She was, she said, only a little sad to know that she would not live long enough to see the experiment's outcome. To her audience's excitement and the amazement of Macadam (who could never imagine being anyone but the Scotswoman she was), Rathbone confessed that if she 'believed in the transmigration of souls and could choose the place of my next resurrection', she might well 'choose to be a Jew in Palestine'.[118]

Two years earlier, at the end of one of the Round Table conferences, Eleanor's half-brother Harry had written to her brother-in-law Hugh to lament the project of Indian constitutional reform. The whole exercise was just 'putting into the heads of the callow youths all sorts of half-digested and impractical ideas ill suited to the orient', ideas that would probably just lead to 'nihilism or sovietism'. And Eleanor, he complained, was aiding and abetting the whole thing. The dangers seem to have escaped her. She is 'such an uncompromising Britisher and has always British ideas and Democracy at the back of her head and I do not think is gifted with a very vivid imagination'. She would never back down, 'and we shall never see things eye to eye'.[119]

Harry was quite right about Eleanor's attachment to 'democracy', but he was wrong about her lack of imagination. True, she was not attracted to the novel or exotic; as we know, she had little interest in cultural or religious variation. What she had, however, was empathy – and when it was engaged, her imagination was quite powerful enough. Even as a young woman, Rathbone had admitted to Hilda Oakeley her 'curious' tendency to find her thoughts dominated by images of human suffering; travelling through Sicily in 1906, she was oppressed by the knowledge that every inch in the country must have been 'drenched again and again with blood and tears'.[120] When she read Mayo's book, she again had no trouble visualizing young girls' helplessness and suffering, nor could she believe it different or less because their skins were not white. A body in pain was to her a body in pain – wherever hidden, however hushed. Evie, who knew Eleanor so much better than Harry, understood this, and as the 1930s served up ever more terrible tragedies, worried about her sister's stamina and health. In 1932 Eleanor turned sixty, but she had, like her father before her, no intention at all of slowing down. The decade that followed would be the most taxing of her life.

Coda

Miss Rathbone has her Portrait Painted

24. Portrait by James Gunn, 1933.

When Eleanor Rathbone arrived back in London from her India trip in early March 1932, she found an odd request awaiting her. In her absence, her friends had decided to have her portrait painted. Four co-conspirators – Rathbone's girlhood friend Oliver Lodge, the Vice-Chancellor of Liverpool University H.J.W. Hetherington, Eva Hubback and an old Liverpool friend L.M. Mott – had dreamt up the plan, but colleagues from every part of her life gladly pledged their support. That group now asked Rathbone for permission to gather contributions and choose an artist.

Rathbone was at once touched and taken aback. 'I do not believe that I belong to the small class of persons who justify public portraits,' she protested in a letter; nor should one really be spending money on such frivolous things during hard times. And what would one do with the finished product? 'A spinster does not want to gaze on her own portrait in her own home.' The societies she had worked with most closely were necessarily 'temporarily and modestly housed', and her claim on more permanent institutions was not very strong. 'I can foresee discussions, fifty, twenty, even ten years hence, as to "What is to be done with *this*?" ' she wrote. And the answer was likely to be ' "Oh, put her in – " (mentioning some dark passage or unfrequented chamber.)'

But the friends wanted to go ahead anyway, and Rathbone was gratified enough to let them do so. A subscription list was opened in May; soon, with more than £200 in the kitty, the committee began to search for an artist. Rathbone's preference for a 'slight water-colour or pastel sketch, or even a photograph' was quickly brushed aside, and the commission given to the prominent portrait painter James Gunn.[1] It was an excellent choice. Gunn presented Rathbone as a woman of determination and intellect – clear-eyed, unsmiling, soberly clad, with a book resting on her knee. Something about her pose – the pressed lips, the clenched hand, the fact that one thumb is book-marking a place – suggests impatience, a kind of restless energy held almost painfully in check. She wants to be up and doing, this woman; at the very least, she wants to get back to her book.

This is one view of Eleanor Rathbone at sixty, but by publishing the list of contributors the 'portrait committee' left us with a second view as well. For the lines of Rathbone's public image can easily be discerned from this list of more than 270 names. Those names were mostly provincial and even more heavily female: 80 per cent of those who gave money were women, and the majority of those were spinsters. The women MPs were well represented, and there was a good showing from the Liberal intellectuals who supported Rathbone's candidacies and causes, but local worthies predominated. Liverpool's Unitarian and philanthropic elite and the remnants of the constitutional suffragist movement joined together to salute her, the most perfect representative of the reforming bluestocking 'type'.

They were so proud of her, Liverpool's most famous daughter – but even as they honoured her, she was leaving them behind. Eleanor tried to make it back to Liverpool for City Council and housing committee meetings, but those trips became harder and harder to sandwich into her busy London schedule. As regular weekly trips dwindled to a couple of days a month, the Liverpool house – with its secretary and staff – seemed an extravagance, and in the early 1930s Eleanor rented it out. Elizabeth convinced her, on the other hand, to expand the cramped London establishment by buying the house next door. Throughout the thirties, then, Eleanor would stay with Evie and Hugh at Greenbank when in Liverpool, but since Evie had never much liked Elizabeth, and Hugh rather resented

Eleanor's growing fame (although he would never have said so), that arrangement had its tensions. Although returned unopposed to the City Council again in 1932, Rathbone's attendance became sporadic, and in November 1935 she decided not to stand again. She had sat on the Liverpool Council for twenty-six uninterrupted years.

And as Eleanor slipped out of Liverpool's grasp, her relationship to the women's movement began to change as well. True, she kept a vigilant eye out for women's interests in the Commons; she remained the only woman MP proud to call herself a feminist. But in 1933, the year Gunn did his work, the world changed utterly, and Eleanor's world changed with it. Many in Britain would see Hitler as just a German nationalist of a particularly uncouth stripe, but Rathbone was not one of them: from the outset, she saw him as the avatar of a coherent and repellent world-view, as the leader of a movement with which democracy could not compromise. 'The Nazi revolution,' she wrote to her constituents in her 1934 annual letter, 'had an effect on the political atmosphere like some frightful volcanic eruption on a city untouched but near-by. It was difficult to get the stench out of one's nostrils, the sights of horror out of one's mind, or to feel as if anything else mattered.'[2] For the next twelve years, Rathbone would circle the volcano, trying to pull a few living bodies from the flames.

PART IV

A WORLD TO SAVE

25. SS *Stanbrook* off Oran, loaded with Spanish Republicans seeking refuge, 1939.

It is just as though one stood hour after hour, day after day, with a small group of people outside the bars behind which hordes of men, women and children were enduring every kind of deliberately inflicted physical and mental torture. We scrape at the bars with little files. A few victims are dragged painfully one by one through the gaps. And all the time we are conscious that streams of people are passing behind us unaware of or indifferent to what is happening, who could if they united either push down the bars and rescue the victims, or – much more dangerously – stop the torturers.

Rathbone, 'A Personal View of the Refugee Problem',
New Statesman and Nation, 15 April 1939, p. 568.

Chapter 14

Prophet without Honour

On 13 April 1933, less than three months after Hitler's accession to power, Rathbone rose to take part in a debate in the Commons about how Britain should respond to the new German regime. Many in the House felt guilt and compunction towards Germany. The harsh terms of the Versailles treaty were widely deplored in the twenties; successive British governments had come think revision necessary to European stability and peace. But now, prominent MPs of all parties spoke up to warn the National government against a conciliatory stance. The Labour Party did support revision, Clement Attlee said, but not revision under the threat of force. Given current German treatment of minorities, other vulnerable populations could not be placed under Hitler's rule. Austen Chamberlain, who as Foreign Secretary had worked so hard to bring a newly democratic Germany into the League, concurred. 'What is this new spirit of German nationalism?' he asked. 'The worst of the all-Prussian imperialism, with an added savagery, a racial pride, an exclusiveness which cannot allow to any fellow-subject not of "pure Nordic birth" equality of rights and citizenship within the nation to which he belongs. . . . That is not a Germany to which we can afford to make concessions.' Rathbone, the only woman to speak in this debate, expressed her 'passionate agreement'. Given Hitler's racial ideas and treatment of the Jews, it would be a crime to accede to German requests for mandates or to purchase its good will by allowing a measure of rearmament.[1]

Rathbone recalled this debate as a rare moment of agreement – a moment when the House spoke across party lines and with a single voice.[2] Not until 1940 would it do so again. Divisions emerged not because some were uncommitted to peace, for everyone – from Winston Churchill on the Conservative right to George Lansbury on the Labour left – wished fervently to avoid another war. What they could not agree on was just how to prevent that calamity. Churchill had one answer: for two centuries, Britain had not allowed the emergence of a dominant power on the continent, whatever its political stripe, and should not do so now.[3] Lansbury had another: as a Christian and a pacifist, he clung to hopes of disarmament even as the world changed. But for the vast mass of people and politicians in the middle, the matter was not so simple. To assess the extent of the threat, and to decide how Britain should respond, required a fine mix of political and strategic judgement. Whether the new German regime was inherently aggressive or simply seeking specific territorial concessions, whether ideological solidarity would inevitably outweigh strategic considerations and force Italian fascism into the Nazi camp, whether indeed the 'collective security' arrangements of the League provided a workable foundation for Britain's security and Europe's peace, were in 1933 all open questions.

It took Rathbone two years to work out her answers. She was convinced from the outset that the Nazi regime was not only internally autocratic but a potent foreign threat – a fact that, she wrote in the *Manchester Guardian* that May, made the Nazi persecution of Jews and socialists 'intimately our own affair'. The German government would happily turn the hatred and revenge being visited on these vulnerable groups against France, Poland and its other former enemies; indeed, if Britain turned a blind eye, such attempts were simply a matter of time. 'No one who has studied the evidence can doubt that Germany wants peace just until she has completed the preparations for war,' Rathbone said in a public speech that same month, but if 'Hitlerism and Fascism secured the leadership of Europe at which they so plainly aim', how long would free democracy in any country survive?[4] 'Must we not frankly realise,' she asked the Commons in early 1934, 'that oil and water cannot mix, and that . . . the best kind of security would be one which there does not seem much opportunity of obtaining from any Disarmament Convention that is at present possible? That security is in the drawing together of the free democracies of the world in defence of something which is even a greater cause than the cause of peace, the cause of the liberties and freedom of the world.'[5]

'Liberty' and 'freedom': here, unapologetically, Rathbone reiterates her democratic creed. As a younger generation was coming to see the world through the lens of class and to divide nations into rival communist and capitalist camps, Rathbone still judged all states by their record on civil liberties and political rights. Having grown up before enfranchisement, she wrote in a letter to the *Inquirer* in June, she would always place 'liberty . . . first of all', and those who would treat it lightly should consider whether they really would 'rather be an Italian in Fascist Italy or a Russian under the dictatorship of the proletariat'.[6] But if Rathbone was already sceptical of those who thought it possible to conciliate either Mussolini or Hitler and worried by what she saw as a lack of realism and commitment especially among the young, she remained for a time uncertain what to do – whether, for example, to support the government's rearmament plans despite its hesitations about the League, or to ally herself with Labour, which was firmly behind the League but entirely opposed to rearmament. In 1934, Rathbone still came down on the Labour side,[7] but a year later she had concluded she could no longer do so. Britain must *both* sustain its military power and unambiguously uphold the principles of collective security under the League. There were risks to that policy, of course, but the risks of either unpreparedness or ambivalence were surely greater. Look at what happened in Abyssinia, Rathbone would say – a tragedy that weighed on her mind for the rest of her life.

The Abyssinian crisis hit home in Britain in late 1935 but arose almost a year earlier, when Italian troops clashed with Ethiopian soldiers on the border between Ethiopia and Italian Somaliland. Mussolini, eager to revenge the 1896 débâcle at Adowa and hungry for an empire of his own, complained hotly of Ethiopian aggression and began shipping in troops; Haile Selassie, the newly crowned Abyssinian emperor, declared his wish for peace and appealed to the League. In the summer of 1935, as the Italians mobilized, Rathbone, like the rest of the British public, woke up to the fact that the 'test' of the League might come here, of all places – and that Britain and France might be required to come to Abyssinia's defence. The foreign policy establishment in the two countries viewed this prospect without enthusiasm. The British Foreign Office had always thought Abyssinia an unsettled warlord state with an unpleasant habit of slave-trading and had opposed its 1923 bid for membership; the French, desperately worried by German revanchism, were determined to avoid offending Italy. But could they abandon Abyssinia without destroying the authority of the League?

Rathbone was sure they could not. Listening to ministers' half-hearted language in the Commons, however, she worried that they might wish to try. France and Britain had made clear their wish to retain Italy's friendship at Stresa in April 1935; while they had gone on to ban arms sales to both sides in May, this move had hurt only lightly armed Ethiopia.[8] British public opinion would favour 'a more vigorous British initiative', Rathbone wrote to Lloyd George; couldn't his 'Council of Action' do something to mobilize that feeling?[9] He was noncommittal, but she did what she could on her own. She had already lent her name to a boycott of goods from (and tourism to) Germany; now, she urged economic sanctions to hamper Italian preparations for war.[10] Baldwin's accession as Prime Minister in June 1935 and his appointment of Sir Samuel Hoare as Foreign Secretary in place of the ineffectual Sir John Simon had been a hopeful sign, but when Hoare finally reaffirmed Britain's commitment to the League in an important speech in Geneva on 11 September, Rathbone felt a mixture of relief and frustration. 'The great majority of thoughtful citizens' she later told the Commons, must have reacted – as she had – by saying 'first "At last" and then "Too late"'. Some 200,000 Italian troops were massed on Ethiopia's borders by that point; when the attack came three weeks later (and, finally, brought economic sanctions against Italy in its train), Rathbone was not surprised. Hoare might insist that he had warned Mussolini against such action, she told the House on 22 October, but 'after all, the adequacy of those warnings must be judged by the results'. The government was fighting the current election with a promise to uphold the principles of the League; should it fail to do so, its supporters would feel 'bitter disillusion and a sense of betrayal'.[11]

Not for the last time, Rathbone's words proved prophetic. The Baldwin government came out of the November 1935 election with a comfortable majority, but within weeks its handling of the Abyssinian crisis had caused a political storm. On 10 December, Members of Parliament awoke to read in the papers that Hoare and his French counterpart Pierre Laval, meeting in Paris two days earlier, had agreed on a plan to appease Italy with substantial territorial concessions. Harold Nicolson, just elected to Parliament as a 'National Labour' member, went to the House that evening to find it 'seething', and to listen to 'a very noble speech' by Rathbone expressing its sense of indignation and betrayal.[12] Rathbone was usually a logical rather than an eloquent speaker, but that evening outrage gave her wings. Much of Rathbone's thinking on foreign policy was captured in that speech, so let us listen to her excoriating words.

She began rather nervously. Backbenchers, she noted, were at a disadvantage speaking in such a debate: they hadn't even the full terms of the offer to Abyssinia in front of them; they had had no time to prepare. And yet, anyone who had read the morning papers and then listened to the statement of the Minister for League Affairs (Viscount Cranborne) must have had their misgivings deepened rather than lightened. Six months ago, the House had urged the government to make it clear to any aggressor that the authority of the League could not be flouted; instead, France and Britain had colluded to reward Mussolini with 'terms incomparably better . . . than he was offered before he went to war at all'. Abyssinia – 'the one independent nation left in Africa, whose independence and integrity the League is pledged to protect' – was to be asked to cede almost half its territory: but what if Abyssinia refused – as it surely *should* refuse? Would the League *then* defend Abyssinia's sovereignty, or would it wash its hands of the matter and stand aside? The government was behaving, she charged, like a man who, having discovered a highwayman in the act of robbing a passenger, 'said to the man who had been attacked, "I was coming to your rescue but this highwayman has kindly consented to let you go if you give him all you possess. You are perfectly free to refuse, but if you do refuse, he will cut your throat and I will not interfere."' 'Is that carrying out our obligations to Abyssinia?' she asked. 'I say it is treachery to Abyssinia. It is a betrayal of Abyssinia.'

And why, Rathbone then asked, was Britain 'forced into this disgraceful surrender?' It was not because Italy had been so successful in the war, for news reports showed that Ethiopia was vigorously resisting; it was not because sanctions had failed, for really effective sanctions – such as the oil embargo that she and others had been urging – had not even been tried. Instead, the government must have decided that 'if we do not make this tremendous surrender to Italy, we shall have war with Italy and Germany too' – and have concluded that such a risk was not worth running. Rathbone flatly disagreed. Concessions to Italy would embolden and not conciliate Germany; they would frighten and not reassure other vulnerable League states; they would lose Britain the respect 'of all the coloured peoples of the world'. Whatever the risk of war, that risk was heightened by a policy of weakness. If Italy could get what it wanted by defying the League, 'what cannot Hitler get if he takes similar action?'[13]

Rathbone's voice was only one among many, a chorus loud and outraged enough to force the resignation of Hoare. And yet, as the *Times* coverage makes clear, her views were noticed.[14] Even before the December crisis Rathbone had emerged – as one historian who has studied this conflict writes – as 'the strongest sanctionist among the M.P.s';[15] in its wake, she began a barrage of parliamentary questions about Britain's failure to embargo oil. The government had failed to impose such sanctions out of fear they would lead to war, but 'which is really the greater risk – the risk of Italy going to war with Great Britain and with a united League . . . or the risk of showing fear before a bully'? Germany's remilitarization of the Rhineland that March she saw as proof that Hitler had taken heart from the League's pusillanimous behaviour.[16] In spring 1936, as Abyssinian resistance began to crumble and reports of Italy's use of poison gas emerged, she joined a small 'Abyssinian Association' formed by Herbert Stanley Jevons to keep the emperor's cause alive; when he fled and Italy proclaimed victory, she urged that sanctions be continued, if only to punish Mussolini for his actions.[17] What public opinion so resented, she told the Commons in May:

> is the idea that because Italy has triumphed she must be allowed to take her place at the Council table of the League as though nothing had happened; that with hands still red with the blood of innocent civilians who have been slaughtered with bombs and poison gas in open defiance of the League she should be invited to co-operate in future with the League in providing means of defence against other aggressors and safeguards against other violations of international law.[18]

By this point, however, the game was up. The government withdrew its sanctions on Italy on 18 June, surviving an opposition vote of censure a few days later.[19]

The Abyssinian crisis damaged the government's credibility but not beyond repair: Abyssinia was too exotic and its war too brief to have the lasting impact on British politics that the Spanish and Czech crises had. For a few MPs, however, Abyssinia was decisive. It was the revelations of the Hoare–Laval pact that launched the maverick Conservative Vyvyan Adams into a career of root-and-branch opposition to 'appeasement', while the decision to end sanctions on Italy six months later led Harold Macmillan to resign the Conservative whip and spend two years in the wilderness. And for Rathbone as well, Abyssinia struck home. She had disagreed with the National government plenty of times before: she found its social policies regressive, its colonial policies inadequate, its ministers lacking in zeal. But its Abyssinian policy she thought actually dishonest: Britain had reneged on its commitments, costing many thousands of innocent people their security and even their lives. 'What could be a worse dishonour,' she asked the audience at a major League of Nations Union rally at the Albert Hall in May 1936, 'than to have encouraged a weak nation to trust in the League; to bind itself to the League by solemn obligations which it has faithfully observed; to lead it on step by step to resist aggression; and then to do nothing effectively to restrain the aggressor but much that has effectually weakened his victim?'[20] She felt personally implicated, for, as she wrote to Jevons (enclosing a cheque to help support the emperor in exile), 'the Government's responsibility is ours also'. 'That's the penalty of belonging to a democracy.'[21]

Rathbone would feel that sense of guilt and obligation until her death. She pleaded unavailingly for a government pension for Selassie during his exile, she opposed League and government recognition of Italian rule, and – when the war finally forced a change in policy – worked with Philip Noel-Baker and others to extract a pledge to restore Ethiopia to full independence.[22] But the Abyssinian crisis did more than turn Eleanor into a warm admirer of Selassie, it also shifted her priorities permanently in a new direction. Rathbone had spent most of 1934 and 1935 on domestic and imperial questions – on child welfare, child marriage, and, in 1934, a campaign against a new sedition bill which would have given magistrates wide powers to issue search warrants against anyone they thought might be 'inciting disaffection' in the armed forces.[23] In 1935, she was absorbed in her campaign to widen Indian women's franchise, and in early 1936 was planning to visit some of the African colonies and make 'the conditions of native women' her special political concern.[24] Mussolini's war and Hitler's remilitarization of the Rhineland pushed those plans aside. For the next year, Rathbone would spend much of her time trying to persuade the public of the need to stand up to what she saw as a unified fascist menace.

Unfortunately, few in Britain saw the Rhineland crisis and the Abyssinian dispute in quite the same way.[25] The invasion of Abyssinia had produced a wave of public protest; in March 1936, by contrast, most Britons seemed to feel, as Lord Lothian declared, that Hitler was just marching into his own back garden. Rathbone's mailbag confirmed that impression. She had received hundreds of letters thanking her for her stand on Abyssinia; now, she found her constituents (she told Churchill) 'deplorably pro-German' and worryingly muddled in their views.[26] Writing in the *Manchester Guardian*, she tried to enlighten them. Out of a mistaken belief that Germany was the 'underdog' menaced by a belligerent France, public opinion 'seems now to be throwing its weight on the wrong side'. But in doing so, it was ignoring evidence of Germany's recent military build-up (for which Rathbone gave chapter and verse) and making light of the destruction of the Locarno treaty, which Hitler's unilateral action had left in shreds. But the system of international treaties and alliances was not a menu, from which one could pick and choose, but a set of solemn pledges on which both Britain's honour and European security depended. 'The hope that Britain would not stand by her word precipitated the Great War and the Abyssinian war,' she wrote. 'It may easily precipitate another.'[27] European security now required that Britain make clear its commitment to resist all acts of aggression, however 'reasonable' they might seem.

Throughout the summer and autumn of 1936, Rathbone wrote article after article and made speech after speech laying out this point of view. (Macadam, who agreed with her but preferred doing to speaking, went off in July to help Philip Noel-Baker fight a by-election on a platform of defence of the League.) Rathbone targeted left-leaning audiences in particular, among whom her credibility was highest and her gadfly role most likely to be effective. At the Independent Labour Party summer school in August, for example, and in the pages of the *Manchester Guardian* a few weeks later, Rathbone offered an acute analysis of the reasons for current National government policy and a plea for new political alignments. Although usually cast as a spectrum running from right to left, she argued, in foreign-policy terms the parties were best seen as a circle, for imperial isolationists on the right joined hands with pacifists on the socialist left in their hostility to granting any real powers to the League. Worse, the extreme dislike of communism felt by most of the Conservative Party left that group sympathetic to German territorial ambitions in the East and inclined to hope that Germany and Russia would fight the matter out between them. But such a hope of 'limiting commitments' left Czechoslovakia – 'the one peaceful, prosperous, genuine democracy left in East-Central Europe' – 'peculiarly exposed'. A European crisis was likely to start in Czechoslovakia, Rathbone warned, with a 'rebellion of [its] German minority, secretly fostered by Hitler'. And should this occur with the current government in power, it was all too likely that neither Britain nor France would come to Czechoslovakia's defence.[28] 'If we are determined to have peace at any price, even at the price of sacrificing the world's security on the altar of our own security, let us say so,' she advised the government at the opening of Parliament that November. 'But whether we shall secure peace even for ourselves permanently by a policy of continually truckling to dictators, yielding step by step, many of us doubt.'[29]

Was another policy possible? Rathbone discerned a new cross-party compact emerging. Against this unholy alliance of pacifists and Conservatives bent on the emasculation of the League, she detected a 'League Front' spanning forces from Churchill and the Duchess of Atholl on the right, through the great bulk of the Labour and Liberal parties, to the Communists on the far left. True, that incipient alliance was riddled with inconsistencies and mutual suspicion. The Labour Party, for example, both professed its commitment to defend the authority of the League *and* consistently voted against all defence estimates – a position that was, Rathbone charged, not merely tactically stupid but a 'real inconsistency', since (as she told her own constituents at the end of 1936, when justifying her own pro-rearmament votes) 'if collective security is to be made a reality, the loyal League States must together have a preponderance of armed strength over any likely combination of aggressors'.[30] She also knew that few on the left liked or trusted Churchill, but urged them to look at him with new eyes. She listened attentively to Churchill's speeches on rearmament and drew on his figures in her letter on the Rhineland crisis; when those figures were challenged, the two began to share information.[31] Churchill's renewed activism was, Rathbone told the ILP, the single most hopeful event of 1936. If he put the same energy into his new 'pro-League' stance that he put into his campaign against Indian self-government, 'I believe he may be the future Prime Minister, with something like a real National Government at his back.'[32]

Brave words: but when Rathbone tried to enlist cross-party internationalist and pro-League organizations behind this 'united front', she found little support. In 1935 Rathbone had joined Lloyd George's newly created 'Council of Action', seduced by his promise of 'New Deal' economics and of a vigorous defence of European peace and security. She was thus worried to learn that Lloyd George had delegated the task of mapping out the Council's foreign policy to Lord Lothian, formerly Rathbone's ally on Indian women's franchise, but who in May 1935 was trying to serve as a conduit for negotiations between Hitler and Ribbentrop on the one hand and John Simon and Baldwin on the other. When Lothian predictably argued that if democracies wanted peace 'a more ample "place in the sun" must be found today for Germany, Italy and Japan' and that Abyssinia – being 'uncivilized' and under a 'primitive form of government' – could be carved up to further such appeasement, Rathbone told Lloyd George just how much she disagreed.[33] Worse was to come. In March 1936, Rathbone could not stir up the Council of Action to take much interest in German remilitarization of the Rhineland;[34] a few months later, Lloyd George made his famous pilgrimage to Hitler at Berchtesgaden. Reading an interview in which he acclaimed Hitler a 'great man' and lauded his many achievements, Rathbone felt sick with shame. 'What must be the effect of his and similar tributes to Hitler?' she asked in a letter published in some half-dozen papers. Not only would they help 'to shut the door of hope on every prisoner in a concentration camp and on every wretched Jewish child who is treated like a pariah in his Fatherland', but they would also convince Hitler and Mussolini that Britain was 'either so gullible or so terrified of their supreme power . . . that they may safely proceed to overthrow the remaining European democracies one by one, to subjugate native populations with poison gas – to do anything so long as they do not menace British skins and money interests'. She was herself a member of the executive committee of the Council of Action, Rathbone admitted, but if that body shared Lloyd George's views, it was clearly no place for her.[35] Superficially, the quarrel was patched up, for Rathbone had long admired Lloyd George and he gallantly (if untruthfully) insisted he didn't mind criticism.[36] But her hope that the Council of Action would serve as the foundation for a revitalized democratic stance had vanished.

What then of the League of Nations Union, ostensibly the body most committed to a vigorous defence of the principles of the Covenant? Through its participation in the 'Peace Ballot' of 11 million British adults in the winter and spring of 1934–5, the Union had helped to document overwhelming public support for those principles; when they were abandoned during the Abyssinian crisis, it became sharply critical of the government. With hundreds of branches, more than a third of a million members in 1936, and a leadership of well-connected politicians and public intellectuals (Lord Cecil, the Oxford classicist Gilbert Murray, and Rathbone's old friend Kathleen Courtney among them), the League of Nations Union felt well placed to influence British foreign policy. Yet the stance of the Union was, like that of the left in general, incoherent: it too was committed to both 'collective security' and disarmament, and in its eagerness to serve as a 'broad church' for internationalist opinion, had many out-and-out pacifists in its ranks.[37] Rathbone, who joined the Union's executive committee in the wake of the Abyssinian débâcle, was determined to force the question. Europe's vulnerable democracies would hardly be protected by thousands of individual Britons professing their own unwillingness to take up arms, she told a meeting of its General Council in December 1936; the Council should, therefore, straight-forwardly state that the 'Peace Pledge' movement (now sweeping the universities) was likely only to encourage 'aggressively-minded nations to commit aggression'. But such open acknowledgement of the incoherence of their position was more than the Union's leadership could stand. Members of the Peace Pledge Union were among their most devoted supporters, Lord Cecil and Clifford Allen pointed out, and should not be made to feel unwelcome.[38] Divided, enormous and ineffective, the League of Nations Union mirrored only too well the international body it was created to defend.

By the end of 1936, then, Rathbone had little to show for her labours; worse, new international conflicts seemed to be making any hope of a 'united front' even more remote. In July 1936, a military uprising led by General Francisco Franco pledged to rid Spain of a newly elected Popular Front government and of the spontaneous social unrest and anti-clerical violence that had followed; by early August, the worried French and British governments had agreed to try to prevent the conflict from spreading by urging a common European policy of 'non-intervention'. Rathbone disagreed with the plan from the outset. Whatever the inadequacies of the Popular Front government, it had been freely elected and hence deserved the democracies' support. But what really aroused her ire was the evidence that Germany and Italy had – although ostensibly supporting the pact – from the outset provided troops and materiel to the rebels, and that the Non-Intervention Committee headquartered in Britain showed little interest in restraining them. 'Non-intervention' thus turned very quickly into what Rathbone feared it would be: a rhetorical smokescreen justifying French and British inaction, while German and Italian aid to the insurgent forces proceeded apace.[39]

Rathbone was sufficiently disgusted by this charade to agree to chair a small Communist-inspired 'Committee of Inquiry into Breaches of International Law relating to Intervention in Spain' which met publicly to hear eyewitness evidence (from Arthur Koestler among others) and review documents captured from Italian forces.[40] The Non-Intervention agreement, that committee concluded in October, had served only to deny the Spanish government the arms it needed while failing to block supplies to the rebel forces.[41] Perhaps the government had decided to support non-intervention in order to prevent the Spanish conflict from escalating, Rathbone said in the Commons that December, but 'in its actual working-out the Non-intervention Agreement . . . has repeated the irony of the Abyssinian crisis last year. Just as then the one really effective thing the League did was by an embargo nominally applied to both parties to prevent the victim of aggression from defending itself, so today the practical effect of the Non-intervention Pact has been to prevent the legitimate Government from arming itself.' It was not enough to point to recent Russian intervention, for such intervention only happened after the massive German and Italian breaches had become apparent and the democracies had washed their hands, and in order to prevent Madrid from falling to the rebels. Ironically, then, Britain and France were creating just the ideological polarization they deplored, for by 'limiting our commitments and keeping safe ourselves, what we are doing is to throw one by one of [sic] the surviving democracies of Europe into the arms of either Fascism or Communism. What can these weaker countries think when they find democratic States huddled into the corner of the fold, hoping that the wolf will feed on smaller lambs than themselves, and so will leave them alone, whereas the dictatorships protect their own?'[42]

For the next six months, Rathbone lost no opportunity to expose the farcical nature of 'non-intervention'. She kept Anthony Eden, Hoare's replacement as Foreign Secretary, well supplied with evidence of Italian breaches; she bombarded ministers in the Commons with questions about Italian airmen, German arms and Francoist atrocities; with her little 'Committee of Inquiry', she issued a second report giving evidence of German and Italian activities – including, by this point, the infamous bombing of Guernica.[43] And yet, when she tried to interest the League of Nations Union executive, she once again faced foot-dragging and ambivalence. The Union was in such a state of mind about 'reds' that he could not publicly support her committee, Gilbert Murray wrote; Lord Cecil, for his part, thought the government should be persuaded to make the non-intervention pact effective.[44] Rathbone could hardly disagree, but she had no confidence at all in the government's good faith. In light of its past failure to set up any machinery to investigate breaches and its habit of ignoring any evidence brought to its attention, she told the House in July 1937, one month after the Basque Republic had fallen to the rebels, 'the Government are not justified in resenting, with an air of injured innocence', the suspicions with which she and others viewed their new proposals to monitor the pact.

> If the proposals are worked courageously and impartially they might not be too bad, but the British Government have never yet shown courage, or even impartiality. They have subordinated everything to their desire to avoid provoking Germany or Italy. In pursuit of that end they have not merely flouted the League of Nations . . . but they have smirched the honour of Great Britain in the eyes of the world. A nation is not behaving honourably if it observes strictly with both sides its own international agreements, but at the same time connives at, by glossing over, the persistent breach of international agreements by others.[45]

Rathbone had wanted the democracies to defend a legal government in Spain. Instead, but they were turning a blind eye to German and Italian actions likely to bring that government down.

Worst of all, the Spanish conflict made Rathbone's sought-for 'united front' of Conservative anti-appeasers and left-liberals more remote than ever. Many Liberals were inclined to favour non-intervention, and while the bulk of the Labour Party supported the Republic, sensitivity about communist infiltration made the leadership reluctant to participate in any cross-party or 'popular' organizations. Churchill, whom Rathbone had begged in 1936 to rally the public for 'an equally strong front towards both Germany and Italy', thought the Spanish conflict an irrelevant sideshow and felt himself by birth and affinity 'naturally . . . not in favour of the Communists'.[46] Moreover, when Neville Chamberlain succeeded Baldwin as Prime Minister in May 1937, the cost of dissidence for discomfited Conservatives suddenly became much higher. For Chamberlain – sensitive, secretive, and frankly contemptuous of the intelligence of most members of the House – had none of Baldwin's emollient bonhomie or canny receptivity to opposition or backbench unease.[47] Accustomed to rely on Halifax, Hoare (now back in the government as Home Secretary) and Thomas Inskip for advice, the Chief Whip David Margesson for parliamentary management, and the right-wing newspaper proprietors to keep public opinion on his side, he reacted to criticism with irritation and resentment.[48] No one could have been less susceptible to appeals for open consultation or democratic accountability.

Rathbone clearly understood this, for by 1937 we can detect a new stridency in her parliamentary interventions and a new daring, almost a recklessness, in her political campaigns. In the House, she asked ever more parliamentary questions – 89 in 1936–7, 100 in 1937–8 – in a determined effort to extract as much damaging information as she could. Her speeches she reserved mostly for extra-parliamentary (and now usually left-wing) audiences, willingly travelling the country to lay out her views. In July 1937 she also wrote to the left-wing publisher Victor Gollancz, asking whether he would be interested in a short book on foreign policy; when he said that he would be, she wrote a 200-page tract at white heat during the summer parliamentary recess and the autumn, delivering the manuscript to Gollancz, as promised, on 1 December.[49] Rathbone could write this quickly because most of what she said in *War Can Be Averted*, published as a Left Book Club book in January 1938, she had said so many times before. In simple, declarative prose, Rathbone summarized the sorry history of Britain's abdication of its professed League principles in the cases of Abyssinia and Spain and laid out the costs of the government's *de facto* policy of conciliation and appeasement. Since that policy had only made the dictators more arrogant, the weaker states more vulnerable, and Britain and France less secure and respected than ever before, it was time to reverse course. Now, Britain and France must rebuild and arm the League, guarantee the security of the weaker states, and come to a pragmatic alliance with the Soviets – who, she argued perceptively, if not dealt with straightforwardly would make their own peace with the Nazis. Such a policy was not without risks, but it offered more hope of averting war than any other – and if war did come, Britain would face it at least with its alliances and values intact.[50]

26. Eleanor and Elizabeth in the garden of the holiday cottage in St Margaret's Bay, August 1937, where Rathbone wrote *War Can Be Averted*.

But here, as well, we can detect a change in tone. Her attack on the pacifist movement is particularly stinging, and her appeal to a younger generation shaded by bitterness and doubt. In *War Can Be Averted*, perhaps for the first time, Rathbone identified herself as an 'elderly Victorian' and admitted that she found the 'readiness with which the post-war generation . . . throws up the sponge' to be 'incomprehensible and baffling'. That generation, she pointed out, had, after all, 'the weapons which the real fighters of the past won for them with their bare hands – adult franchise, universal if limited education, free organs of the Press' – and yet it seemed to view all ideals cynically and to give way so easily to defeatism. But surely, Rathbone wrote, 'there is little hope for freedom, justice and peace unless there can be roused in the peoples of the surviving democracies as vigorous a faith and as self-sacrificing a devotion to these great ends as the Dictators have succeeded in mobilising for their false ends'.[51] Had a kind of rot set in? Was the democratic idealism of her Edwardian young womanhood as out-dated as hoop skirts?

Through her long years in the suffrage movement, Rathbone had never been tempted by militancy. She had been willing to wear away at the rock of parliamentary prejudice or inaction, secure in the knowledge that a democratic public supported her cause. In 1937, however, she had trouble taking such a long view. 'Public opinion' seemed stubbornly indifferent, and time was running out: a crisis could come at any moment, whenever Hitler or Mussolini decided to lay their paws on another tempting plot of land, another vulnerable population. And before this threat to liberty and life, some niceties of constitutional practice must give way. Between 1937 and 1939, then, Rathbone came as close as she ever would to militancy – to political disruption and theatricality, to taking the law into her own hands. Yet she did so in the name of Democracy, still claiming legitimacy from a 'public opinion' she insisted (but could not quite be certain) was on her side. If the Chamberlainites would not defend democracy, Rathbone thought, she would do so. She would mount her own 'foreign policy', defending states and peoples vulnerable to fascist aggression.

This was an ambitious plan for a spinster politician in her late sixties, but Rathbone found some allies. One, especially, stands out: Katharine Marjory Stewart-Murray, the Duchess of Atholl and Conservative MP for West Perth. Atholl might seem an odd collaborator for Rathbone.[52] She had been an anti-suffragist before the war, and, in the early 1930s, a 'diehard', following Churchill into his wilderness of opposition to cross-party agreement on Indian constitutional reform. And yet, for all her seeming right-wing extremism, Atholl was in many ways very like Rathbone: she too was independent-minded and unwilling to take party orthodoxies on faith; she too was fearless and highly principled. Rathbone had admired her competent performance as the first woman Conservative minister in Baldwin's 1924 government and teamed up with Atholl in 1929 to raise the issue of the subjection of women in Britain's African colonies. In 1933, the two women began to correspond privately about the dangers of German rearmament and found themselves often in agreement.[53] In late 1935, Atholl read *Mein Kampf* in its original German and was shocked to find that the most blatant passages had been excised from the English version; she thus arranged for the first unexpurgated English translation and for the publication of key extracts in pamphlet form.[54] Rathbone was one avid reader (as was Churchill): her letter on Hitler's military build-up also warned of that expurgation; her forceful denunciation of Lloyd George's visit pointed readers to the translated extracts.[55] Atholl wrote to thank Rathbone for this letter ('I am so glad you, as a member of his Council of Action, are making a stand').[56] By this point, the usually formal Rathbone was calling the Duchess 'Kitty'.[57]

But what, beyond their usual writing and public speaking, could the two women do? In November 1936, after giving a major speech in the Commons on the need to sustain the independence of the Eastern European states, Atholl had an idea. She had been surprised to learn that her speech had been widely reported in Romania and to find herself deluged with invitations to visit the country. She consulted with Robert Vansittart, Permanent Under-Secretary at the Foreign Office and strongly opposed to any conciliation of Hitler, who thought she should accept. The 'Little Entente' countries, he pointed out, were under constant pressure to throw in their lot with Germany and needed to be assured of Britain's friendly interest in their fate.[58] Would Rathbone like to come along? Indeed she would: she had already been trying to interest the newspapers and the BBC in a campaign to increase public interest in Czechoslovakia.[59] Dorothea Layton, another League of Nations Union stalwart (and the wife of Sir Walter Layton, the editor of the *Economist* and proprietor of the liberal *News Chronicle*), agreed to come too. They would go in February, they decided, and make the long train journeys mostly by night to save the days for meetings. Briefed by the scholar of Eastern Europe Hugh Seton-Watson, they made their way from Zagreb and Belgrade to Bucharest and Cluj, completing the trip in Prague. Although careful to say that they had come as sympathetic visitors only and not as governmental envoys, their visit generated much excitement – a duchess, no less! In Romania they were welcomed with flowers, singing children, royal carriages and enormous formal receptions – rather to their embarrassment, since they had brought only the simplest travelling clothes for the journey. They visited universities and schools, talked to social workers and consular officials, and met with as many political figures as they possibly could – among them Prince Paul in Yugoslavia, Princess Cantacuzene in Romania, and President Beneš and Prime Minister Dr Hodza in Czechoslovakia.[60] Rathbone, sending off their findings to the Foreign Office, noted both the strength of Nazi propaganda in all three countries (and of anti-Semitic sentiment in Romania in particular), and, paradoxically, a tremendous eagerness for British ties.[61] Whether Romania and Yugoslavia would stand

27. Rathbone (second from left), Atholl (fifth) and Layton (sixth) in Cluj, Romania, February 1937.

up to German influence, Atholl added in a separate report, 'was mainly a question of whether we showed ourselves resolute in this matter'.[62] In the Commons, the two teamed up to deplore the extensive Nazi propaganda in Eastern Europe and the inadequate British Council efforts, prompting one disgusted Conservative member to label them a 'feminine United Front'.[63]

They needed one another's support, for by this point their bridges were burning merrily behind them. Their trip to Eastern Europe a success, they went on, two months later, to Spain, this time with the Labour MP Ellen Wilkinson and Dame Rachel Crowdy, the former director of the Social Welfare Section of the League. They were going to assess the operation of the relief organizations and the condition of refugees, they explained, for in late 1936 Atholl had accepted the chairmanship and Rathbone the vice-chairmanship of a new National Joint Committee for Spanish Relief now operating in Republican areas (while Macadam, active behind the scenes as always, took on the job of honorary organizing secretary until the new committee got off the ground). But their visit was one of solidarity, and included meetings with Prime Minister Largo Caballero and other important government figures. The fact that they were shelled during dinner one evening in Madrid didn't hurt publicity ('British Women MPs under Fire,' reported *The Times*),[64] and on their return they gave speeches and published accounts of their visit. The Republic was coping admirably with the needs of children, refugees and even political prisoners, they reported, but was desperately short of medical supplies and food.[65]

The National Joint Committee (NJC) tried to meet these needs, employing its own agent in Spain to organize distribution. It never achieved quite the coordinating role to which it aspired, for Catholic and pro-Francoist relief organizations preferred to operate on their own and the Labour Party insisted on autonomy, but it did raise more than £100,000 on its own account and distributed an even larger amount on behalf of other organizations.[66] Much of that money came in small contributions raised locally, for 'aid to Spain' quickly became a *cause célèbre* within leftist and working-class communities, but Rathbone and Atholl were much more than mere figureheads. Together with the Labour MP David Grenfell, the Liberal MP Wilfrid Roberts (the honorary secretary, who took on the lion's share of the coordination), and one or two others, they set the committee's policy, spoke at its fundraising events, and sought to manage its often tricky relations with the government. Those negotiations were by no means easy, for while Rathbone, Roberts and Atholl had enough clout to force ministers and officials to see them, they were also seen as troublesome, partisan, and not to be counted on to play by the rules.

Some of this hostility came from the fact that the National Joint Committee did not hesitate to work with communists: the charismatic Isabel Brown was one of its most effective speakers and organizers, and at a local level communist supporters could play an important role. Labour party headquarters thus tended to give the committee a wide berth, and its leadership – especially Atholl, whom the papers tended to label the 'Red Duchess' – could be tarred with the communist brush. Such charges were frankly ludicrous: Atholl had no sympathy at all with communism, wrote an early exposé of the Soviet system of forced labour, and had to be deterred from making anti-communist comments at the pro-Republican rallies at which she spoke. Nor was Rathbone a more reliable 'fellow traveller', insisting even at meetings urging a Soviet alliance that there was 'much that we may legitimately fear and dislike there'.[67] Atholl's stance, instead, was founded on a close calculation of British strategic interests, while Rathbone was grateful to 'Spain' for having awoken ordinary *British* citizens from cynicism and pacifism. Yet the simple fact that the NJC made no effort to police the affiliations of its staff and supporters put both women – but especially the Conservative Atholl – at some political risk.[68] Both nevertheless played a major role in the committee's two most memorable campaigns: its removal of some 4,000 children from the combat zone during the spring offensive against the Basque Republic in 1937, and its dispatch of dozens of 'food ships' to the Republic's famished and blockaded cities in 1938.[69]

That first effort is especially significant in light of the British government's opposition to the admission and public funding of Spanish refugees, and of Rathbone's later campaigns. A particular confluence of events – pressure from the NJC and the Trades Union Congress, genuine public shock over the bombing of Guernica and other Basque towns, and Eden's discomfort with the government's ungenerous stance (although he and Baldwin overcame Hoare and Chamberlain's reservations to allow British naval protection for ships taking Basque refugees to safety) – combined to make this early experiment in child evacuation possible. In this environment, Roberts, Rathbone, and Victor Tewson of the Trades Union Congress were able to persuade the government to allow in 2,000 child refugees (a figure that soon doubled): the children would, they promised, come to Britain only temporarily, and the NJC would assume all responsibilities for their selection, evacuation and care.[70] But if the removal of the Basque children and their escort by Navy destroyer to Southampton was a major achievement, the scheme was also a political minefield. Because the Catholics would not work with the NJC, a new Basque Children's Committee was quickly formed, once again with Atholl, Rathbone and Roberts but supplemented now by representatives from the Catholic Church and the Trades Union Congress. That group worked harmoniously for a time, sorting out the formidable logistical challenges involved in caring for some 4,000 children in a country not their own, but once the Basque Republic had fallen and both Francoist authorities and the British government began pressing for the children to be sent back, fissures predictably opened. The Catholic and Conservative members of the committee were eager to comply, but the pro-Republican members held out for independent verification of the parents' wishes. Only about half the children had been repatriated by the outbreak of the Second World War, and some hundreds whose parents could not be traced or could not care for them remained in Britain permanently – a diaspora that spawned its own associations and that affected the lives of thousands of British and Spanish families for many decades.[71]

Four thousand might seem a small number, but the rescue of the Basque children taught Rathbone two important lessons. First, if public pressure was great enough and organizers imaginative and brave, it was possible to get people out of war-torn countries. Second, if refugees managed to make it to Britain, the British people would come generously to their aid. From the day the children landed she tried to build upon those lessons. Throughout summer 1937, she followed the situation in Santander, then flooded with refugees from the fallen Basque Republic. On behalf of the NJC and with the help of Ann Caton, a colleague from suffragist days now active in Spain, she was trying both to deliver humanitarian aid and to get Republican refugees out before the city fell to the rebels. She kept in close touch with a Commander Pursey, who was willing to take his ship into Santander to load refugees, but who cabled that rebel forces were shelling outside Spanish territorial waters, and that the British Navy vessels patrolling the area appeared more interested in *preventing* British merchant ships from entering Spanish waters than in protecting them. Rathbone documented these attacks, wrote letters to the press, and repeatedly raised the matter in the

House in the weeks before the summer recess in an effort to force the Admiralty and the Foreign Office to protect ships carrying refugees or humanitarian aid; in August, she even travelled to France to try to work out the details of an evacuation.[72] To no avail: the British government had agreed that it would not protect ships inside Spanish territorial waters after Franco declared a blockade of the Northern ports in April, and would agree to remove only those refugees whom *both parties* agreed should be removed – a policy unlikely to aid Republican refugees at risk from Franco's advance.[73] The night before Santander fell, as many as 100,000 people packed the quays, desperate to get away. Some took to the sea in small boats; many drowned.[74]

Two months later, these scenes were replayed along the Asturian coast. When the offensive against Asturias began, Atholl and Rathbone had brought their accounts of reprisals and executions following the fall of Bilbao and Santander to the Executive of the League of Nations Union, and a deputation was quickly organized to Lord Plymouth, Under-Secretary at the Foreign Office, to ask the Navy to protect ships removing refugees within Spanish territorial waters.[75] But the government refused, prompting one of Rathbone's bitterest speeches. 'It was a stormy night' last Thursday, Rathbone told the Commons on 26 October, 'and from the ships could be witnessed the scenes which these merchant captains have described – Gijon in flames, people rushing to the sea and people struggling in the water where small boats had capsized owing to the storm and other people clinging to rafts. But these merchant seamen did not dare to enter the three-mile limit because they had received strict orders from the owners of the vessels that they must not do so without the promise of protection' – which the government had insisted it could not, as a 'neutral' pledged to 'non-intervention', give them. But the Hague Convention allowed rescue of the endangered, Rathbone pointed out, going on to lay responsibility for that danger at the British government's door. 'The bombing of Guernica; the fall of Bilbao and Santander and Gijon and the ports along the north of Spain; the ruthless mass executions of prisoners' – none of these would have happened were it not for its policy of preventing Spain's legitimate government from arming while ignoring the continuing fascist intervention. 'In that sense the Government are responsible for the drowning of these men, women and children. It would never have happened but for their policy.'[76] When the Nationalists followed up their conquest with executions and reprisals, Rathbone thought Chamberlain bore a measure of blame for these deaths as well.[77]

She felt nothing but detestation now for the Prime Minister, and in the House was unable to hide her scorn. In July 1937, when Chamberlain refused appeals to keep Parliament in session, Rathbone asked him whether the government might find it more convenient to suspend Parliament indefinitely; in February 1938, when he suggested the press should exercise 'restraint' in reporting on foreign affairs, she asked whether Hitler might be appeased if he set up 'a concentration camp for British journalists'. In March, when Chamberlain promised to have a copy of the League Covenant placed in the Commons Library, she asked whether he was aware that one could get a pocket edition for a penny.[78] She heckled and interrupted ministers freely during the debates on Spain, and, since her own speeches on the supply of British news abroad or protection of British shipping tended to turn into root-and-branch denunciations of the government's foreign policy, once again found herself in constant trouble with the Speaker.[79] But she was whistling in the dark, and she knew it. On 20 February 1938, Eden and his junior minister Cranborne resigned over the conditions of the Anglo-Italian agreement, thus cementing Chamberlain's grip on foreign policy. Rathbone sent Eden a supportive note, but she could hardly contain her anxiety.[80]

On 22 February, Chamberlain told the Commons that the Eastern European states should not count on the League for protection; three weeks later, Hitler's troops marched into Austria. All eyes then turned to Czechoslovakia, on which Hitler had obvious designs, and where the minority German population was emboldened and restive. In Spain, too, the Nationalists were once more resurgent, bombing and sinking with impunity British merchant ships trading with Republican ports. Considerable anger was voiced in Parliament about these attacks, with Churchill, Attlee, Noel-Baker and others saying that the government was treating the matter much too lightly, but Chamberlain refused to intervene.[81] 'The Prime Minister,' Rathbone said in a bitter speech on 26 July 1938, as the House broke up for the summer recess, 'can scarcely conceal his anger that the Spanish Republic, like King Charles, has been so long a'dying, and consequently he vents that anger on his own countrymen who, in a legitimate way, have been helping the Spanish Republic to survive.'[82]

But why, Rathbone asked, was the government behaving in such a cowardly fashion? What could it possibly hope to gain? In a speech that became a sustained attack on the whole policy of appeasement, Rathbone answered:

The Government have permitted these various acts of weakness because of fear of the aggressor countries – Japan, Germany and Italy – and a desire to conciliate them, or, to put it more crudely, to buy them off by encouraging them to vent themselves on weak nations, in the hope that, having become sated, they will leave us and our possessions alone. What we fail to see and what is the cause for the deep anxiety which gnaws at our hearts, is any sign that this policy, ignoble at best, is even succeeding. True, it has kept us out of war so far, and the Government are fighting by-elections on that claim; but can the country be kept permanently out of war by those means, and if so, at what cost? One country after another which might have been our ally in a system of collective security is subjected either by force or by diplomatic pressure, and the balance of power in Europe is steadily being shifted to our disadvantage and to the disadvantage of all the other surviving democratic powers. We should gain something if there were any signs of real appeasement, but are there any signs of that?

The future, she felt, was bleak; she could see almost no way out.

> When freedom has been submerged all over Europe, will our freedom survive; or alternatively, at some point in that intolerable descent into the valley of humiliation, will the point be reached at which we shall fight, but – what is only too likely – fight alone, or with insufficient allies, because, by reason of the selfishness of our present policy, we have been left practically alone.

She could not help but feel, she concluded, that 'the right hon Gentleman the Member for Epping' – Churchill – was in fact right, and that the only way forward was, however belatedly, to rally the democratic states and the Soviet Union in a pragmatic and rearmed League.[83] But it was the summer, and the House dispersed. Eleanor and Elizabeth went off for a much-needed holiday in Sussex; Atholl to raise money for the Basque Children's Committee in America. And Sir Walter Runciman went as the government's envoy to Czechoslovakia, to see whether he might be able to reconcile the Sudeten Germans – and, by extension, Hitler – to the continued existence of a multi-ethnic Czechoslovakia.

We must turn to the famous Munich crisis, of course, but let us first pause before the figure of Rathbone berating Chamberlain, accusing him of cowardice, symbolically laying the corpses of executed Spanish prisoners and drowned British seamen at his feet. There is something remarkable here, echoes of Cassandra and Judith, of the woman visionary or warrior chastising the men around her for their failure of will. How do we account for such passion and conviction, such militancy and rage? Atholl's position seems easier to explain: she was, after all, a Churchillian, determined to defend British imperial and strategic interests, whether in India or on the continent. But Rathbone was, by analysis, affiliation and thirty years of political practice, a feminist – and a feminist of a particular kind. Always concerned about what most women were thinking, always sensitive to the hardships of their everyday lives, she urged women to bring their own insights and ideals into political life. Most issues, she thought, could be illuminated by women's humane sensibilities and practical cast of mind.

When she turned to questions of war and peace, however, Rathbone's approach seems to have changed. Her speeches addressed men and women equally; her writing was done for general periodicals and not the 'women's press'. Breaking with a lifetime of single-sex political work, she expended her efforts on the League of Nations Union, the Council of Action and other mixed-sex organizations; the women's civic organizations she had been instrumental in starting attracted her not at all. And her analysis seems, as well, to have become universalist rather than 'gendered'. *War Can Be Averted* and other writings never assume that women have some innate connection to pacifism and consistently refuse to treat women as a class apart. This stance seems at odds not only with Rathbone's history but also with the opinions of many women at the time – for 'appeasement' was, in fact, popular among women voters, whom Baldwin, Chamberlain and Conservative Central Office watched with a careful eye.

She was at odds, moreover, with that most significant woman writer, Virginia Woolf. Woolf, too, felt compelled to write a book on how to avert war; when the Spanish Civil War took the life of her nephew Julian Bell, that book held her up 'like a spine'.[84] Published in June 1938, Woolf's *Three Guineas* offered just that 'gendered analysis' Rathbone now eschewed. War and fascism, Woolf insisted, were but the public and international expression of a power first exercised at home; through the domination of sisters and wives and the craving of honours and adulation, men learn the lessons that lead to fascism and to war. Women's best contribution to peace was, then, to break that cycle of domination: to resist private patriarchy by earning their own bread and public patriarchy by refusing competition, honours and position. By cherishing her status as 'outsider', a woman will hear appeals to patriotism with indifference. She will understand that 'she has no good reason to ask her brother to fight on her behalf to protect "our" country'. She will be able to say, 'As a woman, I have no country. . . . As a woman, my country is the whole world.'[85]

Rathbone shared Woolf's dislike of political honours but not her scorn for academic distinctions. Her Oxford tutors had preached the duties of active citizenship, not of blind loyalty: ever grateful for those lessons, she was greatly pleased when the university recognized her fidelity with an honorary DCL in June 1938. Her ideas about patriotism remained framed by these early lessons and were, as a result, very far from those espoused by Woolf. Of course women should eschew a patriotism of race or national aggrandizement, but should women not show their allegiance to liberal political systems and democratic forms? Woolf's easy equation between 'fascism at home' and 'fascism abroad' Rathbone would have found slippery and false, for Britain and Germany did not share the same political system – and in only one of those systems could women have a stake. That stake was painfully achieved and partial, she knew – equal suffrage was only ten years old, and women's rights in many areas still fragile. But Rathbone, who could remember only too well the years before the vote, could not take those achievements lightly. Only those who have been deprived of liberty can truly understand its value, Rathbone wrote after the Nazi seizure of power, and 'one had to be a woman or else a member of a subject race to have experienced that'.[86] But with liberty came obligation: the obligation to use those citizenship rights, the obligation to defend the political system on which their very freedom depended. Rathbone's newly gender-blind language was not a sign of political amnesia but a conscious choice, rooted in her conviction that, in a democratic state, women too had much to lose.

And yet there are tensions and ironies here, for the political system to which Rathbone was so staunchly loyal was much less loyal in return. Women's enfranchisement notwithstanding, British politics remained riddled with networks of family, friendship and political dependence, networks that left women in general, and Rathbone in particular, in the cold. Chamberlain's secretive style deepened that tendency towards intrigue and conspiracy: after Eden's resignation, even the Cabinet was divided into shifting factions, with an 'inner circle' of Chamberlain, Halifax, Hoare, Simon and Inskip and a small group of moderate critics (Hore-Belisha, Oliver Stanley, Walter Elliot, Lords Winterton and de la Warr) ringed by others of no fixed ideological abode. Beyond them, of course, were those other groups of ex-ministers or would-be ministers: the 'Eden Group', and Churchill's tiny 'Old Guard'. By summer 1938, discontent with Chamberlain's policies permeated several of those cabals (and was intense within the Labour Party and among Archie Sinclair's Liberals), but for Conservatives the cost of dissent remained high. Most sceptics contented themselves with the illusion of 'consultation', trading their votes for the privilege of being taken into confidence by someone more genuinely 'in the know'.

A stubborn prime minister, a divided Cabinet, an untried opposition – and, crucially, a parliamentary recess – opened up the catastrophic path to Munich.[87] Under considerable pressure from London, in early September the Czech government agreed to the Sudeten German demands, but for Hitler – who had advised his Sudeten allies to make their demands so great as to be unacceptable and who was openly fomenting insurrection – this was by no means good enough. Tried beyond bearing, and hopeful of French willingness to support them, the Czechs were increasingly inclined to fight. In this context, Chamberlain's unconventional decision to seek a meeting with Hitler and try to resolve the crisis on his own startled even his closest cabinet colleagues – but they, at least, were consulted, while the full Cabinet was simply informed of his intentions on 14 September, on the eve of his first German trip. Members of Parliament, like the public, had even less information, and had to judge the full seriousness of the situation from Chamberlain's press statements, the issue of gas masks, and the sight of workmen digging trenches in the London parks. Small wonder, then, that Chamberlain's dramatic announcement in the reconvened House on 28 September that Hitler had agreed to a four-party conference in Munich was greeted by jubilation. Who would not feel relieved to know that the gas masks might not, in fact, be necessary? Chamberlain heard those cheers, those cross-party wishes of Godspeed, as blessings on his policy – but how many who rose to acclaim him imagined what was at hand?[88]

A few people are thought to have remained seated – Churchill, Harold Nicolson, Leo Amery, and the Communist William Gallacher among them. And Rathbone? I do not know, for – and this is itself illuminating – she is elusive, almost invisible, at this moment. 'There is a great longing for leadership,' she had written to Churchill on 10 September as the crisis unfolded, 'and even those who are far apart from you in general politics realize that you are the one man who has combined full realization of the dangers of our military position with belief in collective international action against aggression.'[89] But while Churchill thanked her for her letter, he seems to have felt no need to include her. Nicolson and Amery's famous accounts of those terrible late September days, when they and a few dozen dissidents met together nightly to discover how many among them would be willing to oppose the government, do not mention her.[90] Only a few women with impeccable dynastic credentials – Asquith's daughter Violet Bonham-Carter, Balfour's niece Blanche Dugdale – played any role in such confabulations, and even their influence was limited. Dugdale tried to convince her close friends Walter Elliot and Buck de la Warr to resign from the Cabinet over Munich but without success;[91] Bonham-Carter berated Sinclair for his support for Chamberlain's third mission and stiffened him up to oppose further concessions.[92] Rathbone and Atholl, upright and unclubbable, lacked such easy access and may not have even sought it. Nicolson, who admired both women, nevertheless thought Rathbone so 'self-contained' as to be almost unapproachable and Atholl 'probably the worst bore that I have ever known'; Duff Cooper, the sole cabinet minister to resign over Munich, simply thought the House of Commons 'no place . . . for women'.[93] Yet the fact that Rathbone does not figure in records of those private conversations that produced the Conservative abstentions after the four days of debate over Munich in the House on 3–6 October does not mean that she was silent – but that she spoke in public and not in the bar of the Savoy. Deprived of the luxury of conspiracy, we find her denouncing the Munich pact as a 'peace without honour' at a 2,000-strong meeting of the National Committee of Peace and Friendship with the Soviet Union, at which Bob Boothby and Dugdale also spoke, on the very day of its agreement.[94] If there was a price to be paid for such unsuitable honesty, such unwomanly belligerence, she was prepared to pay it.

But it was Atholl, not Rathbone, who paid. Already in trouble with her constituency party over her stance on Spain, when Atholl returned from the United States in October she found herself charged with disloyalty for statements she had made there about Munich and told that she would not be asked to stand for West Perth again. The soul of honour in such matters, she duly resigned her seat, deciding to try to regain it as an Independent. Under pressure from Sinclair, a popular Liberal candidate reluctantly stood down, and the by-election quickly became a referendum on the Munich accords. It was one that Conservative Central Office could not afford to lose. Boothby and other 'Tory renegades' were persuaded to stay away from the constituency (although Macadam, an old hand at electioneering, made the long drive from London to help), and on the icy December polling day, fleets of cars sent by Conservative Central Office brought Conservative voters to the polls. To Chamberlain's great delight ('a grand wind up to a very difficult session,' he crowed to his Chief Whip),[95] Atholl lost by 1,313 votes. An MP for fifteen straight years and the Conservative Party's first woman minister, Atholl had run political risks that no male anti-appeaser would run. Churchill admired her grit, but never found her another parliamentary seat.

Rathbone, for her part, lived through the days of the Munich crisis caught between horror and shame. Like many of her countrymen and women, she found the prospect of war agonizing – and yet, how much worse that innocent foreigners should be sacrificed to keep her safe! Once the terms were known, and before the fateful Commons debates, she sat down to write her own pledge to the Czech people. 'The sacrifices to which your Government has been forced to consent . . . lie heavily upon our hearts and consciences', imposing on us 'a solemn obligation to do our utmost to mitigate the suffering of your people and to safeguard the future welfare and security of your State'.[96] Seventy-five MPs joined Rathbone in signing that statement, which she delivered to the Czech Legation. For most, probably, it was only a gesture, salve to an aching conscience. But Rathbone felt it as a promise – to the Czechs in general, and to the helpless people caught in the crossfire of territorial transfers and 'regime changes' in particular. From October 1938, Rathbone would live day and night with the 'refugee question', an issue she found more of a 'Heartbreak House' than any she had encountered before.[97]

To understand the context within which Rathbone operated, we need to recall the nature of the refugee problem in the 1930s and the British government's response.[98] The group most in need of refuge in the mid-thirties was, obviously, German Jews, for Hitler made no bones about his determination to expel all Jews from his Reich. And yet, they were hardly the only people seeking a haven. As many as half a million Spaniards took refuge in France as Republican areas fell to the Nationalists; Nazi annexations in Austria and Czechoslovakia placed at risk almost a million more Jews; moreover, other East European states – notably Poland – made clear their desire to follow Hitler's lead and reduce the size of their Jewish populations. Few countries wished to receive them. British policy was guided by two principles: the principle that Britain itself was not a country of immigration and could not, in a time of high unemployment, accept any considerable number for permanent settlement; and the principle that no refugee would be allowed entry into Britain unless a voluntary organization accepted financial responsibility for them. (To this, of course, one might add a third principle: that immigration to Palestine, although possible for some tens of thousands, must be restricted in light of Arab sensitivities and tightly controlled.) Voluntary organizations both adjusted to and chafed under these restrictions. From 1933 the Central British Fund for German Jewry, the Society of Friends and a host of other organizations worked to raise money and provide financial guarantees for refugees (both Jewish and non-Jewish) from the Reich; Rathbone's National Joint Committee for Spanish Relief gave a similar pledge of maintenance on the entry of the Basque children. But the Nazi practice of forcing German Jews to emigrate while stripping them of the assets that might help them do so made the work of the organizations aiding Jewish refugees especially difficult. When the annexation of Austria was followed by another wave of pogroms, property seizures and violence against Jews, they found themselves stretched past breaking point. At the suggestion of the Home Office, they set up a new coordinating committee to pool their efforts – but what they really needed, they told the Home Office, was some relaxation of the stringent British rules and some help in finding territories willing to receive potential migrants. Rathbone's letter to the *Manchester Guardian* on 23 May 1938, calling for a new, 'thought-out and coordinated policy – national, imperial, and international', was only one of many such pleas.[99]

Two months earlier, the United States had in fact proposed setting up an international committee to facilitate the emigration of German and Austrian refugees. The Foreign and Home Offices had looked at that proposal dubiously, preferring to introduce a new visa requirement for German and Austrian passport holders in order to regulate the influx into Britain. Winterton, a touchy, undistinguished minister passionate only about fox-hunting, was nevertheless duly dispatched to Evian to take part in an international conference in July, after which an intergovernmental committee was established. Under the chairmanship of George Rublee and then Sir Herbert Emerson, that committee tried to locate possible places of refuge and to moderate Nazi policies of asset-stripping, without much success – especially since it was not empowered to ask participating states to alter their immigration quotas and requirements. Policy-making remained the prerogative of individual governments. Britain responded to the worsening situation with a mixture of bureaucratic rigidity and spurts of individually motivated humanitarianism. Thus, after *Kristallnacht*, Chamberlain pressed the Home Office to relax financial and visa requirements and allow the entry of specific classes of refugees, notably unaccompanied Jewish children, while Baldwin raised the funds to support them by launching (with a BBC broadcast) the Lord Baldwin Fund for Refugees.[100] But the cornerstones of British policy – pre-selection by voluntary organizations and the requirement of a British visa – remained.

Until the Czech crisis, Rathbone had played only a small role in the widening refugee crisis. She had joined a deputation to ask for some relaxation of the immigration rules; she had lent her name to a memorial sent to the delegates to the Evian conference.[101] But she was closely involved only with refugees from Spain (some quarter of a million of whom were now in camps in France), whose plight she saw as a direct consequence of the British government's 'fatal support for the policy of non-intervention'.[102] The Czech crisis struck exactly the same chord. Britain had (with France) handed over the Sudetenland to Hitler – and when that transfer turned into a rout, with Nazi storm-troopers seizing property unimpeded and thousands of Czechs, anti-Nazi Sudeten Germans, and Austrian and German Jewish refugees fleeing eastward towards the Czech heartlands (and, in the case of the non-Czechs, being turned back), she once again thought Britain directly responsible. With Sir John Hope Simpson – who was rapidly becoming the recognized expert on refugees – she appealed to Halifax and the Home Office for 2,000 visas immediately; by 20 October, however, when the League of Nations Union Executive Committee met, the Foreign Office had granted only 100 visas for German social democrats and 250 for Austrians in Czechoslovakia.[103] (Too many of those on the Czech 'danger list' were communists, Special Branch reported, warning that Rathbone was knowingly collaborating with British communists to try to get them out.)[104] Her pride in her sleeve, she then wrote to a valiant Czech friend, Senator Plaminkova, begging her to do what she could to stop the deportations of ethnic Germans. Plaminkova was understandably outraged. 'England', Plaminkova said, had handed over Czechoslovakia's territories to Germany and Poland; it was now up to England to succour those they had deprived of their homes. With hardly room in the 'small hut left to us' for the impoverished Sudetenland Czechs streaming over the new border, they could not be asked to support many thousands of Germans as well.[105]

Rathbone actually agreed with her; to a degree (and under pressure) the government did so as well. In meetings over the Munich accords, Chamberlain had promised the Czechs help during the transition: in December 1938 and January 1939, then, British officials hammered out the terms of a Czech loan. Concerns over Czech deportations, they assured Rathbone privately, would figure in their calculations.[106] The Czechs were asked not to send any more refugees from the Sudetenland back, and some £4 million of a total sum of £10 million was designated for use in facilitating their emigration. Once again, Britain envisaged taking relatively few refugees itself, although it did allow temporary entry for those with a visa for a final destination. Consular officials and representatives of voluntary organizations moved into Prague to arrange the visas; a new refugee organization was set up to raise funds and guarantee maintenance; voluntary workers – usually women – went out from London to help potential refugees get their papers in order and make their case.

Rathbone responded as well, setting up a new organization of her own. As an MP, she had excellent access to information and officials, and, especially after *Kristallnacht*, she and many other MPs were inundated with mail from refugees or British citizens seeking to drag some friend or family member out of the German net. In December, she and three other MPs formed a 'Parliamentary Committee on Refugees' – a body that, despite its official-sounding name, was entirely voluntary and that Rathbone funded out of her own pocket. Two of her collaborators – the Labour MP David Grenfell and the Independent University of Oxford member Arthur Salter – were old allies, Grenfell from the National Joint Committee for Spanish Relief and Salter from the League of Nations Union. The fourth, Victor Cazalet, was different: a Conservative, he had supported the Nationalists in the Spanish conflict – so much so that Rathbone had added him to a list she kept of politically vulnerable pro-Franco MPs. But Cazalet was repelled by anti-Semitism, genuinely hated cruelty, and wanted to do what he could for Germany's threatened Jews. By Christmas that group of four was meeting almost daily.[107]

The Parliamentary Committee's period of greatest activity would come during the war itself, when it would take the lead in arranging the release – often case by case, refugee by refugee – of those 'friendly aliens' who were interned as German nationals during the invasion scare of 1940. From its inception, however, it combined lobbying 'in favour of a more generous and comprehensive policy on the refugee question' with 'casework', willingly responding to individual requests for help.[108] This made it unusual among MPs' organizations but ideally suited to Rathbone, whose social work background and experience in running the system of separation allowances in Liverpool had prepared her well for the job of keeping track of a shifting maze of regulations and policies on the one hand and what became many thousands of individual cases on the other. She had, as Harold Nicolson remarked, 'an astonishing capacity for dull work', and – being immune to flattery and almost indifferent to abuse – was willing to go beyond the limits of good manners and make herself a nuisance.[109] She would importune any friend or acquaintance on behalf of her charges: she had revived the flagging embers of her friendship with Astor (a strong Chamberlainite) to get her to intercede on Arthur Koestler's behalf when he was in a Spanish prison; she repeatedly appealed on visa questions to Rab Butler (who had replaced Cranborne as Under-Secretary at the Foreign Office and with whom she had worked on the Committee for the Protection of Coloured Women); during the war she would remind Lothian (now Ambassador to the United States) of their old collaboration on India and try to bury the hatchet with Hoare (now Ambassador to Spain) to interest them in those International Brigaders still rotting in Franco's jails.[110] Only some of her work for refugees was done on behalf of the Parliamentary Committee, for Rathbone had many disguises and was as likely to pop up on deputations by the National Council of Civil Liberties (whose refugee sub-committee she chaired), the League of Nations Union, the Abyssinia Association or any one of three or four committees on Spain. But the Parliamentary Committee on Refugees was, even more than these others, her political tool and creation. Now, she had 100 MPs – by the outbreak of the war it would be 200 – pledged to support her efforts.

What those efforts entailed becomes clear if we follow her work in two campaigns: one to aid people threatened by the Nazi attacks on the Czech state, and the other to remove those at risk during the Spanish Republic's last days. As we have seen, in October 1938 Rathbone had already become involved in efforts to rescue social democrats and Jews threatened by the Nazi takeover of the Sudetenland. In January 1939, she had even flown to Prague to look into the condition of the refugee camps and – fearing a further German attack – to see whether anything could be done to speed up the visa process.[111] When that attack came (as she expected) that March, and Alec Randall of the Foreign Office refused to allow her to send money by diplomatic bag to refugees now in hiding, she simply blew up over the phone. She had been warning the government of the approaching fate of Czechoslovakia for the past two and a half years, she pointed out, and now found it hard to care about Foreign Office procedures when people she knew personally in Prague were being picked up by the Gestapo. 'It is difficult to persuade people like Miss Rathbone that the consciousness of the necessity for an all-round view, and for maintaining good faith or at least good relations between us and the Germans, is not cynical, inhuman indifference,' Randall minuted sourly.[112] Rathbone placed her faith, instead, in the indomitable Beatrice Wellington of the Czech Refugee Trust, who was still in Prague arranging visas despite Gestapo interrogation, and tried to get the Home Office and the Trust's officials in London to put fewer obstacles in her way. Couldn't consular officials in Prague be instructed to issue visas on her recommendation without approval from London?[113] (Instead, Randall passed on a query to E.N. Cooper at the Home Office asking him to check whether practices so 'contrary to the regulations' were in fact happening.)[114] If the Home Office was demanding guarantees on maintenance before admission, why didn't the Trust just give such guarantees, whether or not it had the funds in hand? The National Joint Committee for Spanish Relief had always worked on the principle of 'doing what seemed necessary and trusting that the money would come somehow – and it has,' she wrote to Sir Henry Bunbury of the Trust. 'Need the Czech Committee be quite so terribly genteel?'[115]

She was not troubled by such scruples. If funds were the problem, why not use the £10 million promised to the Czech government but impossible to turn over after the Nazi invasion? Four million of that loan had been converted into a free gift and earmarked for refugee resettlement in January, but surely the government didn't intend simply to make 'a nice little economy' out of the disaster and pocket the other six million?[116] In fact, neither shortage of funds nor some penny-pinching desire for economy was driving the behaviour of the government and the Czech Trust; rather, both were using the claim of penury to try to delimit the categories of individuals they were willing to help. In October 1938, it was German social democrats, German and Austrian Jews who had taken refuge in Czechoslovakia, and to a degree Sudeten Jews, who were considered particularly at risk; Czech Jews, it was assumed, were simply Czechs and were not in the same danger. After the German takeover of the rump state the matter was, of course, quite different. Yet while individual voluntary workers and consular officials in Prague did make an effort to help Czech Jews as well, the British government hardly wished to see the tens of thousands of refugees for whom it had acknowledged at least some responsibility swollen to include a Czech Jewish population that numbered hundreds of thousands. Thus, while the government allowed the Czech Refugee Trust to draw on the £4 million earmarked for refugee resettlement, it refused to make the remaining funds available. Rathbone made a great deal of noise about this, writing letters to the press, asking questions in Parliament, and taking an all-party deputation to plead with the Chancellor and Home Secretary, but to no avail.[117]

She had more luck on Spain, but only by resorting to some unorthodox methods. In October 1938, Rathbone and her allies had convinced the government to break with past policy and protect ships transporting food to the famished Republican towns;[118] in early spring 1939, as those cities began to fall, she begged for similar protection for ships taking refugees out. W.H. Montagu-Pollock, her one real ally in the Foreign Office, gave what help he could. The government was under pressure both from MPs and from a very worried Spanish government, he minuted; although Britain had been unwilling to evacuate refugees in the past, there was a clear humanitarian argument for a change in policy.[119] Chamberlain and Halifax disagreed – and the French, no longer under a Popular Front government, were also unwilling to help. Rathbone and Wilfrid Roberts, however, simply circumvented them, approaching the Mexican Ambassador with a plan to hire a ship and run the blockade on their own.[120] The National Joint Committee did in fact succeed in bringing several shiploads of refugees out; they also managed to get the British government to intercede with the French to grant landing rights to the *Stanbrook*, a packed and reeking refugee ship chartered by the Spanish government.[121] But only a fraction of Republicans at risk actually got away, and when Rathbone found her predictions of summary executions and reprisals amply fulfilled, she wrote to Butler with some bitterness. By delaying embarkation at Gandia and diverting refugees to Alicante, the actions of British consular officials had cost several thousand lives. Butler responded imperturbably but was in fact rather shocked, minuting privately that the government had been fortunate that this charge had not been raised on the floor of the House.[122]

At these moments we see Rathbone in full battledress and can begin to understand her mode of operation. On both the Spanish and Czech issues, Rathbone drew on independent information and a wide array of political and even international contacts to force ministers and officials to hear her; in both cases, when they failed to do as she wished, she broadcast their failings energetically or sought to go behind their backs. Small wonder Harold Nicolson thought of her as one of Edmund Spenser's valiant warrior queens ('the Britomart of 1939') and – much as he admired her – felt a pang of sympathy for those junior ministers who would duck behind pillars when they saw her coming.[123] Her niece Nancy's son Michael Warr, trying to work his way up in the Foreign Office hierarchy, learned to give his aunt a wide berth: 'she used people,' he explained to his wife; 'she didn't care who she bored as long as she got her way'.[124] And when she did sense a chink in the armour – a glimmer of conscience or sympathy, or simply a weary inclination towards concession in the hope of making her go away – she pursued her advantage relentlessly. Montagu-Pollock, the rare Foreign Office official who sympathized with her cause, found himself regarded as 'the guardian angel of refugees' and inundated with 'my daily bunch of letters from Miss Rathbone, MP'.[125] She was, simply, implacable; and, since she was well-placed, impossible to shut up, and immune from party discipline, officials and ministers had no alternative but to deal with her. But when they did so, they often found, to their surprise, that she was neither fanatical nor impractical, but flexible, imaginative and terrifyingly good on the details. Thus, when Butler told her that the government would find it easier to consider requests for admission of prominent Republican officials if there were a voluntary committee dealing only with this group, Rathbone set up in short order a 'British Committee for Refugees from Spain' which selected, arranged passage for, and guaranteed support of the few hundred refugees the government would allow to enter.[126] If officials had spent more time trying to help her, and less trying to outwit her, there is no knowing what she could have done.

And yet, for all Rathbone's energy and practical bent, the record of those early months of 1939 does leave us with a question. Why, exactly, did she focus so closely on those threatened with political retribution? Why did she think – as she said repeatedly in the Commons and the press – that the cases of politically active refugees in conquered fascist or Nazi territory were the 'most urgent of all?'[127] In part, her implicit hierarchy of suffering reflected her estimate of the level of Britain's guilt, for on Spain and Czechoslovakia she felt that responsibility without bounds. Yet it also reflected her estimate – from the standpoint of 1939 and without the benefit of hindsight – of the immediacy of different communities' risks and dangers. She knew that Jews were being subjected to terrible privation and brutality simply on the grounds of their Jewishness, but Sudeten German social democrats were also likely to be sent straight to concentration camps and Spanish Republicans to face reprisals as Franco's troops advanced. Rathbone could not have imagined all the horrors in store for Jews as the Nazis extended their control; she was not wrong, however, in her fears for the fate of the Republican officials and supporters, tens of thousands of whom were executed after the Republic fell.[128] Britain accepted only a few hundred Republican refugees, while hundreds of thousands remained confined to camps in France. During the war, unavailingly, Rathbone would try to prevent the Laval government from sending trainloads upon trainloads of them eastwards to 'forced labour' or death.[129]

Moreover, while Rathbone did pay particular attention to those displaced in Spain and the Sudetenland, she was one of the few British politicians to see the refugee issue as a whole – and, crucially, to add the Jewish populations of Eastern Europe as well as those in the Reich to the tally of those needing or likely to need evacuation. On 6 April 1939, in a prominent article damning the government's policy of 'selfish isolationism', Rathbone totted up the numbers: only some 200,000 Jews had escaped from Germany thus far, she thought; another million Jews and 'non-Aryans' needed to be removed from Hitler's expanded Reich immediately, while another four and a half million Jews in Poland, Hungary, Romania and Lithuania were also enduring persecution. Britain could only begin to cope with a problem of this magnitude if it ceased to use international consultation as an excuse for inactivity and began to craft an independent and generous response. Here, and in a memo to the government prepared for the Parliamentary Committee on Refugees, Rathbone sketched out what a policy might look like. The first and most important thing was to 'break with the fatal policy' of restricted quotas and voluntary financing agreed at Evian: even if it did not intend to accept refugees permanently, the government could set up reception centres in Britain where refugees could wait for visas before proceeding further; rather than requiring voluntary organizations to raise money for financial guarantees, the government should subsidize their efforts out of public funds. And, most importantly, Britain should take a lead on the question, appointing a minister and staffing a department in order to carry through an activist, forward-looking policy.[130]

This would indeed have been a generous response. Essentially, Rathbone was suggesting that Britain accept responsibility for the victims of fascism everywhere in Europe, and for the threatened Jews in particular, and take practical steps to rescue as many as it could. Nor did she see such a policy as simple benevolence, but rather as a moral obligation about which there should really be no debate at all. But why, exactly, did she think this? Why did she think individual Britons not merely *ought* but were *obliged* to do all they could, alone and in concert, to aid foreign populations? In the past, Rathbone had grounded her sense of responsibility in politics: Britain was responsible for India's suffering children because of its two centuries of imperial rule; Britain should rescue Spanish Republicans because their peril stemmed from its misguided support for 'non-intervention'; it should rescue Sudeten Germans and Czech Jews because their danger was the consequence of Chamberlain's fatal policy of appeasement. But in calling for a comprehensive effort to save the Jews, Rathbone was urging Britain to take responsibility for populations not tied to it by political obligation or control. Nor, for all her admiration for Jewish culture and for the idealistic Zionists she had met in Palestine, was her conviction grounded in some foundational sense of communal identity. How, then, did she explain her stance?

In an article written for the *New Statesman* in April 1939, we find our answer. In this piece, Rathbone sketched out the horrors to which Jews and other hunted people were now subject, and the inability of the hard-pressed, desperate voluntary organizations to save even a fraction. The government must know 'that the backs of the voluntary organisations are simply breaking under the burden cast upon their workers'.

> Ring up one of the principal workers before 9 a.m. and one usually finds that she (it is usually she) has already gone to her office. Ring up again at 11 p.m. and she has not returned. Worse than overwork to the sensitive must be the knowledge that correspondence unavoidably delayed for weeks, or perhaps mislaid, has often meant that a victim for whom rescue was possible, even under the rigid official restrictions, has been driven to suicide, or seized by the Gestapo, or is in Dachau enduring some of the refined tortures of that hell, or is believed to be hiding by night in empty drain pipes and by day in the forests and is untraceable. (These are actual instances.)

Yet, faced with such stories, government ministers simply repeated their unwillingness either to accept financial responsibility or to allow large-scale temporary refuge, leaving the voluntary organizations to struggle on, inadequately, as best they could. She found it hard to forgive this policy.

> A Cabinet is a collective entity, and such an entity has proverbially neither a body to be kicked nor a soul to be damned. Yet sometimes as I gaze across the House at the serried row of rather uninspiring personalities upon the Treasury Bench, I am tempted to wish that they had indeed a collective soul, which could be condemned to spend eternity in seeing and feeling the torments which their policy has caused others to continue enduring, while their individual souls reposed blissfully in some insipid Paradise, listening to music played upon antiquated instruments.

And yet, for all that, was the responsibility the government's alone? This was the crux of the matter.

> As to responsibility, some people apparently feel it only for the evil they actually do; others feel guilty of *every bit of evil in the world* which they or their nations – with which they identify themselves – fail to prevent, provided it was possible to prevent or try to prevent it without creating a greater evil or neglecting a more important duty.[131]

Such was the evil of suffering, the preciousness of life, that every single individual must do all they could to save those victims threatened with annihilation.

Here it is, again, that transformed faith, the ethos of philosophical idealism, of T.H. Green and Rathbone's Oxford teachers. We are all interdependent – and being part of one another, are called to mutual service. We strive to do right, planning our actions by their likely consequences, aware – as Rathbone had lectured her pacifists – that in a complex social world 'political policies must be judged not by their aims and intentions but by their actual results'.[132] This is a difficult rule to live by, even if one delimits that circle of mutual obligation narrowly: as a neighbourhood, city or even nation. Rathbone, raised in this ethos, had made that progression, expanding her sympathy and her recognition of mutual obligation from city to nation, from nation to empire. Now, however, she expanded that circle yet further: 'every bit of evil in the world' was her responsibility; every suffering soul had equal claim.

But how can one bear such a burden? How can any individual person take responsibility for such a world and for its crimes? When one refugee worker returned from Prague to tell Rathbone that she had nineteen suicides on her conscience, Rathbone willingly absolved her – but it is clear that those suicides weighed on her conscience as well.[133] That burden made her work all the harder, but it also made her even less able to pay much attention to the little worries and cares of the ordinary mortals living around her. Certainly her faithful secretary, Doris Hardman, found Rathbone's combination of humanitarian anguish and personal reserve somewhat frustrating. 'I never felt I could ever get in any way close to her,' Hardman recalled. 'She really had this absolutely genuine feeling for people who suffered, but she could not express herself in relation to people who were just around and obviously not suffering much anyway.'[134] Eleanor's niece Noreen (Frank's youngest child, born in 1923), agrees. 'She was a kind woman, but not, I think, an understanding one'; absolutely concentrated on her causes, she simply had no interest in ordinary human frailties and didn't want to know about other people's private lives. (Noreen would go off, instead, in search of Elizabeth Macadam, who was 'highly approachable' and always ready with a sympathetic ear.)[135] Even the unquenchable human need for diversion and pleasure seemed to Rathbone, in those dreadful pre-war months, almost an affront. In late May, she had rung up Osbert Peake, the junior minister at the Home Office, to try to arrange visas for some German and Austrian International Brigaders facing repatriation to the Reich, but found he had left on holiday – holiday weekends seemingly being, she told her ally Lord Listowel, 'of much more importance in these cabinet ministers' eyes than human lives'.[136] As they went off to enjoy their own holidays, she told the House as it adjourned on 4 August, they should spare some thought for those 'hundreds of thousands of men and women who are wandering about in utmost destitution, many of them hiding by day, many of them already in the hands of the Gestapo'.[137]

Only her work, now, could comfort her. This was why her industry, as Nicolson remarked, was 'insatiable', why she showed an 'infinite capacity for taking pains'.[138] 'Those of us who have found the spectacle of the Spanish tragedy almost unbearable and, because of our nation's share in it, a heavy weight on our consciences, can at least reflect that we have done just a little to mitigate distress,' Rathbone wrote to her constituents in 1939.[139] But Rathbone had turned to practical work before, of course, when searching for comfort and meaning, for a way to reconcile conscience and ambition. 'If one's large schemes fail,' she had written to Hilda Oakeley in defence of 'friendly visiting' some forty years earlier, 'it will be a satisfaction at the end of life to know that, at any rate, some poor bicycle-maker and his wife and children were set on their legs and saved from the House and made respectable citizens through my agency.' Once again, large schemes had failed – the Spanish Republic lay in ruins, Eastern Europe's last democracy had been crushed in the Nazi fist – but the knowledge that she had helped to bring a few threatened Spanish Republicans, a few German social democrats and a few Czech Jews to safety was comfort of a kind.

There was another comfort Rathbone could have claimed. Having predicted almost all the evils to which Chamberlain's policies had led, from the Czech subjection to the destruction of the League, she had (as she told a number of local League of Nations Unions in February 1939) 'the gloomy satisfaction of having been a true prophet'. She would so much rather have been wrong. Now, one could only try for a pragmatic alliance – to draw closer to France and the United States and to seek a new treaty with Russia – while building up Britain's armaments and armed forces as quickly as possible.[140] She was relieved that, after the fall of Czechoslovakia in March, the government finally guaranteed Poland's borders, but doubted its willingness to pursue a Soviet alliance effectively. That summer, she stoked the fires of a press campaign to bring Churchill into the Cabinet so as to convince the Soviets 'that Great Britain at last really means business'.[141] She also supported the government's legislation reintroducing conscription, against her constituents' wishes.[142] In the current situation, no other stance was possible.

On 4 August, the House adjourned for the eight-week summer recess, despite pleas from Churchill, Attlee and others to keep it in session. They were, again, right: on 24 August, Chamberlain was forced to recall it to discuss another crisis – the Nazi pact with the Soviets, announced the previous day. Two years earlier, Rathbone had warned that this might happen; now, with her worst fears realized, she stood up in the Commons to say what many members must have been thinking. They had been wrong to let the government believe that it had the confidence of the House, she said; change at the top was long overdue. 'The leaders of the Opposition cannot ask for changes which affect themselves,' she said, but everyone had their names, and that of Churchill, in their minds. No, she told Nancy Astor, who was trying to interrupt her, she would not allow Astor to put a question, she would not give way. 'Are we going to let the very men who made those mistakes in neglecting our military preparations, and mistakes in their attitude towards Russia, and in misunderstanding the mind of Herr Hitler, which have brought us to this pass, carry on the affairs of the country or will they, before it is too late, form a Government which really represents the people, the whole people and nothing but the people?'[143] One week later, Churchill was in the government and Britain at war.

Chapter 15

A War Worth Fighting

Those who heard Rathbone's fierce criticisms of appeasement in the 1930s sometimes thought her militaristic. Miss Rathbone, one Council of Action member wrote angrily to Lloyd George during the Rhineland crisis, was a 'pest' and a 'fury'. She and her ally Margery Corbett Ashby 'both want to fight Germany and discuss throwing away millions of young lives as if they were ordering a chicken to be killed for dinner'.[1] But B.L. Rathbone, invited to take tea with his aunt in the Commons soon after war was declared, knew otherwise. Everything she had done had been done to prevent this calamity. Dissolving into tears, she told him she only wished she could fight and young men's lives be spared.[2]

Easy words, perhaps, but she truly meant them. She wanted desperately to serve, to share every risk and danger. Soon she would share a few. A quarter of the London population fled or were evacuated during the blitz of autumn 1940, when German bombers pounded London for seventy-six straight nights (less one, when the weather attacked instead), but Eleanor wouldn't budge. Instead, she, Elizabeth and Mrs Wilson carted their bedding over to the secure basement shelter next door. They slept peacefully, but 50 Romney Street fared less well. A particularly fierce raid on the night of 30 October knocked in the two top rooms, driving the three women into new quarters at 5 Tufton Court, a ground-floor utility flat in a secure modern building around the corner. Tufton Court's iron girders and narrow hallways made it as secure as any shelter for sleeping, so Eleanor and Elizabeth could stay at home through the intermittent raids of 1941. 'Things were pretty awful last Saturday with fires blazing all round but we were quite unhurt,' Eleanor wrote to Evie after the terrible night of 10 May, which left the St John Smith Square in flames and the Commons Chamber in ruins.[3] She wasn't unaware of the danger, but she didn't want to duck it. This was her war, fought for her ideals and her home.

But what, beyond risking her life, was she to do? Elizabeth had no trouble finding a way to serve. She had remained active in the National Council for Social Service and now returned to practical social work, assisting in a shelter for those rendered homeless by the war. Eleanor, for her part, added her name to the Ministry of Labour's register of women with high professional and administrative experience available for work. On the register's five-by-eight card she dutifully listed her qualifications. She was good at writing reports and at running organizations, she recorded: her work as the chief officer of the Liverpool Soldiers' and Sailors' Families' Association during the war 'justifies my saying that I am good at directing staff and getting much work out of them without friction'. But with her excellent health and 'exceptionally strong constitution', she was willing to do 'any work (voluntary or paid) not in competition with my duties as an MP'. In the tiny space provided for listing any additional qualifications ('e.g. nautical, aeronautical, languages'), she recorded proudly: 'Can drive a car.'[4]

The Ministry did not in fact employ sixty-seven-year-old Members of Parliament as part-time chauffeurs, although Rathbone did send off her car ('Jane Austen') to do war work without her. Instead, she was asked to serve on the Advisory Committee to the Ministry of Pensions, where her extensive knowledge of military allowances came in handy. But while she attended this committee faithfully for the whole of the war, it couldn't hold her interest. After ten years in the Commons, the last four battling Conservative ministers on every possible front, she was after bigger prey. This war could be won, Rathbone thought, only if the whole population were mobilized and the world constantly reminded of the purposes for which Britain fought. But could Chamberlain – the man who 'lost the peace' – be trusted with those tasks? Her behaviour in the Commons tells us her answer. From the outbreak of the war until Chamberlain's fall eight months later, Rathbone asked question after question (eighty-five in all) on subjects ranging from air raid precautions, to war aims, to the mobilization of manpower, to the provision of news to soldiers serving abroad. She was active behind the scenes as well. In August 1939 Rathbone had warned that she and other anti-appeasers would never forget or forgive the mistakes of the late thirties. Now she would do what she could to help bring Chamberlain down.

On 4 September, the day after war was declared, a circular letter went out from Romney Street. It bore six signatures – those of Bob Boothby, Graham White, David Grenfell, Harold Nicolson, Arthur Salter and Eleanor Rathbone. Boothby and Nicolson had collaborated with Rathbone on child welfare; White, Grenfell and Salter had worked with her on refugees. Now, the six wrote to ask other parliamentary cross-party allies whether they would like to meet regularly as a group. Such an incipient coalition of Independents, Liberals, refugee advocates and dissident Conservatives had already met with Admiral Sir Roger Keyes, a close ally of Churchill, on 6 August to discuss Britain's naval preparedness; most returned for the meeting on 14 September that constituted the 'All Party Parliamentary Action Group'. The Liberal MP Clement Davies agreed to serve as chairman, Boothby as honorary secretary, and Rathbone as convener. Subcommittees on foreign policy, economic warfare and home defence were established, and by late September the group was meeting weekly.

It was, already, a hotbed of anti-Chamberlain feeling. After its second meeting on 20 September, the group asked Chamberlain to discuss the government's war policy in secret session; when he refused, they began to call in the war experts on their own. In September, they invited Lloyd George to lead a discussion of war aims; in October, they heard from Viscount Trenchard, Marshal of the R.A.F., on air warfare, Sir Stephen Tallents on broadcasting, and Beveridge on the war economy. By early November, they had defined their objects and had more than 50 members – 25 National government MPs, 8 Liberals, 16 Labour members, and 4 Independents. That winter, the group discussed the government's prosecution of the war and met with experts – including, significantly, Keynes, who presented a proposal to use family allowances to protect civilian health without generating an inflationary wage spiral.[5] Leo Amery, who went to this and many other meetings of the group, recalled that it offered 'a useful forum for more informal and confidential discussions than were advisable on the floor of the House'.[6] Here, out of the newspapers' hearing and away from the whips' prying eyes, were formulated cross-party agreements and policies that would bear fruit in Churchill's wartime government.

In his memoirs, Boothby stressed the importance of this cross-party pressure group during those uncomfortable months of the 'phoney war'. He and Clem Davies, he recalled, ran the group together and 'went into action' in May after the fiasco of the Norway campaign.[7] But Boothby's recollections are not quite accurate. For it was Rathbone and not Davies who first convened the Parliamentary Action Group, Rathbone whom Boothby consulted when first drafting a statement of the group's aims, Rathbone who approached Lloyd George about possible collaboration, Rathbone who organized most of the group's meetings and invited most of its speakers. And it was Rathbone who, being free of party ties and (as she put it) 'someone who cannot possibly be regarded as seeking office', made the argument Boothby and his ambitious friends could not. On the debate on adjournment on 11 April 1940, a week after Chamberlain's latest cabinet reshuffle and as news began coming in about the Germans' successful attack on Norway, Rathbone rose to question Chamberlain's choices. None of the 'coming young men' of the Conservative Party had been brought into the government, she pointed out; indeed, 'those who have shown courage in opposition and independence of mind, who have criticised where they thought criticism was needed . . . have been blackballed'. Chamberlain was, she said, 'too influenced by his personal likes and dislikes', too determined 'not to allow anyone to come into the Ministry who has ever opposed or criticised, especially on the question of the Munich Pact'. When 'we are fighting for our lives' and 'know that national unity is important', this was no way to run a government.[8]

By this point even a good number of Conservatives agreed. A week earlier, Lord Salisbury and Amery had constituted a small committee of government supporters to 'watch' the government; throughout April, as Norway slid into German hands, that watching committee and the Davies group met regularly. By early May, the two committees were collaborating openly, and on the night of 7 May, after Amery's famous speech quoting Cromwell's dismissal of the Long Parliament, they met to discuss their response should the Labour leadership decide (as it did) to ask for a confidence vote. Ultimately, Churchill's emergence as Prime Minister was contingent on Labour's refusal to serve under Chamberlain and Halifax's decision to give way to Churchill's ambition. But Amery and Davies's work in consolidating cross-party opposition made even Margesson, the Chief Whip, realize that Chamberlain had to go.[9]

Conspirators, of course, tend to reap the rewards of disloyalty. Key Labour members were brought into the new Cabinet (Attlee as Lord Privy Seal, Morrison as Minister of Supply); Amery, by contrast, had to be content with the non-cabinet position of Secretary of State for India and Davies got nothing at all. The less prominent 'dissidents' did better, as junior ministerial posts rained down. Boothby went to the Ministry of Food as Lord Woolton's parliamentary secretary, Nicolson to the Ministry of Information as Duff Cooper's junior, and Dingle Foot to the Ministry of Economic Warfare to second Hugh Dalton. Harold Macmillan became parliamentary secretary at the Ministry of Supply; Salter had already been named parliamentary secretary at the Ministry of Shipping. Grenfell was sent to the Mines Department of the Board of Trade. 'Dined with what was originally the Economic sub-Committee of Clem Davies' Action Group at the Reform Club,' Amery reported in his diary on 30 May, 'but now consisted almost entirely of Ministers!'[10] The All-Party Action Group had done its work well.

Rathbone rejoiced in these appointments and especially in Churchill's accession. For the first time she was utterly content with her nation's leader – almost, indeed, in thrall. Churchill was just the sort of person she liked. Herself incapable of dissimulation or irony, she loved his very bluster and obviousness and thrilled to his defiant speeches. Through those anxious days of late May and early June, as French resistance crumbled and an invasion of England began to look likely, she – like so much of the country – took heart from his bulldog manner and implacable tones. On 5 June, the day after he announced in the House that the bulk of the British army had, miraculously, been rescued from Dunkirk, Rathbone actually quoted much of that 'we shall fight on the beaches' speech to a gathering of the Lambeth League of Nations Union. 'What a leader,' she said, 'and, oh! if he had been sooner.'[11]

That admiration and loyalty never faltered: although Rathbone would disagree with some of Churchill's decisions and appointments, and became a strenuous critic of his government's policies towards aliens and refugees, she believed (as she told him honestly) 'that not only this nation but the world owes more to you than to any other British statesman who has ever lived'.[12] So great was her gratitude that she could hardly bear to hear him criticized, and in 1943 would transfix a packed House with an unpremeditated and virulent attack on Aneurin Bevan in Churchill's defence. That moment lived in her fellow MPs' minds and reveals something of Rathbone's parliamentary standing, so let us join MPs as they pushed their way into the chamber on 23 May. One week earlier, the Labour Party firebrand Aneurin Bevan had questioned the Prime Minister about the regulations governing the behaviour of serving members (and, in particular, about whether a certain MP had violated army regulations in writing to the papers about military matters that had been discussed in the House); now he had given notice that he intended to raise the matter again. Not, one might think, a riveting subject: but the MP in question was Churchill's own son Randolph, and the House, predictably, was packed with members at once intrigued and appalled by the prospect of a personal attack. Bevan, predictably, insisted that the issue was one of principle and independent of the personalities involved, but Churchill clearly felt that Bevan was simply scandal-mongering. As the exchanges about whether Randolph had cleared his letter properly with the censors went on, many members grew embarrassed and uneasy.[13]

Then Eleanor burst in. She knew nothing at all about the disputed letter, she admitted, but she wanted 'to say very bluntly a thing which I think needs saying'. This was that Bevan entertained 'a malicious and virulent dislike of the Prime Minister'. His decision the previous week to raise a matter 'which would embarrass and perhaps pain the Prime Minister the very first time at which he was able to attend the House after a long illness, following upon a long and dangerous journey undertaken in the interests of the nation' already showed 'what I thought most of us must have thought to be an example of bad taste'. Today, then, she thought the House ought not to break up 'without someone saying, and perhaps I may say it because I am so completely outside this issue, and not a member of the Prime Minister's party, and that is with what disgust and almost loathing we watch this kind of temperament, these cattish displays of feline malice'. Her intervention was (as Churchill's secretary wrote to Randolph) 'shattering': she was cheered loudly from all sides of the House, Bevan sat down, and the press delightedly reported on her attack.[14] Eleanor, however, was mortified, telling A.V. Hill that she went home to apologize for her aspersion on the feline temperament to Smuts, her cat.[15] The next day's post relieved her, for Churchill wrote to thank her for her 'dramatic' and 'effective' intervention, and the following day Clementine sent a note praising her 'flaming words' as well.[16] (She only said what the whole House had been thinking, she replied.)[17]

This was only the most vivid manifestation of Rathbone's susceptibility to Churchill's magnetism – as well as of her ability, on rare occasions, to articulate the 'sense of the House'. That susceptibility did not, however, prevent her from

28. Rathbone chastising
Bevan, as seen by *Punch*, 31
March 1943.

watching his government – as she had watched all governments – for laziness or
incapacity. Herself so eager to serve, she worried about the government's attitudes towards women in particular. Whatever else Churchill might be, he was
certainly no feminist, and Ernest Bevin (Rathbone's old opponent on family
allowances) at the Ministry of Labour also seemed uncertain about women's usefulness in times of war. Thus Rathbone, along with the other women MPs, mobilized. They had begun meeting at Nancy Astor's house in the spring of 1940 to
discuss women's role in the war effort; in late June, six weeks after Churchill took
office, that group agreed – in a meeting at Rathbone's house – to become a formal
organization. This 'Woman Power Committee' (as it came to be known) quickly
emerged as the most important wartime feminist lobby. It met regularly for the
rest of the war, usually at the House of Commons, organized the crucial debates
on 'womanpower' in 20 March and 2 December 1941, pressed for an expansion
of nursery places so that married women could take up paid work, and eventually launched a campaign for post-war legislation on equal pay.[18]

Rathbone went along on the committee's deputations and gave some money
to keep it afloat, but she quickly ceased to be one of its moving spirits. For once,
the claims of 'equality' didn't really move her; or rather, she thought of those
claims only in terms of women's equal right to sacrifice, their equal right to
serve. It was because she was a '100 percent feminist', Rathbone said in that first

'womanpower' debate on 20 March, that she favoured conscription of women as well as men and had no tolerance for 'shirking'; young women who wrote asking her to prevent the Ministry of Labour from sending them to work in factories hundreds of miles from home were told shortly that 'equal citizenship should bring with it equal responsibilities' and that, had they been men, they might well find themselves in Singapore or Tobruk.[19] Women had the right to serve even in dangerous or combatant positions, she told BBC listeners in July 1940, and she responded angrily to one MP's claim that women over forty-five were too deranged by the 'considerable internal stresses and strains' of menopause to be fit for National Service.[20] During wartime, the only criterion relevant was aptitude for the job, and she denounced forthrightly the prejudice ('I used to call that feeling the Turk complex, but I think that may be uncomplimentary to our gallant Ally') against placing women in positions of any authority at all. Take the case, she said in August 1943, of a forty-year-old stockbroker outraged at being supervised in carpet-sweeping by a nineteen-year-old recruit to the Women's Auxiliary Air Force (WAAF). But what was wrong with this arrangement? 'A WAAF of 19 would almost certainly have more experience of carpet sweeping than a stockbroker. I am sure the WAAF would not mind being supervised by the stockbroker if the job had been the buying of shares.'[21]

29. Eleanor Rathbone speaking about 'Women and the Call Up' with Miss Mary Smieton of the Ministry of Labour on the BBC Home Service, 18 November 1941.

Not everyone agreed with her. The service ministers worried early in the war about the impact of married women's conscription on their husbands' morale, and even the Woman Power Committee, discussing a memo by Rathbone supporting conscription of women in the autumn of 1941, found itself divided. And so a careful balance prevailed. While Britain did enlist most single women and childless married women in war work, women who were fully occupied at home were never called up and women over fifty never even registered. Soon, Rathbone was too preoccupied with other issues to pay much attention. On 29 June 1940, when she asked Sir Edward Grigg, her collaborator on the 'Children's Minimum' campaign and now Under-Secretary at the War Office, for a bit of time to talk about the Women's Service Auxiliaries, she mentioned another issue that was worrying her even more. 'It is hard to exaggerate the amount of confusion, destitution, despair and panic which are arising out of the hasty sending out and execution of Orders either (a) extending the protected areas from which all aliens are being driven out, and (b) rounding up fresh groups of aliens for internment.'[22] Could he spare her ten minutes to talk about that?

The Churchill government's decision in May 1940 to intern 'enemy aliens' *en masse* returned Rathbone to the issues that had preoccupied her in the late 1930s, and kept her busy for the next two years of the war. For who were these 'enemy aliens'? As the Home Secretary, Sir John Anderson, was well aware, most of the more than 70,000 'aliens' of German or Austrian nationality present in Britain at the outbreak of the war were Jewish refugees who had fled the Nazi system; others were long-term residents, often with British spouses. Knowing this, Anderson did not want to repeat the policy of the First World War, when 29,000 hapless individuals were interned; he did, however, agree that all 'enemy aliens' should appear before local tribunals, be questioned about their background and loyalties, and be categorized. In the autumn of 1939, some 120 tribunals – usually chaired by a local barrister or magistrate – got to work. Of the almost 72,000 Germans and Austrians interviewed, a mere 569 were considered 'dangerous', placed in 'Category A', and interned; a further 6,782 were denoted worth watching (Category B) and subjected to restrictions on movement; and a final 64,244 were judged friendly or harmless, placed in Category C, and left at liberty. The tribunals were also asked to record whether the particular alien was a 'refugee from Nazi oppression'. Some 55,460 people, or 77%, met that condition.[23]

The Home Office was well satisfied with this outcome. It had no desire to intern tens of thousands of people, but could now reassure the Cabinet, the House and a (potentially) panicky public that it had any threat to Britain's security well under control. Volunteers and organizations helping refugees prepare for their tribunal appearances viewed the system more sceptically. The local magistrates who chaired the tribunals sometimes knew little about the Nazi system and less about the hardships of the refugees; unsurprisingly, plenty of odd decisions were made. Some distinguished anti-Nazis were placed in Category A; some tribunals, distrustful of foreigners and eager to be on the safe side, simply put most cases in Category B. As early as November, one month after the tribunals began their work, Rathbone was asking whether their decisions could be reviewed and mistaken assignments to Category B overturned.[24]

Matters soon took a turn for the worse. Two factors – the priority given to military arguments and authorities in the early days of Churchill's administration and a press-stoked panic about possible 'fifth column' activities – transformed the refugees' already vulnerable situation. In April 1940 Anderson had assured the Cabinet that the tribunals had done their work well and with a bias towards internment in doubtful cases; further internment would simply be a waste of manpower and 'difficult to reconcile with our policy of trying to secure support from such sections of German opinion as may be opposed to the Nazi creed'.[25] But the service chiefs, fed dubious intelligence reports about threats of spies and subversion, pressed for wider internment, and once Churchill acceded to the premiership the Home Office was forced to concede. On 11 May all German and Austrian men between the ages of 16 and 60 living in the coastal counties were ordered to be interned, and on 15 May – after Churchill stated his own support in Cabinet for a 'very large round-up' of aliens – all those in Category B were taken in as well.[26] Anderson argued against going further. Even in the Dutch case, he pointed out, 'fifth column' subversion had come from Nazi Germany and not from refugees, and while public opinion might welcome further round-ups now, a reaction would certainly set in if large numbers of friendly refugees were detained.[27] To no avail: the War Office now wanted internment of all enemy aliens (men and women) and restrictions on neutrals, and Churchill himself, his views 'greatly hardened', expressed himself 'strongly in favour of removing all internees out of the United Kingdom'. On 24 May the Cabinet agreed to intern all German and Austrian women in Category B, and on 11 June, the day after Italy entered the war, to round up all male Italians between 16 and 70 – a move that deprived London's restaurants of some of their most famous chefs. On 21 June, police were told that the government had decided to intern all German and Austrian men in stages. Distinguished refugee scientists and writers, prominent exiled politicians and journalists, nurses and domestic servants, not to mention some thousands of long-term residents, all of whom had already been before tribunals and pronounced 'safe', now found the police at their doors.[28]

Looking back at this shameful episode from the vantage point of more than sixty years, it is important to keep the wartime context in view. These were the weeks when France fell, the British army was evacuated, and Britain braced (and Hitler planned) for invasion. But those interned at the time did not have the benefit of hindsight. Usually arrested at night, held in prisons or public buildings, separated from their families and often without access to mail or news, they were frightened and anxious, hungry and cold. The camps set up at short notice to hold them – among them an unfinished housing estate at Huyton near Liverpool and blocks of hotels and boarding houses hastily encircled with barbed wire on the Isle of Man – were undersupplied, overcrowded, and manned by soldiers accustomed to dealing with prisoners of war. Rumours about their fate and fears for the progress of the war abounded. 'Our position is desperate,' one Austrian refugee at Huyton (who had been interned seven weeks earlier) recorded in his diary. 'Separated from those we love, with the fear that they might be victims of an Air Raid, with the uncertainty whether we will live tomorrow and with the darkness of our future. Will we fall into the hands of Hitler again? What is happening to our wives, children and parents? Will we never get out of this situation unworthy of a human being?' New groups of internees kept arriving, but hundreds were also being sent on – some to the Isle of Man, but others, terrifyingly, to unknown destinations. On 2 July an elderly internee at Huyton who had already spent two years in German concentration camps committed suicide; four days later there would be a second suicide.[29] And between these events came the news that the *Arandora Star*, a cruise ship that had been requisitioned to take a first shipload of Category A Germans and Italians to Australia, had been torpedoed by a German U-boat, with the loss of hundreds of lives.[30]

On 7 July, the day after that second suicide, Professor K. Weissenberg, the 'Camp Father' elected by the Huyton internees to represent them, sent a telegram to the Parliamentary Refugee Committee pleading for an end to compulsory deportations and an immediate visit.[31] And here Rathbone returns to the story, for that telegram would have been opened by her – the 'parliamentary committee' being not the official body many internees no doubt imagined but Rathbone's personal creation, albeit one backed by some 200 members of the House. Rathbone was already perturbed by the reports reaching her. From late May, she and other concerned MPs had been asking questions about camp conditions and demanding timetables for release, and on 12 June she convened a joint meeting of the Parliamentary Committee on Refugees and the major refugee organizations to discuss the situation.[32] When the categories subjected to internment were widened in late June she began buttonholing ministers and following up individual cases; yet, loath to criticize Churchill's new government at a moment of national crisis, publicly she held her fire. But something – the sinking of the *Arandora Star*? Weissenberg's telegram? – pushed her over the edge. On 10 July, the House was detained for a long debate on the topic of the government's policy towards refugees. Victor Cazalet, chairman of the Parliamentary Committee, opened, but his very first remarks made clear where the source of the pressure lay. 'For some years I have been interested in this question,' he said, 'but any humble or slight contribution which I may have made to this problem is only a tithe of the really great work which the hon. Lady the Member for the English

Universities has done for refugees. All refugees in this country, and indeed many refugees in other countries as well, owe her a deep debt of gratitude, and I am glad to have an opportunity to pay tribute to her work to-day.'[33]

Almost six hours of speeches and debate followed. Most of the usual 'friends of the refugee' spoke, among them Graham White, Philip Noel-Baker, Josiah Wedgwood, Wilfrid Roberts, and the Labour members Reginald Sorenson, Sidney Silverman and George Strauss. A few backbenchers opposed them, most notably Mavis Tate, who insisted volubly that even Jewish refugees could be Nazi agents and defended internment as essential to national safety. For the most part, however, speakers agreed that internment was unnecessary, out of keeping with British traditions, and counterproductive in a war of liberal ideals against brute totalitarian force. It was, Rathbone pointed out, both cruel and wasteful to put behind barbed wire refugees, many of whom had 'undergone tests in their devotion to the cause of freedom and humanity for which we are fighting, such as not one of us has had to bear', many with linguistic skills and cultural knowledge Britain could use.[34] Even Osbert Peake, the uninspiring junior Home Office minister deputized to respond for the government, spent more time reciting how long his Ministry had held out against public pressure for internment than he did defending internment itself. Peake's transparent ambivalence, and Sir Edward Grigg's blunt statement that the War Office (while administering the camps) was not responsible for the policy decisions either, simply heightened critics' suspicion. Why, Rathbone asked, can we never find out who is responsible? If the military wasn't ordering the deportations, who on earth was doing so? Under persistent questioning, Peake admitted that decisions about internment and deportation were made by a cabinet committee under the chairmanship of the Lord President of Council – Chamberlain again, not present at the debate, and a man many now viewed with loathing. This, of course, was not really fair, for the security services had insisted on internment, and Churchill, not Chamberlain, had urged deportation: Chamberlain, for once, was simply carrying out government policy. Yet the revelation that a special committee headed by Chamberlain, and not the Home Office, was responsible for these decisions scarcely spoke in their favour. Anyone listening to the debate – although few ministers were – would have concluded that Rathbone and her allies had won.[35]

One minister was, however, there, at Rathbone's express request. Rathbone had known Clement Attlee, the often underestimated leader of the Labour Party, since their days in the settlement house movement before the First World War. She had asked him to come to this debate on refugee policy, and he had done so. In Cabinet the very next day, in his usual unemotional way, he reported the House's disquiet about internment and was invited to suggest some reforms.[36] His proposals, submitted a week later, could have been written by Rathbone. 'In a war of ideals every effort should be made to enlist on our side all those who are opposed to Nazism and to utilise their services to the full against the common enemy,' Attlee wrote. Interned aliens should be scrutinized not by nationality but for their loyalty, and those useful to the war effort put to work. Still more radically, he suggested that the tasks of reviewing cases and finding work be taken out of government hands and delegated to a 'really strong committee' that would include such established refugee advocates as Graham White, Noel-Baker and Rathbone.[37] This was more than the Cabinet could stomach: Attlee was asked to redraft his proposal so that overall control remained in Home Office hands. But the drive to 'collar the lot' was over. On 15 July, five days after the Commons debate, the round-ups were halted and never resumed. Control was returned to the Home Office and two advisory committees appointed, one to recommend categories for release, chaired by Mr Justice Asquith, and one – the Advisory Council on Aliens, chaired by Lord Lytton, to which Rathbone, Graham White and Noel-Baker were all appointed – to advise on individual cases and to make recommendations about the camps.[38] Three White Papers defining categories of release were issued between July and October 1940, and slowly, too slowly, the internees began returning home. In August 1940, before releases started, some 26,700 enemy aliens had been interned – a figure comprised of almost 19,000 German and Austrian men, 4,000 German and Austrian women, and 4,000 Italian men. Three months later, more than a quarter, or 7,200, had been released.[39] And who made the case for their freedom?

Minutes after the Commons debate on 10 July ended, Rathbone answered Professor Weissenberg's telegram. His appeal had been read in the Commons, she reported; she would try to arrange a visit to Huyton as well.[40] We have two vivid accounts of that visit, one given to Stocks in 1948 by Graham White, who made the trip with Rathbone, another published in *The Times* after her death by someone there interned. Graham White recalled that he and Rathbone met with the overburdened but capable camp commandant and then privately (with the commandant's consent) with a representative committee of internees to discuss what might be done to improve conditions. When they left that meeting, they found that word of their visit had blazed through the camp and the entire population of internees waiting silently in the driving rain before them. Eleanor, Graham White recalled, rose nobly to the occasion. Addressing the men in simple, heartfelt tones, she assured them of MPs' concern for their plight and of their determination to do all they could to relieve it. She begged for their patience and trust: the muddle and coercion were deplorable, yes, but also understandable at a moment when England lived in daily fear of invasion. H. Redlich, one of the men in that crowd, remembered that gathering vividly. What stayed with him, he recalled in 1946, were four simple words – 'You are not forgotten' – and the sight of Rathbone's face, flanked by soldiers with fixed bayonets, beaten by the pouring rain. The men dispersed with 'her face, her voice . . . nursing the gleam of hope left in their hearts'.[41]

Recommendations for improving camp conditions soon made their way from Rathbone's Parliamentary Committee and from Lytton's Advisory Council on Aliens to the Home Office.[42] More overwhelming, however, was the deluge of mail Rathbone received from refugees and their families throughout the land. Even in the debate on 10 July Rathbone had spoken less of the principles involved and more of individual cases that had come to her attention – of the employer whose internment had deprived many British workers of jobs, of the famous German Jewish research chemist (and former concentration camp inmate) who had killed himself rather than face another internment. After that debate she became, among refugees, famous – the person to write to with a grievance or a complaint, the woman who would always answer a letter, always do what she could. Once again, that First World War experience in setting up separation allowances came in handy. Literally within days the Parliamentary Committee had a capable paid secretary in Vera Craig (who came from the Central Committee for Refugees at Bloomsbury House) and an office in Marsham Street (which was really just the living room of Craig's two-room flat. Friends, refugees and a single paid clerk-typist, helpel out with that work.

Many years later, Helga Wolff, a young refugee girl who took over the job of clerk-typist in 1942, vividly recalled the moment of her hiring. She was eighteen at the time, on her own in London, and working as an invoice clerk at John Lewis – a job she found 'soul-destroying' and which paid her an entirely inadequate thirty shillings a week. When a friend studying at Morley College heard through Eva Hubback that Rathbone was looking for a German-speaking assistant, she decided to apply – even though she knew no shorthand, could hardly type, and thought her chances of getting the job so poor that she wondered whether she should spend the bus fare (which she could ill afford) to go to the interview. Craig, she recalled, took one look at the undernourished and exhausted young girl and made her something to eat; after being given a typing test (which she duly failed), she was sent across the street to Tufton Court to meet Rathbone. The distinguished Member of Parliament reminded Wolff of her grandmother ('such a *generous* face'), and she was almost overwhelmed by the intensity of Rathbone's focus on her. Miss Rathbone was often vague and abstracted, Wolff (like others) recalled, but when she turned on an individual that concentration she usually reserved for her work, she was penetrating and often shrewd. Something about Wolff – her youth, her bravery – clearly touched Rathbone's heart, for after consulting with Rathbone Craig hired her, doubling her meagre previous wage. For the next two and a half years, her typing gradually improving, Wolff worked all hours for Rathbone and Craig; when she left towards the end of the war, Rathbone got Rab Butler to make an exception in the rules barring aliens from eligibility and give Wolff a government teacher-training grant.[43]

The Committee had plenty to do. Although the government had interned refugees *en masse*, it declined to release them *en masse*, nor would it accept as grounds for release the determination of 'friendliness' towards the Allied cause made by tribunals during those early months. When Lord Lytton realized that he would not be able to force the Home Office to accept new, broader categories for release he resigned as chairman of the Council on Aliens.[44] However, the Parliamentary Committee, seeing no alternative, began the painstaking work of helping refugees' relatives and friends assemble documents that would fall within the Home Office criteria. If being Jewish or having already been accorded the status of refugee from Nazi oppression were not accepted as grounds for release, long-standing residence in Britain, employment on work of national importance, a record of opposition to the Nazi system, enrolment in the Pioneer Corps, and various other attributes or actions, were. Thus while Rathbone, Craig and (later) Wolff sent out circular letters advising correspondents on how to contact interned relatives and send comforts or food,[45] they spent most of their time on 'the files'. References would be gathered from employers or other reputable sources about the individual refugee's character and employability, a file built up, and then the case sent off to the Aliens Department at the Home Office, which would either approve it and grant the release or reject it. Between 15 July 1940 and 6 September 1941 they submitted 1,693 cases for release and passed on a further 1,750 to another appropriate committee; of those they took themselves, 1,069 were granted, a further 571 were still (in September 1941) pending, and only 53 had been turned down.[46]

Rathbone's committee was not the only body doing this work, of course. In Oxford and Cambridge, Beveridge, A.V. Hill, and the Society for the Protection of Science and Learning were busy arranging for their sponsored scholars' release; in Euston Road the German Emergency Committee of the Society of Friends worked for those refugees they had supported – and there were many other such groups. But Rathbone's Committee bore that crucial adjective 'Parliamentary': it was, then, the organization the truly friendless could approach, the one that remembered the insignificant or forgotten, that would take on hard cases. It was Rathbone, for example, who told A.V. Hill to ask a question that led the Home Office to designate artistic and scientific work as 'work of national importance',[47] Rathbone who got aliens long resident in Britain but too poor to apply for naturalization specified as a category eligible for release (although not before 'their humble little businesses had been ruined while they were maintained in over-crowded camps at the cost of the taxpayer, and their families by charity'),[48] Rathbone who took the trouble to check the situation of refugees now interned in Australia, write articles explaining their anti-Nazi credentials, and urge their release.[49] And in December 1940 she put up a major fight in the Commons on behalf of a small, demoralized group of aliens who, because they possessed a criminal record (usually for minor crimes like pilfering), had been placed in Category A and held in secure prisons for months without charge. How can the Home Secretary 'justify the indefinite imprisonment of unconvicted men without any opportunity of self-defence?' Rathbone wrote to Noel-Baker in a rage. 'Are not these exactly the methods of the Gestapo, of French *lettres de cachet* under the *Ancien Régime*, of banishment by administrative order under the Czar?'[50] Memos went to the Home Office and the Advisory Council urging that internees be allowed to make the case for release, and a circular was sent to the imprisoned men themselves instructing them in how to do so. When she learned that they had been forbidden to write to MPs or other persons of 'high standing', she cleverly suggested that they send a copy of their case not to her but to 'Miss Craig' at 35 Marsham Street: 'a lady interested in refugees but who cannot, I think, be regarded as coming within the restriction'.[51]

All this took time and, increasingly, it took money as well. From June 1940, when Rathbone revived the Parliamentary Committee, she had met its costs; by the autumn of 1941 office rent, two full-time salaries, several telephones and almost unlimited supplies of paper and postage were straining even Rathbone's considerable private means. She wasn't sure she could keep paying the bills entirely on her own – or rather, she could afford to do so, but not without doing what good Rathbones never did and spending her capital. Probably in passing, she mentioned her worries to Cazalet and Professor A.V. Hill, who had entered the House in February for a Cambridge University seat and was also involved in refugee questions. Cazalet and Hill were shocked: they had had no idea that Rathbone had been paying all expenses herself and did a quick whip-round for funds among their own friends and organizations.[52] Less wisely, perhaps, Hill had the secretary of the Society for the Protection of Science and Learning write to some prominent refugees, asking whether they might be able to contribute to Rathbone's work. A number based in Cambridge, although anything but well-off, did so gladly, but her Oxford friends kept from Rathbone other refugees' angry response to the request that, having suffered internment without cause, they now contribute their meagre resources to what most assumed was an official body seeking only to undo an official wrong. Rathbone, in fact, would have agreed with them. She had voiced some discomfort when she heard of the Society's appeal, since many refugees, she knew, had slender resources 'and I wouldn't like any of them to feel that pressure was being put on them to give money to a British body for carrying out work which is really a British responsibility'.[53] Thus, while Rathbone gratefully accepted donations to the committee's work, she never used these to refund her own subventions, instead digging ever deeper into her (admittedly deep) pockets to keep the committee afloat.

For the whole of the war, Rathbone never gave the internees up, although the nature of the Parliamentary Committee's work changed. By March 1942, more than 20,000 people had been released, and of the 8,858 still interned more than half were in Australia and Canada. Rathbone and Craig continued to take cases, but these were now much more complicated, and in 1942 much of Craig and Wolff's time was spent either trying to arrange employment for internees or acting as advocates for those with complex problems or records.[54] They were in constant contact with the Home Office, and especially with its Under-Secretary, Osbert Peake. Rathbone, like other refugee advocates, was well aware of the need to keep officials and ministers on her side – hence their praise of the Ministry's staff and of Peake in particular in the debate on 10 July. Rathbone was also careful thoroughly to investigate cases for which she advocated before bringing them to the Home Office and was proud of the fact that officials tended to trust Craig's word.

Yet, as contacts between the Home Office and the refugee advocates multiplied – and, ironically, once Herbert Morrison replaced Sir John Anderson as Home Secretary in October 1940 – friction developed. For Morrison – ambitious, authoritarian and eager to make his mark – resisted almost on principle anything that felt to him like a concession. He gladly applied (and was usually given credit for) the release policy worked out under Anderson, but saw no reason to widen greatly the criteria for release or to speed matters up.[55] The civil libertarian and humanitarian arguments that Rathbone and her friends routinely brought before the House simply annoyed him, and by December he and Rathbone were clashing regularly. When Rathbone pointed out that the new release procedures were likely to be time-consuming and ponderous he asked whether she 'enjoys being pessimistic'; when she urged him to provide free legal advice to poor people detained under Regulation 18B (under which supposed fascist sympathizers were held), he said sarcastically that he was being asked to provide 'legal assistance for Sir Oswald [Mosley] if he wants it'.[56] Morrison's officials and juniors took the cue: when Rathbone approached Peake about the internees in prison in December 1940, she found his response 'evasive and unimaginative, to put it mildly'; Council on Aliens meetings were marked by battles between Rathbone and Frank Newsam, the Deputy Under-Secretary at the Home Office (a man Noel-Baker called privately 'that beast, Newsam').[57] Rathbone and Craig's meticulous casework meant that they could still win concessions; throughout 1942 Rathbone remained the most effective advocate of refugees and internees in Parliament. In late 1942, however, a bitter quarrel over Britain's response to reports of deportations of Jews from France to Poland would damage Rathbone's relationship with Morrison beyond repair and leave her desperately worried that those she sought to help might actually be jeopardized by her intervention.

Rathbone's work on behalf of refugees and internees was her personal 'finest hour', the moment when her liberal principles and her impressive organizational abilities came most fruitfully and productively together. Painstaking, unglamorous and usually conducted behind the scenes, this work received little public attention. 'Nothing like justice has ever been done to Miss Eleanor Rathbone's work for the interned refugees,' the *Manchester Guardian* correspondent wrote in December 1940, when a Commons debate forced the subject briefly into the public eye.[58] Only those closest to her – Macadam, Cazalet, Stocks, her new secretary Joan Prewer (who recalled that Rathbone worked through black-outs and air raids with the aid of a bicycle lamp shrouded under a blanket and slept at night with a pad of paper next to her bed)[59] – knew how much work it all was.

When we follow Rathbone's activities in those early years of the war, we might have a sense, almost, of *déjà vu*. As in the First World War, we see her rallying wholeheartedly to the war effort while working almost day and night for the victims – that time soldiers' wives, this time refugees – of the push for 'total war'. And, once again, she refused an honour for her work. 'I hope it will not sound ungracious if I ask respectfully to be excused,' Rathbone wrote to Churchill's secretary in December 1943 on being told that he wished to submit her name for a DBE in the New Year's honours. 'The truth is that I have – perhaps as an inheritance from my Quaker ancestors – a distaste for titles, except where they denote in the bearers a long historic tradition. Further, this feeling of mine is especially strong in wartime, when it is impossible for public honours to be conferred on more than a very few of the millions who are daily risking their lives in dangerous services in which I cannot take part.'[60]

And yet there are differences between these wars, especially in the starkness with which problems of obligation and coercion, freedom and authority, were now posed. During the First World War the state had been pressed, almost inadvertently, to take on extensive powers; during the Second, Churchill's government seized those powers with alacrity. Those who in peacetime were most vigilant for civil liberties acquiesced in, even demanded, those restrictions. For Labour supporters, participation in government acted as a guarantee against abuse; for a broad swathe of liberal opinion, too, the ascendancy of Keynesianism and faith in the efficacy of 'planning' generated enthusiasm for centralized control. And for progressives of all parties (including Rathbone), the fact that this was a 'just war', a war in defence of liberty itself, legitimized unprecedented levels of coercion. For those raised on the dictates of philosophical idealism – as Keynes, Beveridge and Rathbone had been – arguments about the duty of individuals to the state came naturally. Recall the words of David Ritchie, Rathbone's philosophy tutor at Somerville: 'The Athenian citizen should be ready to die for Athens, because Athens offers so glorious a life of freedom to the Athenian citizen.'[61]

But what if that sacrifice were not made freely? Could one impose such service on those excluded from English liberties and lacking political voice? Just how much trouble Rathbone had even in admitting that war service could be – for some – a corvée and not a cause is revealed by her rather blundering appeal in May 1941 to Indian nationalists. This overture repays some attention. Relations between Congress nationalists and the British government were then at a low point, for Congress, offended by the Viceroy's lack of consultation before bringing India into the war, had demanded immediate post-war independence as the price of cooperation and – when that was refused – had withdrawn their ministers from provincial governments and begun a campaign of mild civil disobedience. At the India Office, Leo Amery cast about in vain for a plan capable of reconciling Congress opinion but acceptable to Churchill; the Viceroy simply reverted to 'direct rule' and began clapping dissident nationalists, including Jawaharlal Nehru, in jail. The Muslim League, for its part, used the crisis as a means of advancing its own claim to speak for all Indian Muslims and to broker their fate. And to the east, Japan built up its military might.

Rathbone had paid little attention to Indian affairs since 1935 but now anger and unhappiness about the Congress stance seized her. What was really needed, she wrote to Amery, was an 'appeal to the emotions of non-cooperators'. That should come from him or from Churchill, but if they were not able to do it, perhaps 'those of us who had smaller, limited spheres of influence in India – especially among left-wingers – might possibly try that line'.[62] In May 1941, then, she sat down to write an indictment of non-cooperation. The nationalist movement had forthrightly condemned the Nazi and fascist powers: why then, were they obstructing Britain in its most desperate hour of need? True, England had dragged India into the war without her consent, but 'was the absence of formal consultation, even if a bad mistake, so inexcusable under the stress of great emergency that it should condition your whole attitude and turn you from potential allies of ours into actual allies of the aggressors, for that is what in effect you are?' Why, she asked Nehru in particular, did he refer constantly to such injuries as Amritsar, 'a horror of which most progressive Englishmen are deeply ashamed', while ignoring his and other nationalists' evident debt to English political thought and the recent efforts to extend self-government to India? Such an 'overmastering obsession with your country's wrongs' not only laid Indian nationalists open to the charge of opportunism, of a selfish desire to reap tactical advantage from Britain's plight, but was also morally indefensible given the politician's ethical responsibility, always, to count the cost. For what if 'non-cooperation' proved to be the factor that persuaded Japan to enter the war, or gave Hitler the edge needed for victory? 'Since the cause for which Britain bears the main responsibility is a world cause and there will be no freedom or independence for India if it is lost', hadn't Indian nationalists a duty to try to forget their grievances and join hands against the common foe, secure in the knowledge that they would thereby strengthen their claim 'to shape the destinies of India and of the world you will have helped to save?'[63] Amery, reading a draft of the letter in his office on 27 May, found it 'pretty effective'.[64] He arranged for it to be sent to Nehru in prison, and, under the deceptive title of 'An Open Letter to Some Indian Friends', to be published in the pro-government Indian papers.

But when the responses started coming in a few weeks later, Rathbone discovered that she had – as in 1929 – rubbed salt in an open wound. India's most prominent man of letters, Rabindranath Tagore, rose (he said) from his sickbed to protest against her 'gratuitous' and 'impertinent' sermon. 'It is sheer insolent self-complacency,' he thundered, 'for so-called English friends to assume that had they not taught us we should have remained in the dark ages.' British rule should be judged not by the 'pretensions of its spokesmen' but by the condition of India's masses – an indictment before which any 'decent Britisher' should at least have the grace to hold their tongue.[65] Nehru's masterful response, which ran to some 8,000 words, probably discomfited Eleanor still more. For in two ways – in tone and in argument – Nehru managed to turn her indictment on its head. Rathbone had meant to 'appeal to non-cooperators' emotions', but Nehru would not be drawn. To that 'anger and passion of a war mentality' he detected in her letter, he counterposed a tone of surprised regret, of pained, more-in-sorrow-than-in-anger forbearance. Taking care to point out that he was the one in prison, he nevertheless expressed sympathy for the sufferings of Britain's people and (no doubt to Rathbone's fury) excused her patronizing claim that he should feel 'gratitude' for Britain's teachings with the schoolmasterly remark that her 'knowledge of the course of events in India appears to be very limited'. He was more than happy to acknowledge his debt to English liberal thought; the problem was that England – with its lust for empire – was betraying those very liberal ideals. India's jails were full of the detained and unconvicted; 'if there is any difference, in theory or practice, between Hitler's *Gauleiters* and those whom we have to suffer as Viceroys and Governors, I am not aware of it'. These were the men with whom she expected him to make common cause?

Rathbone's political argument, her charge of Indian nationalists' selfishness and opportunism in the face of a world crisis, Nehru adroitly turned around as well. For in a war against fascism, imperialism had no place: if anyone merited that stricture, it was a government that preferred 'to risk defeat in this war, with all its terrible consequences, rather than give up willingly the domination of India'. By contrast, 'India' (with which Nehru equated the Congress movement) had by its very 'non-cooperation', by its refusal to consent to its own subjugation, upheld the integrity of that anti-fascist cause. After all

> what would you think of England if she compromised away her own freedom and honour? We are human beings also, with the same urges and desires. To ask us to present this claim or that for the beneficent consideration of England, now or later, is to insult us. India is not an appendage of England, even though we may have been forcibly subjected to her rule for many years. India is a great country with a magnificent tradition, with resources, with ability, and a will to freedom which nothing in the world will finally overcome.

Apologizing for the length and frankness of the letter, he closed, brilliantly, by pointing out that he could not know whether it would reach her. 'A prisoner can only hand a letter to the Superintendent of the Prison.'[66]

In fact Rathbone did receive the letter, although it went to Amery and the India Office first. Amery read it in disgust. 'Can even the best good will in the world prevail against such a passionate inferiority complex hatred and such a complete disregard of truth in favour of the worked up legend?' he recorded in his diary. 'A blend of De Valera and Hitler but on a more cultivated plane.'[67] His officials, however, had enough awareness of its power to forbid its publication, and Eleanor was uneasy as well. She could not accept Nehru's account of British rule but knew that his incarceration made it ever more plausible. So long as the Congress Party leadership was kept in prison, she said in the Commons on 1 August, 'they will never be changed from the introverts which they are now – with their eyes always turned inwards upon themselves and upon India – to extroverts who for the first time see the world, the war, and all that it means as they really are'. Locked up without term, 'what can they do but sit and brood; what can imprisonment do but confirm that terrible obsession with past grievances, wrongs and affronts which is the curse of the Indian situation?' If Congress leaders could be released, even brought to London – or, alternatively, if Churchill could reach out to disperse the 'cloud of suspicion' through which Indians viewed him – could they not be persuaded to play their part in the 'common effort to help save the world?' And yet, for all her support for a fresh appeal to Congress, she could not bring herself to endorse, without safeguards or guarantees, a fixed timetable for the granting even of dominion status. 'What Indians have to be taught to learn, what they have not already realised yet, is the inevitability of gradualness.' This, she insisted, was the British way: 'in asking them to accept independence, freedom, step by step, we are only asking them to submit to the process through which we have gone, which has made us the most firmly based, because the most deeply rooted, democracy'.[68] In a second letter to Nehru written later that month she repeated precisely this point, lecturing him rather tactlessly on the virtues of gradualism.[69]

But about his other points – his claims of police and prison brutality, his pessimistic view that there was so little common ground between them that rational conversation had become almost impossible – she confessed herself deeply uneasy. Her conversations with some Quaker friends made her more so. She had consulted Agatha Harrison of the pro-Congress India Conciliation Group before she had sent that first letter, and while she had dismissed Harrison's warning that it would only 'inflame an already tense situation', when that prediction was proven right she had the decency to share Tagore's and Nehru's responses with Harrison and her colleagues William Paton and Carl Heath.[70] Heath found Nehru's letter 'tragic', and Rathbone's reactions to it surprisingly insensitive and naïve. 'To be hurt because a prominent political leader *in prison*, and after many years in prison, doesn't say he loves you, or even tolerates you is somewhat infantile,' he wrote to Harrison.[71] Irritated and annoyed, he took it on himself to try to *make* Rathbone comprehend the evils of imperial rule. 'I venture to suggest,' he wrote to her,

> that the root trouble is that English people, and will you pardon me if I include yourself, do still most firmly believe that if *they* do things *for* India which *they* think are good for India, they deserve to be met with thankfulness. They dislike the idea that this well-wishing and well-doing towards India should be regarded as imperialism and resented as it certainly is. . . . British people seem unable to realise how baffling and infuriating this insistent paternalism is to grown-up India right in the midst of the other grown-up and free members of the Asiatic family of nations.
>
> For this paternalism is ever interfering, always keeping a tight hand, always claiming gratitude for paternal goodness, annoyed at the lack of filial loyalty, making promises quite sincerely of a little more freedom and a little more self-government right through eighty or ninety years, but ending in 1941 with one of the ablest leaders India possesses in prison for four years, and 7,000 others – Cabinet Ministers, Members of Legislatures, etc. –, and quite unwilling to admit that the paternal actions must be wrong somewhere to produce such results in the family. And too always putting the blame, like so many Victorian parents, on the unreasonable and unruly children.[72]

Nehru, in his second letter, was equally pointed. 'As we grow older, most of us, I suppose, believe in the inevitability of gradualism where human progress is concerned. . . . To raise an individual, a community, a nation, in any real and fundamental sense requires ceaseless and often long-continued effort.' But gradualism is not an appropriate response to human catastrophes or dangers, or to the denial of that fundamental human freedom on which any hope of progress must be based. India was not a land colonized by British people looking to the mother country to grant it dominion status or rights, but rather a 'mother country' of its own, albeit one suffering under foreign rule. 'Try to imagine a foreign government established in England,' he suggested. 'Your whole mind and soul would rebel against this.'[73]

Nehru may have been right, but Rathbone could not make this imaginative leap – or rather, while she would indeed have rebelled against even the suggestion of foreign rule, she could never quite see British rule in India in these terms. Precisely because she was more of a liberal universalist than a cultural nationalist, or, more accurately, because she could never quite see the national uses to which those universalist claims could be put, a Millian model of liberties gradually bestowed on deserving and well-instructed children, and not a republican model of rights seized by an awakened band of brothers, held first claim on her heart. Thus while Rathbone – now to Amery's disapproval – continued to worry about the treatment of political prisoners and urge fresh attempts at conciliation, she found the civil disobedience and 'Quit India' movements unjustifiable. Even the suffragettes had renounced militancy at the outbreak of the last war, she pointed out during one Commons debate on India – an observation that characteristically overlooked the fact that in this case British women could make such a choice on the strength of (and not against) their nationalist feelings.[74]

For so many years, Rathbone had written to Nehru in that first letter, she and her internationally minded countrymen and women had felt 'ashamed for our country': 'We hated the policy of appeasement, thinking it – as we think your policy – shortsighted, selfish and ungenerous.' Now, 'in spite of the dangers and suffering around us', they were 'happier than [they] have been for years'; now, finally, they could feel 'no longer ashamed, but passionately proud'.[75] That pride in Britain's stance did not make Rathbone any less of a humanitarian, but it did channel her empathy along particular paths. For if Britain was *not* like Germany, if India's viceroys and governors, however rigid or unimaginative, could *not* be compared with the *Gauleiter* in the German-occupied lands, then those concerned for human life and liberty could quite justifiably put the struggle against Hitler first. A commitment to rescue Hitler's victims took precedence over any obligation to conciliate rebellious subjects. Terrifying news from the continent confirmed her belief in a hierarchy of challenges and crimes. In 1942, Rathbone – along with many other Britons – began hearing reports of mass exterminations of Jews in Poland. On its response to this terrible test, Rathbone thought, would Britain's claims to internationalism and humanitarianism be judged.

Chapter 16

'Rescue the Perishing'

On the night of 3 December 1942, deeply perturbed, Rathbone sat down to write to the Archbishop of Canterbury William Temple. For some time she had been hearing terrible accounts of Nazi atrocities against the Jews; now her very worst fears were confirmed. The World Jewish Congress and the Polish government in exile had just issued reports giving details of a systematic campaign of extermination. Jews were being forced to dig their own mass graves and were then shot by firing squads; they were being murdered by electric shock and poison gas at the death camps of Treblinka, Belzec and Sobibor; as many as two million were thought to have been killed already.[1] Already deluged by frantic letters from refugees fearful of the fate of their relatives still on the continent,[2] Rathbone had no doubts about these accounts' truthfulness. What troubled her, she wrote to Temple, was the relatively muted public response. Almost no attention was being paid to this calamity. 'One would think that the mass extermination of "the chosen people," or a few millions of them, was quite a minor incident, tragic but impossible to influence and entirely the responsibility of the German perpetrators.' She could not agree. 'Thousands of those people might have been saved if our own and other Governments had been less mean and cautious and entirely self-regarding in their treatment of the Jewish and refugee problems before and during the War.' Even at this late stage, what was needed was not just sympathy and recognition but determination and action – an effort to think through what could be done to combat this abominable plan and rescue all who could be saved from its clutches.[3]

From December 1942 until virtually the end of her life, Rathbone would give herself heart and soul to this effort. She emerged quickly as the most significant non-Jewish campaigner for 'rescue'. She was the moving spirit behind the National Committee for Rescue from Nazi Terror, founded in March 1943, and became the most relentless critic of official inaction.[4] Her efforts brought her a measure of official opprobrium, for ministers and civil servants thought her demands unreasonable and her arguments too emotional, and were soon conspiring to outwit her. Yet Rathbone would not be silenced, for after 1942 she saw the whole world differently. All other political questions, even her beloved campaign for family allowances, seemed unimportant, even self-indulgent, when placed alongside this overmastering tragedy. Hers was not a typical reaction. During the Holocaust, Yehuda Bauer remarks, 'countless individuals received information and rejected it, suppressed it, or rationalized about it, were thrown into despair without any possibility of acting on it, or seemingly internalized it and then behaved as though it had never reached them.' Such behaviour was so prevalent that Bauer and other scholars stress the great gulf between 'knowledge' and the transformation of that knowledge into genuine 'understanding'[5] – a gulf perfectly embodied by Anthony Eden, who received much information on Nazi atrocities and even read out the joint Allied declaration acknowledging and condemning the extermination campaign against the Jews in the House of Commons in December 1942, but nevertheless managed to write to Temple some six months later regretting that the government could not promise to help find new homes after the war for Jewish children given refuge in Sweden 'since in many cases their parents will no doubt be remaining on in Europe and will want them back'.[6]

Rathbone never made ludicrous statements of this kind. From the outset, she somehow managed to translate 'knowledge' into 'understanding' – to grasp the extent of the calamity confronting Europe's Jews and to recast her priorities in light of that understanding. Just why she was able to make this leap when so many did not is itself an important question. Her close personal contacts with refugees may have been part of it: unlike most politicians, she now had many friends with relatives on the continent, and could see this tragedy through their eyes. But the other reason surely has to do with Rathbone's character itself, with that special 'receptivity to human suffering' that had also driven her powerful reaction to Katherine Mayo's exposé of child marriage in India. The cost of such identification was high. 'As the war progressed,' Thelma Cazalet-Keir, Megan Lloyd George and Irene Ward remembered, 'she came to wear a tragic, haunted look, as though she was carrying the entire sufferings of all refugees on her shoulders.'[7] Evie, at least, was convinced that the 'rescue' campaign shortened Eleanor's life. 'So you're the man who killed my sister,' she said to Victor Gollancz at Eleanor's memorial service shortly after the war.[8] Eleanor, for all her family feeling, would have been mortified at this remark, for who was she to live when so many were being helplessly slaughtered? But one can see Evie's point. Eleanor was the only sister she had, and if she was called upon to lose her, she wanted to know that the sacrifice had at least had some meaning. What, then, did Eleanor's years of painful activism amount to? Where did the 'rescue' movement come from, and what – if anything – could it accomplish?

In the search for its origins, one moment stands out. This was not Eden's reading of the Allies' solemn declaration in the House on 17 December 1942 but a deputation of eminent churchmen and politicians to Herbert Morrison at the Home

Office on 28 October, some seven weeks earlier. The churchmen were there, at Rathbone's instigation, to plead the case of Jewish children in France threatened with deportation. From July 1942, with Vichy Head of Government Pierre Laval's full support, police had begun raiding refugee camps in the unoccupied zone and rounding up foreign Jews. Although Vichy officials and police collaborated in this activity, some sections of the French population voiced their horror and distress, and Quaker refugee workers witnessing the deportations sent reports to Britain and the USA. By September, accounts of unaccompanied children shipped eastwards and of rafts of suicides among men faced with deportation had appeared in the British and American press, and Jewish and refugee organizations had begun pressing those governments to try to save them.[9]

Rathbone was one of these voices. She knew those refugee camps well. The National Joint Committee for Spanish Relief had supplied them with funds and refugee workers before the war, and as France fell – and again in the autumn of 1941 – she had approached the Foreign Office to try to get intellectuals and political refugees interned in them out of France.[10] Throughout 1941, her efforts foundered on the rock of the wartime Home Office policy of granting entry into Britain only to those who would be useful for Britain's war effort, but when news of the French deportations broke, even ministers and officials began to think twice. Pressed by Jewish organizations, in late September Home Secretary Herbert Morrison secured cabinet permission to admit Jewish children with a near relative in Britain – although the Cabinet, seeing (as Frank Roberts of the Foreign Office put it) 'no reason why Jews as such should receive preferential treatment', decided that only children with parents in Britain could enter, and children of nationals of the Allied governments-in-exile equally with Jews.[11]

Morrison saw this as a concession, especially when the Cabinet – having been told that there were probably fewer than twenty Jewish children in France with parents in the UK – agreed that orphans and children of deported parents were admissible as well.[12] But to the Jewish and refugee organizations, the offer seemed, as Rathbone put it, 'niggling and parsimonious'.[13] Since the purpose of deportation appeared to be mass murder, the only hope was to get all interned foreign Jews – tens of thousands at least, adults as well as children – out of France, with or without Laval's permission. Neutral countries should be approached and asked to take as many as possible; the Swiss should be granted concessions to take the refugees in; and Britain – partly as a sign of good faith – should offer a fixed number of visas for children and the old. True, the Vichy authorities might refuse exit permits, but with places of refuge available, the Latin American states could perhaps pressure Laval to let them go. At least it was worth a try. Throughout the second half of October, Rathbone gathered support for this plan from church leaders and refugee organizations, and met with Latin American ambassadors – the Mexican Minister was especially helpful – to gather pledges of support.[14] 'To the Argentine Embassy with Eleanor,' Victor Cazalet recorded in his diary on 27 October; he would stay up in London that night because Morrison had agreed to receive a deputation the next day.[15]

That deputation could scarcely have been more illustrious. William Temple, the Archbishop of Canterbury, introduced its members, who included Cardinal Hinsley, the Roman Catholic Archbishop of Westminster, a number of other eminent churchmen and public figures, representatives from the major refugee and relief organizations, and members of the Commons and the Lords.[16] The churchmen opened by stressing the depth of feeling on the subject, but then turned to Rathbone to present their case. Possessed by outrage, she began aggressively. Britain had made only a small contribution to the problem of refugees in France, she told Morrison, and 'she had been largely hampered in her negotiations with the South American States by the lack of a generous policy here'. Would the Home Office, then, grant 2,000 visas to threatened children and relatives of men serving in the British forces? She outlined the horrors of the deportation process – the sealed cattle trucks, the abandoned and dying children – and virtually instructed Morrison to grant their request.

Rathbone's peremptory tone set Morrison on edge and was, in purely strategic terms, a bad miscalculation. Of all members of the Cabinet, Morrison was probably the man least likely to tolerate lectures from a spinster politician, most likely to resent meddlesome 'humanitarian' appeals by the great and the good. Britain had already shown itself generous in this matter, he retorted, detaining the deputation with a lengthy recital of the pre-war statistics on admission of refugees throughout the empire. In wartime he could do no more: Britain was small, in danger of invasion, and menaced by an anti-Semitic reaction all its own. One member of the deputation, writing an account the next day from memory, recalled that Morrison discoursed at length on this point, warning that 'anti-Semitism was just under the pavement and that if we let in large numbers of Jews this would cause an anti-Semitic outburst that we would be incapable of controlling'. In any case, Morrison stated, if the Germans were bent on deportation, 'where was it to end?' 'If he gave in and allowed 2,000 children in now, we would be back badgering him again as the position got worse – oh yes, Miss Rathbone, whatever you say, I know you would – and it simply couldn't be done.' As Rathbone protested and Cazalet and the churchmen chimed in, Morrison stated that his decision was inalterable and warned the deputation against further activism. There had been mention of approaches to the South American republics, but the government could be placed in an awkward position if private individuals took diplomacy into their own hands. 'I should be extremely careful what you do, Miss Rathbone.'[17] Shaken and indignant, the deputation withdrew.

This was a decisive moment – the moment when concern transformed itself into outrage, and an alliance was born. 'In forty years I haven't seen a worse handled deputation,' Margery Corbett Ashby commented';[18] Rathbone was so angry that she refused even to thank Morrison for receiving them. Temple, the much-loved 'people's Archbishop', thought Morrison's arguments 'so trifling as to be almost profane'[19] and wrote to Rathbone the next day promising to help her in any way he could.[20] The deputation lingered in people's minds – and made its way into the public record – as the epitome of official insensitivity and the justification for action. It was mentioned in an article by the Labour Party intellectual Harold Laski in the *Daily Herald* and in Victor Gollancz's famous pamphlet, *'Let My People Go'*, and still deplored in an important speech by Temple six months later.[21]

Sadly, that galvanizing anger did nothing to change the fate of Jewish children in France. Although Rathbone continued to badger the Foreign Office and Temple raised the matter in the Lords, it was much too late.[22] Laval's willingness to let the children go had never been sincere, and in November, when the Allies landed in North Africa and German troops moved into the unoccupied zone, the delicate negotiations over exit visas being conducted by Quaker refugee workers and the US representative to Vichy came apart. Jewish rescue organizations and others managed to save many thousands of Jewish children by hiding them or spiriting them over the border to Switzerland or Spain, but more than 10,000 were deported and killed.[23] And yet, the mobilization over the Vichy deportations was significant, for it meant that a network of sympathizers now existed, already deeply concerned about the fate of the Jews, already determined to pursue all possibilities of rescue, and already sceptical of their own government's commitment to this cause, as the new information about the workings of the extermination system in the East made its way to Britain and the United States in the autumn and winter of 1942.

Not that awareness of the character of the Nazi campaign against the Jews descended at a single moment. German atrocities in Poland and the Soviet Union had been reported sporadically in the papers all along; British intelligence officers knew from decoding German police transmissions after the invasion of the Soviet Union in June 1941 about the systematic massacre of Jews.[24] In the summer of 1942, Jewish organizations in the United States and Britain had begun to receive detailed information, especially from the World Jewish Congress, of German plans to deport all European Jews and murder them in death camps in Poland. As evidence mounted, Jewish organizations in Britain had become more critical of the government's unwillingness to recognize Jews as uniquely endangered and victimized. 'The attitude of the Foreign Office . . . is somewhat out of accordance with the actual circumstances prevailing on the Continent,' Joseph Hertz, the Chief Rabbi, had written bitterly to the Colonial Secretary, Lord Cranborne, on 30 October, the day after a massive meeting held at the Albert Hall (with both Temple and Rathbone on the platform) organized to protest Nazi atrocities against the Jews. 'Jews are not being merely maltreated, starved or shot as hostages; a policy of total extermination is pursued.'[25]

The Polish information, gathered in part by Jan Karski, the underground courier who arrived in London in late November 1942, brought the Jewish organizations back to the Foreign Office.[26] This time, Parliamentary Under-Secretary Richard Law minuted, he thought the government would have to respond. The Labour MP Sidney Silverman had been to see him to press for a United Nations declaration, and while he doubted such a declaration would do much good, he thought 'that we would be in an appalling position if these stories should prove to have been true and we have done nothing whatever about them'.[27] In late November and early December, then, the Foreign Office began the process of consultation – with Jewish organizations, with the Polish government, with the Cabinet, with the Americans – that would culminate in the declaration of 17 December 1942.

Those discussions were complex and delicate, for it quickly became apparent that different groups and individuals had very different responses in mind. Certainly the Jewish organizations were eager for some official acknowledgement of the extent of the suffering and slaughter of European Jews. Yet, they saw such a declaration only as part of a broader response to the unfolding tragedy, and hoped that it might be accompanied by – even catalyse – concrete efforts at rescue. Silverman thought a declaration might induce ordinary people in occupied countries to give shelter; Alex Easterman and Noah Barou of the British Section of the World Jewish Congress wanted it to include a call to protection and aid.[28] On 3 December, representatives of the major Jewish organizations, including the Board of Deputies of British Jews, the World Jewish Congress, the Jewish Agency for Palestine and Agudas Israel, met to come up with proposals to facilitate escape; the following day, Lewis Namier, Berl Locker and Blanche Dugdale of the Jewish Agency went to see the Colonial Secretary about possibilities of bringing Jewish children to Palestine.[29] That emphasis on rescue was taken up and elaborated by the refugee advocates as well – among them, Eleanor Rathbone.

For Rathbone was already emerging as a pivotal person in this mobilization. There were reasons for her prominence. Although known as a progressive, her record as an anti-appeaser had given her credibility and contacts across the House. Churchill (and, still more, Clementine) actually liked her; Eden and Law found her tiresome but respected her knowledge and commitment. She had a high reputation among refugee organizations, independent sources of information within the refugee community, and an insider's knowledge of Home Office regulations. Although not Jewish, she had excellent working relations with Selig Brodetsky of the Board of Deputies of British Jews, and hence could play an important alliance-building role. She had independent contacts from pre-war days with numerous ambassadors and foreign diplomats, a confidential relationship with the editor of the *Manchester Guardian*, and easy access to great numbers of liberal intellectuals. She had, finally, time. The Archbishop of Canterbury had the Anglican Church to oversee; Gollancz a publishing house to run; Cazalet the sometimes difficult relations between the British government and its Polish ally (to which he was now liaison officer) to manage. Rathbone, by contrast, could devote herself entirely to whatever she felt to be the most pressing cause.

By 3 December, she was in touch with the principal Jewish organizations, the Archbishop of Canterbury, and her allies on the Parliamentary Committee on Refugees.[30] The next day, she contacted the BBC about a publicity campaign and wrote to W.P. Crozier, the editor of the *Manchester Guardian*.[31] After Temple wrote to *The Times* urging Britain to offer refuge to any Jews who could manage to reach its shores, Rathbone followed up on 9 and 10 December with parliamentary questions calling for revision of the stringent visa regulations 'so as to facilitate the rescue of the few who do have a chance of escaping massacre'.[32] She also began thinking through the suggestions made by the Jewish organizations. On 14 December she sent the first of her many notes on a possible practical policy of rescue off to the Foreign Office, which was in the final stages of its preparations for the declaration.[33]

On 17 December, in answer (as arranged) to a question from Sidney Silverman, the Foreign Secretary Anthony Eden rose in the House to confirm that the government did have evidence that the Nazis were bent on a plan of total extermination, that that plan was already well advanced, and that the United Nations – Britain, the United States, and the other Allies – joined together in deploring this terrible crime and in promising retribution. There were a few brief speeches, and then the House, in an unprecedented gesture, rose to stand in silence for the Jewish dead. It was all, Harold Nicolson noted, 'rather moving'.[34] Yet, as the archival records make clear, officials were worried. A 'rescue' lobby was clearly forming, and if those MPs questioned Eden about what efforts were being made to facilitate escape, officials feared they 'may be difficult to satisfy'. Richard Law transparently hoped that Morrison would finally budge. When he met with the Council of Christians and Jews on 16 December he had been 'very impressed by their anger against the Home Secretary, which quite clearly has not abated'. He felt 'very doubtful myself whether we shall be able to stand much longer on the very strict line that the Home Office is adopting. It has always seemed to me that the apprehensions of the Home Office have been exaggerated and that it would be very difficult for us to go on confining ourselves to denunciation of the German action while refusing to take any alleviating action ourselves.'[35]

In fact, the government survived the declaration without such parliamentary harassment. Silverman and other rescue advocates thought further questions would seem anticlimactic after the 'moment of silence' and so asked Rathbone to hold her fire.[36] But neither she nor the Jewish organizations intended to let the matter drop. The Jewish representatives thought the declaration impressive but by no means sufficient and within days were back at the Foreign Office,[37] and Rathbone was also anything but contented. 'I feel that the result may be that politicians and the public may feel that something substantial has been done by

the Declaration and that they can relieve their consciences of the whole unpleasant business,' she wrote to Crozier on 18 December. 'There is nothing more dangerous than a relieved conscience.' When she had approached Eden after the
debate to ask for assurances about rescue, he had 'charged me with ingratitude
for his efforts. . . . He said "wasn't it better to do something for the whole of
Jewry than for fifty or so escaped victims who might conceivably be got into
safety?" As though the two were alternatives!'[38] Instead of quietening critics, Law
thought that the declaration had 'created a new situation in which it might prove
to be impossible for the Home Secretary to maintain the *non possumus* attitude
which hitherto has come so easily to him'.[39] The argument over 'rescue' had
begun. In a sense, it has never ended.

We must turn to that quarrel and to Rathbone's part within it, but it is necessary
first to clarify the issues at stake. Underlying arguments over the Allied response
to the Holocaust are, of course, painful questions of moral responsibility – and
yet, particularly because the subject is difficult and the stakes high, it is important to keep crucial points about context and timing in mind. War, conquest, and
a deliberate change in Nazi policy transformed beyond recognition the danger to
Europe's Jews. Before 1939, the Nazis had concentrated on oppressing, impov-
erishing and expelling the Jewish population within the Reich itself (and, as those
territories were annexed, in Austria and the Czech areas), and Western Jewish
communities and to a degree Western governments made an effort to receive
them. In 1939, the situation changed utterly. Arrangements for Jewish emigration from the Reich came to a halt as Britain and France went to war; while the
Nazis were still eager to expel Jews, few places could or would take them. Britain,
fighting almost alone and fearful of invasion, could scarcely organize a massive
evacuation of impoverished refugees from enemy territory; France and much of
the continent were soon overrun; the neutrals were anxious and hard-pressed;
the United States isolationist and far away. Palestine was an escape-hatch of a
kind, although only for a few in light of Britain's determination to stick by
the quotas on Jewish immigration set by its White Paper of 1939. Yet, as Nazi-
controlled territory expanded, further Jewish populations, most importantly the
great communities in Poland, came under Nazi rule. The Nazis first planned to
make these territories *judenrein* by massive population transfers and deportations, concentrating Polish Jews in enormous ghettos for transfer to reserves over-
seas or beyond the Reich, but during the course of 1941, in the context of
confrontation with the Soviet Union, the more radical plan for a 'final solution'
was developed and extended.[40] From late 1941, then, most Jews under Nazi rule
were trapped – and by the end of 1942, when the agitation for 'rescue' began,
the majority were already dead. According to Raul Hilberg, by the end of 1942
perhaps three-quarters of all Jews who would die in the Holocaust – including
the vast majority of Poland's great Jewish population – had been murdered.[41] 'At

the core of the Holocaust,' Christopher Browning writes, 'was an intense eleven-month wave of mass murder', centred in Poland, from mid-March of 1942 until mid-February of 1943.[42]

By late 1942, then, scholars agree (and even 'rescue' campaigners at the time recognized) that – given the war, the accelerated machinery of destruction, and Hitler's implacable determination to kill every Jew – any action taken in the democracies could affect only a minority of Europe's Jews. But substantial Jewish communities remained in the satellite states, the neutrals, and in territories occupied by Italy; the majority of Hungary's Jewish community, as we know, was destroyed on the eve of Allied victory. What was fiercely contested at the time, and remains hotly debated to this day, was whether the American and British response to the Nazi campaign of mass extermination was appropriate or at any rate inevitable in wartime (as officials insisted), or fell terribly short (as the 'rescue' lobby contended); and, if it did fall short, to what degree genuine practical difficulties, or countervailing political imperatives, or bureaucratic sclerosis, or a misplaced liberal universalism, or implicit or explicit anti-Semitism was to blame. Almost as much attention and debate has been devoted to the 'rescue' campaigners, Jewish and non-Jewish, who have been seen alternately (both then and now) as pragmatic compromisers or unrealistic utopians, as 'incorporated' and trusted government interlocutors or incompetent outsiders easily outwitted by Whitehall mandarins.[43] Rathbone was the most indefatigable of these campaigners, the person who forged the Commons-based 'rescue' alliance, represented it before ministers and officials, thought through the campaign's demands, wrote the literature in which they were explained, badgered ministers and officials, and briefed the speakers before major deputations or debates. Any assessment of the 'rescue' campaign must come to terms with her tireless efforts.

On 18 December, the day after Eden's declaration, Rathbone took stock. She had urged the Jewish organizations to prepare a plan for rescue and was now reviewing their suggestions. One particularly intrigued her: the proposal that the Allies simply make an offer to Hitler to accept all Jews. She had little hope that they would be willing to do this, but it did seem 'the only means of possible rescue for any but those who escape over the frontiers or are in hiding and later escape – a few thousands at most'. If Hitler refused, he refused. But if the Allies were really afraid he might accept, 'that means that you really prefer that these people should be tortured to death than that you should be faced with the inconvenience of providing for them, even for limited numbers of them'.[44] Rathbone was right to think no government would or could contemplate an 'offer to Hitler'; probably she (like Gollancz) damaged her credibility with the government simply by airing the question. The Allies were committed to utterly defeating Hitler, not talking to him; they were fighting a war (and in the midst of the North Africa campaign), not organizing humanitarian aid. When a cabinet committee got around to considering suggestions that the Allies negotiate for the release of Jews some two months later, they turned the suggestion down flat.[45] But the idea that some massive exit of Jews from Nazi territory just might be possible made its way into Rathbone's earliest speeches and writings and featured in Gollancz's 'Let My People Go'.

Victor Gollancz, the idiosyncratic left-wing publisher, had had an uneasy relationship with the Anglo-Jewish establishment and indeed with his own Jewishness. But the news from the continent in 1942 evoked in him (as it had in Rathbone) a powerful emotional identification. That December he wrote, at breakneck speed, the pamphlet that not only captured his own painful response but that struck a mass chord, selling a quarter of a million copies within a few months. Reports of mass murder seem abstract, Gollancz wrote; to understand what they truly involved readers needed to try to 'be just one of those human beings' concealed by 'the abstraction of numbers'. 'Be the mother flinging her baby from a sixth-story window: be a girl of nine, torn from her parents and standing in the dark of a moving truck with two corpses pressed close against her: be an old Jew at the door of the electrocution chamber. And only then, when you have been each of these for a few short moments, do the multiplication.' But even such identification was not enough. 'What you have to do is, in Miss Rathbone's words, to ask yourself, "What can I do to influence the Government, the Press, my MP, my political party, Church, Trade Union or other organisation to make it plain that the Democracy, much as it cares for its own social security, cares even more immediately for the immediate problem of how many of these innocent men, women and children can be rescued from torture and death?"'[46] Within days, the mail was coming in – a deluge so overwhelming that Gollancz was forced to rent an office and hire a secretary and typist to deal with it, that the Foreign Office found itself answering letters from housewives offering to take in refugees and pensioners pledging their life savings; a stream that, six months later, still made up a part of the forty or fifty letters the National Committee for Rescue from Nazi Terror received each day.[47]

The government had to respond. On 23 December the Cabinet appointed a Committee on the Representation and Accommodation of Jewish Refugees comprised of Morrison, Eden, the Colonial Secretary Oliver Stanley and the relevant officials to consider arrangements for Jewish refugees able to make their way out of enemy territory. One such plan was already in the works, for Stanley had been trying to bring a contingent of Bulgarian Jewish children to Palestine as part of the immigration quota. But when the new committee met for the first time on 31 December, it agreed, on Morrison's insistence, that Jewish refugees should be seen as a common Allied problem (especially since, in his view, Britain could itself take at most a further one or two thousand) and that no distinction should be made between Jewish and non-Jewish refugees. Having essentially repudiated just that recognition of the particular extremity of Jewish suffering that Eden had declared

337

in the Commons, the following week the committee – now with Attlee as a member as well – expressed some anxiety about the possibility of being burdened by Europe's Jews. As some Axis countries, such as Romania, appeared to wish 'to extrude Jews from their territories as an alternative to their policy of extermination', it was imperative that the quota on Jewish immigration to Palestine 'be strictly adhered to'.[48] On 11 January, the Cabinet approved a telegram to the United States proposing consultation and a common approach, and on 19 January Attlee announced that plan in the Commons.[49] Now, the cabinet committee need do nothing but wait for the American response and manage the parliamentary pressure. Its third meeting, on 27 January, thus considered how to answer an all-party deputation on 'rescue' which would be received the next day. Since the Allies could not handle hundreds of thousands of refugees during wartime, it was 'essential to kill the idea that mass immigration to this country and the British colonies was possible'. The deputation should be given no numbers on likely admissions to Palestine and (if necessary) asked bluntly whether they wished to burden the United Nations – as the Allies were beginning to be called – with a problem that might make them lose the war.[50] Already the committee's main purpose had been established: it would consider not 'rescue' but rather how to manage the pressure for rescue.

Rathbone could not know of the committee's deliberations, but she was not naïve. The government might have questions of rescue 'under really "active consideration"', she wrote to Crozier on 13 January, but that consideration might be 'too much in the hands of the over-burdened Mr. Eden and the not very sympathetic Herbert Morrison'.[51] She thus kept up her barrage of parliamentary questions about the government's visa policies (even though MPs cheered when Herbert Morrison called her 'grossly unfair') and lobbied for individual refugees stuck in Spain or Portugal,[52] but she also tried to think through the issue of rescue for herself. Her hope of 'an offer to Hitler' was clearly a non-starter: many of those attending a meeting of Jewish leaders and Commons refugee supporters convened on 7 January thought such an offer unwise.[53] But it might, she thought, be possible to get at least some Jews in the satellite states – Bulgaria, Romania, Hungary – out of Europe through Turkey. Stanley's announcement in the Commons on 3 February of his hopes of removing some 4,000 Bulgarian Jewish children and 500 accompanying adults to Palestine heartened her. On 8 February she asked for a few minutes of Philip Noel-Baker's time to talk about the problem of transport (he was now parliamentary secretary at the Ministry of War Transport), and on 12 February Sir Wyndham Deedes took her to see the Turkish Ambassador, who was friendly but insisted that Turkey could admit Jews only if they were to be removed immediately elsewhere. These discussions brought home to her the complexity of any such efforts. Given the fragmentation of ministerial responsibilities and the number of countries involved, how could such efforts ever be given priority? Noel-Baker, in conversation, told her what she was after – a

'new Nansen', with the authority to override departmental and national juris-
dictions, arrange transit, and offer refuge. Noel-Baker had worked under Dr
Fridtjof Nansen, the High Commissioner for refugees under the League of
Nations, arranging refuge for displaced persons after the First World War, and
had already written to Law recommending a similar sort of appointment.
Rathbone professed herself 'in love with' the suggestion.[54] The problem was that
the League of Nations still had a 'high commissioner', Sir Herbert Emerson, director of the Inter-Governmental Committee set up at the Evian conference in 1939
to organize reception of refugees from the Reich. Emerson sat with Rathbone on
the Co-ordinating Committee on Refugees and the Home Office's Advisory
Council on Aliens, and she knew he was not what she had in mind – 'too much
the typical Civil Servant, who always sees difficulties more than possibilities'.[55]

By mid-February 1943, Rathbone had written up her thoughts on five separate questions. The note on an offer to Hitler had been put aside, but she had
written a note giving examples of the harsh workings of the Home Office's visa
regulations, a note on possible plans for rescue and a note on a 'new Nansen',
and she had put together a short digest of resolutions, offers of help, and other
'evidence of public concern'.[56] These notes were dispatched to Crozier, Temple,
Cecil and other sympathizers;[57] she also sent them to the Foreign Office and, individually, to Attlee and Morrison – merely to be told, again, that the government
was giving 'very close attention' to the matter.[58] But two months had passed since
the December declaration, and the United States government had still not even
responded to the British offer of consultation.[59] 'I suspect you think us pestering
busybodies,' Rathbone wrote to Randall at the Foreign Office (enclosing more
notes), '[b]ut as long as "official channels" discharge nothing but an icy flow of
discouraging answers to parliamentary questions, what can we do but go on
prodding?'[60] Unless the government adopted the 'new Nansen' idea, she wrote
despairingly to Robert Cecil, 'I don't see any hope that all our agitation will have
saved a single Jewish life.'[61]

Her dismay deepened when the American response finally came. The United
States suggested meeting at Ottawa, but thought the whole issue best addressed
by reviving the Inter-Governmental Committee on Refugees.[62] This would, of
course, mean yet more leisurely consultation and then a reference to Sir Herbert
Emerson's organization, which had done (Rathbone thought) such an inadequate
job before the war. On 9 March, she convened a joint meeting of the Jewish and
refugee organizations at the Commons to discuss the situation 'off the record'.
She didn't want to blame any individual or government, she said, but three
months after the declaration, and in spite of the fact that 277 MPs had signed a
motion in favour of strong action, nothing had been done. Perhaps, then, a new
pressure group was needed. Emerson, who had come to the meeting (and would
report back to the Foreign Office) demurred, but most of those present
wouldn't listen to him.[63] In the Commons the next day, Rathbone, Silverman,

Graham White and others extracted from Eden the statement that massacres of Jews ('and of Polish and Yugoslav nationals other than Jews') were continuing and that the matter of rescue would be treated as urgent.[64]

A week later, the National Committee for Rescue from Nazi Terror (as it soon decided to call itself) was in operation. It was an alliance of activist clergy, the main Jewish leaders, and the parliamentary advocates for refugees. The Executive Committee included the powerful foursome from the Parliamentary Committee on Refugees (Cazalet, Rathbone, Grenfell and Roberts), Selig Brodetsky for the Board of Deputies of British Jews, Berl Locker for the Jewish Agency, Lady Reading for the World Jewish Congress, Ian White Thomson representing the Archbishop of Canterbury, Henry Carter for the Free Churches, the Chief Rabbi Joseph Hertz, Victor Gollancz, and a shifting roster of others. The committee had a healthy group of supporters in the Lords, including the elderly Gladstonian Lord Crewe (who accepted the presidency), Herbert Samuel (since 1937 Lord Samuel), Robert Cecil, and Eric Drummond (now Lord Perth), the former Secretary-General of the League. It could use the office at 30 Maiden Lane rented by Gollancz; Mary Sibthorpe left the Friendly Aliens Protection Committee to take on the job of honorary secretary; Gollancz, and then increasingly Rathbone, paid the bills. But it was Rathbone who gathered the 206 signatures of eminent people for the cable the committee sent to Eden (then in Washington) assuring him of their support for energetic efforts at rescue, Rathbone who convened the meetings and prepared the notes, Rathbone who briefed the speakers for a full-dress debate in the Lords on 23 March, and Rathbone who drafted the committee's 'Twelve Point Programme', adopted in April. That programme once again emphasized the need to revise the United Kingdom's own visa regulations, to offer guarantees and encouragement to the neutrals to admit any Jews who could manage to cross the border, to try to ease the pressure on those neutrals by removing refugees to camps in North Africa or other Allied territory, to open Palestine to any who could proceed through Turkey, and to appoint a United Nations High Commissioner (that 'new Nansen') to deal with the whole matter. This time, however, it also asked for warnings to the satellite states not to engage in persecution and for the creation of a new instrument for rescue within the British government itself. Finally, the government was urged to adopt the principle that, whatever other nations did, the British contribution should be 'the speediest and most generous possible without delaying victory'.[65]

Rathbone then buttonholed Eden, just back from Washington, to give him copies of this programme. She managed to waylay Richard Law, who had been named one of the British representatives to the Allied conference to be held in mid-April in Bermuda (and not Ottawa, the Canadian government having no desire to signal any willingness to accept Jewish refugees). 'We have no doubt of your sympathy,' Rathbone wrote to Law – but would he be able 'to convey the sense of urgency which possesses us . . . and to insist that it shall be translated into immediate measures of rescue for all – whether few or many – who could possibly be rescued'?[66] The committee then cabled the delegates at Bermuda, hoping to stiffen them up.[67] The opening speeches at the conference, reported on 20 April, gave them no comfort: Law's in particular seemed crafted to lower expectations ('we must take great care to see that we are not betrayed by our feelings of humanity and compassion into courses of action which at best would postpone the day of liberation, and at worst might make liberation forever impossible') and went out of its way to avoid the use of the word 'Jew'.[68] Cazalet, for the National Committee, wrote to *The Times* in disgust: 'a mounting wave of indignation' would meet the government if it continued to show such an utter lack of 'vigorous determination'.[69] The government then said that, in the interests of the refugees themselves, it could not make the report of the conference public.[70]

Rathbone and the National Committee now found themselves in an extraordinary situation. They had been trying to secure parliamentary time for a debate on 'rescue' for two months; now they would get their debate, but didn't even know what policy the government had adopted. Rathbone prepared as best she could. In April, she had written a new pamphlet – *Rescue the Perishing* – updating the information on Nazi extermination, explaining the committee's programme, and answering objections. Ten thousand copies were printed (at her own expense) and distributed widely. The National Committee held a press conference the week before the debate and marshalled its speakers. But there were worrying signs. The press conference was poorly attended; Eden refused to receive a deputation.[71] Worse, some of the National Committee's own members were uncomfortable with its 'aggressive mood': it was 'swayed at almost every point by Mr Gollancz', Henry Carter wrote to Temple, and had a 'strong bias' against Emerson, whom the refugee organizations centred at Bloomsbury House had come to trust.[72] And the Cabinet made plans of its own, asking the whips to line up speakers with 'a more balanced point of view' to counterbalance the 'extreme' demands it expected to hear from Rathbone and her allies.[73]

At that debate, held on 19 May 1943, the government played every card it had. Osbert Peake, who opened, pointed out that the Allies could do 'little or nothing . . . for the vast numbers now under Hitler's control'. An 'offer to Hitler' would be useless, given the Nazis' unwillingness to let people go; indeed, given the ongoing extermination campaign, the most important thing was to win the war as quickly as possible. It followed that any diversion of resources – shipping, food – to efforts at rescue would not be in the interests of those 'suffering under German tyranny' themselves. Peake then raised the temperature by dismissing the demands of the rescue campaigners. The request that Britain make available blocks of visas in the neutral countries to help Jews escape (made repeatedly by Rathbone) came in for particular attack: such visas would be useless, given the Nazis' unwillingness to give exit permits; worse, such a policy would open Britain to infiltration by German secret service agents. To drive this point home, Peake cited a case, discussed in Rathbone's *Rescue the Perishing*, of a Jewish refugee in Britain whose brother, a naturalized Turk, had told her that he could secure permission for their parents in Berlin to enter Turkey, provided a British visa would await them. That visa, Rathbone pointed out, had been refused, and the parents had now been deported to Poland. 'I shall be very sorry, but I shall also be very surprised,' Peake told the Commons, if that deportation had really happened. For the brother was employed in a firm acting as the agent in Turkey for Krupp – and, no doubt, also made it his business 'to obtain information about the arms supplied by other countries and to forward this information to his masters in Germany'. 'We at the Home Office cannot bring ourselves to believe that the parents of a man occupying an important position in a firm which acts for Krupps in Constantinople are in serious danger, or that we ought to facilitate their escape from German territory by promising them visas to this country.'[74] The Bermuda conference had come up with some more practical proposals, but these could not be talked about without compromising their effectiveness.

Rathbone had to follow Peake, but his invocation of secrecy and personal attack made her understandably defensive. She responded effectively to his charge of ignorance about visas. She knew perfectly well that people had trouble leaving enemy territory, she said – but the point was to facilitate such clandestine attempts as were made, and to foster receptivity within the neutral states. 'Does the Under-Secretary really mean to deny that refugees do not sometimes have secret ways of communication with their relatives in enemy territory? I do not know how they do it but they do it. . . . [D]oes he tell me that it does not make a difference, when a refugee arrives at the border if the authorities of that country have been informed beforehand that a visa is awaiting the refugee? It is common sense that it makes a difference. . . . The right hon. Gentleman also mocked at the suggestion that block visas would make any difference. Of course, they would make a difference.' But Rathbone, frustrated and angry, could also not refrain from personal attack. The problem was not just that the government seemed unwilling to recognize the urgency of the matter and devote real attention to it (she suggested a Ministry for Refugees), it was also that some members of the government, and the Home Secretary in particular, responded to all requests by hardening their hearts. 'It seems that he wants to show that he is a strong man by refusing to make even the smallest concession and that his attitude has been influenced sometimes less by the merits of the case than by his dislike of yielding anything to his critics.' Why did Morrison always make them feel that the whole question was 'a bore and an irritation to him and that he was transferring to refugees the dislike which he quite openly feels for ourselves?' Did she sound too bitter, she asked?

I tell you . . . there is not one who would not feel bitter if he or she had my postbag and read the letters I receive by every post from agonised people who

feel that the one chance left for their relatives is slipping from them and that
they may soon have to take that awful journey to the Polish slaughter-house
and who beg me to rescue them, not realising how impotent I am. I shall be
told that in these dreadful days, anxiety is the common lot. There is not one
of us who does not suffer it, more or less. Many have already suffered cruel
bereavement. But there is a difference. The sacrifices which British people and
our Allies are asked to make and for the most part are making so bravely are
worth while sacrifices for a great and noble end. They are the only means of
ridding the world of a monstrous tyranny and of opening up a brighter future
for mankind. We must not and dare not grudge them. But the deaths, of which
we are thinking to-day, are so utterly useless, squalid and unspeakably cruel.
They serve no purpose, except to gratify one man's lust for cruelty, for wrecking [sic] vengeance on the weak when he cannot reach the strong. Only victory
will put an end to it all. But meantime let no one say: 'We are not responsible.'
We are responsible if a single man, woman or child perishes whom we could
and should have saved.[75]

Having begun in anger, the debate continued at a high pitch. Of the eight
speakers who made arguments on behalf of 'rescue', four explicitly defended
Rathbone (in Cazalet's words, an 'honourable and noble Lady – I use those adjec-
tives not in the Parliamentary sense, but in the ordinary sense').[76] Cazalet and
A.V. Hill also backed up her charges about Morrison; Grenfell deplored the 'deri-
sive note' that crept into Peake's voice when he mentioned the National
Committee's work. As best they could, the campaigners tried to explain why, for
all their own universalist ideals, the government needed to pay particular attention to Jews. It might be true that a hundred million people were suffering under
the Nazis and only victory would free them, Cazalet pointed out, but only the
Jews were being simply exterminated: 'The stories of the horrors of the massacres
at a camp called Treblinka would put to shame the massacres of Genghis Khan
or the sufferings of the Albigenses.'[77] The speakers mobilized by the government
then came to Peake's defence, resurrecting Morrison's claim that the admission
of Jews – indeed, almost any recognition of the extremity of Jewish suffering –
would arouse anti-Semitism. 'I can conceive nothing more likely to create anti-
Semitism in this country than to let the feeling get abroad that every Jew or Jewess
is to have a special measure of relief which is not open to the Norwegian pastor,
the Dutch politician or the French trade unionist,' Sir Herbert Butcher insisted.[78]
A.V. Hill dismissed this argument as a 'gross insult to the intelligence, good nature
and commonsense of the normal citizen'; Cazalet argued that refugees were not
a burden and that 'no country has ever lost' by admitting them anyway.[79] But by
painting efforts at rescue not only as 'impractical' but as somehow a violation of
the British belief in 'perfect equality of treatment for every race and every creed'
(as Butcher put it), the government had placed the rescue lobby, and Jewish MPs

like Daniel Lipson and Silverman in particular, in a difficult position.[80] Eden, wrapping up, poured oil impartially over all the hurt feelings while managing to avoid saying anything at all.[81]

The debate over, the government drove its advantage home. Lord Winterton, Britain's unimpressive representative on the Inter-Governmental Committee, wrote to the *Daily Telegraph* to support Eden and Peake's 'admirable' statement of the government's case; Peake sent Rathbone a lengthy defence of its record on refugees and of his own attack on her pamphlet.[82] The Cabinet closed ranks. Even though Eden and Peake had told the Commons that more was happening than could be divulged in open session, when Rathbone wrote to ask Eden to receive a private deputation to discuss those actions, the Cabinet told him to put her off.[83] Randall, instead, met with Rathbone and Lord Perth each individually to assure them that the situation of Jews in the Balkans was being gone into, and to ask them to abstain from further pressure.[84] Uncertain about the right course of action, and troubled by the contention that publicity was likely to make rescue harder, Rathbone agreed to quieten down. She, Gollancz and Perth all felt 'that we had rather come to a stage when we wanted to work privately rather than publicly', she wrote on 2 June to Clement Davies (who had proposed a debate in the Lords); they would 'give the Government a chance to get on with its Bermuda measures, such as they are, and avoid recriminations about the past'.[85]

For six months, Rathbone and her allies had made a considerable amount of noise, and the government had gone to considerable lengths to contain them. They had seen some official response: the government had agreed to the 17 December declaration; it had tried (if without success) to bring some Bulgarian children to Palestine as part of the immigration quota; in early June the Cabinet decided that Jews escaping to Turkey (a tiny trickle) could be transported to camps in Palestine and then released as legal immigrants against the quota.[86] But the main response to the agitation had been to redefine the question as an international one: henceforth, not only the formulation of policy but specific requests for action (such as the request in April 1943 that Britain promise to help with post-war resettlement should the Swedes approach the Nazis to ask for some 20,000 Jewish children) would be dealt with through time-consuming international consultation.[87] The 'rescue' campaigners were highly critical of that collaborative approach, but – partly through a personal attack on Rathbone's credibility – the government regained the upper hand. The first phase of the 'rescue' campaign was over.

During the next period, from June 1943 until December, Rathbone would again move from attempted collaboration with the government to open antagonism. This time, however, she did so largely on her own. She was still inundated with frantic personal appeals; telegrams from an anguished Palestine Jewish community were addressed to her.[88] Yet public interest appeared to be waning and the

National Committee itself was under strain. At the end of June Gollancz, who had been plagued by mysterious pains and rashes and having trouble sleeping, had a nervous breakdown.[89] And on 3 July Victor Cazalet and General Sikorski, head of the Polish government-in-exile, died off the coast of Gibraltar in a plane crash. 'The Victors', as Rathbone's secretaries called them, had been (after Rathbone) the most outspoken advocates of 'rescue'; although Perth, Grenfell, Quintin Hogg, and in time Harold Nicolson would now support Rathbone on deputations and in debates, none played as important a role. In a complex political landscape, she had trouble finding her way.

For she was painfully conscious of both the ongoing slaughter and the inability of her committee – by now pretty much a one-woman show – to do much about it. As she wrote to the members of the National Committee's executive on 28 June, they seemed 'to have reached a stalemate or dead end'. Six months had now passed since the declaration, but little had been accomplished. The Bermuda conference appeared simply to have been an exercise in lowering expectations; the Inter-Governmental Committee, to whom the whole question was now to be referred, had not even been reconstituted. Perhaps some efforts were being made to remove refugees from Spain and Portugal, but none seemed to have been made to protect the Jews of the satellite states. 'The implication of it all seems that the Government has very little sense of urgency over the whole matter, very little hope of doing anything for rescue except on a small scale and a strong desire to avoid pressure.'

The committee's own position was as weak as could be imagined. Ministers appeared to be avoiding them. Eden had promised to meet with them after the May debate but had now transferred the deputation to Law. Accurately summarizing the government's views, Rathbone wrote:

> We are treated kindly and courteously, but kept at arm's length as much as possible. The Jewish Agency has a semi-official connection with the Colonial Office, but the rest of us are regarded as amateurs and troublesome outsiders. We are continually warned – with good reason – that parliamentary or press publicity on certain aspects of the subject may do actual harm in frustrating the efforts they are making, as it probably did in the case of the children from Bulgaria. Yet if we refrain from publicity and from organised pressure, there is real danger that the Government will assume that public interest has weakened and their present tendency to dismiss a painful subject from their own minds will be encouraged.
>
> What, if anything, can we do about it?[90]

She tried to chart a middle course. On the one hand, the National Committee devoted some energy, in collaboration with the Board of Deputies of British Jews and other sympathetic organizations, simply to publicizing the Nazis' actions. They printed an occasional newsletter (*News from Hitler's Europe*) about conditions in the occupied lands and distributed tens of thousands of pamphlets, including a new edition of Rathbone's *Rescue the Perishing*, brought up to date to include an account of the Warsaw ghetto uprising. They arranged for BBC broadcasts to the Balkans, and – having concluded that pressure was still necessary – went ahead in late July with another debate in the Lords.[91] On the other hand, Rathbone made a real effort to collaborate with the government, refraining from her usual raft of parliamentary questions and instead ringing up Randall at the Foreign Office or buttonholing Law in the House when she wanted to get information or to pass some along. To a degree, they brought her into their confidence; Law, for example, told her about the plan – the sole practical measure agreed at Bermuda – to establish a camp in North Africa to receive refugees from Spain, but then warned her 'that if she drew any attention to it the blood of thousands would be on her head'. Yet, when civil servants realized that their need to deal with the 'refugee pressure groups' just 'really means Miss Rathbone', Rathbone was left vulnerable and exposed.[92]

The Foreign Office wondered whether to co-opt or exclude her. Perth, in a meeting with Randall in early June 1943, had made the argument for inclusion. If 'rescue' was to be referred to the Inter-Governmental Committee, why not appoint Rathbone an assessor, a practice that had worked well when he had been Secretary-General of the League? 'If she were on the inside,' Perth wrote, 'I do not think she would raise difficulties unnecessarily, while her contacts with various societies and individuals might prove of considerable value.'[93] Some at the Foreign Office were receptive: 'it seems a good idea to draw the dragon's teeth by taking it into our confidence,' Alan Walker minuted.[94] Randall, knowing Emerson, doubted it would work, but at the end of July Rathbone's friends and admirers tried again. Churchill had plenty on his mind (not much of it to do with either rescue or refugees) but he thought well of Rathbone, and when his old friend Violet Bonham-Carter sent him a note urging her appointment to the Inter-Governmental Committee Churchill told Eden that he thought 'at first sight . . . she might be useful there'.[95] This was more serious, but when the Foreign Office approached Emerson about making her an assessor, he flatly refused.[96] The National Committee might want to collaborate, Walker noted on 12 August, 'but if by collaboration is meant collaboration with Miss Rathbone there is the personal factor, which may be termed lack of mutual esteem between Sir Herbert Emerson and Miss Rathbone on the one hand and Lord Winterton and Miss Rathbone on the other which is not conducive to the smooth conduct of affairs'.[97]

Perhaps not – but Rathbone didn't want 'smooth conduct'. She wanted action, and two days earlier had marched over to see Law at the Foreign Office to deliver herself, in person and in print, of her most vehement diatribe yet. 'It seems that all the best chances – they were never more than good chances – of rescuing considerable numbers of threatened victims have been thrown away by the failure of the United States and British Governments to take sufficiently prompt and

vigorous action and by the atmosphere of defeatism, half-heartedness and infinite leisureliness with which they have surrounded the whole subject,' she wrote.
'This could hardly have been better devised if it were intended to show the whole
world, including enemy and neutral states, how little importance these two
Governments really attach to the question.' A raft of examples followed. Instead
of simply giving the Swedes the guarantees they had asked for before approaching the Germans, the government had begun consultations with the Americans –
consultations that took so long that the situation changed and the Swedes now
declined to proceed. The Swiss had not been promised that refugees they had
taken in would be accommodated after the war; the Turks had not been pressed
to facilitate passage out of the Balkans. 'As to the Axis satellites, who must be
trembling at the approach of an Allied victory, has enough been done to warn
them against further persecutions and deportations of Jews?' Even more ludicrous
were the decisions on how to address the question. It was bad enough that the
matter had been referred to the Inter-Governmental Committee, but to leave the
committee with its existing executive was even worse. That executive had 'an
incompetent chairman – Lord Winterton – who lacks judgment, discretion and
any real interest in the subject', a director – Sir Herbert Emerson – 'of such
intensely cautious and conservative temperament that he instinctively distrusts
every large and bold proposal', and included representatives of states with no
interest in the subject while excluding many closely concerned. Moreover, far
from being appointed as assessors, 'outside experts' were to be allowed only to
submit written memoranda – a procedure, Rathbone predicted, that would simply
mean 'that Sir Herbert Emerson as Director would explain to his Committee
that anything worth while in the proposals submitted had already been put in
train and was being carried out as far as possible and that the remainder of the
proposals were either impracticable or undesirable'. 'To speak frankly,' she
concluded, 'I feel that we outside experts have been very badly treated'. They had
loyally cooperated with the government, avoiding press or parliamentary publicity whenever told that this would impede rescue attempts, but the government had not cooperated in return.[98]

Richard Law patiently went through all of Rathbone's charges with her,
although he thought her (he minuted privately) 'extremely unfair'.[99] But since
Rathbone had asked him whether Churchill and Roosevelt couldn't perhaps be
asked to take some interest in rescue and refugee questions themselves (they were
too busy 'with matters directly affecting the conduct of the war', he told her), he
did at least send Eden a note. Eden's response highlights, once again, the distance
between officials' and campaigners' understanding of the whole question. 'What
questions are there?' Eden asked. 'If there is anything I can do, please let me have
a note and I will do my best.' But neither Law nor Walker (who prepared the
note) could really think of anything: they were at work on the North Africa camp;
the 4,000 Bulgarian children were still not allowed to go; the Swedish initiative

was now stalemated. The Bermuda conference had recommended that they guarantee help to the neutrals with the post-war refugee situation, and so Britain had now approached the Soviets for agreement on this: perhaps they could tell Miss Rathbone that?[100] Their very thinking confirmed Rathbone's analysis: they were following up the individual suggestions forced upon them, but they had not defined either the Nazis' campaign as a problem or 'rescue' as a goal and hence were giving no independent attention to the question. Moreover, although she had no way of knowing this, the Cabinet had no forum for such consideration. The Cabinet Committee on Refugees, having gratefully turned over the whole question in June 1943 to the Inter-Governmental Committee, had stopped meeting, and would not reconvene until Roosevelt's appointment of the War Refugee Board created a new situation in early 1944.

Law, moreover, had lost patience with Rathbone. When she asked him in mid-August to press the Swedes to try again, he met with Winterton and Emerson to discuss her. Henceforth, they agreed, she would be referred to the Inter-Governmental Committee – a solution that, given Emerson and Rathbone's mutual dislike (Rathbone thought Winterton beneath notice), effectively froze her out.[101] She tried to extract information about the Inter-Governmental Committee's action (or inaction) in Parliament, but officials told Law not to give in to such 'nagging'.[102] ('Is it not time this House was told something of what the Committee are doing? . . . May I have an answer?' The speaker just called the next question.)[103] Worse, when she did – as directed – approach Emerson about guarantees to the neutrals, he told her that this was a diplomatic question which should be addressed to the Foreign Office.[104] The whole question of 'rescue', in other words, had been referred to the Inter-Governmental Committee, but the IGC would accept responsibility only for 'refugee' questions. 'Rescue' seemed to be no one's responsibility at all.

Unwelcome but indefatigable, Rathbone tried again to persuade the government that addressing the German persecution was a Foreign Office responsibility and that any response must (given Nazi policy) focus on Jews. She was unhappy to see that the armistice terms agreed with Italy had made no mention of the need particularly to protect Jews, she told the Foreign Office in late September 1943 (and would have been still more unhappy had she known how the Foreign Office had dithered over a Vatican proposal a few weeks earlier to try to remove Jews from Italian-occupied territories before ceding them to the Germans).[105] Jewish victims were of course included by implication in the recent three-power declaration on Nazi atrocities, the National Committee said in a letter to Churchill (which was signed by Lord Crewe but written by Rathbone), but Jews should have been mentioned by name, since 'the Jewish persecutions are in a class by themselves, as being aimed at the extermination of a whole race'. Could he, then, consider warnings to satellites and guarantees to neutrals, in the hope that this might protect some Jews? (Churchill need not see this letter, his private office decided.)[106] A few days later, Rathbone stopped by the Foreign Office to discuss those same questions, but while G.H. Hall, the new Under-Secretary, gave her a patient hearing, he would not promise to put the matter before the Cabinet. 'You may think me too impatient,' Rathbone wrote to Law, 'but it does seem that – even in wartime – the continuing deportations and murders of thousands of men, women and children every week and the possibility of rescuing even a few thousand of them, was a question deserving more attention from the Cabinet than it seems to be getting.' The committee might raise the matter again in Parliament, Rathbone warned.[107]

Not a good idea, Hall and Randall retorted: the British government was doing more than it could disclose in Parliament, and public protests in Britain 'stimulated rather than deterred Nazi persecutions'. These claims left Rathbone and the National Committee 'perplexed and uneasy'. 'On the one hand we recognise the strength of these objections. . . . On the other hand, we fear that to ignore the subject in the Debate on the Address – the biggest annual opportunity for the discussion of important issues – would convey the impression that both the Government and Parliament had lost interest in the subject.'[108] 'We get nowhere,' Rathbone wrote to Crozier at the *Manchester Guardian* in frustration, '& there is an atmosphere of "hush-hush" which is very hard to estimate at its real value, i.e. however justified or as excuse'.[109] After discussion with the National Committee, Rathbone wrote to Hall offering not to press the government for specific information, but proposing that they be allowed to make three or four speeches and that the government then respond with a statement. Hall bargained her down: after a government statement they could make *one* speech and the speaker had best be her – a proposal that gave the committee a platform, but that (once again) also set Rathbone up.[110]

She did as well as she could, reminding the House that a year had passed since the declaration and that persecution of the Jews had not abated. Constrained by government hints of action behind the scenes, she did not press for further information. And yet, she pointed out, she and others who lived with this question 'on our consciences all the time' did not feel satisfied that 'the utmost has been done for rescue'. She did not underestimate the difficulties: 'We know that the vast majority of the victims are outside our reach. They can never be relieved nor rescued except by final victory, and that may come too late to save them.' But was the government really doing all it possibly could? 'Consider the timing of such action as has been taken. Five months elapse between the declaration of last December and the calling of the Bermuda Conference. Then another three months elapsed before the Inter-Governmental Committee to which the whole matter was referred began to meet. Even now the Committee as a whole has not met; only its small and curiously composed executive. . . . That is not the way to tackle a task on which the lives of thousands of innocent people depend.' There were things, independent of the Inter-Governmental Committee, that Britain could do.

Matters would enter a new phase as the Allied victory came closer. Britain could encourage action by the neutral states and possibly even change behaviour in the satellites by promising to give refuge after the war to any Jews who managed to get away.[111]

This was, for Rathbone, all very moderate. For six months, fearful that she might indeed compromise government efforts, she had kept her criticism within bounds. But that December, as she reviewed the whole situation, she realized she had little faith in those assurances of government action. If she had been privy to internal Foreign Office correspondence she would have had even less. The Cabinet Refugee Committee had not met for six months; when the US government (now under pressure at home) asked for a joint statement on actions taken since Bermuda, Randall had to admit that 'there is not much straw for this particular piece of brickmaking'.[112] But she knew enough to be worried. She knew deportations were continuing, that allies had still not offered the neutrals help settling post-war refugees, and that the government was determined to treat even Jewish refugees as repatriable.[113] 'Public opinion', Rathbone concluded, must again be mobilized. Gollancz, now recovered, agreed: an 'extremely militant attitude' was needed.[114] The final phase of the refugee campaign was at hand.

In the winter of 1943–4, as the Allies prepared for an attack on the continent, Rathbone mobilized again on behalf of Europe's Jews. At Crozier's request, she wrote a summary of the past 'disappointing twelve months' for the *Manchester Guardian*; in early 1944, her pamphlet *The Continuing Terror* was published; in late February she spoke at a mass meeting in Westminster.[115] Early in January, she and Gollancz redrafted their programme to take into account the changing military situation. Allied commanders in the field should be instructed to make special efforts to protect Jews in hiding or in camps; refugee workers should be sent to liberated areas immediately; the UK's visa regulations should be revised to allow immediate entry to surviving relatives of Britain's Jewish refugees.[116] The proposed United Nations policy of treating all displaced persons as repatriable was impractical and inhuman, Rathbone said in the Commons. How could surviving Polish Jews be expected to go back 'to a place which is one vast mortuary, where their wives and children and parents have been done to death?'[117] A deputation led by Grenfell and including Hogg, Nicolson, Rathbone and Lords Horder, Lytton and Perth called on Eden to repeat these points.[118] 'It was a fine deputation,' Nicolson noted. 'Poor Anthony . . . received us with great cordiality. . . .' It was true 'that Anthony is apt to hide behind his own charm. One goes away thinking how reasonable, how agreeable and how helpful he has been, and then discovers that in fact he has promised nothing at all.'[119] Of course not: the War Office, having been sent Rathbone's suggestions, said shortly that continental commanders couldn't be burdened with instructions about Jewish refugees; the Home Office chimed in to point out that it had already asked that commanders not, under any circumstances, send persons liberated by the Allied advance to Britain.[120]

The government clearly had no intention of responding to the National Committee. On 22 January 1944, however, Roosevelt appointed a new body, the War Refugee Board, charged with pursuing all possible rescue efforts at all possible speed. Rathbone, Crozier, Silverman and the other British rescue advocates immediately urged the creation of a comparable British body,[121] and while the government demurred, pressure from the Americans did force a more vigorous response.[122] Thus, when the German occupation of Hungary in March 1944 aroused desperate fears about the fate of Hungary's 800,000 Jews (the largest relatively intact Jewish community left on the continent), and Roosevelt warned the Hungarians to refrain from persecution, the Foreign Office allowed Temple to broadcast an appeal on the BBC and followed up on Rathbone and Chief Rabbi Hertz's request to ask the Vatican to intervene. (Rathbone also drafted a two-sentence 'warning' for possible inclusion in Churchill's 26 March radio broadcast, but it was not used.)[123] Trainloads of Hungarian Jews were sent daily to Auschwitz in May and June anyway, and efforts by Jewish organizations within Hungary to involve the Allies in direct negotiations with the SS (the still-controversial 'blood-for-trucks' offer) failed.[124] The Cabinet remained consistently hostile to 'deals' of this kind, being convinced that such offers were designed to frustrate the war effort or sow dissension between the Western powers and the USSR. Eden thus worked hard to persuade the USA that, while they would accept specific categories (Jews who fell within the Palestine quota, the 4,000 Bulgarian children), the Allies should do nothing 'which would invite bargaining over the fate of the Jews'.[125] By July there would be fewer to bargain over, for only the Budapest Jews were still alive.

News of the deportations and killings brought renewed appeals and warnings from the Allies and the Vatican, but Rathbone and the National Committee played little role. For Rathbone's body was finally protesting about its relentless punishment. Eleanor had cut her shin badly on a piece of debris while making her way to Westminster Underground station during a black-out early in 1941 and had had to spend several weeks in hospital. The shin had slowly healed but remained weak, and Eleanor, absent-minded and clumsy, could not remember to take care of it. She had hurt it again in the summer of 1941 (climbing out of a window on holiday); now, in mid-April 1944, she banged into an electric radiator in her own study and once again couldn't walk. This time, not even a fortnight in Westminster Hospital could mend it. Although she was discharged on 1 May, a week later she was back in the hospital and would stay there for seven weeks. On 1 July she was finally let go, but that very day a V-2 rocket hit Tufton Court, blasting out the windows and doors, and sending Eleanor and Elizabeth to Eva Hubback's house in Golders Green for refuge.[126]

Rathbone and her secretary tried to work in hospital, first in a private room and then with screens around the bed in a general ward. But injury and homelessness put a limit even to Rathbone's industriousness, and the National Committee, during her three-month absence, lost its momentum. Public meetings were planned, but few members of the Executive pitched in to help; there was a serious deficit, but an appeal brought in only a tenth of the necessary funds. In June, Rathbone (from hospital) tried to stir up the Executive to approach the Soviets about the Hungarian situation, but they never quite managed it.[127] Not until she returned on 19 July did action resume. After intensive pressure, Admiral Horthy, the Hungarian Regent, had stopped the deportations on 7 July and made an offer to the Red Cross to release certain categories of Jews; Rathbone immediately organized a deputation to Eden to urge Britain to accept.[128] Characteristically, they left believing he had agreed to do so, only to discover, when Rathbone followed up with G.H. Hall, that the Hungarians had not been told anything.[129] The Americans were causing the delay, she was told, but this was not quite true. In fact, it was the Cabinet Committee on Refugees (and later the Cabinet) that, alarmed by the American proposal that the Allies agree to accept 'all Jews', were negotiating with the United States for some practical limit to the British commitment.[130] The Germans, in any case, refused to let the Budapest Jews go. What Allied pressure had won them was a pause before a final terrible round of persecution after Horthy's fall.

As the Allied armies advanced in 1944, the National Committee went into decline. The Executive continued to meet every few months in late 1944 and 1945. It published circulars giving information on the numbers and conditions of Jews who had survived the Nazi occupation and made recommendations (including to the United Nations' founding conference in San Francisco) about the post-war treatment of refugees.[131] In the Commons, Rathbone kept up her criticisms of any forcible repatriation of Jews, and urged the government to pay special attention to the needs – and claims for entry – of camp survivors.[132] (They should pay no attention to such arguments, Morrison told the Cabinet Committee on Refugees on 16 May 1945. If Jewish refugees were allowed to remain in Britain 'they might be an explosive element in the country, especially if the economic situation deteriorated'.)[133] But the 'rescue' campaign was over. The wave of public revulsion and horror brought on by the first photographs and accounts from the death camps in April 1945 was not set off by the National Committee.

Rathbone, in any case, was not shocked by these revelations. She had 'known' since 1942; she had not needed pictures and Allied news stories to comprehend the Nazi crimes.[134] To put it differently, unlike most of her compatriots, Rathbone began living in the post-Holocaust world in 1942 and not in 1945. As the death camps were liberated, she was neither transfixed by horror nor obsessed with retribution: to the contrary, with so much of Europe 'one vast mortuary', she wanted only to avoid more bloodletting. To the amazement of the Foreign Office (but not of those who knew them), she and Gollancz were worrying now about *Germans*. Rathbone's final campaign was at hand.

It remains, of course, to ask what the pressure for 'rescue' all amounted to. No historian who has studied the British response to the Holocaust has questioned Rathbone's energy and commitment, passion and persistence. Where disagreements arise is on the practicality and the impact of her work. Tony Kushner, on the one hand, insists that Rathbone's plans for rescue were 'penetrating and prophetic'.[135] W.D. Rubinstein, by contrast, calls the National Committee's twelve-point programme 'as pathetic a confession of helplessness and bankruptcy as can possibly be imagined'. 'Not one of these proposals,' Rubinstein insists, 'would have saved the life of a single Jew in Nazi-occupied Europe.'[136]

Before one pronounces on such a dispute, one should recall what Rathbone thought 'rescue' meant and could do. She was not credulous or unrealistic: except briefly in December 1942 and January 1943, when she and Gollancz urged an 'offer to Hitler', she never dared to imagine that any Allied action – except winning the war – could save millions of lives. She understood by 1943 that almost the whole of Polish Jewry had been lost: indeed, pragmatically, she refrained in May 1944 from joining the Independent left-wing MP Tom Driberg in denouncing anti-Semitism in the Polish army because she thought the British should do nothing to offend those Poles who might be harbouring surviving Jews.[137] The best that one could do for those in lands actually occupied by the Nazis would be to broadcast appeals, especially by religious leaders, and to work with the neutrals to further clandestine efforts to get Jews into their lands.[138] Indeed, because she recognized that the scope for action was limited, she focused more on Hungary, Romania and Bulgaria, all formally sovereign and with substantial Jewish populations, than on Nazi-occupied territory itself. 'Rescue', for her, was more about preventing those threatened populations from falling into Nazi hands (as so many did) than about somehow reaching those who had already been sent to Poland.

From this perspective, her proposals were not utopian but pragmatic and sane. They were grounded in the best information she could gather. She met with Jan Karski in early 1943 and the negotiator of the Swedish proposal to take in threatened children that May; she kept in touch with refugee workers in Spain and Portugal. Because, as she told the Commons, she 'lost no opportunity of making contact with everybody – with visiting foreigners, with responsible diplomats, with returned refugees, with anyone and everyone', she was better informed than ministers on this question.[139] Her proposals that Britain collude with (or pressure) the neutrals to try pre-emptively to remove Jews from states vulnerable to Nazi invasion may have been unacceptable but were not unworkable; this is why she thought Stanley's efforts for the Bulgarian children such a hopeful precedent. And other proposals were, after all, essentially what was (albeit belatedly) tried, and what did (albeit for too few) make a difference. Warnings by the Allies and by the Vatican did help to arrest deportations in Slovakia in 1942 and Hungary in 1944; Eden's fear that repeating such warnings somehow 'debased the currency', given that the default position was mass murder, was ridiculous.[140] Intervention or reception by the neutrals was also critical: Sweden ran some risks and incurred German displeasure by taking in Denmark's Jews and some of Norway's; some Jews did manage to make their way to Switzerland and Spain throughout the war; in the Swiss case, Allied pressure could and probably did affect how many were let in.[141] Even the idea of handing out 'block visas' to the neutrals, on which Peake poured such scorn, mattered, for some Jews were saved in Budapest in 1944 by Swedish and Swiss officials handing out not only their own papers but also – on Britain's behalf – Palestine immigration certificates. Although the Gestapo never allowed those Jews to leave Budapest, the documents themselves provided a measure of protection.[142] To argue that earlier and more wholehearted efforts along the same lines would have made no difference runs against the scholarly consensus and strains credulity.

Such arguments, moreover, would have troubled Rathbone deeply, for the simple reason that she was not, and refused to be, distracted by speculation about how few or many might be saved. In line with Jewish tradition, if from different roots, she too thought 'that he who saves one life saves a world'.[143] Morrison's response at the Vichy deputation that the government could not deal with individuals, like Eden's argument that it was better to do something 'big' for all Jews rather than fuss about the fifty affected in one case, made no sense to her. If years of social work and refugee casework had taught Rathbone anything, it was that all change happens, all lives are saved or lost, individual by individual, one by one. No one in touch with individual refugees, many of whom had left relatives behind on the continent, could say that rescue measures weren't worth undertaking because the return in lives saved might be small.

She pursued her goals, moreover, using every ounce of the political skill she had learned over forty years. Scholars have argued about whether rescue campaigners were too deferential or not deferential enough, impossibly idealistic or impractical and lacking in skill. But such a debate again makes little sense for Rathbone, for she tried every approach, judging them entirely by their effectiveness in producing results. She could stir up publicity but could also, when necessary, keep secrets; she would press ministers mercilessly but desist if she felt the pressure had gone too far. She had her weaknesses, of course: she overestimated the importance of rational argument in politics and underestimated the importance of personal ties; although she tried to tone them down, her vehemence and her hectoring tone could put people off. But she was a good judge of character – Morrison really was autocratic, Emerson over-cautious and self-important, Peake (in Rathbone's devastating words) 'a well-intentioned and kindly man naturally but completely weak and under Morrison's thumb; also stupid'[144] – and tried to take account of people's frailties. And her greatest strength was that she (unlike them) had no ego to speak of: she disliked personal attack but would take it without flinching; she knew ministers thought her a nuisance but she simply didn't care. She was, then, importunate beyond the bounds of all decency, assuming she had every right to ring up Foreign Office officials or waylay ministers at any time of the day or night. She was plagued by the thought that there was something else she could have done, but no one could have done more.

Except, of course, for ministers: they, Rathbone thought, could have done much more. For the crux of her criticism was not of policy but of motive and 'machinery' – and here, too, she was perceptive. The problem, she thought, was not that the government declined to pursue this or that specific policy, but rather that they had neither defined rescue as a goal nor created an agency to deal with it – and from that failure of understanding and initiative so many other difficulties flowed. This is why she spent so much time criticizing the government's willingness to leave the issue to the 'few fag ends and tag ends and scraps and leavings of [ministers'] already overburdened minds',[145] why she called for a 'new Nansen' or a British executive agency that could act independently. The Inter-Governmental Committee was not this: instead, it simply took all the delays individual governments were subject to and multiplied them many times over. So obvious was it that the IGC was a recipe for delay and obstruction that the Americans explicitly told the British that the Horthy offer 'should not (repeat not) be handled through the Inter-Governmental Committee'.[146]

When it came to 'rescue', Rathbone knew – and Emerson in fact admitted – only individual governments could effectively act.[147] But for that to happen, and as Rathbone understood, 'saving Jews' would have to be, as it were, a war aim: a central plank of government policy, for which officials would work and to which resources and energies would be turned. Had that been the case, politicians would no doubt still have concluded that 'winning the war' was the only real remedy (as indeed it was), but their approach to the question would not have been completely reactive; they might have examined whether more immediate efforts might be possible and might even have decided that not every single one would compromise the war. But consideration, as Rathbone suspected, never really got that far, for 'rescue' continued to be seen as a distraction from, and never as a part of, the war effort – so much so that whenever the question of removing large numbers of Jews came up the Foreign and Home Offices moved quickly to insist on its impossibility, and not only because they were certain that Hitler or the satellite powers would not release Jews, but also because in some instances they feared the burden and (in the Middle East) political damage that would result if they did. There is no doubt that British officials and politicians felt genuine revulsion at Nazi atrocities and (often) genuine sympathy for the Jews; what they did not feel, however, was any immediate responsibility on this issue. Rathbone's arguments that many refugees could have been safe in Britain or Palestine had pre-war policies not been so restrictive, or even that the war might not have happened had Chamberlain not been so craven, cut no ice with them. Britain, they insisted, had responded generously to the pre-war refugee crisis, but could do little for – indeed, could not be saddled with – a victimized foreign population in the midst of war.

'Rescue', as a result, became simply a problem of politics: not 'saving Jews' but managing the political pressure to save Jews became the goal.[148] Key policy decisions – the decision to draw in the Americans after the declaration of 1942, the decision to reconstitute the Inter-Governmental Committee – were taken not because they offered the best prospect for 'rescue' but because they would, as Rathbone charged, 'buy off public agitation as cheaply as possible'.[149] Likewise, while it would have been entirely reasonable for the government to warn 'rescue' campaigners (as it consistently did warn them) against publicity had they had plans afoot that could have been compromised by such attention, as far as one can tell they made this appeal not to protect activity, but to give the illusion of it.[150] The repeated ministerial pledges that the matter was receiving their energetic attention verged on deception of Parliament.

The question remains why the government responded in this way. For the officials, perhaps, the answer is simple. Civil servants in many instances have seen it as their job to deflect external pressure for action or even to point out the many disadvantages of internal proposals, so the fact that they did so in this case is perhaps not so surprising. But that ministers also responded so unimaginatively and inadequately to a profound human tragedy is more troubling. Certainly that fragmentation of ministerial responsibility that Rathbone thought such a problem had something to do with it. In each case 'rescue' would be weighed against, and could possibly compromise, long-standing departmental goals: Oliver Stanley thus adamantly opposed any measure that could undermine Britain's fragile authority in Palestine; Herbert Morrison would always resist proposals that might cause any hardship or disaffection at home (although in Morrison's case secretiveness and obsession with his own authority surely played a role as well). In the absence of a cabinet decision that 'saving Jews' was itself a priority, ministers held to their established responsibilities and goals. Even after the declaration of December 1942, no minister tried to break through this bureaucratic impasse. Churchill, the only person who showed much genuine human sympathy on this question and who had no qualms about causing trouble, was utterly absorbed in the military side of the war; Eden's preoccupation with the damage any large influx of Jewish refugees to Palestine might cause to Britain's position in the Middle East may have prevented him from entirely grasping the scale and significance of the tragedy. The slaughter was not their responsibility, and they put it out of their minds.

Of all the reasons officials gave for why they could not do more to rescue Jews, nothing upset Rathbone more than the claim that to do so would provoke domestic anti-Semitism. Publicly she met such arguments with scorn, telling Morrison at that ill-fated deputation of October 1942 that she simply could not accept that ordinary Britons would greet Jewish refugee children with racial hatred.[151] But with newspapers reporting black-market activity as if it were the preserve of Jews, with MPs in the Commons painting rescue efforts as an un-English plea to give the Jews 'special treatment', and with a trickle of anti-Semitic letters posted to her own door, she grew worried.[152] After the disastrous Commons debate of May 1943, Brodetsky feared that sympathy for the Jews was declining but thought a campaign to rebuild it would be successful only if under-taken by the National Committee.[153] Rathbone agreed, telling the committee in July that it should issue a short pamphlet combating anti-Semitism.[154] One was drafted by the Reverend James Parkes, probably the clergyman most interested in Jewish studies and inter-faith relations, but was so severely criticized by Gollancz that Rathbone herself decided to write a short pamphlet entitled *Falsehoods and Facts about the Jews* over the autumn parliamentary recess.[155]

Gollancz didn't like this one much better. Her psychology was all wrong, he told her. Rathbone had listed a set of common prejudices – 'the Jews control the banks'; 'the Jews shirk military service'; 'foreign Jews are stealing our jobs' – and presented facts and figures to rebut them. But anti-Semitism wasn't based on inad-equate information, Gollancz pointed out, but on 'something much more primi-tive, instinctive and irrational'. 'I am not sure that you *can* combat this deeper thing by appeals to fact and logic' – and because that 'deeper thing' took so little to feed upon, 'even the smallest reinforcement of this instinct will weigh more than the strongest logical argument'. Rathbone had told Gollancz that she would try to win over the 'ordinary' reader by not sounding 'fanatically pro-Jew' and by 'admitting those faults which are almost universally attributed, exaggeratedly but not *entirely* without basis', but that psychology, Gollancz replied, was all wrong: 'If 99% of your pamphlet is an irrefutably logical attack on anti-Semitism, but 1% is a reinforcement of anti-Semitic prejudices, then, I myself feel quite certain, the whole thing does more harm than good: because the number of people, already anti-Semites, whom you will convince by your logic is very small, whereas every existing anti-Semite, or potential anti-Semite, you will reinforce by the 1% in their anti-Semitism.' Gollancz identified some of the more unfortunate gestures towards impartiality needing excision ('some dislike Jews because some of them are flashy . . . ostentatious . . . clannish . . .') and then published the pam-phlet in January 1945.[156] A first run of 10,000 copies quickly sold out.[157]

It is hard to imagine that it had much impact. But if Rathbone was (as Gollancz understood) far too psychologically unsophisticated to be an effective propagan-dist on such questions, the little pamphlet does give us a window into her own heart and mind. Gollancz found the pamphlet distressing because, as he wrote to Eleanor, had he not known her personally he would have concluded that the author was a 'terrifically humanitarian woman' with 'an extremely strong sense of decency and justice' but who 'in her heart of heart . . . really dislikes the Jews'.[158] After witnessing her tireless work for refugees, her persistent kindness to individual Jews, he couldn't think that, and so put that odd tone down simply to a kind of psychological ineptitude. But had he read more carefully, or himself showed more psychological insight, he might have grasped the truth. For while Rathbone was certainly moved by suffering of all kinds, her particular response to the Jews was also grounded in identification. In Palestine in 1935 Rathbone had admired the Jewish settlers' energy and idealism; when Hitler began persecuting German Jews, she was struck by the generosity with which the Anglo-Jewish community had responded; even the faults attributed to 'Jews' – clannishness, tight-fistedness – were ones that this daughter of a provincial merchant dynasty could scarcely see as flaws. That impartial, almost apologetic tone that startled Gollancz was, then, Rathbone's attempt to rein in identification – but in her last few pages she let her true feelings show. It was just jealousy, she wrote, that drove anti-Semitism: people simply resented Jewish achievement and resisted acknowledging 'what the world owes to this wonderful people'.[159] A catalogue of Jewish achievement followed, but it was an idiosyncratic one, since Rathbone – Victorian liberal that she was – couldn't bring herself to laud the accomplishments of either Marx or Freud.

Identification and not simply humanitarian universalism (although that too) inflected all of Rathbone's responses to questions involving Jews. The British had never been 'what Hitler wanted – a pure race', Rathbone told the Commons during a debate on population in July 1943 (right before she drafted *Falsehoods and Facts*): 'If ever there was a mongrel race, it was ours.' Immigration had strengthened and enriched Britain; if anything, the nation had been too slow to take advantage of 'an opportunity which Hitler's lunacy offered us of getting some of the cream of European culture'. When the war was over Britain should let in more foreign immigrants, Rathbone thought, and should offer – in its own interest, and not simply out of generosity – a particular welcome to Jews.[160] Of course, they should open the gates of Palestine as well: Britain's promise of a 'national home' was still unfulfilled; the limitations on immigration set by the White Paper of 1939 had, she was certain, cost tens of thousands of Jewish lives. But if Rathbone, by 1945, was quite strongly Zionist, planting parliamentary questions and working with the Board of Deputies of British Jews to try to force a more generous immigration policy to Palestine,[161] she never thought Jewishness and nationalism were necessarily linked. There was as much of an elective affinity, she thought, between Jewishness and liberalism, Jewishness and feminism – a perception that undergirded her own identification.

Chapter 17

Miss Rathbone in Victory

From 1935 until 1945 Rathbone spent almost all of her time on international questions. True, she made a point of defending women's interests in the House; she was the obvious person to speak at the twenty-first and twenty-fifth 'birthday parties' for women's suffrage held in 1939 and 1943. But if she had entered the Commons with a reputation for 'extreme feminism', by 1945 she was known and respected for her expertise on social policy, her work for refugees and her unimpeachable record as an anti-appeaser.

Contrary to what one might expect, that absorption in other issues did the cause of family allowances nothing but good. It was inconceivable that Britain would have introduced a comprehensive system of family allowances in the 1930s; dogged concentration on this question would have branded Rathbone as a crank and won her nothing but scorn. But in the 1940s, when conditions finally changed and comprehensive social reform became possible, the ties and credibility she had amassed through those years became important. For by the mid-forties not only had Rathbone built up ties through her international, imperial or social work with Attlee, Amery, Butler, Woolton, Eden, Wilkinson and other members of the wartime government, but literally hundreds of MPs had played some role (if only to sign a resolution) in one of her backbench pressure groups and come to trust her judgement and impartiality. The 1935 Parliament, remember, was in session for ten years, five under a professed 'national' government and five under a genuine cross-party coalition – long enough for this group of 615 men (and women) to come to know one another fairly well, for cross-party alliances to evolve, and even – sometimes – for the division between the front and back benches to have an unexpected importance.

If we appreciate that parliamentary context and Rathbone's place within it, we can better understand the passage of the Family Allowances Act. Journalists, politicians and officials at the time certainly saw the Act as Rathbone's personal achievement; by contrast, historians (myself included) have paid more attention to the wartime context. The Act was only one part of the family-centred meliorist reform articulated in the Beveridge Plan, some of us have argued; family

30. Rathbone speaking at the 25th anniversary of women's suffrage, 20 February 1943. Margaret Bondfield is first from the left, Nancy Astor third from the right.

allowances became attractive to the Treasury because they were linked to efforts to restrain wages, others of us contend. Yet, insofar as they overlook that unusual parliamentary context, those explanations fall short.[1] For, at the most basic level, the Family Allowances Act was passed because the wartime House of Commons insisted upon it, against Treasury wishes and despite ministerial indifference. Eleanor Rathbone had much to do with that insistence.

By the late 1930s, Rathbone already saw the prospects for family allowances brightening. The 'poverty studies' of the thirties had proliferated, establishing beyond challenge the degree to which child dependency and family poverty were locked in a tight embrace. Experts on public health, social insurance and child welfare were, by this point, almost uniformly favourable, and even Rathbone's warnings of population decline, which had been greeted with laughter in the Commons in 1936, gained a hearing as war loomed.[2] Leo Amery was no longer a lone Conservative supporter, for Rathbone's younger anti-appeasement colleagues (Boothby, Macmillan, Sandys, even Eden) had converted as well, while a growing number of forward-looking industrialists had introduced private schemes. For the first time the issue was moving without her prodding.

Although absorbed in her refugee work, Rathbone tried to promote and channel that interest. In the spring of 1938 she asked the government to set up a Royal Commission (and was refused); with Eva Hubback, she revived the languishing Family Endowment Society.[3] And in August 1938 she prepared for a new parliamentary campaign by asking Allen & Unwin to publicize *The Disinherited Family* again. Fearing that the firm hadn't found the book 'a very profit-making proposition' (there were still considerable numbers in stock), she offered to bear the cost of advertising herself. Raymond Unwin wouldn't hear of it. It was true that they had not 'become rich over the publication of *The Disinherited Family*', he wrote to Rathbone, but they had 'nevertheless at no time regretted the privilege of association with your work'. They would be happy to publicize the book again – which, judging from the pick-up in discussion, found new readers.[4]

It was the war, however, that really made the difference. Those child poverty and populationist concerns immediately became more pressing,[5] and the war generated some new arguments all its own. The most important of these was made by John Maynard Keynes who, although unwell, spent the autumn of 1939 working out his ideas on war finance. The danger, Keynes thought, was that wartime full employment (and hence increased purchasing power) would simply lead to inflation, as it had in the First World War. In November 1939, in two influential articles in *The Times*, he thus proposed that the government capture that growth in purchasing power for the war effort by taxing higher incomes and compulsorily 'deferring' earnings on lower incomes, while at the same time protecting living standards by holding free of tax a minimum income that would vary with family size.[6] But how much simpler it would be, Leo Amery responded, to protect living standards amid wartime financial stringency by introducing a universal system of children's allowances.[7] Keynes, who met with Rathbone and Hubback to discuss the question on 17 January 1940, soon thought so as well.[8] By February, when he published *How to Pay for the War*, that proposal for a tax-free minimum had metamorphosed into a straightforward scheme of universal family allowances, a proposal he presented to Rathbone's All-Party Parliamentary Action Group that same month.[9]

Keynes's proposals aroused some interest in the Treasury but were received with such hostility by Labour and trade union leaders that they were quickly dropped, especially when Treasury officials concluded that price rises were levelling off and that food subsidies, rationing, and extended milk and meals schemes would be a better way to maintain living standards anyway.[10] Yet his conversion brought new respectability to the cause and helped Rathbone and Amery consolidate an emerging cross-party backbench alliance. Throughout the winter and spring of 1940 she and Amery – not yet a minister and rather at a loose end – did a considerable amount of writing, public speaking and lobbying in favour of allowances, and in spring 1940 Rathbone summarized the anti-poverty, demographic, feminist and wartime arguments in a hundred-page Penguin Special, *The Case for Family Allowances*.[11] The fall of the Chamberlain government and the

Battle of Britain lowered that level of activism, as Amery moved into government and Rathbone turned her attention to the trials of interned refugees, but by this point the issue had a momentum of its own. Labour members, embarrassed to find their movement cited as the main stumbling block to allowances, were pressing the TUC to revisit their 1930 veto, and in January 1941 Seebohm Rowntree, still the foremost poverty expert, endorsed a universal scheme.[12] In April 1941, then, when Rathbone and the Conservative MP and RAF officer John Allan Cecil Wright gave notice of a motion that the House 'would welcome the introduction of a national state paid scheme of allowances for dependent children, payable to their mothers or acting guardians, as a means of safeguarding the health and well-being of the rising generation',[13] the resolution quickly gained the support of more than 150 members, including more than fifty Labour MPs.

Confronted by such backbench mobilization, the Chancellor of the Exchequer, Sir Kingsley Wood, agreed to draw up an estimate of the cost of a scheme of allowances and to receive a deputation.[14] At that June 1941 gathering, Rathbone voiced considerable impatience with the government, challenging Wood 'to produce a single expert in economics, in industrial welfare, in sociology, who has really studied it who has not come down in favour of family allowances'. The Cabinet, she charged, was simply hiding behind 'a small but vocal number of Trade Union leaders' who were 'jealous that the wage-earning classes should obtain anything except through their method of collective bargaining'. But while Wood did retort that the government could not go forward without the 'whole-hearted support' of the trade union movement,[15] by spring 1941 the General Council itself was having trouble holding out. Anyone following the issue knew that the Labour Party Executive was favourable; there were fierce debates at the party and Trades Union Congress conferences that summer. In this situation, the TUC's General Secretary Sir Walter Citrine, in 1930 a decisive voice against family allowances, began to think it prudent for the labour movement to come round. Ernest Bevin remained hostile to any attempt to adapt wages to needs (or, as he always put it, to pay workers on a 'fodder basis'), but Bevin was now Minister of Labour and presumably well placed to guard against adverse effects on wages. In March 1942, then, after the Labour Party Executive asked them again to reconsider their views, the General Council decided (not unanimously) to support a state-paid scheme of family allowances.[16]

With the acquiescence of the TUC, parliamentary pressure became impossible to resist. On 7 May 1942, the government's White Paper providing information on the cost of allowances (which had been ready for more than a year) was finally published, and on 23 June Wright and Rathbone's long-tabled motion urging immediate consideration of 'a national scheme of allowances for dependent children' passed the Commons easily.[17] But if family allowances were by June 1942 (as The Times put it) 'an agreed principle', they were one the Treasury hoped to fend off for as long as possible.[18] With the danger of inflation minimized, and substantial sums already being spent on food subsidies, social services, and allowances for soldiers' dependants and evacuees, the Treasury saw no case at all for the introduction of allowances in wartime. Wood thus played for time, acknowledging the merits of the anti-poverty case for allowances but insisting that government consideration must wait not only upon a formal TUC decision (expected that summer) and further financial review, but also upon the recommendations of the recently appointed committee headed by Sir William Beveridge to review social insurance.[19] This latter requirement was purely a delaying tactic, for Beveridge was known to be strongly in favour; Wood can hardly have been surprised when family allowances emerged as an 'assumption' of his comprehensive social insurance plan.[20] For the Treasury, however, the entanglement of children's allowances in the general consideration of the Beveridge Report usefully ensured that the financial cost of such allowances would be considered against other parts of that wider scheme and delayed legislation for two years.

During that long pause, control of the issue slipped out of Rathbone's hands. It wasn't just that she was, after December 1942, almost entirely caught up in the campaign to rescue Europe's threatened Jews – so much so, indeed, that she found the attention given to the Beveridge Report disproportionate and almost unseemly. It was also that, once Beveridge and (still more) the experts and actuaries from the Ministry of Pensions got involved, she and other activists were inevitably pushed aside. She and Hubback presented evidence to the Beveridge Committee, kept up a stream of letters to the newspapers, and led another deputation to Wood and Sir William Jowitt (who was coordinating the government's response to the Beveridge proposals),[21] but once the Cabinet decided in February 1943 to accept the principle of family allowances without an income limit for all children beyond the first, and civil servants began concentrating on such technical questions as whether the family should be defined by ties of blood or maintenance, Rathbone's strident arguments about population decline, or poverty, or women's rights seemed beside the point.[22] Sir Thomas Sheepshanks, who was coordinating the officials' work, made time to see Rathbone and Hubback ('I do not see how one can readily decline to see Miss Rathbone')[23] but emerged from the meeting unimpressed. The two ladies might have studied the question, he said, but they had 'only the most nebulous ideas' about the technical difficulties. His impression was that they were 'so delighted at having the principle accepted that had not worried much about the details'.[24]

But the devil is in the detail, and as officials worked those out they pared down the scheme's size and scope. Beveridge himself had decided to cut costs by omitting the first child but had insisted that the allowance for all other children be set at a 'subsistence' rate of nine shillings per week (eight shillings in cash and one in services); officials and ministers, however, were eager to make it clear that allowances were *not* intended to meet all needs and whittled that rate down to five shillings. By 1944, this was not much money, less than half the amount paid for a child under the scheme of army separation allowances, but Rathbone was not well placed to object to such cheese-paring. The five-shilling rate was the one the Family Endowment Society had tended to use as their baseline for two decades, while in *The Case for Family Allowances* Rathbone herself had pointed to omitting the first child as the most palatable means of reducing costs.[25] She had always been a gradualist, had always urged women to say, when told they could not have moon, '[a]t least let us have that little star, just near the horizon'.[26] But Rathbone did have one absolute requirement, on which she would not compromise – as officials discovered, when they decided to cross her.

This was that the allowance be paid to the mother. Rathbone's campaign had begun, after all, as an effort to combat the personal dependence of women on men; early schemes thus focused on the endowment of *mothers* and only secondarily of children. Pragmatism, and then the economic depression and the decline in the birth rate, had led Rathbone to jettison the demand for a separate allowance for the mother and to stress anti-poverty or pro-natalist reasons to introduce children's allowances; certainly she was, by the 1940s, allied with people for whom payment to the mother mattered not at all. And yet, even in 1942, when Wright opened the debate in the Commons by summarizing three arguments for allowances – the anti-poverty argument, the pro-natalist argument, and the anti-inflation argument – Rathbone was quick to jump in with a fourth. 'We want children and their mothers to be recognized not as dependants hung around the necks of their fathers and husbands,' she said, 'but as human beings, with their own feet on the floor of God's earth and their heads in the sunshine – and more sunshine than is allowed now to trickle through the windows of their dingy and overcrowded homes.'[27] Politicians, officials and other MPs all knew how much this meant to her: when Rathbone and Hubback had called on him, Sheepshanks minuted, the two women were most emphatic on this point.[28]

Perhaps this is why officials simply couldn't bring themselves to concede. Had payment to the mother been defined simply as a practical matter, it might perhaps have been palatable. But because Rathbone saw it as *meaningful* – as, indeed, the heart and soul of the whole scheme – officials and ministers balked. It didn't seem to matter that virtually all foreign countries paid allowances to the mother (without any reference to women's rights), or that maternity benefit was already paid to the mother, or that both men and women (when surveyed) strongly favoured payment to the mother, or even that the General Council of the TUC, when asked point-blank, rather grumpily endorsed it as well.[29] Somehow, officials and ministers simply could not take this step. The committee of officials reviewing the Beveridge proposals considered the choice of recipient a policy question and left the matter to the Cabinet Committee on Reconstruction Priorities; that committee discussed the question twice in 1943 but simply recorded its disagreement; in early 1944 the matter went to the Cabinet's Reconstruction Committee, which also found itself divided with a 'slight preponderance in favour of payment of the allowances to the father'.[30] Jowitt, although himself favourable to payment to the mother, in some frustration allowed the White Paper to confirm that majority view.

In mid-1944, Rathbone learned how the wind was blowing. The forthcoming White Paper on social insurance was likely to include a scheme of family allowances, she wrote in *The Times* on 26 June (from Westminster hospital), but might well not include payment to the mother. This would be 'a disaster', for while changes could be made in rates later on, a decision of this kind, once made, might prove impossible to undo. Payment to the mother would 'raise the status of motherhood' and reduce the likelihood of the money being diverted to other purposes; it was the common practice in other countries and backed even in Britain by a consensus.[31] *The Times* agreed, and the women's societies, alerted by Rathbone, began mobilizing as well.[32] When the White Paper on social insurance, published in September 1944, stated that the allowance belonged to the father (while stipulating that it would be 'natural and appropriate' for him to deputize his wife to draw it),[33] Rathbone, Hubback and Violet Bonham-Carter led a deputation from about twenty-five of the main women's organizations to Sir William Jowitt in protest.[34] But the government, now well into its planning process, paid little attention. When the Family Allowances Bill was published in February 1945, it stated simply that where the man and wife were living together, the allowance would belong to the man.

Neither ministers nor officials were prepared for the response. Not until 6 March, two days before the bill's second reading, did the Cabinet wake up to the fact that it was facing a cross-party backbench rebellion. Sir William Jowitt had that day received an all-party deputation insisting that the allowance be made the property of the mother, Anthony Eden reported, and all evidence was that the claim would be widely supported in the House. The Labour Party, now aware of the strength of public opinion on the question, might also move an amendment to change the word 'man' to 'woman'. At this point, the Cabinet – with a long self-justifying statement about how the Reconstruction Committee had simply been following the legal advice given it – agreed that it could not force a solution 'on a matter where public sentiment was so closely engaged'. The question would be left to a free vote.[35]

Jowitt, in introducing the bill's second reading on 8 March, tried to calm tempers down. There were reasonable practical arguments in favour of payment to either the mother or the father, and in the normal happy family 'it really will not matter very much . . . what is done'.[36] But Rathbone, who had been allowed to initiate the debate in light of her standing as 'the grandmother of this proposal', refused Jowitt's implicit offer of victory at the cost of agreeing to the whole matter's insignificance. She was not exaggerating the significance of payment to the mother, she said; it truly was 'of immense importance'. For the first time, the state would accept that the maintenance of children should be in part a public charge, yet it proposed to do so in such a way as to limit its likely effectiveness and weaken the social and familial standing of those who actually had the care of children in their hands. True, the great majority of fathers, being 'kindly, responsible men', would no doubt turn the money directly over to their wives, but if even one in ten appropriated it for themselves – or reduced the house-keeping allowance in consequence – a very substantial number of children would be harmed. Still more damaging, however, would be the consequences for women's standing and self-respect. The Cabinet, being composed of men, 'cannot be expected to realise how women think on this question', but she wanted to warn them of 'the intensity of women's feelings'. By its thoughtless action, the government was allowing 'sex antagonism' again 'to raise its ugly head'; if they had to, the women's societies would make sure every woman knew how her representative had voted at the forthcoming election. Indeed, if it were not amended, she herself would not vote for the final bill, 'although I have worked for this thing for over 25 years'.[37]

Shocked by Rathbone's vehemence, the next few speakers did their best to shove the genie of sex antagonism back into the bottle. Good, decent working-class fathers would certainly wish the allowance to be paid to the mother, insisted the Labour MP James Griffiths; even to discuss the relative merits of husband and wife was 'the wrong way of approach'. Labour women, Jennie Adamson agreed, did not 'take a purely feminist attitude', but looked at the matter as house-wives handling family budgets, from 'the commonsense point of view'. The first Conservative speaker chimed in to agree that payment to the mother should be based on such 'constructive and practical arguments and not, if I may say so without disrespect, the arguments put forward by the hon. Lady the Member for the Combined English Universities', and even Rathbone's ally Wright thought it 'a great pity to discuss the question of whether fathers or mothers are more suitable'.[38] But Mavis Tate, Nancy Astor, Arthur Salter, William Beveridge and especially Edith Summerskill all spoke up to insist that the issue was indeed fun-damentally one of women's rights. Questions of status were not unaffected by parliamentary enactments, Salter pointed out, and Rathbone was quite right to insist that payment to the father would have an unfortunate impact on the posi-tion of women: 'It would have thrown us back from the conception of marriage as a partnership into patriarchy.'[39] Since there was virtually no support in the House for payment to the father ('the women have decided that they are going to get the 5s., and all of us accept that,' said the Labour MP George Buchanan),[40] in the committee stage the bill was quietly amended to make the allowance the property of the mother.

This was Rathbone's victory – but then, so was the Family Allowances Act itself. Family allowances never had any real support in Cabinet (Amery, the only governmental enthusiast, was not in Cabinet), were disliked by the Treasury and the Ministry of Labour, won the support of the three major parties only in 1941 and 1942, and were viewed by most employers and trade unionists with grudging tolerance at best. At every stage, it was backbench enthusiasm, organized by Rathbone, that forced the policy forward. This was especially true in May 1945, when, following the withdrawal of the Labour ministers from the government, cross-party pressure was put on Churchill's caretaker administration to put the bill through its final stages before a new election. The passage of the Act was not, then, a victory of Treasury inflation-fighters over trade union activists, nor even really a victory of feminists over defenders of male rights. It was, rather, a victory of Parliament over officialdom, of backbenchers over ministers, and of cross-party feeling over party loyalty. And it was a victory, especially, for the woman who incarnated that cross-party, backbench spirit.

During those final stages, MPs showed a real awareness of the ways in which Rathbone's 'independence' and the 'independence' of the House had productively reinforced each other. There were the usual attempts at partisan point-scoring, of course. Both Labour and Conservative MPs insisted that their party had been more vigorous in support, and Rhys Davies, Rathbone's most vituperative trade unionist antagonist from the late 1920s, even asserted volubly (and mendaciously) that the trade union movement had never opposed a state-funded scheme. But whenever such claims were made, from some corner of the House a voice would come, pointing out that family allowances had emerged outside the context of party politics and had gained support only through Rathbone's 'indefatigable work'.[41] It was nice to know, those backbenchers said, that there was 'still a place in English politics and in English political life for those rare persons like the hon. Lady', persons who – against party indifference and popular prejudice – could take an important idea and, with perseverance, bring it to fruition.[42] Nancy Astor, herself such a very bad party woman, put it best. 'When family allowances were first mooted people on this side of the House said that it would break up the home, and the Labour Party and the trade unions would not have them at all,' she said during the second reading. 'We have come a great way since then, and all because of one revolutionary woman. It is very difficult, when we look at the hon. Lady the Member for the English Universities, to think of her as a revolutionary, but she is, and it is her work, and her vision and courage, that have really brought us where we are to-day.'[43]

For Rathbone, those parliamentary debates were something of an ordeal. She was still not very well: her legs kept acting up, and she had to attend the third reading in a wheelchair. The other Rathbone now in parliament – Beatrice Rathbone, widow of William Gair's grandson John Rankin Rathbone, who had (with Eleanor's encouragement) taken over her airman husband's seat when he was killed on a raid over Germany – wheeled Eleanor to the bar of the Commons.[44] She sat there, Harold Nicolson recalled, 'flustered and surprised' as the tributes and cheers rained down.[45] 'It might seem rather ungracious, when somebody is being congratulated upon her baby, to point out the defects of the baby,' she said, after thanking everyone. 'Yet I feel I must point out that this baby is a very little one. . . . [I]t will have to be a good deal fattened and cossetted before it reaches its proper stature.'[46] She must have hoped that that 'cossetting' could be left, finally, in someone else's hands.

In early 1945, as her long campaign appeared to be heading for victory, Rathbone considered standing down at the next election. She was almost seventy-three, the oldest of the sitting women MPs, and thought she should give younger people a chance. There were also personal reasons to consider. Late in the war, Elizabeth Macadam was diagnosed with the cancer that would ultimately kill her. We know nothing about the doctor's prognosis, or about how Eleanor and Elizabeth took this news, but Elizabeth's illness must have had something to do with the tiredness and strain that friends noticed in Eleanor in 1944 and 1945. For a time she and Macadam considered retiring to the countryside, but then decided instead to look for a more comfortable London house. The Tufton Court arrangement had been ramshackle and *very* cramped, with the 'best bedroom' used as a secretary's office and the dining room turned into a 'bed-sit' for Eleanor (who often wrote at night). Now, with the war drawing to a close and her beloved friend unwell, Eleanor finally sold Oakfield, her Liverpool house (which she had rented out for years), and bought the kind of house a woman of her means might have been expected to have. Twenty-six Hampstead Lane in Highgate, to which she and Elizabeth moved in April 1945, had big sunny rooms, a large garden, a two-car garage for 'Jane Austen' (now back from war service) and a view of Kenwood. 'We reconcile our consciences to its size by having a married couple with three children to look after us,' Rathbone would write to her wartime secretary Joan Prewer ('Prue'), of whom she was very fond; by the end of the year they had also taken in a Polish couple expecting a baby.[47]

Hampstead Lane would have been a comfortable house for Eleanor and Elizabeth in retirement, but by the time they moved in Eleanor had abandoned her plan to stand down. She was still absorbed in refugee and international questions, and her political position, reinforced by the family allowances victory, had never been stronger. The few friends she consulted told her that if her health were up to it she should certainly carry on, and Elizabeth raised no objection.[48] In late June and early July, Eleanor thus spent a week speaking at the civic universities for what she was certain would be her last electoral fight. In a sense, she needn't have bothered, for the contest was a rout. Of 20,973 first preference votes cast for six candidates, Rathbone gained 11,176 – more than all her five opponents put together and almost 8,000 more than the second-place candidate. Every single one of those opponents, lemming-like, also claimed to be an 'independent', and the one closest to Rathbone's own politics, Kenneth Lindsay (formerly General Secretary of Political and Economic Planning), won the second seat on the strength of her transferred superfluous votes.

She was gratified by her win, of course, but Labour's landslide victory in the 1945 election aroused more mixed emotions. 'Leftish' though she felt herself, her enthusiasm for economic reconstruction and social reform had always been tempered by her commitment to voluntary effort and civic activism, ideals that found little place in Labour's statist plans. In her election address she had hoped openly for a renewed cross-party coalition. Who better to determine labour policy than Bevin; who better to entrust with social reform than the author of the Beveridge Plan?[49] She had less confidence, however, in Attlee or Morrison's ability to cope with the complicated problems of the post-war European settlement, and it is a sign of how completely she had become absorbed in international matters that she put these issues first. Two worries possessed her. Before the war, Rathbone had been among those most eager to ally with the Soviets against Hitler, but she had no illusions about Stalin's democratic principles, and in 1944 and 1945 was one of the few left-leaning MPs to denounce the deportations of Polish officers to the Soviet Union. (She even persuaded Clementine Churchill to raise the issue with Ivan Maisky, the Soviet Ambassador to Britain from 1932 to 1943, on a trip to Russia in early 1945.)[50] The prospect that Britain would have 'a new Government without Mr Churchill and Mr Eden in it to "stand up to Stalin"', she wrote to Clementine, filled her with dismay.[51]

Soviet score-settling and repression in the East was one worry, but Allied policy towards Germany – for which she felt more directly responsible – preoccupied her still more. Not only were the Western Allies giving way to Soviet claims for territory and hegemony in the East and colluding in the wave of brutal 'ethnic cleansing' through which the Poles and Czechs drove their German minorities into the shrunken Reich,[52] but Britain itself seemed poised to repeat all the mistakes of 1918. Ever since his retirement from the Foreign Office in 1941, Sir Robert Vansittart (now Baron Vansittart) had been writing articles and giving speeches ascribing Nazism to an aggressive, militaristic spirit deeply rooted in the German character and recommending that Germany be administratively decentralized, partially de-industrialized, permanently disarmed, and occupied for a very long time.[53] Rathbone disagreed, but in 1945, as the full horror of the extermination camps finally entered the public mind, she could not (nor did she wish to) argue her case simply on pragmatic grounds. If Germany was to be rebuilt and not permanently 'broken', still more if individual Britons were to sacrifice a share of their own scarce amenities to that rebuilding, questions of guilt and innocence, of collective and individual responsibility, would have to be faced. In 1945, she and Victor Gollancz faced them together.

At first glance, the two seem an odd couple: the enthusiastic but overbearing left-wing publisher and the indomitable but emotionally distant spinster MP. Yet, as their collaboration in the 'rescue' campaign showed, when it came to humanitarian questions, they saw exactly eye to eye. Both had responded as radical moral individualists. Gollancz, we recall, urged the readers of 'Let My People

Go' to apprehend the precious individual life within 'the abstraction of numbers'. Rathbone reminded Britons to ask themselves always 'what can *I* do'?

The maelstrom of revenge and misery that was Germany's lot at the war's end elicited the same response. Already in late 1944, in a Commons debate on war crimes, Rathbone had argued against the idea of collective guilt. She was not some sort of sentimentalist seeking to pardon Germans for their crimes, she told MPs. Almost every night it was her 'painful duty to read almost unreadable accounts of the brutal cruelties committed by Nazis against innocent victims, Jewish and others'; she believed absolutely in the need to bring their perpetrators to justice. But it was neither just nor prudent to generalize: some Germans had resisted Hitler, and if MPs felt that resistance had been too little, they should ask themselves whether, in a repressive regime, 'we should have been quite as courageous in open opposition as we now feel ought to have been the case'.[54] Gollancz, in April 1945, pressed that argument further. In *The Meaning of Buchenwald*, a pamphlet that, like *'Let My People Go'*, sold more than 150,000 copies within weeks, he not only drew attention to the fact that Germans had been brutalized there as well but also suggested that those living in democratic countries who had done nothing for Jewish rescue were now ill-placed to throw stones. Small wonder some readers found the pamphlet slippery and enraging in its claim that shared nationality and proximity did not bring with it a special measure of responsibility for crimes committed in one's name.[55] But to Rathbone, for whom sins of omission were always of the darkest hue, Gollancz's arguments made sense. She was planning to write a second pamphlet on similar lines, she told the National Committee for Rescue from Nazi Terror at a meeting in June 1945.[56] Bringing perpetrators to justice was one thing, but the columns of sick and starving old people and children making their way westwards were not Nazi murderers and needed help now.

In August 1945, officials at the Foreign Office were thus perplexed to receive from the National Committee not only the usual pleas for special rations or visas to Britain for Jews who had survived the camps, but also a request that Britain release emergency food stores to cope with the waves of famished refugees pouring into Germany. Officials were not persuaded. Most of the problems were in the Eastern zone where they had no authority, they minuted privately, so unless public opinion in the United Kingdom and the United States became too agitated, the matter should be left to the Soviets.[57] Gollancz was already doing his best to stir up just such an 'agitation'. Early in September, he, Rathbone and another six of the 'usual suspects' (the churchmen Henry Carter, Sidney Berry and Bishop Bell; the academics and intellectuals A.D. Lindsay, Bertrand Russell and Gilbert Murray) printed an appeal in the *Daily Herald*, the *News Chronicle* and the *Manchester Guardian*. Two paragraphs detailed the wretched conditions of the 'horde of Germans . . . struggling daily into Berlin' and estimated that in the Eastern zone altogether there could be as many as 13 million 'homeless nomads' wandering in search of food. A third paragraph urged the Allied armies to release their stocks of food and to solve the transport problem. It was the last bit, however, that carried the punch. The British government probably felt it could not ask its people, after six years of war, to sacrifice their rations to avert mass starvation on the continent, but 'we do not think that the Government need feel such hesitation'. 'It is not in accordance with the traditions of this country to allow children – even the children of ex-enemies – to starve', and many Britons would surely wish to make 'some voluntary sacrifice in this cause'. Any who might share this view, the appeal closed, should send a postcard to 'Save Europe Now' (as the campaign called itself) at 144 Southampton Row.[58]

Within the month 30,000 postcards had come in; by the end of the year there would be 60,000. Gollancz, who thrived on just such public approbation, was soon in his element, hiring Peggy Duff (who would run many such campaigns) to organize an office and recruiting an impressive roster of the great and the good. Bishop Bell, Violet Bonham-Carter and Richard Crossman were among the speakers at a major public meeting held on 8 October in London's Conway Hall – a meeting so successful that Rathbone, at the last minute, had to take the chair for an overflow meeting down the road. Those audiences enthusiastically called on the government to negotiate with the Soviets, the Poles and the Czechs to stop the mass expulsions, to develop an Allied policy for the reception of refugees, to revive production on the Ruhr as soon as possible, to release food reserves, and – most importantly – to allow Save Europe Now to go ahead with a voluntary scheme to send food parcels to Germany.[59]

But when Gollancz, Rathbone and a host of distinguished supporters (among them Beveridge, Crossman, Boothby and Quintin Hogg) called on Prime Minister Attlee on 26 October and a second deputation waited on Ben Smith, Labour's new Minister of Food, two weeks later, they met with a frosty reception. Almost all their proposals were impractical, Smith's private secretary wrote to Gollancz on 20 November. The suggestion that individuals be allowed voluntarily to surrender points would upset the distribution of rationed food; proposals to collect soap, unused adult confectionery rations or restaurant points were essentially proposals to cut general rations and could not be entertained. A plan to collect used clothing was not the business of the Ministry of Food; the request that they be allowed to send individual food parcels would only feed the black market. Save Europe Now could raise money for relief societies if it liked, but those relief societies would not be allowed to purchase foods or goods that were in short supply. Britain had already sent 850,000 tons of food to Europe since the end of the war, he pointed out, beside which any voluntary effort would be quite insignificant. Too much emphasis was being given to enabling voluntary contributions.[60]

'Really, Sir Ben, we don't like this Führer attitude,' Rathbone hit back in a speech at a major rally in the end of November at the Albert Hall.[61] Since (as she had told the Commons in October) 'all suffering is individual suffering, . . . all

responsibility is individual responsibility', voluntary action was never superfluous but mattered in ways that – if hard to quantify – were crucial to civic health.[62]
Voluntary effort – that 'gift of self' – ennobled the giver as much as the recipient, cultivating those sentiments of caring and compassion on which any humane
society (or indeed any humane international order) must be based. The 60,000
individuals who had volunteered to spare rations were not ignorant idealists who
should just leave everything to the government, she said at the Albert Hall rally,
especially since many of them were housewives, ever mindful of their children's
welfare and 'accustomed to struggling with the mysteries of coupons and points'.
Reading through the letters and postcards those women sent, she felt 'prouder
than ever of being an Englishwoman', impressed less by the generosity they
showed, great as that was, than by their sense of individual responsibility.

> They did not say, 'The Germans brought it on themselves.' They did not say,
> 'The Americans have far more to spare than we. Let them feed Europe.' They
> did not say, 'The Government has done much already. It is doing its best. We
> leave it to the Government.' They said in effect: 'There is starvation in Central
> Europe and perhaps even beyond it. There is cold and hunger just short of
> starvation, what can *I* do about it?'

This was the voice of '*real* democracy', to which politicians should give way.[63]
Attlee, however, had no intention of giving way. Voluntary schemes such as those
proposed by Save Europe Now, he wrote Gollancz shortly in a letter of 17
December, 'could not make an effective contribution to the solution of this
problem in Europe, even though they might satisfy the consciences of particular
individuals'.[64] Their campaign, he implied, was simply a form of self-indulgence
– a way to salve their own conscience without improving the lot of Germans in
any measurable way.

One can understand Attlee's position. He was the Prime Minister of Britain, a
country that had exhausted its wealth and its people in a just war it had neither
desired nor caused. He had been elected to salvage a decent life for its common
people from that wreckage, and could be forgiven for thinking it his job, when
resources were scarce, to put those people first. Patient, self-effacing, and a 'party
man' to a fault, Attlee doubtless also found the flamboyant and oppositionalist
Gollancz profoundly irritating. Gollancz's campaigns, Peggy Duff recalled (albeit
affectionately) were run autocratically and dominated by his personality; moreover, being 'frequently contrapuntal', he always 'had the urge to help those who
had the least claim on his concern'.[65] Moved to tears by starving Germans,
he had (as his biographer remarks) 'neither the will nor the ability to put
himself less dramatically in the shoes of the majority of his countrymen –
physically healthy but sick to death of spam fritters'. Nor, as one friend
truthfully pointed out (ending the friendship by this observation), had Gollancz

any idea what it actually meant to live on one's rations, since he ate many of his meals in restaurants. He was not a hypocrite, for his responses were emotional and utterly genuine (hence his effectiveness), but to a man like Attlee, and indeed to the Labour Cabinet, his holier-than-thou needling must have been hard to take.[66]

Rathbone, however, admired Gollancz greatly. His very excess and ebullience made him attractive to her; he was, like Churchill, just the sort of person she liked. She had faith in his good-heartedness and didn't mind that he wasn't, always, entirely consistent. Predictably, she was far harder on herself. No more than Gollancz did Rathbone know what it meant to manage on her rations, since she left all that to Elizabeth, but the 'rescue' campaign and then the desperate news from the continent seem to have put her off her food. Even as a girl Eleanor had had trouble remembering meals; now she didn't even try. The photographs from the mid-1940s tell the story. In middle age Eleanor was an imposing physical presence: her secretaries described her as 'large', 'stout' ('North-country sort of stout') and recalled her 'sort of floating' into the room when she wanted something done.[67] But between 1942 and 1945 Eleanor must have lost a substantial amount of weight, for in photographs taken towards the end of the war she looks much thinner, much older, and drawn. Some of that loss may have been deliberate, for Elizabeth always worried about Eleanor's weight, but only after 1942 did the pounds begin to fall off.[68] Eleanor was not Simone Weil, starving herself out of painful fellow-feeling, but nor was she someone who could urge sacrifices on others that she was not willing to make. Smoking was now the only vice left to her, and it hardly improved her health.

Through the desperate years of 1946 and 1947 Gollancz and Peggy Duff kept Save Europe Now going. They deluged Attlee and his two successive Ministers of Food with pleas to allow their voluntary schemes, raised money for relief efforts, and, in late 1946, finally extracted permission from a reluctant government for individuals to send food parcels to Germany. Unfortunately, the parcel post to Germany had not yet opened, so for six weeks Save Europe Now organized shipments themselves – an effort that involved working out a special franking scheme, setting up depots all over London and the provinces, lining up volunteers to handle the queues of donors, wrapping and arranging transport for many tens of thousands of parcels (the Air Ministry gave them 1,000 pounds' transport per day for three weeks), and establishing contacts to arrange distribution within Germany itself. It was, Peggy Duff recalled, 'a tremendous strain on a small organisation', but an accomplishment of which Rathbone would have been extraordinarily proud.[69] In the grand scheme of things, those food parcels may have been only a drop in a well of need, but they did more (as Rathbone would have predicted) to re-knit bonds of humanity and fellow-feeling between Britons and Germans than many larger, more institutional, efforts.

Sadly, Rathbone was not there to see it. On the evening of 2 January 1946, after a morning spent writing an appeal for Save Europe Now and an afternoon at the dentist, Eleanor sat down to dinner with Elizabeth in the new Highgate house. She had been complaining of headaches over the past weeks; now, she cried out in sudden pain. It was a brain aneurysm, probably, or possibly a stroke. She died instantly. Eva Hubback, across town, received a distraught phone call and hurried to Elizabeth's side; Gollancz, shocked and saddened, sent out that last circular. Across London, pressure groups and lobbies – the Abyssinia Association, Save Europe Now, the Parliamentary Committee on Refugees, the Family Endowment Society – gathered together to decide what to do now that one of their animating spirits was gone.

One of these was the National Committee for Rescue from Nazi Terror. The 'Nazi Terror' was over but the committee was still at work, pressing the government to admit Jews and intervening in debates over post-war refugee policy. It was, however, a shadow of its former self. Victor Cazalet had died in 1943; the Archbishop of Canterbury at the end of 1944; Lord Crewe in 1945. Now Eleanor Rathbone, its founder and moving spirit, was gone as well. On 10 January 1946, its main supporters met to discuss the committee's future, but without her, of course, it wouldn't have one. The meeting stood in silence in memory of Miss Rathbone.[70]

The Lady Vanishes

FIRST pay-day under the Family Allowances Act took place yesterday. For more than 20 years Eleanor Rathbone advocated financial aid for parenthood. Before she died last January, aged 73, she saw her major proposals accepted and about to become law.

But if she were alive today it is likely that her voice would be heard in protest against one aspect of the new Act. That is the decision to reduce relief payments for tuberculosis and public assistance from families receiving family allowances. A selection of letters below shows what readers think of this new Means Test.

31. The spectre of Eleanor Rathbone presides over the first payout of family allowances, cartoon by 'Vicky' (Victor Weisz), 1946.

In July 1939, as the war clouds gathered, Eleanor wrote a few lines about what should be done with her body after death. The best thing, she thought, would be to send it to a medical school for dissection, 'preferably one where women students are taken'. How unfair that only the poor and friendless ended up on the dissecting table! They would dislike it so much if they knew; she, on the other hand, didn't mind a bit. 'My own feeling is that whether the soul survives the body or not, and of that I am not sure, *my body is not me* and of no more importance than a cast-off garment. I have no sentiment whatever about it, except that I should rather like to feel that it is being useful to the last. The body of some one who has been well fed and healthy throughout many years would be a novelty to dissectors.'

But Elizabeth just couldn't face it – and the medical student served up with Miss Rathbone, MP, might have balked as well. Eleanor had anticipated that. 'But my dear, dearest people do just as you like,' she instructed Elizabeth and Eva. 'You have been so good to me in life, don't let me be either more trouble than necessary or a cause of hurt feelings after death.'[1] So the body was cremated and the memorial services held – one for the great and the good at St Margaret's, Westminster, another for family and friends in Liverpool Cathedral, a third at Bloomsbury House for co-workers in the refugee cause. Tributes from MPs, suffragists and grateful refugees filled the pages of the *Manchester Guardian* and *The Times*. Lord Horder, Victor Gollancz and Barbara Ayrton-Gould launched an appeal to build a cultural centre for refugee children in Rathbone's memory in Israel. Churchill, Lord Cecil, Lord Derby and Graham White lent their names to a second appeal to endow a memorial lecture at the civic universities.

But privately, as so often happens, the arguments had already begun. These were not about the money, for Eleanor – good Rathbone that she was – had tied up her substantial capital neatly in charitable trusts. About a quarter of Rathbone's almost £100,000 would be left to Macadam and her various nephews and nieces, but the bulk of the estate went to aid refugee organizations and to establish an 'Eleanor Rathbone Trust' that (now under the chairmanship of Eleanor's great-niece Jenny Rathbone) supports social schemes for the under-privileged to this day. But who would take over the legacy – the name, the causes, the university seat? Macadam, heir to all manuscripts and copyrights, struggled to keep everything in her own hands. Eva Hubback was *not* to be trusted to draft letters about the appeal, she instructed Graham White; Stocks was *not* to refer to Macadam when she wrote the Life.[2] Together, Macadam and Stocks sorted the papers, putting aside a selection for Stocks to use.[3] Macadam then moved to Edinburgh, taking the faithful Mrs Wilson with her. 'I miss her terribly and life can never be the same again,' Macadam wrote, but she had friends and family in Edinburgh and by mid-1947 was 'beginning to feel at home'.[4] She returned to London that winter to clear the Hampstead house – 'a sad business but with many happy memories'.[5] Much of Rathbone's substantial political archive must have vanished in that 'clearing'.

Thus the body, thus the archive – but what of that parliamentary plum, Eleanor's staunchly progressive university seat? There was a by-election, of course, and Stocks – encouraged by Macadam – stood as her colleague and heir. But then, so too did Ernest Simon, former Lord Mayor of Manchester and Eleanor's old ally from her housing campaigns of the twenties; so too did Stanley

Wormald, who promised to carry on Rathbone's legacy from an 'Independent Socialist' point of view. Divided into almost equal thirds, Eleanor's rock-hard majority crumbled, and H.G. Strauss, the single Conservative candidate, won by a hair. Most of Eleanor's constituents were appalled, and the Labour Party took notice as well. Population changes and wartime cross-party consultations had made a new Representation of the People Act necessary, and when Labour introduced a measure in 1948, it included abolition of the university seats. There was an immediate public outcry, but the scathing newspaper comments and parliamentary speeches did no good. Macadam, now bedridden much of the time, was touched to find Eleanor cited 'as the ideal member *over and over again*' but recognized that she would now have no successor.[6] Stoical to the end, Macadam died in Edinburgh on 25 October 1948.

By then, even the causes had suffered a decline. The Family Endowment Society had achieved its object and melted away. Save Europe Now had been founded to deal with immediate hunger and distress: as the situation on the continent eased, Victor Gollancz and Peggy Duff wound the organization up. When Stocks's biography appeared in 1949, a kind of amnesia had already set in. Who was this Eleanor Rathbone, who had stormed with such vigorous feminism, such democratic conviction, through the pre-war world? No party could claim her, and a public tired of causes put her out of its mind. In the 1970s, when chronic unemployment put child poverty back on the agenda, Rathbone's ideas about family policy would gain a new hearing; in the eighties, feminist historians would recover her works and name. But that public in which she had such faith forgot her. Today, few people passing the little blue plaque in Tufton Court or James Gunn's portrait in the National Gallery know anything of the woman there recalled.

Rathbone would not have cared. She wanted to be useful, not famous, and found her busy life of committee work and lobbying, information-gathering and advocacy its own rich reward. In the late 1930s, working all hours to bring aid to Spain, milk to hungry children and Czech refugees to Britain, she was, in her own way, happy. 'If any other desired the credit, let him have it,' Sir Arthur Salter recalled at her memorial service; 'for her it sufficed to have the drudgery of preparation, of persuasion and following up.' She was, he thought, 'the most selfless humanitarian I have ever known'.[7]

She was that, but she was something more. In dark times, Eleanor Rathbone kept faith with politics. For fifty years, Rathbone held to the belief that purposive collective action in a democratic state could improve human life, could prevent the world from foundering on the shoals of untrammelled selfishness, mutual hatred or apathy. That commitment grew from varied roots – from her abandoned childhood faith and her substitute Oxford faith, from her long apprenticeship in the suffrage movement and her painstaking achievement of dozens of piecemeal reforms. It was tested by the economic crises and burgeoning rival ideologies of the thirties, and redeemed (if only partly) by the struggles of the Second World War. And yet, for all her consistency, Rathbone was never sentimental or unrealistic: she knew that the achievements won through democratic politics were always partial and tainted by compromise; she knew exactly what Max Weber meant when he likened political work to 'the strong and slow boring of hard boards'. But for all that (she would have said), what might be the alternative? Unless we cede to the market, to bureaucrats or to strongmen the task of determining our common fate, we have no other means through which to work the redemption of our world.

Appendix 1

Principal Writings by Eleanor Rathbone, by Date

'Women Cigar Makers in a Large Provincial Town', *Women's Industrial News*, 12 (Sept. 1900), pp. 185–90.

Report of an Inquiry into the Conditions of Dock Labour at the Liverpool Docks. Liverpool: Northern Publishing Co., 1904.

William Rathbone: A Memoir. London: Macmillan & Co. 1905.

How the Casual Labourer Lives: Report of the Liverpool Joint Research Committee on the Domestic Condition and Expenditure of the Families of Certain Liverpool Labourers. Liverpool: Northern Publishing Co., 1909.

'Statement on Casual and Dock Labour in Liverpool, and on the Unemployment of Women', in Royal Commission on the Poor Laws, Appendix Vol. VIII, *Minutes of Evidence*. PP. 1910, XLVIII, Cmd. 5066, pp. 261–7.

(with E. McCrindell), *Technical Education of Women and Girls in Liverpool*. Liverpool: Liverpool Women's Industrial Council. 1910.

(with Emma Mahler), *Payment of Seamen: The Present System*. Liverpool: C. Tinling, 1911.

Disagreeable Truths about the Conciliation Bill. Liverpool: Northern Publishing Co. [1912].

The Problem of Women's Wages: An Enquiry into the Causes of the Inferiority of Women's Wages to Men's. Liverpool: Northern Publishing Co., 1912.

'The Economic Position of Married Women', *Common Cause*, 3: 143 (4 Jan. 1912), pp. 674–5.

What Anti-Suffrage Men Really Think about Women: Sir Almroth Wright and His Critics. Liverpool: Lee & Nightingale, 1912.

Report on the Condition of Widows under the Poor Law in Liverpool. Liverpool: Lee & Nightingale, 1913.

The Muddle of Separation Allowances. [For private circulation, 1915].

'Separation Allowances: An Experiment in the State Endowment of Maternity', I, *Common Cause*, 7: 359 (25 Feb. 1916), p. 611; II, *Common Cause*, 7: 362 (17 Mar. 1916), p. 648.

'The Remuneration of Women's Services', *Economic Journal*, 27: 105 (Mar. 1917), pp. 55–68. Rpt. in *The Making of Women: Oxford Essays in Feminism*, ed. Victor Gollancz. London: George Allen & Unwin, 1917, pp. 100–27.

'The Industrial Outlook for Women after the War', *The Englishwoman*, 100 (Apr. 1917), pp. 1–10.

(with K.D. Courtney, H.N. Brailsford, A. Maude Royden, Mary Stocks, Elinor Burns and Emile Burns) *Equal Pay and the Family: A Proposal for the National Endowment of Motherhood*. London: Headley Brothers [1918].

Wages Plus Family Allowances: A Practical Way of Reducing the Costs of Production without Lowering the Standard of Life of the Workers. Printed for Private Circulation, 1921.

'Family Endowment in its Bearing on the Question of Population', *Eugenics Review*, 16 (Apr. 1924–Jan. 1925), pp. 270–5.

The Disinherited Family: A Plea for Direct Provision for the Costs of Child Maintenance through Family Allowances. London: Edward Arnold, 1924; 3rd edn, London: George Allen & Unwin, 1927.

(for the Family Endowment Society), 'Memorandum of Evidence', in Royal Commission on the Coal Industry, *Report*, vol. 2, *Minutes of Evidence*. London: HMSO, 1926, pp. 862–79.

'The Old and the New Feminism', *Woman's Leader*, 13 Mar. 1925, pp. 51–2.

(for NUSEC), *Widows', Orphans', and Old Age Contributory Pensions Bill*. London: NUSEC, June 1925.

The Ethics and Economics of Family Endowment. London: Epworth Press, 1927.

The Poor Law Proposals and Women Guardians. London: NUSEC, Dec. 1928 [rpt. from *Nation and Athenaeum*, 24 Nov. 1928].

Milestones: Presidential Addresses at the Annual Council Meetings of the NUSEC. Liverpool: Lee & Nightingale, 1929.

'Has Katherine Mayo Slandered "Mother India"?' *Hibbert Journal*, 27 (Jan. 1929), pp. 193–214.

(for NUSEC), 'Memorandum on the Condition of Women of the Coloured Races, in British Crown Colonies and Dependencies', submitted to the Colonial Conference, 1930.

Memorandum on the Problems of Child Marriage and Maternal Mortality in India. London, n.p. 1930.

'Memorandum on Certain Questions affecting the Status and Welfare of Indian Women in the Future Constitution of India.' Submitted to the Round Table Conference, Dec. 1930.

The Goal of Our Housing Policy. Liverpool: Lee & Nightingale [1930].

'Child Marriage in India', *Hibbert Journal*, 29: 4 (July 1931).

Memorandum on the Use and Abuse of Housing Subsidies. London, n.p., Nov. 1931.

(with the Duchess of Atholl and Josiah Wedgwood), 'Memorandum on Female Slavery within the Family,' May 1932, copy in RP XIV. 2.1 (40).

'Evidence Concerning the Status of Women in the Future Indian Constitution', Memorandum 9, in Joint Committee on Indian Constitutional Reform, vol. 2a, *Minutes of Evidence*, PP, 1932–3, VI, pp. 343–61, and 'Supplementary', Memorandum 84, in Joint Committee on Indian Constitutional Reform, vol. 2c, *Minutes of Evidence*, PP, 1932–3, VIII, pp. 1794–55.

(for the Children's Minimum Campaign Committee), *Memorandum on the Scale of Needs Suitable for Adoption by the Unemployment Assistance Board in Assessing Assistance to Applicants under Part II of the Unemployment Act, 1934*. London: CMC, July 1934.

Child Marriage: The Indian Minotaur: An Object Lesson from the Past to the Future. London: George Allen & Unwin, 1934.

The Harvest of the Women's Movement. London, 1935.

'Changes in Public Life.' In *Our Freedom and its Results*, ed. Ray Strachey. London: Hogarth Press, 1936, pp. 13–76.

Foreword to *The Tragedy of Abyssinia: What Britain Feels and Thinks and Wants*. London: League of Nations Union, June 1936.

(with Lord Faringdon, John Jagger, J.B. Trend, R. McKinnon Wood and E.L.O. Mallalieu), *Report and Findings of Committee of Inquiry into Breaches of International Law relating to Intervention in Spain*. London, Oct. 1936.

(with Lord Faringdon, John Jagger, J.B. Trend, R. McKinnon Wood and E.L.O. Mallalieu), *Evidence of Recent Breaches by Germany and Italy of the Non-intervention Agreement*. London: P.S. King & Son, May 1937.

(with the Duchess of Atholl, Dame Rachel Crowdy and Ellen Wilkinson), *Report of a Short Visit to Valencia and Madrid in April, 1937*. London: National Joint Committee for Spanish Relief, 1937.

War Can Be Averted. London: Victor Gollancz, 1938.

The Case for the Immediate Introduction of a System of Family Allowances. London: FES, Jan. 1940.

The Case for Family Allowances. Harmondsworth: Penguin Books, 1940.

Rescue the Perishing. London: National Committee for Rescue from Nazi Terror, Apr. 1943.

(for the National Committee for Rescue from Nazi Terror), *The Continuing Terror*. London: NCRNT, Feb. 1944.

Falsehoods and Facts about the Jews. London: Victor Gollancz, Jan. 1945.

Appendix 2

Municipal Election Results,
Granby Ward, Liverpool

Note: Granby Ward had three representatives, each elected for a staggered term of three years. One seat is up for re-election each year.

Polling Date	Candidate (Party)	Result	Electorate	Other two Granby reps
7 Oct. 1909 (by-election)	E.F. Rathbone (Ind.) J. Welland (Lab)	1,066 516		Cons., Lib.
1 Nov. 1910	Rathbone (Ind.) R. Richards (Cons.)	1,211 769	3,556	Cons., Lib.
1 Nov. 1913	Rathbone (Ind.)	no contest	3,645	2 Cons.
	– no elections 1915–1918 –			
1 Nov. 1920	Rathbone (Ind.)	no contest	8,623	Cons., Lib.
1 Nov. 1923	Rathbone (Ind.)	no contest	9,075	Cons., Lib.
1 Nov. 1926	Rathbone (Ind.) K.F. Graham (Cons.)	2,581 1,587	9,360	Cons., Lab.
1 Nov. 1929	Rathbone (Ind.)	no contest	9,932	2 Lab.
1 Nov. 1932	Rathbone (Ind.)	no contest	9,858	Cons., Lib.
1 Nov. 1935	C.E. Burke (Lab.) H.H. Jones (Lib.)	2,191 1,949	9,760	Cons., Lib.

Source: *Election Record Books*, Liverpool City Libraries

Parliamentary Election Results, Combined English Universities, 1918–46

Date	Candidate	Party	First Preferences	Final Count	Size of Electorate
Dec. 1918	Fisher*	Coalition Liberal	959	665	2,357
	Conway*	Coalition Unionist	303	777	
	Hobson	Independent	366	481	
Nov. 1922	Conway*	Unionist	968	983	3,967
	Fisher*	National Liberal	815	1,009	
	Strong	Liberal	571	813	
	Woolf	Labour	361	—	
	Faraday	Ind. Unionist	141	—	
	Lawrence	Ind. Unionist	90	—	
Dec. 1923	Conway*	Unionist	1,711		5,008
	Fisher*	Liberal	1,316		
	Findlay	Labour	850		
Oct. 1924	Conway*	Conservative	2,231	1,476	5,655
	Fisher*	Liberal	1,333	2,064	
	Findlay	Labour	861	885	
Mar. 1926 by-election on the retirement of Fisher					
	Hopkinson*	Conservative	2,343		6,513
	Ramsay Muir	Liberal	2,000		
May 1929	Conway*	Conservative	2,679	4,321	13,775
	Rathbone*	Independent	3,331	3,394	
	Conway, R.S.	Liberal	2,231	2,281	
	Selby-Biggs	Conservative	1,762	—	
Oct. 1931	Craddock*	Conservative	3,633	4,858	19,108
	Rathbone*	Independent	5,096	4,567	
	Jowitt	National Labour	2,759	3,632	
	Williams	Conservative	1,748	—	
	Nicolson	New Party	461	—	
Nov. 1935	Craddock*	Conservative	unopposed		26,809
	Rathbone*	Independent	unopposed		
Mar. 1937 by-election on the death of Craddock					
	Harvey*	Independent Progressive	6,596		28,808
	Lindley	Conservative	4,952		
	Brackenbury	Independent	2,373		

Appendix 3 Parliamentary Election Results

Continued

Date	Candidate	Party	First Preferences	Final Count	Size of Electorate
July 1945	Rathbone*	Independent	11,176	6,992	42,312
	Lindsay*	Independent	1,923	5,826	
	Wormald	Ind. Labour	3,212	4,675	
	Arden	Independent	2,433	—	
	Richardson	Independent	1,124	—	
	Foxall	Independent	1,105	—	
March 1946 by-election on the death of Rathbone					43,438
	Strauss*	Conservative	5,483		
	Stocks	Independent	5,124		
	Simon	Independent	4,028		
	Wormald	Socialist	3,414		
	Oddie	British Peoples	239		

* elected

Appendix 4

Rathbone's Major Parliamentary Speeches and Questions

Session	PQs	of which	Speeches	of which
1929–30	35	8 housing 12 colonial women	14	5 housing 3 colonial women
1930–1	23	9 colonial women 7 various women	23	11 various women* 3 colonial women
1931–2	25	7 colonial women	14	5 various women
1932–3	21	7 colonial women 5 arms/foreign policy	12	4 housing 3 various women
1933–4	35	10 housing 8 various women	32	13 unemployment insurance 6 civil liberties
1934–5	29	10 foreign policy 7 India bill	44	31 colonial/India
1935–6	76	31 Abyssinia 14 various women	14	5 various women 3 Abyssinia
1936–7	89	48 Spain 14 other Europe**	12	4 various women 3 Spain
1937–8	100	27 Spain 34 other Europe	14	7 Spain
1938–9	119	33 Spain 31 refugees	11	2 Spain 4 Czechoslovakia
1939–40	100	28 refugees/aliens	13	2 family allowances
1940–1	59	26 refugees/aliens	5	2 refugees/aliens
1941–2	47	10 refugees/aliens 9 women's work	10	4 budget/tax 3 women's work
1942–3	52	15 refugees/aliens 11 Jews	7	2 refugees/aliens 2 women's work
1943–4	52	10 social welfare 9 refugees/Jews	10	2 refugees/Jews
1944–5	65	20 UN/post-war 12 social welfare 10 family allowances	9	5 family allowances
1945–6	24	11 aliens/Jews 6 European situation	4	4 European situation

* 'various women' excludes speeches/questions on women in India and the colonies
** 'other Europe' includes speeches/questions on Italy, Abyssinia and the League

Appendix 5

A Note on Sources

I have drawn heavily on Eleanor Rathbone's writings, letters and speeches; on the Rathbone Family Papers at the University of Liverpool; and on articles by and about Rathbone in the feminist, provincial and national press. Yet much of the life, and in particular the details of Rathbone's manifold political campaigns, had to be pieced together from parliamentary debates and papers, from the records of relevant government ministries, and from correspondence and records scattered in many dozens of archives. Relevant Public Record Office materials (and especially the extensive India Office, Foreign Office and Home Office records dealing with Rathbone's campaigns on child marriage, Indian women's franchise, Spain, and refugees) are cited fully in the notes. The following collections also provided useful material on various aspects of Rathbone's life; I am grateful for permission to quote from them.

Papers of Individuals

Vyvyan Adams papers (anti-appeasement), London School of Economics
Leo Amery diaries (family allowances and child welfare), Churchill Archives Centre, Churchill College, Cambridge
Norman Angell Papers (Abyssinia), Ball State University, Bracken Library, Muncie, Indiana
Nancy Astor Papers (feminist issues), Reading University Library
Katharine Atholl Papers (Spain), Blair Castle, courtesy of Lady Warner.
Katharine Atholl Papers, India Office Library
George Bell (Bishop Bell) Papers (refugees and the Holocaust), Lambeth Palace Library
William Beveridge Papers (family allowances), British Library of Political and Economic Science
Walter Lyon Blease diary (suffrage), University of Liverpool Library, courtesy of Mrs. Jane MacLachlan
Bonar Law Papers (World War I), House of Lords Record Office
R.A. Butler Papers (India), Trinity College, Cambridge
Victor Cazalet Papers (refugees), courtesy of Sir Edward Cazalet
Viscount Cecil of Chelwood Papers (anti-appeasement, refugees, Holocaust), British Library
Winston Churchill Papers, Churchill Archives Centre, Churchill College, Cambridge
Selina Cooper Papers (suffrage), Lancashire Record Office
Margery Corbett Ashby Papers (feminist issues), Women's Library
W.H. Dickinson Papers (suffrage), Greater London Record Office
Edith Eskrigge Papers (suffrage), Women's Library
Millicent Garrett Fawcett Papers (feminist issues), Women's Library
Millicent Garrett Fawcett Papers (feminist issues), Manchester Central Library
Margery Fry Papers (friendship), courtesy of Ms. Annabel Cole
Victor Gollancz Papers (Holocaust, Save Europe Now), Modern Records Centre, University of Warwick

J.L. and Barbara Hammond Papers (friendship), Bodleian Library
A.V. Hill Papers (refugees), Churchill Archives Centre, Churchill College, Cambridge, courtesy of Mrs. Maggie Bell
Durning Holt Family Papers (Liverpool), Liverpool Record Office
Herbert Stanley Jevons Papers (Abyssinia), National Library of Wales
Walter Layton Papers (India, anti-appeasement), Trinity College, Cambridge
Lloyd George Papers (anti-appeasement), House of Lords Record Office
Oliver Lodge Papers (friendship), Birmingham University Library
Lothian Papers (India), Scottish Record Office
Margaret MacDonald Papers (social welfare), British Library of Political and Economic Science
Harold Macmillan Papers (child welfare, anti-appeasement), Bodleian Library
Violet Markham Papers (social welfare), British Library of Political and Economic Science
Catherine Marshall Papers (suffrage), Cumbria Record Office
Katherine Mayo file (India), India Office Library
Katherine Mayo Papers (India), Beinecke Library, Yale University
Melly Family Papers (Liverpool), Liverpool Record Office
Gilbert Murray Papers (foreign affairs), Bodleian Library
Philip Noel-Baker Papers (Spain, refugees), Churchill Archives Centre, Churchill College, Cambridge
James Parkes Papers (Holocaust), University of Southampton Library
Passfield Papers (social reform), British Library of Political and Economic Science
Alice Paul Papers (feminist issues), Schlesinger Library, Radcliffe Institute for Advanced Study, Harvard University
Eleanor Rathbone Papers (India), Women's Library
Eleanor Rathbone file (India), India Office Library
Herbert Reynolds Rathbone Papers (Liverpool), Liverpool Record Office
Rathbone Family Papers, Special Collections and Archives, Sydney Jones Library, University of Liverpool, courtesy of the Rathbone family
Wilfrid Roberts Papers (Spain), Modern Records Centre, University of Warwick
John Simon Papers (India), India Office Library
Hannah Whitall Smith Papers (feminist issues), Lilly Library, Indiana University
Jane Norman Smith Papers (feminist issues), Schlesinger Library, Radcliffe Institute for Advanced Study, Harvard University
Cornelia Sorabji Papers (India), India Office Library
Doris Stevens Papers (feminist issues), Schlesinger Library, Radcliffe Institute for Advanced Study, Harvard University
William Temple Papers (refugees and the Holocaust), Lambeth Palace Library
Viscount Templewood (Sir Samuel Hoare) Papers (Spain), Cambridge University Library
Viscount Thurso (Sir Archibald Sinclair) Papers (anti-appeasement), Churchill Archives Centre, Churchill College, Cambridge
Henry Graham White Papers (refugees), House of Lords Record Office

Papers of Organizations and Corporate Bodies

Allen & Unwin Archives, Reading University Library
Anti-Slavery Society Papers, Rhodes House, Oxford
BBC Written Archives Centre, Talks scripts
Board of Deputies of British Jews Papers, Greater London Record Office
British Association for the Advancement of Science Papers, British Library of Political and Economic Science
British Council Papers, Churchill College, Cambridge
Central British Fund for World Jewish Relief Archives (Microfilm)
Confederation of British Industries Predecessor Archive, Modern Records Centre, University of Warwick

Consultative Committee on Women's Suffrage Papers, Women's Library
Family Endowment Society Papers, British Library of Political and Economic Science
For Intellectual Liberty, Cambridge University Library
Girls' Public Day School Trust Records, at the Girls' Public Day School Trust, London
Gollancz/Cassell Company Archive, held by Cassell, London
Hogarth Press Archive, Reading University Library
Institute for Personnel Management Papers, Modern Records Centre, University of Warwick
Joint Committee on the Living Wage Papers, Congress House
League of Nations Archives, Geneva
League of Nations Union Papers, British Library of Political and Economic Science
Liverpool Central Relief Society Papers, Liverpool Record Office
Liverpool Child Welfare Association, Merseyside Record Office
Liverpool Council of Social Service Newscuttings, Liverpool Record Office
Liverpool Council of Voluntary Aid Papers, courtesy of the Liverpool Council of Voluntary Aid
Liverpool Personal Services Society, Merseyside Record Office
Liverpool Vigilance Association, Merseyside Record Office
London Society for Women's Service Papers, Women's Library
Macmillan Archive, Reading University Library
Manchester Guardian Archives, John Rylands Library, Manchester University
National Council for Civil Liberties Papers, Hull University Library
NUSEC Papers, Women's Library
NUWSS Papers, Women's Library
School of Social Science and of Training for Social Work Papers, Special Collections and Archives,
    Sydney Jones Library, University of Liverpool
Society for Psychical Research Papers, Cambridge University Library
Society for the Protection of Science and Learning Papers, Bodleian Library
Society of Authors Archive, British Library
Society of Friends Germany Emergency Committee Papers, Friends House Library, London
Society of Friends India Conciliation Group Papers, Friends House Library, London
Somerville College Archives
Trades Union Congress Archives, Congress House
Victoria Settlement Papers, Special Collections and Archives, Sydney Jones Library, University of
    Liverpool
Woman Power Committee Papers, British Library of Political and Economic Science
Women's Library Autograph Letter Collection, Photograph Collection, Scrapbooks, and Brian
    Harrison Oral History Tapes
Women's Local Government Society Papers, Greater London Record Office
Women's University Settlement Papers, Women's Library

Notes

Abbreviations Used in the Notes

People

EFR	Eleanor Florence Rathbone
OJL	Oliver J. Lodge
WGR	William Gair Rathbone
WR	William Rathbone

Publications

HC Deb.	*House of Commons Debates*
HL Deb.	*House of Lords Debates*
PP	*Parliamentary Papers*

Repositories and Collections

BL	British Library
BLPES	British Library of Political and Economic Science, London School of Economics
Bodleian	Bodleian Library, Oxford
BUL	Birmingham University Library
CAC	Churchill Archives Centre, Churchill College, Cambridge
CRO	Cumbria Record Office
GLRO	Greater London Record Office
HLRO	House of Lords Record Office
IULL	Indiana University, Lilly Library
JRL	John Rylands Library, University of Manchester
LPL	Lambeth Palace Library
LRO	Liverpool Record Office
MRC	Modern Records Centre, University of Warwick
PRO	Public Record Office
RP	Rathbone Papers, Special Collections and Archives, Sydney Jones Library, University of Liverpool
SCA	Special Collections and Archives, Sydney Jones Library, University of Liverpool
SRO	Scottish Record Office
USL	University of Southampton Library
WL	Women's Library, London Metropolitan University

Introduction

1. RP XIV.2.15 (29), Eleanor F. Rathbone, 'Refugees from Czechoslovakia: A Government Economy at their Expense' (20 July 1939).
2. Eleanor F. Rathbone, 'Equal Wages for Equal Work', *The Times*, 26 Aug. 1918, p. 9.
3. *Manchester Guardian*, 3 Jan. 1946, p. 3.
4. Mary D. Stocks, *Eleanor Rathbone: A Biography* (London: Victor Gollancz, 1949), p. 14.
5. BUL, OJL 1/324/6, EFR to OJL, 5 May 1892.

Chapter 1   Snares of Wealth and Virtue

1. Eleanor F. Rathbone, *William Rathbone: A Memoir* (London: Macmillan & Co., 1905). [Augustine Birrell], *Records of the Rathbone Family*, ed. E.A. Rathbone (Edinburgh: R. & R. Clark, 1913).
2. On Quarry Bank, and the role of the Rathbones as suppliers of cotton and (later) of capital, see Mary B. Rose, *The Gregs of Quarry Bank Mill: The Rise and Decline of a Family Firm, 1750–1914* (Cambridge: Cambridge University Press, 1986), esp. pp. 20, 45–6, 67–8.
3. The best source of information on the early William Rathbones is Birrell's commissioned *Records of the Rathbone Family*, which was edited by Emily Rathbone and printed for private circulation.
4. For the history of the house, see Adrian Allan, *Greenbank: A Brief History* (Liverpool: University of Liverpool, 1987).
5. On this interesting controversy, which led to a landslide Tory victory and blackened the name of William Rathbone in the town, see Frank Neal, *Sectarian Violence: The Liverpool Experience, 1819–1914* (Manchester: Manchester University Press, 1988), ch. 2; and, for a hagiographic account, R.V. Holt, *The Unitarian Contribution to Social Progress in England* (London: Allen & Unwin, 1938), pp. 236–9, 259.
6. Lucie Nottingham, *Rathbone Brothers: From Merchant to Banker, 1742–1992* (London: Rathbone Brothers Plc, 1992), pp. 11–12.
7. For the most clear-sighted account of the politics of the Roscoe-Rathbone circle, see Ian Sellers, 'William Roscoe, the Roscoe Circle and Radical Politics in Liverpool, 1787–1807', *Transactions of the Historic Society of Lancashire and Cheshire*, 120 (1968), pp. 45–62.
8. N.G. Annan, 'The Intellectual Aristocracy', in J.H. Plumb, ed., *Studies in Social History: A Tribute to G.M. Trevelyan* (London: Longmans, Green, 1955).
9. [Birrell], *Records of the Rathbone Family*, p. 225.
10. This account is based on Sheila Marriner's excellent study of Rathbones' strategies and performance during the period of William and Sam's control. See Marriner, *Rathbones of Liverpool, 1845–73* (Liverpool: Liverpool University Press, 1961).
11. On the Rathbone ships, see esp. Nottingham, *Rathbone Brothers*, pp. 61–8.
12. William cites these figures for his personal income in his memo entitled 'Principles of Expenditure', RP IX.9.45.
13. For these figures, see Marriner, *Rathbones*, pp. 61, 227–30.
14. For Thom's teachings, see R.K. Webb, 'John Hamilton Thom: Intellect and Conscience in Liverpool', in P.T. Phillips, ed., *The View from the Pulpit: Victorian Ministers and Society* (Toronto: Macmillan of Canada, 1978), pp. 210–43; and for his influence on William Rathbone, see especially Eleanor F. Rathbone, *William Rathbone*, pp. 65–70.
15. RP IX.9.45, WR, 'Principles of Expenditure'.
16. RP IX.9.39a, WR, 'What Fools We Are', n.d.
17. RP IX.9.45, WR, 'Principles of Expenditure'.
18. RP IX.4.47, Samuel Greg Rathbone to WR and H.W. Gair, 10 Aug. 1854.
19. RP IX.4.188, WR to Elsie, 12 Aug. 1866.
20. RP IX.4.53, Sam to WR, 15 July 1878.
21. Rather a different explanation for restricting economic growth than the 'gentrification' argument offered by Martin J. Wiener, *English Culture and the Decline of the Industrial Spirit, 1850–1980* (Cambridge: Cambridge University Press, 1981), ch. 7.

22. RP IX.9.45, WR, 'Principles of Expenditure'.
23. Eleanor F. Rathbone, *William Rathbone*, p. 456.
24. On William Rathbone's involvement with district nursing, see *ibid.*, pp. 155–86; Gwen Hardy, *William Rathbone and the Early History of District Nursing* (Ormskirk: G.W. & A. Hesketh, 1981).
25. RP XXV.1.104 (6), Elsie to WGR, n.d. (spring 1872). There would have been ten children by this point, had Cyril Charles lived.
26. John Vincent, *The Formation of the Liberal Party, 1857–1868* (London: Constable, 1966), pp. 35, 39. Vincent is well off the mark, however, in labelling Rathbone an 'astute machine politician' (p. 35), just as he is quite wrong to believe that the Liberal Party's new radicals 'lacked any theory as to *what* they were dealing with' (p. 30) simply because they did not approach society from the viewpoint of Cobdenite radicalism. J.P. Parry, more appropriately, places Rathbone at the heart of the attempt to forge a new, cross-class politics designed to promote both efficiency and public morality. See *The Rise and Fall of Liberal Government in Victorian Britain* (New Haven: Yale University Press, 1993), ch. 10.
27. See, e.g., RP IX.5.2, WR to his mother, 11 May 1873; RP IX.4.122, Ashton to Emily, 9 June 1875.
28. Eleanor Rathbone provides a general account of her father's local government proposals in *William Rathbone*, pp. 234–51; see also William Rathbone, Albert Pell and F.C. Montague, *Local Government and Taxation* (London: Swan Sonnenschein & Co., 1885).
29. For the University of Liverpool, see David R. Jones, *The Origins of Civic Universities: Manchester, Leeds & Liverpool* (London: Routledge, 1988) and Thomas Kelly, *For Advancement of Learning: The University of Liverpool, 1881–1981* (Liverpool: Liverpool University Press, 1981), which covers William Rathbone's role in the founding in some detail. For the University College of North Wales, see Eleanor Rathbone, *William Rathbone*, pp. 346–57.
30. The doyen of the revisionists being, of course, Peter Gay, in his multi-volume opus, *The Bourgeois Experience: Victoria to Freud*, esp. vol. 1, *Education of the Senses* (New York: Oxford University Press, 1984). For an account that reveals the degree of variation possible within a single family, see, e.g., Barbara Caine, *Destined to Be Wives: The Sisters of Beatrice Webb* (Oxford: Clarendon Press, 1986); and José Harris's acute comments in *Private Lives, Public Spirit: A Social History of Britain, 1870–1914* (Oxford: Oxford University Press, 1993), p. 92.
31. Michael Mason, *The Making of Victorian Sexuality* (Oxford: Oxford University Press, 1994), p. 7.
32. RP IX.9.8, WR, 'Memorandum on the character of Lucretia'.
33. RP IX.4.183, WR to WGR, 16 July 1861.
34. RP IX.9.9, WR to Elsie, 6 Sept. 1861.
35. Eleanor Lodge, *Terms and Vacations* (Oxford: Oxford University Press, 1938), p. 67; RP XXIIA, Diary of Hugh Reynolds Rathbone, 1918.
36. RP IX.4.80, WR to Emily, 12 Mar. 1883.
37. Eleanor Lodge, *Terms and Vacations*, p. 68.
38. For which, see RP X.1.209–16.
39. RP IX.9.9, WR to Elsie, 6 Sept. 1861.
40. Pat Jalland, *Women, Marriage and Politics, 1860–1914* (Oxford: Clarendon Press, 1986), esp. ch. 7; M. Jeanne Peterson, *Family, Love and Work in the Lives of Victorian Gentlewomen* (Bloomington: Indiana University Press, 1989), p. 104.
41. RP IX.5.2, WR to Emily, 20 Aug. 1871.
42. RP IX.4.182, WR to WGR, 16 Nov. 1856.
43. RP IX.4.188, WR to Elsie, 12 Aug. 1866.
44. RP IX.4.185, WR to Ashton, 29 Mar. 1872.
45. RP IX.4.121, WGR to WR, 8 Feb. 1890.
46. RP IX.4.126, Ashton to Emily, 23 Oct. 1877.
47. RP IX.9.9, WR to Elsie, 6 Sept. 1861.

48. RP IX.4.184, WR to WGR, 27 May 1861. William Rathbone wrote this letter two years after his first wife's death and in fearful apprehension of his own demise. It is not clear when he sent it, but as it has been copied over in William Gair's hand, presumably it was eventually received.

49. RP IX.5.3, WR to Emily, 30 May 1875.

50. RP IX.4.122, Ashton to Emily, 9 June 1875.

51. For the eyes, RP XXV.1.91 (36), Alice Rathbone to WGR, 1 Oct. 1874; RP IX.5.3, WR to Emily, 5 Dec. 1875.

52. See, e.g., RP X.1.184c–d, Lyle to Emily, and 184e, Lyle to Teddy; IX.4.122, Ashton to Emily, 9 June 1875.

53. These comments from letters from Emily's sister Augusta (Lyle) Rathbone to Emily, undated (and almost illegible), RP X.1.85 and X.1.99.

54. See Eleanor's contribution to the memoir of Sidney Ball, the academic socialist and Fabian who tutored the Rathbone children one summer at the house in Bassenfell, in Oona H. Ball, *Sidney Ball: Memories and Impressions of 'An Ideal Don'* (Oxford: Basil Blackwell, 1923), pp. 36–7.

55. RP X.1.133, Augusta to Emily, n.d.

56. P.J. Waller, *Democracy and Sectarianism: A Political and Social History of Liverpool, 1868–1939* (Liverpool: Liverpool University Press, 1981), pp. 33–5.

57. See Eleanor F. Rathbone, *William Rathbone*, pp. 346–62, 397–426. Kenneth Morgan notes William Rathbone's disaffection with Welsh Home Rulers (and vice versa); see his *Wales in British Politics, 1868–1922* (Cardiff: University of Wales Press, 1970), esp. p. 117.

58. William Rathbone's behaviour on Irish Home Rule was, in a word, prevaricating: he raised objections to the bill but voted for it in 1886; in 1893, by contrast, he simply stayed away from Parliament for the vote. For the Rathbone–Gladstone correspondence, see RP IX.6.41–65; also Eleanor Rathbone, *William Rathbone*, pp. 412–16, 418–20.

59. Quoted in Nottingham, *Rathbone Brothers*, p. 71.

60. *Ibid.*, p. 74.

61. RP IX.5.3, WR to Emily, 2 Mar. 1884.

62. E.g., RP IX.4.68 and 69, WR to Emily, 10 and 13 Dec. 1882; IX.4.83, WR to Emily, 12 Mar. 1884; IX.4.87, WR to Emily, 14 Oct. 1885.

63. RP XXIIA.167, Hugh to Evie, 14 Sept. 1886.

64. RP XIV.3.92, Margery Fry, 'Eleanor Rathbone' [BBC script], 18 May 1952.

65. RP XXIIA.17, Ashton to 'dear Pest', 1 Sept. 1886.

66. RP XIV.3.73, 'Speech notes – Somerville College, Sunday, 17 January 1943'.

67. RP IX.4.99, WR to Emily, 13 May 1888.

Chapter 2   Mothers and Mentors

1. RP XIV.3.35, EFR, 'Prizegiving, Kensington High School, 16 March 1937 – Notes for Speech.' For a contemporary view of the new high schools, see Alice Zimmern, *The Renaissance of Girls' Education in England: A Record of Fifty Years' Progress* (London: A.D. Innes & Co., 1898); also, Laurie Magnus, *The Jubilee Book of the Girls' Public Day School Trust, 1873–1923* (Cambridge: Cambridge University Press, 1924).

2. *The Times*, 10 May 1890, p. 14.

3. For an account of presentation at Court in the late Victorian period, see Hilary and Mary Evans, *The Party That Lasted 100 Days* (London: Macdonald & Jane's, 1976), pp. 131–8; and, for the rituals of courtship in high society more generally, see Pat Jalland, *Women, Marriage and Politics, 1860–1914* (Oxford: Clarendon Press, 1986), ch. 1; Leonore Davidoff, *The Best Circles* (1973; rpt. London: Century Hutchinson, 1986).

4. According to Oliver Lodge's young sister, Eleanor. See her *Terms and Vacations* (Oxford University Press, 1938), pp. 66–8.

5. BUL, OJL 1/326/4, WR to OJL, 21 July 1891.

6. Oliver Lodge, *Past Years* (London: Hodder and Stoughton, 1931), pp. 167–8. Lodge's autobiography gives the mistaken impression that this trip took place in 1889.

7. Eleanor Lodge, *Terms and Vacations*, p. 67.

8. Oliver Lodge, *Past Years*, p. 121.

9. *Ibid.*, p. 167.

10. BUL, OJL 1/322/1, OJL to Emily, 25 Sept. 1891.

11. For an insightful discussion of such friendships, see M. Jeanne Peterson, *Family, Love and Work in the Lives of Victorian Gentlewomen* (Bloomington: Indiana University Press, 1989), esp. pp. 68–72.

12. BUL, OJL 1/326/33, Emily Rathbone to OJL, 29 Sept. 1891.

13. BUL, OJL 1/324/1, EFR to OJL, 2 Nov. 1891.

14. BUL, OJL 1/322/15, Emily to OJL, 14 Oct. [1891?].

15. BUL, OJL 1/326/78, Emily to OJL, 17 Oct. [1891].

16. BUL, OJL 1/324/1, EFR to OJL, 2 Nov. 1891.

17. BUL, OJL 1/324/5, EFR to OJL, 20 Apr. 1892.

18. BUL, OJL 1/326/66, Emily to OJL, 17 Nov. [1891?].

19. BUL, OJL 1/324/3, EFR to OJL, 6 Mar. 1892.

20. BUL, OJL 1/324/5, EFR to OJL, 20 Apr. 1892.

21. BUL, OJL 1/324/3, EFR to OJL, 6 Mar. 1892.

22. On Lodge's engagement with psychical research, see especially Janet Oppenheim, *The Other World: Spiritualism and Psychical Research in England, 1850–1914* (Cambridge: Cambridge University Press, 1985), esp. pp. 371–90.

23. Eleanor Lodge, *Terms and Vacations*, pp. 38–9.

24. Oliver Lodge, *Past Years*, p. 168.

25. Cambridge University Library, Society for Psychical Research Papers, WR to OJL, 30 Dec. 1893.

26. Alex Owen, *The Darkened Room: Women, Power and Spiritualism in Late Victorian England* (Philadelphia: University of Pennsylvania Press, 1990).

27. BUL, OJL 1/324/5, EFR to OJL, 20 Apr. 1892.

28. BUL, OJL 1/324/4, EFR to OJL, 24 Mar. 1892.

29. BUL, OJL 1/324/3, EFR to OJL, 6 Mar. 1892. Broughton had a *succès de scandale* with *Belinda*, a *roman-à-clef* based on Mark Pattison's marriage to the young art student Emily Strong. *Nancy* is a sunnier book, but dwells – intriguingly – on the ways in which Nancy's 'innocence' prevents her from comprehending or responding to her husband's love. Eleanor, reading the novel, may well have understood the reasons (both in terms of protection and in terms of plot) for that innocence, and have realized that it was something of a pose. See Rhoda Broughton, *Nancy* (London: R. Bentley & Son, 1873).

30. BUL, OJL 1/324/6, EFR to OJL, 5 May 1892.

31. BUL, OJL 1/324/5, EFR to OJL, 20 Apr. 1892.

32. Case is mentioned regularly in Virginia Woolf's diaries and letters after their meeting in 1902; see also Quentin Bell, *Virginia Woolf: A Biography* (1972; rpt. London: Hogarth Press, 1990), vol. 1, esp. p. 68.

33. BUL, OJL 1/324/6, EFR to OJL, 5 May 1892.

34. Girls' Public Day School Trust (London), Kensington School Log Book, p. 57.

35. Rita McWilliams-Tullberg, *Women at Cambridge: A Men's University – Though of a Mixed Type* (London: Victor Gollancz, 1975), *passim*.

36. BUL, OJL 1/326/61, Emily to OJL, 29 Sept. 1893.

37. Although Eleanor did not seem to know it, this was true of Newnham as well. 'The brother of one is not the brother of all,' one Newnham principal reminded students. McWilliams-Tullberg, *Women at Cambridge*, p. 104.

38. BUL, OJL 1/324/9, EFR to OJL, 27 July 1893.

39. RP IX.9.9a, WR to EFR, 6 Sept. 1893.

40. BUL, OJL 1/326/60, Emily to OJL, 7 Sept. 1893.

41. BUL, OJL 1/326/58, Emily to OJL, 19 Sept. 1893.

42. *Ibid.*

43. BUL, OJL 1/326/61, Emily to OJL, 29 Sept. 1893.

44. B.A. Crackanthorpe, 'The Revolt of the Daughters', *Nineteenth Century*, 35: 203 (Jan. 1894), pp. 23–31; 35: 205 (Mar. 1894), pp. 424–9; and replies *ibid.* by M.E. Hawes, pp. 430–6; Kathleen Cuffe, pp. 437–42; and Alys Pearsall Smith, pp. 443–50. David Rubinstein discusses this debate but, interestingly, does not mention that it is *mothers* who are the focus of the 'strike'. Rubinstein, *Before the Suffragettes: Women's Emancipation in the 1890s* (Brighton: Harvester, 1986), pp. 12–15.

45. Olive Banks, *Becoming a Feminist: The Social Origins of 'First Wave' Feminism* (Brighton: Wheatsheaf, 1986), pp. 25–31.

46. For an insightful look at some of the tensions between mothers and daughters, see Carol Dyhouse, *Girls Growing Up in Late Victorian and Edwardian England* (London: Routledge & Kegan Paul, 1981), esp. ch. 1.

47. Virginia Woolf, quoted in S.P. Rosenbaum, *Victorian Bloomsbury: The Early Literary History of the Bloomsbury Group* (New York: St Martin's Press, 1987), p. 82.

48. Crackanthorpe, 'Revolt of the Daughters', Mar. 1894, p. 426.

49. Jalland, *Women, Marriage and Politics: 1860–1914, passim.*

50. Barbara Caine, *Destined to Be Wives: The Sisters of Beatrice Webb* (Oxford: Clarendon Press, 1986), p. 141; Katherine Chorley, quoted in Dyhouse, *Girls Growing Up*, p. 160.

51. On this debate, see Dyhouse, *Girls Growing Up*, pp. 158–61.

52. BUL, OJL 1/324/9, EFR to OJL, 27 July 1893.

53. BUL, OJL 1/324/8, EFR to OJL, postmarked 15 July 1893.

54. BUL, OJL 1/324/33, EFR to OJL, n.d.

55. BUL, OJL 1/324/8, EFR to OJL, postmarked 15 July 1893.

56. BUL, OJL 1/324/27, EFR to OJL, n.d. [July 1893].

57. BUL, OJL 1/324/28, EFR to OJL, n.d. [July 1893].

Chapter 3   Philosophy and Feminism

1. The two preceding paragraphs rely upon John Sutherland's *Mrs Humphry Ward: Eminent Victorian, Pre-eminent Edwardian* (Oxford: Clarendon Press, 1990).

2. Mrs Humphry Ward, *A Writer's Recollections*, quoted in Sutherland, *Mrs Humphry Ward*, p. 65.

3. Charles Edward Mallet, *A History of the University of Oxford*, vol. 3, *Modern Oxford* (London: Methuen, 1927), p. 432.

4. Vera Brittain, *The Women at Oxford: A Fragment of History* (London: George G. Harrap & Co., 1960), p. 87.

5. Muriel St Clare Byrne and Catherine Hope Mansfield, *Somerville College: 1879–1921* (Oxford: Oxford University Press [1922]), p. 20.

6. For Miss Maitland's reign, see Pauline Aclams, *Somerville for Women: An Oxford College, 1879–1993* (Oxford: Oxford University Press, 1996), ch. 3; also Vera Farnell, *A Somervillian Looks Back* (Oxford University Press, 1948), pp. 21–30.

7. L.T. Meade, 'English Girls and their Colleges. No. V. Somerville Hall, Oxford', *Lady's Pictorial*, 2 Jan. 1892. 'L.T. Meade' is the pen name of Elizabeth Thomasine Meade Smith, who published *A Sweet Girl Graduate*, her novel of college life, in 1892.

8. RP XIV.3.73, 'Speech notes – Somerville College, Sunday, 17 January 1943'.

9. Somerville College Archives, College Meeting Minutes, 25 Jan. 1895.

10. *Ibid.*, 30 Jan. 1895.

11. RP XIV.3.73, 'Speech notes – Somerville College, Sunday, 17 January 1943'.

12. RP, Dec. 2002 accession (being catalogued), Transcript of letter from Lettice Fisher to Mary Stocks, *c.* 1947.

13. BUL, OJL 1/324/38, EFR to OJL, n.d.

14. For which see G.R. Searle, *The Quest for National Efficiency: A Study in British Politics and Political Thought, 1899–1914* (Berkeley: University of California Press, 1971).

15. Robert Latta, 'Biographical Memoir', in David G. Ritchie, *Philosophical Studies* (London: Macmillan, 1905), pp. 4–5.
16. On the Greats school, see especially Melvin Richter's useful discussion in *The Politics of Conscience: T.H. Green and His Age* (Cambridge, Mass.: Harvard University Press, 1964), esp. pp. 59–63.
17. RP XIV.4.40, Lucy Kempson to Mary Stocks, 8 May 1947.
18. Hilda Oakeley, *My Adventures in Education* (London: Williams & Norgate, 1939), esp. pp. 58–9, 62.
19. Somerville College Archives, Reports of Collections, E.F. Rathbone, Comments by Mr Ritchie, Lent Term 1894; Professor Pelham, Summer Term 1895; and the Master of Balliol, Michaelmas Term 1895.
20. Stefan Collini, *Public Moralists: Political Thought and Intellectual Life in Britain, 1850–1930* (Oxford: Clarendon Press, 1991), pp. 82–3.
21. The literature on idealism, conflicts within late Victorian liberalism, and the origins of the settlement house movement is immense, but see especially, in addition to Collini's *Public Moralists* and Melvin Richter's study of Green, Peter Clarke, *Liberals and Social Democrats* (Cambridge: Cambridge University Press, 1978); José Harris's chapter on 'Society and Social Theory' in her *Private Lives and Public Spirit: A Social History of Britain, 1870–1914* (Oxford: Oxford University Press, 1993), pp. 220–50; and Standish Meacham, *Toynbee Hall and Social Reform, 1880–1914: The Search for Community* (New Haven: Yale University Press, 1987). Mary Ward's *Robert Elsmere* is discussed in all of these books, but for the background to the novel, see especially John Sutherland's account in his *Mrs Humphry Ward*.
22. Latta, 'Biographical Memoir', in Ritchie, *Philosophical Studies*, pp. 7–8.
23. On these divisions, see especially, Christopher Harvie, *The Lights of Liberalism: University Liberals and the Challenge of Democracy, 1860–1886* (London: Allen Lane, 1976), esp. chs 8–9; and John Roach, 'Liberalism and the Victorian Intelligentsia', in Peter Stansky, ed., *The Victorian Revolution: Government and Society in Victoria's Britain* (New York: New Viewpoints, 1973), pp. 323–53.
24. Latta, 'Biographical Memoir', p. 5.
25. William Beveridge, *Power and Influence*, quoted in José Harris, *William Beveridge: A Biography* (Oxford: Clarendon Press, 1977), p. 41.
26. David G. Ritchie, *Plato* (New York: Charles Scribner's Sons, 1902), p. 162.
27. John MacCunn, 'The Political Idealism of Thomas Hill Green', in *Six Radical Thinkers* (1907; rpt. New York: Arno Press, 1979), pp. 242–3.
28. The term is MacCunn's: *Six Radical Thinkers*, pp. 243–4.
29. David G. Ritchie, *The Principles of State Interference* (London: Swan Sonnenschein & Co., 1891), pp. 102, 107.
30. *Ibid.*, p. 144.
31. *Ibid.*, p. 104.
32. Richter, *Politics of Conscience*, p. 283.
33. *Ibid.*
34. Ritchie, *Principles*, p. 108.
35. Collini, *Public Moralists*, p. 65.
36. The story is told by Ritchie, *Principles*, p. 131.
37. F. Haverfield, 'Biographical Note', in Henry Francis Pelham, *Essays* (Oxford: Clarendon Press, 1911), p. xxi; Sir Henry Jones and John Henry Muirhead, *The Life and Philosophy of Edward Caird* (Glasgow: Maclehose, Jackson & Co., 1921), pp. 93–125. For dons' civic action more widely, see Anthony Howe, 'Intellect and Civic Responsibility: Dons and Citizens in Nineteenth-Century Oxford', in R.C. Whiting, ed., *Oxford: Studies in the History of a University Town since 1800* (Manchester: Manchester University Press, 1993), pp. 12–52.
38. Ritchie, *Principles*, p. 101.
39. Oakeley, *My Adventures in Education*, p. 67.
40. *Ibid.*, pp. 62–3; see also Jones and Muirhead, *The Life and Philosophy of Edward Caird*, p. 145, and RP XIV.4.40, Lucy Kempson to Mary Stocks, 13 May 1947.

41. Somerville College Archives, Lettice Ilbert to her sister Olivia, 21 Oct. 1894.
42. RP XIV.4.38, Mildred Pope to Mary Stocks, 4 Apr. 1947.
43. On women's college friendships, see especially Martha Vicinus, *Independent Women: Work and Community for Single Women, 1850–1920* (Chicago: University of Chicago Press, 1985), esp. pp. 144–5.
44. RP XIV.4.40, Lucy Kempson to Mary Stocks, 8 May 1947.
45. Somerville College Archives, Minute Book of the A.P.s.
46. *Ibid.*
47. RP XIV.3.92, BBC script, 18 May 1952.
48. Somerville College Archives, Minute Book of the A.P.s.
49. Margery Fry Papers courtesy of Ms Annabel Cole, Oakeley to Fry, n.d.
50. This account of the campaign for degrees relies on Annie M.A.H. Rogers, *Degrees – by Degrees* (Oxford: Oxford University Press, 1938), and Vera Brittain, *The Women at Oxford*. Somerville students discussed petitioning the university to grant degrees on 11 and 12 May 1895; see Somerville College Archives, College Meeting Minutes.
51. RP IX.4.108, WR to Emily [n.d., probably 1895]; and for an uncharacteristic avowal of pride in his daughter's efforts, see RP IX.5.4, WR to EFR, 9 May 1896.
52. Although no figures are available for the occupational breakdown of the vote, Rita McWilliams-Tullberg, analysing Cambridge University's decision against degrees for women in 1897, found that churchmen and doctors tended to oppose women and teachers clearly to support them. See Rita McWilliams-Tullberg, *Women at Cambridge: A Men's University – Though of a Mixed Type* (London: Victor Gollancz, 1975), p. 224.
53. For an account of the debate, see, *Manchester Guardian*, 11 Mar. 1896, p. 3.
54. Numbers of candidates are from Mallet, *A History of the University*, III, p. 472ff.
55. Somerville College Archives, Reports of Collections, E.F. Rathbone, Comments by Mr Pelham and Mr Cannan, Hilary Term 1895, Summer Term 1895 and Summer Term 1896.
56. Margery Fry Papers, 'Cherub' [Lucy Kempson] to Margery Fry, 15 July 1896.
57. Mary Stocks, *Eleanor Rathbone: A Biography* (London: Victor Gollancz, 1949), p. 47.
58. BBC Broadcast, 26 Mar. 1956, quoted in Enid Huws Jones, *Margery Fry: The Essential Amateur* (London: Oxford University Press, 1966), p. 47.
59. RP, Dec. 2002 accession (being catalogued), Miss Maitland to Eleanor Rathbone, 3 Aug. 1896; Charles Cannan to EFR, 7 July 1896.
60. Huws Jones, *Margery Fry*, p. 47.
61. See the brief mention of this 'anonymous' gift in the centenary pamphlet, *Somerville College Oxford, 1879–1979* (Oxford: Somerville College, 1978), p. 11; Maitland thanks Rathbone for her contribution in an undated letter [probably 1897], RP Dec. 2002 accession (being catalogued).
62. Somerville College Archives, College Meeting Minutes, 15 June 1895; Adams, *Somerville for Women*, p. 126.

Chapter 4   Her Father's Daughter

1. RP IX.4.102, WR to Emily, 2 Jan. 1891, and RP IX.4.104, WR to Emily, 8 Feb. 1891.
2. SCA, Photocopy of a diary kept by Winifred Richardson Evans, later wife of Herbert Reynolds Rathbone, Christmas 1907; see also Lyle's letters to 'Pup' [Francis Warre Rathbone] during his honeymoon, esp. RP IX.4.178, 6 Jan. 1899.
3. RP IX.4.160, Francis Warre Rathbone to WR, 20 Sept. 1899.
4. RP IX.4.189, WR to Elsie, 1 Jan. 1887.
5. For this crisis in the family firm, see Lucie Nottingham, *Rathbone Brothers: From Merchant to Banker, 1742–1992* (London: Rathbone Brothers Plc, 1992), pp. 71–7.
6. Letters between William and William Gair, between William and Blanche, and between Blanche and William Gair, reveal considerable conflict and resentment over William Gair's declining circumstances; see esp. RP IX.8.45b–e.
7. RP XV.3.4, Hugh to Emily, 28 Aug. 1908.

8. RP, Dec. 2002 accession (being catalogued), Maitland to EFR, 3 Aug. 1896.
9. On William Rathbone's work with the Central Relief Society, see especially, Margaret Simey, *Charity Rediscovered: A Study of Philanthropic Effort in Nineteenth Century Liverpool* (1951; rpt. Liverpool: Liverpool University Press, 1992), esp. ch. 7.
10. Mary Stocks, *Eleanor Rathbone: A Biography* (London: Victor Gollancz, 1949), pp. 50–1.
11. RP, Dec. 2002 accession (being catalogued), EFR to 'my dear Father', 24 Mar. 1897.
12. LRO, Liverpool Central Relief Society Papers, Executive Committee Minutes, 14 Oct. 1897, 3 Nov. 1897.
13. Central Relief Society, *Annual Report*, 34 (1896–7), p. 19; 35 (1897–8), p. 20.
14. *Ibid.*, 34 (1896–7), pp. 18–19; 35 (1897–8), pp. 19–21.
15. *Ibid.*, 35 (1897–8), p. 20.
16. Most brilliantly (for the London Charity Organisation Society) by Gareth Stedman Jones, *Outcast London: A Study in the Relationship between Classes in Victorian Society* (1971; rpt. New York: Pantheon, 1984).
17. Margery Fry Papers, courtesy of Ms Annabel Cole, Oakeley to Fry, 16 Jan. [1898].
18. These passages are taken from two letters from Rathbone to Oakeley, written – I believe – in the summer of 1901 and December 1901. The letters are quoted at length by Stocks, *Eleanor Rathbone*, pp. 52–6; her copies of the originals are in RP, Dec. 2002 accession (being catalogued).
19. RP, Dec. 2002 accession (being catalogued), EFR to Oakeley, n.d. [summer 1901].
20. RP IX.9.37, WR, 'Memo on Experience as to Hard Work', 4 Apr. 1899.
21. Eleanor F. Rathbone, *William Rathbone: A Memoir* (London: Macmillan & Co., 1905), p. 489.
22. RP IX.5.3, WR to Emily, 11 May 1901.
23. RP, Dec. 2002 accession (being catalogued), Eleanor to 'my dear Papa', 15 May 1901.
24. *Ibid.*
25. Eleanor F. Rathbone, *William Rathbone*, p. 485.
26. *Women's Suffrage Journal*, 17: 204 (1 Dec. 1886), p. 160.
27. See W.R. Rubinstein, *Men of Property: The Very Wealthy in Britain since the Industrial Revolution* (New Brunswick, NJ: Rutgers University Press, 1981), pp. 31, 41, for statistics on size of estates.
28. The following summary of the provisions of the will and ultimate disposal of the property has been pieced together from the will and probate of William Rathbone, dated 15 Aug. 1898, Somerset House, and the estate duty registers held at Kew (PRO IR 26/8363, Folios 1221–1238).
29. See William's correspondence with his cousin Richard Rathbone prior to Hugh and Evie's marriage in 1888, in RP IX.8.46–52; Pat Jalland also discusses William Rathbone's determination to ensure Evie's right to dispose of her own income freely after marriage in *Women, Marriage and Politics, 1860–1914* (Oxford: Clarendon Press, 1986), pp. 60–1.
30. The records on the children's settlements and trusts are complicated, but correspondence between Emily and Hugh, both of whom were executors of the will, makes it clear that they understood that each of the children had received a total of £15,000. See RP XV.3.1–7.
31. Lucretia's settlement was divided fairly equally among her four children in 1893–4, at which point its total value was over £78,000. See Note f., in the Estate Duty Registers on the Estate of William Rathbone (PRO, IR 26/8363).
32. RP IX.9.9b, dated Mar. 1892.
33. RP, Dec. 2002 accession (being catalogued), EFR to Hilda Oakeley, n.d. [1903?].
34. RP XXV.1.111 (5), Emily to WGR, 28 July 1903; RP XXV.1.103 (3), EFR to WGR, 30 Sept. 1903.
35. RP XXV.1.103 (2), EFR to WGR, date unclear.
36. *Ibid.*
37. Eleanor F. Rathbone, *William Rathbone*, p. 493.
38. *Ibid.*, p. v.
39. Noel Annan, *Leslie Stephen: The Godless Victorian* (New York: Random House, 1984).

40. Eleanor F. Rathbone, *William Rathbone*, pp. 25, 358.
41. WR to OJL, quoted *ibid.*, p. 434.
42. Eleanor F. Rathbone, *William Rathbone*, p. 53.
43. *Ibid.*, pp. 34–5.
44. *Ibid.*, pp. 39–40.
45. *Ibid.*, p. 72.
46. *Ibid.*, pp. 493, 470–1.
47. *Ibid.*, p. 454n.
48. *Ibid.*, pp. 183, 222, 266–7.
49. *Ibid.*, p. 187.
50. RP XIX.1.3 (1).
51. Enid Huws Jones, *Margery Fry: The Essential Amateur* (London: Oxford University Press, 1966), p. 3; RP XIX.1.4 (6), A.C. Bradley to EFR, 11 Apr. 1905.
52. *The Times*, 21 Apr. 1905; *Evening Standard*, 2 Mar. 1905; *Charity Organisation Review*, 20: 118 (Oct. 1906), pp. 190–7.
53. Quoted in Huws Jones, *Margery Fry*, p. 61.

Coda to Part I: Emily Alone

1. RP IX.4.107, WR to Emily, 30 June 1895.
2. RP XXV.1.111 (1), Emily to WGR, 13 Mar. 1900.
3. Her obituary notes that she played no role in public life after William's death: *Liverpool Post and Mercury*, 20 Mar. 1918.
4. RP, Dec. 2002 accession (being catalogued), 'Cherub' [Lucy Kempson] to Margery Fry, n.d., forwarded by Fry to Mary Stocks, 6 May 1947.
5. Hugh recorded Emily's trips in his diary, RP XXIIA.

Chapter 5   Enter Miss Macadam

1. Letter (now lost), n.d., quoted in Mary D. Stocks, *Eleanor Rathbone: A Biography* (London: Victor Gollancz, 1949), p. 58.
2. *Ibid.*, p. 8.
3. General Register Office for Scotland, Edinburgh, Registers of Births, Marriages and Deaths.
4. G.F. Barbour, *The Life of Alexander Whyte, D.D.* (London: Hodder & Stoughton, 1923), p. 140.
5. Lizzie died in 1885, when Elizabeth was aged fourteen and Margaret twelve; *ibid.*, p. 269.
6. Communication from Ms Silviane Dubois, Archivist, Literary and Historical Society of Quebec, 16 Sept. 1993; also, Laura Isobel Bancroft, 'Morrin College: An Historical and Sociological Study', Bachelor's Memoir, Department of Sociology, University of Laval, 1950, Appendix D.
7. Although Elizabeth Macadam listed Morrin College as the school from which she obtained her BA (SCA, *University of Liverpool Students' Handbook*, volumes for 1911 and 1913–14), Morrin College records list Margaret – but not Elizabeth – as a BA graduate in 1893.
8. National Archives of Canada, Census of 1891, Microfilm Reel T–6415, District 178, p. 8.
9. Macadam's death date is given in his entry in W. Ewing, ed., *Annals of the Free Church of Scotland* (Edinburgh: T. & T. Clark, 1914). Barbour, on the other hand, insists that Alexander Whyte's nieces came to live with him after Macadam's death, and remained there for several years prior to Margaret's marriage in 1897. It is possible, then, that Thomas Macadam died in 1894; certainly his daughters left for Scotland around this year.
10. The quotation describes Margaret's interests, although we know Elizabeth shared them. For this, and for the Reverend John Murdoch Ebenezer Ross, as Ian was formally known, see James Moffatt, 'A Sketch of John M.E. Ross', in J.M.E. Ross, *The Tree of Healing: Short*

Studies in the Message of the Cross, preface by Elizabeth Macadam (London: Hodder & Stoughton, n.d.), pp. xviii–xix.

11. General Register Office for Scotland, Will and Probate of Elizabeth Macadam.

12. Interviews with Dr B.L. Rathbone, Liverpool, 18 Mar. 1993 and 26 July 1994, and with David and Diana Hopkinson, Godalming, 18 Aug. 1994.

13. Interview with Margaret Simey, Liverpool, 7 Jan. 1993.

14. SCA, *University of Liverpool Students' Handbook*, volumes for 1911 and 1913–14.

15. WL, Archives of the Women's University Settlement, 5/WUS/2, Minute Book 1891–9, Meeting of 4 Feb. 1898.

16. *Ibid.*, List of Pfeiffer Scholars.

17. WL, Women's University Settlement, *Annual Report*, 15 (Mar. 1902), pp. 19–25.

18. On the Women's University Settlement, see especially, Elizabeth Macadam, *The Equipment of the Social Worker* (London: George Allen & Unwin, 1925), ch. 2 (by Margaret Sewell); also Seth Koven, 'Culture and Poverty: The London Settlement House Movement, 1870–1914', PhD Diss., Harvard University, 1987, esp. pp. 404–19; Martha Vicinus, *Independent Women: Work and Community for Single Women, 1850–1920* (Chicago: University of Chicago Press, 1985), pp. 211–46 *passim*; Jane Lewis, *Women and Social Action in Victorian and Edwardian England* (Stanford: Stanford University Press, 1991), pp. 66–70.

19. WL, 'Special Report on District Visiting by Miss H.J. Gow', WUS, *Annual Report*, 13 (Mar. 1900), pp. 16–22.

20. Margery Fry Papers courtesy of Ms Annabel Cole, Oakeley to Fry, 25 June (probably 1898 or 1899).

21. WL, WUS, *Report*, 16 (Mar. 1903), p. 18.

22. WL, WUS, *Report*, 15 (Mar. 1902), p. 25.

23. The above paragraph draws on the WUS *Reports*, which list volunteers under each branch of work.

24. On population, see especially, R. Lawton, 'The Population of Liverpool in the mid-nineteenth Century', *Transactions of the Historic Society of Lancashire and Cheshire*, 107 (1955), pp. 89–120; D. Caradog Jones, ed., *The Social Survey of Merseyside*, vol. 1 (Liverpool: Liverpool University Press, 1934), pp. 59–65.

25. Howard Channon, *Portrait of Liverpool* (London: Robert Hale & Co., 1970), pp. 74–5.

26. Lawton, 'Population of Liverpool', pp. 101–4. For Welsh and Irish immigration more generally, see P.J. Waller, *Democracy and Sectarianism: A Political and Social History of Liverpool, 1868–1939* (Liverpool: Liverpool University Press, 1981), esp. pp. 7–10.

27. Carlton Eugene Wilson, 'A Hidden History: The Black Experience in Liverpool, England, 1919–1945', PhD Diss., University of North Carolina, Chapel Hill, 1992, ch. 1; Maria Lin Wong, *Chinese Liverpudlians: A History of the Chinese Community in Liverpool* (Birkenhead: Liver Press, 1989).

28. Eric Midwinter, *Old Liverpool* (Newton Abbot: David & Charles, 1971), chs 5–6; Derek Fraser, *Power and Authority in the Victorian City* (New York: St Martin's Press, 1979), ch. 2.

29. Waller, *Democracy*, pp. 82–90.

30. Gervas Huxley, *Both Hands: An Autobiography* (London: Chatto & Windus, 1970), p. 118.

31. 'The White Slave Traffic', *Liverpool Daily Post*, 6 Nov. 1908.

32. For which, see especially Frank Neal, *Sectarian Violence: The Liverpool Experience, 1819–1914* (Manchester: Manchester University Press, 1988).

33. The above paragraph draws largely on Margaret Simey, *Charity Rediscovered: A Study of Philanthropic Effort in Nineteenth Century Liverpool* (1951; rpt. Liverpool: Liverpool University Press, 1992), *passim*. On the first appointment of women sanitary inspectors, see Susan Turnbull Shoemaker, *'To Enlighten, Not to Frighten': A Comparative Study of the Infant Welfare Movement in Liverpool and Philadelphia, 1890–1918* (New York: Garland, 1991), pp. 51–4.

34. The story of the establishment and early years of the settlement is told in Simey, *Charity Rediscovered*, pp. 130–2, and in Michael Rose, 'Settlements of University Men in Great

Towns: University Settlements in Manchester and Liverpool', *Transactions of the Historic Society of Lancashire and Cheshire*, 139 (1990), pp. 137–60. Records of the Victoria Settlement are held by the University of Liverpool: SCA, D. 45; the appeal for a cart and donkey is in Victoria Settlement, *Report*, 1 (1898), pp. 11–17. Local papers watched the early efforts of the settlement closely; for Hamilton's romantic past, see 'Liverpool Women's Settlement: A Famous Lady Doctor in Liverpool', *Liverpool Post*, 15 Apr. 1898, and for sketches of Mrs Booth and other patrons see Sarah A. Tooley, 'Ladies of Liverpool', *The Woman At Home*, 4: 21 (June 1895).

35. For the dispensary, see SCA, D. 45, Victoria Settlement, *Report*, 4 (1901), p. 13; for the evolution of work with invalid children, see Mrs Frank Fletcher, 'Trades for Invalid Children', *Charity Organisation Review*, new ser., 16: 93 (Sept. 1904), pp. 152–60.

36. Royden to Courtney, 2 Nov. 1900, quoted in Sheila Fletcher, *Maude Royden: A Life* (Oxford: Basil Blackwell, 1989), p. 31.

37. *Ibid.*

38. Royden to Courtney, 21 Feb. 1901?, quoted *ibid.*, p. 36.

39. Royden to Courtney, 5 Dec. 1900, quoted *ibid.*, p. 31. (Fletcher has the passage as 'laughed like anything'; but see Koven, 'Culture and Poverty', p. 389.)

40. Royden to Courtney, 29 Jan. 1901, quoted *ibid.*, p. 32.

41. Royden to Courtney, 5 Dec. 1900, quoted *ibid.*

42. Royden to Courtney, 29 Jan. 1901, quoted *ibid.*, p. 36.

43. Royden to Courtney, 5 Dec. 1900, quoted *ibid.*, p. 35.

44. For Macadam's outreach to students, see 'University Settlement', *The Sphinx*, 13: 5 (13 Dec. 1905), pp. 74–7; SCA, *University of Liverpool Students' Handbook*, 1908–9, entries for 'settlements'. For numbers of women at Liverpool University, see Julie Sims Gilbert, 'Women at the English Civic Universities: 1880–1920', PhD Diss., University of North Carolina at Chapel Hill, 1988, p. 70.

45. SCA, D. 45, Victoria Settlement, *Report*, 6 (Jan. 1904), p. 3.

46. RP XXIIA, Diary of Hugh Rathbone, entry for 1902.

47. Stocks, *Eleanor Rathbone*, p. 58.

48. Much of this giving was virtually anonymous. Although the subscriptions and smaller donations of all the Rathbone women were listed in the settlement's reports, later more substantial donations – such as the £500 that Elsie gave to support an office for friendly visiting, the £5,000 that Evie gave to endow Macadam's lectureship at Liverpool University, and the sizeable amounts Eleanor gave towards the salaries of the secretaries of several organizations – emerge only through the archival records.

49. SCA, D. 45, Victoria Women's Settlement, *Annual Reports*, 1901 and 1910, *passim*.

50. SCA, D. 45, Leaflet, 'Victoria Women's Settlement' (Nov. 1904), p. 3.

51. Macadam (*Equipment of the Social Worker*, p. 33) states that the school was founded in January of 1904, and certainly some regular instruction began during that year. The first General Meeting was held only in March 1905, however, and an organizing committee established to set up the rules of the school. The first serious course of lectures was given in 1905, and a name chosen in 1906. See SCA, P. 826, Minute Book of the Committee of the SSSTSW.

52. Macadam, *Equipment of the Social Worker*, pp. 33–4.

53. SCA, P. 826, Minute Book of the SSSTSW, Entry for July 1906, for the 1906 course of lectures. For the founding of the school, see SCA, P. 826, 'School of Social Science', MS history; also Simey, *Charity Rediscovered*, pp. 135–6; Thomas Kelly, *For Advancement of Learning: The University of Liverpool, 1881–1981* (Liverpool: Liverpool University Press, 1981), pp. 143–5.

54. This paragraph draws on two lectures by John MacCunn, 'Motives to Social Work', and 'Social Motive and Democratic Education', in *Liverpool Addresses on Ethic of Social Work* (Liverpool: The University Press, 1911).

55. For an account of one year's programme of 'practical work', see SCA, D. 45, Victoria Settlement, *Report*, 11 (1908), pp. 8–9; and for one student's recollections, see SCA, P. 826, 'School of Social Science', MS history, pp. 8–10.

56. Elizabeth Macadam, 'The Universities and the Training of the Social Worker', *Hibbert Journal*, 12 (Jan. 1914), p. 292; Macadam reiterated the absolute centrality both of 'practical work' to the training of social workers, and of contact with independent working-class organizations, in her 1925 book, *The Equipment of the Social Worker*, esp. ch. 6.

57. Macadam, 'Training for Social Work', paper given at the Annual Conference of Charity Organisation Societies, 13–16 June 1910, *Charity Organisation Review*, new ser., 28: 163 (July 1910), p. 78.

58. See especially SCA, P. 826, SSSTSW Minutes, 13 Mar. 1908.

59. SCA, S. 135, Faculty of Arts Reports Book, 'Report of the Committee on Relations of Faculty to the School of Social Science', 11 Feb. 1911.

60. SCA, P. 826, Attendance figures appended to a report, 'The Provision of Training in Social Science'.

61. SCA, P. 826, SSSTSW, *Report*, 1913–14, p. 2.

62. SCA, D. 45, Victoria Settlement, *Report*, 1 (July 1898), p. 6.

63. SCA, D. 45, Victoria Settlement, *Report*, 7 (1904), p. 6.

64. SCA, D. 45, Victoria Settlement, *Report*, 13 (1910), p. 7; also Macadam's speech to the settlement's workers' association, *ibid.*, pp. 30–1.

65. Neither the dispensary operated by the settlement, nor the 'Poor Man's Lawyer' which provided free legal advice on their premises, would provide services to those able to pay for private doctors or solicitors (see SCA, D. 45, Victoria Settlement, *Annual Report*, 9 [1906], p. 6; 12 [1909], p. 26), and while they arranged holidays for families and vacation schools for children, they did require that families pay for these services.

66. SCA, D. 45, Victoria Settlement, *Annual Report*, 11 (1908), esp. pp. 7, 9.

67. SCA, P. 826, SSSTSW Minute Book, Executive Committee Meeting, 20 Nov. 1908; also LRO, Liverpool Central Relief Society Papers, Executive Committee Minutes, 7 Jan. 1909. For the Office of Friendly Help, see SCA, D. 45, Victoria Settlement, *Report*, 12 (1909), p. 6.

68. SCA, D. 45, Victoria Settlement, *Report*, 13 (1910), pp. 9–11.

69. See, for example, Daniel H.C. Bartlette, Letter, 'Inquisitorial Spirit Abroad', *Liverpool Post*, 1 June 1912; 'Pooling of Charity', *Liverpool Courier*, 31 May 1912.

70. 'Select Vestry. Divergent Views on Voluntary Aid', *Liverpool Courier*, 24 Aug. 1910.

71. For these figures, see Liverpool Council of Voluntary Aid, *Annual Report* 4 (1913), pp. 30–1; for a complete history of the Council, see H.R. Poole, *The Liverpool Council of Social Service, 1909–1959* (Liverpool: Liverpool Council of Social Service, 1960).

72. For their work, see especially the Archives of the Liverpool Council of Voluntary Aid Courtesy of the Council, Minute books of the Executive Committee, the Committee on Relief in the Homes of the Poor, and the Social Improvement and Education Committee.

73. SCA, D. 45, Victoria Settlement, *Annual Report*, 9 (1906), pp. 10–13.

74. Macadam, 'Training for Social Work', pp. 72–82.

75. The three women members established a sewing room for unemployed women, and cooperated with the Victoria Settlement in efforts to find them more permanent work. See the minute book of the Distress Committee in the Liverpool Record Office, 352 MIN/DIS/1/1.

76. SCA, D. 45, Victoria Settlement, *Annual Report*, 12 (1909), p. 5.

77. SCA, D. 45, Victoria Settlement, *Annual Report*, 13 (1910), p. 8.

78. The rules governing eligibility were complicated; whereas anyone could stand for the School Board, only substantial ratepayers could stand for election as a guardian, a distinction that retarded women's entry into this work. For a detailed account of the local franchises and qualifications, and for women's gradual entry into different realms, see, Patricia Hollis, *Ladies Elect: Women in English Local Government, 1865–1914* (Oxford: Clarendon Press, 1987).

79. SCA, D. 45, Victoria Settlement, *Report*, 11 (1908), pp. 7–8. There were, by 1909, some 1,165 women guardians serving on 412 boards in England and Wales; there were 638 boards with 24,600 guardians altogether. See Women's Local Government Society *Annual Report*, 1909–1910, p. 23.

80. Letter from Harry Green, *Liverpool Daily Post*, 6 Oct. 1909, p. 9; also 4 Oct. 1909, p. 9.

81. RP, XIV.1.2, EFR to Emily Rathbone, 5 Oct. 1909.

82. 'Liverpool's Lady Councillor', *Liverpool Daily Post*, 8 Oct. 1909, p. 8.
83. Women's Local Government Society, *Annual Report*, 1909–1910, p. 31. Granby had an electorate of 3,600 on 1 Nov. 1909; according to figures published in *Common Cause* (4: 192, [13 Dec. 1912], p. 619), there were only 679 women on the register in 1910. Even if Rathbone received most of the votes of the 500 or so women who voted, she still must have won more votes from men than did her opponent.
84. For the Conservatives' view that Rathbone was, in fact, a Radical, see 'Municipal Elections', *Liverpool Courier*, 28 Oct. 1910, p. 5.
85. 'Granby Ward', *Liverpool Daily Post*, 26 Oct. 1910, p. 7.
86. See Appendix 2 for Rathbone's local election contests.
87. Rathbone stressed this point in her speeches before the 1910 election; see 'Granby Ward', *Liverpool Daily Post*, 26 Oct. 1910, p. 7; for her efforts on women's pay, see also City Council meeting of 10 Nov. 1913 summary in *Liverpool Red Book* (1914), p. 641.
88. WL, Brian Harrison interviews with Mary Stocks, 21 May 1974 and with Doris (Hardman) Cox and Marjorie (Green) Soper, 15 Mar. 1977; my interview with Mrs Joan (Prewer) Gibson, London, 6 Jan. 1996.
89. Harrison interview with Marjorie (Green) Soper, 15 March 1977.
90. SCA, S. 135, Faculty of Arts Reports Book, C.S. Loch to E.K. Gonner, appended to the Report of the Committee on Relations of Faculty to the School of Social Science, 11 Feb. 1911.
91. SCA, D. 45, Victoria Settlement, *Report*, 13 (1910), pp. 5–6.
92. Quoted in Enid Huws Jones, *Margery Fry: The Essential Amateur* (London: Oxford University Press, 1966), p. 48.
93. Quoted in Stocks *Eleanor Rathbone*, p. 181.
94. RP X.1.221, Elizabeth Macadam to Emily Rathbone, 7 July 1912.
95. For the trip to Greece, RP XXIIA, Diary of Hugh Rathbone, entry for 1907; for the trip to the Lake District, RP X.1.222, Florence MacCunn to Emily Rathbone, n.d.
96. Interviews with B.L. Rathbone, Liverpool, 18 Mar. 1993 and 26 July 1994, and with David and Diana Hopkinson, Godalming, 18 Aug. 1994.
97. Telephone interview with Noreen Rathbone, 2 Aug. 2003; for the Romney Street arrangements, see RP, Dec. 2002 accession (being catalogued), inventory of 50 Romney Street, Feb. 1938.
98. RP XIX.3.13, Diary of Winifred Rathbone (née Evans), Christmas 1907.

Chapter 6 Must Mothers be Poor?

1. Entry for 2 July 1886, *The Diary of Beatrice Webb*, ed. Norman and Jeanne MacKenzie, vol. 1, *Glitter around the Darkness Within* (Cambridge, Mass.: Harvard University Press, 1982), p. 173.
2. Margery Fry Papers courtesy of Ms Annabel Cole, EFR to Fry, 7 Aug. 1898.
3. On the Women's Industrial Council, see Ellen Mappen, *Helping Women at Work: The Women's Industrial Council, 1889–1914* (London: Hutchinson, 1985); Liselotte Glage, *Clementina Black: A Study in History and Literature* (Heidelberg: Carl Winter, 1981).
4. There is some discussion of this episode in Krista Cowman, 'Engendering Citizenship: The Political Involvement of Women on Merseyside, 1890–1920', D.Phil. thesis, University of York, 1994, pp. 101–6.
5. E.F. Rathbone, 'Occupations of Girls after Leaving School', *Women's Industrial News*, 11 (Mar. 1900), pp. 163–4.
6. E.F. Rathbone, 'Women Cigar Makers in a Large Provincial Town', *Women's Industrial News*, 12 (Sept. 1900), pp. 185–90.
7. The Women's Industrial Council, *What the Council Is and Does* (London: Morton & Burt, 1909); rpt. in Mappen, *Helping Women at Work*, p. 63.
8. The women's workroom was open from January 1907 until September 1912, and it operated under the personal supervision of Rathbone and her two colleagues. For this work, see LRO, 352/MIN/DIS/1/1, Minute Book of the Distress Committee.

9. SCA, D. 45, Victoria Settlement, *Report*, 11 (1908), pp. 12–15, quoted at p. 14.

10. E.F. Rathbone and E. McCrindell, *Technical Education of Women and Girls in Liverpool: Report of an Inquiry for the Liverpool Women's Industrial Council* (Liverpool: Liverpool Women's Industrial Council, 1910).

11. Royal Commission on the Poor Laws and Relief of Distress, *Appendix*, Vol. VIII, *Minutes of Evidence, PP* 1910, XLVIII, Cd. 5066, p. 271.

12. 'Liverpool Women's Industrial Council Report,' in SCA, D. 45, Victoria Settlement, *Report*, 13 (1910), p. 11.

13. Rathbone referred to this failed effort twice, once in her evidence to the Royal Commission (p. 272), and once at the 1907 Conference of the National Union of Women Workers, for which see below.

14. National Union of Women Workers, *Women Workers* (London: P.S. King, 1907), p. 93.

15. *Ibid.*, pp. 93–5.

16. This summary cannot do justice to the subtle and carefully thought out positions of both Black and MacDonald, for which see especially, Ellen F. Mappen, 'Strategies for Change: Social Feminist Approaches to the Problems of Women's Work', in Angela V. John, ed., *Unequal Opportunities: Women's Employment in England, 1800–1918* (Oxford: Basil Blackwell, 1986), pp. 235–59.

17. Under Rathbone's leadership, the Liverpool Women's Industrial Council took a strictly egalitarian stance on such issues as factory legislation, declining to sign one council memorial on women's work because of its endorsement of separate regulations for women. See, BLPES, Margaret MacDonald Papers, I.13, EFR to MacDonald, 5 Apr. 1900; also BLPES, British Association for the Advancement of Science Papers, Coll. Misc. 486/2/9.

18. For an account stressing Booth's Liverpool connections and his early revulsion from the society of its merchant class, see T.S. and M.B. Simey, *Charles Booth: Social Scientist* (Oxford: Oxford University Press, 1960). For the history of dock labour and of attempts at its regulation, I have relied on Gordon Phillips and Noel Whiteside's comprehensive study, *Casual Labour: The Unemployment Question in the Port Transport Industry, 1880–1970* (Oxford: Clarendon Press, 1985).

19. For Booth's decasualization scheme, and his efforts in Liverpool, see Phillips and Whiteside, *Casual Labour*, pp. 47–55; and for reasons behind employers' and workers' opposition, see Eleanor F. Rathbone, *Report of an Inquiry into the Conditions of Dock Labour at the Liverpool Docks* (Liverpool: Northern Publishing Co., 1904), pp. 41–3.

20. See RP IX.5.4, WR to Charles Booth, 16 May 1896, WR to Mr Hughes, 17 Dec. 1896, and WR to Mr Hughes, 14 Jan. 1897; also Eleanor F. Rathbone, *William Rathbone: A Memoir* (London: Macmillan & Co., 1905), pp. 389–94.

21. Rathbone, *Dock Labour*, p. ii.

22. For one historian's high assessment of its accuracy and value, see, E. Taplin, 'Dock Labour at Liverpool: Occupational Structure and Working Conditions in the Late Nineteenth Century', *Transactions of the Historic Society of Lancashire and Cheshire*, 127 (1978), pp. 133–54, esp. p. 150.

23. Rathbone, *Dock Labour*, pp. 21–2, 30.

24. *Ibid.*, p. 43.

25. For which, see Liverpool Central Relief Society *Annual Report*, 42 (1904–5), p. 10; 44 (1906–7), pp. 18–19.

26. For the introduction of the scheme in Liverpool, see Phillips and Whiteside, *Casual Labour*, ch. 3, esp. pp. 89–96; also Richard Williams, *The Liverpool Docks Problem* (Liverpool: Northern Publishing Co., 1912).

27. Royal Commission on the Poor Laws, *Minutes of Evidence*, p. 268.

28. *Ibid.*, pp. 262–4.

29. *How the Casual Labourer Lives: Report of the Liverpool Joint Research Committee on the Domestic Condition and Expenditure of the Families of Certain Liverpool Labourers* (Liverpool: Northern Publishing Co., 1909), p. vi.

30. B. Seebohm Rowntree, *Poverty: A Study of Town Life* (London: Macmillan, 1901). And for

Rowntree more generally, Asa Briggs, *Social Thought and Social Action: A Study of the Work of Seebohm Rowntree, 1871–1954* (London: Longmans, Green & Co., 1961).

31. Lady Bell, *At the Works: A Study of a Manufacturing Town* (1907; rpt. London: Virago, 1985).

32. *How the Casual Labourer Lives*, pp. ix–x.

33. *Ibid.*, p. xx.

34. *Ibid.*, p. xxiv.

35. *Ibid.*, p. ix.

36. *Ibid.*, p. xiv.

37. *Ibid.*, p. xv.

38. Paul Johnson, *Saving and Spending: The Working-Class Economy in Britain, 1870–1939* (Oxford: Clarendon Press, 1985), p. 170; and for pawnbroking more generally, see also, Melanie Tebbutt, *Making Ends Meet: Pawnbroking and Working-Class Credit* (Leicester: Leicester University Press, 1983).

39. *How the Casual Labourer Lives*, p. xvi.

40. Mary D. Stocks, *Eleanor Rathbone: A Biography* (London: Victor Gollancz, 1949), p. 121.

41. *How the Casual Labourer Lives*, p. xvi.

42. *Ibid.*, p. xxiii.

43. Maud Pember Reeves, *Round about a Pound a Week* (1913; rpt. London: Virago, 1979), esp. ch. 9.

44. It is worth mentioning, as historical research by Ellen Ross has confirmed, that Lady Bell recognized that the wives did not consider such physical abuse to be exceptional, showing 'not so much forbearance as a sort of dogged acceptance of the matrimonial relation with its rough as well as its smooth side'. Lady Bell, *At the Works*, p. 239; and, for the meaning of domestic violence in working-class culture before the First World War, see Ellen Ross, *Love and Toil: Motherhood in Outcast London, 1870–1918* (New York: Oxford University Press, 1993), pp. 84–6.

45. *How the Casual Labourer Lives*, p. xxxiv.

46. *Ibid.*, p. xxvi.

47. Jane Lewis, 'Social Facts, Social Theory and Social Change: The Ideas of Booth in relation to those of Beatrice Webb, Octavia Hill and Helen Bosanquet', in David Englander and Rosemary O'Day, eds, *Retrieved Riches: Social Investigation in Britain, 1840–1914* (Aldershot: Scolar Press, 1995), p. 59.

48. *How the Casual Labourer Lives*, pp. xxviii–xxxii.

49. Royal Commission on the Poor Laws, *Minutes of Evidence*, p. 264.

50. Eleanor F. Rathbone, *The Problem of Women's Wages: An Enquiry into the Causes of the Inferiority of Women's Wages to Men's* (Liverpool: Northern Publishing Co., 1912), p. 5.

51. *Ibid.*, p. 8.

52. *Ibid.*, pp. 20–1.

53. *Ibid.*, p. 21.

54. *Ibid.*

55. *Ibid.*, p. 22.

56. *Ibid.*, p. 23.

57. Eleanor F. Rathbone, 'The Economic Position of Married Women', *Common Cause*, 3: 143 (4 Jan. 1912), p. 675.

58. Rathbone, *The Problem of Women's Wages*, p. 22.

59. *Ibid.*, p. 23.

60. *Ibid.*

61. Anna Martin in particular raised the problem of married women's inability to enforce their legal claim to maintenance; see her influential articles, 'The Mother and Social Reform', *Nineteenth Century and After*, I, 73: 435 (May 1913), pp. 1060–79; II, 73: 436 (June 1913), pp. 1235–55. For the early endowment proposals, and Wells's advocacy, see esp. Susan Pedersen, *Family, Dependence, and the Origins of the Welfare State: Britain and France, 1914–1945* (Cambridge: Cambridge University Press, 1993), pp. 42–6.

62. And, for this view, Cicely Hamilton, *Marriage as a Trade* (London: Chapman & Hall, 1909).

63. Rathbone, *The Problem of Women's Wages*, p. 22.

64. Editorial postscript to Rathbone, 'The Economic Position of Married Women', p. 675.

65. Letters by W.A. Elkin and A. Maude Royden, *Common Cause*, 3: 144 (11 Jan. 1912), pp. 688–9, and by Ada Nield Chew, *Common Cause*, 3: 146 (25 Jan. 1912), p. 724.

66. Eleanor F. Rathbone, Letter, *Common Cause*, 3: 145 (18 Jan. 1912), p. 710.

67. For which see Catherine Hakim, 'Census Reports as Documentary Evidence: The Census Commentaries, 1801–1951', *Sociological Review*, 28: 3 (Aug. 1980), pp. 551–80.

68. Women's Co-operative Guild, *28th Annual Report* (1911), p. 27.

69. E. Mahler and E.F. Rathbone, *Payment of Seamen: The Present System* (Liverpool: C. Tinling, 1911), p. 10.

70. See the pamphlet cited above; also Eleanor F. Rathbone, 'Women's Need of the Vote: A Practical Illustration. The Wives of Seafaring Men', *Common Cause*, 2: 99 (2 Mar. 1911), pp. 761–2; 'The Method of Payment of Seafaring Men as it Affects their Wives and Children: Investigation and Legal Committees', *Women's Industrial News*, 55 (July 1911), pp. 107–9; E. Mahler and E.F. Rathbone, 'Payment of Seamen', I, *Liverpool Courier*, 23 Jan. 1911, II, *Liverpool Courier*, 24 Jan. 1911.

71. 'Payment of Seamen', *Liverpool Courier*, 10 Jan. 1912.

72. 'Seamen's Wages. The Allotment Question. From the Men's Standpoint', *Liverpool Courier*, 18 Jan. 1912.

73. The settlement's visiting arrangements are mentioned in the Liverpool Central Relief Society's *Annual Report*, 41 (1903–4), p. 21; 42 (1904–5), p. 24; 44 (1906–7), p. 34, and in SCA, P. 826, SSSTSW Minute Book, Executive Committee Meeting, 8 Feb. 1906.

74. For one characteristic account of the frustrations of this work, see SCA, D. 45, Victoria Settlement, *Report*, 10 (1907), pp. 9–10.

75. Royal Commission on the Poor Laws, *Minutes of Evidence*, p. 273.

76. *Ibid.*, p. 274.

77. See Royal Commission on the Poor Laws, *Appendix*, Vol. IV, *PP* 1909, XLI, Cd. 4835, Evidence of Harris Cleaver, Clerk to the Guardians of the West Derby Union, esp. p. 19; Evidence of Henry Ball, Superintendent Relieving Officer for the parish of Liverpool, pp. 1–8, Evidence of Miss J.S. Thorburn, Member of the Liverpool Select Vestry, esp. p. 11.

78. A.M. McBriar, *An Edwardian Mixed Doubles: The Bosanquets versus the Webbs: A Study in British Social Policy, 1890–1929* (Oxford: Clarendon Press, 1987), pp. 242–6, 294–7.

79. E.F. Rathbone, *Report on the Condition of Widows under the Poor Law in Liverpool* (Liverpool: Lee & Nightingale, 1913), p. 29.

80. 'Guardians Resent Attack', *Liverpool Courier*, 20 Mar. 1914.

81. Liverpool Council of Voluntary Aid Papers, Executive Committee Minutes, 20 Mar. 1914.

82. Eleanor F. Rathbone, 'Position of Widows under the Poor Law in Liverpool' (letter), *Liverpool Post*, 26 Mar. 1914.

83. Eleanor F. Rathbone, 'The Position of Widows under the Poor Law', II, *Common Cause*, 5: 260 (3 Apr. 1914), p. 1021.

84. Rathbone, *Condition of Widows*, p. 32.

85. *Ibid.*, p. 33.

86. *Ibid.*, p. 32.

87. Rathbone, 'The Position of Widows under the Poor Law', II, p. 1022.

Chapter 7   Claiming Citizenship

1. The best account of the suffrage movement in Liverpool, albeit comprehensive only for the militant side, is Krista Cowman, 'Engendering Citizenship: The Political Involvement of Women on Merseyside, 1890–1920', D. Phil. thesis, University of York, 1994; see also Marij van Helmond, *Votes for Women: The Events on Merseyside, 1870–1928* (Liverpool: National Museums and Galleries on Merseyside, 1992). There is no adequate account of the work of

the LWSS. Reports of early meetings of the Society can be found in the *Englishwoman's Review*, 25: 1 (17 Jan. 1894), pp. 23–5; 27: 2 (14 Apr. 1896), p. 95; 29: 1 (15 Jan. 1898), pp. 24–5; 32: 1 (15 Jan. 1901), pp. 17–18; 34: 3 (15 July 1903), p. 164.

2. For brief biographical sketches of these three, see Sarah A. Tooley, 'Ladies of Liverpool', *The Woman At Home*, 4: 21 (June 1895).

3. *Liverpool Daily Post*, 13 April 1905; Cowman, 'Engendering Citizenship', pp. 200–1.

4. Van Helmond, *Votes for Women*, p. 24.

5. For figures on NUWSS affiliation, see Leslie Parker Hume, *The National Union of Women's Suffrage Societies, 1897–1914* (New York: Garland, 1982), pp. 57, 229.

6. Lancashire Record Office, DDX 1137/3/87, Rathbone to Amalgamated Society of Carpenters and Joiners, 5 Mar. 1907; on Cooper's Liverpool work, see also Jill Liddington, *The Life and Times of a Respectable Rebel: Selina Cooper, 1864–1946* (London: Virago, 1984), pp. 186–9.

7. For these meetings, see SCA D. 55/16, Transcript of entries in the Diary of Prof. W. Lyon Blease, and coverage in *Common Cause*, 1: 2 (22 Apr. 1909), p. 30, and 1: 4 (6 May 1909), p. 62.

8. *The Times*, 7 Sept. 1908, p. 15b.

9. 'Women and the Vote', *Liverpool Courier*, 20 June 1910, p. 7.

10. 'A Lady of Liverpool: Miss Cicely Leadley-Brown, M.B.E.', *Liverpolitan*, Nov. 1951, p. 2.

11. Edith Eskrigge, 'National Union Van Tour', *Common Cause*, 4: 177 (29 Aug. 1912), p. 364.

12. Royden as quoted in Sheila Fletcher, *Maude Royden: A Life* (Oxford: Basil Blackwell, 1989), p. 94.

13. Eleanor F. Rathbone, Letter, *The Times*, 16 Aug. 1910, p. 10.

14. 'By-Election', *Common Cause*, 2: 68 (28 July 1910), p. 260.

15. 'Kirkdale', *Liverpool Courier*, 19 July 1910, p. 7; 'Granby Ward', *Liverpool Courier*, 29 Oct. 1910, p. 8.

16. Eleanor F. Rathbone, 'By-election', *Common Cause*, 2: 67 (21 July 1910), p. 243.

17. Eleanor F. Rathbone, Letter, *The Times*, 16 Aug. 1910, p. 10; van Helmond, *Votes for Women*, pp. 37–8.

18. For these three incidents, see Andrew Rosen, *Rise up Women!* (London: Routledge & Kegan Paul, 1974), pp. 122, 129–30; van Helmond, *Votes for Women*, pp. 39–40, 49–50.

19. RP XIV.1.15, Christabel Pankhurst to EFR, 4 Feb. 1910.

20. SCA, D. 55/16, Blease Diary, entries for 20 July 1910, 16 Oct. 1910, 20 Oct. 1910, 22 Oct. 1910, and 22 Jan. 1911.

21. Harry Green, Letter, *Liverpool Daily Post*, 4 Oct. 1909, p. 9; 'Kirkdale', *Liverpool Courier*, 19 July 1910, p. 7; 'Granby Ward', *Liverpool Courier*, 29 Oct. 1910, p. 8; 'Alderman Salvidge and Lady Candidates', *Liverpool Daily Post*, 28 Oct. 1910, p. 4.

22. 'Kirkdale', *Liverpool Courier*, 19 July 1910, p. 7.

23. For Flatman's leadership, see esp. Cowman, 'Engendering Citizenship', pp. 213–20.

24. The complex manoeuvres over the Conciliation Bill are covered in detail by Hume, *National Union of Women's Suffrage Societies*; for Brailsford's crucial role, see also F.M. Leventhal, *The Last Dissenter: H.N. Brailsford and his World* (Oxford: Oxford University Press, 1985), ch. 5.

25. Eleanor F. Rathbone, Letter, *The Times*, 26 Dec. 1910, p. 6; also her debates with the National League for Opposing Women's Suffrage, *Manchester Guardian*, 10 Jan. 1911, p. 5; 13 Jan. 1911, p. 8; 17 Jan. 1911, p. 4.

26. See especially the reports of the demonstration on 18 June 1910, before the vote on the second reading in the *Liverpool Daily Post*, 20 June 1910, pp. 6, 9; *Liverpool Courier*, 20 June 1910, p. 7; *Common Cause*, 2: 63 (23 June 1910), p. 174. The LWSS also held a special service in St Margaret's Anfield on the night of the second reading of the 1912 version of the Conciliation Bill, with the Vicar of Wakefield taking as his text: 'And they marvelled that he should speak with the women'. *Common Cause*, 4: 158 (18 Apr. 1912), p. 27.

27. For the July 1910 demonstration, see *Common Cause*, 2: 66 (14 July 1910), pp. 219–21; for the June 1911 procession (the 'Women's Coronation Procession'), see *Common Cause*, 3: 114 (15 June 1911), p. 175; Hume, *National Union of Women's Suffrage Societies*, p. 109; and

especially Lisa Tickner, *The Spectacle of Women: Imagery of the Suffrage Campaign, 1907–14* (Chicago: University of Chicago Press, 1988), pp. 122–31.

28. City Council meeting of 1 Feb. 1911, summary in *Liverpool Red Book* (1912), p. 580; and, for more detail, Liverpool City Council, *Proceedings, 1910–11*, vol. 1, *Minutes*, Entry for 1 Feb. 1911, pp. 177–80.

29. *Common Cause*, 3: 111 (25 May 1911), p. 122.

30. A record of the Federation's activities must be compiled from its reports – usually by Leadley-Brown or Eskrigge – in *Common Cause*.

31. *Common Cause*, 4: 192 (13 Dec. 1912), pp. 619–20.

32. The NUWSS's budget also grew; the Union collected some £40,000 during ten months in 1912 alone. *Common Cause*, 4: 204 (7 Mar. 1913), p. 816.

33. The militants argued, with some justification, that a woman's suffrage amendment, lacking government support, would have no chance of success, but would destroy the Conciliation Bill. Christabel Pankhurst, *Unshackled: The Story of How We Won the Vote* (London: Hutchinson, 1959), p. 187; see also Emmeline Pethick-Lawrence, *My Part in a Changing World* (London: Victor Gollancz, 1938), pp. 256–7.

34. On hostility to the suffragettes, see Brian Harrison, *Separate Spheres: The Opposition to Women's Suffrage in Britain* (London: Croom Helm, 1978) ch. 9; on declining membership and defections from the WSPU, see Rosen, *Rise up Women!*, pp. 146–7, 157fn, 211, 223–6.

35. Cowman asserts that militancy revitalized the Liverpool movement after 1912, with donations and meetings continuing ('Engendering Citizenship', pp. 347–53), but also gives figures showing a serious decline in the average number of monthly meetings in the years before the war (p. 399).

36. 'Mrs. Fawcett and the Suffragettes', *Liverpool Daily Post*, 23 Nov. 1911.

37. *Common Cause*, 4: 171 (25 July 1912), p. 266.

38. Dr Alice Ker to her daughters, 19 Mar. 1912, reprinted in van Helmond, *Votes for Women*, p. 64.

39. SCA, D. 55/16, Blease Diary, see especially entries for March–June 1912, and 9 July 1913.

40. *Common Cause*, 3: 108 (4 May 1911), p. 62.

41. *Common Cause*, 3: 156 (4 Apr. 1912), pp. 887–8.

42. *Common Cause*, 5: 236 (17 Oct. 1913), p. 489; note also the discussion at the Federation's quarterly meeting in Colwyn Bay in May 1913 of the disastrous effects of militancy on the cause. *Common Cause*, 5: 214 (16 May 1913), p. 94.

43. See the photographs in van Helmond, *Votes for Women*, pp. 27, 83.

44. The Federation, for example, held some 90 meetings in support of the Labour candidate at one East Carmarthenshire by-election in the summer of 1912; the WSPU did not appear. *Common Cause*, 4: 177 (29 Aug. 1912), pp. 362–3.

45. *Common Cause*, 4: 184 (17 Oct. 1912), p. 483.

46. *Common Cause*, 5: 214 (16 May 1913), p. 94.

47. *Common Cause*, 5: 230 (5 Sept. 1913), p. 378.

48. See the reports on the Pilgrimage in *Common Cause*, 5: 219 (20 June 1913); 5: 222 (11 July 1913); 5: 223 (18 July 1913) and 5: 224 (25 July 1913); also Tickner, *Spectacle of Women*, pp. 141–7.

49. See CRO, Catherine Marshall Papers, 3/MAR/3/21, Jessie Beavan to Catherine Marshall, 27 Apr. 1913; *Common Cause*, 2: 254 (20 Feb. 1914), p. 892.

50. For the LWSS especially, see *Common Cause*, 6: 271 (19 June 1914), pp. 235–6.

51. Eleanor F. Rathbone, 'Methods of Conciliation', *Common Cause*, 4: 178 (5 Sept. 1912), pp. 373–4.

52. Max Weber, 'Politics as a Vocation', in *From Max Weber: Essays in Sociology*, ed. H.H. Gerth and C. Wright Mills (New York: Oxford University Press, 1946), pp. 77–128.

53. Quoted in Rosen, *Rise Up Women!*, p. 189.

54. Mrs Humphry Ward, Letter, *The Times*, 11 July 1910, p. 11, and Rathbone's response, *The Times*, 12 July 1910, p. 11.

55. See Rathbone's arguments in favour of petitions, canvasses and open-air meetings: WL,

2/NWS/B/1/1, Annual Council Minutes, 19 Mar. 1910; Eleanor F. Rathbone, Letter, *Common Cause*, 2: 73 (1 Sept. 1910), pp. 343–4; WL, 2/NWS/A/1/4, EC Minutes, 17 Apr. 1913, 15 May 1913.

56. For example, Rathbone had a pamphlet summarizing the Federation's work printed at her own expense; see WL, 2/NWS/A/1/4, EC Meeting, 17 Apr. 1913.

57. Letter, *Common Cause*, 1: 51 (31 Mar. 1910), p. 724.

58. RP XIV.3.89, *Liverpool Daily Post* clipping, n.d. [Aug. 1913].

59. *Common Cause*, 6: 271 (19 June 1914), pp. 235–6; 'Women and the War: Liverpool', *Common Cause*, 6: 279 (14 Aug. 1914). See also SCA, [E. Warhurst], 'Liverpool Women Citizen's Association' (typescript, 1944); CRO, Marshall Papers, D/MAR/3/24, Eleanor F. Rathbone, *A New Form of Suffrage Propaganda: The Liverpool Association of Women Citizens* (n.p., Nov. 1913).

60. On Mrs Fawcett and militancy, see David Rubinstein, *A Different World for Women: The Life of Millicent Garrett Fawcett* (Hemel Hempstead: Harvester Wheatsheaf, 1991), esp. p. 175; for Balfour, see Martin Pugh, *The March of the Women: A Revisionist Analysis of the Campaign for Women's Suffrage, 1866–1914* (Oxford: Oxford University Press, 2000), pp. 182–3.

61. Eleanor F. Rathbone, *The Harvest of the Women's Movement* (London, 1935), pp. 12–14.

62. RP XIV.3.35, Speech, Kensington High School, 16 Mar. 1937.

63. Rathbone, *Harvest*, p. 14.

64. E.g., 'National Union Deputation to the Prime Minister', *Common Cause*, 6: 24 (30 June 1910), p. 182; also Rathbone's notes on West Lancashire MPs for Union lobbying efforts, in CRO, Marshall Papers, D/MAR/3/14, EFR to Marshall, 9 Mar. 1912.

65. Historians have paid considerable attention to the last phases of the suffrage agitation and to the National Union's emerging alliance with Labour in particular, especially in view of the emerging historical consensus about the WSPU's pre-war decline. Sandra Holton's *Feminism and Democracy: Women's Suffrage and Reform Politics in Britain, 1900–1918* (Cambridge: Cambridge University Press, 1986) sees the NUWSS–Labour alliance as a reflection of a wider commitment to 'democracy' shared by feminists and socialists; Jo Vellacott's detailed study, *From Liberal to Labour with Women's Suffrage: The Story of Catherine Marshall* (Montreal: McGill-Queen's University Press, 1993), pays close attention to the strategic calculations made by the Union's leadership as well. Martin Pugh summarizes the strengths, weaknesses and likely consequences of that alliance in *The March of the Women*, ch. 10.

66. *Manchester Guardian*, 27 Nov. 1911, p. 9.

67. Eleanor F. Rathbone, *Disagreeable Truths about the Conciliation Bill* (Liverpool: Northern Publishing Co., n.d. [1912]), p. 3.

68. Ibid., p. 8. See also, Rathbone, 'The Enfranchisement of Married Women', *Common Cause*, 3: 140 (14 Dec. 1911), p. 629.

69. Rathbone mentioned that some members of the Executive viewed the proposal as a 'fancy franchise' in *Disagreeable Truths*, p. 3, and remembered this response again, many years later, in an essay entitled 'Changes in Public Life', in Ray Strachey, ed., *Our Freedom and Its Results* (London: Hogarth Press, 1936), p. 26n.

70. Millicent Garrett Fawcett, *What I Remember* (1925; rpt. Westport, Conn.: Hyperion Press, 1976), pp. 201–2.

71. This complex legislative history is best summarized by Hume, *National Union of Women's Suffrage Societies*, chs 4–5.

72. WL, 2/NWS/A/1/4, EC Minutes, 2 May 1912.

73. CRO, Marshall Papers, D/MAR/3/33, EFR to Fawcett, 10 May 1912.

74. 'Special Council Meeting', *Common Cause*, 4: 163 (23 May 1912), pp. 103–4; see also Vellacott, *From Liberal to Labour*, pp. 166–7, and Mrs Fawcett's strong retrospective defence of the policy, *What I Remember*, pp. 206–8.

75. Eleanor F. Rathbone, 'Methods of Conciliation', *Common Cause*, 4: 178 (5 Sept. 1912), pp. 373–4.

76. There is a copy of Rathbone's memorandum, ' "The Gentle Art of Making Enemies": A

Criticism of the Proposed Anti-Government Policy of the National Union', Feb. 1913, in WL, 2/NWS/B/1/3.

77. 'The National Union Annual Council Meeting', *Common Cause*, 4: 204 (7 Mar. 1913), pp. 817–18; see also Vellacott, *From Liberal to Labour*, pp. 211–13.

78. Hume, *National Union of Women's Suffrage Societies*, pp. 203–7.

79. CRO, Marshall Papers, D/MAR/3/19, Marshall to EFR, 14 Apr. 1913.

80. Evidence of local dissent must be pieced together from EC minutes and letters in the Marshall and H.W. Smith papers. The best summary of these tensions is provided by Holton, *Feminism and Democracy*, pp. 97–115.

81. CRO, Marshall Papers, D/MAR/3/21E, Eleanor Acland to Marshall, 7 May 1913; see also D/MAR/3/24, Eleanor Acland to Marshall, 20 Nov. 1913.

82. CRO, Marshall Papers, D/MAR/3/19, Dickinson to Marshall, 24 Apr. 1913.

83. Indiana University, Lilly Library, H.W. Smith Papers, Box 14, Ray Strachey to Oliver Strachey, 29 Jan. 1914.

84. WL, 7/MGF/88, 'The Policy of the National Union with regard to Labour Candidates', Jan. 1914; see also Vellacott's account of the Glasgow negotiations: *From Liberal to Labour*, pp. 316–21.

85. WL, 2/NWS/A/1/5, EC Minutes, 15 Jan. 1914 and 5 Feb. 1914.

86. WL, 2/NWS/B/3/2, EFR and Olivia Japp, LWSS, Circular dated 7 Feb. 1914 [copy], contained within Rathbone, Haverfield and Cross's statement to the EC; see also WL, 2/NWS/D/5, Final Agenda for the Annual Council Meeting, 12–13 Feb. 1914.

87. Rathbone reminded her fellow committee members of the narrowness of this vote; see WL, 2/NWS/A/1/5, EC Minutes, 5 Mar. 1914.

88. *Ibid.*

89. WL, 7/MGF/89, Fawcett to EFR, 8 Mar. 1914.

90. WL, 2/NWS/A/1/5, EC Minutes, 19 Mar. 1914.

91. WL, 2/NWS/A/1/5, EC Minutes, 5 Mar. 1914.

92. WL, 2/NWS/A/1/5, EC Minutes, 15 Jan. 1914.

93. See Marshall's arguments to the 5 March Executive Committee meeting (WL, 2/NWS/A/1/5, EC Minutes, 5 Mar. 1914) and Fawcett's statement to the leaders of the Liberal Women's Suffrage Union (CRO, Marshall Papers, D/MAR/3/32, Typescript transcript of conference between Liberal Women's Suffrage Union and the NUWSS, 27 July 1914); also Vellacott, *From Liberal to Labour*, pp. 323–4.

94. Hume, *National Union of Women's Suffrage Societies*, pp. 161, 206.

95. Jill Liddington and Jill Norris make a case for the importance of working-class 'radical suffragists' in *One Hand Tied Behind Us* (London: Virago, 1978), but their account pays too little attention to the links between the radical movement and the parliamentary work of the national suffrage organizations. This link is explored by Sandra Holton, *Feminism and Democracy*; see also June Hannam, *Isabella Ford* (Oxford: Basil Blackwell, 1989).

96. Nearly all historians agree that what legislative progress may have been made after 1912 was made by the NUWSS, the WSPU having become a purely negative force. Holton, Pugh and Vellacott all argue that Liberal opposition to a government measure was in fact weakening in that last year, quite possibly because the Union's alliance with Labour led it to employ more democratic arguments and the Liberals to see women's suffrage as a democratic measure. This is possible, but if so, it was the Union's increasing populism, and not specifically the electoral strategy, that brought about this change of view. Hume argues, rightly in my view, that while the Union was very strong in terms of funds and members on the eve of the war, its legislative momentum had been lost (Hume, *National Union of Women's Suffrage Societies*, pp. 221–3).

97. In addition to her protest against the pledges made to the ILP in January of 1914, Rathbone argued that the Executive had misinterpreted the Council's decisions on the Election Fighting Fund twice in 1912 (WL, 2/NWS/A/1/4, EC Minutes, 20 June 1912 and 19 Sept. 1912; see also Vellacott, *From Liberal to Labour*, p. 166); early in 1913, she also objected that policy

announcements had appeared in *Common Cause* without the Council's authorization (*ibid.*, pp. 210–11).

98. Macmillan alone voted with Rathbone's allies in the Executive Committee meeting on 19 March, and argued in a letter to Marshall that Rathbone's charge that the action of the Executive in ratifying the Glasgow decisions had been *ultra vires* 'inasmuch as it altered the policy of the Union by further determining it without the sanction of the Council' was 'so obvious as to require no argument' (CRO, Marshall Papers, D/MAR/3/36, Macmillan to Marshall, 8 Apr. 1914). George Armstrong, a member of Rathbone's short-lived committee, likewise objected in a letter to Fawcett that the committee should hardly be accused of trying to limit the NUWSS's freedom of action when its whole aim had been to try to *prevent* any further determination of the Union's general election policy without discussion by the Council (WL, 2/NWS/B/3/2, George Armstrong to Fawcett, 17 Apr. 1914).

99. CRO, Marshall Papers, D/MAR/3/54, Marshall to Arthur Henderson, 14 Oct. 1912; see also Holton, *Feminism and Democracy*, p. 87.

100. WL, 2/NWS/A/1/5, EC Minutes, 2 Apr. 1914.

101. WL, 2/NWS/B/1/4, 'NUWSS Proceedings of the Half-Yearly Council, Chelsea ... April 28–9, 1914'; also Vellacott, *From Liberal to Labour*, pp. 331–3.

102. For evidence of continued unhappiness, see, e.g., the letter from the Highgate Branch of London Society for Women's Suffrage to Marshall, 1 July 1914, reporting that the Society could scarcely survive if asked to oppose the prominent suffragist Liberal MP W.H. Dickinson at the election (CRO, Marshall Papers, D/MAR/3/32), and the report by Mrs Alderton of the Colchester Branch – where Liberal women had succeeded in forcing the Party to replace an anti-suffragist candidate with a suffragist – of her society's demise upon learning they would be unable to support this new candidate at the election (D/MAR/3/32, Typescript transcript of conference between Liberal Women's Suffrage Union and the NUWSS, 27 July 1914); also letters by Liberal women to *Common Cause*, 6: 263 (24 Apr. 1914), p. 56, and 6: 265 (8 May 1914), p. 105; and Holton, *Feminism and Democracy*, pp. 112–15.

103. CRO, Marshall Papers, D/MAR/3/32, NUWSS, EC Minutes, 2 July 1914.

104. WL, Edith Eskrigge Papers, 7/EES/8, EFR to Eskrigge, n.d.

105. Fawcett to Caroline Marshall, 1 May 1914, quoted in Vellacott, *From Liberal to Labour*, p. 333.

106. *Ibid.*

107. RP, Dec. 2002 accession (being catalogued), Marshall to EFR, 2 Nov. 1914; Ashton to EFR, 28 Sept. 1914; Courtney to EFR, 20 June 1914.

108. CRO, Marshall Papers, D/MAR/3/39, EFR to Marshall, 14 Nov. 1914.

Chapter 8   Time of Trial

1. For wartime Liverpool, see P.J. Waller, *Democracy and Sectarianism: A Political and Social History of Liverpool, 1868–1939* (Liverpool: Liverpool University Press, 1981), pp. 270–4.

2. 'The War Cloud in Liverpool: Provision Panic Threatened', *Liverpool Daily Post*, 5 Aug. 1914.

3. CRO, Marshall Papers, D/MAR/3/48, EFR to Marshall, 4 Sept. 1915.

4. Diary notes of Archibald Salvidge for November 1920, in Stanley Salvidge, *Salvidge of Liverpool: Behind the Political Scene, 1890–1928* (London: Hodder & Stoughton, 1934), p. 186.

5. Mary Stocks, *My Commonplace Book* (London: Peter Davies, 1970), p. 117.

6. Eleanor F. Rathbone, 'Our Common Cause', *Common Cause*, 10: 472 (26 Apr. 1918), p. 15.

7. For Rathbone's organization, see Liverpool Council of Voluntary Aid, *Annual Report* 5 (1914), pp. 14–15; 'Liverpool's Part in the War: LXV. The Town Hall Soldiers' and Sailors' Families Relief Organisation', *Liverpool Courier*, 13 Apr. 1920.

8. The bitter, unpleasant wrangle between Herbert and the local Tories was exhaustively publicized in the Liverpool papers and shadowed the early months of the organization's work. See especially Derby's letters to Herbert of 23–29 Oct. 1914, in LRO, Acc. 4593, Herbert R. Rathbone Papers. The conflict was publicized by the Conservative *Liverpool Courier* on 23, 24, 26, 27, 28 and 29 October; the Liberal *Liverpool Post* weighed in to defend Rathbone on 27 October. Eleanor wrote a brief account of Herbert's wartime work – and of this controversy – in her contribution to a compilation in his honour, *Herbert Reynolds Rathbone, 1862–1930* (Liverpool: C. Tinling & Co., 1931), pp. 20–2.

9. The national working of the allowance system is fully discussed in Susan Pedersen, 'Gender, Welfare and Citizenship in Britain during the Great War', *American Historical Review*, 95: 4 (Oct. 1990), pp. 983–1006.

10. HLRO, Bonar Law Papers, 36/1/6, Derby to Bonar Law, 5 Jan. 1915.

11. Select Committee on Naval and Military Services (Pensions and Grants), *Special Report, Second Special Report, Proceedings, Minutes and Appendices*, PP 1914–15, IV, pp. 90–103, here at p. 94.

12. *Ibid.*, p. 112.

13. *Ibid.*, pp. 102, 111, 98.

14. 'Report of a Conference of the SSFA . . . 6 April 1916', in SSFA *Report* (1915–16), p. 1794.

15. 'Voluntary War Work. Miss Rathbone on Fine Record in Liverpool', *Liverpool Post*, 4 Nov. 1919.

16. Eleanor F. Rathbone, 'Separation Allowances: An Experiment in the State Endowment of Maternity', I, *Common Cause* 7: 359 (25 Feb. 1916), p. 611.

17. Emma Mahler, 'The Social Effects of Separation Allowances', *The Englishwoman*, 36: 108 (Dec. 1917), pp. 194, 195.

18. *Ibid.*, p. 198.

19. Eleanor F. Rathbone, 'Separation Allowances: An Experiment in the State Endowment of Maternity', II, *Common Cause*, 7: 362 (17 Mar. 1916), p. 648.

20. CRO, Marshall Papers, D/MAR/3/39, Minutes of Special Executive Committee, 4 Nov. 1914.

21. See CRO, Marshall Papers, D/MAR/3/45, Fawcett to Marshall, 6 Mar. 1915, and D/MAR/3/45, EC Minutes of 18 Mar. 1915.

22. CRO, Marshall Papers, D/MAR/3/39, EFR to Marshall, 14 Nov. 1914.

23. IULL, Hannah Whitall Smith Papers, Box 14, Ray Strachey to Mary Berenson, 21 Apr. 1915.

24. *Common Cause*, 7: 320 (28 May 1915), p. 104.

25. *Common Cause*, 7: 324 (25 June 1915), p. 158.

26. *Ibid.*

27. IULL, Hannah Whitall Smith Papers, Box 14, Ray Strachey to Mary Berenson, 20 June 1915.

28. *Common Cause*, 7: 324 (25 June 1915), p. 162.

29. IULL, Hannah Whitall Smith Papers, Box 14, Ray to Mary Berenson, 21 Apr. 1915.

30. IULL, Hannah Whitall Smith Papers, Box 2, Oliver Strachey to Ray Strachey, 21 Apr. 1915.

31. This question caused much dispute both on the Executive and on the EFF committee – on which the resigners were still represented – throughout 1915 and 1916; see the records of both committees in the Women's Library, 2/NWS/A/1/7–8 and CRO, Marshall Papers, D/MAR/3/48–50.

32. WL, 2/NWS/A/1/8, EC Minutes, 4 May 1916; CRO, Marshall Papers, D/MAR/3/51, EC Minutes, 19 Apr. 1917.

33. WL, 2/CSS, Consultative Committee Minutes, esp. 4 Aug. 1916, and 2/NWS/A/1/8, EC Minutes, 15 August 1916.

34. WL, 2/NWS/A/1/9, EC Minutes, 3 Nov. 1916.

35. WL, 2/NWS/A/1/9, EC Minutes, 16 Nov. 1916, 7 Dec. 1916.

36. WL, 2/NWS/A/1/9, EC Minutes, 17 Jan. 1917.

37. GLRO, W. H. Dickinson Papers, F/DCK/52/23, Dickinson to Miss Barry, 20 Jan. 1943, attaching his handwritten notes taken on the day of the conference.

38. GLRO, Dickinson Papers, F/DCK/52/14, Strachey to Dickinson, 6 Feb. 1917.

39. WL, 2/NWS/A/1/9, EC Minutes, 12 Feb. 1917.

40. IULL, Hannah Whitall Smith Papers, Box 14, Ray Strachey to Oliver Strachey, 14 Nov. 1916.
41. *The Times*, 23 May 1917, p. 9.
42. *The Times*, 26 May 1917, p. 11.
43. Rathbone supported conscripting young women rather than men over forty in *The Times*, 6 Apr. 1918, p. 9; for her refusal of an OBE for her work with soldiers' wives in the First World War, see her letter of 25 Dec. 1918 describing her war contribution as 'trivial', in RP, Dec. 2002 accession (being catalogued).
44. CRO, Marshall Papers, D/MAR/3/51, Open letter from Rathbone, 31 Mar. 1917.
45. 'Municipal Votes for the Married Women', *Common Cause*, 9: 430 (6 July 1917), p. 164.
46. Eleanor F. Rathbone, 'Changes in Public Life', in Ray Strachey, ed., *Our Freedom and Its Results* (London: Hogarth Press, 1936), p. 26.
47. CRO, Marshall Papers, D/MAR/3/51, EC Minutes, 19 Apr. 1917.
48. The Women's Local government Society held a special meeting of their Council on 3 April 1917 to consider Rathbone's request for support; see the minutes in GLRO, Women's Local Government Society Papers, A/WLG/12. Also, for a complete summary of the Society's initial opposition and final turnaround, see, Women's Local Government Society, *Report 3*, (1917–18).
49. GLRO, Women's Local Government Society Papers, A/WLG/25, Parliamentary and Legal Subcommittee, Minutes, 4 Apr. 1917.
50. WL, 2/CSS, Consultative Committee Minutes, 18 Apr. 1917; CRO, Marshall Papers, D/MAR/3/51, EC Minutes, 19 Apr. 1917.
51. GLRO, Women's Local Government Society Papers, A/WLG/12, Council Minutes, 12 July 1917, and A/WLG/25, Parliamentary and Legal Subcommittee, Minutes for 17 May 1917, 25 June 1917, and 15 Oct. 1917.
52. WL, 2/CSS, Consultative Committee Minutes, 6 July 1917, 21 Sept. 1917; also Mrs Fawcett, 'Can We Safely Try to Improve the Women's Clauses of the Representation of the People Bill?' *Common Cause*, 9: 443 (5 Oct. 1917), pp. 302–3.
53. GLRO, Dickinson Papers, F/DCK/52/16/11, EFR to Dickinson, 20 Oct. 1917; GLRO, Women's Local Government Society Papers, A/WLG/25, Parliamentary and Legal Subcommittee, Minutes, 19 Nov. 1917.
54. 'Deputations on the Municipal Franchise of Women', *Common Cause*, 9: 430 (23 Nov. 1917), pp. 339–40.
55. 'The Representation of the People Bill', *Common Cause*, 9: 450 (23 Nov. 1917), p. 391.
56. WL, 2/NWS/A/1/10, EC Minutes, 22 Nov. 1917.
57. E.M. [Elizabeth Macadam], 'The Training of the Welfare Worker', *The Englishwoman*, 93 (Sept. 1916), p. 248; 'A New Profession. Welfare Workers in the Making. Interview with Miss Macadam', *Liverpool Courier*, 25 Sept. 1916. For Macadam's leave arrangements, SCA, P. 826, 'School of Social Science', manuscript history, pp. 15–16; also, SSSTSW, *Report*, 1915–16, p. 4; SSSTSW EC Minutes, 17 Dec. 1915 and 3 Nov. 1916.
58. Eleanor Rathbone, 'The Remuneration of Women's Services', *Economic Journal*, 27: 105 (Mar. 1917), pp. 55–68; rpt. in Victor Gollancz, ed., *The Making of Women: Oxford Essays in Feminism* (London: George Allen & Unwin, Sept. 1917; second edn, Jan. 1918).
59. *Equal Pay and the Family: A Proposal for the National Endowment of Motherhood* (London: Headley Bros. [1918]), quoted here pp. 9, 10.
60. Imperial War Museum, War Cabinet Committee on Women in Industry, Minutes of Evidence, Family Endowment Committee, 14 Oct. 1918; some form of family endowment was also supported by James Beard of the Workers' Union, Mary Carlin of the Dockers, Clementina Black of the Women's Industrial Council and Barbara Drake of the Fabian Women's Group.
61. Eleanor F. Rathbone, 'Equal Wages for Equal Work', *The Times*, 26 Aug. 1918, p. 9.
62. Beatrice Webb, Entry for 8 Dec. 1918, in *The Diary of Beatrice Webb*, vol. 3, 1905–1924: 'The Power to Alter Things', ed. Norman and Jeanne MacKenzie (Cambridge, Mass: Belknap Press, 1984), p. 325.
63. War Cabinet Committee on Women in Industry, *Report*, PP 1919, XXXI, Cmd. 135, esp. Majority Report at pp. 176–9, Minority Report, pp. 279, 306.

Coda to Part II: Elsie Makes her Will

1. See, e.g., RP IX.9.10a, Willie to Elsie, 29 Nov. 1870, apologizing for forgetting her birthday and neglecting to write.
2. RP XXV.1.104 (12), Elsie to WGR, [1877].
3. RP XXV.1.342 (3), Henry Gair Rathbone to Elena Richmond, 7 Dec. 1920.
4. On this scandal, RP XXV.1.338 (8), Elsie to Elena Richmond, 14 Nov. 1918; RP XXV.1.200 (94), Dora Rathbone to Blanche Rathbone, 17 July 1919.
5. Somerset House, Will and Probate of Elizabeth Lucretia Rathbone; also, for Elsie's property under her mother's settlement, see PRO IR 26/8363, Estate Duty Registers, Probate of William Rathbone, Folio 1223, note F.
6. Somerset House, Will and Probate of Eleanor Florence Rathbone.

Chapter 9   Choosing Elizabeth

1. Enid Huws Jones, *Margery Fry: The Essential Amateur* (London: Oxford University Press, 1966), p. 50.
2. RP XXIIA, Diary of Hugh Rathbone, entry for 1918.
3. Emily left an estate valued at £22,695 to be divided equally between her four living children, Evie, Lyle, Eleanor and Frank, and her household effects equally between Evie and Eleanor. Residual property was left to Evie, to help her maintain Greenbank. Somerset House, Will and Probate of Emily Rathbone.
4. RP, Dec. 2002 accession (being catalogued), E.R. [Eleanor Rathbone] to 'My dearest' [Elizabeth Macadam], 5 Mar. [1919?].
5. Documents in the possession of Diana Hopkinson, EFR to Eva Hubback, 2 Sept. 1941.
6. Interview with Dr B.L. Rathbone, Liverpool, 16 Aug. 1989.
7. Interview with Lady Warr and Mrs Warr, London, 20 Jan. 1993.
8. RP XXIIA, Diary of Hugh Rathbone, entries for 1919 and 1920.
9. RP XXV.1.342 (2), Henry Gair Rathbone to Elena, 9 Oct. 1920 and 22 Dec. 1920.
10. RP XXIIA, Diary of Hugh Rathbone, entry for 1920.
11. RP XXIIA.539, Nancy to Evie, 4 July 1944.
12. Elizabeth Macadam, *The Equipment of the Social Worker* (London: George Allen & Unwin, 1925).
13. Visitors' book kept by Elizabeth Macadam, held by Jenny Rathbone (in 2003).
14. Diana Hopkinson, *The Incense-Tree: An Autobiography* (London: Routledge & Kegan Paul, 1968), p. 55; Diana Hopkinson, *Family Inheritance: A Life of Eva Hubback* (London: Staples Press, 1954), p. 105; also RP XXIIA, Diary of Hugh Rathbone, entry for 1922.
15. WL, Brian Harrison interview with Doris [Hardman] Cox, 15 Mar. 1977.
16. BLPES, Violet Markham Papers 26/23, EFR to Markham, 30 Dec. 1918; Mary D. Stocks, *Eleanor Rathbone: A Biography* (London: Victor Gollancz, 1949), pp. 78–9.
17. WL, Brian Harrison interview with Marjorie [Green] Soper, 15 Mar. 1977.
18. Stocks, *Eleanor Rathbone*, p. 121.
19. Interview with David and Diana Hopkinson, Godalming, 18 Aug. 1994.
20. RP XIV.3.92, Margery Fry, 'Eleanor Rathbone', BBC script, 18 Mar. 1952.
21. For Rathbone's forgetfulness, see especially Stocks, *Eleanor Rathbone*, pp. 121–2; RP XIX.3.13, Diary of Winifred Rathbone (née Evans), Christmas 1907; and Rathbone's correspondence with the family of Professor Frank Smith, with whom she often stayed on her visits to Leeds, retrieving some forgotten possession, RP XIV.5.
22. Stocks, *Eleanor Rathbone*, p. 122.
23. Ibid., pp. 121–2.
24. RP XXIIA.115, EFR to Evie, 12 Sept. 1934.
25. See RP XIV.2.9(6), [Atholl], 'Details of Proposed Trip', and RP XIV.2.9 (21), 'Tour in Yugoslavia, Roumania and Czechoslovakia, February 1937'.

26. Interview with Lady Warr and Mrs Warr, London 20 Jan. 1993.

27. RP XIV.3.92, Margery Fry, 'Eleanor Rathbone', BBC script, 18 Mar. 1952.

28. WL, Brian Harrison interview with Mary Stocks, 21 May 1974.

29. Elizabeth Macadam, *The New Philanthropy: A Study of the Relations between the Statutory and Voluntary Social Services* (London: George Allen & Unwin, 1934). Macadam also brought out a new edition of the 1925 book on training for social work in 1945: *The Social Servant in the Making: A Review of the Provision of Training for the Social Services* (London: George Allen & Unwin, 1945).

30. Interview with Lady Wright, London, 18 Jan. 1993.

31. For Wilkinson and these other examples, see Martin Pugh, *Women and the Women's Movement in Britain, 1914–1959* (London: Macmillan, 1992), pp. 158–9.

32. WL, Brian Harrison interview with Doris [Hardman] Cox, 15 Mar. 1977.

33. WL, Brian Harrison interview with Marjorie [Green] Soper, 15 Mar. 1977.

34. RP XIV.2.5, EFR to O.W.R. Williams, Colonial Office, 1 Sept. 1934.

35. Telephone interview with Noreen Rathbone, 2 Aug. 2003; obituary of Elizabeth Macadam, *Manchester Guardian*, 12 Nov. 1948.

36. WL, Brian Harrison interview with Mary Stocks, 21 May 1974, and with Marjorie [Green] Soper and Doris [Hardman] Cox, 15 Mar. 1977; my interview with Mrs Joan [Prewer] Gibson, London 6 Jan. 1996.

37. WL, Brian Harrison interview with Mary Stocks, 21 May 1974.

38. Interview with B.L. Rathbone, Liverpool, 18 Mar. 1993.

39. For which, see especially Michel Foucault, *The History of Sexuality*, vol. 1 (New York: Vintage, 1980).

40. For prevailing late nineteenth-century views of female friendship, see especially Martha Vicinus, *Independent Women: Work and Community for Single Women, 1850–1920* (Chicago: University of Chicago Press, 1985), pp. 187–99; Lucy Bland, *Banishing the Beast: English Feminism and Sexual Morality, 1885–1914* (Harmondsworth: Penguin, 1995), pp. 168–71.

41. Much has been written on the rise of sexology and the concomitant attack on spinsters and 'new women'; for one view, see Sheila Jeffreys, *The Spinster and Her Enemies* (London: Pandora Press, 1985); also Bland, *Banishing the Beast*, passim.

42. On Stopes and the new rhetoric of conjugal relations after 1918, see especially Roy Porter and Lesley Hall, *The Facts of Life: The Creation of Sexual Knowledge in Britain* (New Haven and London: Yale University Press, 1995), pp. 202–23.

43. Alison Neilans, 'Changes in Sex Morality', in Ray Strachey, ed., *Our Freedom and Its Results* (London: Hogarth Press, 1936), pp. 221–2. And, for some discussion of the ways in which different generations of feminists responded to new sexual attitudes, see Martin Pugh, *Women and the Women's Movement*, pp. 257–63.

44. Winifred Holtby, *Women and a Changing Civilization* (1935; rpt. Chicago: Academy, 1978), pp. 125–33.

45. Miss N.D. to M.C.S., 10 Apr. 1919, quoted in Ruth Hall, ed., *Dear Dr. Stopes: Sex in the 1920s* (Harmondsworth: Penguin Books, 1981), p. 168.

46. Clemence Dane [Winifred Ashton], *Regiment of Women* (New York: Macmillan, 1917); Dorothy L. Sayers, *Unnatural Death* (London: Ernest Benn, 1927); Radclyffe Hall, *The Well of Loneliness* (London: Jonathan Cape, 1928).

47. Much has been written about the Holtby–Brittain friendship, and especially about whether it should in fact be categorized as 'lesbian'. Jean Kennard, citing the depth of its emotional intensity, argues that it should be accepted as, in a broad sense, lesbian; Deborah Gorham, noting that Brittain 'found lesbian sexuality repellent' and that Holtby felt that all passions should be controlled, argues that it should not. Both accept that, at the root of this quarrel, lies the definition of lesbianism – for Gorham, unlike Kennard, argues that (as today) only explicitly erotic relations between women should be termed lesbian. In this debate, in my view, Gorham has had the better of the argument, not because 'romantic friendships' cannot be seen as lesbian, but because the Brittain–Holtby relationship did not conform to this essen-

tially nineteenth-century mould. Indeed, by the 1920s, I would argue, it was difficult for female friends to preserve that 'romantic' model: the invention of the category of lesbian meant that these women were, unfairly, forced to confront the issue of sexuality directly. See Jean E. Kennard, *Vera Brittain and Winifred Holtby: A Working Partnership* (Hanover: University Press of New England, 1989), pp. 4–8; Deborah Gorham, *Vera Brittain: A Feminist Life* (Oxford: Blackwell, 1996), pp. 162–5.

48. Edith Picton-Turbervill, *Life is Good: An Autobiography* (London: Frederick Muller, 1939), p. 94.

49. Telephone interview with Noreen Rathbone, 2 Aug. 2003.

50. WL, Brian Harrison interview with Mary Stocks, 21 May 1974.

Chapter 10   What Future for Feminism?

1. RP XXV.1.338, Elsie to Elena Richmond, 3 Nov. 1918.

2. *Ibid.*

3. BLPES, Violet Markham Papers 26/23, Macadam to Markham, 6 Dec. 1918, and EFR to Markham, 7 Dec. 1918.

4. Violet Markham, *Return Passage* (London: Oxford University Press, 1953), p. 157.

5. IULL, Hannah Whitall Smith Papers, Box 14, Ray Strachey to family, 24 Feb. 1918.

6. BLPES, Markham Papers 26/23, EFR to Markham, 30 Dec. 1918.

7. WL, NUSEC, *Annual Report* 1 (1920), p. 26.

8. Rathbone remains a controversial figure for historians writing explicitly as feminists. Suzie Fleming, for example, claimed Rathbone as the foremother of the Wages-for-Housework movement in 'Eleanor Rathbone: Spokeswoman for a Movement', introduction to a new edition of *The Disinherited Family* (London: Falling Wall Press, 1986), pp. 9–120. Sheila Jeffreys, by contrast, writing from the standpoint of 1980s radical separatism, condemns Rathbone for having 'submerged all the interests of all women in the glorification of repro-duction' (Jeffreys, *The Spinster and her Enemies* [London: Pandora, 1985], p. 153), a view largely shared by Susan Kingsley Kent in *Making Peace: The Reconstruction of Gender in Interwar Britain* (Princeton: Princeton University Press, 1993), ch. 6. Hilary Land, by con-trast, stresses (rightly in my view) Rathbone's foundational feminist concern with women's independence: she wished to 'endow' mothers not in order to push women into the home but in order to free those women already there from painful subjection to men. See Land, 'Eleanor Rathbone and the Economy of the Family', in Harold Smith, ed., *British Feminism in the Twentieth Century* (Amherst: University of Massachusetts Press, 1990), pp. 104–23.

9. Eleanor F. Rathbone, 'The Future of the National Union', *Common Cause*, 9: 462 (14 Feb. 1918), p. 573.

10. CRO, Marshall Papers, D/MAR/3/52, Courtney to Marshall, 5 Mar. 1918.

11. *Common Cause*, 9: 467 (22 Mar. 1918), pp. 660–1.

12. For which, see especially Kenneth O. Morgan, *Consensus and Disunity: The Lloyd George Coalition Government, 1918–1922* (Oxford: Clarendon Press, 1979), ch. 3.

13. For this hounding of women claimants, see especially Alan Deacon, *In Search of the Scrounger: The Administration of Unemployment Insurance in Britain, 1920–1931* (London: G. Bell & Sons, 1976).

14. Figures in *Common Cause* and NUSEC *Annual Reports* suggest that the number of affiliated societies fell from a pre-war high of 600 to 200 by the end of the war. The NUSEC's dilem-mas and strategies are discussed in three studies of inter-war feminism: Johanna Alberti, *Beyond Suffrage: Feminists in War and Peace, 1914–28* (London: Macmillan, 1989); Cheryl Law, *Suffrage and Power: The Women's Movement, 1918–1928* (London: I.B. Tauris, 1997); Martin Pugh, *Women and the Women's Movement in Britain, 1914–1959* (London: Macmillan, 1992).

15. *Common Cause*, 2: 13 (30 Apr. 1920), pp. 290–1; also Pamela M. Graves, *Labour Women:*

Women in British Working-Class Politics, 1918–1939 (Cambridge: Cambridge University Press, 1994), pp. 119–20.

16. Vera Brittain, 'Why Feminism Lives' (1927), rpt. in *Testament of a Generation*, ed. Paul Berry and Alan Bishop (London: Virago, 1985), pp. 97–9.

17. 'The Uses of Unpopularity' (8 Mar. 1921), in Eleanor F. Rathbone, *Milestones: Presidential Addresses at the Annual Council Meetings of the National Union of Societies for Equal Citizenship* (Liverpool: Lee & Nightingale, 1929), p. 7.

18. Eleanor F. Rathbone, 'Equal Citizenship' (9 Mar. 1920), in *Milestones*, p. 3.

19. See the works by Sheila Jeffreys and Susan Kingsley Kent, cited in note 8 above.

20. P.J. Waller, *Democracy and Sectarianism: A Political and Social History of Liverpool, 1868–1939* (Liverpool: Liverpool University Press, 1981), pp. 283–5.

21. For these activities, see especially, LRO, H352 COU, *Proceedings of the Council*, Minutes for 1 Mar. 1922, 5 Apr. 1922, 20 Feb. 1924, 2 Jan. 1930, 2 Apr. 1930, 4 July 1934.

22. For the work of the Personal Services Society, see Dorothy Keeling, *The Crowded Stairs: Recollections of Social Work in Liverpool* (London: National Council of Social Service, 1961); Rathbone's crucial role in its establishment can be traced through the minutes of the Executive Committee of the Liverpool Council of Voluntary Aid, still held by the Council, and those of the Liverpool Personal Services Society, Merseyside Record Office, 364 PSS.

23. Interview with Margaret Simey, Liverpool, 7 Jan. 1993.

24. Eleanor F. Rathbone, Letter, *Common Cause*, 11: 555 (28 Nov. 1919), p. 432.

25. *Ibid.*

26. Rathbone, 'The Uses of Unpopularity', pp. 8–9.

27. 'Election Address', *Woman's Leader*, 13: 4 (25 Feb. 1921), p. 60.

28. 'Impressions of the National Union Council Meeting. By A Delegate', *Woman's Leader*, 13: 7 (18 Mar. 1921), p. 104.

29. For Eva Hubback, see especially the biography written by her daughter: Diana Hopkinson, *Family Inheritance: A Life of Eva Hubback* (London: Staples Press, 1954); also Brian Harrison, *Prudent Revolutionaries: Portraits of British Feminists between the Wars* (Oxford: Oxford University Press, 1987), pp. 273–300.

30. WL, Brian Harrison interview with Marjorie [Green] Soper and Doris [Hardman] Cox, 15 Mar. 1977. For Stocks, see her memoir, *My Commonplace Book* (London: Peter Davies, 1970); also Barbara Hooper, *Mary Stocks, 1891–1975: An Uncommonplace Life* (London: Athlone Press, 1996).

31. For Rhondda, see Shirley M. Eoff, *Viscountess Rhondda, Equalitarian Feminist* (Columbus, Ohio: Ohio State University Press, 1991).

32. WL, Brian Harrison interview with Mary Stocks, 21 May 1974.

33. WL, Brian Harrison interview with Corbett Ashby, 23 Nov. 1976.

34. IULL, Hannah Whitall Smith Papers, Ray Strachey Diary, entry for 26 Mar. 1924.

35. Vera Brittain, 'Committees versus Professions' (1929), in *Testament of a Generation*, p. 107.

36. WL, NUSEC, *Annual Report 1920*, 2 (1921), p. 5.

37. WL, 2/NSE/A/1/3, EC Meeting, 8 May 1924.

38. Rathbone summarized the extent of these changes, and the nature of NUSEC's work, in her retrospective account of 'Changes in Public Life', in Ray Strachey, ed., *Our Freedom and Its Results* (London: Hogarth Press, 1936), pp. 13–76. Johanna Alberti, Cheryl Law and Martin Pugh, cited in note 14, above, all find this record quite impressive, but it is worth noting – with Harold Smith – that these legislative reforms were often alternatives to (rather than enactments of) feminist proposals, and that feminists found themselves almost entirely unable to improve women's employment status. Harold L. Smith, 'British Feminism in the 1920s', in Smith, ed., *British Feminism in the Twentieth Century*, pp. 47–65.

39. Eleanor F. Rathbone, 'The Old and the New Feminism' (11 Mar. 1925), in *Milestones*, p. 26.

40. PRO, PIN 4/98, Record of NUSEC deputation, 8 June 1925, and associated correspondence; see also *Widows', Orphans' and Old Age Contributory Pensions Bill. Memorandum by Eleanor F. Rathbone* (NUSEC, June 1925).

41. Rathbone, 'The Old and the New Feminism', pp. 25–30.

42. The endowment resolution passed by 111 to 42, with only two members of the Executive Committee voting against it; see 'Family Endowment', *The Times*, 13 Mar. 1925, p. 7; 'Family Endowment', *Manchester Guardian*, 13 Mar. 1925, p. 7; 'Women in Council', *Woman's Leader*, 17: 8 (20 Mar. 1925), pp. 61–2.

43. Millicent Fawcett, 'The Case against Family Endowment', *Woman's Leader*, 17: 1 (30 Jan. 1925), pp. 3–5.

44. RP, Dec. 2002 accession (being catalogued), Fawcett to EFR, 14 Dec. 1924; see also, David Rubinstein: *A Different World for Women: The Life of Millicent Garrett Fawcett* (Hemel Hempstead: Harvester Wheatsheaf, 1991), pp. 269–71.

45. This formulation comes from 'Quo Vadis', *Woman's Leader*, 18: 54 (4 Feb. 1927), p. 459.

46. For the 1926 Council, see 'Equal Citizenship', *Woman's Leader*, 18: 6 (5 Mar. 1926), pp. 48–9.

47. 'The "New Feminism",' *Time and Tide*, 7: 10 (5 Mar. 1926), p. 220.

48. 'The "New Feminism" of the NUSEC', *Time and Tide*, 7: 11 (12 Mar. 1926), p. 254.

49. The conference was held from 26 May until 8 June 1926, and its proceedings were covered in detail by both the *New York Times* and the *Christian Science Monitor*. See their continuing coverage, and for the inside story, Harvard University, Radcliffe Institute for Advanced Study, Schlesinger Library, Jane Norman Smith Papers, Box 12, Folder 221, 'Report on Morning Session of Tenth Congress of IWSA . . . May 31st, 1926'. The conference is covered briefly in the context of a discussion over the emerging rift on protective legislation in Leila J. Rupp, *Worlds of Women: The Making of an International Women's Movement* (Princeton: Princeton University Press, 1997), pp. 141–2.

50. 'Women Seeking Equal Rights in Air With Men', *Christian Science Monitor*, 2 June 1926.

51. 'World Suffragists Bar American Group; British Party Quits', *New York Times*, 1 June 1926.

52. 'Feminists Meet the Woman's Party', *New York Times*, 3 June 1926.

53. 'The "New Feminism"', *Woman's Leader*, 18: 7 (12 Mar. 1926).

54. Winifred Holtby, 'Family Endowment' (letter), *Time and Tide*, 6: 7 (13 Feb. 1925), p. 158.

55. Winifred Holtby, 'Feminism Divided', *Yorkshire Post*, 26 July 1926, rpt. in *Testament of a Generation*, pp. 47–50.

56. Rose Macaulay, 'Problems of a Woman's Life', in *A Casual Commentary* (New York: Boni & Liveright, 1926), p. 236.

57. Holtby, 'Feminism Divided', p. 48; Virginia Woolf, *Three Guineas* (1938; rpt. New York: Harcourt, Brace, Jovanovich, 1966), pp. 101–2.

58. Vera Brittain, ' "Semi-Detached" Marriage', *Evening News*, 4 May 1928; 'Nursery Schools', *Manchester Guardian*, 29 Mar. 1929; 'I Denounce Domesticity', *Quiver*, Aug. 1932; all rpt. in *Testament of a Generation*, pp. 130–2, 136–44; see also Holtby's sympathetic discussion of an American inquiry into such two-career marriages in 'Counting the Cost', *Manchester Guardian*, 23 Nov. 1928; rpt. in *ibid.*, pp. 54–7.

59. Debate on 'What is Equality?' *Woman's Leader*, 19: 1 (11 Feb. 1927), pp. 3–4 (for Rathbone and Abbott), and 19: 3 (25 Feb. 1927), pp. 20–1 (for Ward and Balfour); and *Time and Tide*, 8: 9 (4 March 1927), p. 218 (for How-Martyn).

60. *Manchester Guardian*, 16 Mar. 1925, p. 3.

61. The controversy at the Council is covered from somewhat different angles in a letter signed by Rathbone, Corbett Ashby, Courtney and Stocks, in *Woman's Leader*, 19: 5 (11 Mar. 1927), pp. 36–8; and 'A Deep Cleavage', *Time and Tide*, 8: 10 (11 Mar. 1927), p. 229.

62. As they did each year, *The Times* and the *Manchester Guardian* carried daily articles throughout the conference, and reported the split in some detail.

63. 'Voteless Women', *The Times*, 8 Mar. 1927, p. 12.

64. 'Statement by the Eleven Resigning Members', *Woman's Leader*, 19: 5 (11 Mar. 1927), p. 38; also, 'Sex Equality', *Manchester Guardian*, 7 Mar. 1927, p. 3.

65. 'A Deep Cleavage', *Time and Tide*, 8: 10 (11 Mar. 1927), p. 229.

66. WL, 2/NSE/A/1/5, EC Minutes, 26 Apr. 1927.

67. Quoted in Alberti, *Beyond Suffrage*, p. 171.

68. 'A Deep Cleavage', *Time and Tide*, 8: 10 (11 Mar. 1927), p. 229.

69. Helen Ward, Letter, *Woman's Leader*, 19: 7 (25 Mar. 1927), p. 59.
70. *Common Cause*, 7: 324 (25 June 1915), p. 155.
71. 'Equal Suffrage', *The Times*, 9 Mar. 1928, p. 16.
72. PRO, HO 45/13020 pt 1. Cabinet. Equal Franchise Committee, 3rd Meeting (21 Feb. 1927).
73. The Cabinet first confirmed that commitment on 18 February 1925; see PRO, Cab. 23/49, Cabinet 9 (25), (18 Feb. 1925) Conclusion 11. Joynson-Hicks's statement to the House came two days later.
74. Churchill made this argument at the meeting of the Equal Franchise Committee; see PRO, HO 45/13020 pt 1, Cabinet Equal Franchise Committee, 2nd Meeting (14 Feb. 1927). When the Cabinet agreed to go ahead anyway, he placed his dissent on the record; see PRO, Cab. 23/54, Cabinet 26 (27) (12 Apr. 1927), Concl. 4.
75. PRO, Cab. 23/54, Cabinet 27 (27) (13 Apr. 1927), Concl. 7.
76. 'Statement by the Eleven Resigning Members', *Woman's Leader*, 19: 5 (11 Mar. 1927), p. 38.
77. *Time and Tide*, 9: 11 (16 Mar. 1928), pp. 239–40; WL, NUSEC, *Annual Report 1928–9* (1929).
78. WL, 2/NSE/B/3/1, 'Proposed Lines of Expansion for the NUSEC', Confidential leaflet (Dec. 1928); WL, Brian Harrison interview with Corbett Ashby, 23 Nov. 1976.
79. For the decline of both NUSEC and the egalitarian organizations, see Pugh, *Women and the Women's Movement*, pp. 236–44.
80. WL, 2/NSE/D/2/2, Abbott to Ward, 2 Dec. 1927.
81. WL, 2/NSE/D/2/2, EFR to Miss Auld, 31 Oct. 1927.
82. Winifred Holtby, 'King George V Jubilee Celebrations', *Time and Tide*, 4 May 1935, rpt. *Testament of a Generation*, pp. 90–1.
83. Holtby, 'Feminism Divided', p. 48.
84. Rathbone, 'Changes in Public Life', p. 34.
85. Eleanor F. Rathbone, *The Harvest of the Women's Movement* (London, 1935), pp. 10, 12, 18.

Chapter 11   Feuds about the Family

1. David J. Dutton, ed., *Odyssey of an Edwardian Liberal: The Political Diary of Richard Durning Holt* (Liverpool: The Record Society of Lancashire and Cheshire, 1989), entry for 24 July 1921, p. 71.
2. Rankin was the brother of Dora Rankin, estranged wife of William Gair's son Bill (the 8th William Rathbone). Bill had deserted Dora and his children at the end of the war, and relations between the Rathbones and the Rankins presumably were not good (for which, see RP XXV.1.200 [94]). When Eleanor learned that Rankin planned to contest East Toxteth again, she tried to persuade Holt to let her have the much more attractive constituency of Wavertree instead, in order to 'escape opposing Captain Rankin, which for personal reasons I very much dislike doing'. Holt would not help. See LRO, 920 DUR, EFR to Holt, 17 Aug. 1921 and 24 Aug. 1921.
3. 'David v. Goliath. Battle with the Tory Giant', *Liverpool Daily Post*, 1 Nov. 1922.
4. *The Times*, 27 Oct. 1922.
5. RP XXIIA, Hugh Rathbone's Diary, entry for 15 Nov. 1922.
6. Paraphrase of an undated latter from EFR to Hubback, n.d., quoted in Diana Hopkinson, *Family Inheritance: A Life of Eva Hubback* (London: Staples Press, 1954), p. 165.
7. RP XXV.1.337 (1), Elizabeth Macadam to Elena Richmond, 31 Oct. 1922.
8. RP, Dec. 2002 accession (being catalogued), 'Family Endowment' [leaflet], scrapbook on the 1922 election campaign.
9. 'An Electioneering Dodge' [leaflet], *ibid.*; Eleanor F. Rathbone, 'Family Allowances' [letter], *Liverpool Echo*, 14 Nov. 1922; 'Miss E. Rathbone Misrepresented. An Eleventh-hour Leaflet', *Liverpool Daily Post*, 14 Nov. 1922.

10. 'An Insult to Bachelors', *Liverpool Courier*, 15 Nov. 1922.

11. 'Liverpool Returns', *Liverpool Courier*, 16 Nov. 1922.

12. Rathbone, Letter, *Manchester Guardian*, 3 Feb. 1921, p. 3

13. Rathbone, Letter, *Woman's Leader*, 13: 11 (15 Apr. 1921), p. 172.

14. 'Kirkdale', *Liverpool Courier*, 19 July 1910, p. 7.

15. 380 *HC Deb.*, 23 June 1942, col. 1876.

16. Eleanor F. Rathbone, 'The Standard of Life: Wages and Family Allowances', *The Times*, 4 May 1921, p. 6; Askwith, 'The Standard of Life', *The Times*, 5 May 1921, p. 6.

17. MRC, CBI Predecessor Archive, MSS 200 B/3/2/C262, EFR to J. Forbes Watson, 20 June 1921, enclosing Eleanor F. Rathbone, *Wages Plus Family Allowances: A Practical Way of Reducing Costs of Production without Lowering the Standard of Life of the Workers* [1921].

18. RP, Dec. 2002 accession (being catalogued), leaflet signed by a dozen MPs, announcing meeting in the Commons on 5 July 1921.

19. BL, Add. Ms 56786, Society of Authors Papers, EFR to the Society, 28 July 1926.

20. Hugh Dalton, 'To Each According to His Need: Grants for Children', *New Leader*, 13: 6 (15 Jan. 1926), p. 9.

21. Eleanor F. Rathbone, *The Disinherited Family: A Plea for Direct Provision for the Costs of Child Maintenance through Family Allowances* (1924; rpt. 3rd edn London: George Allen & Unwin, 1927), p. viii. References are to this edition unless otherwise specified.

22. *Ibid.*, p. 17.

23. This was the subtitle of Rathbone's book.

24. *Ibid.*, p. 176. Much has been written on the Australian inquiry into a 'living wage' in 1919 and on subsequent child endowment policies, but see especially Morris Graham's biography of the main advocate, *A.B. Piddington: The Last Radical Liberal* (Sydney: University of New South Wales Press, 1995).

25. Rathbone, *Disinherited Family*, p. 40.

26. *Ibid.*, p. 56.

27. *Ibid.*, pp. 88–9.

28. *Ibid.*, p. 84.

29. *Ibid.*, p. 270.

30. *Ibid.*, p. 271.

31. *Ibid.*, p. 273.

32. Eleanor F. Rathbone, *The Ethics and Economics of Family Endowment* (London: Epworth Press, 1927); *The Case for Family Allowances* (Harmondsworth: Penguin Books, 1940).

33. Mary Stocks, in *Time and Tide*, 8: 11 (18 Mar. 1927), pp. 267–8. Hilary Land makes the same point about Rathbone's importance as a feminist theorist; see, Land, 'Eleanor Rathbone and the Economy of the Family', in Harold Smith, ed., *British Feminism in the Twentieth Century* (Amherst: University of Massachusetts Press, 1990), pp. 104–23.

34. Eleanor F. Rathbone, *Family Allowances* (London: Allen & Unwin, 1949); Rathbone, *The Disinherited Family*, new edn, London: Falling Wall, 1986).

35. Feminist writings that have drawn on Rathbone are now too extensive to cite fully, but see especially Heidi Hartmann's early perceptive article, 'Capitalism, Patriarchy and Job Segregation by Sex', in Zillah Eisenstein, ed., *Capitalist Patriarchy and the Case for Socialist Feminism* (New York: Monthly Review, 1979), pp. 1–42; and, most recently, Shirley Burggraf, *The Feminine Economy and Economic Man: Reviving the Role of Family in the Post-industrial Age* (Reading, Mass.: Addison-Wesley, 1997) and Ann Crittenden, *The Price of Motherhood: Why the Most Important Job in the World Is Still the Least Valued* (New York: Metropolitan Books, 2001).

36. Rathbone, *Disinherited Family*, p. xi.

37. Alexander Gray, *Family Endowment: A Critical Analysis* (London: Ernest Benn, 1927); D.H. MacGregor, 'Family Allowances', *Economic Journal*, 36: 141 (Mar. 1926), pp. 1–10; see also BBC Written Archives Centre, Talks File on Eleanor Rathbone, for Rathbone's debate over family allowances with D.H. MacGregor, broadcast on 19 Feb. 1929; *The Listener*, 27 Feb. 1929, pp. 237–8.

38. Beveridge to Wallas, 29 Apr. 1924, quoted in José Harris, *William Beveridge: A Biography* (Oxford: Clarendon Press, 1977), p. 343.

39. The best account of this movement remains John Macnicol, *The Movement for Family Allowances, 1918–1945: A Study in Social Policy Development* (London: Heinemann, 1980). Macnicol argues for the movement's lack of success until the development of a conservative, wage-restraint case in the 1930s; I would retort that the feminist perspective prevented that conservative case from ever becoming hegemonic.

40. Constitution of the FES, in BLPES, FES, *Report* (1924).

41. A good sampling of this literature can be found in the Family Endowment Society papers held by the BLPES (which also holds a copy of the Society's *Monthly Notes*). Mary Stocks and Joseph L. Cohen also both wrote small books on family endowment; see Stocks, *The Case for Family Endowment* (London: Labour Publishing Co., 1927); Joseph L. Cohen, *Family Income Insurance: A Scheme of Family Endowment by the Method of Insurance* (London: P.S. King & Son, 1926).

42. BLPES, William Beveridge Papers, IIb 23, EFR to Beveridge, 20 May 1924.

43. For Rathbone's appointment, see League of Nations Archives, Geneva, Box 189, 12/42088/34652, and 12/42971/34652, EFR to Crowdy, 31 Mar. 1925.

44. See League of Nations Archives, Geneva, Box 693, for collaboration between the League and the International Labour Organization on this subject.

45. BLPES, FES, *Report* (1926).

46. *Britain's Industrial Future* (1928; rpt. London: Ernest Benn, 1977), pp. 190–2.

47. BLPES, FES, *Report* (1930).

48. Rathbone, *Disinherited Family*, pp. 232–48.

49. Rathbone, 'Family Endowment in its Bearing on the Question of Population', *Eugenics Review*, 16 (Apr. 1924–Jan. 1925), pp. 270–5.

50. 'Discussion', *ibid.*, pp. 276–8. The chilling metaphor of 'the tiller of maternity' was first used by Rathbone, *Disinherited Family*, p. 237.

51. For the Eugenics Society's consideration of allowances, see especially Richard A. Soloway, *Demography and Degeneration: Eugenics and the Declining Birthrate in Twentieth-century Britain* (1990; new edn Chapel Hill: University of North Carolina Press, 1995), pp. 292–301.

52. Rathbone, *Disinherited Family*, pp. 250, 252.

53. For developments in France, see esp. Susan Pedersen, *Family, Dependence, and the Origins of the Welfare State: Britain and France, 1914–1945* (New York: Cambridge University Press, 1993), ch. 5.

54. Rathbone, *Disinherited Family*, pp. 192–219.

55. BLPES, Beveridge Papers, IIb 24, Beveridge to EFR, 19 Oct. 1925; see also William Beveridge, *Power and Influence* (London: Hodder & Stoughton, 1953), pp. 220–1.

56. See Rathbone's letters to *The Times* on the coal industry of 4 May 1921, p. 6, 5 July 1921, p. 6, and 9 Oct. 1922, p. 13; also her 'Children First!', *New Leader*, 13: 33 (28 May 1926), p. 6.

57. Royal Commission on the Coal Industry, *Minutes of Evidence* (London: HMSO, 1926), pp. 862–7.

58. Royal Commission on the Coal Industry, *Report*, PP 1926, XIV, Cmd. 2600, p. 164.

59. BLPES, Beveridge Papers on the Coal Commission, Vol. X, Rathbone to Beveridge, 5 Feb. 1926; for the FES's initiative in the coal areas, see BLPES, FES Papers, R. Coll. Misc. 9, 33–40.

60. Miners' Federation of Great Britain, *Annual Conference Report* (1928), pp. 37–42.

61. Sidney B.M. Potter, 'The ILP Summer School', *New Leader*, 8: 8 (22 Aug. 1924), pp. 3–4.

62. The Commission's proposals emerged gradually throughout 1926 in articles and an interim report, and were fully embodied in their final report published that September; see H.N. Brailsford, John A. Hobson, A. Creech Jones and E.F. Wise, *The Living Wage* (London: ILP, 1926).

63. Labour Party, *Report*, 26 (1926), pp. 259–61, 274–5.

64. Labour Party, *Report*, 28 (1928), pp. 167–8.

65. Congress House, TUC Archives, File 117.32, Joint Committee on the Living Wage, Rathbone Evidence, 26 Jan. 1928, p. 4.
66. *Ibid.*, p. 6.
67. *Ibid.*, p. 18.
68. *Ibid.*, p. 11.
69. Rathbone made roughly the same case earlier in 'Child Allowances', *New Leader*, 13: 18 (29 Jan. 1926), p. 6.
70. This paragraph summarizes my discussion of the Joint Committee in *Family, Dependence*, pp. 197–208. It is worth noting that the committee's various twists and turns were covered fully in the press, and especially by the *Manchester Guardian*, whose correspondent was clearly privy to details of discussions within the General Council.
71. Congress House, TUC Archives, File 117.13, EFR to Milne-Bailey, 26 July 1928.
72. See the following articles in *FES Monthly Notes*: 'The Trades Union Congress', 6: 57 (June 1929), pp. 1–2; 'Trades Unions', 6: 59 (Aug.–Sept. 1929), pp. 1–2; 'The Labour Party and the Report', 7: 66 (Apr. 1930), pp. 1–2; 'Another "Leakage"', 7: 68 (June 1930), pp. 10–11.
73. BLPES, Coll. Misc. 9, Rathbone to Beveridge, 22 May 1930; the FES's letter was published in the *Manchester Guardian* on 12 June 1930.
74. Congress House, TUC Archives, File 117.11, Milne-Bailey to Margaret Bondfield, 27 Aug. 1928.
75. Congress House, TUC Archives, File 118.1, Memorandum by E.P. Harries, 17 July 1930.
76. Congress House, TUC Archives, File 118.2, General Council, 'Report of a Special Meeting held on March 18, 1942, to discuss the question of Family Allowances'.
77. Ellen Wilkinson, *Peeps at Politicians* (London: Philip Allan, 1930), p. 114.
78. Rhys Davies, 'Family Allowances – Good or Bad', *New Leader*, 15: 106 (2 Nov. 1928), p. 8.
79. Rathbone, *Disinherited Family*, p. 85.
80. *Ibid.*, p. 84.

Chapter 12   Most Independent Member

1. For the jockeying between the parties prior to the 1929 election, see especially Philip Williamson, *National Crisis and National Government: British Politics, the Economy and Empire, 1926–1932* (Cambridge: Cambridge University Press, 1992), ch. 1.
2. *The Times*, 20 July 1928.
3. Just how carefully Rathbone and her supporters planted these seeds can be seen from the collection of election material which she sent in 1938 to the Duchess of Atholl, who was contemplating contesting a Scottish university seat. Blair Castle, Atholl Papers, File 18/1.
4. 'A University Constituency', *Woman's Leader*, 21: 19 (14 June 1929), p. 149.
5. *Manchester Guardian*, 4 June 1929, p. 5; RP XXV.1.337 (2), EFR to Elena Richmond, 10 June 1929.
6. WL, Brian Harrison interview with Marjorie (Green) Soper and Doris (Hardman) Cox, 15 Feb. 1976; and for Rathbone's distress at Picton-Turbervill's lack of secretarial help, see Edith Picton-Turbervill, *Life is Good: An Autobiography* (London: Frederick Muller, 1939), pp. 185–6.
7. Thelma Cazalet-Keir, *From the Wings: An Autobiography* (London: The Bodley Head, 1967), p. 126.
8. Pamela Brookes, *Women at Westminster: An Account of Women in the British Parliament, 1918–1966* (London: Peter Davies, 1967), p. 22.
9. Cazalet-Keir, *From the Wings*, p. 126; Mavis Tate, speaking to the British Commonwealth League conference, 26–28 May 1937, *Report* (1937), pp. 37–8.
10. On women in the House in this period, see especially, Brookes, *Women at Westminster*, and Brian Harrison, 'Women in a Men's House: The Women M.P.s, 1919–1945', *Historical Journal*, 29: 3 (1986), pp. 623–54; Beverly Parker Stobaugh, *Women and Parliament,*

1918–1970 (New York: Exposition Press, 1978); Elizabeth Vallance, *Women in the House: A Study of Women Members of Parliament* (London: Athlone Press, 1979).

11. Brookes, *Women at Westminster*, p. 36.

12. 'The Combined Universities: Miss Rathbone's Address', *Manchester Guardian*, 23 May 1929.

13. *Time and Tide*, 10: 23 (7 June 1929), p. 670; 'Miss Eleanor Rathbone', *Manchester Guardian*, 4 June 1929.

14. 310 *HC Deb.*, 1 Apr. 1936, col. 2033, 370 *HC Deb.*, 20 Mar. 1941, col. 369.

15. For Rathbone's participation in the BBC's 'The Week in Westminster' series, see BBC Written Archives Centre, Talks File, Eleanor Rathbone.

16. 233 *HC Deb.*, 11 Dec. 1929, cols 604, 606–8; 237 *HC Deb.*, 31 Mar. 1930, cols 1027–9.

17. For this one instance, see 281 *HC Deb.*, 9 Nov. 1933, col. 391.

18. Ellen Wilkinson, *Peeps at Politicians* (London: Philip Allan, 1930), p. 112.

19. Picton-Turbervill, *Life is Good*, pp. 233–4.

20. 301 *HC Deb.*, 15 May 1935, col. 1793.

21. Enid Huws Jones, *Margery Fry: The Essential Amateur* (London: Oxford University Press, 1966), p. 49.

22. Cicely Leadley-Brown, in *Common Cause* 2: 68 (28 July 1910), p. 260.

23. 'Impressions of Parliament', *Punch*, 204 (31 Mar. 1943), p. 270; 'Miss Rathbone's Attack', *Star*, 24 Mar. 1943.

24. Wilkinson, *Peeps*, p. 113.

25. Conservative MP Captain Alan Graham, at 406 *HC Deb.*, 15 Dec. 1944, cols 1513–14; *Manchester Guardian*, 20 Dec. 1940, p. 6, and 23 Dec. 1942, p. 6.

26. 281 *HC Deb.*, 9 Nov. 1933, col. 389.

27. WL, Brian Harrison interview with Marjorie (Green) Soper and Doris (Hardman) Cox, 15 Mar. 1977.

28. For these difficulties, see esp. Williamson, *National Crisis*, pp. 92–132.

29. 230 *HC Deb.*, 22 July 1929, cols 972–80.

30. Cazalet-Keir, *From the Wings*, p. 141.

31. See, e.g., 237 *HC Deb.*, cols 2092 et seq.; 245 *HC Deb.*, cols 1176–8.

32. RP XIV.2.3 (4), Rathbone, 'The Case for University Representation' (Dec. 1930).

33. 247 *HC Deb.*, 3 Feb. 1931, cols 1715–25; also Rathbone, letter, *The Times*, 16 Mar. 1931, p. 13.

34. RP XIV.2.3 (2), Correspondence between EFR and Vice-Chancellors, giving statistics on students' educational background and financial status.

35. 247 *HC Deb.*, 3 Feb. 1931, col. 1724.

36. 252 *HC Deb.*, 20 May 1931, cols 2012–18.

37. 'Cross Bench' [Eleanor F. Rathbone], 'Notes from Westminster', *Woman's Leader*, 23: 7 (20 Mar. 1931), p. 52.

38. RP XIV.4.23–32, for correspondence and documents relating to honorary degrees.

39. D.E. Butler, *The Electoral System in Britain since 1918*, 2nd edn (Oxford: Clarendon Press, 1963), p. 150.

40. Eleanor F. Rathbone, Letter, *Manchester Guardian*, 12 Mar. 1937, p. 24.

41. RP XIV.3.46, Durham graduates (London) dinner, 27 Jan. 1938.

42. A.P. Herbert, *Independent Member* (London: Methuen & Co., 1950), p. 108.

43. Arthur Salter, *Slave of the Lamp* (London: Weidenfeld & Nicolson, 1967), p. 141.

44. 406 *HC Deb.*, 15 Dec. 1944, col. 1512.

45. Thelma Cazalet-Keir, Megan Lloyd George and Irene Ward, Letter to *The Times*, 8 Jan. 1946, p. 7; Obituary, *Manchester Guardian*, 3 Jan. 1946, p. 3.

46. For Rathbone's arguments for maintenance grants for all children compulsorily kept in school, see 245 *HC Deb.*, 25 Nov. 1930, cols 1176–8; also *The Times*, 14 Nov. 1929, p. 8.

47. Her gadfly role comes out clearly in the reports of the Council's meetings found in the *Liverpool Red Book*; see especially the volume for 1925, reports of the council meetings of 2 January, 6 February, and 4 June 1924. The Council was also under attack during these years by the Ministry of Health, whose auditors had uncovered a tangled mess of kickbacks

and corruption in housing contracts. For houses built by 1930, see L.H. Keay, Director of Housing, 'Housing Work in Liverpool', in *Liverpool Red Book*, 1932, pp. 90–2.

48. Eleanor F. Rathbone, 'Drift Back to the Slums', *Liverpool Post*, 2 Jan. 1929; 'Drift Back to Slums: Criticism of Housing Policy in Liverpool', *The Times*, 3 Jan. 1929, p. 8.

49. Report of the council meeting of 5 Feb. 1930, in *Liverpool Red Book*, 1931, p. 575.

50. See Rathbone's and Simon's letters to *The Times*, 18 Jan. 1930, p. 6; 29 Jan. 1930, p. 10; and 4 Apr. 1930; also 'The Housing Bill', *The Times*, 9 July 1930; Eleanor F. Rathbone, *The Goal of Our Housing Policy* (Liverpool: Lee & Nightingale, 1930).

51. On maintenance allowances, see *The Times*, 16 Dec. 1930, p. 8.

52. For her first attempt, see 248 *HC Deb.*, 20 Feb. 1931, cols. 1641–704; for her comments on the final passage, see 335 *HC Deb.*, 29 April 1938, esp. cols 465, 482.

53. *The Times*, 17 Apr. 1930, p. 9.

54. 247 *HC Deb.*, 6 Feb. 1931, cols 2310–17.

55. WL, 2/NSE/5/5, Parliamentary Subcommittee, 13 July 1931.

56. *Woman's Leader*, 23: 25 (24 July 1931), p. 195.

57. 255 *HC Deb.*, 15 July 1931, cols 667–80.

58. *Woman's Leader*, 23: 26 (31 July 1931), p. 203.

59. For the Anomalies Act, see Susan Pedersen, *Family, Dependence and the Origins of the Welfare State: Britain and France, 1914–1945* (Cambridge: Cambridge University Press, 1993), pp. 297–307; also, J.D. Tomlinson, 'Women as "Anomalies": The Anomalies Regulations of 1931, Their Background and Implications', *Public Administration*, 62 (Winter 1984), pp. 423–37. David Howell, discussing this episode, notes that it brought out Rathbone's 'distance from, and perhaps antipathy towards, the institutions and ethos of the labour movement'. See Howell, *MacDonald's Party: Labour Identities and Crisis, 1922–1931* (Oxford: Oxford University Press, 2002), pp. 369–79, here at p. 373.

60. 251 *HC Deb.*, 16 Apr. 1931, cols 363–490.

61. *Woman's Leader*, 23: 29 (2 Oct. 1931), p. 227.

62. 256 *HC Deb.*, 18 Sept. 1931, cols 1192–7, 1943–9; *The Times*, 19 Sept. 1931, p. 9; 257 *HC Deb.*, 30 Sept. 1931, cols 255–8.

63. *The Times*, 17 Oct. 1931, p. 8.

64. This is Rathbone's account of the spirit of the House during its final days, *Woman's Leader*, 23: 25 (24 July 1931), and 23: 27 (7 Aug. 1931), p. 211.

65. RP XIV.2.26, Speech to Leeds University Old Students' Association, London Branch, 22 Nov. 1935.

66. RP XIV.3.10, Speech, 'The Place of the Voluntary Worker in the New Social Order', Birmingham, 28 Apr. 1933.

67. PRO, HLG 101/23: EFR to Hilton Young, 8 Dec. 1931, enclosing EFR, *Memorandum on the Use and Abuse of Housing Subsidies* (Nov. 1931); Memorandum of a meeting with Miss Rathbone, 26 Apr. 1932; and EFR to Hilton Young, 7 May 1932. See also 273 *HC Deb.*, 15 Dec. 1932, cols 589–97; 302 *HC Deb.*, 20 May 1935, cols 135–44; and 314 *HC Deb.*, 16 July 1936, col. 2228; also John Macnicol, *The Movement for Family Allowances: A Study in Social Policy Development* (London: Heinemann, 1980), pp. 62–4.

68. 285 *HC Deb.*, 1 Feb. 1934, col. 616; see also, 279 *HC Deb.*, 11 June 1933, cols 427–31.

69. 265 *HC Deb.*, 11 May 1932, cols. 1977, 1980.

70. See, e.g., 304 *HC Deb.*, 10 July 1935, cols 327–8; 307 *HC Deb.*, 19 Dec. 1935, col. 1919; 311 *HC Deb.*, 21 April 1936, cols 17, 26, 27; 331 *HC Deb.*, 1 Feb. 1938, col. 28.

71. Harold Macmillan, *Winds of Change, 1914–1939* (London: Macmillan, 1966), p. 310.

72. The findings of these social surveys are well summarized by John Stevenson and Chris Cook, *The Slump* (London: Quartet, 1979), ch. 3.

73. A great deal has been written on the social policies of the National government. I have drawn especially on Stevenson and Cook, *The Slump*, chs 4 and 5; and Bentley B. Gilbert, *British Social Policy, 1914–1939* (London: B.T. Batsford, 1970), ch. 4.

74. Harold Macmillan agreed to be a convener for the meeting; see Rathbone's correspondence with him in Bodleian, Macmillan Papers dep. c. 81, fols 78, 80–1, and dep. c. 84, fols 279–80.

75. 286 HC Deb., 26 Feb. 1934, cols 767–90.
76. See esp. PRO, MH 55/688, *Memorandum on the Scale of Needs Suitable for Adoption by the Unemployment Assistance Board in Assessing Assistance to Applicants under Part II of the Unemployment Act, 1934*, submitted on behalf of the Children's Minimum Campaign Committee by Eleanor F. Rathbone; and PRO, AST 7/32, Green to Thomas Jones, 17 Sept. 1934 and 11 Oct. 1934, enclosing CMC pamphlets giving evidence of malnutrition.
77. For the CMC's 12 March 1934 deputation to the Prime Minister, see PRO, PREM 1/165; to the Ministry of Health on 23 March, see PRO, MH 55/275; to the Board of Education on 26 March, see PRO, ED 50/78. See also Rathbone's speech in the Commons criticizing the Board of Education's method of detecting malnutrition and arguing for free provision of milk and meals for children below a simple poverty line, 292 HC Deb., 17 July 1934, cols 1055–62.
78. 296 HC Deb., 18 Dec. 1934, col. 1025.
79. PRO, AST 12/15, UAB 5th meeting, 31 July 1934, and 9th meeting, 9–12 Oct. 1934.
80. Rathbone accused the government of misleading the Commons in implying that its scales were up to the British Medical Association's standards, and challenged the Minister and the Board to explain the foundations of their scale: 297 HC Deb., 28 Jan. 1935, cols 77–82.
81. Macnicol, *The Movement for Family Allowances*, pp. 62–6.
82. 296 HC Deb., 18 Dec. 1934, cols 1932–3.
83. 292 HC Deb., 17 July 1934, cols 1061–2.
84. PRO, ED 24/1215, Inter-Departmental Committee on Milk Consumption, 'The Milk in Schools Scheme', Paper MC No. 12 (1935).
85. PRO, ED 24/1215, Inter-Departmental Committee on Milk Consumption, 'Note for Deputation from the Children's Minimum Organising Committee, 18 December 1935'.
86. PRO, ED 50/216, Minutes and records of a CMC deputation 27 Mar. 1939, and 'Board of Education and Nutrition: Deputation from the Children's Minimum Council', *Education*, 7 April 1939.
87. PRO, AST 12/15, UAB 5th meeting, 31 July 1934.
88. For the development of this argument, see esp. Macnicol, *The Movement for Family Allowances*, ch. 5.
89. CAC, Leo Amery diaries AMEL 290, *passim*.
90. *The Next Five Years: An Essay in Political Agreement* (London: Macmillan, 1935), and for these groups, see especially Arthur Marwick, 'Middle Opinion in the Thirties: Planning, Progress and Political "Agreement"', *English Historical Review*, 79: 311 (Apr. 1964), pp. 285–98; Daniel Ritschel, *The Politics of Planning: The Debate on Economic Planning in Britain in the 1930s* (Oxford: Clarendon Press, 1997).
91. RP XIV.3.106, Nicolson's review of Mary D. Stocks, *Eleanor Rathbone: A Biography* (London: Victor Gollancz, 1949).
92. RP, Dec. 2002 accession (being catalogued), EFR to Stocks, n.d. (early 1920s).
93. Interviews with Diana Hopkinson, Godalming, 18 Aug. 1994; with Dr B.L. Rathbone, Liverpool, 18 Mar. 1993 and 26 July 1994; with Nancy Warr, London, 20 and 27 Jan. 1993; with Jenny Rathbone, London, 25 Jan. 2003; with Noreen Rathbone, 2 Aug. 2003; also Diana Hopkinson, *Family Inheritance: A Life of Eva Hubback* (London: Staples Press, 1954), p. 105.
94. Eleanor F. Rathbone, *The Disinherited Family*, (1924; rpt. 3rd edn. London: George Allen & Unwin, 1927) p. 50.
95. Eleanor F. Rathbone, 'Victory – and After?' (6 Mar. 1929), in *Milestones: Presidential Addresses at the Annual Council Meetings of the National Union of Societies for Equal Citizenship* (Liverpool: Lee & Nightingale, 1929), pp. 44–9.

Chapter 13   The Difference Empire Makes

1. WL, Brian Harrison interview with Doris (Hardman) Cox and Marjorie (Green) Soper, 15 Mar. 1977.

2. WL, 2/NSE/A/1/5, EC Minutes, 27 Sept., 25 Oct. and 22 Nov. 1927; *ibid.*, NUSEC *Annual Report 1927* (1928), p. 17.

3. RP XXV.1.337 (2), EFR to Elena Richmond, 10 June 1929.

4. 276 *HC. Deb.*, 28 Mar. 1933, col. 941.

5. Katherine Mayo, *Mother India* (New York: Harcourt, Brace, 1927), p. 22.

6. Mrinalini Sinha is completing a major, much-needed study of the Mayo controversy. For early instalments of that work, see 'Reading *Mother India*: Empire, Nation, and the Female Voice', *Journal of Women's History*, 6: 2 (Summer 1994), 6–44; and her introduction to a new edition of selections from *Mother India*, published by Kali for Women and the University of Michigan Press, 1998. Earlier significant articles on the controversy over child marriage include: Geraldine Forbes, 'Women and Modernity: The Issue of Child Marriage in India', *Women's Studies International Quarterly*, 2 (1979), pp. 407–19; Barbara Ramusack, 'Women's Organizations and Social Change: The Age-of-Marriage Issue in India', in Naomi Black and Ann Baker Cottrell, eds, *Women and World Change: Equity Issues in Development* (London: Sage, 1981), pp. 199–216.

7. Yale University, Beinecke Library, Mayo Papers 5/40, EFR to Mayo, 14 Nov. 1927; 6/41, EFR to Mayo, 6 Dec. 1927.

8. Eleanor F. Rathbone, 'Has Katherine Mayo Slandered "Mother India"?' *Hibbert Journal*, 27: 2 (Jan. 1929), p. 197.

9. *Ibid.*, p. 214.

10. There is now a considerable literature on these ties, but for an early and still useful survey see Barbara Ramusack, 'Cultural Missionaries, Maternal Imperialists, Feminist Allies: British Women Activists in India, 1865–1945', in Margaret Strobel and Nupur Chaudhuri, eds, *Western Women and Imperialism: Complicity and Resistance* (Bloomington: Indiana University Press, 1992), pp. 119–36.

11. For which see especially, Antoinette Burton, *Burdens of History: British Feminists, Indian Women, and Imperial Culture, 1865–1915* (Chapel Hill: University of North Carolina Press, 1994).

12. 'Women in India Conference', *Manchester Guardian*, 9 Oct. 1929, p. 17.

13. 'British Women and India: Our London Letter', *Indian Daily Mail*, 23 Oct. 1929. See also Rama Rao's recollections of the conflict in Dhanvanthi Rama Rao, *An Inheritance* (London: Heinemann, 1977), pp. 166–73.

14. 'Women in India', *The Times*, 22 Oct. 1929, p. 12.

15. Ibid.

16. WL, 7/ELR/2, Benn to EFR, 15 May 1930.

17. WL, 7/ELR/2, EFR to Benn, 8 July 1930.

18. Reading University Library, Astor Papers 1416/1/1/1012, EFR to MPs, 17 July 1930; *The Times*, 24 Sept. 1930, p. 8.

19. WL, 7/ELR/5, EFR to Lady Hartog, 26 May 1930.

20. See Rathbone's favourable comments on Reddi in WL, 7/ELR/8, EFR to Sankey, 26 Mar. 1931.

21. On Subbarayan, see Padmini Sen Gupta, *Pioneer Women of India* (Bombay: Thacker & Co., 1944), pp. 160–6.

22. WL, 7/ELR//1, Reddi to EFR, 29 July 1931.

23. 247 *HC. Deb.*, 26 Jan. 1931, col. 714.

24. RP XXV.1.319 (1), Katherine Mayo to Elena Richmond, 24 May 1926.

25. India Office Library, Cornelia Sorabji Papers, Mss Eur. F165, File 161, Copy of a letter from Mayo to EFR, marked personal, n.d. [November 1927?].

26. Reading University Library, Astor Papers, 1416/1/1/1012, Astor to Mayo, 16 April 1931.

27. Beinecke Library, Mayo Papers, 11/97, EFR to Mayo, n.d.

28. Eleanor F. Rathbone, 'Child Marriage in India', *Hibbert Journal*, 29: 4 (July 1931), p. 610.

29. *Ibid.*, p. 609.

30. 260 *HC Deb.*, 2 Dec. 1931, col. 1190.

31. For this campaign, see Susan Pedersen, 'The Maternalist Moment in British Colonial Policy:

The Campaign against 'Child Slavery' in Hong Kong, 1917–1941', *Past and Present*, 171 (May 2001), pp. 171–202.

32. For this campaign, see Susan Pedersen, 'National Bodies, Unspeakable Acts: The Sexual Politics of Colonial Policy-making', *Journal of Modern History*, 63: 4 (Dec. 1991), pp. 647–80.

33. For the meetings and evidence of the Committee for the Protection of Coloured Women, see RP XIV.2.1.

34. PRO, CO 323/1067/1.

35. WL, Brian Harrison interview with Doris (Hardman) Cox and Marjorie (Green) Soper, 15 Mar. 1977.

36. 233 *HC Deb.*, 11 Dec. 1929, col. 608.

37. 'Retrospect', *Woman's Leader*, 21: 48 (3 Jan. 1930), pp. 369–70.

38. 'Feminist Politics', *Woman's Leader*, 22: 4 (28 Feb. 1930), p. 27.

39. Coverage of the February conference can be found in the *Woman's Leader*, 22: 3 (21 Feb. 1930), p. 22, and in the *Manchester Guardian*, 13 Feb. 1930. The Colonial Office prudently dispatched a civil servant to attend the meeting 'unofficially'; his report is in PRO, CO 323/1071/8.

40. PRO, CO 323/1071/8, 'Notes of a meeting held in the Secretary of State's Room . . . Tuesday, the 8th of April, 1930'.

41. PRO, CO 323/1071/8, Note by Gilbert Grindle, 4 Apr. 1930.

42. *Papers Relating to the Health and Progress of Native Populations in Certain Parts of the Empire*, Colonial Office publication no. 65 (1931).

43. WL, Brian Harrison interview with Doris (Hardman) Cox and Marjorie (Green) Soper, 15 Mar. 1977; also RP XIV.2.1 (39), EFR to Hardman, 7 Sept. 1932.

44. Atholl, Rathbone and Wedgwood, 'Memorandum on Female Slavery within the Family' (May 1932), copies in RP XIV.2.1 (40) and Reading University Library, Astor Papers, 1416/1/1/1088.

45. PRO, CO 1177/1, 'Note of a meeting in the Secretary of State's room on Tuesday, the 10th May [1932], with a deputation from the National Union of Societies for Equal Citizenship'.

46. WL, 7/ELR/24, EFR to Amrit Kaur, 9 Jan. 1935.

47. 'Women of the Coloured Races', *Woman's Leader*, 22: 24 (18 July 1930), pp. 183–4; see also the copy in RP XIV 2.1 (52).

48. 'Women Slaves', *Manchester Guardian*, 13 Feb. 1930.

49. Reading University Library, Astor Papers 1416/1/1/797, Astor to John Harris (refusing to sign an appeal for colour-blind colonial franchises), 13 June 1929; Astor likewise refused to sign a memo authored by Rathbone, Atholl and Josiah Wedgwood. See 1416/1/1/1088.

50. R.J. Moore and Carl Bridge both see the 1935 Act as an instrumental attempt to fragment Indian political identities and prevent Congress dominance; see Moore, *Endgames of Empire: Studies of Britain's Indian Problem* (Delhi: Oxford University Press, 1988), and *The Crisis of Indian Unity, 1917–1940* (Delhi: Oxford University Press, 1974); and Bridge, *Holding India to the Empire: The British Conservative Party and the 1935 Constitution* (New Delhi: Sterling Publishers, 1986). Andrew Muldoon's recent dissertation, 'Making a "Moderate" India: British Conservatives, Imperial Culture and Indian Political Reform, 1924–1935' (PhD dissertation, Washington University, St Louis, 2000) dissents to a degree from this view, arguing that while its Conservative supporters certainly intended to undercut Congress, they nevertheless saw the Act as a progressive measure.

51. See, for example, evidence of Rathbone's coaching in the Astor Papers at Reading University Library, esp. 1416/1/1/1013, 'Suggested Points for speech to a conservative audience on women in the New Indian constitution', typescript, n.d., marked 'Miss Rathbone's notes'.

52. See, e.g., 301 *HC Deb.*, 14 May 1935, cols 1633–5.

53. India Office, Katharine Atholl Papers, Mss Eur. D 903/1, [Rathbone], 'A Summary of the more salient facts respecting the status and conditions of Indian women and of some of the proposals for improving and safeguarding their well-being' (29pp., typescript, Mar. 1930). Rathbone sent this memo to Simon and discussed it with him: see India Office, John Simon

Papers, Mss Eur. F 77/86, EFR to Simon, 4, 11 and 24 Mar. 1930; Simon to EFR, 21 Mar. 1930.

54. *Report of the Indian Statutory Commission*, vol. 1, *Survey*, PP 1929–30, XI, Cmd. 3568, p. 53.

55. *Report of the Indian Statutory Commission*, vol. 2, *Recommendations*, PP 1929–30, XI, Cmd. 3569, pp. 78–9, 93–4.

56. India Office Library, L/P&J/9/48: see especially, Eva Hubback (NUSEC) to Benn, 15 Oct. 1930, Women's National Liberal Federation to Benn, 15 Oct. 1930, and British Federation of University Women to Benn, 8 Nov. 1930.

57. Trinity College, Cambridge, Layton Papers, File 106, 'Abstract of Proceedings of a Deputation ... on 27th February 1931'.

58. WL, 7/ELR/7, Subbarayan to EFR, 1 May 1931. Mrinalini Sinha has written cogently about the debates among Indian and British women over suffrage; see her 'Suffragism and Internationalism: The Enfranchisement of British and Indian Women under an Imperial State', *Indian Economic and Social History Review*, 36: 4 (1999), pp. 461–84, rpt. in Ian Fletcher et al., eds, *Women's Suffrage in the British Empire: Citizenship, Nation, and Race* (London: Routledge, 2000), pp. 224–39; see also Barbara N. Ramusack, 'Catalysts or Helpers? British Feminists, Indian Women's Rights, and Indian Independence', in Gail Minault, ed., *The Extended Family: Women and Political Participation in India and Pakistan* (Columbia, Missouri: South Asia Books, 1981), pp. 109–50, and Geraldine Forbes's comprehensive survey of campaigns for women's rights in her *Women in Modern India* (Cambridge: Cambridge University Press, 1996), pp. 92–120.

59. Reading University Library, Astor Papers, 1416/1/1/1012, Memorandum of the National Council of Women, All–India Women's Conference and the Women's Indian Association, to the Round Table Conference, May 1931.

60. WL, 7/ELR/1, EFR to Reddi, 1 May 1931.

61. Indian Round Table Conference, 12 Nov. 1930–19 Jan. 1931, *Proceedings*, PP 1930–31, XII, Cmd. 3778, pp. 385–8.

62. WL, 7/ELR/7, EFR to Subbarayan, 8 Jan. 1932.

63. RP XIV.1. All quotations taken from EFR's circular letters to her family, Jan.–Feb. 1932.

64. RP XIV.1.8 and XIV.1.9, EFR to her family, 3 and 7 Feb. 1932.

65. WL, 7/ELR/9, EFR to MacDonald, 8 Apr. 1932, and 7/ELR/11, Hoare to EFR, 12 May 1932 and EFR to Hoare, 18 June 1932.

66. 265 *HC Deb.*, 29 Apr. 1932, cols 744–9.

67. RP XIV.1.12, EFR to family, Benares to Lucknow train, 23 Feb. 1932; XIV.1.13, EFR to family, Lahore, 6 Mar. 1932.

68. WL, 7/ELR/13, EFR to Lothian, 9 April 1932.

69. Trinity College, Cambridge, Butler Papers, Box F43, Minutes of the Indian Franchise Committee, Apr. 1932, p. 24; also Indian Office Library, L/P&J/9/63, 'Declaration [of the All-India Women's Conference], n.d. [Spring 1932].

70. Indian Franchise Committee, *Report*, PP 1931–2, VIII, Cmd. 4086, pp. 81–90, 206–9.

71. India Office Library, L/P&J/9/83, Rajwade to Ramsay MacDonald, 19 July 1932.

72. British Commonwealth League, *Report* (1932), pp. 61–2, 64.

73. WL, 7/ELR/21, EFR to Mrs P.K. Ray, 9 March 1933; WL, 7/ELR/19, EFR to Begum Shah Nawaz, 24 Jan. 1933; WL, 7/ELR/7, Subbarayan to EFR, 6 Feb. 1933, and EFR to Subbarayan, 16 Feb. 1933.

74. WL, 7/ELR/21, Sarala Ray to EFR, 28 Apr. 1933.

75. Catherine Candy pays close attention to the conflicts among Indian feminists and to competing cross-national feminist alliances (among them the Subbarayan/Rathbone alliance) in 'Competing Transnational Representations of the 1930s Indian Franchise Question', in Fletcher et al., eds, *Women's Suffrage in the British Empire*, pp. 191–206.

76. WL, 7/ELR/1, EFR to Reddi, 9 Feb. 1933; also 7/ELR/17, EFR to Mrs Irving, 8 Sept. 1932.

77. India Office Library, L/P&J/9/94, Government of India, Reforms Department, to Sir Samuel Hoare, No. 13, 24 Sept. 1932, esp. pp. 7–9.

78. *Proposals for Indian Constitutional Reform*, PP 1932–3, XX, Cmd. 4268, pp. 94–5.

79. SRO, Lothian Papers, GD40/17/166, Lothian to Hoare, 8 Mar. 1933.

80. Ibid., Hoare to Lothian, 9 Mar. 1933.

81. WL, 7/ELR/7, EFR to Subbarayan, 15 May 1931.

82. WL, 7/ELR/1, EFR to Reddi, 1 May 1931.

83. WL, 7/ELR/2, EFR to Wedgwood Benn, 27 Mar. 1931.

84. IULL, Hannah Whitall Smith Papers, Box 15, Ray Strachey to Mary Berenson, 26 July 1933.

85. Evidence of Ray Strachey, 26 July 1933, Joint Committee on Indian Constitutional Reform, *Minutes of Evidence*, PP 1932–3, VIII, p. 2268.

86. Rathbone's old ally Maude Royden came to understand that this was the real analogy. The situation in India, she reported after a brief visit in 1935, reminded her forcibly of the suffrage years: 'people not interested in politics giving their whole energy to the political struggle'; 'men and women apologizing for the fact that they had not been in prison'. Friends House Library, Society of Friends Indian Conciliation Group Papers, Box 41/2, 'Notes of meeting held on Feb. 15th 1935 for Dr. Royden'.

87. WL, 7/ELR/1, EFR to Reddi, 12 Mar. 1931.

88. WL, 7/ELR/24, EFR to Amrit Kaur, 29 Feb. 1934.

89. WL, 7/ELR/18 and 7/ELR/24, EFR to Amrit Kaur and Mrs Hamid Ali, 14 Oct. 1933.

90. WL, 7/ELR/1, EFR to Reddi, 13 Apr. 1933.

91. Rajkumari Amrit Kaur and Mrs Hamid Ali used this language explicitly in their evidence to the Joint Select Committee.

92. WL, 7/ELR/1, Reddi to EFR, 31 Mar. 1933; WL, 7/ELR/24, Amrit Kaur to EFR, 7 Dec. 1933 and 2 Apr. 1934.

93. Evidence by Rajkumari Amrit Kaur and Mrs Hamid Ali to Sub-Committee C of the Joint Committee on Indian Constitutional Reform, 29 July 1933, and to the full committee on 2 August 1933, in Joint Committee on Indian Constitutional Reform, *Minutes of Evidence*, pp. 1617–22, 2288–324.

94. WL, 7/ELR/24, 'Statement of the Standing Committee of the All-India Women's Conference held at Poona on the 28th July 1935'.

95. WL, 7/ELR/7, Subbarayan to Rathbone, 16 Sept. 1932; WL, 7/ELR/19, Shah Nawaz to EFR, 17 Sept. 1934.

96. WL, 7/ELR/24, Amrit Kaur to EFR, 11 Feb. 1935.

97. WL, 7/ELR/24, EFR to Amrit Kaur, 9 Jan. 1935.

98. WL, 7/ELR/24, Amrit Kaur to EFR, 11 Feb. 1935.

99. Reading University Library, Astor 1416/1/1/1256, *Mother India's Daughters: The Significance of the Women's Movement* (Women's International League, n.d.), and 1416/1/1/1257, 'Bulletin of the Indian Women's Movement', No. 4 (Feb. 1935).

100. Ramusack, for example, defines Rathbone as a 'maternal imperialist' in her article, 'Cultural Missionaries', while Sinha stresses (rightly) the ways in which Rathbone's rhetoric of some unified women's interest both depended upon and elided imperial power. To my mind, however, both understate the degree to which Rathbone's language and actions were forged not simply in an imperial field-of-force but in the more constrained world of Whitehall and Westminster, and hence varied considerably with audience and context.

101. WL, 7/ELR/24, Amrit Kaur to EFR, 11 Feb. 1935; 298 *HC Deb.*, 19 Feb. 1935, col. 314; see also WL, 7/ELR/34, EFR to N.M. Joshi, 20 Feb. 1935, explaining her vote.

102. WL, 7/ELR/34, EFR to N.M. Joshi, 20 Feb. 1935.

103. Again, she explained her considerable reservations, but hoped that the new constitution would enable Indian politicians to extract that promise of dominion status she was convinced they deserved; 302 *HC Deb.*, 4 June 1935, cols 1810–15.

104. WL, 7/ELR/14, EFR to Hutton (Office of the Census Commissioner for India), 9 July 1932.

105. 'Politics or Social Reform?' *Lucknow Pioneer*, 17 May 1934.

106. WL, 7/ELR/24, EFR to Amrit Kaur, 29 Feb. 1934.

107. *Spectator*, 6 Apr. 1934.

108. *Stri Dharma*, May 1934.

109. WL, 7/ELR/24, Amrit Kaur to EFR, 2 Apr. 1934.
110. WL, 7/ELR/1, Reddi to EFR, 29 Mar. 1934.
111. See, e.g., WL, 7/ELR/24, EFR to Amrit Kaur, 29 Feb. 1934, 15 June 1934; Amrit Kaur to EFR, 5 July 1934 and 3 Sept. 1934; 7/ELR/30, EFR to Lakshmi Menon, 15 June 1934; 7/ELR/29, EFR to Mrs Brijlal Nehru, 8 June 1934.
112. WL, 7/ELR/18, Mrs Hamid Ali to EFR, 8 Aug. 1934.
113. WL, 7/ELR/34, EFR to N.M. Joshi, 23 Jan. 1935.
114. For this conflict, see, Rathbone's correspondence with Margery Corbett-Ashby and with Jewish feminists in RP XIV.2.5; also Ruth Abrams, ' "Pioneering Representatives of the Hebrew People": Campaigns of the Palestinian Jewish Women's Equal Rights Association, 1918–1948', in Fletcher et al., eds, *Women's Suffrage in the British Empire*, pp. 121–37.
115. RP XIV.2.5 (8), Cunliffe Lister to EFR, 21 Feb. 1933.
116. RP XIV.2.5 (23), Welt Strauss to EFR, 21 June 1933 and XIV.2.5 (32), 7 July 1933.
117. For Rathbone's trip to Palestine, see RP XIV.2.5 (45), Macadam's account, and RP, Dec. 2002 accession (being catalogued), Margaret Nixon to Mary Stocks, 30 July and 5 Aug. 1948.
118. RP XIV.2.5 (44), 'The Women's Movement: At Home and In the British Commonwealth', typed, with handwritten addenda.
119. RP XXIIA.159, Henry Gair Rathbone to Hugh Rathbone, 11 Nov. 1932.
120. RP, Dec. 2002 accession (being catalogued), EFR to Hilda Oakeley, n.d. (1906).

Coda to Part III: Miss Rathbone has her Portrait Painted

1. Correspondence relating to the portrait, including the circular letters sent by the committee and by Rathbone, can be found in the Beveridge Papers at the BLPES, II b, 31.
2. RP XIV.3.4.

Chapter 14   Prophet without Honour

1. 276 *HC Deb.*, 13 Apr. 1933, cols 2737–822; quoted material at cols 2757, 2762, 2764–5.
2. RP XIV.3.4, Letter to constituents, Mar. 1934.
3. For Churchill's thinking on foreign policy, I have found R.A.C. Parker's recent book, *Churchill and Appeasement* (London: Macmillan, 2000), especially useful, along with Churchill's own classic, if tendentious, account, *The Gathering Storm* (Boston: Houghton Mifflin, 1948).
4. Eleanor F. Rathbone, 'Democracy's Fight for Life', *Manchester Guardian*, 2 May 1933; RP XIV.3.11, speech to the Proportional Representation Society, Caxton Hall, 10 May 1933; see also Eleanor F. Rathbone, 'Nazis and Jews', *The Times*, 11 Apr. 1933, p. 10.
5. 285 *HC Deb.*, 6 Feb. 1934, col. 1087.
6. RP XIV.2.6 (4), EFR, Letter to the *Inquirer*, 21 June 1933.
7. Rathbone supported, for example, the joint Liberal and Labour motion deploring the government's rearmament plans after the failure of the disarmament conference. See 292 *HC Deb.*, 30 July 1934, vote at cols 2443–8.
8. For the run-up to the war, see especially Harold G. Marcus, *A History of Ethiopia* (Berkeley: University of California Press, 1994). The British government's treatment of the crisis is meticulously chronicled in Maurice Cowling, *The Impact of Hitler: British Politics and British Policy, 1933–1940* (Cambridge: Cambridge University Press, 1975), pp. 79–102.
9. RP, Dec. 2002 accession (being catalogued), EFR to Lloyd George, 13 July 1935, and HLRO, Lloyd George Papers, G/141/38/2, EFR to Lloyd George, 7 Sept. 1935.
10. On the boycott of German goods see RP XIV.2.6 (5), Letter, *The Times*, 11 Aug. 1933; RP XIV.2.6 (14), British Anti-Nazi Boycott, *Report*; and for Italy, Eleanor F. Rathbone, 'An Alternative to War: Economic Sanctions', *Manchester Guardian*, 23 Apr. 1935, p. 16; also 304 *HC Deb.*, 29 July 1935, col. 2306.

11. 305 *HC Deb.*, 22 Oct. 1935, cols 127–30.

12. Harold Nicolson, Entry for 10 Dec. 1935, *Diaries and Letters, 1930–1939* (London: Collins, 1966), p. 230.

13. 307 *HC Deb.*, 10 Dec. 1935, cols 844–50. Rathbone's assessment of politicians' and officials' motives was accurate. In his autobiography, Hoare recalled Vansittart's insistence on the need to retain the friendship of Italy, the service chiefs' strong opposition to any course of action that might lead to war, and Laval's collusion with Mussolini. The 'so-called Hoare-Laval plan' was, he insisted 'the only practicable basis for a compromise' given the common public and governmental opposition to the prospect of war. Viscount Templewood, *Nine Troubled Years* (London: Collins, 1954), pp. 149–92, quoted here at p. 191.

14. 'Abyssinia', *The Times*, 11 Dec. 1935, p. 9.

15. Daniel Waley, *British Public Opinion and the Abyssinian War, 1935–6* (London: Maurice Temple Smith, 1975), p. 45; and see EFR's letter, 'Oil and Coal for Italy: The Most Vital Sanction', *Manchester Guardian*, 28 Nov. 1935, p. 18.

16. 310 *HC Deb.*, 6 Apr. 1936, col. 2544; *The Times*, 7 Apr. 1936, p. 9. In her election address, Rathbone had admitted that a strong stand against aggression did carry some risk of war, but thought that 'almost negligible compared with the practical certainty that a collapse of collective security will lead within a few years to a far more general and terrible war'. RP XIV.3.4, 'Miss Eleanor Rathbone's Election Address' (1935).

17. Records of the small and quite ineffective Abyssinian Association are in the H.S. Jevons Papers, National Library of Wales; for Rathbone's speech at the LNU meeting at the Albert Hall on 8 May 1936, see RP XIV.3.32, and Waley, *British Public Opinion*, p. 78. Rathbone also wrote the introduction to (and may have compiled) a collection of speeches and letters documenting the outcry against the betrayal of Abyssinia. See *The Tragedy of Abyssinia* (League of Nations Union, June 1936).

18. 311 *HC Deb.*, 6 May 1936, col. 1809; *The Times*, 7 May 1936, p. 9.

19. 313 *HC Deb.*, 23 June 1936, cols 1605–734.

20. RP XIV.3.32, 'LNU Meeting at Albert Hall, 8 May 1936'.

21. National Library of Wales, Jevons VI 236, 'Emperor of Ethiopia's Fund. Abyssinia Association' (leaflet, 1938).

22. On the May 1938 fight at the League, see Trinity College, Cambridge, Walter Layton Papers, I (13)(I), EFR to Layton, 3 May 1938, and Ball State University, Norman Angell Papers, Angell to EFR, 6 May 1938; on the Anglo-Italian agreement, see 340 *HC Deb.*, 2 Nov. 1938, cols 307–11, and for wartime promises, see PRO, FO 371/27521, File J 2603/15/1, Deputation by Mander, Rathbone and Noel-Baker to Richard Law, 8 Aug. 1941, and Jevons VI 239, Abyssinia Association, EC Meeting, 9 Oct. 1941.

23. According to its most recent historians, the sedition bill in its original form 'represented a calculated attempt to render a whole segment of radical political opinion vulnerable to arbitrary police action'. See K.D. Ewing and C.A. Gearty, *The Struggle for Civil Liberties: Political Freedom and the Rule of Law in Britain, 1914–1945* (Oxford: Oxford University Press, 2000), p. 243. The fierce cross-party campaign against the bill, which also led to the founding of the National Council of Civil Liberties, succeeded in amending the bill and making it largely irrelevant. See the coverage in *The Times*, 1 Nov. 1934, pp. 7, 8, and 3 Nov. 1934, p. 6.

24. WL, 7/ELR/28, EFR to Mona Hensman, 3 Feb. 1936; RP XIV.3.4, 'Miss Eleanor Rathbone's Election Address' (1935), p. 2.

25. Only in retrospect, R.A.C. Parker points out, did historians and politicians see the Rhineland crisis as the moment when Hitler could have been stopped. At the time, they concentrated instead on reining in the French, who wanted a strong Anglo-French response. See R.A.C. Parker, *Chamberlain and Appeasement: British Policy and the Coming of the Second World War* (New York: St Martin's Press, 1993), pp. 58–79; also Cowling, *Impact of Hitler*, pp. 102–8.

26. RP XIV.4.4, EFR to Churchill, 22 Apr. 1936.

27. 'British Public Opinion and the Crisis: Throwing Its Weight on the Wrong Side?' *Manchester Guardian*, 28 Mar. 1936, p. 7.

28. RP XIV.3.34, 'The Future of European Peace, Liberty and Democracy' (speech notes), 3 Aug. 1936 (this speech was thought important enough to merit coverage in *The Times*, 4 Aug. 1936, p. 7) and Eleanor F. Rathbone, 'The "League" and "Anti-League" Fronts: Non-Party Alignments', *Manchester Guardian*, 2 Sept. 1936. See also Rathbone's speech to the House, 315 *HC Deb.*, 31 July 1936, cols 1935–8. Macadam's work for Noel-Baker is mentioned (and condemned by Nancy Astor) in Reading University Library, Astor Papers, 1416/1/1/1409, Astor to Hubback, 15 July 1936.

29. 317 *HC Deb.*, 5 Nov. 1936, col. 336.

30. RP XIV.3.4, Letter to constituents, Dec. 1936; see also Rathbone's criticism of the Labour Party's stance in her speeches of 31 July and 3 August, note 28 above.

31. RP XIV.4.1, Churchill to EFR, 13 Apr. 1936, and RP XIV.4.4, EFR to Churchill, 22 Apr. 1936; also in CAC, Winston Churchill Papers, CHAR 2/274/12.

32. RP XIV.3.34, 'The Future of European Peace, Liberty and Democracy' (speech notes), 3 Aug. 1936. Rathbone urged Churchill to lead such a front, but his 'Arms and the Covenant' campaign was derailed by the abdication crisis. See CAC, Churchill Papers, CHAR 2/260/109, EFR to Churchill, 18 Nov. 1936.

33. For Lothian's approaches to Hitler, see SRO, Lothian GD 40/17/201–4; for his memorandum and Rathbone's reactions, see HLRO, Lloyd George Papers, G/141/23/17, and G/141/38/1, Lloyd George to EFR, 3 Sept. 1935, and G/151/38/2, EFR to Lloyd George, 7 Sept. 1935; also, Stephen Koss, 'Lloyd George and Nonconformity: The Last Rally', *English Historical Review*, 89: 350 (Jan. 1974), p. 97.

34. HLRO, Lloyd George Papers, G/11/6/61, A.P. Laurie to Frances Stevenson, 31 Mar. 1936.

35. Eleanor F. Rathbone, 'Mr. Lloyd George's Views on Germany: What Must Be the Effect of His Tributes to Hitler?' *Manchester Guardian*, 25 Sept. 1936, p. 20. For a judicious recent account of Lloyd George's visit, see Antony Lentin, *Lloyd George and the Lost Peace: From Versailles to Hitler, 1919–1940* (London: Palgrave, 2001), ch. 5.

36. See RP, Dec. 2002 accession (being catalogued), EFR to Lloyd George, 28 Sept. 1936.

37. Martin Ceadel, 'The First British Referendum: The Peace Ballot, 1934–5', *English Historical Review*, 95: 377 (Oct. 1980), pp. 810–39.

38. BLPES, LNU.I.3, General Council meeting, 15–17 Dec. 1936, and 'Pacifists and the League', *The Times*, 17 Dec. 1936. For the Union's conflict-ridden debates over rearmament more generally, see Donald Birn, *The League of Nations Union, 1918–1945* (Oxford: Clarendon Press, 1981), ch. 10.

39. For the incompetent and half-hearted administration of the non-intervention pact, see especially Gerald Howson's recent well-researched book, *Arms for Spain: The Untold Story of the Spanish Civil War* (New York: St Martin's Press, 1998), pp. 114–19.

40. According to Koestler, the committee was orchestrated by the Party's Comintern propaganda chief for Western Europe, based in Paris, and had party members as its two secretaries. The implication that this collection of MPs and academics was dancing, puppet-like, to strings pulled from afar is, however, nonsense: the committee behaved in much the same manner as countless other fact-finding bodies coping with distance and complex webs of interest and intrigue (the Bryce Commission springs to mind here). See Koestler, *The Invisible Writing* (New York: Macmillan, 1954), pp. 313–14, 323–4.

41. *The Times*, 25 Sept. 1936; Eleanor Rathbone et al., *Report and Findings of the Committee of Inquiry into Breaches of International Law relating to Intervention in Spain* (London, 3 Oct. 1936).

42. 318 *HC Deb.*, 1 Dec. 1936, cols 1121–7; and see 'Arms for Spain', *The Times*, 2 Dec. 1936, p. 8. There is an extensive historiography on military assistance to both sides in the Spanish Civil War. John Coverdale's *Italian Intervention in the Spanish Civil War* (Princeton: Princeton University Press, 1975) documents the considerable Italian involvement; in *Spain Betrayed: The Soviet Union in the Spanish Civil War* (New Haven: Yale University Press, 2001), Ronald Radosh, Mary R. Habeck and Grigory Sevostianov plumb newly opened

Russian archives to show the extent to which the Republic was infiltrated and undermined by the Soviets. Yet the conclusions of Jill Edwards's older study of British policy and the impact of non-intervention, *The British Government and the Spanish Civil War, 1936–1939* (London: Macmillan, 1979), still hold. Howson, in *Arms for Spain*, confirms that the non-intervention agreement gave an enormous advantage to the fascist-supplied rebels, leaving the Republic at the mercy of arms traffickers and the penny-pinching and duplicitous Soviets.

43. See Rathbone's correspondence with Eden in November 1936 and June 1937 in PRO, FO 371/29584, FO 371/20586, and FO 371/21342; for representative parliamentary questions, see 321 *HC Deb.*, 17 Mar. 1937, col. 2166, 322 *HC Deb.*, 12 Apr. 1937, col. 596; also RP XIV.2.13 (25), *Evidence of Recent Breaches by Germany and Italy of the Non-intervention Agreement* (London: P.S. King & Son, May 1937); Eleanor F. Rathbone, 'The Fiasco of Non-Intervention', *Manchester Guardian*, 3 June 1937. It is worth noting that Eden did try in January 1937 to bring the Cabinet to support more effective enforcement of non-intervention but was not successful. See Parker, *Chamberlain*, pp. 84–5; Cowling, *Impact of Hitler*, pp. 164–6.

44. Bodleian, Gilbert Murray Papers 79/207, Murray to EFR, 23 Oct. 1936; BL, Add. MS 51141, Cecil Papers, fol. 272, Cecil to EFR, 13 May 1937, and see BLPES, LNU.II.15, Executive Committee meetings, 6 and 24 May 1937.

45. 326 *HC Deb.*, 19 July 1937, col. 1899.

46. RP XIV.4.4, EFR to Churchill, 22 Apr. 1936; Churchill, *Gathering Storm*, p. 214.

47. Philip Williamson's recent study stresses Baldwin's concern to conciliate Labour and unite the country by emphasizing common constitutional and national values. By the late 1930s, Baldwin underlined the need for spiritual resistance to totalitarianism of all kinds, and worried that Chamberlain's combative style was compromising national unity. See Philip Williamson, *Stanley Baldwin: Conservative Leadership and National Values* (Cambridge: Cambridge University Press, 1999), esp. pp. 313–26.

48. In August 1939, Duff Cooper captured this difference perfectly. Chamberlain, he wrote to Baldwin, 'believes public opinion is what *The Times* tells him it is – and he believes Conservative opinion is what the Chief Whip says it is', thus turning the Party rightward in ways Baldwin 'so bravely and brilliantly avoided'. See Cooper, *Old Men Forget* (1953; New York: Carroll & Graf, 1988), p. 255.

49. Gollancz/Cassell Company Archive, File on *War Can Be Averted*, EFR to Gollancz, 30 July 1937 and 30 Nov. 1937; and Gollancz to EFR, 3 Aug. 1937.

50. Eleanor F. Rathbone, *War Can Be Averted: The Achievability of Collective Security* (London: Victor Gollancz, 1938).

51. *Ibid.*, pp. 92–3, 110–11, 165–6, 192–3.

52. For Atholl, see her own memoir, *Working Partnership* (London: Arthur Barker, 1958), and S.J. Hetherington, *Katharine Atholl, 1874–1960: Against the Tide* (Aberdeen: Aberdeen University Press, 1989).

53. RP, Dec. 2002 accession (being catalogued), Atholl to EFR, 23 Apr. 1933, and EFR to Atholl, 27 Apr. 1933.

54. Hetherington, *Katharine Atholl*, pp. 169–70.

55. See Rathbone's letters to the *Manchester Guardian*, 2 April and 25 Sept., 1936.

56. RP, Dec. 2002 accession (being catalogued), Atholl to EFR, 26 Sept. 1936.

57. *Ibid.*, Atholl to EFR, 10 Sept. 1936.

58. RP XIV.2.9 (6), Atholl, 'Reason for Proposed Journey to Rumania'.

59. Trinity College, Cambridge, Layton Papers 9 (6) (1), EFR to Layton, 3 Nov. 1936, enclosing Eleanor F. Rathbone, 'Proposal Concerning Czecho-Slovakia as affected by the Government Policy of "Limiting Commitments" to Western Europe', 3 Nov. 1936. Rathbone also sent this to Gilbert Murray (see Bodleian, Murray Papers, 80/12, Murray to EFR, 4 Nov. 1936), and tried to interest the BBC (see BBC Written Archives Centre, Talks file 'Eleanor Rathbone', correspondence in Nov. 1936).

60. On the trip, see RP XIV.2.9 (21), 'Tour in Yugoslavia, Roumania and Czechoslovakia, February 1937', and Atholl, *Working Partnership*, pp. 204–7.

61. RP XIV.2.9 (22), EFR, 'Notes on Cultural Relations' (Apr. 1937).
62. Atholl Papers, Blair Castle, File 16/1, Confidential Report by Atholl for the Foreign Office (1937).
63. 321 HC Deb., 25 Mar. 1937, col. 3136.
64. The Times, 19 Apr. 1937.
65. The Duchess of Atholl, Miss Eleanor Rathbone, Miss Ellen Wilkinson and Dame Rachel Crowdy, Report of Our Visit to Spain (National Joint Committee for Spanish Relief, 1937); The Duchess of Atholl, My Impressions of Spain (Southend-on-Sea: H.F. Lucas & Co., 1937); Betty Vernon, Ellen Wilkinson (London: Croom Helm, 1982), pp. 164–6.
66. MRC, Wilfrid Roberts Papers, MSS 308/3/NJC,1, 'Report on the Work of the National Joint Committee' (n.d., probably 1938), gives the amount of money raised by the NJC as £150,000. Rathbone estimated a figure of almost £300,000 for the NJC and the Basque Children's Committee together by early 1939. See RP XIV.3.4, Letter to Constituents, Mar. 1939.
67. Hetherington, Katharine Atholl, pp. 150–1; Jim Fryth, The Signal Was Spain: The Spanish Aid Movement in Britain, 1936–39 (London: Lawrence & Wishart, 1986), pp. 201–2; RP XIV.3.58, Speech on the Czech and German Crisis, Friends House, 30 Sept. 1938.
68. In the Commons, for example, both women were accused of recruiting for the International Brigades, in violation of the Foreign Enlistment Act (The Times, 30 July 1938, p. 7).
69. Some records of the NJC are in the Wilfrid Roberts Papers, but for the fullest account, see Tom Buchanan, Britain and the Spanish Civil War (Cambridge: Cambridge University Press, 1997), ch. 4, and Fryth, The Signal Was Spain, chs 14, 16.
70. For negotiations over admission of the children, see PRO, FO 371/21370/W9147, W9446, W9496 and W9705. Eden's support was clearly critical.
71. For arguments over repatriation in 1937 and again in 1939, see MRC, Roberts Papers, MSS/308/3/RO/46–7, and 308/3/FO, 11, 13, 20, 24, 29, 35; also, for Foreign Office discomfort over the unwillingness of the Basque Children's Committee to repatriate children, see FO 371/21372. The evacuation of the Basque children is covered in depth by Fryth, The Signal Was Spain, ch. 15; see also Kevin Myers, 'History, Migration and Childhood: Basque Refugee Children in 1930s Britain', Family and Community History, 3: 2 (Nov. 2000), pp. 147–57, and Lord Layton, Dorothy (London: Collins, 1961), pp. 113–15. It is important, of course, to keep this evacuation in perspective. As Rathbone persistently reminded the government, it had allowed in 4,000 children whose maintenance was guaranteed by private funds at a time when France was supporting somewhere between 50,000 and 100,000 Spanish refugees.
72. Rathbone had persuaded Attlee and Sinclair to raise the issue of Britain's failure to protect ships bringing refugee ships out of Bilbao in early June; see R.P. XIV.2.13 (26), Telegram, Rathbone to Attlee, 19 June 1937, and CAC, Sinclair Papers THRS II 39/5, Telegram, Rathbone to Sinclair, 19 June 1937. She asked parliamentary questions on the possibility of evacuating refugees from Santander on 29 June, and on 1, 5, 8, 14, 19, 26 and 30 July. See also RP XIV.2.11 (11) for Rathbone's correspondence with Pursey; RP XIV.2.12 (5), for letters to the News Chronicle and the Birmingham Post, 8 and 9 July 1937, on the situation in Santander; FO 371/21356, Rathbone to Eden, 7 July 1937 and FO 371/21374, Rathbone to Halifax, 16 Aug. 1937; and MRC, Roberts Papers, MSS 308/3/NJ/9, Miller to Roberts, 27 Aug. 1937 on Rathbone's trip to Paris.
73. PRO, FO 371/21374, Memo by Shuckburgh, 23 Aug. 1937.
74. For which, see Hugh Thomas, The Spanish Civil War (1961; rev. edn New York: Modern Library, 1989), pp. 696–71.
75. BLPES, LNU.II.16, EC Minutes, 21 Oct. 1937.
76. 328 HC Deb., 26 Oct. 1937, cols 64–8.
77. PRO, FO 371/22610, EFR to Butler, 11 June 1938.
78. 326 HC Deb., 21 July 1937, col. 2198; 332 HC Deb., 28 Feb. 1938, col. 746; 332 HC Deb., 10 Mar. 1938, col. 2103.

79. For interruptions, see e.g., 333 *HC Deb.*, 16 Mar. 1938, cols 502, 519–20, 528, 532; and for efforts by the Speaker to restrain her, 331 *HC Deb.*, 16 Feb. 1938, cols 1963–8; 337 *HC Deb.*, 23 June 1938, cols 1371–6.

80. RP, Dec. 2002 accession (being catalogued), EFR to Eden, 2 Mar. 1938, noting 48 letters, nine telegrams and three resolutions signed by over 400 people, all urging her to support Eden and oppose the government – and no mail urging the opposite.

81. The issue of the sinking of British ships was raised by Rathbone in a debate on adjournment on 20 May – see 336 *HC Deb.*, cols 793–6 – and was taken up by other speakers in June; see 337 *HC Deb.*, 14 June 1938, cols 41, 44, 46, 47 (Attlee), 21 June 1938, cols 922–35 (Noel-Baker) and 23 June 1938, cols 1381–8 (Churchill).

82. 338 *HC Deb.*, 26 July 1938, col. 3017.

83. *Ibid.*, cols 3018–20. For the significance and context of this speech, see Parker, *Churchill and Appeasement*, p. 171.

84. Entry for 12 Mar. 1938, *The Diary of Virginia Woolf*, ed. Anne Oliver Bell, vol. 4 (London: Hogarth, 1984), p. 130.

85. Virginia Woolf, *Three Guineas* (New York: Harcourt, Brace, Jovanovich, 1938), here at pp. 108–9.

86. RP XIV.2.6 (4), Eleanor F. Rathbone, Letter to *The Inquirer*, 21 June 1933.

87. Few subjects have attracted as much scholarly attention as the Munich crisis. In addition to the memoirs and diaries mentioned below, I have relied especially on Parker, *Chamberlain*, pp. 156–81.

88. For that famous House session on 28 September, there is no better record than Harold Nicolson, *Diaries and Letters, 1930–1939*, pp. 368–71. Other accounts are simply too numerous to mention, but one that captures the many misunderstandings about what was at stake is Vyvyan Adam's pseudonymous chapter on Chamberlain, drafted immediately after the outbreak of war: 'Watchman', *Right Honourable Gentlemen* (London: Hamish Hamilton, 1939), esp. pp. 34–40. Nicolson and Adams were, of course, both critics of Chamberlain, but the diary of Sir Cuthbert Headlam, a more typical Conservative backbencher, also reveals considerable unease. See *Parliament and Politics in the Age of Churchill and Attlee: The Headlam Diaries, 1935–1951*, ed. Stuart Ball (London: Royal Historical Society, 1999), pp. 133–42.

89. CAC, Churchill Papers, CHAR 2/331/60, EFR to Churchill, 10 Sept. 1938, from Garthdale.

90. Nicolson, *Diaries and Letters 1930–1939*, pp. 371–6; *The Empire at Bay: The Leo Amery Diaries 1929–1945*, ed. John Barnes and David Nicholson (London: Hutchinson, 1988), pp. 508–28.

91. *Baffy: The Diaries of Blanche Dugdale, 1936–1947*, ed. N.A. Rose (London: Vallentine, Mitchell, 1973), pp. 109, 112.

92. *Champion Redoubtable: The Diaries and Letters of Violet Bonham-Carter, 1914–1945*, ed. Mark Pottle (London: Weidenfeld & Nicolson, 1998), pp. 190–1.

93. Harold Nicolson Diary (Harvester Microfilm), 17 Mar. 1938; RP XIV.3.106; Cooper, *Old Men Forget*, p. 251.

94. RP XIV.3.58, Speech Notes for a Meeting on the Czech and German Crisis, Friends House, 30 Sept. 1938; and entry for 30 Sept. 1938, *Baffy*, pp. 109–10.

95. Chamberlain to Margesson (Conservative Chief Whip), quoted in Parker, *Chamberlain*, p. 190; and see Robert Rhodes James, *Bob Boothby: A Portrait* (London: Hodder & Stoughton, 1991), pp. 184–9; Hetherington, *Katharine Atholl*, pp. 201–9.

96. RP XIV.2.15 (3), Letter, dated 3 Oct. 1938.

97. Rathbone used this phrase in 'A Personal View of the Refugee Problem', *New Statesman and Nation*, 17: 425 (15 Apr. 1939), p. 568.

98. There is a very extensive literature on British government policy towards refugees in the 1930s. I have relied especially on A.J. Sherman's classic account, *Island Refuge: Britain and Refugees from the Third Reich, 1933–1939* (1973; new edn Ilford: Frank Cass, 1994), supplemented by Louise London's recent, comprehensive study, *Whitehall and the Jews*,

1933–1948: British Immigration Policy and the Holocaust (Cambridge: Cambridge University Press, 2000).

99. Eleanor F. Rathbone, 'Great Britain and the Refugees: The Government's Niggardly Policy', *Manchester Guardian*, 23 May 1938, p. 16; also 336 *HC Deb.*, 23 May 1938, cols 834–6.

100. The Baldwin fund raised about £500,000, half of which was allocated to Jewish refugees and spent largely on children. For this, and for Chamberlain's crucial role, see London, *Whitehall and the Jews*, pp. 105–8, 122.

101. BLPES, LNU.II.16 EC meeting, 24 Mar. 1938; *Manchester Guardian*, 9 July 1938, p. 18.

102. PRO FO 371/21356, EFR to Eden and Cranborne, 7 July 1937.

103. BL, Add. Ms 51141, Cecil Papers, fol. 278, Telegram, EFR to Cecil, 10 Oct. 1938; PRO, FO 371/21585, Telegram, EFR to Hoare, 10 Oct. 1938; FO 371/21584, Draft communiqué regarding deputation to Halifax, 19 Oct. 1938; BLPES, LNU.II.17, EC 20 and 27 Oct. 1938.

104. PRO, FO 371/21587/C14473, Special Branch report, 5 Nov. 1938.

105. RP XIV.2.15 (5), Plaminkova to EFR, 28 Oct. 1938.

106. PRO, FO 371/24074, Note by Reilly, 13 Jan. 1939.

107. Victor Cazalet diary, n.d. (post-Munich, before Christmas), courtesy of Sir Edward Cazalet.

108. Central British Fund for World Jewish Relief Archives (microfilm), Reel 21, File 113, fols 6–9, Statement of Objects of the Parliamentary Committee on Refugees.

109. RP XIV.3.106.

110. On Koestler, see RP XIV.2.12 (28), EFR to Viscountess Astor, 8 Apr. 1937 and Koestler to EFR, 31 May 1937; Koestler, *The Invisible Writing*, pp. 366–7. For Rathbone and Butler, see, e.g., PRO, FO 371/21587, EFR to Butler, 10 Nov. 1938 and Butler to EFR, 11 Nov. 1938, raising the case of four communists barred from entry into Britain. Butler did intercede and they were given permission to come; see *ibid.*, McAlpine to Makins, 21 Nov. 1938. For Hoare, Lothian and the International Brigaders, see Cambridge University Library, Templewood Papers, XIII: 5 (14), Hoare to EFR, 3 May 1943; Scottish Record Office, Lothian Papers, GD 40/17/404, pp. 105–7; and numerous Foreign Office files, esp. FO 371/29172, 31232, and 31921.

111. RP XIV.2.15 (4), 'Notes on Visit to Prague, 14–20 Jan. 1939'. These recommendations were passed on to the Foreign Office, see PRO, FO 371/24081/W4984, and to the Home Office (see London, *Whitehall and the Jews*, p. 148).

112. PRO, FO 371/24081/W4984, EFR to Randall, 23 Mar. 1939 and Minute by Randall, 28 March 1939.

113. RP XIV.2.15 (16), (18) and (19): Courtney to EFR, 28 April 1939; 'Recommendations agreed on at a conference . . . 15 May 1939'; EFR to Butler, 17 May 1939.

114. PRO, FO 371/24083/W8047, Randall to Cooper, 6 June 1939.

115. RP XIV.2.15 (36), EFR to Bunbury, 21 July 1939.

116. 350 *HC Deb.*, 4 Aug. 1939, col. 2894.

117. See the extensive documentation of these efforts in RP XIV.2.15 (24)–(37), and, on the deputation, RP XIV.2.15 (43), 'Memorandum on the need for further financial provision . . . , 2 Aug. 1939'.

118. PRO, FO 371/22654, see esp. records of the deputation by the Parliamentary Committee for Spain, 4 Oct. 1938; notes by Bullock, 24 and 26 Oct. 1938; Despatch No. 878 to Sir Robert Hodgson, British Agent in Nationalist Spain. For the foodships, see Fryth, *The Signal Was Spain*, ch. 16.

119. PRO, FO 371/24153, Note by W.I. Mallet, 3 Feb. 1939; Butler to EFR, 21 Feb. 1939; FO 371/24154, EFR to Butler, 23 Feb. 1939; FO 371/24155: EFR to Sir George Mounsey, 2 Mar. 1939; records of a deputation, 6 Mar. 1939; note by W.H. Montagu-Pollock, 6 Mar. 1939.

120. RP XIV.2.12 (8), EFR to Mexican Ambassador, Paris, 11 Mar. 1939.

121. For the NJC's rescue ships, see Fryth, *The Signal Was Spain*, p. 293; correspondence on the *Stanbrook* is in PRO, FO 371/24155.

122. RP XIV.2.12 (55), Foreign Office, 'Memo on Policy of H.M. Government in regard to evacuation of refugees from Republican territory', 20 Mar. 1939; PRO, FO 371/24154, EFR to Butler, received 4 Apr. 1939, and Butler to EFR, 18 Apr. 1939.

123. Nicolson, 'People and Things', *Spectator*, 20 Jan. 1939; Nicolson, 'Marginal Comment', *Spectator*, 11 Jan. 1946.

124. Interview with Lady Warr and Mrs Warr, London, 20 Jan. 1993.

125. PRO, FO 371/24153, Montagu-Pollock to E.N. Cooper, 7 Mar. 1939.

126. PRO, FO 371/24153, Butler to EFR, 21 Feb. 1939; FO 371/24154, EFR to Butler, 23 Feb. 1939; and Fryth, *The Signal Was Spain*, pp. 297–8.

127. EFR, 'British Government and the Refugee Problem', *Manchester Guardian*, 6 Apr. 1939, p. 20.

128. Thomas, *The Spanish Civil War*, p. 899.

129. For these efforts, see BL, Add. Ms 51141, Cecil Papers, fols 286–95.

130. Eleanor F. Rathbone, 'British Government and the Refugee Problem', *Manchester Guardian*, 6 Apr. 1939, p. 20; and see RP XIV.2.15 (20), Parliamentary Committee on Refugees, 'Note Submitted by the Parliamentary Committee on Refugees', July 1939.

131. Eleanor F. Rathbone, 'A Personal View of the Refugee Problem', *New Statesman and Nation*, 17: 425 (15 Apr. 1939), pp. 568–9, emphasis mine.

132. BLPES, LNU.I.3, General Council meeting, 15–17 Dec. 1936, and 'Pacifists and the League', *The Times*, 17 Dec. 1936.

133. Rathbone included this story in an article she wrote, RP XIV.2.15 (29), 'Refugees from Czechoslovakia' (20 July 1939).

134. WL, Brian Harrison interview with Doris [Hardman] Cox, 15 Mar. 1977.

135. Telephone Interview with Noreen Rathbone, 2 Aug. 2003.

136. RP XIV.2.14 (31), EFR to Listowel, 26 May 1939.

137. 350 *HC Deb.*, 4 Aug. 1939, col. 2893.

138. Nicolson, 'Marginal Comment', *Spectator*, 11 Jan. 1946, p. 34.

139. RP XIV.3.4, Letter to constituents, Mar. 1939.

140. RP XIV.3.59, 'Is it too late for collective security?' (Speech notes), 1–3 Feb. 1939.

141. BL, Add. MS 51141, Cecil Papers, fols 280–1, EFR to Cecil, 26 June 1939; and see Parker, *Churchill*, pp. 232–6.

142. RP XIV.3.4, Letter to constituents, 11 May 1939.

143. 351 *HC Deb.*, 24 Aug. 1939, col. 35.

Chapter 15   A War Worth Fighting

1. HLRO, Lloyd George Papers, Box 11, File 6, G/11/6/61, Laurie to Stevenson, 31 Mar. 1936, and G/11/6/70, Laurie to Miss Stevenson, 18 May 1936.

2. Interview with Dr B.L. Rathbone, Liverpool, 16 Aug. 1989.

3. Quoted in Mary D. Stocks, *Eleanor Rathbone: A Biography* (London: Victor Gollancz, 1949), p. 282.

4. RP, Dec. 2002 accession (being catalogued).

5. Information about these meetings can be found in RP XIV.2.16; also Paul Addison, *The Road to 1945* (1975; rpt. London: Quartet, 1977), p. 67.

6. L.S. Amery, *My Political Life*, vol. 3, *The Unforgiving Years, 1929–1940* (London: Hutchinson, 1955), p. 339; see also L.S. Amery, *The Empire at Bay: The Leo Amery Diaries, 1929–1945*, ed. John Barnes and David Nicholson (London: Hutchinson, 1988), p. 558.

7. Robert Boothby, *Boothby: Recollections of a Rebel* (London: Hutchinson, 1978), pp. 136, 143–4.

8. 359 *HC Deb.*, 11 Apr. 1940, cols 762–4.

9. Andrew Roberts provides a judicious account of the negotiations within the cabinet leadership in *The Holy Fox: A Life of Lord Halifax* (London: Weidenfeld & Nicolson, 1991), ch. 21. This account of the machinations of Amery and the 'Davies group' has drawn on Amery's diary entries and Barnes and Nicholson's commentary in *The Empire at Bay*; see also Addison, *Road*, pp. 91–102.

10. Amery, *The Empire at Bay*, p. 620.
11. RP XIV.3.65, Speech to Lambeth LNU, 5 June 1940.
12. CAC, Churchill Papers CHAR 20/102/74, EFR to Churchill, 26 Mar. 1943.
13. *HC Deb.*, 23 Mar 1943, cols 1585–98.
14. CAC, Churchill Papers, CHAR 20/102/16, John Martin to Captain Randolph Churchill, 26 Mar. 1943; 'Impressions of Parliament', *Punch*, 204 (31 Mar. 1943), p. 270; 'Miss Rathbone's Attack', *Star*, 24 Mar. 1943.
15. CAC, A.V. Hill, 'On Cat Fights', in his unpublished autobiography, 'Memories and Reflections', vol. 2, p. 305.
16. CAC, Churchill Papers, CHAR 20/93A/9, WSC to EFR, 24 Mar. 1943; RP XIV.4.11, Clementine Churchill to EFR, 25 Mar. 1943.
17. CAC, Churchill Papers CHAR, 20/102/74, EFR to Churchill, 26 Mar. 1943.
18. Records of the Woman Power Committee are in BLPES, Coll. Misc. 548; see also Harold Smith, 'The Womanpower Problem in Britain during the Second World War', *Historical Journal*, 27: 4 (Dec. 1984), pp. 925–45.
19. 370 *HC Deb.*, 20 Mar. 1941, col. 369; 378 *HC Deb.*, 5 Mar. 1942, cols 884–5.
20. BBC Written Archives Centre, Talk Scripts, EFR, 'Women in Dangerous Services', BBC talk, 30 July 1940; 392 *HC Deb.*, 24 Sept. 1943, col. 608.
21. 391 *HC Deb.*, 3 Aug. 1943, cols 2130–5.
22. RP XIV.2.19 (17), EFR to Grigg, 29 June 1940.
23. For figures on categorization, see PRO, Cab. 67/6, WP (G) (40) 115 War Cabinet, 'Control of Aliens. Memorandum by the Home Secretary' (29 Apr. 1940). Three fine book-length accounts of internment of aliens exist, and I have drawn on all three. François Lafitte's *The Internment of Aliens*, first published as a Penguin Special in the autumn of 1940 (new edn, London: Libris, 1988) remains useful. In 1980, two books were published that combined research into recently released official papers with vivid accounts by those interned. See, Peter and Leni Gillman's *Collar the Lot!: How Britain Interned and Expelled its Wartime Refugees* (London: Quartet, 1980), and Ronald Stent, *A Bespattered Page? The Internment of His Majesty's 'Most Loyal Enemy Aliens'* (London: André Deutsch, 1980).
24. See 353 *HC Deb.*, 9 Nov. 1939, col. 405; 353 *HC Deb.*, 23 Nov. 1939, cols 1396–7, 1417.
25. PRO, Cab. 67/6, WP (G) (40) 115 War Cabinet, 'Control of Aliens. Memorandum by the Home Secretary' (29 Apr. 1940).
26. For 'fifth column' fears, see PRO, Cab. 66/7, ' "Fifth Column" Activities in the United Kingdom', COS (4) 315, (JIC), 2 May 1940, appended to 20 (40) 153 (10 May 1940). For the key cabinet decisions, see Cab. 65/7, War Cabinet 119 (A) (40), 11 May 1940, and War Cabinet 123 (40), 15 May 1940.
27. PRO, Cab. 67/6, WP (G) (40) 131 War Cabinet, 'Invasion of Great Brtain: Possible Cooperation by a "fifth column." Memorandum by the Home Secretary' (17 May 1940).
28. PRO, Cab. 65/7, War Cabinet 137 (40), 24 May 1940; Cab. 65/7, War Cabinet 161 (40), 11 June 1940; Stent, *A Bespattered Page?*, p. 74.
29. RP XIV.17 (16), 'Diary of an Austrian Refugee at Huyton Camp' (July 1940).
30. For a vivid reconstruction of the voyage of the *Arandora Star*, see especially, Gillman and Gillman, *Collar the Lot!*, chs 1, 17, 18.
31. RP XIV.2.17 (11).
32. 361 *HC Deb.*, 23 May 1940, cols 293–7, 6 June 1940, cols 979–81, and 11 June 1940, cols 1113–14; see also Rathbone's comments in BLPES, LNU.II.18, EC Minutes, 4 July 1940.
33. 362 *HC Deb.*, 10 July 1940, col. 1207.
34. *Ibid.*, col. 1212. Waste of refugee talents was one of Rathbone's major grievances: long before the round-ups began, and again once they were over, Rathbone would approach the BBC, the Foreign Office and well-placed politicians and friends with suggestions for using 'friendly aliens' yet more fully in broadcasts and publications. See, e.g., BLPES, LNU.II.17, EC Minutes, 28 Sept. 1939; PRO, FO 371/23104, EFR to Butler, 18 Sept. 1939; HLRO, Lloyd George Papers, G/16/7/8, EFR to Lloyd George, 20 Feb. 1941; RP XIV.2.19 (53), records of meeting on propaganda at Tufton Court, 20 Aug. 1941.

35. 362 *HC Deb.*, 10 July 1940, cols 1207–306.
36. PRO, Cab. 65/8, War Cabinet 200 (40), 11 July 1940.
37. PRO, Cab. 67/7, War Cabinet, 'Aliens. Memorandum by the Lord Privy Seal' (16 July 1940).
38. PRO, Cab. 65/8, War Cabinet 209 (40), 22 July 1940.
39. PRO, Cab. 67/8, WP (G) (40) 309, War Cabinet, 'Internment of Aliens of Enemy Nationality. Memorandum by the Home Secretary' (20 Nov. 1940).
40. RP XIV.2.17 (11), EFR to Weissenberg, 10 July 1940.
41. Stocks, *Eleanor Rathbone*, pp. 284–6, H. Redlich, 'Eleanor Rathbone', *The Times*, 14 Oct. 1946, p. 5.
42. HLRO, Graham White Papers, GW 14/1/2, EFR, 'Suggestions for improvement in Internment Camps' (17 July 1940).
43. WL, Brian Harrison interview with Helga Wolff, 31 Aug. 1977.
44. For the Council of Aliens' recommendations of 26 Aug. 1940 on new categories for release, and their rejection by the Home Office on security grounds, see PRO, HO 213/565. Lytton carried on until January and then asked to resign; see PRO, FO 371/29174/W1408, Lytton to Eden, 21 Jan. 1941. Churchill objected, stating that he thought MI5's 'witch-hunting' should be curtailed and Lytton's views accepted, but Morrison refused to comply. At Eden's request, Lytton carried on until June, when he finally resigned in frustration. See PRO, FO 371/29178/W7442, Lytton to Eden, 11 June 1941.
45. RP XIV.2.17 (17), EFR, circular letter, Aug. 1940.
46. Bodleian, SPSL Archives, Box 120, File 3, fol. 328, 'Parliamentary Committee on Refugees, period of July 15, 1940 to September 6, 1941. Summary of Work'.
47. CAC, A.V. Hill, 'Retrospective Sympathetic Affection, 1966', in his unpublished autobiography, 'Memories and Reflections', vol. 3, pp. 601–2.
48. Bodleian, SPSL Archives, Box 120, File 3, fol. 328, 'Parliamentary Committee on Refugees, period of July 15, 1940 to September 6, 1941. Summary of Work'.
49. For her efforts on behalf of aliens (mostly refugees) interned in Australia, see LPL, George Bell Papers, vol. 31, part 2, fols 313–24, which includes records of a deputation to the Australian High Commissioner.
50. CAC, Philip Noel-Baker Papers, NBKR 4/580, EFR to Noel-Baker, 2 Nov. 1940.
51. RP XIV.2.17 (31), EFR to internees in prison, circular letter, 14 Nov. 1940.
52. In 1939, Cazalet had elicited two substantial donations of £50 each from Sigmund Gestetner; in 1941, Gestetner again gave money to support the Parliamentary Committee. Records of these transactions are in the archives of the Central British Fund for World Jewish Relief, microfilm reel 21, file 113.
53. Bodleian, SPSL Archives, Box 120, File 3, EFR to Simpson, 14 Nov. 1941. The complex story of the SPSL's efforts to raise money for the Parliamentary Committee can be pieced together through the correspondence in Files 2 and 3 of Box 120.
54. Bodleian, SPSL Archives, Box 120, File 3, fols 520–2, Parliamentary Committee on Refugees, 'Report of Activities for the Current Year' (14 Oct. 1942).
55. PRO, Cab. 67/8, WP (G) (40) 309, 'Internment of Aliens of Enemy Nationality. Memorandum by the Home Secretary' (20 Nov. 1940).
56. 367 *HC Deb.*, 3 Dec. 1940, col. 452; 367 *HC Deb.*, 10 Dec. 1940, col. 874.
57. CAC, Noel-Baker Papers, NBKR 4/580, EFR to Noel-Baker, 2 Nov. 1940 and NBKR 4/581, Noel-Baker to EFR, 16 Apr. 1941; PRO, FO 371/29176/W3589, EFR, 'Black Spots on the Refugee Situation' (Mar. 1941), and PRO, FO 371/29176/W3894, Council of Aliens, Minutes of the 32nd meeting (9 Apr. 1941), discussing Rathbone's memo cited above.
58. *Manchester Guardian*, 21 Dec. 1940, p. 6.
59. Joan Prewer (later Gibson), 'I knew Eleanor Rathbone', copy courtesy Mrs Gibson.
60. RP, Dec. 2002 accession (being catalogued), EFR to T.L. Rowan, 23 Dec. 1943.
61. David G. Ritchie, *The Principles of State Interference* (London: Swan Sonnenschein & Co., 1891), p. 101.
62. India Office Library, L/I/1/1498, EFR to Amery, 21 May 1941.
63. Copies of this correspondence are now in the Rathbone Papers at the University of Liverpool.

Mary Stocks reprinted the entire correspondence in *Eleanor Rathbone*, pp. 337–69; Rathbone's opening letter to Nehru, dated May 1941, is at pp. 337–41.

64. CAC, Leo Amery Papers, AMEL 291, Diary entry for 27 May 1941.
65. India Office, L/I/1/1498, Amery to EFR, 11 June 1941, enclosing decipher of telegram of Tagore's press statement of 4 June.
66. Nehru to Rathbone, 22 June 1941, rpt. in Stocks, *Eleanor Rathbone*, pp. 342–58.
67. CAC, Amery Papers, AMEL 291, Diary entry for 26 July 1941.
68. 373 *HC Deb.*, 1 Aug. 1941, cols 1735–9.
69. Rathbone to Nehru, 28 Aug. 1941, rpt. in Stocks, *Eleanor Rathbone*, pp. 359–62.
70. Friends House Library, India Conciliation Group Papers, Temp. Mss 47/4, Harrison to EFR, 21 May 1941, and EFR to Harrison, 19 June 1941 and 12 Sept. 1941.
71. *Ibid.*, Heath to Harrison, 15 Sept. 1941.
72. *Ibid.*, Heath to Rathbone, 17 Sept. 1941.
73. Nehru to Rathbone, 9 Nov. 1941, rpt. in Stocks, *Eleanor Rathbone*, pp. 363–9.
74. CAC, Amery Papers, AMEL 291, Diary entry 5 Oct. 1942; 338 *HC Deb.*, 8 Oct. 1942, col. 1345; 402 *HC Deb.*, 28 July 1944, col. 1020.
75. Stocks, *Eleanor Rathbone*, p. 340.

Chapter 16   'Rescue the Perishing'

1. For this 'information breakthrough' of late 1942, see especially Richard Breitman, *Official Secrets: What the Nazis Planned, What the British and Americans Knew* (New York: Hill & Wang, 1998), ch. 9. The statement by the Polish government was later published as Republic of Poland, Ministry of Foreign Affairs, *The Mass Extermination of Jews in German Occupied Poland: Note Addressed to the Governments of the United Nations on December 10th 1942, and Other Documents*, copy in JRL, *Manchester Guardian* archives, 223/5/55; also World Jewish Congress (British Section), 'Annihilation of European Jewry. Hitler's Policy of Total Destruction' (1 Dec. 1942), copy in JRL, *Manchester Guardian* archives, 223/5/42.
2. Mention of these voluminous mailbags is made in the Parliamentary Committee on Refugees' 'Report of Activities from Oct. 1, 1942 to Feb. 28, 1943', HLRO, Graham White Papers, GW 10/3/54.
3. LPL, Temple Papers, 54/185–6, EFR to Temple, 3 Dec. 1942.
4. Archival records confirm the absolute centrality of her role. Rathbone's notes on particular crises, her briefings for deputations, her explanations of the reasons for different demands, can be found in the papers of the Foreign Office, the Home Office, the League of Nations Union, the Board of Deputies of British Jews, the Society for the Protection of Science and Learning, the *Manchester Guardian*, the Archbishop of Canterbury, Bishop Bell, the Reverend James Parkes, Lord Cecil of Chelwood, Graham White – and no doubt (could one search long and hard enough) many others.
5. Yehuda Bauer, *Jews for Sale: Nazi–Jewish Negotiations, 1933–1945* (New Haven: Yale University Press, 1994), p. 72.
6. LPL, Temple Papers, 55/23, Eden to Temple, 21 May 1943.
7. Letter, *The Times*, 8 Jan. 1946, p. 7.
8. Interview with Lady Warr, London 27 Jan. 1993.
9. See, e.g., 'Vichy's Jewish Victims', *The Times*, 7 Sept. 1942, p. 3.
10. PRO, FO 371/24326/C7400, EFR to Butler, 24 June 1940, and Butler to EFR, 1 July 1940; PRO, FO 371/29233/W14514, Eleanor F. Rathbone, 'Scheme for the Rescue of Alien Refugees in Unoccupied France and French North Africa', 13 Nov. 1941; also PRO, FO 371/32654, which includes information on an approach by Rathbone to the US Ambassador in February 1942.
11. PRO, Cab. 66/29, WP (42) 427, 'Admission to the United Kingdom of a limited number of Jewish Refugees from Unoccupied France. Memorandum by the Home Secretary' (23 Sept.

1942); PRO, FO 371/32680, Note by Roberts, 25 Sept. 1942; Cab. 65/27, War Cabinet 130 (42), 28 Sept. 1942, conclusion 4.

12. PRO, Cab. 65/28, Cabinet 131 (42), 5 Oct. 1942, conclusion 9.

13. LPL, Bishop Bell Papers, 31/477, EFR to White-Thomson, 15 Oct. 1942.

14. For Rathbone's plans, see *ibid.*; and PRO, FO 371/32680, Eleanor F. Rathbone, 'Refugees in Unoccupied France', 24 Oct. 1942. For Rathbone's ties with the Mexican Minister, see PRO, FO 371/32680, Note by Randall, 28 Oct. 1942.

15. Victor Cazalet diary, 27 and 28 Oct. 1942 (courtesy of Sir Edward Cazalet).

16. JRL, *Manchester Guardian* archives, 223/5/27, Deputation to the Home Secretary, 28 Oct. 1942.

17. LPL, Temple Papers, 54/129–32, Record of the Deputation of 28 Oct. 1942, 'from memory'. The Foreign Office did in fact telegraph their ambassadors in Latin America asking them to make it clear that the appeals had come without government support. PRO, FO 371/32681, Note by Randall, 3 Nov. 1942, and telegram to HM representatives, 5 Nov. 1942.

18. LPL, Temple Papers, 54/135, Corbett Ashby to Temple, 29 Oct. 1942. Alec Randall of the Foreign Office was also struck by their anger, warning that the MPs and churchmen might make a parliamentary issue of it. PRO, FO 371/32680, Note by Randall, 28 Oct. 1942.

19. LPL, Temple Papers, 54/181–2, Temple to Eden, 3 Dec. 1942.

20. LPL, Temple Papers, 54/134, Temple to EFR, 29 Oct. 1942. For Temple's heartfelt response to the persecution of the Jews, see F.A. Iremonger, *William Temple, Archbishop of Canterbury: His Life and Letters* (London: Oxford University Press, 1948), pp. 562–8.

21. Victor Gollancz, *'Let My People Go': Some Practical Proposals for Dealing with Hitler's Massacre of the Jews and an Appeal to the British Public* (London: Gollancz, December 1942), p. 9; 126 *HL Deb.*, 23 Mar. 1943, col. 815.

22. PRO, FO 371/32699/W16002, EFR to Eden, 11 Nov. 1942, and Eleanor F. Rathbone, 'Refugees in or from France', 19 Nov. 1942; LPL, Temple Papers, 54/143–4, Temple to Cranborne, 3 Nov. 1942; 125 *HL Deb.*, 11 Nov. 1942, cols 21–4.

23. The deportations are discussed in Michael R. Marrus and Robert O. Paxton, *Vichy France and the Jews* (New York: Basic Books, 1981), pp. 255–69; for clandestine rescue operations in France, see esp. Lucien Lazare, *Rescue as Resistance: How Jewish Organizations Fought the Holocaust in France*, trans. Jeffrey M. Green (1987; English trans. New York: Columbia University Press, 1996), ch. 11.

24. Much work has now been done on the question of the character and extent of knowledge about the early stages of the Holocaust in Britain and the United States. In an early study, Andrew Sharf emphasized the degree to which accurate coverage of Nazi atrocities against the Jews was available from the early stages of the war, but noted that coverage of 'actual slaughter' became extensive only after 1942, when readers grasped the literal and physical meaning of the Nazi threat to exterminate Jews; see Sharf, *The British Press and Jews under Nazi Rule* (London: Oxford University Press, 1964), pp. 88–100. Richard Breitman assesses the extent of information about the early stages of the Holocaust gathered by British code-breakers at Bletchley Park and points out that they did almost nothing with that information: few ministers or officials had access to the decodes, and once intelligence analysts came to recognize the Nazi pattern of separating out Jews and murdering them forthwith, they stopped passing even that information along. See Breitman, *Official Secrets*, ch. 6.

25. PRO, FO 371/32681, Hertz to Cranborne, 30 Oct. 1942; files on the 29 October protest meeting are in the Papers of the Board of Deputies of British Jews at the Greater London Record Office; see esp. GLRO, BDBJ Papers, 3121/C10/2/9/2, EFR to Chairman, 24 Oct. 1942. Hertz had approached Cranborne about possibilities of rescue, but Randall had insisted that the Foreign Office must 'firmly refuse to recognise the Jews as a separate nationality' and continue to treat Jews only as nationals of particular countries, since any other policy would cause difficulties with Britain's European allies and 'could be represented as discrimination in their [the Jews] favour'. PRO, FO 371/32680, Note by Randall, 7 Oct. 1942.

26. For Karski's critical role, see E. Thomas Wood and Stanislaw M. Jankowski, *Karski: How One Man Tried to Stop the Holocaust* (New York: John Wiley & Sons, 1994).

27. PRO, FO 371/30923/C11923, Note by Law, 26 Nov. 1942.
28. Silverman's suggestions can be found in PRO, FO 371/30923/C11923, Note by Law, 26 Nov. 1942; the World Jewish Congress proposals are in LPL, Temple Papers, 54/185–6, EFR to Temple, 3 Dec. 1942.
29. GLRO, BDBJ Papers, 3121/C11/7/1/1; Martin Gilbert, *Auschwitz and the Allies* (New York: Holt, Rinehart & Winston, 1981), p. 98.
30. For Rathbone's activities, see LPL, Temple Papers, 54/185–6, EFR to Temple, 3 Dec. 1942.
31. JRL, *Manchester Guardian* archives, 223/5/47, EFR to Crozier, 4 Dec. 1942.
32. 'Nazi War on Jews', *The Times*, 4 Dec. 1942, p. 3, and for Temple's letter, 5 Dec. 1942, p. 5; 385 *HC Deb.*, 9 Dec. 1942, col. 1584, and 10 Dec. 1942, cols 1704–5.
33. PRO, FO 371/32682/W16732, Eleanor F. Rathbone, 'Note on a practical policy', 14 Dec. 1942, and EFR to Law, 12 Dec. 1942.
34. 385 *HC Deb.*, 17 Dec. 1942, cols 2082–7; Harold Nicolson, Entry for 17 Dec. 1942, *Diaries and Letters, 1939–1945* (London: Collins, 1967), p. 268.
35. PRO, FO 371/30925/C12711, Note by Roberts, 16 Dec. 1942, and PRO, FO 30925/C12716, Note by Law, 16 Dec. 1942.
36. JRL, *Manchester Guardian* archives, 223/4/78, EFR to Crozier, 18 Dec. 1942.
37. GLRO, BDBJ Papers, 3121/C11/7/1/1, Joint Foreign Committee emergency meeting, 17 Dec. 1942, and Cab. 65/28, War Cabinet 172 (42), 23 Dec. 1942, conclusion 5.
38. JRL, *Manchester Guardian* archives, 223/4/78, EFR to Crozier, 18 Dec. 1942.
39. PRO, FO 371/32682/W17401, Note by Law, 18 Dec. 1942.
40. It is not possible here to summarize the very extensive debate over the timing and sequence of Nazi decision-making on the extermination of the Jews. Many scholars have argued that Hitler made a decision to exterminate the Jews in the spring or summer of 1941; some more recent studies point instead to a gradual radicalization of policy and a systematization of local campaigns of extermination culminating in a clear decision by autumn 1941 at the earliest. For a summary of this historiography, see especially, Ian Kershaw, *The Nazi Dictatorship: Problems and Perspectives of Interpretation* (4th edn, London: Arnold, 2000), pp. 113–33; for an account that emphasizes the great importance of the spring of 1941, Christopher Browning, *Fateful Months: Essays on the Emergence of the Final Solution* (rev. edn, New York: Holmes & Meier, 1991), esp. prologue, ch. 1.
41. Raul Hilberg, *The Destruction of the European Jews*, rev. edn, vol. 3 (New York: Holmes & Meier, 1985), p. 1220.
42. Christopher Browning, *The Path to Genocide: Essays on Launching the Final Solution* (Cambridge: Cambridge University Press, 1992), p. 169.
43. This literature is now very extensive. The early and still authoritative starting point for the British side is Bernard Wasserstein's *Britain and the Jews of Europe, 1939–1945* (1979; rev. edn, Leicester: Leicester University Press, 1999), which pays particular attention to the ways in which British officials' concern to limit immigration to Palestine conditioned their response; Martin Gilbert's useful *Auschwitz and the Allies* discusses government policy and the rescue campaign within the context of available knowledge on the Holocaust (and on Auschwitz in particular) but must now be supplemented by Breitman's *Official Secrets*. More recently, Louise London's well-researched *Whitehall and the Jews of Europe, 1933–1948: British Immigration Policy, Jewish Refugees and the Holocaust* (Cambridge: Cambridge University Press, 2000) discusses the rescue campaign and the government response within the context of Home Office policy on immigration generally. These comprehensive accounts have been supplemented by works surveying the activities of specific individuals or organizations or tracing particular themes. The response of Jewish organizations is treated critically by Richard Bolchover, *British Jewry and the Holocaust* (Cambridge: Cambridge University Press, 1993); Pamela Shatzkes, by contrast, absolves them of charges of 'lack of will' but convicts them, oddly, of 'lack of skill' in her *Holocaust and Rescue: Impotent or Indifferent? Anglo-Jewry, 1938–1945* (London: Palgrave, 2002). The ephemeral National Committee for Rescue from Nazi Terror has not received independent treatment except briefly in Aimée Bunting, 'Representing Rescue: The National Committee for Rescue from Nazi Terror, the British and

the Rescue of Jews from Nazism', *Journal of Holocaust Education*, 9: 1 (Summer 2000), pp. 65–83, but its work (and Rathbone's crucial role) is discussed extensively in Tony Kushner, *The Holocaust and the Liberal Imagination: A Social and Cultural History* (Oxford: Blackwell, 1994), chs 4–6, a study dedicated to Rathbone, which focuses on the ways in which liberal discomfort with Jewish particularity sometimes impeded comprehension and effective response. There is no study of Rathbone's work for refugees and rescue *per se*, but Susan Cohen is writing a PhD thesis on this subject at the University of Southampton.

There is an extensive literature on these campaigns for the United States as well; for a beginning, see Richard D. Breitman and Alan M. Kraut, *American Refugee Policy and European Jewry, 1933–1945* (Bloomington: Indiana University Press, 1987). A very useful collection of essays on responses to the Holocaust in individual countries is David S. Wyman, ed., *The World Reacts to the Holocaust* (Baltimore: Johns Hopkins University Press, 1996).

44. JRL, *Manchester Guardian* archives, 223/4/78, EFR to Crozier, 18 Dec. 1942.

45. PRO, Cab. 95/15, Cabinet Committee on the Reception and Accommodation of Jewish Refugees (hereafter Cabinet Refugee Committee), 4th meeting (19 Feb. 1943).

46. Gollancz, *'Let My People Go'*, pp. 3–4, 8–9; Rathbone's original language was printed in Eleanor F. Rathbone, 'The Horror in Poland', *New Statesman and Nation*, 26 Dec. 1942. For sales, see Ruth Dudley Edwards, *Victor Gollancz: A Biography* (London: Gollancz, 1987), p. 375.

47. Some of those letters to the Foreign Office can be found in PRO, FO 371/36651, and for correspondence with more illustrious individuals, see FO 371/36650. A moving summary of the resolutions and offers of help sent to the National Committee can be found in USL, James Parkes Papers, 60/15/57/2, compilation dated 31 May 1943; and for the numbers of letters, see in the same file National Committee for Rescue from Nazi Terror (NCRNT), 'Short Secretarial Report' (16 June 1943). Rathbone mentioned Gollancz's new office to deal with the correspondence at a meeting of the League of Nations Union, BLPES, LNU.II.19, EC Minutes, 4 Feb. 1943.

48. PRO, Cab. 95/15. War Cabinet Committee on the Reception and Accommodation of Jewish Refugees, Minutes, 1st meeting, 31 Dec. 1942 and 2nd meeting, 7 Jan. 1943.

49. PRO, Cab. 65/33, War Cabinet 6 (43), 11 Jan. 1943, conclusion 4; 386 *HC Deb.*, 19 Jan. 1943, cols 32–3.

50. PRO, Cab. 95/15, 3rd meeting, 27 Jan. 1943, and see Randall's minute for the all-party deputation in PRO, FO 371/36651, 27 Jan. 1943. Eden, a much more emollient figure than Morrison, took that deputation, and it passed off without incident and with reassurances of government interest and efforts. See PRO, FO 371/36651, Note of deputation on 28 Jan. 1943 (29 Jan. 1943).

51. JRL, *Manchester Guardian* archives, 223/5/132, EFR to Crozier, 13 Jan. 1943.

52. 386 *HC Deb.*, 20 Jan. 1943, cols 183–6; 21 Jan. 1943, cols 289–91; 11 Feb. 1943, cols 1446–7; also, 'Britain's Help for Refugees: Home Secretary and M.P.'s "Unfair Observation"', *Manchester Guardian*, 22 Jan. 1943, p. 6. For officials' irate comments on MPs' individual 'lobbying', see PRO, FO 371/32700, notes by Cheetham and Randall, 1 and 4 Jan. 1943, and by Walker, 7 Jan. 1943.

53. GLRO, BDBJ Papers, 3121/E1/74, 'Nazi Extermination Policy Against the Jews', Minutes of meeting of 7 Jan. 1943; JRL, *Manchester Guardian* archives, 223/5/119, Eleanor F. Rathbone, 'Jewish Massacres. The Case for an Offer to Hitler' (7 Jan. 1943), and 223/5/127, EFR to Crozier, 9 Jan. 1943. Selig Brodetsky recalls the 7 January meeting in his *Memoirs: From Ghetto to Israel* (London: Weidenfeld & Nicolson, 1960), p. 223.

54. CAC, Philip Noel-Baker Papers, NBKR 45/578, EFR to Noel-Baker, 8 Feb. 1943, enclosing Eleanor F. Rathbone, 'The Nazi Massacres of Jews and Poles. What Rescue Measures are Practically Possible?' (8 Feb. 1943), and EFR to Noel-Baker, 12 Feb. 1943; PRO, FO 371/36649, Noel-Baker to Law, 8 Jan. 1943. For Stanley's announcement, 386 *HC Deb.*, 3 Feb. 1943, cols 864–5.

55. JRL, *Manchester Guardian* archives, 223/5/171, EFR to Crozier, 12 Feb. 1943.

56. Rathbone updated these notes regularly, and multiple copies with variable dates exist in

various repositories, including the FO, Cecil, Parkes, Temple, and the *Manchester Guardian* archives. See, e.g., Eleanor F. Rathbone, 'Note, with Examples, of the Harsh Workings of the Home Office's Regulations' (2 Feb. 1943), Cecil Papers, BL Add. MS 51141, fols 297–8 and an updated version (24 Feb. 1943) in USL, Parkes Papers, 60/15/57/1; Eleanor F. Rathbone, 'The Nazi Massacres of Jews and Poles. What Rescue Measures are Practically Possible?' (12 Feb. 1943), copy in PRO, FO 371/36652; for the 'new Nansen', see LPL, Temple Papers, 54/244, EFR to Temple, 13 Feb. 1943; Eleanor F. Rathbone, 'Nazi Massacres of Jewish and Other People. Evidence of Public Concern', n.d. [Feb. 1943] and updated (10 Mar. 1943), copy in USL, Parkes Papers, 60/15/57/1.

57. On the 'new Nansen', see LPL, Temple Papers, 54/252, Temple to EFR, 15 Feb. 1943, and BLPES, LNU.II.19, EC Minutes, 18 Feb. 1943.

58. PRO, FO 371/36654/W3891, Attlee to EFR, 26 Feb. 1943. Morrison typically disputed her characterization of Britain's policy on visas and accused her of wanting to divert resources needed for the war effort to 'rescue'. PRO, FO 371/36655/W4400, Morrison to EFR, 9 Mar. 1943.

59. By mid-February, Eden was worried about the delay and the difficult parliamentary situation, but Morrison strongly opposed any unilateral action. See Cab. 95/15, Cabinet Refugee Committee, 4th meeting (19 Feb. 1943) and Cab. 65/33, War Cabinet 33 (22 Feb. 1943).

60. PRO, FO 371/36652, EFR to Randall, 27 Feb. 1943.

61. BL, Add. MS 51141, Cecil Papers, fol. 303, EFR to Cecil, 28 Feb. 1943. For the Jewish organizations' unhappiness with the lack of action, see material in PRO, FO 371/36652, and GLRO, BDBJ Papers, 3121/E1/74, 'Note of an Interview with Mr. F.K. Roberts, Foreign Office', 24 Feb. 1943.

62. For the *aides-mémoire* sent by the two governments outlining conditions of consultation, see Cab. 95/15, JR (43) 13 (28 Feb. 1943). It is worth noting that their reluctance was expressed openly, the British note saying that such discussion might meet the public agitation while also demonstrating 'the practical limitations to which the Allied Governments . . . must at present be inexorably subjected', and the American note dilating on everything the United States had done for refugees already.

63. USL, Parkes Papers, 60/15/57/1, 'Minutes of Conference held at the House of Commons on March 9, 1943'. Correspondence between Emerson and Randall aimed at shaping the behaviour of the NCRNT is in PRO, FO 371/36654 and 36655. A 'Suggested Agenda for Tuesday's Conference' (8 Mar. 1943), clearly drawn up by Rathbone, is in PRO, FO 371/36655/W4262; see also Note by Randall, 19 Mar. 1943.

64. 387 *HC Deb.*, 10 Mar. 1943, cols 638–40.

65. Minutes of meetings of the NCRNT, and the April 12-point programme, are in USL, Parkes Papers, 60/15/57.

66. USL, Parkes Papers, 60/15/57/1, NCRNT, EC Minutes, 13 Apr. 1943; PRO, FO 371/36658/W5673, EFR to Eden, 9 Apr. 1943 and 10 Apr. 1943, and PRO, FO 371/36660/W6801, EFR to Law, 7 Apr. 1943.

67. USL, Parkes Papers, 60/15/57/1, NCRNT, text of cable, 13 Apr. 1943.

68. 'Help for the Refugees', *The Times*, 20 Apr. 1943, p. 3.

69. Victor Cazalet, 'The Bermuda Speeches', *The Times*, 22 Apr. 1943, p. 5; also PRO, FO 371/36660/W6739, EFR to Eden, 26 Apr. 1943.

70. For the best account of the workings and impact of the Bermuda conference, see Wasserstein, *Britain and the Jews*, pp. 169–81.

71. USL, Parkes Papers, 60/15/57/1, NCRNT, EC Minutes, 29 Apr. 1943, and 15/57/2, EC Minutes, 6 May 1943, and circular letters to committee members and the press.

72. LPL, Temple Papers, 54/404, Carter to Temple, 30 Apr. 1943.

73. PRO, Cab. 65/34, War Cabinet 67, 10 May 1943, conclusion 5.

74. 389 *HC Deb.*, 19 May 1943, cols 1117–32.

75. *Ibid.*, cols 1132–43.

76. *Ibid.*, col. 1156. This was Cazalet's last speech in the House. For Cazalet's life, concern for

refugees, and work with the Polish government, see Robert Rhodes James, *Victor Cazalet: A Portrait* (London: Hamish Hamilton, 1976).

77. 389 *HC Deb.*, 19 May 1943, col. 1157. Bishop Bell of Chicester, another man who understood, also criticized Peake's description of the entire European population as in some sense 'refugees' in the Lords on 28 July 1943. He had nothing by sympathy for the Poles, Norwegians, Dutch, Yugoslavs, Czechs and other peoples subjected to Nazi rule, Bell said, but 'none of these people have been singled out by the Nazis for mass murder because of their race, as the Jews have been'. 128 *HL Deb.*, 28 July 1943, cols 846–50.

78. 389 *HC Deb.*, 19 May 1943, col. 1180.

79. *Ibid.*, cols 1162, 1188.

80. *Ibid.*, col. 1180.

81. *Ibid.*, cols 1196–204.

82. *Daily Telegraph*, 24 May 1943; PRO, FO 371/36662/W7963, Peake to EFR, 25 May 1943. Harold Nicolson wrote a forthright defence of Rathbone in his column, 'Marginal Comment', *Spectator*, 28 May 1943, p. 498. Rathbone, who cared passionately about getting the facts right, also sent out a circular letter responding to charges of inaccuracy. For a copy, see HLRO, Lloyd George Papers, G/16/7/9, EFR circular, 26 May 1943.

83. PRO, Cab. 65/34, War Cabinet 77, 24 May 1943, conclusion 6.

84. LPL, Bishop Bell Papers, 32/70–1, EFR to Bell, 11 June 1943.

85. LPL, Bell Papers, 32/69, EFR to Davies, copy to Bell, 2 June 1943.

86. PRO, Cab. 65/35, War Cabinet 92 (43), 2 July 1943, conclusion 3, and WP (43) 277.

87. For these negotiations, see Wasserstein, *Britain and the Jews*, pp. 214–16.

88. See, e.g., GLRO, BDBJ Papers, 3121/E3/536/2, Rokach, Mayor of Tel Aviv, to EFR, 19 June 1943, and Dr Joesph Kruk to EFR, 29 June 1943. Rathbone forwarded these cables to the Foreign Office, PRO, FO 371/36663/W9768.

89. For Gollancz's breakdown, see Edwards, *Victor Gollancz*, pp. 378–83.

90. USL, Parkes Papers, 60/15/57/2, Eleanor F. Rathbone, 'Confidential Note on the Position', 28 June 1943.

91. USL, Parkes Papers, 60/15/57/2, NCRNT, EC Minutes, 1 July 1943, 21 July 1943; 128 *HL Deb.*, 28 July 1943, cols 836–72.

92. PRO, FO 371/36640/W10287, Note by Law, 13 July 1943; PRO, FO 371/36727/W11589, Note by Walker, 12 Aug. 1943.

93. PRO, FO 371/36726/W8828, Perth to Randall, 11 June 1943, also PRO, FO 371/36662/W8192, Note by Randall, 9 June 1943.

94. PRO, FO 371/36726/W8828, Notes by Cheetham and Walker, 17 June 1943.

95. PRO, FO 371/36727/W11245, Prime Minister's personal minute, serial no. M53713, 29 July 1943. Bonham-Carter went to the meetings of the National Committee occasionally. On 19 August she recorded in her diary that except for Perth, Pakenham, herself and Rathbone, those present were 'all Jews'. Mark Pottle, ed., *Champion Redoubtable: The Diaries and Letters of Violet Bonham-Carter, 1914–1945* (London: Weidenfeld & Nicolson, 1998).

96. PRO, FO 371/36727/W11245, Eden to Churchill, 2 Aug. 1943, and PRO, FO 371/36727/W11589, draft memo by Emerson, 9 Aug. 1943.

97. PRO, FO 371/36665/W11961, Note by Walker, 12 Aug. 1943.

98. PRO, FO 371/36665/W11588, Eleanor F. Rathbone, 'Note on the Position regarding Rescue from Nazi Terror and Post-war Refugee Policy' (9 Aug. 1943).

99. PRO, FO 371/36665/W11588, Note by Law, 10 Aug. 1943.

100. PRO, FO 371/36665/W11961, Law to Eden, 10 Aug. 1943, note by Eden, 11 Aug. 1943, and note by Walker, 12 Aug. 1943.

101. PRO, FO 371/36665/W12086, EFR to Law, 19 Aug. 1943, and note by Law, 19 Aug. 1943.

102. PRO, FO 371/36729/W15384, Note by Walker, 26 Oct. 1943.

103. 393 *HC Deb.*, 3 Nov. 1943, col. 638, see also 392 *HC Deb.*, 13 Oct. 1943, col. 861.

104. PRO, FO 371/36730/W15978, EFR to Emerson, 8 Nov. 1943, and Emerson to EFR, 10 Nov. 1943.

105. See the discussion of the Italian offer in PRO, FO 371/36666/W12893, and, for Rathbone's comments about the armistice, PRO, FO 371/36666/W13938, Note by Randall, 21 Sept. 1943.

106. PRO, FO 371/36668/W15982, Crewe to PM, 10 Nov. 1943, Peck to Lawford, 15 Nov. 1943, and Law to Crewe, 26 Nov. 1943.

107. PRO, FO 371/36668/W15983, Eleanor F. Rathbone, 'Points submitted by E.F. Rathbone on behalf of the above committee to Mr. Richard Law', 16 Nov. 1943; PRO, FO 371/36669/W16144, EFR to Law, 18 Nov. 1943.

108. USL, Parkes Papers, 60/15/57/2, Eleanor F. Rathbone, 'Draft letter concerning debate on the address for the consideration of the Executive Committee', 24 Nov. 1943; and copy in PRO, FO 371/36669/W16144, EFR to Hall, 25 Feb. 1943.

109. JRL, *Manchester Guardian* archives, B/R45/9, EFR to Crozier, 3 Dec. 1943.

110. HLRO, Graham White Papers, GW 10/3/80, EFR to White, 7 Dec. 1943.

111. 395 *HC Deb.*, 14 Dec. 1943, cols 1467–73.

112. PRO, FO 371/36669/W16144, note by Randall, 29 Nov. 1943. For the statement, see PRO, Cab. 95/15 JR (43) 26 (3 Dec. 1943), 'Note by the Minister of State'.

113. GLRO, BDBJ Papers, 3121/E3/536/1, EFR to Brodetsky, 13 Dec. 1943.

114. USL, Parkes Papers, 60/15/57/2, NCRNT, EC Minutes, 9 Nov. 1943.

115. JRL, *Manchester Guardian* archives, B/R45/8, Crozier to EFR, 29 Nov. 1943; Eleanor F. Rathbone, 'The Refugees: A Disappointing Twelve Months', *Manchester Guardian*, 17 Dec. 1943, p. 4; [Eleanor F. Rathbone,] *The Continuing Terror* (London: National Committee for Rescue from Nazi Terror, Feb. 1944); USL, Parkes Papers, 60/15/67/3, invitation to public meeting held on 29 Feb. 1944; 'Victims of Nazi Terror', *Manchester Guardian*, 22 Feb. 1944, p. 6.

116. USL, Parkes Papers, 60/15/57/3, NCRNT, EC Minutes, 18 Jan. 1944, and 'Continuing Terror: How to Rescue Hitler's Victims' (draft, Jan. 1944).

117. 396 *HC Deb.*, 25 Jan. 1944, col. 616.

118. GLRO, BDBJ Papers, 3121 E3/536/1, E.F. Rathbone, 'Note on points for submission to the Rt. Hon. Anthony Eden at proposed deputation' (20 Dec. 1943).

119. Nicolson, *Diaries and Letters, 1939–1945*, entry for 11 Jan. 1944, p. 344.

120. PRO, FO 371/36673/W17831, Newling (War Office) to Randall, 8 Jan. 1944; Moylan (Home Office) to Randall, 5 Jan. 1944.

121. JRL, *Manchester Guardian* archives, 223/5/272, EFR to Crozier, 3 Feb. 1944; 396 *HC Deb.*, 9 Feb. 1944, cols 1740–2; 397 *HC Deb.*, 1 Mar. 1944, cols 1457–95.

122. The Cabinet Refugee Committee was not happy about this. Roosevelt, the committee thought, was simply trying to secure the Jewish vote in an election year; the Ministry of Economic Warfare objected that the Board's plans to allocate funds to try to protect Jews on the continent were a violation of the economic blockade. PRO, Cab. 95/15, RF (44) 4, 'Note by the Secretary of State for Foreign Affairs' (10 Mar. 1944), and JR (44) 1st meeting, 14 Mar. 1944.

123. Allied response to the occupation and deportations in Hungary is discussed in Breitman, *Official Secrets*, pp. 202–7. For Temple, see USL, Parkes Papers, 60/15/22/4, Council of Christians and Jews, EC Minutes, 16 May 1944, and LPL, Temple Papers, 55/114, Temple to Easterman, 7 Apr. 1944. For Rathbone, see PRO, FO 371/42723/W4703, EFR to Randall, 23 Mar. 1944 and 24 Mar. 1944; notes by Walker and Randall, 28 Mar. 1944; and FO to HM Minister, Holy See, telegram, 29 Mar. 1944; also CAC, CHAR 9/204 B, EFR to Harvie Watt, 24 Mar. 1944.

124. The Cabinet Committee on Refugees, discussing the Brand offer on 31 May 1944, concluded that they would be unable to manage the evacuation of up to a million Jews, that they could not maintain them in Palestine, and that they could not allow goods to go to Germany that might aid the war effort (Cab. 95/15, 2nd meeting, 31 May 1944). This was confirmed in Cabinet, Cab. 65/42, War Cabinet 71 (44), 1 June 1944, conclusion 3.

125. PRO, Cab. 95/15, JR (44) 15, 'Overtures relating to the evacuation of Jews in return for supplies of war material' (29 June 1944); Cab 95/15 JR (44) 19, 'Present State of the Brandt

[sic] discussions. Note by the Foreign Office' (12 July 1944); Cab. 95/15, JR (44) 3rd meeting, 13 July 1944.

126. Rathbone's accidents and convalescences are discussed in Mary D. Stocks, *Eleanor Rathbone: A Biography* (London: Victor Gollancz, 1949), pp. 292–3.

127. USL, Parkes Papers, 60/15/57/3, NCRNT, EC Minutes, 10 May 1944, 18 May 1944 and 27 June 1944.

128. USL, Parkes Papers, 60/15/57/3, NCRNT, EC Minutes, 19 July 1944.

129. GLRO, BDBJ Papers, 3121 E3/536/2, NCRNT, EC Minutes 27 July 1944, with copies of EFR's letters to Eden, 27 and 31 July 1944; and USL, Parkes Papers, 60/15/57/3, NCRNT, EC Minutes, 2 Aug. 1944.

130. Committee and cabinet considerations can be found in PRO, Cab. 95/15, JR (44) 21, 'Note by the Secretary of State for Foreign Affairs' (3 Aug. 1944); Cab. 95/15, JR (44) 4th meeting, 4 Aug. 1944, and Cab. 65/43, War Cabinet 104 (44), 9 Aug. 1944, conclusion 6 and War Cabinet 107 (44), 16 Aug. 1944, conclusion 2.

131. USL, Parkes Papers, 60/15/57/3, 'Note on the future of the National Committee for Rescue from Nazi Terror' [n.d., Oct. 1944]; NCRNT, EC Minutes, 19 Dec. 1944, 14 Mar. 1945 and 5 June 1945, and General Committee minutes, 30 Jan. 1945.

132. 413 *HC Deb.*, 20 Aug. 1945, cols 360–5; 414 *HC Deb.*, 18 Oct. 1945, cols 1340–1; 416 *HC Deb.*, 29 Nov. 1945, col. 1516; and PRO, FO 371/51099/WR2439, EFR to Bevin, 4 Aug. 1945.

133. PRO, Cab. 95/15, JR (43), 2nd meeting, 16 May 1945.

134. Unlike, for example, Selig Brodetsky, who – even though he led the Board of Deputies of British Jews during a period when they were seeking relentlessly to publicize the crimes of the Nazis – says that he and his allies 'still did not realize the terrible extent of the annihilation of the Jewish populations of Europe'. Brodetsky, *Memoirs*, p. 218.

135. Kushner, *The Holocaust and the Liberal Imagination*, p. 173.

136. W.D. Rubinstein, *A History of the Jews in the English-Speaking World: Great Britain* (London: Macmillan, 1996), p. 354. These charges are elaborated in his *The Myth of Rescue: Why the Democracies Could Not Have Saved More Jews from the Nazis* (London: Routledge, 1997).

137. RP XIV.18 (7), EFR to Wilfrid Roberts, 1 May 1944.

138. It is true that Rathbone's thinking about the Nazi persecution of the Jews, like that of virtually all other 'rescue' campaigners and indeed the government, remained caught in a pre-war framework. That is, she focused on task of removing endangered individuals from harm, rather than on the possibility – the famous issue of bombing Auschwitz – of targeting the actual machinery of their destruction. Rubinstein is right to stress this limitation, but it is one that virtually everyone shared.

139. 389 *HC Deb.*, 19 May 1943, col. 1138. For Rathbone's involvement in the (Swedish) Adler-Rudel scheme, see LPL, Temple Papers, 55/7–8, 'Note of Discussions at Miss Rathbone's Flat . . .' (5 May 1943).

140. On Slovakia, see Livia Rothkirchen, 'Czechoslovakia', in Wyman, ed., *The World Reacts to the Holocaust*, p. 170. On Hungary, see Randolph Braham, *The Politics of Genocide: The Holocaust in Hungary*, vol. 2 (New York: Columbia University Press, 1981), ch. 31. For Eden's comment, PRO, Cab. 95/15, RF (44) 4 (10 Mar. 1944) 'Note by the Secretary of State for Foreign Affairs'.

141. In 1996 Switzerland appointed a five-year Independent Commission of Experts to research and report on issues relating to Switzerland's response to the Holocaust, including its treatment of Jews seeking refuge. For information on the Commission's work and to access its reports, see its website, *http://www.uek.ch*.

142. On the importance of protective documents in the final Hungarian crisis, see Wasserstein, *Britain and the Jews*, pp. 238–41, and Jean-Claude Favez, *The Red Cross and the Holocaust*, ed. and trans. John and Beryl Fletcher (1988; English trans. Cambridge: Cambridge University Press, 1999), pp. 242–50.

143. Bauer, *Jews for Sale*, p. 60.

144. CAC, A.V. Hill Papers, Box 4/69, EFR to Hill, 16 September 1944.

145. 389 *HC Deb.*, 19 May 1943, col. 1137.

146. The US comment about the IGC is in telegram 4118, Washington to Foreign Office, 1 Aug. 1944, contained in PRO, Cab. 95/15, JR (44) 21, 'Note by the Secretary of State for Foreign Affairs' (3 Aug. 1944).

147. Emerson said as much to Pehle of the War Refugee Board; see PRO, Cab. 95/15, JR (44) 12, 'Note by the Chairman' (31 May 1944).

148. This is a point also made by London, *Whitehall and the Jews*, p. 221.

149. 389 *HC Deb.*, 19 May 1943, col. 1138.

150. An exception being Eden's concern not to draw attention to the Pyrenees, through which British intelligence sources (and, fortunately, also some Jews) passed. See PRO, Cab. 65/34, War Cabinet 69, 17 May 1943, conclusion 5.

151. LPL, Temple Papers, 54/129–32, Record of the Deputation of 28 Oct. 1942.

152. When Violet Bonham-Carter tried to get the BBC to make a broadcast commemorating the December 1942 declaration, that too was scotched with 'the usual excuse – fear of arousing Anti-Semitism'. See her diary, 11 Nov. 1943, in Pottle, ed., *Champion Redoubtable*, p. 285. A few letters from anti-Semites are preserved in Rathbone's papers; see RP XIV.2.17 (62).

153. GLRO, BDBJ Papers, 3121/C11/7/1/1 Joint Foreign Committee, Emergency Consultative Committee, 26 May 1943.

154. USL, Parkes Papers, 60/15/57/2, NCRNT, EC Minutes, 21 July 1943.

155. GLRO, BDBJ Papers, 3121/E3/536/1, EFR to A.G. Brotman, 21 Sept. 1943.

156. Victor Gollancz/Cassell company archive, File on *Falsehoods and Facts about the Jews*, EFR to Gollancz, 19 Aug. 1944 and Gollancz to EFR, 22 Aug. 1944. The Revd. W.W. Simpson of the Council of Christians and Jews had a similar response to Gollancz to the pamphlet, as did James Parkes, who noted perceptively that titles purporting to state the truth while identifying others as liars ('Falsehoods and Facts') always create 'a suspicion of objectivity of the author'. See USL, Parkes Papers, 60/15/22, Simpson to members of the publications subcommittee, 1 Jan. 1944; Parkes, 'Some Comments on Miss Rathbone's proposed pamphlet' (Jan. 1944); Simpson to Parkes, 13 June 1944.

157. Eleanor F. Rathbone, *Falsehoods and Facts about the Jews* (London: Victor Gollancz, 1945). An accounting note in the Gollancz file on 'Falsehoods and Facts' gives revenue amounting to £149 4s. 4d., suggesting that – given a price of threepence, discounted to booksellers – probably 30,000 copies were printed.

158. Gollancz/Cassell company archive, File on *Falsehoods and Facts about the Jews*, Gollancz to EFR, 22 Aug. 1944.

159. Rathbone, *Falsehoods and Facts*, pp. 13–14.

160. 391 *HC Deb.*, 16 July 1943, col. 561; also EFR letter, *The Times* 21 Aug. 1945, p. 5.

161. See the collection of material from 1945 on Palestine, including drafts of parliamentary questions and correspondence with Jewish organizations, in RP, Dec. 2002 accession (being catalogued), as well as Rathbone's speech supporting Zionist claims in the Debate on the Address, 413 *HC Deb.*, 20 Aug. 1945, cols 363–5.

Chapter 17   Miss Rathbone in Victory

1. The wartime movement for family allowances is discussed most thoroughly in Hilary Land, 'The Introduction of Family Allowances: An Act of Historic Justice?' in Phoebe Hall et al., *Change, Choice and Conflict in Social Policy* (London: Heinemann, 1975), esp. pp. 179–230; John Macnicol, *The Movement for Family Allowances, 1918–45: A Study in Social Policy Development* (London: Heinemann, 1980), pp. 169–213; Susan Pedersen, *Family, Dependence and the Origins of the Welfare State: Britain and France, 1914–1945* (Cambridge: Cambridge University Press, 1993), pp. 327–56. Land and Macnicol both emphasize the degree to which hopes of restraining wages lay behind the government's final acceptance of family allowances. I have disagreed and pointed to the continued ambivalence

of both the Treasury and the TUC (much the two most important actors) about allowances, but have also paid too little attention to the role played by an activist wartime Commons.

2. For that laughter, see 308 *HC Deb.*, 12 Feb. 1936, cols 1001–9. In 1938, Leo Amery provided a comprehensive summary of those child welfare and populationist arguments in 'The Worker and His Family: A National Issue', *The Times*, 24 June 1938.

3. Rathbone summarized the changed situation in her March 1939 letter to her constituents, RP XIV.3.4.

4. Reading University Library, Allen & Unwin Archives, MS 3282, File on Eleanor Rathbone, EFR to Unwin, 23 Aug. 1938, and Unwin to EFR, 25 Aug. 1938.

5. Note, for example, the *Times*'s intensely sympathetic summary of the 'anti-poverty' case for family allowances, 'Family Poverty: How the Children Suffer', *The Times*, 11 Dec. 1939.

6. John Maynard Keynes, 'Paying for the War', *The Times*, 14 Nov. 1939, p. 9, and 15 Nov. 1939, p. 9.

7. Leo Amery, 'Family Allowances: A Precaution against Inflation', *The Times*, 14 Dec. 1939.

8. Robert Skidelsky, *John Maynard Keynes*, vol. 3, *Fighting for Freedom, 1937–1946* (New York: Viking, 2000), p. 61.

9. John Maynard Keynes, *How to Pay for the War: A Radical Plan for the Chancellor of the Exchequer* (New York: Harcourt, Brace, 1940).

10. Macnicol, *Movement*, pp. 170–5; Skidelsky chronicles Keynes's heroic efforts to persuade working-class leaders and Treasury officials to support his proposals in *Fighting*, ch. 2.

11. CAC, Leo Amery diaries, AMEL 290, diary entries for 9 Nov. 1939; 25 Jan. 1940; 15, 26 and 29 Feb. 1940; and 2 and 6 Apr. 1940; Eleanor F. Rathbone, *The Case for Family Allowances* (Harmondsworth: Penguin, 1940).

12. B. Seebohm Rowntree, 'Wages in Wartime: The National Finance and the Public Health', *The Times*, 4 Jan. 1941.

13. 'Family Allowances', *Manchester Guardian*, 25 Apr. 1941, p. 6.

14. 371 *HC Deb.*, 29 May 1941, col. 1991 and 372 *HC Deb.*, 12 June 1941, col. 363; PRO, ACT 1/664, EFR to G.S.W. Epps, 5 May 1941, and Minutes by Maddox, 17 May 1941 and 29 May 1941.

15. PRO, PIN 8/163, HM Treasury, 'Notes of a deputation received by the Chancellor of the Exchequer . . . 16 June 1941'.

16. For the debate within the labour movement, see Pedersen, *Family, Dependence*, pp. 330–5.

17. *Family Allowances. Memorandum by the Chancellor of the Exchequer*, PP 1941–2, IX, Cmd. 6354; 380 *HC Deb.*, 23 June 1942, cols 1853–944.

18. 'An Agreed Principle', *The Times*, 11 June 1942.

19. 380 *HC Deb.*, 23 June 1942, col. 1941.

20. *Social Insurance and Allied Services: A Report by Sir William Beveridge*, PP 1942–3, VI, Cmd. 6404, pp. 154–8.

21. PRO Cab. 87/77, SIC (42), 12th meeting, 2 June 1942; and Cab. 87/79, SIC (42), 42, 'Evidence by Mrs. E.M. Hubback on behalf of the Family Endowment Society' (Apr. 1942); PRO PIN 8/16, HM Treasury, 'Notes of a Deputation organised by the Family Endowment Society . . . 14 January 1943'.

22. PRO, Cab. 87/13, PR (43) 13, Committee on Reconstruction Priorities, 'The Beveridge Plan: Interim Report' (11 Feb. 1943); Cab. 65/33, WM 43 (28), 12 Feb. 1943; 386 *HC Deb.*, 16 Feb. 1943, cols 1666–7. It is worth noting that the Cabinet was far from united. The Committee on Reconstruction Priorities first favoured only a minimal scheme for low-income families with more than two children but then agreed to include the second child and remove the income cap; the Cabinet – in Churchill's absence – favoured accepting Beveridge's three assumptions, but at its next meeting qualified that considerably. In the Commons, Sir John Anderson (now Chancellor of the Exchequer) announced the government's acceptance of allowances but refused to give a timetable.

23. PRO, PIN 8/16, Rathbone to Jowitt, 4 June 1943; Sheepshanks to Daish, 5 June 1943.

24. PRO, PIN 8/16, Sheepshanks to Daish, 8 June 1943.

25. Rathbone, *The Case for Family Allowances*, pp. 59, 63.

26. Eleanor F. Rathbone, *The Harvest of the Women's Movement* (London, 1935), p. 9.
27. 380 *HC Deb.*, 23 June 1942, col. 1863.
28. PRO, PIN 8/16, Sheepshanks to Daish, 8 June 1943.
29. The Ministry of Information survey is in PRO PIN 17/4, Stephen Taylor to M.A. Hamilton, 28 Dec. 1943 and reproduced in Pedersen, *Family, Dependence*, p. 347; the TUC opinion is recorded in PRO, PIN 8/7, TUC, 'Deputation to Sir William Jowitt' (12 Aug. 1943).
30. PRO, PIN 8/115 and 8/116, Minutes and memoranda of the committee on the Beveridge Report [Phillips Committee]. For the Committee on Reconstruction Priorities, see PRO, Cab. 87/12, PR (43) 14th meeting, 26 July 1943; Cab. 87/13, PR (43) 77, 'Social Insurance and Allied Services: Outstanding points on which decisions are needed' (3 Oct. 1943); for the Reconstruction Committee, see PRO, Cab. 87/7, R (44) 36, Reconstruction Committee, 'Report of the Sub-Committee on Social Insurance', p. 2.
31. Eleanor F. Rathbone, 'Allowances for Children: Payment to the Mother', *The Times*, 26 June 1944.
32. 'Children's Allowances', *The Times*, 4 July 1944.
33. *White Paper on Social Insurance*, PP 1943–4, VIII, Cmd. 6550, p. 14.
34. Correspondence and papers relating to this deputation of 12 October 1944 are in PRO, PIN 8/68.
35. PRO Cab. 65/49, WM (45) 26, 6 Mar. 1945.
36. 408 *HC Deb.*, 8 Mar. 1945, col. 2267.
37. *Ibid.*, cols 2275–83.
38. *Ibid.*, cols 2287, 2293, 2295, 2304.
39. *Ibid.*, col. 2323.
40. *Ibid.*, col. 2327.
41. 411 *HC Deb.*, 11 June 1945, col. 1415 (Group-Captain Wright).
42. *Ibid.*, col. 1417 (Kenneth Lindsay).
43. 408 *HC Deb.*, 8 Mar. 1945, col. 2332.
44. Interview with Lady Wright, London, 18 Jan. 1993.
45. RP XIV.3.106, Nicolson, 'Devoted Pioneer', n.d.
46. 411 *HC Deb.*, 11 June 1945, col. 1418.
47. RP, Dec. 2002 accession (being catalogued), EFR to Joan Prewer, Christmas 1945, enclosed in Prewer to Elizabeth Macadam, 25 July 1946.
48. RP XIV.3.3 (37) and (38), EFR to Leonard Behrens, 29 Jan. 1945, and Behrens to EFR, 30 Jan. 1945.
49. RP XIV.3.3, Election address, 1945.
50. Rathbone was alerted to the Polish deportations by Atholl and Thelma Cazalet-Keir; her papers contain correspondence with both women, and later with Rose Macaulay, on this subject. See RP XIV.2.18 (5) and (6), Atholl to EFR, 1 Mar. 1944, and EFR to Atholl and Cazalet-Keir, 4 Mar. 1944; RP XIV.2.18 (28), Macaulay to EFR, 18 Feb. 1945; this file also contains correspondence with H.N. Brailsford and others attempting to arrange newspaper articles on the subject. For parliamentary interventions, see 406 *HC Deb.*, 15 Dec. 1944, cols 1510–13; 407 *HC Deb.*, 17 Jan. 1945, col. 136; 408 *HC Deb.*, 21 Feb. 1945, col. 768; 408 *HC Deb.*, 7 Mar. 1945, col. 1999; for the meeting in the House on 14 Feb. 1945, see RP XIV.2.18 (23). For Clementine Churchill's interventions with Maisky, see RP XIV.4.12–14, EFR to Mrs Churchill, 31 Mar. 1945, and Clementine Churchill to EFR, 28 May 1945. Rathbone also took her concerns to the Foreign Office in early December 1944. See PRO, FO 371/39420/c17492, Minute by Roberts, 6 Dec. 1944.
51. RP XIV.4.15, EFR to Clementine Churchill, May 1945.
52. Rathbone was particularly upset by Czech plans to expel the Sudetenlanders, for she had close ties both to Beneš and Masaryk and to exiled German Social Democrats from the Sudetenland. For her fears about these plans, see BL Add. MS 51141, Cecil Papers, Rathbone to Cecil and Lytton, 14 Feb. 1944, fol. 308; RP XIV.2.15 (47), A.P. Peres to EFR, 13 Apr. 1944 and 10 May 1944, and EFR to Peres, 23 June 1944; BLPES, LNU.II.21, EC Minutes, 7 June 1945; and 411 *HC Deb.*, 13 June 1945, cols 1633,

1686–7. For these deportations, see Norman M. Naimark, *Fires of Hatred: Ethnic Cleansing in Twentieth-Century Europe* (Cambridge, Mass.: Harvard University Press, 2001), ch. 4.

53. For a good account of Vansittart's views, see Aaron Goldman, 'Germans and Nazis: The Controversy over "Vansittartism" in Britain during the Second World War', *Journal of Contemporary History*, 14: 1 (Jan. 1979), pp. 155–91; for Rathbone's response, see RP XIV.3.76, 'Anti-Vansittart Meeting at Birmingham on Sat. 12 Feb. 1944. Speech Notes'.

54. 604 *HC Deb.*, 10 Nov. 1944, cols 1725–31.

55. For the controversy over Gollancz's pamphlet, see Ruth Dudley Edwards, *Victor Gollancz: A Biography* (London: Victor Gollancz, 1987), pp. 401–9.

56. USL, Parkes Papers, 60/15/57/3, NCRNT, EC Minutes, 5 June 1945.

57. PRO, FO 371/46813/C993, EFR to Noel-Baker, 25 Aug. 1945, and civil servants' notes.

58. The appeal is reprinted in Edwards, *Gollancz*, pp. 410–11, which is the best source for the Save Europe Now campaign. I have drawn on Edwards's account throughout.

59. MRC, Gollancz Papers, MSS 157/3/SEN/1/6/1, Resolutions from Conway Hall Meeting, 8 Oct. 1945; also Edwards, *Gollancz*, pp. 414–15. It is not clear whether the food parcel scheme was first dreamed up by Rathbone, but she had plenty of experience from her Spanish 'food ships' days and was asking Churchill's government as early as March 1945 to relax restrictions on food parcels to the continent. See 409 *HC Deb.*, 21 Mar. 1945, col. 805.

60. MRC, Gollancz Papers, MSS 157/3/SEN/2/6, G.S. Bishop to Victor Gollancz, 20 Nov. 1945.

61. RP XIV.3.84, 'Speech Notes – "Save Europe Now," Albert Hall, 26 Nov. 1945'.

62. 414 *HC Deb.*, 26 Oct. 1945, cols 2416–17.

63. RP XIV.3.84, 'Speech Notes – "Save Europe Now," Albert Hall, 26 Nov. 1945'.

64. MRC, Gollancz Papers, MSS 157/3/SEN/2/8, Attlee to Gollancz, 17 Dec. 1945.

65. Peggy Duff, *Left, Left, Left: A Personal Account of Six Protest Campaigns, 1945–1965* (London: Allison & Busby, 1971), p. 13.

66. Edwards, *Gollancz*, pp. 429–30.

67. WL, Brian Harrison interview with Doris [Hardman] Cox and Marjorie [Green] Soper, 15 Mar. 1977.

68. Telephone interview with Noreen Rathbone, 2 Aug. 2003.

69. Duff's recollections are quoted by Edwards, *Gollancz*, pp. 439–40; also Duff, *Left*, pp. 19–20.

70. USL, Parkes Papers, 60/15/57/3, NCRNT, General Committee Minutes, 10 Jan. 1946.

Coda to Part IV: The Lady Vanishes

1. RP, Dec. 2002 accession (being catalogued), Eleanor F. Rathbone, 'Directions for disposal of my body after death' (9 July/12 Aug./17 Sept. 1939).

2. HLRO, Graham White Papers, GW17/2/13, Macadam to Graham White, 15 Feb. 1947; Mary D. Stocks, *Eleanor Rathbone: A Biography* (London: Victor Gollancz, 1949), p. 8.

3. This is the selection that now forms the bulk of the Eleanor Rathbone materials in the Rathbone Papers at the University of Liverpool. These papers appear to have gone to Evie after Stocks finished her draft, except for a small collection of personal material, which Stocks gave to B.L. Rathbone. B.L. Rathbone turned a portion of that over to the university in the early 1990s, but some crucial private letters were still in his possession (although he allowed me access) in 1993. Those papers were finally given to the Library by his daughter Jenny Rathbone following his death in 2002.

4. RP XIV.5.47, Macadam to Mrs Smith, 26 Nov. 1946, and RP XIV.5.49, Macadam to Smith, 5 May 1947.

5. RP XIV.5.50, Macadam to Mrs Smith, 21 Dec. 1947.

6. RP XIV.5.51, Macadam to Mrs Smith, 25 Feb. 1948. On the 1948 Act, see D.E. Butler, *The Electoral System in Britain since 1918* (2nd edn, Oxford: Clarendon Press, 1963), ch. 5, and for tributes to Rathbone, 447 *HC Deb.*, 17 Feb. 1948, cols 1014–15, 1017, 1037–8, 1085.

7. RP XIV 3.88d, 'Copy of the Address by The Right Hon. Sir Arthur Salter, M.P. on the occasion of the Memorial Service to Miss Eleanor Rathbone, M.P.'

Index

Works by Eleanor Rathbone (EFR) appear directly under title; works by others under author's name.

Titles and ranks are generally the highest mentioned in the text.

Page numbers in *italic* indicate illustrations.